D1596989

DATE DUE

SPLENDID LAND
SPLENDID PEOPLE

SPLENDID LAND
SPLENDID PEOPLE

The Chickasaw Indians to Removal

JAMES R. ATKINSON

THE UNIVERSITY OF ALABAMA PRESS
Tuscaloosa

Typeface: Minion

∞

The paper on which this book is printed meets the minimum requirements of American
National Standard for Information Science–Permanence of Paper for Printed Library
Materials, ANSI Z39.48-1984.

Library of Congress Cataloging-in-Publication Data

Atkinson, James R.
    Splendid land, splendid people : the Chickasaw Indians to removal / James R. Atkinson.
        p.   cm.
Includes bibliographical references and index.
    ISBN 0-8173-1339-7 (cloth : alk. paper) — ISBN 0-8173-5033-0 (pbk. : alk. paper)
1. Chickasaw Indians—History—Sources. 2. Chickasaw Indians—Government relations.
3. Chickasaw Indians—Wars. 4. Tombigbee River Valley (Miss. and Ala.)—History—Sources.
I. Title.
    E99.C55A75 2004
    976.004'973—dc21

                                                                2003008300

Dedicated in memory of my father, Robert F. Atkinson (1915–1993), and to my mother, Evelyn House Atkinson

Contents

Illustrations

Preface and Acknowledgments

In 1492 when Christopher Columbus and some of his subordinates walked a sandy island beach in the West Indies, one of the numerous native populations of the present southeastern United States was occupying territory on an ancient river that flowed south into the Gulf of Mexico. Eventually the Chickasaw chiefdom people would learn of the alien arrival via word of mouth, and those still alive in A.D. 1540 would actually meet, communicate, and cooperate with the strangely dressed humanoids from another world. By then the Chickasaw people had learned that the alien world lay far to the east, on the other side of what they and other indigenous people called the "Great Lake."

This is a story of the Chickasaw people gleaned from the historical and archaeological records left behind as they traveled through the centuries. It is a story of conflicts in culture, the detrimental consequences of European contact, and remarkable survival to the present.

ACKNOWLEDGMENTS

Because I began this work over twelve years ago and went several years at a time without returning to it, there may be some people now forgotten who provided assistance. I remember well, however, Pat Galloway's reading of my first draft in 1990 and her making valuable comments and suggestions and encouraging me to lengthen it into a book rather than the article I initially intended it to be. I finally took her advice in late 1999. To her I offer a belated "thank you."

As always when I write papers of a historical nature about the Old Southwest, Jack D. Elliott, Jr., has been of assistance with regard to clarifications of some of the numerous inaccuracies in the secondary literature and in bringing to my attention a few obscure sources. Others who have contributed varying amounts of assistance include, especially, Joseph Peyser, Jim Knight, Princella Nowell, Alexander Moore, Richard Colbert, Joyce Bushman, and Mary Ann

Wells. The latter appears to be the first researcher in Mississippi to discover that an obscure but extremely valuable French map of some of the early eighteenth-century Chickasaw villages had been published in a general history book in 1967.

I also wish to thank the Natchez Trace Parkway library at Tupelo, Mississippi, for being just across the hall from my office between 1984 and 1997 when I was employed by the National Park Service as a prehistoric and historic archaeologist. The collections of copies of early documents and maps located there were invaluable, as were the thousands of research note cards and typed reports written over the years by people who had worked there, such as Dr. Dawson A. Phelps and Dr. Jesse D. Jennings. Other libraries that provided assistance through having books I needed, or by acquiring them through interlibrary loan, include the Lee County, Mississippi, Public Library, the Mitchell Memorial Library at Mississippi State University, and the Fant Memorial Library at Mississippi University for Women. With regard to the MSU library, special thanks are due Mattie Sink of Special Collections, as well as others in that division. Assistance of personnel at other libraries and archives is also much appreciated, such as the National Archives depositories at Suitland, Maryland, and Washington, D.C., the Library of Congress, the United States Court of Claims in Washington, Mississippi Department of Archives and History, and the Tennessee State Library and Archives, especially Susan Maszatos. I also appreciate the constructive comments provided by reviewers Patricia K. Galloway, Jay K. Johnson, and Tony Paredes. Lastly, I extend my sincere gratitude to Kathy Cummins for her laborious and excellent editorial work on the manuscript.

SPLENDID LAND
SPLENDID PEOPLE

1
Land of the Bones

The "splendid and fertile" land on the upper Tombigbee River (Figure 1) in present-day northeast Mississippi contains the bones of the vast majority of the many thousands of Chickasaw people who have lived upon the earth to the present. Some of the progenitor people of the population that evolved into this sociopolitical entity, originally written "Chicasa," may have migrated from west of the Mississippi River in remote prehistoric times. Unless such people were so numerous and superior militarily that they forced a mass exodus of the indigenous people, these possible westerners more likely would have joined and amalgamated with the indigenous people, who are archaeologically documented to have been present there on a consistent basis since at least 6000 B.C. It really makes no difference. The Chickasaw, whose name meaning has become obscure, came to be and continue to be.[1]

Nearly all of the various origin myths of both the Chickasaw and Choctaw give an unspecified trans–Mississippi River location for the earlier home of both of these groups, and they were supposedly one people until separating after arriving east of the river. Most historians and anthropologists have asserted that this is evident as a result of alleged similarities in their cultural manifestations. This is not the case, however, because archaeological evidence and ethnographic descriptions show a marked disparity between their pottery, burial customs, hairstyles, physical characteristics, and other traits. The only significant similarity was their language.[2]

The Tombigbee River (Figure 1) flows slightly southeast from the Chickasaw area into the present-day state of Alabama and on to Mobile Bay after its juncture with the Alabama River. Today, that part of the river north of the juncture is known as the Tombigbee and the remainder from there to Mobile Bay is known as the Mobile River, but the entire source from the bay to the Chickasaw villages was referred to by the Europeans as the Mobile River, the River of the Chickasaw, or the River of the Choctaw.

1. Locations of Indian groups and sites in the present-day states of Mississippi, Alabama, Tennessee, and Louisiana (by author)

From remote times the native people of the southeast built secure homes, obtained sustenance from the land, made comfortable clothing, and constructed efficient tools, weapons, adornments, and household items from natural resources. In winter they lived in secure, well-insulated round houses constructed by placing closely spaced posts in the ground, weaving cane or sapling strips horizontally among them, and plastering the resulting walls with wet mud, which was allowed to dry. The cone- or dome-shaped roofs were covered with thick layers of long grass oriented toward the ground. The summer houses were usually square or rectangular with peaked roofs. The winter houses had fire basins in the centers of the earth floors, and other fire basins for cooking were located outside the houses. Trash was thrown away near the houses or buried in dug or natural pits. If houses were located near streams, water was procured from them in large earthen jars and transported to the houses for storage and use. In instances similar to the customs of the historic Chickasaw whose houses were usually built on ridge tops far from springs or flowing streams, pit cisterns with clay linings were constructed to catch rainwater. Sometimes small erosional ravines on the sides of ridges were dammed to create small reservoirs. Clothing and footwear were made from animal skins, and cordage was made with inner fibers of the bark of trees. After European cloth woven from cotton, flax, and wool became available, clothing was made from these materials. In historic times blankets purchased from European traders supplemented their animal-skin wraps and bed coverings. Food was partially procured from wild-growing plants and trees until domestic fruit trees such as peach were introduced by the Europeans. Fish, shellfish, turtles, and crustaceans were captured from streams, rivers, and natural ponds. After about A.D. 500 domesticated crops such as maize (corn) were introduced and planted near villages or isolated houses. Nearly all species of mammals and large birds were hunted for food, especially deer, bears, raccoons, opossums, rabbits, squirrels, turkeys, geese, and ducks. Introduction in about A.D. 500 of the stringed bow with arrows tipped by small chipped stone points had made hunting more efficient and less time consuming. Tools, weapons, and personal adornments were made from local Tombigbee River chert and exotic stone and from wood, bone, and shellfish. Baskets were made from cane and sapling strips. Pottery, made from local clays by hand molding, made its appearance in the southeast around 2000 B.C. Numerous changes in decoration techniques, motifs, and other elements of pottery making occurred through the centuries. Examples of native seventeenth-century and eighteenth-century cultural materials related directly to the Chickasaw are shown in Figure 2, and a Chickasaw warrior wearing archaeologically documented ornaments is shown in Figure 3.[3]

Religious beliefs and practices of the native southeastern people, especially belief in an afterlife, extended into remote prehistoric times, as demonstrated by burial thousands of years ago of personal possessions with the dead. Religious ceremonies in various forms were conducted, and funeral rites of various types were performed. The Chickasaw sometimes buried their dead inside the house and under the frame bed belonging to the deceased individual. Those who died at home or nearby were buried soon after death, but those who died too far away to carry home immediately were normally either placed on elevated scaffolds or covered with tree branches, logs, or stones; normally the bones were later retrieved and given a typical funeral at his or her home. With regard to the historic Chickasaw, the deceased was buried either in a round or oblong grave large enough to accommodate an extended on the back, flexed on the side, or bundle (disarticulated) position. The flexed position was sometimes referred to by early Euro-Americans as "in a sitting position."[4]

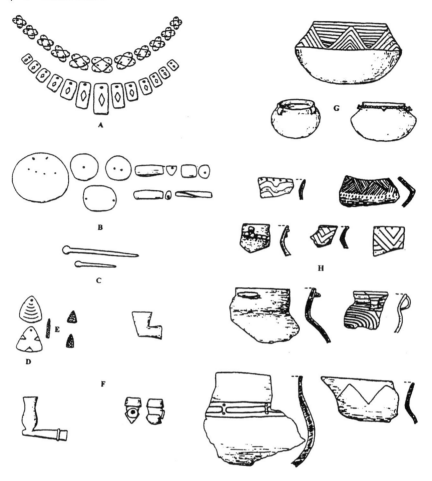

2. Examples of seventeenth- and eighteenth-century Chickasaw cultural material: *A*, Engraved marine shell necklace ornaments; *B*, marine shell gorgets and beads; *C*, marine shell ear pins; *D*, engraved stone ornaments; *E*, chipped chert punch and arrow points; *F*, clay pipe bowls and stone pipe bowls; *G*, whole pottery vessels; *H*, decorated pottery fragments (from Atkinson, "Historic Chickasaw Cultural Material," 1987; courtesy of *Mississippi Archaeology*)

In general, early social organization among southeastern native Americans consisted of extended family clans led by headmen; one of these might also serve as overall "chief" of the village in which he resided. There were peace chiefs and war chiefs, but only a man belonging to a hereditary line could advance to "great chief" or "king" over the entire tribe, as further addressed below. Each village had a head war chief, a position acquired through personality and

3. Recent painting of a Chickasaw warrior as one might
have appeared wearing only native-made shell ornaments
in the late seventeenth and early eighteenth centuries (by
author)

personal accomplishment. One of them could rise to the position of head war
chief over the entire tribe. A more complex feature of social organization was
the moieties, among which the clans were divided. In most tribes, descent of
an individual was through the female lineage rather than the male, meaning
that children became members of their mother's clan and were the responsibility of the mother and her blood relatives. A resigning or deceased great chief
or king (an alternate title applied by Europeans) was nearly always succeeded
by a maternal nephew.[5]

By around A.D. 1200 the early Chickasaw had probably accepted most or all
of the widespread cultural practices and customs of a lifestyle known archaeologically as the Mississippian Tradition, named after the Mississippi River where
it appears to have originated. Its most prominent physical remains to be seen
today are the small to very large rectangular, flat-topped earthen pyramids,
which when in use had wooden temples or important officials' houses on their

tops. Such pyramids had actually been constructed on a limited scale in the Mississippi drainage several hundred years prior to the appearance of the Mississippian Tradition, but erection of them fell by the wayside until the practice was rejuvenated in about A.D. 1000. Once introduced prior to A.D. 1000, corn and its extensive cultivation seems to have been instrumental in giving rise to larger populations, which in turn necessitated more sophisticated and complex government, the hallmark of the Mississippian Tradition. Social evolution, however, resulted in the governments of the Tradition becoming somewhat totalitarian, with religion and politics enmeshed. It is believed that hereditary priest rulers in some areas of the southeast came to be overlords, with authoritarian power that allowed only limited personal freedoms. Some of the Tradition societies became so powerful that other smaller Mississippian societies located far away were brought under their control. Resulting were Mississippian "chiefdoms" made up of as many as three or four societies, or towns, each sometimes having its own similar customs and sometimes ceremonial pyramids, but each subject to a central government and its subordinating, powerful officials who had control of the military.[6]

In the present northeast quadrant of Mississippi there is only one classic Mississippian mound group, the Owl Creek site in present-day Chickasaw County on a third-rank tributary of the Tombigbee River (Figure 1). It originally had seven small to medium-sized mounds in addition to a large pyramidal mound, which has survived almost intact. A site with only one mound (Lyon's Bluff) is present on the south side of Line Creek in present-day Oktibbeha County between Columbus and Starkville, Mississippi. In addition, there are several pyramidal mound sites along the upper Tombigbee River proper south of Columbus, Mississippi, with only one mound each (Coleman Mound, Butler Mound, and two Chowder Springs Mounds). Partially as a result of almost no archaeological excavations at these river sites, possible political and temporal affiliations with one or both of the two sites that have seen limited investigation (Owl Creek and Lyon's Bluff) are undetermined. At least one pyramidal mound is also found farther south near the city of Macon, Mississippi. A prominent mound in that area is located on the south side of the Noxubee River near the southwest part of the city. The Owl Creek site, partly because of its relative closeness to a huge Mississippian settlement area located in Lowndes, Clay, and Oktibbeha Counties and the documented settlement of the eighteenth-century Chickasaw north of there, was once assumed by lay people to be one of the sites visited by the famous Hernando De Soto Spanish expedition in 1540 (discussed below), but evidence for such has yet to be found. In fact, recent acquisition of a number of radiocarbon dates strongly indicates that the mounds were built prior to A.D. 1200 and abandoned by A.D. 1400. In any case, it seems reasonable to assume that at least some of the documented Chickasaw discussed below were descendants of at least some of the people who were affiliated with some of these mound sites.[7]

A site likely occupied in 1540 is the aforementioned Lyon's Bluff site on the upper course of Tibbee Creek (called Line Creek in that area), which has produced native ceramics typical of the fifteenth and sixteenth centuries and where a piece of orange micaceous earthenware typically associated with the sixteenth-century Spanish colonies of the circum-Caribbean area has been recovered. At Harmon Lake just to the north of Lyon's Bluff was found a non-Indian artifact strongly resembling Damascene metal clothing buttons documented to have been in common use in Europe during the sixteenth century. This and other archaeological evidence indicate that the core area of the mid-sixteenth century Chickasaw was probably located on the west side of the Tombigbee River within a general area formed by drawing imaginary lines connecting the present-day cities of Columbus, Okolona, Starkville, and Macon, Mississippi.[8]

At the time of the De Soto expedition, the Mississippian chiefdom system was still distinctively in place, although it was probably in decline in some areas of the southeast visited by the Spanish. Although the Chickasaw were apparently no longer maintaining, building, or using Mississippian mounds by the beginning of the eighteenth century, trader James Adair recorded that they had a word, "Aiambo Chaah," for their "old round earthen forts." Because most early writers described Indian mound sites as "forts," Adair's reference is undoubtedly to artificial earthen mounds or defensive earthworks built by the Mississippian ancestors of the Chickasaw. The defensive earthworks usually encircled compact villages or ceremonial centers possessing one or more pyramidal mounds. Such applies at least to the Cotton Gin Port mound site on the west side of the Tombigbee River in present-day Monroe County, Mississippi, and the aforementioned Owl Creek site. Although the encircling earthworks are now obliterated at these sites by cultivation and erosion, they were still present through the late nineteenth century, as attested to by early white visitors such as Dr. Rush Nutt, who described the Owl Creek Mounds and earthworks in 1805. Although definite archaeological evidence has yet to be discovered, quite possibly the Lyon's Bluff site also originally had an encircling earthwork prior to modern cultivation and resulting erosion. An early visitor to the Chickasaw, Englishman Thomas Nairne, recorded in 1708 that some "old men here show the way [the Spaniards of 1540] Entered and Departed out of their Nation with the Hill where they Encampt." Unfortunately, he gave no indication as to even the general location of this hill.[9]

After wintering in present-day Tallahassee, Florida, among the Apalachee, the De Soto expedition left there in early 1540 and traversed parts of the present-day states of Georgia, South Carolina, North Carolina, Tennessee, and Alabama prior to spending the winter of 1540–1541 among the Chicasa/Chickasaw on the Tombigbee River in present-day northeast Mississippi. Arriving at the river in December, the populous expedition was confronted across the water by Indians, but no communication ensued. The Spaniards built rafts and later crossed the river, arriving after dark of the same day at an abandoned village called "Chicaca" by the Spaniards. This village, situated on a ridge, may have contained one or more pyramidal mounds, but the sketchy writings of the chroniclers do not mention any. The chief of the "Chicaca province," which had a dispersed population, was brought to meet with De Soto by attendants carrying him on a litter. The chief presented little dogs, rabbits, deer hides, and blankets to the Spaniards, and other Chicacas brought many rabbits and other foods in the days following. While encamped at the village, the almost 500 Spaniards undoubtedly put a strain on the food resources of the Chicaca and as well those of another group called the "Saquechuma," which was subject to the former, thus indicating that a chiefdom existed. Because the Saquechuma would not pay tribute to the Chicaca, some Chicacas and a force of Spaniards marched to a village of the former but found it abandoned; the Chicacas then set it afire. Little else was recorded about the four-month stay of the Spaniards, but when preparing to continue the expedition De Soto "asked" the probably already disgruntled Chicaca chief for 200 people (undoubtedly both men and women) to help carry baggage and perform other jobs (earlier, De Soto had punished a Chicaca for stealing pigs by cutting off his hands). In early March the Chicaca launched a ferocious night attack on the camp, burned its structures, killed about twelve Spaniards, wounded many others, and killed or captured as many as sixty horses (some died in their burning stalls) and 300 to 400 pigs. Only one Chicaca warrior was killed; he was said to have been lanced by De Soto. Apparently fear of loose horses running all about during the mayhem of battle caused the Chicaca warriors to retreat, believing that Spaniards were riding them. Thereby the expedition was saved from total destruction, as admitted to by the chroniclers of the expedition. The army then moved less than two miles away to another village called Chicacilla, where an encampment was established on an adjacent slightly sloping hillside. The Chicaca chief had lived at Chicacilla prior to its apparent abandonment after the battle.[10] Because the chief had lived here, this village was more likely to have had a pyramidal mound or mounds than the first. The Lyon's Bluff site may well have been Chicacilla.

At Chicacilla the Spaniards repaired as best they could their weapons burned in the battle and made new shields, saddles, and lances, but before they could leave the Chicaca territory, the Chicacas launched another attack. This time the Spaniards were alert and repulsed them with some loss of life. In April the expedition headed northwest toward the Mississippi River after camping for a few days at a nearby small village of the Alimamu, or Alibamu, a group apparently part of the Chicaca chiefdom. While there they ravaged the countryside for provisions. Soon after leaving the camp, however, they had to do battle at a palisade fort of the Alimamu, which was captured. The expedition escaped from the area to continue its exploration for two more years on the west side of the Mississippi River.[11]

The Spaniards left behind a Chickasaw culture whose participants, as a result of meeting the alien Spaniards, had a different perspective on themselves and their rigid social/political system, a circumstance that is speculated to have eventually resulted in notable changes. Devastating loss of life through the diseases introduced by the Spaniards is also speculated to have further altered the Mississippian system. The same was applicable to most other native American cultures encountered directly or indirectly by the De Soto expedition. Just as the American civil war disrupted the cotton/slavery social system of the southern United States in the nineteenth century, European contact and its negative effects are believed to have contributed greatly to the disruption of Mississippian society. In both cases a more egalitarian society eventually evolved.[12]

In the 144 years following the De Soto expedition, during which there were no European incursions into present-day northeast Mississippi, Chickasaw society underwent the changes mentioned above, and the primary settlement area shifted northward to the headwater creeks of the Tombigbee River (Figure 1). By 1690 the southernmost village or settlement area was Yaneka, as recorded by English trader James Adair. This settlement was primarily located in present-day southeastern Pontotoc County on Chiwapa Creek (earlier labeled Yaneka Creek on French maps) and probably also on the nearby much smaller Tubbalubba Creek in present-day Lee County. According to Adair, Yaneka was the habitation area first settled by the Chickasaw upon moving into the upper Tombigbee River drainage. The other villages were located to the northeast on present-day Old Town Creek and its northwest-oriented tributaries of Coonewah, Little Coonewah, and Kings Creeks in present-day Lee County in the northernmost part of the Black Prairie physiographic zone that extends south into Monroe, Chickasaw, Clay, Oktibbeha, and Noxubee Counties and on into Alabama.[13] At this time the tribal name was usually spelled "Chickasah" or "Chickasaw" by the Europeans.

Prior to the Baron de Crenay map of 1733, which first located most or all of the villages, habitation locations in the upper Tombigbee River basin had not been recorded with any significant specificity, but many names had been recorded by 1702. The earliest known list of Chickasaw villages or towns appears on a map of the Mississippi Valley by Vicenzo Coronelli in 1684. These villages/towns, some of which are recognizable in later lists, were Fabatchaous (Falatchao), Malata (Amalata), Archebophoni (Apeony?), Totchinaske (Tonasqui), Chichafalara (Choukafalya), Ontcha Patafa, Pakaha (Ackia?), and Chik-oualika (Chuckalissa). Of interest is the apparent absence of the Yaneka settlement discussed by Adair, who may have rendered the name incorrectly. In 1702 Pierre Le Moyne d'Iberville listed eighteen villages, some of which were undoubtedly minor subdivisions of major habitation locales. Most do not subsequently appear in historical records. A total of 588 houses are tabulated for the eighteen villages. In another 1702 document d'Iberville stated that in addition to the main Chickasaw settlement the "Chicacha have additional people on the Ouabache [Wabash] River, in two villages where they have about 120 men." In those days, before an understanding had been acquired of the various confluences of the many streams and rivers, the Ohio River was often referred to as the Wabash River, and sometimes the Tennessee River was referred to as the Wabash as well. In this case the Tennessee is probably the river addressed. According to a relation from five traveling Canadians in 1701, there was a "Chicacha" village on the Wabash, which in this case was definitely the Tennessee. Also, a map dated 1701 by Guillaume de Lisle shows four unnamed "Petit village des Chicachas" below villages of other Indian tribes on the Tennessee, apparently in present-day north Alabama. Another map by de Lisle dated 1703 is similar but shows only two unnamed villages that are labeled similarly to those on the 1701 map. Significantly, both of these maps and a third (apparently prepared prior to 1697), which shows no "Chickasaw" villages on the Tennessee, depict the Chickasaw settlement in present-day northeast Mississippi. Probably the mysterious "villages" on the Tennessee were actually base camps occupied intermittently by Chickasaw hunters. Some of the eighteen village names reported by d'Iberville could be applicable to these possible camps or villages. Possibly the occupants of the villages on the Tennessee River were not actually Chickasaw, for this name also appears among other Muskhogean Indian groups. For example, a village of Choctaw-affiliated people living near the Gulf Coast was called Chickasahay.[14]

Choctaw research by Patricia Galloway led her to contend in two publications that the Chickasaw had not yet moved into the Lee–southeast Pontotoc County area by 1700. However, her contention is based on what I consider a flawed interpretation of where Frenchman Henri de Tonti visited the Chickasaw in 1702 after traveling from Mobile Bay. She had used Tonti's leagues traveled per day, as recorded by him, to calculate where certain natural features, Indian sites, and other places were located, including his northernmost point of travel, the Chickasaw villages. Using 2.5 miles to a league, as Galloway had done, my subsequent figuring of the Tonti route based on my previous research placed the historic period Chackchiuma Old Fields in the Starkville-Columbus area and the Chickasaw villages no farther south than present-day adjacent southern Lee and Pontotoc Counties, whereas she had placed the Chackchiuma

Old Fields some forty miles south of there in Kemper County, Mississippi, and the Chickasaw villages in Clay County, some forty miles south of present-day Lee County.[15]

By the turn of the eighteenth century the Chickasaw villages appear to have been scattered over a large area of the extreme northern part of the Black Prairie, which terminates just north of present-day Tupelo in Lee County. Thomas Nairne wrote from the villages in 1708 that the "Chicasaw Tribe at present consists of about 700 men devided in 8 villages, the chief whereof is that of Hollatchatroe."[16] Nairne went on to say that the villages were located within fifteen miles of the head of navigation on the Tombigbee, and he described the country as being "pleasant open forests of oake chesnuts and hickery so intermixt with savannas as if it were a made lanskape. These savanas are not perfectly Levell, like our's in Carolina, but full of gentle Ascents, which yet are not too steep for the plough, on the Top of these knowlls live the Chicasaws, their houses a Gunn or pistole shot asunder, with their improved ground peach and plum trees about them."[17] The fifteen miles mentioned by Nairne with regard to the head of navigation on the Tombigbee is significant in that all early historic documents and maps that mention this place locate it just below the fork of the Tombigbee River and its western branch, present-day Old Town Creek, on which most of the Chickasaw resided. The documented southern end of the main part of the Chickasaw settlement in the Tupelo area west of Old Town Creek is about fifteen miles from the fork, and the site of the southernmost part of the settlement on present-day Chiwapa Creek, Yaneka, is about seventeen miles slightly northwest of the fork.

A dispersed configuration of the Chickasaw settlements apparently continued until the early 1720s when frequent attacks from the Choctaw to the south began. For mutual protection the villages were thereafter consolidated into a relatively small area in present-day Lee County that became known as the Chickasaw Old Fields on present-day Old Town Creek and its tributaries (Figures 4 and 5). This entailed the abandonment or relocation of outlying settlements such as Yaneka. The sizes of the villages were also reduced because the previous dispersed configurations of the houses that made up the village areas were not conducive to safety from surprise attacks. Moreover, by 1724 the Chickasaw population had been significantly reduced as a result of European diseases and intensified warfare, the latter also a repercussion from European interactions. Thus clusters of villages came to characterize the now consolidated Chickasaw settlement. After the French-Chickasaw-Choctaw wars ended in the mid-1760s, the settlement retained its same general location on the Old Town Creek drainage until the late 1790s. The groups of villages that made up the settlement were called towns by the English. As an example with regard to village constriction, archaeological evidence shows that the Choukafalya

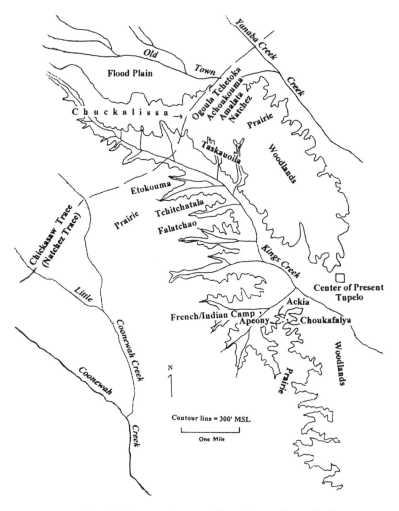

4. Locations of the Chickasaw settlement villages by 1736 (by author)

settlement/town area in present-day south Tupelo had extended for at least three miles south from the compact village by that name that was present by 1736. Such was also the case with the Chuckalissa settlement/town in northwest Tupelo, which had earlier extended northwest into the edge of present-day northeast Pontotoc County.[18]

The Chickasaw people who lived upon this land were generally described in glowing terms by nearly all of the Europeans who associated with them in the eighteenth century. Le Page du Pratz, for example, said, "The men have regular features, well shaped and neatly dressed; they are fierce, and have a high opinion of themselves." Jean-Bernard Bossu stated that the "Chickasaws are tall,

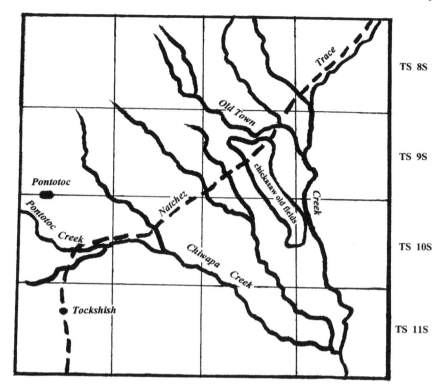

TS 8S

TS 9S

TS 10S

TS 11S

Trace

Old Town

Pontotoc

chickasaw old fields

Creek

Natchez

Pontotoc Creek

Chiwapa Creek

Tockshish

5. Pen tracing of part of Henry Lusher's U.S. Land Office survey map of 1835, showing the Chickasaw Old Fields (by author, after copy at Mississippi Department of Archives and History)

well made, and of an unparalleled courage." John F. D. Smyth opined that they "are a very brave and respectable nation, not for their numbers, for they are few, but for their virtue, and unconquerable spirit." With regard to Chickasaw women, Major Robert Rogers described them in 1762 as "far exceeding in beauty any other nation to the southward," and with regard to the men and possibly the women also, he wrote that they were "tall, well-shaped and handsome featured." Thomas Nairne, writing in 1708, stated that the "Chickasaws are to the Talapoosies as men of Quality among us are to the peasants, look much more brisk, airy and full of life . . . ; add to that both sexes of the Chickasaws are proper handsom people, exceeding the others."[19]

Although Chickasaw adult males are normally perceived as the military defenders of the homeland and the only sex to engage in attacks against an enemy in their territory and in external raids, the participation of women in such activities seems to have at least occasionally occurred in the eighteenth century.

In 1708, Thomas Nairne reported the following: "The Chickasaws ussually carry 10 or Twelve Young women with them to the Warrs, whose business is to sing a fine Tune, dureing any action. If their own men succeed, they praise them highly and Degrade the Enimy but if they give Back [retreat] the singers alter their praises into reproaches, Thus changing notes according as their party advance or give way." During a French and Indian attack on a Chickasaw village in 1736, singing women with hatchets in their hands are reported to have led the reinforcements from a nearby village. In the late eighteenth century women sometimes, at least, were still accompanying men on war parties, as illustrated by documentation that the wife, named Wayther, of mixed-blood William Colbert always went with him to war and on other travels.[20] Thus Chickasaw women were valuable in boosting the morale of the warriors, in addition to their numerous other roles and tasks of bearing and raising children, planting, tending, and harvesting crops, fishing, gathering wild plant foods and firewood, cooking, making clay pottery and wooden baskets, and so on.

Prior to 1734, according to Le Page du Pratz, five Yazoo River tribes had become so depopulated that they joined the Chickasaw and "make now but one nation with them." These were the Yazoo, Koroa, Chackchiuma, Ofogoula, and Tapoussa. Du Pratz was not entirely accurate, however, for not all of the populations of some of these tribes joined the Chickasaw, especially those of the Chackchiuma, Ofogoula, and Koroa. By 1736 the northwest villages constituted the area known by the French as the "large prairie" and those located to the southeast were in the "small prairie." The three villages in the southern division, or town, of the large prairie were named Tchitchatala, Falatchao, and Etokouma. Those in the northern division, collectively called the town of Chuckalissa by the Chickasaw and English, were Amalata, Taskaouilo, Achoukouma, and Ogoula Tchetoka. Chuckalissa was also referred to as "great town" by 1771, as recorded by Bernard Romans. It later came to be called Big Town and Old Town as well. Following dispersal of the Natchez Indians by the French in 1730, a sizable contingent of that nation was given asylum by the Chickasaw. Most of them became established in a separate village for which no name other than "Natchez" has been recorded; it was located just east of Amalata in the large prairie (Figures 6 and 7). Numerous Natchez pottery sherds have been recovered on the east side of the large prairie in the approximate area where the Natchez village is shown on the de Batz map of 1737. By 1736 the compact small prairie town was made up of the villages named Choukafalya, Ackia, and Apeony. This town was in the northern part of a once larger settlement referred to by Adair as "the Long House." Eventually the area exclusively came to be called Long Town. The prairie area in which all these villages lay was called the Chickasaw Old Fields as early as 1752 and was delineated and labeled as such on the official Chickasaw Cession survey map dated 1835 (Figure 5). All of

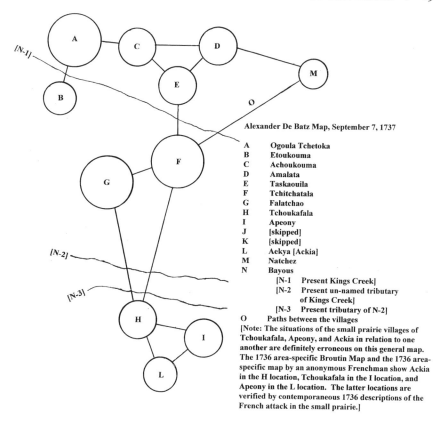

[N-1]

Alexander De Batz Map, September 7, 1737

A   Ogoula Tchetoka
B   Etoukouma
C   Achoukouma
D   Amalata
E   Taskaouila
F   Tchitchatala
G   Falatchao
H   Tchoukafala
I   Apeony
J   [skipped]
K   [skipped]
L   Aekya [Ackia]
M   Natchez
N   Bayous
        [N-1   Present Kings Creek]
        [N-2   Present un-named tributary
                of Kings Creek]
        [N-3   Present tributary of N-2]
O   Paths between the villages
[Note: The situations of the small prairie villages of
Tchoukafala, Apeony, and Ackia in relation to one
another are definitely erroneous on this general map.
The 1736 area-specific Broutin Map and the 1736 area-
specific map by an anonymous Frenchman show Ackia
in the H location, Tchoukafala in the I location, and
Apeony in the L location. The latter locations are
verified by contemporaneous 1736 descriptions of the
French attack in the small prairie.]

6. The Chickasaw settlement villages in the large and small prairies by 1736 (by author, after the 1737 Alexander de Batz map in Archives Nationales, Paris, France)

these towns in present-day Lee County are now archaeologically documented,
and portions have been infrequently excavated by professional archaeologists
over the years from 1935 to the present.[21] Professional excavations, however, no
longer occur except with the consent of the present Chickasaw government in
Oklahoma when a site is threatened by development. Digging of graves by local
artifact collectors in search of valuables, however, has been ongoing regularly
for over a hundred years. Such digging is now illegal, but it continues.

Of interest is that after focused historical and archaeological studies conducted in the 1930s and 1980s regarding the specific location of the early to late
eighteenth-century Chickasaw settlement had been completed, a unique primary source never used before by amateur or professional historians and archaeologists came out of obscurity to verify the accuracy of the studies. Totally
supporting the conclusions of the location studies is the following quote from
Malcolm McGee, a white resident of the Chickasaw nation between 1767 and

7. Present view of approximate site of the Natchez village, looking south from new Highway 78 (by author)

1848, who served as Chickasaw interpreter for dozens of years after becoming an adult: "The 'Old Fields' lay on the Southern bank of Old Town Creek, stretching from some four or 5 miles above [northwest] to down four or five miles below Long Town—making it some 13 or 14 miles long by about 4 broad, with here & there a copse of wood to dot the wide & long extended expanse. Long Town was 4 miles down Town Creek from Old Town, & the Post Oak Town was about the same distance in a southerly direction on Coppertown viz Techatulla creek [present-day Coonewah Creek]."[22]

The village called Achoukouma by 1737 may have originated as a result of the documented incorporation of part of the Chackchiuma, whose population and settlement became fragmented in the early eighteenth century. Romans reported that the "Ashuck hooma" village name meant "red grass." The name spelled this way indeed means red grass, but the original meaning of the village name could have been "red crawfish," the English translation of the Chackchiuma Indian tribal name. This is supported, in fact, by the de Crenay map of 1733, which spells the village name "Chochuma." Romans also states in his book that in 1771 all the villages of the Chickasaw were in an irregular area about one mile and a half in length, but this is undoubtedly an error on his part. He probably only meant to be referring to the Chuckalissa/Old Town settlement. In fact, the description is contradicted in notations on the Roberts map of circa 1773, which was made using data obtained by Romans. The notation states that the villages "do not take up more than 2 1/2 miles in length & about half that Breadth."[23] Still, the areal size was somewhat understated.

That all of the upper Tombigbee River Chickasaw villages were in the present-day Tupelo area by 1736 is proved by French governor Bienville's statement that the Natchez village in the large prairie was only one league (about 2.5 to 3 miles) from Choukafalya and Ackia in the small prairie. The Natchez village was only a short distance from Ogoula Tchetoka, as shown on the de Batz map of 1737 (Figure 6). Moreover, and as substantiating proof, a map drawn in 1740 by Ignace Francois Broutin, Louisiana's chief engineer and surveyor, shows one or more of the large prairie villages and the route of d'Artaguette's attack on them in 1736. As translated by Joseph Peyser, who brought the map out of obscurity in the late 1980s, a notation along a watercourse just south of the villages shown states "small branch of the Mobile River which passes between these villages and those attacked in 1736." This small stream is present-day Kings Creek, which indeed flows southeast from the large prairie to the north side of the small prairie and on to its junction with Old Town Creek in present-day east Tupelo.[24]

In addition to various writers of history in the nineteenth century and first half of the twentieth century, even some modern professional historians, including Arrell Gibson (*The Chickasaws*), have presented highly erroneous locations for the early Chickasaw villages. The cause in all cases was reliance on an undocumented statement by H. B. Cushman in 1899. In his poorly documented writings in *History of the Choctaw, Chickasaw, and Natchez Indians,* Cushman made the totally erroneous statement that "Pakitakohlih," supposedly the original version of the present name Pontotoc, "was a town known to the French . . . by the name Chickasahha" and afterward to the English as "Chickasaw Old Town" and then to the Americans as "The Chickasaw Old Fields." As if that were not enough, he further stated that it was "the same 'Old Town' in which De Soto wintered with his army in 1540." In fairness to Cushman, I must point out that he conceived these notions without having seen pertinent early French and English maps and numerous eighteenth-century French, English, and Spanish documents and without knowledge of modern archaeological data that prove that the Chickasaw had no villages until the late eighteenth century in that part of present-day Pontotoc County. These mistakes have been perpetuated in subsequent historical literature even to the present by history writers unaware of the numerous modern anthropological/ archaeological studies of the Mississippi Chickasaw. Moreover, with regard to Gibson's 1971 history of the Chickasaw, both published and unpublished twentieth-century scholarly archaeological and historical research that contradicts Cushman and others was either overlooked or ignored. Gibson's work contains other frequent misinterpretations and factual errors but is otherwise a scholarly overview of Chickasaw history. Unfortunately, because Gibson's history is a modern work, his erroneous locations for the Chickasaw are being assumed correct and repeated by scholars unfamiliar with some of the pertinent sources.[25]

Apparently associated with reopening of official trade with the English following the disruptive Yamasee War to the east in 1715, a group of Chickasaws migrated in about 1717 to near Fort Moore (on the site of an old Shawnee village called "Savannah Town") on the South Carolina side of the Savannah River. Motivated by the desire for protection of the western part of the colony, the South Carolina government encouraged Chickasaw migrations to near the New Windsor township area (where Fort Moore was located), and in 1722 proposed that the entire Chickasaw nation "settle at the place they desire, and we will assist them with all the corn we can from the Savannah Town." Others indeed soon migrated to the Savannah River, but the main nation rejected the proposal, stating that they resolved "to maintain themselves on that Spot of Ground, where their fore Fathers had kindled their Fires & laid their Bones for so many generations." The second group of migrants, led by a chief known as Squirrel King, formed a separate village about ten miles from the first at the mouth of Horse Creek. In 1739 the South Carolina government set aside 21,774 acres for Chickasaw settlement in New Windsor township. By 1748 the second group was the largest, comprising about seventy men and their families. The first group was composed of about twenty men and their families.[26]

The Chickasaws who moved to South Carolina were undoubtedly some or all of that part of the population who had found intolerable the Choctaw and northern Indian attacks instigated by the French in Louisiana and in New France in the region of what is now southern Canada and the northern United States. Distressed by the killings associated with the conflicts, these Chickasaws saw South Carolina as a refuge far removed from the violence. That their leader was called Squirrel King is significant in this regard. According to Thomas Nairne, writing in 1708, the Chickasaw had a custom whereby any family so inclined could choose a man from another family as its protector. This man was nearly always an esteemed and respected warrior, who after being chosen for the duty was expected to take steps to ward off potential harm to the family by other Chickasaws or by people from other tribes. Upon being bestowed with this duty, he was thereafter referred to as a "Fane Mingo or Squirrell king."[27] Thus it seems clear that the noted leader of the South Carolina Chickasaws named Squirrel King had been persuaded by at least the second group of migrants to accept the invitations of the colony whites and lead them out of the main nation to a safer location. Alternatively, perhaps the Squirrel King himself instigated migration of the family he had been chosen to protect. It is possible that some of the migrants were from the same family as the Squirrel King.

Some of the Carolina Chickasaws became disgruntled and moved across the river into Georgia, where a man named Roger Lacy "had run out a little town near him" for their habitation in gratitude for the Chickasaws' helping him establish the town of Augusta by assisting in building a fort in 1737. This was not a permanent move; a disastrous flood in 1741 is probably what caused them to move back to South Carolina. Later, all of Squirrel King's Chickasaws moved from Horse Creek to the Ogeechee River in Georgia, but all except ten returned in 1747. However, by 1752 and as late as 1762 the eastern Chickasaws were living about ten miles below Augusta on the Georgia side of the river at a place called New Savannah. In 1758 an aging Chickasaw leader called "The Doctor" by the English stated that they had exchanged their land with Lachlan McGillivray and were then occupying and planting land that belonged to him in both Georgia and South Carolina, the location in Georgia being at New Savannah. South Carolina officials were perturbed over this unauthorized and unfair exchange of land (the Chickasaw got only 1,000 acres, 500 on each side of the river). In 1756, McGillivray had caused the land he obtained from the Chickasaw to be surveyed and had allotted parcels to other white men besides himself. Edmond Atkin, a colony official, scolded the Chickasaw for exchanging so much land for so little and tried unsuccessfully to recover the Horse Creek property by canceling McGillivray's original title. By 1766, the Georgia settlement may have been abandoned; some or all Chickasaws were occupying South Carolina land at that time. At least some of the eastern Chickasaw moved to the Creek territory, where they resided for a time before all or some of them joined the main Chickasaw in present-day northeast Mississippi. Although John Swanton determined that some eastern Chickasaw joined an old ally in the Creek country, the Kashita, possibly others went to the Chickasaw village called the Breed Camp near the Coosa River (discussed below). In early 1772 a Chickasaw group possibly from South Carolina was in the process of making a settlement in the same general area as the Breed Camp, as discussed by David Tait: "Chickasaws are making a settlement on the side of a creek called Caimullga about 15 miles north from this [a Natchez and Creek village called "Natchie"] and falling into the Coosa River at the Chickasaw Trading path." Some Chickasaws, however, could have earlier (prior to 1767) left South Carolina and founded the mysterious settlement located at a place on the north side of the Tennessee River in present-day Madison County, Alabama, that was later referred to (in the late eighteenth century and early nineteenth century) as "Chickasaw Old Fields." The Chickasaw living there had been attacked by Cherokees, supposedly in 1766. Although the attack was repulsed, the Chickasaws evidently abandoned the site because of continuing hostilities from that nearby tribe. As discussed in Chapter 5, however, the old fields on the Tennessee may have been settled earlier by Chickasaws documented to have migrated to the Cherokee domain in the 1740s and 1750s to escape the violence occasioned by war with the Choctaw and French. The Chickasaw were still claiming that area, as were the Cherokee, as late as 1805; in that year the former relinquished claim to it. Efforts in the first half of the 1790s by Chickasaw leaders to reclaim some of the old South Carolina property or be compensated for it were fruitless.[28]

Squirrel King apparently only maintained limited association with the main population in the interior. The western Chickasaw who chose to remain and bear the hardships of the conflicts with the Choctaw and other groups instigated by the French apparently had little or no respect for the colony Chickasaw who had abandoned their homeland. Governor Glenn of South Carolina stated in 1750 that the eastern Chickasaw who "live upon lands given them by this Province upon Savannah River and sometimes stroll over to the Georgia side . . . dare not return to their own Nation." The next year he stated, quite probably inaccurately, that they had been "banished [from] their own country." In 1756 after depletion of the western population as a result of war and disease, the headmen and warriors of the western Chickasaw requested that the South Carolina colony send back the eastern Chickasaws to help them "keep our lands from the French and their Indians." Such did not occur, although it is possible that some Chickasaws rejoined the nation.[29]

According to Edmond Atkin, writing in 1755, Squirrel King was "reputed to have killed more men with his own Hands, than any other Indian on the continent." This statement is probably much exaggerated, and another Atkin reference to Squirrel King that indicates he was the man "who opened the Indian War in 1715" seems to be totally unfounded. However, Atkin's contention that Squirrel King had "more Personal Weight and Authority than any other; his talks being listened to attentively by other Nations as well as his own" is probably true, but only with regard to the eastern Indians. Subchiefs under Squirrel King included Tuski Suki, Captain Coates, and Mingo Stobi (or "Mastobey"). All four of these men tried in mid-1746, with the blessing of the South Carolina House of Commons, to gain Crown approval for a visit to England on board a man-of-war.[30] They were apparently unsuccessful but support for such a journey by the House of Commons does reflect that the Chickasaw were considered valuable inhabitants of the colony.

The eastern Chickasaw indeed proved valuable to the South Carolina colony. In 1727 Squirrel King and his warriors provided significant aid to South Carolina in warring with the Yamasee. In 1740, during a declared war between Spain and Britain (War of Jenkins' Ear), they assisted the English in a military campaign against and siege of Spanish St. Augustine, during which an English general was highly critical of Squirrel King for presenting him the head of a Spaniard. In 1742 Squirrel King and his warriors aided in the repulse of a Spanish attack on Fort Frederic in Georgia. According to one report they were the major factor in the victory. The eastern Chickasaw also occasionally became enmeshed in Indian conflicts, the Cherokee, Yamasee, Shawnee, and Mohawk being their most common adversaries. During the Cherokee War of the late 1750s and early 1760s, trader James Adair prepared to lead eastern Chickasaws against the Cherokee but withdrew his services when he could not obtain orders to march ahead of the colony army. These Chickasaws, however, joined eleven of the western Chickasaw under the command of Captain James Colbert, a trader who had lived among them since childhood. In 1761 the Chickasaw warriors joined South Carolina governor James Grant's force of regulars and other Indian allies. The forces attacked and destroyed about fifteen middle Cherokee towns on the upper branches of the Tennessee River.[31]

By 1748 the once highly respected Squirrel King had succumbed to the degrading influences of the English and become a drunkard. The aged leader had virtually lost control of the eastern Chickasaw, and one Englishman called them at that time, perhaps unjustifiably, "a pack of renegados." Squirrel King was still alive in 1755 but apparently died prior to the end of 1757. In 1758 the principal leaders were Mingo Mastobey (or "Stoby") and W. B. Nahettaly (or "Nathlettoby"), but "Old Doctor," who also had been born in the original homeland, was described as "headman" in 1757 and as a "beloved man" in 1758 (Mingo Mastobey was referred to as a beloved man in that year and Nathlettoby as the "head warrior"). Also in 1758, Tuccatoby was referred to as the "king" (head chief). According to Swanton and historian C. J. Milling (*Red Carolinians*), a man named Succatabee had "succeeded" the Squirrel King and was head chief in 1765; this man was undoubtedly the same as Tuccatoby.[32]

Chickasaws first moved among the Coosas in the Upper Creek territory in the first half of the eighteenth century. Their Coosa River village, called the Breed Camp by the English, apparently originated as a result of a late 1717 South Carolina government request that the Chickasaw "settle a Trading House, at a Place called the Coosatees . . . which Trade the English might manage and furnish from Savano Town." Because the word *breed* meant mixed-bloods at the time, the inhabitants were primarily the offspring of Chickasaw women and white traders. Consent of the Upper Creeks for the establishment of the trading camp was undoubtedly obtained first. Although proposed in 1717, it may not have materialized until about 1741. In that year, trader Thomas Andrews assisted "in removing some of the Chickasaws to the Coosaws in the Upper Creeks." The name "Breed Camp" began to appear in documents after 1741. It was located east of the river on the noted Upper Creek Trading Path, also called the Chickasaw Trading Path (Figure 1). Anthropologist Charles H. Fairbanks's

research located the village "in the region between modern Talladega and Sy-
lacauga, Alabama . . . on or near the Coosa River." According to the William
Bonar map of 1757, it was several miles east of the Coosa River. In 1757 the chief
was Mucklesa Mingo (possibly a full blood). Other headmen and leading warriors included John Pettycrew (sometimes spelled "Pettycrou" or "Pettygrew"),
William Bean, Ricar (or J. W.) Kowle, Moule Minggs (Mingo?), Opoy Mingo,
and Pastabe Mingo. A trader named John Brown, son of a white man and a
Cherokee, also resided there, at least intermittently. In 1755 Edmond Atkin
wrote that these Chickasaws, consisting of about eighty men and additional
women and children, did not concern themselves with Creek affairs and that
their chief service to the English was "guarding our Traders up and down
in time of any Danger between their Nation and the Creek Country." It is
probable that the Breed Camp village is the "upper western town" in the Creek
territory referred to by Adair as "Ooe-asah." According to Adair, who refers to a
post-1744 visit, that village was settled by Chickasaw and Natchez. This makes
perfect sense, for some of the refugee Natchez who had first joined the Chickasaw after the former's dispersion by the French in 1730 and 1731, later moved to
the Creek territory (see discussions in Chapter 5). John Swanton recorded that
historian Henry S. Halbert suspected that Adair's Ooe-asah was really "Wiha
Ansha," which meant "home of emigrants," and that the village was the Breed
Camp. A 1757 report revealed that some of the Chickasaw living on the Coosa
River moved to near Fort Massac in the Illinois territory.[33]

The Breed Camp Chickasaw and the eastern Chickasaw apparently maintained a cordial relationship that seems to have been cemented by the fact that
the groups had in common their separation from the main nation, in addition
to blood ties. In 1749, for example, James Adair reported that a woman from
the Breed Camp on her way to Charlestown was the daughter of Squirrel King.
Milling (*Red Carolinians*) asserts that "they were at all times on the best of
terms with one another."[34] There indeed seem to be no records to the contrary.

The journal of trader John Buckles illuminates the use of the Breed Camp
as a way station for English traders heading to the Chickasaw settlements on
the upper Tombigbee River. Buckles wrote in his journal on January 18, 1754,
that he had arrived that day at the Breed Camp where he awaited some traders
to come down from the main Chickasaw settlement to assist him to that location. The traders and forty Chickasaws arrived on March 12 when Buckles was
told by one of the assistant traders, Francis Underwood, that they were there
to assist him "up to the Breed with the presents" (Buckles was probably referring to the main settlement in saying "to the Breed"). On the 23rd, Buckles and
the group proceeded to the Chickasaw settlements, where they arrived safely
on April 8. Also under that date he wrote that three days before he arrived "in
the Breed" a popular warrior leader named "the Jockey" had died. Buckles

stated that he was always "a Friend to all white people and is much missed in this Nation."[35]

John Swanton presents almost no information on the Breed Camp but states that a 1761 census showed it "was already said to be broken up." There is a good possibility that at least part of the Breed Camp Chickasaw moved to the upper Tombigbee settlement area between 1757 and 1761. Such could explain the presence of a separate settlement of mixed-bloods depicted on some late eighteenth- and early nineteenth-century maps that show the Chickasaw settlement area. The earliest map, by Victor Collot, dates to the last four years of the eighteenth century. It shows a "Half Breed Settlement" on the upper reaches of Old Town Creek northwest of the two main early settlements; the latter are labeled "Great Village of the Chickasaws" (Old Town/Big Town) and "Long Town." A later map, entitled "Mississippi Territory," may have been drawn with the aid of the Collot map. It displays a loose concentration of five triangles labeled "Half Breed Towns." The location north of the early main settlements at present-day Tupelo is generally similar to that on the Collot map, and the site is shown between the upper reaches of Old Town Creek and 20 Mile Creek, which is what the Tombigbee River was called farther south. Other early maps show an "Underwood Village" on the west side of Bear Creek, also north of the Tupelo settlement area.[36] Possibly all of these maps are attempting to show the same habitations but fail to place them in exactly the same area as a result of the imprecise nature of such maps drawn before instrument land surveys were made. Possibly the "Half Breed Settlements" shown on the late eighteenth-century and early nineteenth-century maps are a result of mostly mixed-blood Carolina and Breed Camp Chickasaws moving to the homeland before and soon after the beginning of the Revolutionary War. Interestingly, the Chickasaw settlement at the so-called "Chickasaw Old Fields" on the north side of the Tennessee River in present-day northeast Alabama is fairly well documented to have been abandoned after an attack by the Cherokee in about 1766.[37] As mentioned above, these Chickasaws may have represented a movement of part of the South Carolina population to the Tennessee River prior to the Revolutionary War. Thus, after becoming endangered by hostile Cherokees, these Chickasaws may have been responsible for at least part of the population living northward of present-day Tupelo by the late eighteenth century. However, as discussed in Chapter 11, these latter settlements could have resulted from a change in the Chickasaw settlement pattern of the early Old Town Creek population, which occurred in the late 1790s.

A new ethnic group became established in the upper Tombigbee area when runaway black slaves occasionally found refuge among the Chickasaw. Later, white traders and other white men residing there brought slaves into the nation to work their farms, afterward selling some slaves to the mixed-blood Chickasaws. Perhaps the primary source of the first Chickasaw-owned slaves was James Colbert, a white trader and resident of the nation since boyhood. He claimed to have owned 150 slaves in 1782. Another main source may have been the British commissary (agent) to the Chickasaw, John McIntosh, who possessed a plantation worked by slaves as early as 1772. Although records regarding slaves are scanty for the preremoval Chickasaw, researchers of the subject have concluded that most were owned by mixed-bloods during that period. However, a sizable number of full-bloods owned at least one or two. Records show that on the eve of removal in the 1830s, at least 1,156 slaves were represented among the total Chickasaw and black population of 6,380. The Chickasaws' slaves also endured the rigors of removal west of the Mississippi River. Unlike with the Creek and Seminole tribes, Chickasaw, Cherokee, and Choctaw sexual intermingling with slaves was rare during the preremoval period and this continued to be the case after removal.[38]

Although on rare occasions some Chickasaw black slaves were mistreated, the vast majority led better lives than those owned by whites elsewhere in the south. The mixed-blood and especially the few full-blood Chickasaw slave owners did not view slaves the same as did the typical white plantation owners outside the Indian territories. The relationship was more symbiotic in that daylight to sundown intensive labor was seldom demanded, causing some whites to refrain from buying slaves formerly belonging to Indians because they were considered spoiled. An ex-slave of the Chickasaw nation, for example, stated that he had not thought of himself as a slave because he felt free, did not have to work much, and always had food and clothing provided. By the late eighteenth century, many of the Chickasaw slaves were able to speak Chickasaw fluently and were found useful as interpreters by missionaries and other whites who visited the nation. Most of the missionaries to the Chickasaw also offered their Christian teachings to the slaves and obtained satisfactory responses.[39]

2
Down a Long Road

By the time France established a foothold along the Gulf Coast in 1699, the Muskhogean-speaking Chickasaw had for a number of years been directly associating with English traders coming into the nation from the Carolina colony. Earlier, however, the first known interior post–De Soto contact had been an encounter of two Chickasaws near the Mississippi River with members of the La Salle expedition down that river in 1682. Even earlier than that, European goods acquired by travel to the Spanish colony in Florida, as well as through Indian middlemen, were undoubtedly the first non-Indian-made materials seen by the Chickasaw since 1540. It is believed that English traders first made their way into the Chickasaw settlement about sixteen years after Henry Woodward visited the Westo Indians on the upper Savannah River in 1674, where he learned of the existence of other Indian tribes to the west, including the Chickasaw. In 1698 the first significant contact with the Tombigbee River Chickasaw since the De Soto expedition occurred when Thomas Welch and his party from South Carolina trekked all the way to the Mississippi River over a trail that came to be called the Upper Trading Path. Welch, a trader, left no known written account of his journey, but it became well documented on early French and English maps. The primary significance of Welch's activities was the establishment of a permanent and consistent trade with the Chickasaw. When the French came in 1699, therefore, they found direct English trade well entrenched, and they were somewhat appalled to discover that in addition to animal skins, trade in Indian slaves was a large part of the interaction. Supplied with guns by the English and motivated by financial rewards (in the form of goods), the Chickasaw began raiding numerous other Indian groups who lacked guns, primarily within a 200-mile radius, including the Choctaw to their south. This ugly and destructive slave trade instigated by the English was the beginning of the end for a number of Indian groups in the south, for the Chickasaw were not the only ones the English had induced to participate in it.[1]

Fascinated by the materials of the English traders, most of the Chickasaw accepted these strangers into their country without having the foresight to visualize the ordeal to which they would be subjected during the first half of the eighteenth century following the establishment of the French colony at Biloxi by Pierre Le Moyne d'Iberville. The Chickasaw were, with their acquiescence, to be exploited prior to 1760 by each of these European powers in a bitter struggle for territorial domination of the interior. Fortunately for the Chickasaw, as well as other groups, the Spanish never attempted to send traders into the Chickasaw country during the first decades of the eighteenth century and were distant enough, in Florida and far west of the Mississippi River, that direct abuse in the form of political warfare at their instigation did not occur. If the Spanish had been in a position to interact with the Chickasaw in a similar manner to that of the English and French, it is unlikely that their autonomy would have survived those tumultuous times.

Before entering into discussion of the late seventeenth-century and eighteenth-century Chickasaw-European interactions, a brief examination of the general nature of Chickasaw attitudes is appropriate. Although the Chickasaw have been characterized by nearly every European writer to come in contact with them as a very warlike people, it is doubtful that they were any more warlike than other southeastern groups prior to the coming of the Europeans in the late seventeenth century. In 1541 the Chickasaw had shown no warlike or "savage" disposition toward the De Soto expedition until the arrogant and ethnocentric Spaniards demanded that the chief furnish them 200 men and women to carry their baggage and perform other favors not specified by the chroniclers of the expedition. Confronted with this insulting demand, the Chickasaw then defended their rights against the strange, uninvited guests by attacking and almost destroying the expedition. Faced with insults and threats from Europeans 160 years later, the Chickasaw were again adamant in defending their rights against infringements from people possessing a system of behavior that made little sense to them. As acknowledged, sometimes unwittingly, by early European visitors to the Chickasaw, the latter's form of government and social system were, in fact, as logical, workable, and just as their own.[2] The values inherent in their religious and social systems were superior in many ways to those of the ethnocentric intruders. Realizing this, at least on a general level, the Chickasaw were also ethnocentric. Thus hatreds and conflicts were inevitable.

A seemingly incongruous attitude existed among the Chickasaw with regard to war and peace. Although the Chickasaw were depicted by the French as enjoying warfare and being a dangerous threat to them, we often find the "Great Chief of the Chickasaw" and other chiefs going out of their way to obtain peace for the nation. The reason for this paradox is directly related to the

Chickasaw form of government, as described by Thomas Nairne and others.[3] Without elaborating further, the following observation recorded in 1708 should suffice to explain why the great chief during the earliest years of European interaction seemed almost always to be in favor of peace while the nation in general was engaged in war.

> [B]y Law the kings [head chief's] power was Limetted to matters relating to peace. He was not to be guilty of shedding the Least Blood, was to oppose all projects of Distroying, was Vigorously to harrangue the Warriers, to keep firme to the Treaties of Peace with their Friends and Neighbours, was not so much as to be present at the Execution of an enemy, and might save hime [unless] the desire of revenge be ever so great. In short his duty obliged him by all wayes and means to promote peace and quiet, and to be a Counterpoise to the fury of the Warriors. He had likewayes charge of the other concerns of the nation, (except war).[4]

European influences, however, were instigating modifications with regard to the traditional role of the great chief. Nairne observed that the great chief of the Chickasaw in 1708, Fattalamee, had become so enthralled with the prospect of quick wealth through acquisition of Indian slaves for sale to English traders that he had "turned Warrior too, and proved as good a man hunter as the best of them." This modification of the role of the great chief, however, did not continue on a consistent basis throughout the entire remainder of the eighteenth century, as illustrated by Ymahatabe, a great chief in the 1730s and 1740s who adhered to the old custom (see following chapters). A dual top leadership developed, as illustrated by the observation of Bernard Romans in 1771: "Their Grand chief is called Opaya Mataha, and it is said he has killed his man upwards of forty times, for which great feate he has been raised to this nominal dignity."[5] Opaya Mataha was not the hereditary great chief, however, but rather the great war chief, an achieved position that had come to carry as much power and prestige, and often more, than the former. Thus by the mid-eighteenth century the head chief was a warrior who had achieved that status through war exploits, and the hereditary chief, although technically the same as the traditional "great chief," held the new title of "king," which obviously originated as a result of European influence. Apparently, however, the modifications described by Nairne in 1708 had created complexity with regard to claims to the king position. In 1765, Mingo Houma ("Red Chief" or "Red King"), an apparent war chief, was claiming to be the king of the Chickasaw and, in fact, was recognized as such by the Chickasaw despite opposition from some quarters. Successors, however, inherited the king position through him, and they were not also war chiefs. Apparently the king position was thereafter held by a peace chief of the ruling family, signifying a return to the pre-English custom for the highest ranking leader (see Chapters 6–12).

As already alluded to, the origin of the bitter hostilities in which the Chickasaw came to be embroiled during the first half of the eighteenth century can be traced directly to the influence of the early English traders, whose trading enterprises were unofficially sanctioned by the British government prior to 1707 and officially sanctioned and regulated after passage of the Indian Trade Regulation Act on July 19, 1707. Although the traders were initially only interested in acquiring animal skins, they eventually began to supply guns to the Chickasaw and to encourage them to capture Indian slaves from other groups for whom the English traders would barter for later sale in the West Indies. In addition to guns and dry goods such as blankets and fabrics, metal kettles, colorful glass beads, knives, iron hatchets, other tools, and ornaments made of silver, copper, and brass were supplied to the Chickasaw by the British officials and traders. The weapons, of course, enabled them to kill more deer and other game, as well as made them more proficient at capturing slaves prior to the end of the slave trade.[6]

The Choctaw, who were located only about sixty miles to the south, were a primary source for slaves and in the late seventeenth century and early part of the eighteenth century, hundreds of Choctaws were killed or captured as a result of Chickasaw slave raids in which the traders sometimes participated. In March 1702 Frenchmen first came face to face with some of the perpetrators of the slave trade. Henri de Tonti reported that two Englishmen were living at the Chickasaw villages, one of whom was away leading a force of 400 warriors to attack the Choctaw during his visit. The number of the attackers may have been overstated, as was likely the case when Jean-Baptiste Le Moyne, sieur de Bienville, governor of Louisiana, later reported that in autumn 1705 the English came "with three thousand Indians to raid the villages of the Choctaws who having been warned of it retired to the woods." After the Indians, probably allied Chickasaw, Alibama, Abeca, and Chackchiuma, ravaged the Choctaw houses and corn, the Choctaw attacked them on their return and killed "many of their men," a circumstance that the Choctaw attributed to the guns that the French had begun to supply them a few years earlier.[7] Thus began a Chickasaw-Choctaw war that continued almost uninterrupted for over fifty years.

By 1702 the Chickasaw were reported to have captured as many as 500 Choctaws through slave raids and to have killed an additional 1,800 people, losing 800 themselves. Although these figures were put in writing by the Louisiana government rather than by a French citizen, they were probably derived from exaggerated hearsay. For the Chickasaw to continue very long engaging in an activity that was costing them more people than they were obtaining would

have been somewhat foolish, but the desire for new wealth in the form of European trade goods could well have overridden such concerns. Indian groups,
however, were very conscious of the need to maintain their populations in order to preserve autonomy and independence, so there is no reason the Chickasaw, who had already undergone a reduction in population (mostly as a result
of European diseases),[8] would have been an exception. Perhaps a more realistic
figure for annual capture of Choctaws was the 100 reported sold to Carolina
merchants by traders among the Chickasaw about ten years later. In any case,
by 1714 the slave raids had ended but the bitterness of the Choctaw toward the
Chickasaw caused by the raids was kept alive by the French who would remind
the Choctaw of it in order to strengthen a so-called alliance they had made
with them. In April 1734, Bienville wrote:

> [W]hen one knows the history of this country one does not fail to know
> that we have a great advantage over the English in the minds of that na-
> tion [the Choctaw]. It is only a question of knowing how to make wise
> use of it by not letting them forget at all that in the past the English had
> armed the Chickasaw and used to send them to make raids on them in
> order to carry off wives and children whom they would buy—they were
> in that condition when I came to explore this country—and that we on
> the contrary have always protected them and put them in a position to
> defend themselves against their enemies.[9]

Perhaps related to Chickasaw aggressiveness in pursuit of slaves, an undocumented but prominent Chickasaw tradition concerns a determined attack by
them against Shawnee settlements located in the area encompassing the Duck
and Cumberland Rivers in present-day Tennessee. Said to have occurred between 1710 and 1714, the Chickasaw attack resulted in abandonment of the area
by the Shawnee, who supposedly fled across the Mississippi and Ohio Rivers.
The Chickasaw are said to have captured all of the Shawnee horses, which
were taken south to the Chickasaw settlements. The area is indeed rich in Mississippian through early historic native American cultural remains, but it was
unsettled by Indians after the early eighteenth century. Both the Cherokee and
Chickasaw considered it part of their hunting territory, and tradition has it that
the displaced Shawnee in present-day Kentucky also returned there to hunt.[10]

Despite the English having already established trade with the Chickasaw by
1699, the French attempted to compete with them. In 1702 Pierre Le Moyne
d'Iberville, a French explorer representing the king of Spain, sent Henri de
Tonti to the Chickasaw for the purpose of establishing rapport with them and
to bring to Mobile a Chickasaw peace delegation. In that same year d'Iberville
promised both the Chickasaw and Choctaw that a trading post would be es-

tablished halfway between them on the Tombigbee River. Apparently the trading post was not established, but by 1706 Bienville had promised the Chickasaw that he would have a "fort" built for them, the purpose of which would be to "maintain peace between [the Chickasaw] and the Choctaw and to prevent them from resorting to the English." Bienville was still planning to build the fort/trading post in 1707. There is no known documentation that it was ever built. Regardless, the French were greatly interested in maintaining peace with the Chickasaw in order to establish viable trade intercourse with them for political and financial benefits to the colony.[11]

During this early period of the Louisiana colony there is no evidence that the French made an aggressive attempt to establish on-site trade with the Chickasaw as the English had done, although the trade did swing in favor of France for about five years as a result of the disruptive Yamasee-English War of 1715, during which most of the southern tribes sympathized with the Yamasee because of the previous arrogant bullying of the Indians by the English traders. The English, unlike the French, allowed private traders to enter the Indian territories whereas the latter opted to carry on trade directly through French military channels. Such tight governmental control greatly limited the number of French traders and the quantity of goods traded. The situation is illustrated by the words of Bienville in 1708 to the "chief of the Chickasaws," from whom he was attempting to get assurances that the Chickasaw would not join in a threatened English attack on the French colony. In this conversation Bienville told the chief that the Chickasaw could "come here [to Mobile] and trade with us for all the necessities as they could with the English." The chief must have found this somewhat nonsensical considering that they did not have to travel to the English colonies to trade with the English. Moreover, the Chickasaw knew from experience that trade merchandise from France was not plentiful and that some items, such as blankets, were inferior to those traded to them by the English. Also, the English were supplying not only the Chickasaw chiefs but the general population as well.[12]

This early failure by the French to aggressively establish a meaningful trade with the Chickasaw nation allowed a gradual strengthening of the English position among them. Observing the growing Chickasaw alliance with the English, Bienville in 1711 had developed a pessimistic attitude about the future French relationship with that nation. To blame, the thirty-one-year-old Bienville declared, was that in the ten years since the founding of the colony, the English had expended on the Indians approximately 100,000 crowns (300,000 livres) and the French only 10,000 livres.[13]

The period between 1712 and 1720 seems to have been a static and apparently neglectful one for the French colony with regard to Indian relations. In 1710 Bienville was replaced as governor by Antoine De La Mothe Cadillac, but the latter did not arrive from France until June 1713. In 1717, following the short terms of Cadillac and his successor, de L'Epinay, Bienville was again appointed governor of the Louisiana colony.[14] The French documents reveal little about the Chickasaw or other Indian groups during this period, the reason for which may be partially explained by a marginal note on one of Cadillac's 1716 letters: "Reply of Mr. [Antoine] Crozat: Mr. Crozat agrees [with Cadillac] that the colony is in horrible disorder, but that is the result of the disunion that Mr. [Cadillac] has brought into it and of the fact that he was unwilling to execute any orders that were sent him to establish the commerce of the Mississippi River, and of his bad conduct toward the Indian nations, with all of whom he has found a way to get into a quarrel."[15]

Apparently de L'Epinay was no great improvement, as indicated in a report by Hubert of St. Malo in 1717:

> The majority of the Indian nations are not pleased with the reception that Mr. De L'Epinay has given them. The Indian wishes stability; besides, the presents that he gave them were of no importance in comparison with the quantity of goods that were taken from Mr. Crozat's warehouse for this purpose. . . . Several are very dissatisfied and they say among themselves that Mr. De L'Epinay was an old mangy dog whom the Great Chief on the other side of the great lake [Atlantic Ocean] had sent to this country, because he was dying of hunger in his village . . . that he made a big noise but that his words did not go beyond the door of his room; these are the Indian expressions. The contempt for [him] is reflected at the same time on the nation. The Indians are savages only in name. They have as much discernment and shrewdness as can be expected from people without education. They talk little, but very much to the point. They have a regular government among themselves . . . and great respect for their chiefs. . . . They love war. They are brave. They despise those who show no indications of being brave. They suffer resolutely hardship, hunger and even death.[16]

By 1720 the stage had been set for the ensuing intensive confrontations between the Chickasaw and the Choctaw and between the French and English in attempts to control those tribes for their benefits. From the English standpoint peace between the Choctaw and Chickasaw was desired so that the Choctaw would allow English traders into their nation. The French, on the other hand, feared that English-Choctaw trade would undermine their perceived alliance with the Choctaw, recognizing the fact that the English could supply cheaper and greater quantities of trade goods than they. This fear led to the greater fear that if the English were allowed to establish trade with the Choctaw on a par with that of the Chickasaw, then these two nations could unite against the French colony at the prodding of the English and cause it great harm. This paranoia, probably justified, of the French resulted in a policy established early by Bienville to encourage Choctaw and Chickasaw hostility as long as the English were present among the Chickasaw. Additionally, the English desire for peace between the Chickasaw and Choctaw only pertained if they possessed exclusive trade with both nations. Because exclusive trade with both was not a reality, the Choctaw must be considered the aggressor after 1720 in the conflicts between the two nations, and the French the antagonists. The English, therefore, were not opposed to hostilities between the Chickasaw and French and apparently encouraged attacks against the latter. Likewise, the French encouraged Choctaw attacks against the English.

The Chickasaw, as well as the Choctaw and other tribes, suffered greatly from these conflicts but were caught up in a situation that defied solution. The Chickasaw were spoiled by the availability of the usually plentiful English goods and refused to adhere to the main French term for peace, that of driving the English from their villages. It is not surprising that the Chickasaw refused to do so, because they had become dependent on European weapons, clothing, and other goods and were no longer content with just their native materials. Since the Chickasaw knew that the French could not adequately supply the Choctaw with these goods, they were not inclined to drive out the English. The Choctaw, on the other hand, desired to trade with the English for their cheaper and more plentiful goods, but they were constantly coerced against it by the French. Thus the last forty years of the Louisiana colony's existence can be characterized as a time when the Chickasaw, as well as the Choctaw, acted out roles written for them by the French and English. The whole scenario was undoubtedly perceived by the Indians as superficial and theatrical, but the French apparently became so engrossed in the fantasy that they believed the final act in the drama would have them triumphant. Instead the entire play, based on unrealistic premises, was a tragedy for all concerned and was partially to blame for the poor success of the Louisiana colony.[17]

During Bienville's second term as governor, the French-Chickasaw estrangement began to express itself in open violence. Bienville asserted that the Chickasaw declared war on the French in 1720 when some warriors pillaged the possessions of and threatened to kill some Frenchmen who were attempting to trade among them. The circumstances of this action by the Chickasaw were not stated, but Bienville went on to say that two Chickasaw chiefs saved the lives of the Frenchmen and then escorted them to the Choctaw country. In 1721, when hostilities began on a large scale between the Chickasaw and the Choctaw/French, Bienville reiterated a policy established in 1706 of paying the

Choctaw for each Chickasaw scalp brought to him and also eighty livres for each captive.[18]

In about April 1722 some of the antagonized Chickasaw killed two Frenchmen and wounded a third who were descending the Mississippi River from the Illinois post. In retaliation the Choctaw, encouraged by the French, reportedly attacked and destroyed three Chickasaw villages, killed 400 people, and took 100 prisoners. The villages destroyed may have at least partially been those that made up the settlement, or town, of Yaneka, described by James Adair as a main settlement and the most southern one in the early years of the eighteenth century. Although the statistics in the reports may be somewhat exaggerated, the incident is significant in its illustration that the Chickasaw had not previously been harassed enough to consolidate and better fortify their settlement in the present-day Tupelo area, as was the case by 1736 when the Chickasaw villages were constricted into a relatively small area.[19]

It is interesting to note that there is no record that the Chickasaw were launching organized attacks against the Choctaw. It is evident that the Chickasaw-Choctaw hostilities were a direct result of Bienville's desire to promote the viability of the Louisiana colony by stirring up the Choctaw against the Chickasaw in order to keep the English from further establishing themselves among the latter, the feared repercussions of which have been discussed above. The Chickasaw, having "discernment and shrewdness," as Hubert wrote of Indians in the passage quoted above, were well aware of these French intrigues, as were the English traders among them. Thus the alleged Chickasaw attack on the Frenchmen on the Mississippi River in 1722 can be considered justified retaliation.

Bienville stated his new policy toward the Chickasaw at a council meeting in July 1723, when he discussed a peace proposal of four Chickasaw chiefs, two of whom were the same men who had delivered the French traders to safety in 1720 and, according to Bienville, were friends of the French.[20] Bienville's no-peace recommendations were accepted and reiterated by each of the council members, one of whom stated,

[O]n the subject of the war that we have stirred up between the Choctaws and the Chickasaws in order to avenge the death of several Frenchmen killed by the said Chickasaws, my opinion is . . . to maintain this war between these two nations and to give the Choctaws, a nation that contains nearly eight thousand men, this bone to gnaw, which since it is naturally warlike might with the assistance of the English disturb us in the future, and it is to be hoped . . . that all these strong nations may one after another become aroused against each other in order that their destruction may make it impossible for them to unite against us as might happen sooner or later.[21]

Earlier, in discussing the aforementioned Choctaw attack on the Chickasaw in February 1723, Bienville had first articulated the new policy in a letter to the council: "This advantage does not fail to be of importance in the situation in which things are so much the more since this affair took place without risking a single Frenchman, all by the care that I have taken to put these barbarians into play against each other, the sole and only way to establish any security in the colony because they will destroy themselves by their own efforts eventually."[22]

Finally, in December 1724, the French decided that the war had lasted long enough, but the peace that ensued was not initiated by them. In late 1724 the Chickasaw sent calumets (peace symbols, sometimes pipes) and presents to the Choctaw with overtures of peace. Upon learning that the Choctaw were willing to accept the peace proposal, Bienville called a council of war at his house at Mobile to discuss the situation. The council voted to grant peace for two major reasons that had not existed before. First, the French warehouses were well stocked with goods with which to keep the Choctaw satisfied and therefore the English out of their villages. Second, convoys were no longer to supply merchandise to the Illinois post, which meant that individuals would have to come to New Orleans to receive it, thereby leaving them endangered on the Mississippi River if the Chickasaw were still at war.[23]

In February 1725 the council cautioned against a proposed abandonment of the Yazoo post because they were "not sure that the Chickasaws will remain quiet," but contrary to this fear the peace lasted. As a result, in April 1726 Diron d'Artaguette obtained an exclusive grant to trade under the auspices of the Company of the Indies for deer hides with the Choctaw and Chickasaw. He soon built establishments among them, which were still operating in October 1729. Possibly the establishment among the Chickasaw was the one referred to by Bernard Romans in 1771 as "where the French formerly had a fortified trading house, about one mile below the mouth of . . . [Old Town] creek, on the west bank [of the Tombigbee River]." However, because this is supposedly the same location where Bienville built a fort and disembarked overland to attack the Chickasaw in 1736 (see Chapter 3), it is possible that Romans was referring to that fort and had his facts wrong about it being a trading house or even about where either one had been located.[24]

With the replacement of Bienville by Perier de Salvert in 1726, maintaining peace between the Indians became a matter of policy rather than a situation-fitting accommodation, as illustrated by the words of Perier in 1728:

One might perhaps offer the objection that it is not an evil that the Indian nations should be at war with each other. It would really not be [war] if we were the only ones who had dealings with them, but the English, who see them as we do, profit by their quarrels to penetrate into the nations that are most attached to us, which can not be prevented except by keeping as we do all the nations in peace among themselves, making them understand that the English are seeking to have them destroyed among themselves in order to be masters of their country. They like this reason above all the others.[25]

Perier's opinions as to how to keep the English at bay were not, however, supported by actual circumstances. For one thing, the French, not the English, were trying to incapacitate the Chickasaw. Following temporary termination of the French-Chickasaw-Choctaw hostilities in December 1724, the English seem to have greatly increased their movements into the Chickasaw and Choctaw nations. Diron d'Artaguette reported that in 1725 Englishmen were passing among the Indian nations in great numbers and that some had planned to develop establishments in the Chickasaw and Choctaw villages but that he had induced some Choctaw to kill those who had refused to withdraw from that nation. To further obviate English incursions within the territory claimed by the French colony, d'Artaguette induced the Kawita to burn the English warehouses among the Shawnee, who were then settled among the Upper Creeks, but he was unable to do anything about the English traders and warehouses among the Alibama, Tallapoosa, Kawita, and Chickasaw. He was, however, able to establish a trade coexistent with that of the English among the Chickasaw, as mentioned above. Also, by threatening to withhold presents from the Choctaw chiefs, he was able to temporarily silence a vocally pro-English Choctaw chief with the title name of Soulouche Oumastabe or, as called by the French, Red Shoe.[26]

Despite Perier's desire to maintain peace between the Indians, continued French and English exploitation of them during his term resulted in an explosion in 1729 that soon resulted in the Chickasaw being referred to by the French as "our enemies" throughout the remainder of the existence of the Louisiana colony. On November 28, 1729, the antagonized Natchez launched a surprise attack on the Natchez post settlement and Fort Rosalie and killed or captured almost the entire French population of men, women, children, and black slaves. The Chickasaw and English were suspected of having been involved, possibly with some Choctaw, in planning the attack.[27]

During the ensuing war between the French and Natchez, some of the Chickasaw did indeed display sympathy for the Natchez by allowing the largest displaced part of the population to settle among them. This occurred in early 1731. In March of that year Regis Du Roullet learned that "the Natchez had escaped to the Chickasaws" and were "at the village of Falatchao." That the Natchez first went to Falatchao is significant, because it was here, as reported by a French trader in July 1729, that Oulacta Tasca, an "honored man" of the Chickasaw, resided. Since the trader had reported that Oulacta Tasca was "the most rebellious of the whole nation" and Du Roullet that he "was the leader of all the seditions organized against the French,"[28] we may in this association have confirmation that some Chickasaw were indeed indirectly involved in the attack on Fort Rosalie. If so, however, the entire nation cannot be blamed for having participated, for there is substantial evidence that not all of the Chickasaw population deserves the reputation of unprovoked aggressor that has been attributed by writers to the whole nation over the years. This evidence will become apparent in the post-1729 Chickasaw-French interactions discussed below.

Believing that the Chickasaw had been involved in the Natchez attack, the French were not long in retaliating against them. Within two months after the attack Perier began trying to have the northern Indians, primarily the Illinois and Huron, attack the Chickasaw.[29] He did not wish to declare war on them until he had finished the Natchez war, but he established a policy toward the Chickasaw to which the French adhered until the abolition of the Louisiana colony: "It is important to destroy that nation as soon as the affairs of the colony permit it, or at least to drive it out of this province, where it is established too near the [Mississippi] river and we must regard it as an irreconcilable enemy. When we win them by presents it will never be for longer than a while. There now remain only three hundred warriors in this nation."[30]

Apparently in response to Perier's request to the governor of New France that he induce the northern Indians to attack the Chickasaw, a band of Hurons, or possibly Illinois, struck in September 1730 and killed or captured between thirty and fifty men. Following this and apparently other attacks by the northern Indians, a Chickasaw chief visited Mobile to ask Perier for relief from the attacks. Perier responded that the French would not attack the Chickasaw but claimed that he had no control over the actions of the northern Indians.[31]

By February 1731 there was sentiment within the Choctaw nation to declare war on the Chickasaw, partially because of a rumor started in January by Regis Du Roullet that the English had applied poison to some Lemberg cloth that they had traded to the Choctaw for the purpose of causing them all to die. At the time there was an epidemic of some sort among the Choctaw that made this ridiculous rumor believable. The Choctaw war parties being formed did not attack, however, primarily because Red Shoe objected and the Great Chief would not give his consent.[32]

At this time, evidence of division among the Chickasaw became apparent. This division seems almost certainly to have come about over the Natchez issue. Although there is no known written record of what had been transpiring in the Chickasaw villages, there must have been long discussions with regard to giving the Natchez sanctuary. On the pro-Natchez side we would expect to find Oulacta Tasca, who, as mentioned above, had already been identified in 1729 and 1730 as the leader of the "seditions organized against the French" and the "most rebellious of the whole nation." He had, in fact, received a peace calumet from two Natchez emissaries in October 1730, which he in turn sent to the Great Chief of the Choctaw, who rejected the peace overture. Another Chickasaw chief or honored man in the pro-Natchez faction was probably Quouatchitabe, who had been planning to go to the Mississippi River and attack pirogues (dugout canoes) descending from the Illinois post. On the anti-Natchez side we find the principal chief, Ymahatabe, or as called by the French, Ymahatabe La Borgne, because he had sight in only one eye; he was referred to by one Englishman as the "Blind King."[33] His name is mentioned either directly or indirectly numerous times in the French documents and always in connection with peace, a circumstance that conforms with Thomas Nairne's previously discussed identification of the traditional role of Chickasaw great chiefs.

Apparently the pro-Natchez faction prevailed, for in February 1731, Ymahatabe went to the Great Village of the Choctaw, Couechitto, to request asylum for himself and four Chickasaw villages: Tchitchatala, Achoukouma, Taskaouilo, and Falatchao. Ymahatabe reported at this time that the "English were in such great numbers at the Chickasaw villages that one could not count the number" and that "four Chickasaws were at the Natchez with the intention of bringing that nation home with them."[34]

Although the villages never moved to the Choctaw country, the fact that the undoubtedly frustrated Ymahatabe even suggested it implies that serious internal disagreements were occurring. That Oulacta Tasca, the pro-Natchez honored man, was from one of these villages (Falatchao) indicates that there was also internal disagreement within the individual villages, possibly as a result of conflicting political positions among the clans. As discussed below, this situation among the Chickasaw continued until 1745 and later.

As mentioned above, a substantial contingent of the harassed Natchez population settled among the Chickasaw in early 1731. The French, determined to destroy the Natchez wherever they might be found, caused the Chickasaw nation to become the object of intensified retaliation. Whereas earlier the Choctaw nation as a whole had been unenthusiastic about declaring war on the Chickasaw as the French wished, the Chickasaw acceptance of the Natchez seems to have reversed this sentiment, at least among the Choctaw of the eastern division. Even Red Shoe had a change of heart, although he was obviously

motivated by French presents and the promise of a medal,[35] as his statements
recorded by Du Roullet show: "You are right to tell me that the Chickasaws have
bad hearts. . . . If I was obligated to them, I am not any longer. . . . I even prevented the warriors from going to attack them. Today, when they have taken
the Natchez into their home, I declare that I wish to attack them; thus I invite
you [the chiefs and warriors of Yowani] to do the same."[36]

At this time the French began demanding of the Chickasaw that they surrender the Natchez, but this demand was refused. In July 1731, therefore, Red
Shoe led a Choctaw attack on a Chickasaw hunting party and took six Chickasaw scalps and eleven prisoners. The Chickasaw then began asking the Choctaw for peace, but surrender of the Natchez was the only condition upon which
the French would allow it.[37]

In November 1732 a Choctaw named Patlaco led a small force against the
Chickasaw but was unable to do any damage. Instead, his force attacked a
twenty-horse train on the road to the Abecas, killing three Englishmen and
one Chickasaw. In that same month Red Shoe led a party of forty men against
the Chickasaw but to no avail, probably because by then the Chickasaw villages were better fortified. The Great Chief and Alibamon Mingo, a prominent
Choctaw chief, promised the French that they would continually send small
war parties against the Chickasaw. The Choctaw, however, were becoming dis-
heartened, primarily because the French would not accompany them in these
attacks as they had promised earlier in 1731. In August 1732 de Cremont reported
that the Choctaw were "getting tired of making war alone."[38]

The Chickasaw and Natchez were not lying back and taking these attacks
without retaliation. At this time the Chickasaw were reported to have 600
warriors and the Natchez 250 to 300, which were probably overestimations. In
December 1732 a Chickasaw war party attacked six French voyagers on the
Ohio River, killed three of them, and captured the other three with the intention of burning them. However, Ymahatabe saved their lives by asking for them
as slaves. The Chickasaw showed considerable restraint in not burning the
Frenchmen in light of the fact that a year earlier Perier had ordered three captive Chickasaws burned.[39]

Because the Chackchiuma, by then a small tribe settled on the Yazoo River
but who had formerly resided between the Choctaw and Chickasaw, were observing neutrality in the French-Chickasaw/Natchez war, a party of 250 to 300
men consisting of Chickasaw, Natchez, and possibly some Yazoo launched a
surprise attack on their village. The attackers killed between eight and fifteen
people, including some children, and captured eleven women, two of whom
were later released by Oulacta Tasca, the probable leader of the force. This attack caused the Chackchiuma to side with the Choctaw-French alliance. At
about this same time, Ymahatabe, who was chief of the Chickasaw village

named Ackia, as well as the Great Chief of the Chickasaw, went to the South Carolina colony for reasons uncertain but apparently to obtain English goods to present to the Choctaw in an effort to make peace with them through Abeca mediation. Although threatened by war with the Abecas if they did not agree to the peace and accept the goods, the Choctaw refused and thwarted this apparent scheme of the English.[40]

During these Chickasaw-Choctaw/French hostilities a conspiracy to drive the Natchez out of the settlement was formulated. According to Perier, the Chackchiuma, wishing to take revenge for the above-mentioned attack, persuaded some "relatives that they had among the Chickasaws to form a party . . . strong enough to kill all the Natchez who were among them."[41] Perier heard that an attack had indeed rid the Chickasaw of the Natchez, but his information was erroneous and there is no supporting documentation that an attack occurred.

In the spring of 1733, soon after Bienville returned from France to begin his third term as governor, at least some of the Chickasaw were inclined toward removing the Natchez in exchange for peace with the French and Choctaw. A Chickasaw chief, whose Indian name is unrecorded but who was called Courcerai by the French, went to the Alibama post called Fort Toulouse and presented the French commander there a letter, written by a French captive, in which two other Chickasaw chiefs (one was probably Ymahatabe) sincerely expressed a desire for peace. They asked that the French prevent the Choctaw and Wea, a group affiliated with the Illinois, from attacking them. Courcerai indicated to the French commander at the post that the Chickasaw "would not be opposed to surrendering . . . the rest of the Natchez to obtain peace" and that the Natchez "were scattered about the cabins of the Chickasaws who were employing them in the most servile tasks." The French commander replied that he had no authority to grant peace but that he would ask of Bienville his permission to have Courcerai come and meet with him on the subject. Courcerai then went home, promising to return in September. There is no further reference to this chief until 1737, when it was revealed that Courcerai had been kept prisoner by Bienville "during the war."[42] Apparently Courcerai had indeed returned in late 1733 and met with Bienville, who threw him in prison. The circumstances of this affair are curiously not recorded in the known French documents, but possibly Bienville had not been satisfied with what Courcerai had to say and decided to hold him prisoner as a response to the capture of two Frenchmen on the Mississippi in 1732.

Another intriguing possibility, and one that seems enhanced by the deafening silence surrounding this affair, is that this chief had the authority as well as the respect and allegiance of enough of his people to accomplish the removal of the Natchez with minimal internal opposition. Could it be that, realizing this, Bienville wished to continue to have an excuse to present to the king for launching his anticipated expedition against the Chickasaw and had imprisoned Courcerai in order to prevent the removal of the Natchez?

That Courcerai was more than an average chief is indicated by the fact that two Frenchmen captured in d'Artaguette's attack in 1736, discussed below, were said to have been expressly spared from execution for the purpose of exchanging them for him. Three years later the Chickasaw were still hoping to have Courcerai returned to them, for in February 1740 a French commander responded to a Chickasaw inquiry about him with the possible false statement that "he did not know where he was."[43] He likely died in prison or was sent to Santo Domingo as a slave.

Meanwhile, the Choctaw and northern Indian hostilities against the Chickasaw continued at the urging of the French in Louisiana and New France. The Chickasaw peacemakers continued to intermittently ask for peace, and Red Shoe again became friendly with the English. Bienville became determined to destroy the Chickasaw by sending a French force against them: "The destruction of the Chickasaw and the Natchez would be an example capable of making these Indians [the Choctaw] reflect, and finally as long as the Chickasaws exist we shall always have to fear that they will entice away the others from us in favor of the English. The Choctaws then leagued with the Chickasaws, who are brave and enterprising, would become formidable for us. The entire destruction of this hostile nation therefore becomes every day more necessary to our interests and I am going to exert all diligence to accomplish it."[44]

The situation within the Chickasaw settlement was characterized by stress and internal strife over the Natchez issue and the war. In April 1734 Bienville learned from some captured Chickasaws that "the Chickasaws are extremely fatigued with the war which has caused them to lose many of their best warriors and several of their principal chiefs; that those who upheld the side of the English are thinking of retiring this summer with the Abecas in the direction of Carolina; and that the others who have always been in our interests are waiting for a favorable moment to attack the Natchez in order to obtain by their destruction peace and permission to settle on our lands."[45] Bienville further noted that "the English traders in the nation, interested in the preservation of the Natchez are offering presents to the others to oppose the designs of these men, and even warned the Natchez who are always on guard against the Chickasaws."[46] Thus by 1736, when Bienville finally launched a French expedition against the Chickasaw, the Natchez were still there.

In the two years prior to the 1736 French campaign (discussed in the next chapter), the French had hoped in vain that the Choctaw could accomplish their dirty work for them. On some occasions a few Frenchmen would even accompany the Choctaw on attacks against the Chickasaw. In August 1734, Jean Paul Le Sueur, under the orders of Bienville, hurriedly assembled nine Frenchmen to march with him at the head of a coerced Choctaw force. However, upon approaching the Chickasaw settlement the extremely animated war songs of the women and the excited cries of the Chickasaws in general discouraged the Choctaws so much that they fled. Le Sueur, unable to control them, decided to attack without the Choctaws with his nine Frenchmen, but the Choctaws pragmatically "opposed it and carried [him] away with them for a long distance."[47]

The retreat of the Choctaws in this incident should not be attributed to cowardice, as the French were wont to do, but rather to the fact that Indians would only attack with vigor following a period of ritualistic preparation for war, usually preceded by a specific affront from the enemy. This probably had not occurred, so the Choctaws were not emotionally agitated at the Chickasaw when they reached the settlement. In fact, this is confirmed with regard to a similar attempt in September 1733 by Le Sueur to march at the head of 500 Choctaws. That expedition also had been a failure for the same reason and Le Sueur even recognized the problem, as shown by the following statement by Bienville: "[Le Sueur] soon had reason to think that complaisance was leading rather than warlike ardor for in proportion as they advanced [the Choctaw] deserted in troops."[48]

Expeditions not organized and impressed upon the Choctaw by Frenchmen, on the other hand, were much more successful. In early 1734 the Great Chief of the Choctaw led a force of about 600 warriors against the Chickasaw village of Choukafalya in order to avenge the death of his brother (or uncle) who had been killed in one of Red Shoe's attacks against this same village. In the Great Chief's attack, the Choctaw used a strategy to induce the Chickasaw to come out of the forts and into an ambush in which about forty-six Chickasaws were killed and scalped. In this much more successful prelude to the famous battle of Ackia/Choukafalya at the same place in 1736, thirty Choctaw were wounded and five killed, including the eldest son of the Great Chief.[49]

Weary of the attacks on their villages, Ymahatabe and three other Chickasaw chiefs were received at Mobile by Bienville in October 1734 to discuss peace. As always, Bienville demanded the destruction of the Natchez as a prelude to peace, but the Chickasaw chiefs presented excuses for why they could not oblige, the main one being that the Natchez were still too numerous and strong for them to attempt to kill, even though some had recently moved east. However, the chiefs finally promised Bienville to kill the Natchez and implored him to stop the Choctaw raids for three months while they planned and carried out the deed. Because the Choctaw were complaining of having to neglect their crops as a result of the war, Bienville agreed to the three-month peace and in a letter to France spoke of ending the war entirely because there were really no punitive reasons for continuing it, for the Chickasaw were always on the defensive and had not attacked the Indian allies.[50]

Bienville, who seemingly wanted to make peace and believed that the Chickasaw were definitely going to kill the Natchez in order to allow it, soon had his optimism shattered. In April 1735 two French commissaries from the Illinois post foolishly left 1,700 pounds of powder at the Arkansas post, and when Pierre d'Artaguette sent Lieutenant Ducoder and ten soldiers back to retrieve it, 240 Chickasaw and Natchez warriors, on their way to attempt to rescue some of their captured women from the Illinois Indians, happened upon them. The French soldiers immediately opened fire and the Indians returned it. The Indians, led by Mingo Houma of the village Ogoula Tchetoka, then killed or captured all the Frenchmen, Ducoder being among the latter, and made off with the powder and other cargo. As a result of this untimely and unplanned incident, Ymahatabe and the other peace delegation chiefs lost all hope of the French being willing to negotiate a peace, and the promise to destroy the Natchez was broken. To show good faith and that peace was still desired, Ymahatabe and the other three chiefs supplied Ducoder with provisions and shoes and had him escorted safely toward the Choctaw settlements. They also saved the lives of three other French prisoners and later had them released.[51]

Following this turn of events, Bienville seriously turned his attention to preparations for the major French offensive against the Chickasaw. First, he took steps to establish Fort Tombecbe on the Tombigbee River, which he had been considering for a year. Next, he induced the Choctaw to have the English traders removed from that nation and also encouraged and excited them to keep the war active until he was in a position to "put himself at the head of all the Frenchmen and Indians whom he would be able to get together."[52]

3
The Long Road Narrows

By the end of March 1736 Bienville had assembled at Mobile all the Frenchmen possible to the number of about 460. He also employed the services of a Swiss company about 100 strong. On April 1 the French force began its ascent of the Mobile/Tombigbee River, arriving at the Fort Tombecbe area on the twenty-third. Here he withdrew from his force a garrison for the fort and also formed from his servants a company of forty-five armed black slaves with freedmen as officers. He also met with the Choctaw chiefs to arrange for a rendezvous with the Choctaw force that was to accompany the French.[1]

While at Fort Tombecbe Bienville learned that a Choctaw scouting party had observed a "great French trail" northwest of the Chickasaw settlement, which he suspected to be that of Pierre d'Artaguette's French and Indian force from the Illinois post, which was supposed to join Bienville's forces to attack the Chickasaw. Having been delayed at Mobile, Bienville had sent a message to d'Artaguette instructing him to delay his march also. However, as Bienville suspected, d'Artaguette did not receive the letter and, in fact, had approached the Chickasaw settlement while Bienville's force was still at Mobile.[2]

Pierre d'Artaguette had left the Illinois post on February 22 with a French force of 145 troops and unenlisted men and an Indian force of 326 Iroquois, Arkansas, Illinois, and Miami. Upon arriving at the Prudhomme Bluff north of present-day central Memphis, he constructed a small palisade fort. Here he left a garrison of twenty-five Frenchmen commanded by a Captain Jolibois. On March 5 d'Artaguette left the Prudhomme fort area along a trail that ran southeast to the Chickasaw villages. When within about forty miles of the Chickasaw settlement, d'Artaguette sent out two scouting parties to look for Bienville and to ascertain the position of the Chickasaw forts and houses. The second party sent, composed of four Iroquois, four Illinois, a Chickasaw adopted by the Miami, and a French Canadian named Framboise, discovered one of the Chickasaw villages and reported back to d'Artaguette. This village

turned out to be Ogoula Tchetoka, one of the villages that formed the Chuckalissa division of the large prairie of the Chickasaw (Figures 4, 6, 8, and 9). As
already mentioned, Chuckalissa was located in present-day northwest Tupelo
on the south side of Old Town Creek, and it was described as the strongest town
in the nation. The other Chuckalissa villages to the east were Amalata, Achoukouma, and Taskaouilo. The main Natchez refuge village bordered Chuckalissa
on the east (Figures 6 and 7).[3]

Meanwhile, the Chickasaw had become aware of impending danger. According to William McMullin, an English trader present among the Chickasaw
at this time, Squirrel King's Chickasaw group settled on the Savannah River
had warned a Chickasaw hunting party, in January 1735, that the French intended to come at about this time with a force strong enough to destroy them.
In response, the Chickasaw placed themselves in a "posture of defence,"[4] possibly by further constricting their northern prairie villages and building additional forts.

On March 8 some Chickasaws heard the ominous sound of gunshots. The
next day three scouting parties went out from Chuckalissa toward the northwest for about half a mile distance. One of the parties found bread on the
ground, causing the Chickasaw to speculate that some of the French Indian
allies had thrown it down to let the Chickasaw know that they were in danger.
If this was the purpose of the discarded bread, the action could have resulted
from disagreements between the French and their Indian allies. Quarreling between them on the march to the Chickasaw was indeed subsequently reported.[5]
Presumably the bread had been left there or lost by the Indian scouting party
sent ahead by the French.

Having finally received the communication from Bienville at about this
time, d'Artaguette held a council with the leaders of the Indian groups. The
Iroquois stated that because nearly all the provisions had been consumed, it
would be prudent to attack the Chickasaw village located by the scouting party,
capture it and its fort, and wait for Bienville while subsisting on captured
Chickasaw provisions. The other Indian leaders agreed and d'Artaguette approved the plan. The march was resumed and at 9 P.M. on March 24, the force
was within three miles of the Chuckalissa villages. After midnight the army
proceeded to within a mile of the nearest one, Ogoula Tchetoka, where their
powder, munitions, and baggage were left under the guard of Sieur de Fron-
tigny, with five French soldiers and fifteen French citizen soldiers. Jesuit Father
Antoine Senat, the chaplain, also stayed with the baggage.[6]

Between six and seven o'clock on the morning of March 25, d'Artaguette
approached Ogoula Tchetoka at the head of his Frenchmen, who now numbered only about seventy-three men. The Iroquois and Miami were on the left
and the Arkansas and Illinois were on the right. As the whole force approached

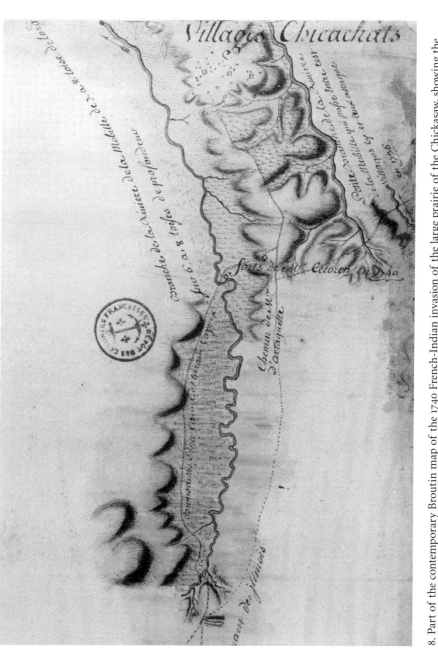

8. Part of the contemporary Broutin map of the 1740 French-Indian invasion of the large prairie of the Chickasaw, showing the 1736 attack route of Pierre d'Artaguette (courtesy of Archives de la Marine, Vincennes, France)

9. Present view of approximate site of Ogoula Tchetoka, looking south from new Highway 78 (by author)

the fort, a Chickasaw chief came out with three peace pipes but was fired upon and killed by the Illinois and Miami. They then gave a war whoop and attacked the hill on which stood the houses and fort of Ogoula Tchetoka. As the French and Indians advanced, most of the Chickasaws stayed in the fort and houses, firing through loopholes. The Iroquois were able to take one scalp and capture a female Tunica prisoner of the Chickasaw. The Miami captured a woman and the Arkansas captured a child. By the end of fifteen minutes, however, a few hundred Chickasaw, Natchez, and possibly some Shawnee who were with the Chickasaw, came swarming from the nearby villages, which caused the Illinois and Miami to flee in fear. An English report asserted that the reinforcements from the nearby villages were led by "singing" women with hatchets in their hands, and that boys with bows and arrows accompanied the men.[7]

With the loss of 250 Indian allies, d'Artaguette retreated to the place where he had left his baggage and munitions. During the retreat he lost three fingers on his right hand to a musket ball. The Chickasaw then surrounded the army, and d'Artaguette received a second ball in the thigh. Leaning against a tree, he tried to verbally rally his troops, but to no avail. The situation was hopeless. One of his servants, Pantaloon, brought his horse, but he refused to mount and continued to call out to his troops and the Indian allies. While doing so he received a third ball in the abdomen. According to a detailed report of the expedition, this third wound killed d'Artaguette instantly, but later it was discovered that he had been alive when captured.[8]

Even after the fall of d'Artaguette some of the French officers, including especially de St. Ange, tried to repulse the Chickasaw forces but, outnumbered, most of them were killed near d'Artaguette's seemingly lifeless body. The small number of Frenchmen remaining, having no leaders, fled for their lives with the Chickasaw and probably the Natchez as well in pursuit. After a few miles, said by McMullin to be eight, a heavy downpour occurred at about 10 A.M. and the Chickasaw ended the pursuit. The Iroquois and Arkansas Indians were instrumental in saving about twenty wounded Frenchmen, whom they aided by helping carry them back to the fort on the Mississippi River. The remnants of the exhausted army arrived at the fort on March 29 and 30.[9]

Questioned after the battle, the Tunica woman related that the total Chickasaw numbered about 1,000 men (undoubtedly much too high an estimate) and that there were about 100 Natchez and eighty Shawnee also present in the settlement area. She also said that there were several English traders in the Ogoula Tchetoka fort. Another report asserted that during the battle two Englishmen emerged from the fort and trampled a flag that an Iroquois had planted in the middle of the village. One French version had it that these two Englishmen were killed by the Iroquois; another that they withdrew to the fort. The former is not likely, for none of the English reports mention the deaths of traders. Mingo Ouma, the chief of Ogoula Tchetoka, later denied other assertions that Englishmen were involved in the battle.[10]

During the battle and retreat the Chickasaw captured the wounded d'Artaguette, Father Senat, and several officers, soldiers, and citizen soldiers. The total captured were twenty-two Frenchmen and two Indians, one of whom was a Chickasaw slave. Various accounts indicate that between twenty-five and forty Frenchmen were killed at the scene. According to McMullin, nine or ten Indian allies of the French were killed. Additionally, some of the fleeing Frenchmen apparently found refuge from the slaughter only to die of wounds, for McMullin reported that several were later found by the turkey buzzards. Others escaped and became permanently separated from the retreating force. Sometime after the battle some Cherokee told an English trader that a group of "upper Indians" had encountered some Frenchmen who had been present. The Indians killed four and captured one they had wounded. The captive related that sixty of his fellow Frenchmen, including d'Artaguette, had been killed.[11]

A detailed French report stated that an estimated sixty or seventy Chickasaw were killed, but this was undoubtedly an extreme exaggeration. McMullin, who remained as a post-battle observer, reported that only eight were killed, consisting of four men, a woman, and three children. However, Claude Drouet de Richardville, a captured Frenchman whose life was spared, reported that twenty were killed and thirty wounded.[12]

The French and Indians necessarily had to abandon their supplies and reserve munitions. English traders reported that ten horses loaded with ammunition and goods were captured by the Chickasaw. The French later acknowledged the loss of at least 450 pounds of powder, 1,200 pounds of musket balls, and thirty jugs of brandy.[13]

Infuriated by the French violation of their homes and the Chickasaw deaths before and during the battle, the Chickasaw men instructed the women of Chuckalissa to build two large fires, said to have been on a prominent hill in the center of the town. Between three o'clock in the afternoon and midnight on the day of the battle, nineteen Frenchmen were thrown into the fires, including d'Artaguette and Father Senat, who had repeatedly led the others in prayer and song in the face of certain death. According to a report from one of the English traders, apparently Augustine Smith, the Chickasaw were merciful and knocked over the head those Frenchmen still conscious, supposedly so as to render them all dead or unconscious prior to hurling them into the fires. This was not supported by other reports, however. Richardville stated in a letter to a Father Vitry that just before he was taken away to another village he saw both Father Senat and d'Artaguette attached to frames. This indicates that both may have been tortured prior to the burnings.[14]

James Adair presents a long discussion of why Indians were inclined to sometimes burn prisoners. In summary, he states that the relatives of people killed by an enemy could not obtain closure and that the ghosts of the dead victims could not rest until revenge was taken on members of the offending group. Burning was a special way of obtaining revenge, for it was also a way of "purifying themselves at home, to obtain victory over their enemies." With regard to the burnings at Chuckalissa, Adair states that two in particular were burned because they "carried the French ark against them." This desire for revenge and closure, states Adair, was so intense that the English traders could not dissuade the Chickasaw from it—could not have even if English goods for the redemption of the Frenchmen had been "piled as high as the skies."[15] Perhaps the burnings were also acts of terrorism for the purpose of discouraging future attacks.

Another prisoner, de Courceras, or Coustillas, was burned in the "grand village" three days later, along with an Iroquois from Sault St. Louis. Courceras, an officer, had been detailed to guard some of the ammunition with thirty-five men but got lost and stumbled upon Chuckalissa, where he was captured after his men retreated. According to a report from one of the English traders, apparently Smith, the captured Iroquois was first tied naked to a stake and tortured. The other Indian captive, undoubtedly the Chickasaw slave, related that if the French had been victorious, any captured English trader would have been turned over to the French Indian allies to suffer a like fate.[16]

Three other Frenchmen, the above-mentioned Claude Drouet de Richardville, Sergeant Louis Gamot, and Pierre *dit* Courteoreille, were spared to be used in a possible future prisoner exchange for the Chickasaw chief named Courcerai (see Chapter 2). Richardville later related that he was kept out of sight for six months in the house of the chief of "Jantalla" (probably Tchitchatala). Richardville and Courteoreille escaped eighteen months after the battle with the aid of an English trader after the Chickasaw finally permitted Richardville the liberty to go about as he pleased and even accompany Chickasaw hunting parties. Louis Gamot was released, apparently after an English trader purchased him.[17]

One of three French prisoners became seriously ill with the "Flux" as trader Thomas Andrews and four Chickasaws were escorting them to Georgia. Because he was unable to travel, the Chickasaws hanged him. This unknown man may have been a captive prior to the battle, as may have been Courteoreille, who escaped with Richardville. The hanged man could not have been Gamot, Richardville, or Courteoreille, for all three made it to Georgia. If the hanged man was with Richardville and Courteoreille, it is strange that Richardville did not mention him in his report. A trader had advised Richardville and Courteoreille of the trail they should take; after going about forty leagues (about 100 miles) they encountered some English traders from Georgia who took them to James Oglethorpe, who thereafter "bought" the Frenchmen from some Chickasaws who had come to Georgia to reclaim them. According to Jean-Bernard Bossu, writing in the 1760s, Gamot was ransomed by an Englishman from Carolina. In a footnote, Patricia Galloway relates that Gamot "escaped en route to Georgia," apparently while being taken there by one or more Englishmen or some Chickasaws.[18]

A French document presents a rare description of the battle from the Indian viewpoint. Part of an interview with Mingo Ouma, chief of Ogoula Tchetoka, was recorded by a Frenchman:

> [I]t was in spite of all the Chickasaw chiefs that those of d'Artaguette's party had been burned . . . they had not had the authority to save their lives . . . the warriors were berserk and took all authority upon themselves . . . they made a big fire and threw into it the living and the dead, not excepting the black robe [Father Senat], who sang from the time he arrived in the village with all the others until the last breath . . . they had really grieved for these Frenchmen because they were true men and they fought with all possible valor in spite of the desertion of the Indians . . . they came as far as the cabins, killing, plundering everything they found

... fortunately for him [Mingo Ouma] the two neighboring villages made a sortie and surrounded the French, killing several, capturing some alive, and pursuing the rest as far as the forest, fighting all the way.[19]

Returning to Bienville at Fort Tombecbe, we find him embarking on May 3 for the final movement up the river. On the 14th, the French force arrived at the mouth of Octibia (present-day Tibbee) Creek, where they may have built a rudimentary fortification. After a few days spent there making arrangements for the rendezvous with the Choctaw, the force left and arrived at what Bienville called the "old portage" (lower portage) (Figure 1). Here were assembled the majority of the Choctaw volunteers, consisting of about 600 warriors and their most notable chiefs, including Red Shoe, Alibamon Mingo, and even the unnamed Great Chief. On the 22nd the French and Indians moved on to the "new portage" (upper portage). The remainder of the Choctaws arrived that day. At the new portage, on May 23, Bienville had a fort with a shed inside constructed of 600 logs to protect his supplies, boats, boatmen, and the sick. The next day twenty soldiers under the command of an officer named Vandereck were left there and, guided by a trader familiar with the area, the force began the overland trip northwest to the Chickasaw settlement, which according to Bienville was a distance of nine leagues from the portage.[20] The distance is no more than twenty miles.

The new portage on the west bank of the Tombigbee River has often been assumed to have been south of the east and west forks, about two miles west of present-day Amory, Mississippi, but such is not certain. Possibly both the fort and the mobilization area were actually several miles north of the portage west of Amory and on the west fork of the Tombigbee River (Old Town Creek). The Baron de Crenay map of 1733, in fact, shows a "portage" in that location while showing another "portage" below the fork to the south where "Petite Portage" is shown on the de Marigny map of 1743 and on another similar, anonymous and undated French map. An Old Town Creek location for the portage where the fort was built is suggested by the report of the Ministry of the Colonies, which states that it was at the "last portage." However, the de Crenay map shows the upper portage to be north of Coonewah Creek. If the army disembarked from that location, it would not have had to cross any creeks before reaching the lower Chickasaw villages. This does not fit well with the words of Bienville: "On the twenty-fifth we had in a space of five short leagues to pass through three deep ravines in which we had water up to our waists." This statement seems to fit the lower portage route. The de Crenay map probably locates the upper portage too far north. If it was actually just south of the mouth of Yaneka/Chiwapa Creek, the crossing of three creeks as stated by Bienville would be applicable. If the upper portage on Old Town Creek was indeed where the fort was built, such could explain why the French had to spend several days cutting fallen trees and sometimes dragging their boats downstream to deeper water, probably below the fork, as a result of the water level receding during the land campaign against the Chickasaw (discussed below). However, the lower portage is shown on the Purcell and Roberts maps as the site of the "Old French Fort." This location, obtained from Bernard Romans, could be a mistake considering the great length of time between 1736 and the early 1770s. Interestingly, Gideon Lincecum, an early nineteenth-century resident of the area, wrote that the disembarkation point and fort were on the "left prong of the river." If the upper portage was indeed the one used by Bienville, it was an imprudent action that must have bemused the Choctaw, Chickasaw, and English traders (if the latter two learned about it), for fast recession of the upper Tombigbee creeks after heavy rains ceased was a well-known occurrence to the Indians and English traders.[21]

Although plagued by rains since leaving Mobile the men made the overland trek to the Chickasaw settlement in two days without getting their powder wet. The French marched quietly in two columns with the Choctaw on their flanks. After camping the night of the 24th and crossing a tributary of Yaneka/Chiwapa Creek, that creek, and Coonewah Creek on the 25th, Bienville encamped the force in a plain about five miles south of the small prairie. At the camps the army was fed pork and biscuits.[22]

As discussed in Chapter 1, in the small prairie lay the major village of Choukafalya and two adjacent minor villages, Apeony and Ackia (Figures 6, 10, and 11). These villages formed the small prairie town on the north end of the area known later as Long Town. As discussed earlier, its 1736 composition probably resulted from the consolidation and reduction of the sizes of villages, which had begun after 1720. Choukafalya was probably the only village there prior to the consolidation.[23]

While the forces were in camp about five miles from the small prairie on May 25, Red Shoe and four of his warriors proposed to go on a scouting trip, but not trusting Red Shoe because of his past actions in favor of the English, Bienville sent two French officers along. During this all-night reconnaissance, Red Shoe's party encountered a group of Chickasaw hunters, who fired on them from a long distance. According to Bienville the encounter warned the Chickasaw of the army's presence, but this is not necessarily so since the hunters only detected the scouting party, which they could not easily have identified in the dark. Being almost totally ignorant of the Chickasaw settlement himself, Bienville had to rely on his Choctaw guides. Apparently the trader guide did not know the current situation of the villages.[24] The initial events on the morning of May 26 are described by Bienville: "The Choctaws . . . set out on the march with us. At the first halt the Great Chief came to ask me what village I

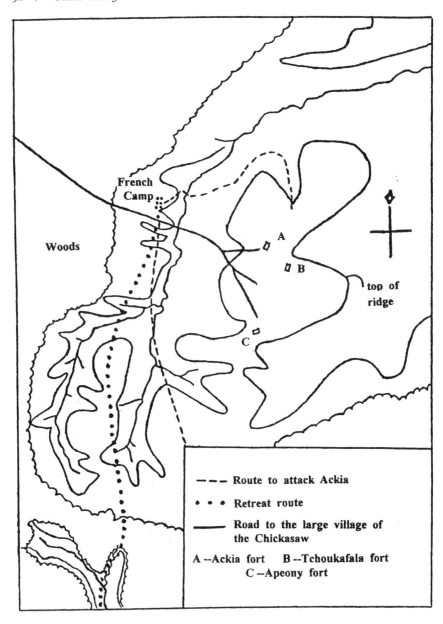

Woods

French
Camp

A

B

top of
ridge

C

– – – Route to attack Ackia

• • • Retreat route

——— Road to the large village of
the Chickasaw

A –Ackia fort   B –Tchoukafala fort
C –Apeony fort

10. Pen tracing of the primary features on the contemporary 1736 Broutin map of Bienville's invasion of the small prairie, showing Ackia, Choukafalya, Apeony, the French-
Indian camp, the attack route, and other points of interest (after Atkinson, "The Ackia
and Ogoula Tchetoka Chickasaw Village locations in 1736 during the French-Chickasaw
War," 1985; courtesy of *Mississippi Archaeology*)

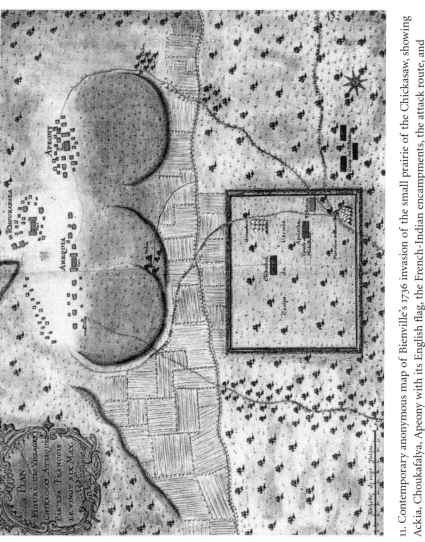

11. Contemporary anonymous map of Bienville's 1736 invasion of the small prairie of the Chickasaw, showing Ackia, Choukafalya, Apeony with its English flag, the French-Indian encampments, the attack route, and other points of interest (courtesy of American Heritage Publishing Company, with permission from Centre des Archives d'Outre-Mer, Archives Nationales, Paris)

wished to attack first. I replied to him that I had orders from the King to go first against the Natchez. . . . He said to me thereupon that he would have wished very much that I might attack Chuckafalaya first; that this village . . . gave them more trouble than all the others; that it was there that he had lost his son and his uncle."[25]

The Great Chief was supported by the other chiefs in the desire to attack Choukafalya, but Bienville insisted on the Natchez, located about three miles to the northwest. However, he promised them that after the attack on the Natchez they would return and attack Choukafalya. Perhaps perceiving that such would not likely occur, the Choctaws pretended to be leading Bienville to the Natchez village. Emerging from the woods, Bienville found himself at the small prairie: "Their guides after having made us march here and there in the woods as if to lead us to the large prairie where is the main part of the Chickasaw and Natchez villages led us at last to a prairie which is possibly a league in circumference in the middle of which we saw three small villages situated in a triangle on the crest of a hill at the foot of which an almost dry stream was flowing. . . . I made them march along the little wood that borders the Prairie in order to reach a small height on which I made them halt to take food. It was then past noon."[26]

While the force halted for lunch, reinforcements coming from the large prairie were observed by the Choctaws, and Bienville asked them to confront the Chickasaws. The Chickasaws imprudently but bravely sent forward five men carrying a peace pipe, but the Choctaws fired on them and murdered two, whose scalps and feathers were presented to Bienville. Excited by these killings, the Choctaws became more and more vocal in their desire to attack Choukafalya. Succumbing to the pressure from the Choctaws and most of his own officers to attack the three tightly clustered villages, Bienville relented. He then established a rudimentary fortification around his encampment (Figure 11). Observing people whom he believed to be Englishmen and an English flag flying at Apeony, the southernmost village, Bienville ordered the attack against Ackia, the northernmost village, in order to avoid firing on the Englishmen. According to later Chickasaw reports there were only about 100 warriors present in the small prairie during the ensuing battle, for most of them were away turkey hunting.[27]

The capture of Ackia would allow the forces to next march against nearby Choukafalya, the Choctaw objective. Ironically, Ackia was the home village of Ymahatabe,[28] who had been devoting himself to obtaining peace for his people to no avail for the previous six years. It seems somewhat fitting, therefore, that his village would bear the brunt of the French attack, the results of which would serve to teach the French that direct warfare against the Chickasaw was not something to be taken lightly. That the French were facing disaster in attempting to storm the villages should have been recognized by Bienville. The northern extremity of the north-south ridge system on which the villages were situated was the best defensive position in the whole nation. Although the area is now mostly altered by twentieth-century construction of the Tupelo Mall and old Tupelo High School, in 1736 there was a very steep bluff on the north end of the ridge where Ackia was located. From the small north-south-flowing drainage stream east of the camp, shown on Figures 10 and 11, to the top of the ridge where the villages' three palisade forts and fortified houses were located was a gradual forty-four-foot elevation increase, the slope almost bare of trees.[29]

The greatly outnumbered Chickasaw warriors placed their women and children inside the forts, stationed themselves within the loopholed forts and fortified huts, and waited for the Frenchmen to ascend the ridge. The attack force left the encampment, which was reported by Augustine Smith to have been protected by an entrenchment in the form of a half moon but was illustrated on a drawing by Dumont du Montigny to have been protected by a crude, rectangular fortification that he refers to as "Defences made of trees." A second French map (Figure 11), discussed below, also shows a rectangular encampment. As the Frenchmen circled around to the steep north end of the ridge and approached its base with drums beating and flags flying, the Chickasaw commenced firing.[30]

The initial attack movement, which began around 3 P.M., was made by a company of fifty grenadiers, 120 soldiers from eight companies, sixty Swiss soldiers, and forty-five volunteers and militiamen, all under the command of Bienville's nephew, Major Chevalier de Noyan. Ahead of them Bienville had sent black servants (slaves) carrying "mantlets" (thick padded mats), which were to serve as protection for the attack force. However, when one of the servants was killed and another wounded, the prudent carriers threw down the mats and fled.[31]

The following French attack force crossed over the small stream east of the encampment, followed the protection of the steep bluff on the north end of the ridge, and ascended it through a ravine (Figure 10). Upon emerging on top of the ridge, the Frenchmen were met with a hail of musket balls. Suffering heavy casualties, the French were able to capture the first two or three structures, which the decimated attack force had to hide behind in order to preserve their lives. By then only a small portion of the officers and soldiers were available to attack the Ackia fort, approximately seventy officers and soldiers having been killed and wounded from the murderous crossfire occasioned by the layout of the forts and fortified cabins of Ackia and Choukafalya. Major de Noyan was among the wounded and Joseph Christophe de Lusser, a Swiss captain of infantry, among those killed. While the attack force was hiding behind the houses and whatever else was available, including, according to du Montigny's drawing, a pile of canes, Bienville considered sending Jadart de Beauchamp with his 150 soldiers from Fort Conde into the fight. De Beauchamp, however, prudently opposed this under the circumstances for "it seemed to him a rather difficult thing to go and attack men who could fire directly at us without our being able to see them and without losing more than half of our men." Bienville agreed and ordered de Beauchamp to assist in a withdrawal. The Chickasaw houses being used for protection were apparently set ablaze. In trying to bring off the dead and wounded, another officer was wounded and several soldiers were killed. The Choctaws then entered into the fracas as they covered the retreat to the camp, themselves losing twenty-two men.[32]

According to du Pratz, the fortification around the encampment was constructed after the battle, which could well be the case. The official French reports are not clear on this subject. Du Pratz also states that on the night of the battle the Chickasaw tore down the houses and other structures that the French had hidden behind so they could not be so used again if another attack on the Ackia fort occurred. He further states that the French were unable to recover the bodies of the dead Frenchmen, which cannot be disputed. They were undoubtedly stripped of their clothing, after which they were probably cremated. Although the reports of Bienville and others are silent with regard to the use of grenades by the grenadiers who participated in the attack, James Adair wrote that some were thrown, but because the fuses were too long, the Chickasaws pulled them out or threw the grenades back at the French. Adair, who apparently lived in the present-day south Tupelo area at least some of the time after his arrival in 1744, had obtained two French grenades that he believed were relics of that battle. Incidentally, I was once told by a citizen of Tupelo that he knew of a person who had found a French grenade in that area.[33]

There are three known maps of the battle area that provide valuable data about the villages and the battle. These include one already cited, by du Montigny, called "Attack of the French Army"; it is of little value because it was drawn years later by an individual not present at the battle. A map produced by Ignace Francois Broutin, Chief Engineer of the Louisiana colony ("Plan a l'estime ou. Scituation de Trois villages Chicachas 1736") is extremely informative and was obviously drawn by, or directed by, someone at the scene, perhaps Broutin himself. This map (Figure 10) shows terrain features at and south of the three villages, which proved valuable in helping locate the battle area in south Tupelo. The ravine used by the French to access the ridge shown on the Broutin map is probably the one still visible behind the old Tupelo High School. The third and most remarkable of the maps of the battle area, entitled "Plan Figure des Villages Chikachas Attaquez Par les Francois le vingt six May 1736" ("Plan of the Chickasaw Villages attacked by the French on May twenty-six 1736"), is much more detailed with regard to the immediate battle area (Figure 11). It shows the three villages, labeled "Ahequia" (Ackia), "Apeony," and "Tchoukafala," on top of the ridge. A flag, undoubtedly the English one mentioned by Bienville, is depicted in the Apeony village flying over a large rectangular structure, probably a trading house. Other large, red-colored rectangles in each village are labeled "Fort." A small, blue-painted square on the left end of the Ackia structures has an illegible label containing two words, the second of which may be *deux* ("two," or "second"). No matter what the words are, the location of the Chickasaw houses captured by the French and used for protection during the battle was probably intended. Across fields and a stream from the villages and the ridge is shown an almost square fortification labeled within (translated to English) "Camps of the Armies." A road running from the camp to the Ackia village is labeled "Chemin des Troupes pour l'Attaque des Chikachas" ("Road used by the troops to attack the Chickasaws"). A road leading from the lower right part of the French encampment to the village of Apeony is labeled "Chemin des Naichez aux Anglois" ("Road from the Natchez to the English"). This road passes through a grove of trees at the foot of the ridge labeled "Piches" (peaches). A second grove on the side of the lower slope of the ridge has the same label. Another road, leading from the French encampment to the right and off the map, is labeled "Chemin de l'Armies au Portage" ("Road [or route] of the armies to the portage"). A fourth road, leading from Ackia and along the left (north) side of the French encampment, is labeled "Chemin des Natchez au Chikachas" ("Road from the Natchez to the Chickasaws"). Locations of French and Indian camps, or chiefs of the latter, are shown inside the French encampment. A cluster of words are, in French, "Apalache," "Tiensa," and "Mobilliens." These are coastal plain remnant tribes that had become closely affiliated with the French. Near a cluster of white symbols for tents is the word "Girnadiers" ("Grenadiers"), while in the lower right corner, also near white tent symbols, are the words "Monsieur de Bienville." A large gray tent, undoubtedly representing Bienville's, is on one end of the group of smaller tents. Another word appears to say, in French, "Tchacto." This is likely the camp of the Great Chief of the Choctaw, who is documented to have been present. The word "Chikachae" is written in the top center of the fortification. Possibly the French had brought some Chickasaw prisoners with them in anticipation of a possible prisoner exchange, but the word more likely represents the camp of the Choctaws from the village of Chickasahay (or its chief), who were with the force. Finally, outside the fortification and near its lower right corner is the camp of the "Tchactas" ("Choctaws"). This colored map is published in *The American Heritage History of the Thirteen Colonies*. A poor-quality black-and-white reproduction of the map had earlier been published in France by Marc de Villiers du Terrage in *Les dernieres Annees de la Louisiane francaise*.[34]

With the exception of the two peace emissaries murdered prior to the battle, no casualties were reported for the Chickasaw. The death of a Natchez, possibly one of the two murdered men mentioned above, was reported second-hand to Samuel Eveleigh through a trader named Spencer (John?), who had heard it from Augustine Smith, who arrived soon after the battle. According to Bienville the French had twenty-four soldiers killed and fifty-two wounded, but according to an unsigned report by an apparent officer and participant, over seventy soldiers, colonists, and volunteers were wounded and possibly 120 were killed. The commandant at New Orleans, however, reported that sixty or eighty were killed, which may be more accurate. An English ship captain named Colcock was told while he was in Mobile in November that the French there acknowledged a final toll from d'Artaguette's battle at Ogoula Tchetoka and the battle of Ackia/Choukafalya of about 200 soldiers and twenty-two commissioned officers killed, and he was told that forty Frenchmen were still in the hospital at Mobile.[35] This mortality figure could well be generally accurate considering that wounds often eventually proved fatal.

The army spent the night at the camp and the next day began the retreat. Bienville had stretchers made for the wounded and after marching all afternoon camped his fatigued Frenchmen only about four miles from the villages. To enhance the retreat, Bienville persuaded the reluctant Choctaw chiefs to have some of the French wounded carried by their warriors. By now the Choctaws, especially Red Shoe, were disgusted with the whole affair and wished to separate from the French, but Bienville persuaded them to stay until the portage was reached. According to recollections told to Malcolm McGee by trader Benjamin Seeley many years later, Seeley saw "the bones of the French scattered for six miles below Long Town," suggesting that some wounded died on the retreat. After embarking at the portage on May 29, the force reached Fort Tombecbe on June 1 and Mobile on June 8, where Bienville received confirmation of the fate of d'Artaguette, of whom he had heard for the first time the day before.[36]

Although there is no record of it, the Chickasaw and the English must have been jubilant over the decisive victory. There must have been apprehension also, especially among wise men of peace like Ymahatabe, who probably feared for the future of his nation in the face of the retaliations that were sure to come.

Back in New Orleans, Bienville began to defend his actions to the king. In doing so he presented legitimate excuses for the disaster but also engaged in some grasping at straws. He blamed his troops for cowardice, when in fact it was his imprudent method of attack that had resulted in the defeat. He even complained about the physical size of the soldiers in the colony, stating that the "wreched blackguards" sent to the colony were with rare exceptions all under four feet, ten inches in height. He also insinuated that the Chickasaw would not have been able to repulse them if it had not been for the English having instructed them on the art of fortification, and he intimated that the English in fact directed and fought with the Indians in both battles. In a rare communication between the French and English colonies, Bienville sent the governor of South Carolina a letter in which he accused the English traders of firing on his troops in the small prairie and encouraging the Chickasaws to burn the prisoners at Chuckalissa. These allegations were denied by the traders, especially Augustine Smith, who assured Samuel Eveleigh that there was not a single Englishman among the Chickasaw when he arrived there soon after the battle of Ackia had ended. Bienville may have indeed seen Englishmen, for Smith was contradicted by Mingo Houma, who stated that four Englishmen at Choukafalya fled to Tchitchatala upon the approach of the French and Indian forces. Thus Bienville may have seen them scurrying around in an effort to remove themselves and their belongings to a safer place.[37]

Bienville was mistaken in attributing the Chickasaw knowledge of fortifications to the English. Although the English may have influenced certain configurations of the palisaded Chickasaw forts, they were basically similar to those that Indians of the southeastern United States had been constructing for several hundred years. The fortified houses, however, may have been an English innovation. The two French drawings of "Chickasaw forts" reproduced in an article by Joseph Peyser are somewhat peculiar. According to a plan of attack, written by Chaussegros de Lery in 1739, the seven-foot-high palisade walls of the Chickasaw forts leaned inward, as depicted in one of the drawings (Diagram 6). De Lery stated that the aforementioned soldier named Richardville, who had escaped from the Chickasaw after eighteen months of captivity, was the verbal source for this configuration of at least one fort. This is the only description known that has fort walls leaning in either direction. Inward-leaning walls may well be true, however, for de Lery's discussion of what Richardville said is the only available detailed recording of an observation of the forts by a longtime observer. It seems to me, however, that if some walls leaned in either direction, they would have leaned outward. In any case, a fort with leaning walls would not have been typical. A second drawing (Diagram 3) in Peyser's article shows a rectangular fort with four triangular bastions at each corner and three smaller rectangular and triangular bastions located in the center of three walls. This fort, drawn to illustrate how approach trenches could be dug, was not discussed by de Lery or addressed by Peyser. The labeling on the drawing does not state that a Chickasaw fort is depicted but rather says it is a "Fort des Sauvages." In fact, de Lery cites Richardville as stating that in 1736 and 1737 none of the Chickasaw forts seen by him had bastions. It seems likely, therefore, that the fort in this drawing is generic and depicted for the primary purpose of showing locations of proposed trenches. Interestingly, however, Bienville stated in December 1737, after the French and Choctaw had found the Ackia, Choukafalya, and Apeony villages deserted in that year, that four forts were present rather than the three that had been there in 1736. He also stated that one of the forts had "small regular bastions." Could it be that the new, fourth fort, possibly built by the English traders, indeed had bastions similar to the European-style fort drawing in Peyser's article? Only archaeological discovery of, and excavation of, all four forts could clarify this question. However, this is not going to happen now because of almost total disturbance of the area by Tupelo development. Incidentally, there seems to be no credible documentation for a notion that trenches were commonly dug around the interior walls of Chickasaw forts. Such a trench is depicted on a display at the archaeologically discovered "Chickasaw Village" fort site on the Natchez Trace Parkway, despite the fact that a trench was not present.[38]

Humiliated by the defeat of the glorious forces of the king, the royal court in Paris reproached Bienville for having failed and instructed him to organize a second expedition. Although the court made no mention of Bienville's assertions with regard to cowardice of the soldiers, the latter wrote back that such was "the sole cause of the poor success."[39] As proof of it, Bienville went on to say that "[t]he death or the wounds of almost all the officers of the detachment indicate that they were abandoned, but those of the soldiers do not prove that they did their duty. They crowded together in large groups behind the cabins protected from the fire of the first fort, but exposed to that of the entire village which was on the left."[40]

In hindsight, and in defense of the soldiers, it must be pointed out that the method of attack used by Europeans in the eighteenth century can only be called stupid, and that used at Ackia was no exception. Customarily attacks were made with the soldiers marching and firing in ranks, and the officers were expected to be at the forefront directing the attacks. Perhaps this seemed logical to the average soldier when the opponent was using the same tactics, but the French at Ackia were not fighting other Europeans. From all reports the French could not even see the Chickasaw because they were out of sight inside the loopholed forts and fortified houses. Why, then, should the soldiers be expected to follow their officers, who were more motivated by the "honor" of their position than by logic, into the face of a murderous fire from opponents whom they could not even see? Rather than being cowards, the soldiers were logical and motivated by self-preservation.

The Choctaw below the ridge top must have been dumbfounded while observing what to them was an unorthodox method of attack. Diron d'Artaguette, in talking to Red Shoe soon after the battle, had the following observations: "This chief [Red Shoe] told me that the French did not know at all the way to carry on war; we had been able to take only a little village of thirty or forty men; that on the contrary we had lost many men without being able to say that we had killed a single one; that our troops heavily clad marched with too slow a step and so close together that it was impossible for the Chickasaws to fire without killing some of them and wounding several."[41]

4
The Road Has No Fork

Having received his instructions from the king to launch a second expedition, Bienville had to decide on the most practical route to reach the villages. His alternatives other than the Mobile/Tombigbee River were to go up the Mississippi to Prudhomme Bluff and march overland or to go up the Mississippi and then up the Yazoo River to the Chackchiuma villages and march overland from there. Because his route depended on the time of year and other more complex variables and he could not judge very far in advance whether logistical conditions would be suitable, Bienville had difficulty establishing an attack plan.

At first, Bienville proposed to move in January 1739, but some conditions became favorable for an earlier date, so he moved his plans forward to January 1738. By June 1737, however, other conditions were not right so he changed the date back to January 1739. Finally, in about July 1739, the second expedition got under way, the Mississippi River route to the Prudhomme Bluff area having been decided upon.[1]

In the meantime, between June 1736 and September 1739, the Chickasaw were subjected to continued harassment from the Indian allies of the French. In February 1737 Bienville reported that he had induced several parties of Choctaw to attack the Chickasaw but that the promise of the Iroquois to come and join the Arkansas to attack them had not been kept. Diron d'Artaguette reported that by May 1737 he had paid the Choctaw for the scalps of about twenty Chickasaw men and women and that "they go [to attack] in little bands of five, ten, twelve, twenty men."[2]

In June 1737 Bienville received assurances from the Choctaw that in August they would go and lay waste to the Chickasaw cornfields. Men from ten villages in the eastern division were to strike the small prairie and men from the remaining villages were to strike the large prairie. Bienville agreed to allow Joseph Chauvin de Lery, two of de Lery's brothers, and two Choctaw interpreters to accompany them. In October 1737 this expedition did in fact occur, but only Choctaws led by the medal chiefs from the western division participated.[3] On October 10, the Choctaw force of 500 men, de Lery, and his brothers assumed a position in front of the Choukafalya, Apeony, and Ackia forts. While "entrenchments" were being made, the Chickasaw launched an attack but were repulsed, losing six or seven men. After forcing the Chickasaws back into their forts, the Choctaws cut the corn growing near the villages (see fields on Figure 11). Later that day de Lery and some of the Choctaws went to the large prairie where the same thing occurred. From the forts the Chickasaws watched as the Choctaws destroyed their cornfields. Getting low on ammunition, the Choctaws returned with ten scalps and a woman prisoner. No Choctaws were killed, but fourteen were wounded.[4]

Upon de Lery's return, the Choctaws of the eastern division became excited when they learned of the success of the western division warriors. Thereupon, de Lery suggested that another attack be made as soon as possible. On October 23 a force of more than 900 Choctaw from both divisions again marched on the Chickasaw. The Choctaws encountered a Chickasaw hunting party several miles from the villages and killed five men. When they reached the small prairie, de Lery and the Choctaws discovered that the villages of Choukafalya, Apeony, and Ackia had been abandoned and burned a few days earlier.[5]

On the ridge where the Chickasaw had won their great victory in 1736, the French found the burned remains of four forts. Bienville attributed the destruction of the forts to the Chickasaw upon desertion of the small prairie and described what they had looked like: "One of their forts had small regular bastions, two were long squares and another was oval in the Indian fashion. These forts each had in their enclosures a fortified cabin which occupied almost all their space leaving only a gallery all around six to seven feet in width between the piles of the cabin and those of the exterior enclosure."[6]

There are no known records of the circumstances of the abandonment and burning of the small prairie villages. Bienville only stated that they were burned by the enemy when they "retired." Possibly the pro-French faction among the Chickasaw destroyed the villages, but this is unlikely unless Ymahatabe, who was still living at Ackia in August 1737, had recently moved to the large prairie. Such a move could have been motivated by the humiliating striking of Ymahatabe by an English trader in August. Ymahatabe possibly caused the small prairie villages to be peacefully abandoned and burned, hoping this would appease the Choctaw and end hostilities. If the villages were evacuated because of destruction by Choctaw or northern Indians, the French and/or Choctaw who found them in that condition would seemingly have already learned about it. That at least Choukafalya continued as a village is evidenced by its mention in a French document in 1739, and in September 1740 there was a reference made with regard to attacking "the two villages of the small prairie." Thus the small prairie was reoccupied after 1737 by reestablishment of Choukafalya and either reconstruction of one of the smaller villages or construction of a new one whose name is unknown. In any case, the southern part of the Chickasaw settlement, usually called Long Town, was thereafter occupied by Chickasaws into the nineteenth century.[7]

After burning the few remaining houses in the abandoned small prairie and destroying everything still intact, the Choctaw inflicted a supreme and rare insult. They disinterred the bodies of two Chickasaws killed in the attack a few weeks earlier, quartered the bodies, and "put them on posts after having carried them about in fine style with all the cries and dances customary among them."[8]

Satisfied with the destruction of the small prairie villages, which had been their objective since at least 1734, the Choctaws wished to return home. However, de Lery talked some of them into accompanying him to the large prairie, and soon the remainder joined them. Tchitchatala, the closest village to the small prairie, was one of those approached in the large prairie. The present-day historical site on the Natchez Trace Parkway called "Chickasaw Village" was apparently part of Tchitchatala, which may also have been the town name. Tchitchatala was probably the scene of the following events: "The Chickasaws did not dare come and attack them and they only fired at each other a great deal on both sides. A Chickasaw was killed near a fort and carried away by his people. Another having been killed also very near the stockade, the Choctaw made determined efforts to get his scalp but they were repulsed with the loss of one of their good warriors. The combat began again more actively for the body of this warrior which the Choctaws finally carried away but they did not get the Chickasaws scalp."[9]

The palisade trench of a rectangular Chickasaw fort measuring eighty-five by eighty feet was discovered during excavations at site MLe14 (22Le524) on the Natchez Trace Parkway property. This could be the fort attacked, for Tchitchatala probably included the MLe14 area. The parkway fort's boundary can be viewed by visitors at the "Chickasaw Village" site, as it is delineated with curbing.[10]

In this expedition the Choctaw killed twelve men and one woman, but more significantly a new approach to weakening the Chickasaw as well as the English was realized by the French. While the fighting was occurring most of the Choctaw began dispersing to chase a herd of horses that appeared on the edge of the prairie, and they subsequently killed more than twenty-five horses and captured twenty-two.[11] From that time on the Choctaw were encouraged by the French to concentrate their attacks against horses as well as to carry out the destruction of corn. During most of the next two years the Chickasaw suffered greatly from Choctaw raids and losses of these two resources. The English traders were no less perturbed, for many of the horses killed and captured were their own.

The Chickasaw must have been severely anguished while watching without recourse the shooting and theft of their beloved horses in 1737 and afterward. By the 1730s, horses had become as much a part of the prairie settlement landscape as were the Chickasaw houses, forts, corn houses, council houses, agricultural fields, and small water ponds. These horses were somewhat smaller than most horses and were apparent descendants of those brought to the New World by the Spanish in the mid-sixteenth century and afterward. These swift and hardy animals were subsequently bred on the prairie grasslands of the Chickasaw into a distinctive subspecies that was later referred to as the "Chickasaw Pony."[12]

Alarmed by the persistent harassment and trade interference, King George instructed the governor of the South Carolina colony to afford protection to the Chickasaw and Natchez. No evidence is known that this protection involved a military force, but in early 1738 the English devised a plan by which they hoped to bring peace and halt the economic disruption within the Chickasaw nation. In carrying it out they utilized the friendliness that Red Shoe had nearly always displayed toward them in exchange for merchandise. In about 1738 the English ransomed a condemned Choctaw prisoner and sent him to Red Shoe, requesting that he meet with them and some Chickasaw chiefs to discuss peace. Red Shoe, who was not blind to the fact that his people were being used by the French, visited the Chickasaw and returned to his village with a ten-man peace delegation. Although not all the Choctaw agreed with Red Shoe's actions, the peace negotiated was not openly opposed, much to the consternation of the French.[13]

The peace, although it did not last long, was a welcome respite to the Chickasaw. As early as mid-1737 tension had gotten so intense in the nation that over 160 Natchez men and women went to live among the Creek and Cherokee, allegedly because of fear of some of the Chickasaw. The ones who went to the Cherokee could be the Cherokee nation Natchez refugees encountered by a Frenchman named Bonnefoy in 1742. Also at about this time, an unspecified number of Chickasaws moved into the Creek nation, thereby resulting in establishment of the Breed Camp discussed in Chapter 1. Others may have joined the eastern Chickasaw on the Savannah River, as had Squirrel King's group in the 1720s. The Natchez established at least one settlement in the upper Creek nation, probably the village referred to as "Natchie" in 1772 and "Nau-chee" in 1798. In July 1737, Ymahatabe was accused of planning to leave secretly with a number of other Chickasaws to settle among the Alibama, a French-allied tribe that managed to remain neutral in the Indian conflicts. Whether this was true or not, Ymahatabe stayed. If true, his staying may have been due to opposition to such a step by Mingo Ouma, who chastised Chickasaws for entertaining ideas like that "at a time when [their nation] needed them," but perhaps he stayed also because of the love and attachment Bienville said the Chickasaw had for their "splendid and fertile country."[14]

The Chickasaw-Choctaw peace had no effect on Bienville's plans to march against the Chickasaw for a second time. In January 1739 a report to the king penned in Paris voiced the opinion that it would "be advantageous if he [Bienville] were able to do without them [the Choctaw] because in addition to the embarrassment and the expense they would cause, the success of the expedition without their assistance would humiliate them and render them more docile." However, in early 1739 the peace was broken by the faction opposed to Red Shoe, who also became disgruntled with the English at about the same time. Upon hearing this, Bienville invited the Choctaw to participate in the expedition, which was drawing close to finally getting under way. Subsequently, Choctaws began making raids on the Chickasaw and bringing back scalps.[15]

A raid in late 1738 or early 1739 was believed to have been made by a group of "Chigassaies" who were settled among the Choctaw. These Indians attacked an English trader convoy about thirty miles east of the nation, and this was followed by an attack on their camp, which was plundered. Eleven Chickasaws who had come to escort the traders were there at the time, four of whom were killed. A trader named Binon had three fingers shot off, and one named Fisher was wounded in both feet.[16]

When news of the French campaign preparations reached the Chickasaw, the English traders there appealed to the South Carolina government for assistance. In early November 1739, John Searjent, who had been sent by horse express with a message for the Chickasaw, arrived back in Charlestown with an alarming letter penned by Thomas Andrews, the trader who had helped establish the Chickasaw settlement among the Upper Creeks. The Commons House of Assembly immediately appointed a committee to consider the matter. The committee recommended the very next day that the Chickasaw be furnished immediately with 500 pounds of powder, 800 pounds of bullets, 200 pounds of "Swan shot," 1,000 gun flints, twenty guns, and six pounds of paint.[17]

In September 1739 Bienville's long-delayed expedition began. This time the French, having received from France enough firepower and troops to theoretically render the Chickasaw helpless, were determined to succeed.

Prior to the campaign Bienville had, in 1739, established at present-day Memphis a depot named Fort Assumption, to which were transported over a period of two or three months hundreds of thousands of pounds of munitions and supplies. Munitions sent from France included four eight-pounder cannon, eight four-pounder cannon, two nine-pounder brass mortars, two six-pounder cannon, twelve small mortars, two thousand grenades, fifty thousand pounds of powder, and sixty thousand pounds of musket balls. Some of the powder and balls were distributed to the various garrisons, however. Also, because Bienville had suggested that tunnels could be dug underneath the villages for the purpose of blowing them up, six miners with a sufficient supply of bombs were included.[18]

Although 550 new troops had been dispatched from France, sickness and deaths resulted in only about 300 French troops disembarking for Fort Assumption in two convoys on July 25 and August 8, 1739. However, these convoys had been preceded by others with unrecorded numbers of troops. From the northern colony came 230 additional French troops and 503 northern Indians from many tribes. Apparently, the army that finally coalesced at Fort Assumption numbered at least 1,000 Frenchmen. At the Choctaw village of Chickasahay, Jean Paul Le Sueur and 1,000 Indians of that tribe, primarily from the eastern division, waited for orders to march up from the south in order to prevent an anticipated escape attempt.[19]

Despite the extensive preparations and assemblage of troops, supplies, and munitions, Bienville's plans were thwarted by the weather, sickness, and desertions of both Indians and Frenchmen. Upon reaching Fort Assumption in November he became aware that there was not a suitable road over which he could transport his artillery and other munitions because of the mud and swollen creeks and rivers resulting from the winter rains. Moreover, of the 300 horses and about 200 oxen that had been acquired from the Illinois and Natchitoches posts, all but thirty of the former and thirty-five yoke of oxen had perished, gotten lost, or become too emaciated for use as a result of the bad weather encountered while transporting them to Fort Assumption.[20]

By February 9, 1740, Bienville had despaired of being able to carry out the campaign as originally planned. Without sufficient oxen and horses he could not transport the artillery, which was considered essential for breaching the forts and fortified houses of the Chickasaw. Ten companies of the army, the grenadiers, and others had been, by January 15, reduced by sickness to no more than 218 Frenchmen. He therefore laid before a council of war an alternate design that included reducing the size of the army to 800 selected Frenchmen (most of the sick having apparently recovered) and carrying only one four-pounder cannon and a nine-inch mortar. Even with these reductions, Bienville stressed that they would "still have left more than one hundred and thirty thousand pounds to transport with the thirty-five yoke of oxen and the thirty horses that [were] in the yard."[21]

Following these disclosures to the council of war, Bienville stated that he was in no condition to go to war. He then asked for each council member's opinion. All ten of the members present voted against continuing the campaign because of the "unforeseen accidents," as Bienville had put it.[22]

By this time the expedition forces had been bivouacked at Fort Assumption for more than two months, and the northern Indians present were restless and undoubtedly disgusted with the French. They had been trying to get Bienville to let them march against the Chickasaw alone, but he had refused them because he thought it might interfere with the French attack. However, at various times since November 1739, small groups of Indians had already launched scouting expeditions to the Chickasaw villages, which sometimes resulted in short conflicts and the deaths of Chickasaw men and women. A few were captured and brought to Fort Assumption, where some were horribly tortured to death by the French Indian allies.[23]

Upon realizing that the campaign had to be terminated and for reasons outlined below, Bienville assigned a detachment of French Canadian soldiers under Pierre Joseph de Celeron to accompany the restless Indians to the Chickasaw villages. On February 2, a force of 337 Indians and 201 Frenchmen set out for the villages. On the 7th, de Celeron, who had been ill on February 2, caught up with the advance force led by an officer whose surname was St. Pierre.[24]

Prior to this, Red Shoe had decided against continuing war with the Chickasaw. Aware of the looming massive French attack, he sent to the Chickasaw, in December 1739, eighteen men of his pro-English faction under the leadership of the chief of Cushtusha. The apparent purpose of the mission was to warn the Chickasaw and English of the French intentions, to assure them of Red Shoe's neutrality in the coming attack, and to urge them to try to make peace with the French. It seems, however, that the English traders were extremely angry with Red Shoe because of the earlier raids that his faction had launched against the Chickasaw, in which many of the English horses had been lost. This, combined with the English-Chickasaw distrust of the delegation, resulted in the assassination, apparently at Choukafalya, of sixteen of them, including the chief of Cushtusha. Learning of this, the Choctaw force waiting for orders under Le Sueur at Chickasahay became even more eager to march against the Chickasaw.[25]

Like the northern Indians, the Choctaw force at Chickasahay had become quite restless by February 1740. In that month a contingent of sixty Choctaw arrived at Fort Assumption to find out when they were supposed to march, arriving there only a few days after de Celeron had left. After the news of the assassination of the sixteen Choctaws was related to Bienville, he gave the angry group permission to join de Celeron's force, which was accomplished prior to its arrival at the Chickasaw villages.[26]

During the two months that the army had been at Fort Assumption, the Chickasaw had made several attempts to enter into peace negotiations. In October 1739, the "Great Chief," undoubtedly Ymahatabe, had caused a letter, written by a French captive, to be delivered to Bienville, in which he proposed peace. Bienville, expecting to make an attack, ignored it as well as subsequent "symbols of peace" (probably white objects). Upon the discontinuation of the campaign, however, Bienville changed his mind, for a peace was now the only way to salvage his dignity in the expensive and futile campaign. He therefore instructed de Celeron to go ahead and "strike a blow" at the Chickasaw but afterward make attempts to confer with them on the subject of peace.[27]

With these instructions de Celeron cautiously moved his force of about 600 Indians and Frenchmen nearer to the Chickasaw, making the approach over the same road used by d'Artaguette in 1736. Much time was spent crossing creeks and rivers and hunting bear, deer, and buffalo. On February 14th, snow fell until midnight.[28]

On February 21, near the Chickasaw settlement, de Celeron encountered the large Choctaw force that had come up from the south. The attack force marched along the Old Town Creek floodplain and reached the border of the prairie near present-day Belden. When the French ascended the prairie hills bordering the floodplain, the Chickasaw fired several shots and retreated. The force then encamped. Gunshots were heard during the rainy night, and the cries of the agitated Chickasaw and beating of their drums kept the anxiety-stricken Frenchmen awake all night.[29] The d'Artaguette fiasco probably bore heavily on their minds, for the situation was exactly the same.

At the crossing of Old Town Creek, approximately where old U.S. Highway 78 crosses today, de Celeron left 100 men to guard the equipment and build a fort (see Figure 8). The main force advanced toward the large prairie villages on February 22 and observed the villages, where both English and French flags were flying. About twenty Chickasaw came forward with a white flag of peace, but the uncontrollable Indians fired upon the group, which returned to its fort. The attack force advanced and came within 200 yards of three forts, all relatively close together (Figure 8). The force surrounded some of the adjacent fortified cabins and began firing on them at about nine A.M. The well-protected Chickasaw returned the fire, and at noon the attack force retreated.[30] The village attacked was undoubtedly Ogoula Tchetoka.

Twice during this action some Chickasaws came out with white flags, but again the Indians fired on them. During this action the fort that flew a French flag did not fire. Likely this was the fort mentioned by a French officer in which two captured Chickasaws said all the women (and children?) were placed.[31] This fort may have been explicitly built for that purpose after the d'Artaguette attack in 1736.

On the 23rd, de Celeron proposed to move closer to the villages and build another fort. The Indian allies were not in favor of this, especially the Missouri and Choctaw. The latter stated that "it was not possible to take their forts"; that they were out of food and "did not wish to eat horse meat." Thereafter, the

Choctaws left for home. This caused the other Indian groups to lose morale, and they would not cooperate with the French in their plan to entrench themselves near the enemy. De Celeron afterward persuaded the Indian allies to refrain from firing in the future on the Chickasaws who had been coming out with white flags.[32]

The rainy night passed quietly on both sides. The next morning the small French fort, which had been built on the floodplain of Old Town Creek, was inundated, so the force moved at about one P.M. to the prairie hills bordering the floodplain and built a new fort (in present-day Belden). This palisade fort (Figure 8) was twice the size of the first fort.[33]

On February 25, after light skirmishing in front of the Chickasaw villages, a Chickasaw carrying a white flag appeared and two adopted Chickasaws of the Iroquois were sent to meet him. One of the adopted Chickasaws entered one of their forts, where he presented the French peace conditions. Suspicious of the French, the Chickasaws insisted that a Frenchman and one man from each Indian nation be sent to them before they would surrender the French prisoners whom they had among them. The adopted Chickasaw left the Iroquois flag with the Chickasaws and they, in turn, gave him one of theirs.[34]

About two hours after dark three Chickasaws were escorted to a cabin where all the chiefs of the Indian allies were assembled. These Chickasaws asked for pity on their wives and children should they suffer a future defeat. The Chickasaw, who had been unable to find all the Natchez whom the French wanted (most had fled) were still fearful of a determined French-Indian attack. They said that they were trying their best to round up the Natchez but they needed more time. The Chickasaws asked that the killing of their horses cease, which had been going on since the arrival of the attack force. The Iroquois gave the Chickasaws two hoops of cheese and the meeting ended.[35]

The next day the Chickasaw requested negotiations with a "French chief." Although wary of doing this, de Celeron sent St. Pierre along with the Indian negotiators. Shortly thereafter St. Pierre met with sixty to eighty Chickasaws and five English traders, who told him that most of the Natchez could not be found. After trading of knives, belts, garters, and some guns, the Chickasaws returned to their village, again promising to turn over the Natchez.[36]

On the 27th, a Chickasaw chief named Tchatamingo, accompanied by four Englishmen, approached the French fort, but they were not allowed to enter. The Iroquois accused the Chickasaws of lying about their promise to turn over the Natchez, which accusation the Chickasaws countered by saying that there were unsettled disagreements about it among the chiefs, but that it would be done. That evening Tchatamingo and others returned and gave one Natchez man and two Natchez women to the Iroquois and promised that the other Natchez and the French prisoners would be turned over the next day. The

Chickasaws related that most of the Natchez were far away hunting, and that ten or twelve had run away. It was also reported that some Natchez had been bound but were released by some young men. The Chickasaws also stated that the English in the villages had participated in the earlier gun battles.[37]

On the 28th, Tchatamingo again returned to the French fort in company with several other Chickasaw chiefs. This time they gave the Iroquois one Natchez and two French prisoners who were turned over to de Celeron. The Iroquois were presented some pottery and a calumet by the Chickasaw chiefs as a sign of reconciliation. Thereafter more trading took place among the Chickasaw and the Indian allies; in the evening a third French prisoner was brought to the fort. Tchatamingo promised that he and others would go to Fort Assumption in four days, where they would ask Bienville for ratification of the peace. De Celeron agreed and the force returned to Fort Assumption.[38]

On March 7 the advance sentinels informed Bienville, at Fort Assumption, that a Chickasaw chief, who turned out to be Ymahatabe, was approaching in the company of four Englishmen, much to the surprise of the French. One of these English traders had earlier caught up with de Celeron on his return and complained about the loss of his horses during the confrontations and asked for their return, which de Celeron refused. The stubborn Englishman then replied that he would later come to Fort Assumption and claim them, to which de Celeron responded that "he was at perfect liberty to do so."[39]

Bienville conferred with the four English traders, these or some others of whom had been accused by the Natchez captives not only of helping other Natchez escape but also of having dressed like Indians and fought in the recent hostilities. When the four could not produce their commissions from the English governor, Bienville had them arrested, a possibility that Ymahatabe had warned them of if they accompanied him.[40]

The traders are probably the four named by Edmond Atkin: Godfrey Harding, Florence Agan, and two men with the last names Clarke and Picket. According to Atkin the men were taken to Mobile where they remained in prison for three or four years under the charge that they had assisted the Chickasaw in a gunfight when invaded by the French. They were then taken to Brest, France, where their imprisonment continued. Picket managed to escape and Clarke, after becoming Catholic, was released; he thereafter married in France. Harding and Agan were still in prison in 1747 when some other Englishmen were imprisoned there during a war between Britain and France. Atkin speculated that Harding and Agan were still in the Brest prison at the time he was writing (1755).[41]

Bienville observed that Ymahatabe did not seem concerned about the arrests of the Englishmen. Perhaps this attitude is understandable for in 1737 an English trader who had obviously gained the favor of the general Chickasaw population, had struck Ymahatabe with his fist when he tried to stop the trader from making derogatory remarks about the French to the captain of Pacana, a pro-French chief of the Alibama Indians.[42]

Prior to the interrogation and arrests of the English traders, Bienville and Ymahatabe had entered into discussions of peace. The latter, in response to Bienville's question as to why he had come alone to confer with him about an affair of such great importance, stated that "the other chiefs had not wished to run the risk of being captured or insulted by [the French Indian allies] on the mere word of an officer whom they did not know, but that the desire that he had always had to procure peace for his nation had made him disregard these considerations and that he had come only to learn . . . what they had to fear or to hope."[43]

Bienville then reminded Ymahatabe of the recent assassination of the sixteen Choctaw emissaries and warned him that he should not expect any assurances of a negotiated peace with the Choctaw. To this Ymahatabe replied that the assassination had occurred because they were expecting an act of treachery from those Choctaws but that the Chickasaw were ready to make reparation for that mistake. Ymahatabe left the next day, promising to return on about March 21 with one or more chiefs from each village to confer again and reach agreements on the peace.[44]

In the meantime, Bienville turned his attention to dismantling the depot at Fort Assumption. Since the Iroquois were still there and becoming a burden he had them return home. At the same time the troops and volunteers from Canada and the Illinois post departed, leaving him with only his regular troops, by that time about 500 men.[45]

By the end of the month Ymahatabe had not returned and Bienville began to break camp. The marine detachment with twelve boats loaded with the munitions and conveyances left on March 30. Remaining troops were busy destroying Fort Assumption and the affiliated buildings when Ymahatabe and six other chiefs appeared. As Bienville had suspected, the Chickasaw peace envoy had been delayed because of Iroquois hostilities. After leaving Fort Assumption the Iroquois had made an attack on the Chickasaw in which they obtained at least four captives and killed four others. Some of them then returned north but about fifty remained behind to launch another attack. The Chickasaw chiefs had set out three times but were forced to return because of these hostile Indians.[46]

Following Ymahatabe's explanation of why the envoy was so late, he proceeded to present the peace solicitations. After presenting Bienville with a Natchez woman and her three children, apparently all who remained, Ymahatabe stated that he had presented to a Chickasaw council the French conditions for peace and that each village was agreeable, as evidenced by the seven representatives who had come, one from each village. He then gave the following speech, as paraphrased by Bienville:

> I can therefore assure you on behalf of all the villages whose envoys you see here that not only will we no longer give asylum to the Natchez, but further that we will follow them in their retreats until we have exterminated the rest of this nation which has cost us so much blood. We do not ask that you restrain the vengeance that the Choctaws wish to exact for their warriors. It is just, but we shall behave in such a way that the French and they will be satisfied. Our purpose is to repair the loss that they have caused, by means of Natchez slaves whom we shall deliver to them. We are then very well satisfied for the present if you restrain the nations of the North and of the Mississippi.[47]

To this speech Bienville replied that he was "quite willing" to have the northern and Mississippi River Indians cease hostilities. With regard to the Choctaw, however, Bienville claimed to have told the envoy that he would continue to supply munitions to that nation and to pay them for Chickasaw scalps until they were satisfied that they had taken revenge for the loss of their sixteen murdered men. According to Bienville the Chickasaw envoy consented and the peace was concluded. A few small presents were given to the Chickasaw chiefs and they parted company with Bienville. On April 1, Bienville departed for New Orleans, where he would once again endure the barbs of his critics, both in France and in the colony.[48]

5
The Road Lengthens

Although the peace negotiated in March 1740 ended direct French participation in the war against the Chickasaw, there was no respite for the Chickasaw; actually, harassment of them increased. Even while the peace negotiations were going on at Fort Assumption Red Shoe arrived at the Chickasaw villages with a force of 450 to 500 warriors. Upon their arrival in front of one of the large villages, possibly Tchitchatala, a Chickasaw chief came out unarmed and spoke as follows: "My brothers we are not your enemies at all. We have always desired peace and at the present time several of our chiefs have gone to ask the great chief of the French for it. . . . If you wish to fight your enemies, fight those two villages [Choukafalya and Falatchao]. Destroy them, if you can; we shall not be sorry because of it. It is they who have always worked to perpetuate the war that is destroying us."[1]

Although the Choctaws did approach the two villages pointed out by the chief, no attack was made other than the usual hit-and-run skirmishing that for centuries had been the custom of southeastern Indians. According to Red Shoe these two villages were the only ones that wanted to continue the war with the Choctaw, and the warriors of the large village stood outside the fort unarmed when they returned. For the next two days Red Shoe's warriors contented themselves with attacking the English and Chickasaw horses, killing more than twenty and capturing sixty.[2]

Apparently the majority of the Chickasaw tried to keep their word with regard to the expulsion of the Natchez. In June 1740 Bienville reported that the Natchez had become aware of the Chickasaw intention to rid their villages of them and that the majority had fled in fear prior to de Celeron's expedition in February. According to Ymahatabe, however, some returned after the Fort Assumption peace, and the Chickasaw were not able to agree to kill them because of the continued hostilities from the Choctaw and from the northern Indians as well. That the northern Indians were continuing to attack "more mercilessly than before" indicated to the Chickasaw that the French did not intend to abide by the peace and wanted the Natchez removed so they could more easily attack and destroy the Chickasaw. This was a perfectly logical assumption on the part of the bewildered and justifiably suspicious Chickasaw. Ymahatabe assured the French, however, that the Chickasaw had treated the returning Natchez so badly that "they had obliged them to flee" and thus "the motive that had led [the French] to declare war on them no longer existed." By the end of 1741 Bienville was convinced that the remaining Natchez had moved out of the nation, which indeed seems to have been the case.[3]

Regardless of the exodus of the Natchez, which Bienville had been demanding since 1733, he still would not entertain the idea of working for a peace between the Chickasaw and Choctaw. With the Natchez excuse no longer available, Bienville reverted to the old pre-Natchez excuse, probably the real one, for refusing to cease the hostilities against the Chickasaw. In September 1741 he wrote: "I do not think that it is good policy in the present circumstances to procure peace with the Choctaws for them [the Chickasaws] because we should always have to fear that the English under cover of this reconciliation might find means to make their way into this latter nation where they would give us more anxiety than ever."[4]

In the meantime, the Choctaw continued their harassment of the Chickasaw. In September 1740 another large Choctaw force returned to cut the Chickasaw corn. Again, as in April, Chickasaws in the large prairie objected to being attacked in retaliation for the death of Red Shoe's sixteen men and directed them to "the two villages of the small prairie who alone were guilty of these murders."[5] This statement may indicate that following the mysterious abandonment of the small prairie in 1737 the village of Falatchao was later moved there and Choukafalya was reestablished in that prairie. This speculation is based on the 1740 confrontation discussed above, when a Chickasaw chief tried to persuade the Choctaws under Red Shoe to attack Choukafalya and Falatchao rather than his village because those two were the ones "who have always worked to perpetuate the war."

Bienville continued to encourage the Choctaw attacks, especially after having realized the importance of the horse raids: "I do not see any better way to ruin the English race at the Chickasaws and consequently to bring this nation to subjection than to have their horses carried away from time to time, without which they can not carry away the peltries and return to their country."[6]

By May 1742 the Choctaw were again eager to send a large force against the Chickasaw, partially because some of the disgruntled Chickasaw had gone on the offensive and in two separate incidents had attacked some Choctaws near their village. In August 1742 a force of between 1,600 and 2,000 Choctaws, consisting of warriors from ten eastern-division villages and all villages of the western division under Red Shoe, marched to Ogoula Tchetoka, accompanied by ten Frenchmen, some of whom were civilian volunteers. Upon reaching the village, the Choctaw chiefs engaged in a long discussion but eventually agreed to attack from the same direction as had d'Artaguette in 1736, the northwest.[7]

Upon perceiving the coming attack, Chickasaws approached the English traders Nicholas Chinnery and James Campbell with demands for ammunition, as the governor of South Carolina had earlier given them permission to do in an emergency. Reluctantly but in fear of bodily harm if they refused, Chinnery and Campbell gave away ammunition worth 486 English pounds. A trader named John McFarland likewise gave up sixty pounds worth of ammunition.[8]

At seven o'clock on the morning of August 25 a vigorous two-hour attack was made against the village and fort but the Chickasaw were not dislodged. The Chickasaws lost five men and seven women and had three people taken prisoner. The Choctaws lost two warriors and had seven wounded. The next day a second attack was made in which the Chickasaws lost two men and the Choctaws had seven wounded. After skirmishing with the Chickasaws for two more days, the Choctaws retreated and returned to their territory, having destroyed as much corn as possible and killing or capturing nine horses. According to Chinnery and Campbell, total Choctaw casualties were about fifty men and those of the Chickasaw about twenty-five men.[9]

At this time the Chickasaw were being subjected to perhaps the worst harassment in their history, apparently as a result of the Choctaw's desire for revenge for the assassination of the sixteen men in late 1739. For the first time since about 1723 the Choctaw were waging a serious war against the Chickasaw that did not seem to need encouragement from the French. Bienville reported that in 1741 the Choctaw killed or captured as many as fifty-four Chickasaw. In February 1742 the Choctaw were "keeping large parties in the field." Some captured English letters turned over to the French stressed that "the Choctaws were pressing them so closely that they did not dare to go out and had killed so many of their horses that they could not carry back their peltries." In September of that year, soon after the August attack, a force of about 1,500 Choctaw "ravaged more than a league of country, killed six men, took 13 prisoners, and carried off 20 horses." In December, eleven Choctaw raiding parties were reported to be in the field. From the north in 1741 and 1742 came raids, encouraged by the governor of New France at the request of Bienville, by Mississague, Ottawa, Pottawatomi, Huron, Kickapoo, Miami, and Mascoutin.[10] In March 1742 Bienville wrote, "never have our allies been so well disposed and never have they acted so effectively to reduce this rebellious nation, and it is not to be doubted that with a little attention to humoring this disposition we shall soon accomplish our purpose in this."[11]

By June 1742 there were consistent reports that some of the Chickasaw had migrated east and that most of those remaining were intending to follow. In late 1742 or early 1743 some Chickasaw prisoners stated that the majority of the Chickasaw had spoken in favor of moving east to Carolina, where they could be protected by the English, but that a Chickasaw chief, described by Bienville as the "author of the war," had prevented such an exodus. The numerous Chickasaw losses during 1741 and 1742 were alarming to the English, who feared they had been reduced to such a condition that they could no longer be depended upon as a barrier between the French and the English colonies.[12]

Although unnamed, the chief who prevented an exodus of the Chickasaw to Carolina was probably Oulacta Tasca, who had favored receiving the Natchez in 1730 and, as discussed in Chapter 2, was described at that time as the leader of the "seditions organized against the French." Another possibility, however, is Mingo Houma of Ogoula Tchetoka, who had been the leader of the band that fought the French convoy on the Mississippi River in 1735, a circumstance that caused Bienville to give up hope of a peaceful settlement.

With the retirement and return to France of Bienville in 1743, the Chickasaw peace chiefs saw an opportunity to find the French colony more disposed to cessation of hostilities. In August 1743 four Chickasaw chiefs sent a letter, written by a French captive, to the new governor, Pierre Francois de Cavagnal et Vaudreuil. In this letter the chiefs stated that they wanted peace with the French, that no Natchez remained, and that the Choctaw were "madmen" to attack them. They then asked for powder, bullets, guns, and coats in exchange for their French captives. In concluding the letter, they threatened to attack the French and Indians on the Mississippi and elsewhere if their wishes for peace were refused. Vaudreuil, being receptive to peace because he believed such would lead to peace with the Cherokee, who had recently become aggressive, replied that he would procure peace for them if they would drive out the English traders and agree to having the Choctaw involved in the peace agreement.[13]

To show good faith the Chickasaw released at different times three Frenchmen, a French woman, and an Indian ally. Subsequently, Vaudreuil caused the Choctaw to cease hostilities. In November, however, some Choctaws pillaged an English convoy, killing three Englishmen and two Chickasaws, which caused Vaudreuil to fear that the Chickasaw would not drive out the English (they undoubtedly did not intend to). While waiting for news he requested again that the Choctaw continue cessation of hostilities and they agreed.[14]

Because the French colony was nearly always low in merchandise, about which Vaudreuil repeatedly complained to Paris, the Choctaw began trading for English merchandise through the Chickasaw during this "pretended peace," as Vaudreuil termed it. Because of the unavailability of French merchandise with which to supply the Chickasaw if they should drive away the English, Vaudreuil, in December 1744, apologetically voiced his decision to declare war on them again, although acknowledging that they could not be blamed for refusing to drive away the English when doing so would deprive them of goods.[15] The beleaguered Chickasaw were still enmeshed in the same impasse that had existed since 1720.

Frustrated by not having the means to establish peace between the Indians within the confines of the English-French struggle for domination, Vaudreuil turned to the course of his predecessor, Bienville. By December 1744 he was busy trying to keep Red Shoe in tow by encouraging him to show his allegiance to the French through attacks on the Chickasaw. In order to control Red Shoe's influence among the Choctaw, he also induced other Choctaw leaders to do the same, thereby demonstrating their opposition to Red Shoe's pro-English leaning.[16] Thus, things had returned to normal for the persecuted Chickasaw.

By late 1745 Vaudreuil's thinking had completely meshed with that displayed earlier by Bienville. In October of that year he wrote to France, "I am still sparing nothing at the present to have [the Chickasaw] harassed on every side, but I fear that in spite of the blows that it will be possible to strike them, it will be very difficult to reduce them except with open force. . . . Besides, our Choctaws are becoming weary of making war on them. . . . I [therefore] propose to you that we make a new attempt to destroy them, without which it will never be possible to make an end of it no matter what raids may be made upon them."[17]

Despite Vaudreuil's solicitations to the king with regard to a third French expedition against the Chickasaw, such never transpired. Accounts of such an expedition, supposedly in 1752, have become embedded in the literature as a result of an undocumented passage by Francois-Xavier Martin in his 1827 work, *History of Louisiana from the Earliest Period.*[18]

From 1745 until the end of the Louisiana colony in 1763, the Choctaw-Chickasaw War continued, but on a more subdued level. The French never attempted a large-scale direct attack on the Chickasaw again, but they continued to induce Choctaw and other allies to harass them. In retaliation the Chickasaw committed acts of violence against the Choctaw. When hostilities against the Chickasaw became intense, certain Chickasaw chiefs asked for peace, as in the past. In late 1744 Ymahatabe had secretly sent a woman to the Choctaw with a proposal of peace between them and the English. Consequently a delegation of pro-English Choctaw came to the Chickasaw nation in January 1745, where trader John Campbell, who had probably initiated the plan, gave talks. The Choctaw agreed to a peace and invited the English traders to come into the Choctaw nation. However, an entire year elapsed before any went, probably because of an occurrence three months later. In April 1745 three Chickasaw chiefs, eleven warriors, and a French captive named Languedocq went toward the Alabama Indians to ratify a treaty between the Choctaw on the one side and the Abeca, Tallapoosa, and Chickasaw on the other. On the way a band of Choctaw under Alibamon Mingo attacked them and killed two of the chiefs and a principal warrior. Afraid to go any farther, the Chickasaws put the French captive in a bark canoe, along with a white flag, a calumet, and a white fan, all symbols of peace. After the canoe capsized, Languedocq arrived at Fort Tombecbe on a floating tree.[19]

The Frenchman relayed a message to Vaudreuil from the Chickasaw that they still wanted peace. Thereupon, Languedocq and Renochon, a Frenchman who had lived with the Chickasaw in about 1728, were sent with seven Alabamas to the Chickasaw village of Taskaouilo. Here Renochon met with six Chickasaw chiefs (Chanstabe Mingo, Okapakana Mingo, Pahe Mingo, Sonachabe Mingo, Oulacta Oupaye, and Tachikeianantla Opaye). Again the major peace term, removal of the English, was presented to the chiefs. At this the warriors present at the assembly became animated, saying that they wanted no peace and that the chiefs alone had asked for it.[20] The warriors then voiced the opinion that had kept, and would continue to keep, the English among the Chickasaw: "But for the English we would all be dead. Those are our genuine Frenchmen. Neither the length of the road nor the difficulty in bringing us the things we need ever rebuffs them. They do not let us lack anything. The red men who are [the French] allies and at their door go without breeches, the women and the children have no blankets to protect themselves against the cold; how would [the French] manage to give us merchandise, are we not far distant from them?"[21]

As on occasion before, the South Carolina Commons House of Assembly responded to the Chickasaws' almost constant need for guns and ammunition in the face of the consistent harassment. In March 1746, the House approved the provision of 250 pounds of powder and 500 pounds of musket balls for the Chickasaw.[22]

Because war had broken out in Europe between France and England (King George's War), merchandise for the Indians became even more scarce than usual in the French colony, the result of which was increased English-Choctaw trade intercourse. Red Shoe, in 1745 and 1746, attempted to negotiate peace with Ymahatabe and English traders without French agreement. Ultimately, dissension between Red Shoe's pro-English faction and the opposing pro-French faction broke out into a bitter and bloody civil war that lasted from 1746 until 1750.[23]

Upon attention being turned away from the Chickasaw because of the internal strife among the Choctaw, Vaudreuil began to encourage the Arkansas to increase attacks on the Chickasaw by having the commander of the Arkansas post pay them for scalps.[24] Overall, however, the Chickasaw enjoyed relatively peaceful times during the civil war.

The Choctaw civil war was at least partially a result of earlier scheming by two English traders, James Adair and John Campbell, to open more trade with the Choctaw. In concert with two Chickasaw leaders, Pastabe and Pahemingo-Amalahta, they persuaded the Chickasaw in June 1746 to send presents to Red Shoe with an offer of peace. Partly because of a recent revelation that a Frenchman allegedly had performed forced sexual relations with his favorite wife, Red Shoe was able to gain the support of a considerable portion of the Choctaw and soon sent a return sixty-man peace delegation to the Chickasaw. Adair and the two Chickasaws mentioned above greeted the delegation with verbose anti-French, pro-English rhetoric and, supplied with numerous presents, the delegation returned home strongly inclined to oppose the French; a peace was thereafter made with the Chickasaw in November 1746. According to Edmond Atkin, writing in 1753, Governor Glenn of South Carolina sent a letter to Adair, dated April 22, 1747, in which he urged Adair, an unlicensed trader at the time, to stir up the Choctaw against the French and to try taking Fort Tombecbe. Adair then went to the pro-English Choctaw at the "seven lower towns which lie next to New Orleans," carrying as much ammunition as he could spare. He presented a number of "red chiefs of war" and some "old beloved men" with silver ornaments and tried to persuade them to go with him to attack Fort Tombecbe, but they refused, citing fear of the dreadful cannon there. Adair told the Choctaw that a trader named Charles McNaire was also coming to them with goods, after which he traveled to Charlestown, where he obtained a trading license and more goods for the Indians.[25]

Adair, James Campbell, and William Newbury (or Newberry) claimed to have incurred financial losses as a result of their personal efforts to establish an entrenched trade with the Choctaw. In a petition to the Commons House, they asked for reimbursement:

> [T]he Petitioners having lived there and constantly supplied the Chickesaws in their hot War (even beyond the Petitioners' Abilities) to harass the French and their Indians, and having by large Presents so bribed and managed the Choctaws as to compleat a firm Peace between them and the English, which had greatly involved the Petitioners in debt, notwithstanding which there were three or four Traders fitting out for that Nation to build upon the Ruins of the Petitioners. And therefore humbly praying that they may be allowed a Permit for the said Nation for the Space of two or three years, that they may thereby be enabled to collect their Debts.[26]

The peace responses of Red Shoe soon resulted in a tragedy for the Chickasaw. Shortly after the return of Red Shoe's peace delegation, a Chickasaw peace envoy arrived at the Choctaw village of Bouctoucoulou Chitto for the purpose of later meeting with Red Shoe at his village, Couechitto. Just as the Chickasaw emissaries were about to leave for Couechitto, however, an attack was made on them by Choctaws opposed to Red Shoe that killed "the two most famous partisans of these Chickasaw," along with a woman. Their scalps were presented to Vaudreuil.[27] Although these "famous partisans" are not identified by name in the known historical documents, one of them may have been the great peacemaker Ymahatabe. His name is noticeably absent in subsequent historical records.

While the French were preoccupied with the Choctaw civil war, English traders and the Chickasaw seized opportunities to strike back at the French in retaliation for recent Choctaw killings of Englishmen and Chickasaws. In May 1749 a group of Abeca and some pro-English Choctaws entered the Chickasaw nation on their way to attack the Arkansas Indians across the Mississippi River. Apparently at the encouragement of James Adair and other English traders, the party was joined by a contingent of Chickasaw under the leadership of Paya Mattaha, the head war chief by that time. The combined force descended the Mississippi River in a fleet of canoes, attacked the Arkansas post, killed six Frenchmen, and captured eight women and children. The Arkansas Indians normally would have been there to protect the post, but they were at this particular time about fifteen miles away planting some new fields. The war party then proceeded downriver to the vicinity of the Natchez post, the news of which terrified the French inhabitants all the way to New Orleans, for it was feared that the Choctaw and Chickasaw had combined forces and were planning to ravage the French settlements on the lower Mississippi. The settlers' fears were reinforced by a report that three Englishmen had been observed in the lead canoes.[28]

After the attack Adair purchased three of the French captives whom Paya Mattaha's force had captured at the Arkansas post. Following notification to come to Carolina with a party of Chickasaws to meet with the governor, Adair gave the French captives back to the war chief so that he might impress the governor by making "a flourishing entrance into Charles-town" with the prisoners in tow. Having learned that they were coming through their country with the French prisoners, the neutral Alibama and Kawita became upset and informed Vaudreuil that they planned to demand that the Chickasaw hand over the prisoners or they would have a Choctaw party take them by force. Accordingly, the leader of the Alibama and his men joined the Chickasaw party and the leader delivered a speech in which he asked Paya Mattaha to turn over the prisoners to him as proof that he desired retightening of the "old friend-knot" that had been loosened by recent events.[29] Paya Mattaha refused to turn over the prisoners and delivered a long speech in which he exalted the English, criticized the French, and admonished the Alabama leader for threatening the Chickasaw-Alabama peace by demanding the slaves. "You have no right to demand of me those ugly French prisoners. We took them in, at the risque of blood; and at home in our national council, we firmly agreed not to part with any of them, in a tame manner, until we got to Charles-town. If the Muskoghe [Creek Indians] are as desirous as we to continue to hold each other firmly by the hand, we shall never loose the friend-knot."[30]

As Adair and the Chickasaws proceeded toward Carolina they were shadowed and occasionally attacked. Finally, at the solicitation of some other English traders on behalf of the French commandant at the Alabama fort (Toulouse; see Figure 1), Paya Mattaha turned over the prisoners, a woman and her two children, and received French presents in exchange.[31]

With the success of the French party in the Choctaw civil war, the gains made among the Choctaw by the English were mostly lost. By 1751 the English traders who had been going among the upper Choctaws were so intimidated that few dared risk going there. Some had been killed while in, as well as outside, the Choctaw nation during the civil war. In September 1750 James Campbell reported that in July a band of "French party Choctaw" had killed a trader named John Legrove in the Chickasaw nation, and in November John Campbell, a possible relative of James Campbell, was killed by Choctaws near the Chickasaw settlement.[32]

Despite termination of most travel to the Choctaw, trade continued by Choctaws coming to or near the Chickasaw settlement. During the 1750s the Chickasaw found this English trade with the Choctaw somewhat distasteful, for the guns and ammunition so obtained were thought to be used against them by raiding bands of pro-French Choctaw, as related in a petition of the Chickasaw head men to the South Carolina governor: "Our enemies, the Chactaws, has had many large supplies of Ammunition, Guns &c. carried threw our Towns by your beloved Men to them which we never attempted hindering, and not long since a large Quantity was delivered them in our Towns, and soon after they came to war with us with the Guns and Amunition you were pleased to give them."[33]

Upon the conclusion of the Choctaw civil war, the relative quiet that the Chickasaw had enjoyed came to an end. The French immediately began coercing both Choctaw factions to demonstrate their good faith and loyalty by attacking the Chickasaw. The result was almost continuous harassment of the Chickasaw during the 1750s by the Choctaw, as well as by pro-French factions of other groups in the Mississippi Valley and elsewhere.

Perhaps the largest Choctaw force to attack the Chickasaw was organized in 1752. As mentioned above, this event has been mistakenly defined by some historians as a third major French campaign, carried out under Governor Vaudreuil. Actually, it entailed an attack on September 6 by a substantial force of Choctaws, said to have been drawn from thirty villages, accompanied by only a handful of Frenchmen. Vaudreuil was not one of them. The all-day gun battle resulted in the deaths of five Chickasaws, including a woman, and the wounding of three others. The Chickasaw were scattered about, firing from erosional gullies, features common in that part of the prairie in which they lived. The attackers left the next day with about forty captured horses.[34]

That the Chickasaws fought from gullies in a scattered fashion could be a response to fear of hand grenades being thrown at them while inside forts or fortified houses. At a July 1736 conference in Savannah, Governor Oglethorpe told some western Chickasaw chiefs who had only recently endured the French attacks that grenades and mortars could be disastrous in confined spaces and that they should fight in open spaces or behind trees. The principal chiefs present and those who did most or all of the talking were "Postubee[,] Chief of the Chickesaws," and chief "Mingobemingo." A "Pastabe Mingo" was a headman or leading warrior at the Breed Camp in 1757 (see Chapter 1), but this man is not likely to be the same one who had gone to Georgia in 1736. More likely Postubee was the same chief whose name was spelled "Pastabe" in 1746 and who assisted traders James Adair and John Campbell with their peace solicitations to Red Shoe in that year. I have seen no other reference to the chief with the peculiar name of Mingobemingo, which would seem to translate to "chief of chiefs" or something similar. Perhaps Postubee was the head war chief, or considered himself so, and Mingobemingo was a chief who considered himself to be the great chief of the Chickasaw from the English viewpoint. As already noted, Ymahatabe had apparently been the great chief (in the eyes of the French at least) since 1730 or earlier.[35]

The years 1755–1758 were especially destructive to the Chickasaw in terms of life and property. Four Choctaw raids occurred in the winter of 1755, resulting in the deaths of twenty Chickasaw warriors and the capture of several women and children. The trader Jerome Courtonne reported that on September 11, 1755, about 1,000 Choctaws carrying four French flags attacked at three different places in the "Old Field." Seven days later a night attack occurred, during which "the best part of one Town" was burned to the ground and eight women and children were captured. During the attacks many horses were captured, including thirteen of Courtonne's. In November 1756, a war leader of the Chickasaw called Pyomingo and his forty companions were attacked at their hunting camp by at least 100 northern Indians, referred to by the traders as "northward" or "back enemy" Indians. The Chickasaw group had two men killed and five men and two women wounded. Alarmed by the establishment of a heavily garrisoned French fort on the lower Cherokee (Tennessee) River, the Chickasaw and the English traders furiously constructed, in eight days, four large additional forts in early 1758.[36]

This prolonged war against the Chickasaw was devastating. Dozens of Chickasaw men, women, and children were killed every year by small to large hit-and-run bands of Indians that attacked Chickasaws wherever they could be found, primarily at their settlement and hunting camps. Of course, the Chickasaw were retaliating. An example of the intensity of the violence is illustrated by the following excerpts from the journal of John Buckles in 1757 and 1758:

28th May. A Gang of Chawcktaws set a House on Fire in the Night, but did no other mischief.

12th June. A Gang of Quapaws [Arkansas] killed and scalped six Chickersaws in the Night at a Hunting Camp.

24th. A small Gang of Chactas came into the Nation in the Night, killed a Fellow and wounded a Child as they were asleep on a Corn House Scaffold.

1st August. Five Chickersaws were killed by the Cherockees being a hunting on the Cherockee River.

14th. The Chactaws [killed?] a young Fellow in the Night.

26th September. Three Chickersaws were killed at their hunting Camp by a Gang of Chactaws.

5th October. Five Chickersaws were killed by the Chactaws at a hunting camp.

15th December. The Chactaws killed a Chickersaw Fellow as he was going out a hunting and carryed off a Woman and two Children Prisoners. The 16th the Chickersaws pursued them, came up with them, killed five and redeemed said Woman and Children.

18th. A Gang of Chickersaws went against the French on the 20th September [and] returned having killed one French Man and brought in his scalp.

19th. A Gang of Chickersaws returned from War with one Chactaw Scalp.

8th February. A Chickersaw Woman was killed in Sight of the Houses by the Chactaws.

14th. A Chickersaw was killed by the Northward Indians.

16th. A Woman was killed and scalped as she was cutting Wood in sight of the Houses by the Chactaws.

2nd April. The second Gang returned from War against the French having killed one Indian and brought in his Scalp.

19th. An Army of Chactaws consisting of about two hundred Men came here . . . [and returned home] after killing several of our Horses and carrying off ten Head.[37]

Because of the hostilities, conditions in the nation for both the Chickasaw and the English traders deteriorated to an extremely stressful level. In all their petitions and letters written to the governor of South Carolina, the Chickasaw leaders emphasized the extreme curtailment of hunting because of fear of the enemy while doing so, as well as the fear of leaving their women, children, and old men unprotected. Thus food was in short supply and hides were not being procured with which to barter for clothing, arms, ammunition, and other goods. This, of course, highly reduced the commercial success of the traders whose income depended on the acquisition of hides. This is best articulated in a petition (undoubtedly penned for them by a trader) from the headmen of the Chickasaw in 1754:

> It's true some Years ago we did not mind how many our Enemies were, but that is not our case at Present, our Number being reduced to a handful of Men, and thereby we are rendered uncapable of keeping our Ground without a Continuance of your friendly Assistance, we not being able to hunt nor are we free from the hands of our Enemies even in our Towns, so that it is impossible for us to kill Dear to buy Cloathing for ourselves, our Wives, and Children, or even to purchase Amunition. This the English Traders that comes amongst us . . . [are aware] of from the small Quantity of Skins they have carried out of this Nation these last two Years to what they used to do formerly. . . . Our Traders is tired out with trusting us with Ammunition and Guns, nor can we be angry with them as it has not been in our Power to pay them for it, and many other Things we had from them, so that we may now say our Lives is in your Power to save or to let the enemy have their Desire off us. It has always been your desire as well as our own that we should keep this Ground from the French [and now] we must either run from it and save our Lives or die upon it.[38]

The stress and fear had indeed become too much for some of the Chickasaw. By this time, 1754, some had moved east to live with the eastern Chickasaw colony groups or other tribes, such as the Creek and Cherokee. Such is acknowledged elsewhere in the petition quoted from above, where it is stated that "a great many of our people has left us; a thing we are sorry at, but young people will rather go from us to live in peace than stay here where they are in danger every day." A census of the males conducted by John Buckles just prior to the petition revealed that the main Chickasaw settlement contained 340 able gunmen, 25 old men between 50 and 70 years of age, and 155 young boys. He estimated that the female adults numbered two or three times as many as the men and that young girls probably about equaled the number of young boys.[39] The adult male population was thus about half what it had been forty years earlier.

As first suggested by Charles H. Fairbanks ("Ethnographic Report on Royce Area 79"), the Chickasaws who migrated to the Cherokee between 1750 and 1754 are probably those who established the controversial settlement on the north side of the Tennessee River in present-day Madison County, Alabama. I am in total agreement with Fairbanks on this logical explanation for the so-called "Chickasaw Old Fields" in that area. After pointing out that this locale eventually found its way into some of the various Chickasaw migration legends, Fairbanks states:

> There is a strong suggestion that the identification of Chickasaw Old Fields with the tribe is of comparatively late origin. This view would hold that the Chickasaw crystalized as a tribe in northern Mississippi and began an eastward extension to Chickasaw Old Fields about 1750. This would be partly a population expansion and partly the result of . . . French pressures from the southwest. The attraction of colonial trade from the Atlantic litoral might also have been a factor. At any rate they were traditionally defeated by the Cherokee at Chickasaw Old Fields in 1766. From that time onward they maintained an interest and some occupancy of the northern, or right, bank of the Tennessee.[40]

Alarmed by potential loss of his Tombigbee River Chickasaw trade clients, John Buckles urged the Chickasaw leaders to intensify their efforts to discourage migration of the inhabitants. He said to them what they already knew: "Indeavour to keep your Warriors together for the Future, and bring back all you can that have formerly left your Land by which means you'l increase and be strong and able to defend yourselves against all your enemies. You may be sure whenever you leave your Lands and settle in other nations you will be no more a People. Besides you'l lose your antient Rights and Customs, and be confined to comply with the Laws and Customs of other Nations whom you live amongst, who perhaps may use you hardly, and you will get no Satisfaction."[41]

Fear that the French might launch another major campaign caused the Chickasaw to seek means of reinforcement. At various times when harassment was intensified, appeals were made to the eastern Chickasaw in Georgia and South Carolina and to the Breed Camp to send warriors back to the homeland. Some may have gone, but there is no known documentation. The Chickasaw also encouraged the Cherokee to send assistance, which was done in February 1753 when forty-six Cherokee arrived almost naked due to having lost all their guns, blankets, and boots when their canoes overturned in river rapids. The fiasco continued when thirteen of them, outfitted by the Chickasaw, went toward the Choctaw settlements only to be attacked on the way by a Choctaw force that killed three of them and wounded another. The remainder threw away their guns and hurriedly retreated to the Chickasaw settlement. The English trader who recorded these incidents did not expect any more Cherokee to attempt war with the Choctaw, which indeed appears to have been the case.[42]

In the face of potential disintegration of their nation, the Chickasaw leaders were often in desperate need of additional guns and ammunition to hold off the merciless onslaught of the Choctaw and other Indian allies of the French. The English traders, with much to lose financially if the Chickasaw were lost, supported with letters and journals the petitions asking the South Carolina colony for aid. In 1754 the governor of South Carolina sent, by trader John Buckles, 75 guns, 600 pounds of powder, 1,200 pounds of musket balls, 4,000 gun flints, 75 white blankets, and 6 pounds of paint. In February of 1756 the House provided the Chickasaw with 75 guns, 600 pounds of powder, 1,200 pounds of musket balls, 3,000 flints, 6 pounds of vermillion, and assorted cloth and clothing. The House reimbursed Jerome Courtonne for carrying twenty-five horse loads of guns and ammunition to the Chickasaw in 1755, and in 1757 the House reimbursed him for carrying presents to the Chickasaw valued at 870 English pounds. In emergencies, during attacks, English traders continued to give ammunition to the Chickasaw that otherwise the Indians would have had to purchase. In January 1754 John Buckles and John Tanner presented to the Commons House an account in the amount of 426 pounds to cover the cost of ammunition "supplied the Chickasaw Indians when attacked [in 1753] in their Nation by the French and Chactaw Indians."[43]

6

A Better Road Traveled

The road to impending possible destruction of the Chickasaw finally came to an end in the early 1760s when the Seven Years' War (French and Indian War) between France and Britain ended. The war had begun in 1754 when Britain resolved to oust the French from America. Following great British victories at Louisbourg and Fort Duquesne in 1758, Fort Niagra, Martinique (West Indies), and Quebec in 1759, and Montreal in 1760, French power in North America was shattered. In the south, the Cherokee sued for peace in 1761 after a bloody war with the southern colonies. As mentioned in Chapter 1, Chickasaw participation in the French and Indian War was confined to limited manpower aid to the colonies during the Cherokee conflict. The Chickasaw contribution to ouster of the French had been of long duration, however, for they had significantly contributed to preventing the northern and southern French colonies from consolidating in the Mississippi Valley and thereby becoming a more formidable adversary for the British.[1]

Fighting between the French and British continued for another three years, but in the Caribbean. By the Treaty of Paris, signed in 1763, France ceded Canada and all territory east of the Mississippi River except New Orleans to Great Britain; New Orleans and the vast territory west of the Mississippi went to Spain, and the latter gave up Florida to Britain. During the last few years of the war, the political situation had changed little with regard to English/French/Chickasaw interactions. The Chickasaw, Choctaw, Creek, and other Indian groups continued to serve as barriers between the French and English, so interior military campaigns were not attempted by either European power. English trade with the Chickasaw continued, as did the usual limited, unorganized English trade with the Choctaw. With the termination of the Louisiana colony, the European powers' long-running tug-of-war with the Chickasaw and other Indian nations ceased. The French-allied Indians in the south, especially the Choctaw, were at first bewildered, for their French trade goods supply had been abruptly cut off, leaving them with no established European ally and no organized access to the only available European goods, those of the English.[2]

The news of the end of the Louisiana colony must have been received with euphoria in the Chickasaw nation, where so much blood had been shed as a result of European politics. The Chickasaw had endured despite irrevocable disruption and alteration of their quite efficient political and social structures that had existed prior to the coming of the Europeans. Although French and English exploitation had resulted in internal stress and division, the Chickasaws' strong allegiance to a common cause, cultural survival, had enabled them to retain their identity as an unconquered nation. Now they were on a new and better road, but one that was to eventually narrow again.

Soon after the war, British officials began to address the problem of unallied Indian groups occasioned by the exodus of France. In 1763, representatives from the Chickasaw, Choctaw, Cherokee, and Creek tribes were invited to a November conference, or "congress," at Augusta, Georgia, for the purpose of assuring them of British friendship and assistance and to discuss trade. The conference was attended by the governors of Virginia, South and North Carolina, and Georgia; almost 900 male and female Indians were present, but only forty-five were Chickasaw. John Stuart, who had been appointed superintendent of Indian Affairs for the southern district (south of the Ohio River) on January 5, 1762, opened the conference as general manager. He spoke of reconciliations and continuance of friendships with the Chickasaw and others. Afterward the Indian leaders began to speak, beginning with principal Chickasaw chief Paya Mattaha, who stated, "You must not look on [me] as on other Indian Nations, for [I am] True and Trusty, [we] are few but faithful." The desire was voiced that the traders who resided among the Chickasaw, Cherokee, and Creek should be honest and responsible, and Paya Mattaha asked that the traders to his nation be limited to John Highrider and John Brown. His motivation in asking for only these two men is unknown, but he apparently felt that some he had dealt with before were unworthy. Regardless, his wishes did not transpire: one among others not named by Paya Mattaha, James Adair, continued to trade in the nation until about 1769 and while there wrote much of his *History of the American Indians*. Creek, Cherokee, and Choctaw representatives had more serious concerns to speak of than did the Chickasaw chief, especially those who represented the disaffected Creek tribes.[3]

In order to establish control over the Indian territories, Britain incorporated them into its North American governmental organization. In 1764 Florida was divided, with West Florida stretching from the Chattahoochee River to the Mississippi River. George Johnstone was appointed governor, with the capital at Pensacola. His judicial district, in which were the Chickasaw, Choctaw, Creek, and other groups, extended north to the Ohio River. As mentioned

above, John Stuart was superintendent of Indian Affairs for that district. Policies were fashioned by Johnstone and Stuart through which they could admin-
ister the Indian nations, particularly with regard to trade regulation and non-
intrusions on the Indian lands guaranteed them by the Royal Proclamation of
1763. In March 1765, Johnstone and Stuart called a council in Mobile with the
Chickasaw and Choctaw, the main purposes of which were to explain the new
system to them and declare friendship and, with regard to the Chickasaw, reaffirm their friendship. The Indians agreed to the terms of a treaty, which was
signed on April 27, 1765. In part the treaty consisted of a peace between the
English and the Chickasaw and Choctaw, as well as between the Chickasaw and
Choctaw. These peace pledges were never broken.[4] Paya Mattaha spoke only
once at the council, in an address to the Choctaws, part of which follows:

> [Y]ou will consider that I am a warrior & not accustomed to make Long
> Speeches. You will therefore not expect a fine Speech from me. My Younger
> Brothers: The Talks we have heard at this meeting have determined me
> to Speak to you in a friendly manner. I shall not therefore call to mind
> old affairs. Let what is past be buried in Oblivion, & Let us only now think
> of what is to Come. Some of you were always my Friends & supported
> the Interest of the English in your Nation. The Red Captain & Chulus-
> tamastabe were of the Same Sentiments with me, they went to Visit the
> English & the Treatment they received confirmed their Attachment to me,
> for it was by my advice that they undertook the Journey at the Risque of
> their Lives yet they did not repent of having performed it. While the
> French were in this Land division and Discord reigned in your Country,
> you fought and killed each other; but now look around & See Peace and
> Plenty; You are all Children of one Family & have but one Father, who
> admonishes & orders you to Live in Unity & Love each other. Let us now
> return to our Village hand in hand rejoicing & carrying with us the Pres-
> ents of our Elder Brothers.[5]

Unfortunately the Creek were not yet pacified, and in 1766 a war broke out
between the Upper Creek and the Choctaw that lasted until 1775. For the first
time in recorded history the Chickasaw and Choctaw became allies when the
former entered the war in 1768. After two years, however, the Chickasaw withdrew and remained neutral thereafter. The British finally interceded and ended
the war because of their desire for the Indian nations to be at peace so they
could be utilized as allies against the revolting Americans.[6]

In enforcing the stipulations of a royal plan for the management of Indian
affairs, which called for licensing of traders under substantial bonds and for-
bidding traders from selling alcoholic drink and certain types of ammunition,

Stuart appointed "commissaries" (Indian agents) to the Chickasaw and other tribes. According to the plan, commissaries were to live in the same town as that resided in by a tribal representative, who was to be appointed by a council made up of one man selected from each town. John McIntosh, the man appointed Chickasaw commissary by Stuart in 1765, had been a soldier under Oglethorpe at the capture of St. Augustine in the 1740s, where he lost a finger at the hands of a sword-swinging Spaniard. In later years he had been a minor British public official. Rather than set up residence in an established Chickasaw town, McIntosh soon developed a homestead on the Natchez Trace about twelve miles west of the nearest prairie town (Old/Big Town) and on the north side of "Paontitack" (present-day Pontotoc) Creek, an upper northern branch of Yaneka Creek (now Chiwapa) in present-day Pontotoc County (Figure 1). He built a house in that location, developed agricultural fields, and eventually kept there a herd of cattle and some black slaves. Alexander Fraser, an Englishman who was living in Campbell Town township, British West Florida, by early 1769, visited him at the commissary in 1766 and later reported to John Stuart that he "need not expect to come at the truth from any Trader but you may safely trust to his information, as I know him to be a man of such honesty that nothing cou'd make him conceal any thing which regards his Majesty's Service." The chief chosen to represent the Chickasaw, Paya Mattaha, had a plantation by 1771 located just north of McIntosh's commissary, both of which are shown on the map made in 1773 by Joseph Purcell. Paya Mattaha may have moved his residence from the large prairie to this isolated woodland location because of McIntosh's establishment of the commissary. In 1771, Bernard Romans discovered that the cattle at the commissary were said by McIntosh to belong to that Chickasaw chief. McIntosh's commissary and farmstead are undoubtedly the origin of the Chickasaw settlement known as "Pontitack" by the turn of the nineteenth century.[7]

The previous literature regarding John McIntosh's commissary, or house, has placed it in the wrong place. Harry Warren originated the error in 1904 by surmising erroneously that agent John McIntosh founded a small settlement in present-day Pontotoc County called Tockshish when he moved to the Chickasaw nation and that this was the British Indian agency. He based this assertion on the fact that a John McIntosh was living there by 1800. However, that John McIntosh was the agent's son. Agent McIntosh died in 1780, a fact unknown to Warren and the subsequent historians who have cited his article. The Purcell map shows "Commissary McIntosh's Plantation" on the north side of the northern headwater tributary (Pontotoc Creek) of present-day Chiwapa Creek. Purcell obtained Chickasaw-area data for his map from Romans, who wrote in his book that he visited "Mr. Commissary" in late 1771 and that he lived at "Paon titack" (not to be confused with the present Pontotoc located five miles to the northwest). On the map compiled by Captain Roberts on which Romans's data were incorporated, a fortlike structure symbol is located on the north side of Pontotoc Creek in the same place shown for McIntosh's plantation by Purcell. These representations of the location of McIntosh's commissary are supported by Malcolm McGee's statement that McIntosh, with whom McGee lived for several years, died in 1780 "at a little fort" on the old Natchez Trace "a little below the union of Pontotoc & other creeks." The site of McIntosh's commissary house is near the site of the nineteenth-century Chickasaw Council House, erected in 1821, where the Chickasaw removal treaty of 1832 (Treaty of Pontotoc Creek) was signed.[8]

By 1771 other plantations and facilities had been established by traders and mixed bloods in the Chickasaw territory. Some of these are listed on the Purcell map (as well as the Roberts map), but not all were specifically located. In addition to the main Chickasaw villages in present-day Lee County and McIntosh's and Paya Mattaha's plantations already discussed, the other sites, as obtained by Romans and listed on the Purcell map, are as follows:

McGillwray & Strathers Plant'
Bubbys Hog Crawle
Latcho Hoa Indian Plantas'
McBeans Hog Crawle
Colbert's Plantations
Late John Highriders Plant'

The "McGillwray & Strathers" plantation is shown on the south side of upper Chiwapa/Yaneka Creek and a few miles east of "Opay Mattahaw's Plantation" (in present-day Pontotoc County). Purcell locates a "Rubby's Hog Craul" on the east bank of Old Town Creek and a few miles north of its mouth (in present-day Lee or Monroe County). This undoubtedly is the same as "Bubbys Hog Crawle," as indeed it appears on the Roberts map. There was an English trader among the Chickasaw by the mid-1760s whose name appears in documents as "Bubby"/"Bubbie" or "James Bubbie/Bubby." According to Malcolm McGee, James Bubby drowned while on a beaver hunt, which would have been at an unknown time after 1771. "McBeans Hog Crawle" was undoubtedly associated with John McBean, a man who was serving as a packhorseman for John Highrider by 1766. Nothing at present is known about these so-called Hog Crawl sites, but possibly the term indicates places where hogs were driven across steep-banked creeks. "McGillwray" was probably John McGillivray, a merchant from Mobile who traded with the Chickasaw and served in West Florida as a colonel in the British army during the American Revolution (see Chapter 7). He was probably the father of mixed-blood William McGillivray, a prominent Chickasaw chief in the very late eighteenth century and early nineteenth century. In 1771, Paya Mattaha spoke of a "John McGuillivray" who had helped him understand measuring procedures and like matters. "Strather" was probably Arthur Strother, presumably the man who owned "Mr. Strother's plantation on Mobile Bay." By early 1769 he was a resident of Campbell Town township in British West Florida and by 1788 he was associated with the New Orleans mercantile/trading firm of Mather and Strother. This firm was trading with the Chickasaw at that time. The man who operated the Chickasaw plantation could also, alternatively, have been the "William Struthers" who attended a Chickasaw and Choctaw congress with the British in Mobile in late 1771 and early 1772. Earlier, in June 1770, a "Mr. Strothers" was described as a trader then in the nation who was violating British trade regulations. The Colbert plantations listed by Purcell were undoubtedly those of trader James Colbert, who lived among the Chickasaw from an early age until his death in very late 1783 while militarily opposing the American revolutionists and the Spanish; he fathered several mixed-blood sons (William, George, Levi, James, and others), some of whom became prominent in Chickasaw affairs in the late eighteenth and early nineteenth centuries. Arrell Gibson (*The Chickasaws*), incidentally, is mistaken in stating that Pitman Colbert was also James the younger. Pitman was actually a son of George Colbert. Colbert's plantations in 1771 and later were probably between Old Town Creek and the Tombigbee River just above their junction, as indicated by the Collot map of about 1796–1800, which shows fields and the word "Colbert" in that location. As discussed above, John Highrider was one of the two traders who Paya Mattaha recommended in 1763 to be exclusive traders to the Chickasaw.[9] The location of the site of his plantation is unknown.

Representing the large prairie Chickasaw villages listed on the Purcell map are three dots along the north side of apparent Kings Creek and south of apparent Old Town Creek. Apparent Old Town Creek is labeled "Ahala Ikalchubbe." The dots are followed by the words "Latcho Hoa," which obviously correspond to "Latcho Hoa Indian [Plantations]" in Purcell's list. Interestingly, Purcell locates, in about the position of old Ogoula Tchetoka, "Chicalaia Opays Matahaw T." The *T* undoubtedly stands for "Town" since the other villages in the large prairie are shown to the east and south. Purcell does not show the existence of old Ogoula Tchetoka, which the French and Indians had harassed so much in the 1730s, 1740s, and 1750s. In his book, however, Romans lists "Chucalissa," the name by which Ogoula Tchetoka and adjoining villages seem to have always been called by the English. "Chicalaia" probably refers to Chukalissa rather than to part of a Chickasaw's name. Probably despite omitting punctuation Purcell was meaning to convey the following: "Chicalaia (or Chukalissa), the town of Opays Matahaw." If so, this Matahaw is probably the same chief (Paya Mattaha) who had a plantation near McIntosh's commissary. Purcell's and Romans's spellings of some of the other Chickasaw villages are quite different from the popular and more accurate French spellings but are similar enough to correlate them with the latter.[10]

After his appointment as commissary, McIntosh was instructed to assist Major Robert Farmar on his expedition up the Mississippi River to visit the Illinois country and meet with the Illinois Indians, who had not yet reacted positively to the English. In the summer of 1765, McIntosh and 125 Chickasaws under Paya Mattaha met Farmar and his British regiment at the mouth of the Margot (now Wolf) River, at present-day Memphis. The Chickasaws killed buffalo, bear, and deer as the expedition moved up the Mississippi River, thus supplying the expedition with meat and thereby enabling completion of the trip. After arriving in the Illinois country, McIntosh and fourteen of the best Chickasaw hunters accompanied Farmar to Fort Chartres, where the latter was able to obtain a favorable response from the Illinois, partly because of the strong impression the presence of Chickasaw English allies made on them. To appease the Englishmen, both the Illinois and Chickasaw agreed to a peace. Either while on this expedition or afterward, Chickasaws burned Fort Massac, a French fort on the Mississippi River in the Illinois country.[11]

An incident regarding opposition to McIntosh by some of the traders is discussed by historian Russell Snapp, who relates that initially the traders who had been undermined by McIntosh's strict enforcement of Stuart's regulations opposed him by aligning themselves with a Chickasaw faction that opposed Paya Mattaha. James Adair reported that in early 1766, traders John Buckles and Alexander McIntosh (probably not closely or at all related to the agent) called a meeting at a chief's house, where they told the Chickasaws present that Stuart had told them that everything he had said to the Indians at Mobile had been revoked and that Stuart did not like McIntosh any more than the Indians. When McIntosh returned from the trip to the Illinois country, he exposed these statements as lies and arrested Buckles and an associate, which so infuriated Alexander McIntosh that he gave a Chickasaw named Piomingo Eulixi (or Elooksee) and other Chickasaws who were opposed to Paya Mattaha a keg of rum and incited them with talk after they became intoxicated. The Chickasaw group then went to McIntosh's house in the middle of the night and broke open the door with a hatchet, but they ran off when McIntosh "bounded up."[12] McIntosh strongly responded to the disruptive situation:

> In my last [letter] I informed you of the obstinate disorderly behavior of Messrs Buckles and Goodwine, that they were spiteful fixt Enemys to all Order & the Quiet of this Nation, and they ought not on any account to be allowed to return here; I likewise said enough of that corrupted Vil-

lain, their Friend, Paheminggo Elookse, that he was the Common Disturber of the Peace of this Nation, utterly despised by the Heads of it &
should be equally despised below, by every gentleman of Power & Friendship to his Country, both to check his desponding villainy & support
Pahemataka [Paya Mattaha] who is an approved steady friend of the English, and made chieftain both by his own War graduation and the most
solemn publick Ceremonies of a long Continuance lately renewed at Mobile. . . . [Buckles's] Associate Goodwin swore before many People, with
the most wrathfull Bitterness that he would make a New Hell of this
Place after his Return to it. . . . As to Mr. Alexander McIntosh, since I
committed his partner & hireling, he has run on in despite to all Law &
Order, just as Devils who despair.[13]

During the 1760s a political power struggle over English-Chickasaw communication mechanisms ensued within the Chickasaw nation between Stuart's
representative, Paya Mattaha, and apparent head chief/king Mingo Houma,
who may have been the same man who had led the pro-Natchez, anti-French
faction in 1730 and afterward. In an address to the Chickasaw-Choctaw-British
congress at Mobile on January 1, 1772, Mingo Houma spoke after a long speech
by Paya Mattaha, saying defiantly, "I am the King of my Nation and Paya Mattaha is my Warrior. I am the last of a Long Race of Kings and am now come to
meet you great chiefs of the white men." That he may not have been the 1730s
Mingo Houma is suggested by his statement that "this is the first time of my
being present at a meeting of white Chiefs." On the other hand, documentation
does not seem to exist that the French-period Mingo Houma had ever attended
a meeting with either upper-level French or English officials.[14]

Snapp writes that a "temporary civil war" occurred in association with this
rivalry, by which he seems to mean that widespread violence occurred. Although some isolated acts of internal hostility did occur, there was by no means
a full-scale civil war. Stuart, with the aid of McIntosh, was able to quiet the
insulted Mingo Houma.[15]

This confrontation is significant in that it demonstrates the practice of Europeans to pay little or no attention to the Chickasaw kings. As will be seen in
Chapter 8, Mingo Houma was indeed considered by the Chickasaw to be their
"king." Stuart, however, obviously found Paya Mattaha, undoubtedly the head
war chief, to be the more competent and cooperative of the two and therefore
support of him to be in the best interest of the goals of the English in its Indian
diplomacy. This Paya Mattaha, who was an elderly man when he died in 1784,
was probably the Chickasaw whose name first appears in a 1736 document containing an interview in Georgia with the Reverend John Wesley. Paya Mattaha
had been given a large medal at the 1765 Mobile conference, a political action

that bestowed upon him the English title of "Great Medal Chief," which further enforced his achieved status position. The situation is illustrated by Stuart's statements at the congress with Chickasaws and Choctaws at Mobile in December 1771 and January 1772. He stated to the Chickasaw delegates, apparently off the record, that "all Correspondence between me and their Nation should be Carried on thro' Paya Mataha during his life," and he further arrogantly stated: "If I should come to Learn that he [Mingo Houma] took part with Traders and disorderly persons in Opposition to his great Chief Paya Mataha and my Commissary I should never afterward look upon him as a man of Consequence." Stuart wrote that Paya Mattaha was so relieved and happy with Stuart's actions in his behalf that he stayed intoxicated for three days, thereby delaying the conclusion of the conference. Stuart apparently convinced Mingo Houma to terminate serious opposition by threatening to deny him support and pacified him to some extent by the award of a small medal, thus giving him the title of "Medal Chief."[16] This manner of attempting to manipulate the Chickasaw and other tribes was continued after the Revolutionary War by the Americans, as well as by the Spanish.

Because the governors of the southeastern seaboard colonies took offense at the British edicts that regulated the Indian trade, which they believed was their responsibility, McIntosh indeed found himself in a difficult situation. Many unlicensed traders continued to come into the Chickasaw country, and some of the licensed ones vehemently opposed him for trying to limit liquor trading and uphold other regulations. The dishonest traders were undoubtedly pleased when the secretary of state for the newly created Colonial Department cut the funds for Indian agents. Stuart discharged all the commissaries and most other interior employees of his department on November 1, 1768. McIntosh was rehired about two years later after Paya Mattaha and chiefs from other tribes complained that commissaries were needed to govern the unruly traders.[17]

McIntosh may have been absent from the nation during the temporary termination of commissaries between 1768 and late 1770. R. S. Cotterill (*The Southern Indians*) states that they were "withdrawn temporarily from the tribes," but this does not necessarily mean that they all abandoned their homes. However, in April 1769 McIntosh (along with John McGillivray and Arthur Strother) was serving as a member of the "Commission of the Peace" in British West Florida. In December 1770, John Stuart reported that he had "sent [the Chickasaws'] former commissary, Mr. John McIntosh, among them who undertook to act without pay till the sense of government should be known." These facts suggest that McIntosh had indeed ceased residing in the Chickasaw nation. Perhaps while absent McIntosh turned his plantation over to Paya Mattaha, whose plantation was nearby. After resuming his office, McIntosh apparently received an official appointment with an annual salary of 150 British pounds.[18]

Bernard Romans had the following to say about the commissary during McIntosh's second term: "This office of Commissary seems to me the most needless expence the crown is at, as it only serves for a subject of ridicule both to the traders and [Indians], which last scruple not often to give the officer in this nation the . . . scandalous epithet of old woman; and he can do but little towards preventing disorders among them, or in regulating the standard of the trade; besides, I am sure that whatever Commissary dared to pretend to be any thing more than a cypher, would run an imminent risque of his life."[19]

The 1771–1772 Mobile congress was held in order to give the Indians an opportunity to express their wishes and complaints with regard to British policies and interaction with Englishmen and for the latter to assure the Indians of friendship and concern for their welfare. Among a number of white men, the conference was attended by West Florida governor Peter Chester, John Stuart and his brother Charles, who was deputy superintendent of Indian Affairs, Paya Mattaha's white son-in-law John Favre, John McIntosh, and some of the traders such as James Colbert. The conference was opened by Stuart's lighting of a pipe, which was smoked by the primary Englishmen and all the Chickasaw and Choctaw chiefs. The proceedings of the second day, however, were opened after the Chickasaws

> produced Fire by friction of a Wooden Apperatus. . . . Paya Mattaha their great Leader lighted his Pipe with it, and holding an Eagles Tail or Calumet in his hand addressed the Superintendent and said This Calumet was given me by the Querpha [Quapaw] Chief (who accompanied me to Pensacola) in Token of Friendship. I now hold it and this Pipe and Tobacco kindled with pure Virgin Fire of which I desire you will Smoke and I desire that the Calumet may remain in your Possession as a memorial of the Faith mutually Pledged by my nation and the Querphas also called Arcanzas.[20]

Paya Mattaha then began to speak, initially saying, "I am a Redman of a Nation once great but now much diminished by Death. I am going to speak of Red men, and if my Talk is not attended to but Falls to the ground I cannot help it." He then continued, "You see me here, I am not a Boy. I have the use of my Reason and Senses, and Remember That I have often made Promises of attachment and Fedility [sic] to the Great King. I now again Repeat and Confirm them. I scorn Duplicity and do not Speak with Two Tongues. I am not a man of many words, but what Little I have to say I will speak openly altho' a Red man like me ought to Speak with Caution before so many great Chiefs assembled together."

Paya Mattaha, who Englishmen sometimes simply called "the Leader," went on to complain that his nation was disrupted, primarily because traders corrupted his people and cheated them by misrepresenting weights and counts of hides, and that many of the traders made them disrespect the old ways, corrupted their manners, and caused them to be difficult to govern. With regard to many of the traders, he stated,

> [M]y Warriors Complained of being Cheated in having short measures, afterwards Shorter and a Third and fourth time Shorter and Shorter still. I advised my people to be easy (for our Commissary was then taken away) and take the Goods as they would give them until we Should have an opportunity of Complaining and making our Case known. . . . [If I were to] enumerate all our Grievances I should never Finish and [I wish] so many disorderly Vagabonds can be prevented from Insulting our Towns. I cannot hope for Redress, they steal our Horses and commit Innumerable Violence and what is worse they have Corrupted the manners of my People and rendered them as bad as themselves so That I cannot govern them; I shall say no more upon this Disagreeable Subject.

After his talk, Paya Mattaha held up a bow and quiver of arrows while stating to the Indians: "Behold the Arms of your Ancestors[—]on such they depended for Food[,] for Raiment and for defence. . . . Think of your Former Situation and be grateful for the benefits you have received from your white Brethren, who have armed you with Guns [and] Clothed you and Supplied all your wants." He then presented the bow and quiver to Stuart with the request that they be sent to the British king as a testimony of his "Gratitude for his goodness and Protection."[21]

Throughout the post-French period, British attempts to regulate the number of traders coming into the Chickasaw nation were generally failures. Soon after the peace of 1763 the number of traders increased significantly. Most were unlicensed and unscrupulous, and many used rum as their primary medium of exchange for hides. Governor Chester voiced his consternation about the situation in a late 1771 letter to Stuart: "I think that the people and traders who supply them with rum are more to blame than the [Indians], and in order to restrain the traders and others from furnishing them with such quantities of rum as they do . . . of which the chiefs complain so often, I think it advisable . . . for commissaries to be appointed in the Creek, Choctaw, and Chickasaw nations, that they might keep those licentious unruly traders under some restrictions."[22]

Although James Colbert also complained about the unscrupulous traders, he did not escape criticism himself. In December 1770, Charles Stuart wrote the following:

I am credibly informed that there are not less than 18 traders and pack-horsemen now out a-hunting on the hunting grounds of [the Chickasaw] nation the same as Indians, which is contrary to all rule and of which the Indians complain much and are so good a people as not to take satisfaction otherwise than by representation. I am informed those hunters are divided into parties and that they are headed by Messrs. [James] Colbert and [James] Bubbie, and that said Colbert is contrary to His Majesty's instructions establishing plantations in that nation and that he has got cattle, negroes, etc. so as even to admit of his having an overseer.[23]

As was the case with all the Indian nations and the non-Indian citizens of North America, the Chickasaw had their share of thieves and short-tempered individuals who broke the laws that governed them. Among the recorded instances of Chickasaw impropriety during the British period, one is especially notable. While visiting the British settlement of Kaskaskia in the Illinois territory in May 1772, an intoxicated Chickasaw warrior patronizing a trading store engaged in disorderly behavior. The fracas resulted in the warrior and the Chickasaw band with him launching an attack on the store. Fortunately for the villagers, the place was garrisoned by a British army contingent commanded by Captain Hugh Lord. The soldiers attacked the rioting Chickasaw band, resulting in its retreat from the town.[24]

By this time, Spain had become well entrenched in New Orleans and its new Louisiana lands west of the Mississippi, and the British began having to compete with that country for the favor of the Indian tribes in the domain of the West Florida district and elsewhere. In the 1770s some Chickasaws, said to be adherents of the old French faction, made occasional trips to New Orleans and St. Louis to meet with Spanish officials. Alarmed by this, the British used the periodic Pensacola and Mobile Indian conferences as forums, stressing upon the Chickasaw and others that the Spanish had evil designs and reminding them of their treaty obligations to Britain.[25] But British authorities were being confronted with more serious internal problems occasioned by citizen discontent within the American colonies. In the spring of 1775 that discontent culminated in the initiation of open rebellion at Lexington and Concord, Massachusetts. The Chickasaw now found themselves approaching a strange road never before traveled or even imagined.

7
A Road Unexpected

In 1775 the average Chickasaw must have been greatly confused upon learning that the English colonies were in revolt against the British Crown, for both the English king and court and the colony officials subject to the king and court had supported the Chickasaw in conflicts with the French to the end that their very existence had been preserved. Did this new turn of events mean that officials John Stuart, John McIntosh, and the others were now enemies of the Chickasaw, or were individual English citizens such as the traders now their enemies instead? The traders among the Chickasaw as well as McIntosh must have been inundated with questions until an understanding of that peculiar political situation evolved.

Prior to the opening of the Revolution the Chickasaw enjoyed unusually peaceful times as a result of the total cessation of Choctaw hostilities and largely those of northern Indians. The decades-long upward spiral of the mortality rate had ended and the Chickasaw population was on the increase. The British nonetheless continued to need Chickasaw assistance in defense against northern Indians, and the Spanish replaced the French as Britain's chief rival for Chickasaw allegiance. The Revolution, however, created a new British rival that, unlike the Spanish, was using firearms to gain its political ends. The British immediately began to take steps to reaffirm and strengthen their alliance with the Chickasaw. A formidable, determined, war-hardened group such as the Chickasaw entirely on the side of the American rebels would be a serious setback for the British in West Florida and the Mississippi Valley in general. The British, therefore, courted the Chickasaw, Choctaw, and other tribes of the southeast to serve as barriers against American incursions into the interior. Resulting British-Indian alliances thereby kept American-British conflicts mostly confined to the eastern seaboard. Henry Hamilton, British lieutenant governor in Detroit, even made plans (which did not materialize) to unite the Chickasaw and Cherokee with northwestern Indians such as the Delaware and Shawnee to raid the American frontiers.[1]

Orders issued from Boston in 1775 resulted in John Stuart becoming a military coordinator for the Old Southwest region. Arms and ammunition collected by him at St. Augustine, Pensacola, and Mobile were distributed to the commissaries in the Indian settlements for the use of the warriors. Three thousand pounds of powder and many pounds of lead were sent to the Chickasaw by pack train in December. The British, however, were disappointed to discover that most of the Indians traditionally loyal to them were not enthusiastic about making war on English-speaking people. John McIntosh, having been instructed to have men loyal to the king of Great Britain form parties of Chickasaws for the purpose of "distressing his enemies," apparently had poor success. The Chickasaw had seemingly agreed to patrol the Tennessee and Mississippi Rivers, but failed to do so in late 1776 during their primary hunting season. As a result, Britain's undeclared second opponent in the early stages of the Revolution, Spain, was able to trade with the Americans via the Mississippi River and its tributaries. Alarmed by this and other apparent lethargic attitudes from other tribes, John Stuart sent his brother, Charles Stuart, into the Choctaw country in early 1777 to encourage loyalty to Britain and to invite delegates to attend a conference in Mobile. John McIntosh was undoubtedly instructed to do the same in the Chickasaw country. The Choctaw refused to promise anything until they determined what the Chickasaw were going to do. This caused John Stuart to fear that the Americans had already obtained Chickasaw pledges of nonaggression. Stuart subsequently placed even more emphasis on the importance of the Mobile conference as a means to dash American hopes of obtaining Chickasaw allegiance.[2]

Concerned about the situation themselves, especially in light of the fact that the British were their primary source of trade goods, the Chickasaw, Choctaw, and Creek tribes enthusiastically sent a combined 2,800 delegates to the Mobile conference, held in May and June. Stuart, playing the trade card, stressed that American military incursions down the Tennessee, Tombigbee, and Mississippi Rivers could result in American footholds in the Chickasaw country that could terminate British trade and cause the Chickasaw severe harm. Showing that they were well aware of such a possibility, the Chickasaw delegates replied that their low attendance (forty delegates) was due to rumors heard about a rebel invasion down the Tennessee River; most warriors had stayed at home "to defend their country . . . to the last extremity." The Chickasaw delegates, partially headed by King Mingo Houma and Taska-Oppaye, went on to speak in favor of a British alliance and vowed that they would risk their lives to maintain it. Such allegiance was not unconditional, however, for the politically savvy delegates stressed that adequate and well-regulated trade must accompany their military assistance, which initially was directed to interrupting Spanish and American communications on the Mississippi River.[3]

Prior to general Chickasaw involvement in the Revolutionary War, James Colbert personally assisted the British in 1776 by delivering from Mobile (as requested by Henry Stuart) a huge pack train of ammunition and goods to the Overhill Cherokee, who had determined to wage frontier war against the American settlers. Although there seems to be no contemporary documentation, Malcolm McGee recalled in the nineteenth century that Colbert and his oldest son, William, fought with part of famed chief Dragging Canoe's Cherokee force at the "Tatum Flats" (same as "Island Flats"; battle site in present-day east Tennessee) in July 1776. Possibly other Chickasaws also participated in that conflict. Although military activities by James and William Colbert with the Cherokee related by McGee do not seem to be verifiable, the former Colbert's association with that tribe in 1776 is documented in letters from Henry Stuart written while among the Overhill Cherokee: "I brought Mr. Colbert with me from the Chickasaws. I thought he might be very useful to me as he understands the Chickasaw and Creek languages, and [is] so much esteemed by their nation and the other nations who go among them."

In that and a second letter, Stuart related that he was sending Colbert to Pensacola with letters requesting goods and more ammunition for the Cherokee. Colbert subsequently traveled to Mobile, obtained 100 horseloads of ammunition and presents, and returned to the Cherokee. The horrific Cherokee violence against the American settlers lasted into 1777, when it was shut down by separate American forces from North Carolina, South Carolina, Georgia, and Virginia. The Cherokee towns were destroyed by the forces, causing the inhabitants to seek refuge in the Creek territory and with the British in West Florida.[4]

In 1777, the Chickasaw began to demonstrate allegiance to the British government after earlier visits to the Chickasaw by both Spanish and American emissaries had failed to generate enthusiasm, no doubt in spite of the efforts of the anti-British faction among the tribe. Almost immediately after the June 1777 Mobile conference, James Colbert initiated significant and official Chickasaw participation in the war when he raised Chickasaw parties to patrol the Mississippi, Tennessee, and Ohio Rivers. The Choctaw also agreed to perform river patrolling. Pleased by Chickasaw indifference to the emissaries and by the patrolling activities that were beginning, Stuart declared in August 1777 that the Chickasaw and Choctaw were once again displaying "their usual good disposition."[5] The trade goods factor, nearly always at the forefront with regard to Chickasaw political directions, undoubtedly played a significant part in obviating the resistance of the anti-British faction in that tribe.

During the winter, Chickasaw and Choctaw parties intercepted and searched Mississippi River vessels and at times fired on Spanish boats from the Chickasaw Bluffs (present-day Memphis) as they descended from the Illinois country. The Mississippi, however, was not continuously monitored by the Indians. As a result, Captain James Willing's American command went uncontested when it descended the Mississippi River in February 1778 and raided loyalist settlements at Walnut Hills (now Vicksburg) and Natchez, as well as settlements to the south. An irritated John Stuart was perturbed at both the Choctaw and Chickasaw for not having been at the river. Such surveillance must have been boring, as indicated by trader Hardy Perry in a letter to Farquhar Bethune on February 4 regarding the Choctaw; Perry stated that the Choctaw were "tired of watching." Stuart qualified his disappointment with the Chickasaw by acknowledging that they had been preoccupied in warring with the trans–Mississippi River Osage, an activity caused by Chickasaws hunting west of that river.

In April, fearful that he was losing his grasp again, Stuart persuaded a man named John McGillivray to command a provincial corps of over 100 men, which he led at Stuart's instruction into the Chickasaw nation with substantial gifts and ammunition for the inhabitants. Stuart, who had commissioned McGillivray a lieutenant colonel, described him as "a gentleman of fortune intimately acquainted with the Choctaw and Chickasaw Indians, their language and customs." This John McGillivray, a prominent Mobile merchant and trader, was probably the "McGillwray" who was a partner in an apparent trading establishment in the Chickasaw nation as early as 1771 (see Chapter 6). In the nation, he recruited an undetermined number of Chickasaws but was unable to persuade many or any at all to accompany his corps to the Natchez District in response to the continuing anxiety there caused by the Willing Raiders, who were still in the lower valley but south of Natchez. With no significant military action forthcoming in the Natchez District, however, McGillivray's command left there after a few weeks, as did a Choctaw force led by Farquhar Bethune, the Choctaw commissary. Meanwhile, the Spanish continued the intrigues begun in 1770, prompting Charles Stuart to resume his consultations with the Indians in June 1778, this time with "medal and gorget chiefs" of the Chickasaw and Choctaw.[6]

Disappointed with the overall performance of the Chickasaw in helping put down the American rebellion, British officials were told that the lack of enthusiasm was due to fear that Chickasaw aggression against the Americans would result in retaliation against their villages, which were greatly exposed to rebel invasions down the Ohio and Tennessee Rivers. A second, more likely reason, John Stuart opined, was probably that traders discouraged the Chickasaw from traveling on military excursions because "it is diametrically opposite to their views of traffic by getting hides in barter for their goods, and consequently must cut them off from the profits by which they propose to live."[7] The latter probably had some merit, for many of the traders undoubtedly had no particular affection for the British empire; after all, most traders were American-born colonists too. Thus their only sincere affinity for the British concerned the British-made trade goods supplied to them, the backbone of their trading enterprises among the Indians. Both of the above reasons are probably applicable to explain the Chickasaws' lack of enthusiasm for war activities, but perhaps another is the same as the one displayed by a band of Choctaw in the first half of the 1700s when they refused to attack the Chickasaw in the absence of a specific affront and therefore a reason for revenge (see Chapter 2). In other words, the Chickasaw were not angry at the Americans, a prerequisite for effective military action. Enmeshed with all these reasons is the underlying one mentioned earlier and cogently articulated by Paya Mattaha to John Stuart in the summer of 1778 and reported by the latter:

> In the course of my conversation with the chief I found that it was with the utmost difficulty he could place in the light of enemies those men whom from his earliest infancy he had been taught to consider as his dearest friends, whom he had assisted and defended upon many occasions at the risk of his life. I had also the greatest difficulty to make him comprehend that they had forfeited their right to the protection of the Great King and the British nation by their apostasy and rebellion; and he at last observed that although these might be considerations of sufficient weight to engage us to make war upon them, yet he could not bring himself to imbrue his hands in the blood of white people without the greatest reluctance, and that he shuddered at the apprehensions of committing some fatal blunder by killing the King's friends instead of his enemies.[8]

Impressed by the chief's feelings and honesty, Superintendent Stuart was left with a "high esteem and respect for his character." Possibly altering his previously conceived plan for use of the Chickasaw, Stuart thereafter assured Paya Mattaha that the Chickasaw role would be strictly defensive with regard to intrusions into their own nation and use of rivers and roads by the rebels to threaten the British settlements. The reassured chief then returned to the upper Tombigbee River settlements "fully determined to take an active part" in the war with the Americans, or so Stuart believed. Governor Peter Chester of West Florida, however, was not optimistic that more enthusiasm was forthcoming. He voiced the opinion that one British regiment assigned to the Mississippi River would be of more use than both the Choctaw and Chickasaw tribes if they were indeed unified in the British interest.[9]

Meanwhile, the Spanish continued to work for influence in the Chickasaw and Choctaw towns, causing Stuart much concern. Accordingly, he instructed John McIntosh to intensify his efforts to counterattack and disrupt Spanish efforts in the nation, and he made up lists of presents, including "a considerable quantity of scarlet coats," to present to the chiefs at anticipated meetings. American efforts to influence the Chickasaw were of little consequence, probably because few or no trade goods would be forthcoming from that quarter. In late 1778, for example, George Rogers Clark proposed peace with the Chickasaw through Kaskaskia emissaries. They were met with "cool" conversation on the subject, however, and the mission was a failure. In 1779, General John Campbell, observing Indian neutrality by some groups with regard to alliances with the British and Spanish in order to obtain goods from both, stated that the Indians "are a mercenary race . . . the slaves of the highest bidder without gratitude or affection." He also added that "Europeans themselves have taught them these principles."[10]

By late 1778, the British had realized the value of James Colbert, which Henry Stuart first recognized in April 1776. By then Colbert had been a resident of the Chickasaw nation for over forty years. As discussed earlier, Colbert had led Chickasaws against the Cherokee in the French and Indian War, assisted the British in supplying the Cherokee with ammunition in 1776, fought with Dragging Canoe's Cherokees in that year, and independently formed military companies of Chickasaws to patrol the rivers in 1777. In November 1780, an action occurred that would eventually contribute to some of Colbert's mix-blood male offspring rising to the forefront of Chickasaw political, social, and economic affairs. By a commission dated November 23, 1780, General John Campbell appointed Colbert "Leader and Conductor of such Volunteer Inhabitants and Chickasaw, Choctaw, Creek or other Indians as shall join you for the purpose of annoying[,] distressing[,] attacking[,] or repelling the King's Enemies, when, where and as often as you shall judge proper for the good of his Majestys' Service, subject always to such further Orders and Instructions as you shall from time to time receive." Colbert thereafter referred to himself as James Colbert, Captain in his Majesty's Service.[11]

Perhaps as a result of his official British military service, Colbert became an honorary Chickasaw "chief," or so he, a relative, or an acquaintance of his related to some Spanish captives in 1782, who later stated: "This Colbert has several sons (whom he has had by Chickasaw women), who are today very important chiefs in that nation, and by consequence their father is also." The oldest of James Colbert's sons, William, was apparently about twenty-two years old in 1782, and the second oldest, George, was only about eighteen.[12]

The Chickasaw in general were now firmly attached to the British and seemingly equally opposed to the Americans and the Spaniards, probably in part because of the influence of James Colbert with his new status as the only British military commander among the Chickasaw. By March 1779, invasion threats had been made against the Chickasaw by the Americans, and in that month the principal chiefs reported that the Spaniards had sent "bad Talks to the Chactaws endeavoring to set them against us & our friends the English." The meddling had motivated unidentified Chickasaw hostilities against the Spanish in the winter of 1778–1779, as emphasized in a letter to the Spaniards signed by the principal leaders, including King Mingo Houma and Paya Mattaha. In response to information that the Spanish and French inhabitants had been supplying ammunition to their enemies, the Chickasaws stated: "therefore shou'd We lose any of our People in their hunting grounds by your red people We shall not go to them for redress as We know what quarter to take Satisfaction in, for it is no New thing to us for We allways knew that the french bought our Hair till lately."[13]

With the Chickasaws now on the offensive, making war-party raids on the Mississippi and Ohio Rivers and elsewhere, the Americans became alarmed. In May 1779, just as a large party of Chickasaws recruited by James Colbert and led by him and a "Mr. Hazle" was leaving to join British lieutenant governor Henry Hamilton at Vincennes, the Chickasaw received a symbol of peace from Virginia with a message informing them that they would be destroyed if American friendship was not accepted. By now the Chickasaw were united against the Americans, having become convinced that there was truth in what the northern Indians had been saying—that the Americans intended to destroy them and take their land. In a letter said to have had the backing of every warrior in the nation, Mingo Houma and brothers Paya Mattaha and Tuskau Pautaupau spared the diplomacy: "We desire no other friendship of you but only desire you will inform us when you are Comeing and we will save you the trouble of Comeing quite here for we will meet you half way, for we have heard so much of it that it makes our heads Ach[.] Take care that we dont serve you as we have served the French before with all their Indians, send you back without your heads. We are a Nation that fears or Values no Nation as long as our Great Father King George stands by us for you may depend as long as life lasts with us we will hold him fast by the Hand."[14]

The Americans had inadvertently ensured that the Chickasaw would not join their ranks by accepting France as an ally in 1778. The Chickasaw bitterness caused by actions of the French prior to the end of the Louisiana colony in 1763 had not dissipated among the majority of the Chickasaws old enough to remember the horrific violence of that period. The chiefs accordingly stated in the same letter just quoted from that if the Americans wanted peace with the Chickasaw they should cease hostilities with the British and open the same with the French, a "people we will never make peace with as long as Oak grows and Water runs." The Chickasaws' extreme anti-American position was punctuated by a request that the Virginians publish the letter in a newspaper so "that all your people may see it and know who it was from . . . [for] We are men & Warriors and dont want our Talks hidden." Earlier, John Stuart, through McIntosh, had motivated the Choctaw and Chickasaw to undertake scouting of the banks of the Ohio and Mississippi Rivers. A large party of Chickasaw had captured eleven Americans, apparently on the Ohio River, whom the party delivered to Mobile where the British obtained them in exchange for "an assortment of goods." The next year, Indians who attacked a boat on the Ohio were supposedly Chickasaws. The boat and numerous goods were captured, and all but one of its passengers, consisting of eight or nine men and one family, were killed. In June 1780, Thomas Jefferson made the observation that the "Chickasaw have entered into war with us."[15]

By mid-1779, the Revolutionary War fighting in the east was more than half over, with such battles as Lexington and Concord, Bunker's/Breed's Hill, Brooklyn Heights, Montreal, Quebec, Trenton, Princeton, Fort Stanwix, Saratoga, Brandywine, and Germantown consigned to history. In the Old Southwest, Indian Superintendent John Stuart died of tuberculosis in March 1779, causing the agent to the Cherokee, Alexander Cameron, to be reassigned to the Chickasaw and Choctaw. John McIntosh, Chickasaw commissary, was still alive, but he would die nearly one year later, in February 1780, at his home on Pontotoc Creek. Cameron soon appointed McIntosh's son, also named John, "to act in his place." Thus contemporary references to a living John McIntosh dated after March 1780 are to the son, whom I will hereafter call John McIntosh, Jr. One of his first actions as commissary was to send a party of Chickasaws to patrol the Mississippi River. Cameron had passed over James Colbert for the position of commissary, stating that he was "illiterate and very extravagant, and the present limitation of the Indian establishments will not afford to employ such men."[16]

In June 1779, Spain declared war against Britain, partially because of alleged British attempts to incite the Chickasaw, Choctaw, and Cherokee to attack Louisiana. With war declared, the Spanish openly intensified efforts to obtain Indian allegiance, and the Choctaw and Chickasaw towns began to play host to Spanish agents with a focused agenda oriented toward gaining the upper hand politically and economically over the British, as well as the Americans. Despite talks and visits from the Spaniards, most of the Chickasaw continued to pay little attention to them, and Paya Mattaha told the wavering Choctaw that if they did not also support the British he would cause some Shawnees and Chickamauga Cherokees lately settled on the Tennessee River near the Chickasaw territory to come and join him in a march on the Choctaw "with powder and ball," as Cameron reported it. With these words by Paya Mattaha, who was highly respected by the Choctaw, the latter indeed returned to the English. After the Spanish sent flags to the Chickasaw by way of Quapaw chief Anguska, James Colbert reported that "the majority of the Nation would not allow them to be hoisted."[17]

The Chickasaw were still further alienated by the Americans. Just as the theater of fighting moved from the northeast to the south, Thomas Jefferson, governor of Virginia, advocated encouraging one of the old enemies of the Chickasaw, the Kickapoos, to make war on them, and he ordered George Rogers Clark to construct a fort five miles below the confluence of the Ohio and Mississippi Rivers on hunting land claimed by the Chickasaw. The fort, unauthorized by the Chickasaw, was to serve as a base for protecting anticipated Mississippi River commerce to and from New Orleans. More irritating to the Chickasaw, however, was its potential use as a depot for the purpose of arming northern Indians who could then travel to the upper Tombigbee to harass the Chickasaw towns. Jefferson and Clark believed that the Chickasaw were the backbone of the British defenses south of the Ohio and that their defeat would lead to destruction of British power in that theater. Fort Jefferson, as it was named, could have easily been called "Jefferson's Folly," for the angered Chickasaw became solidly at war with the Americans and saw to it that the fort had an ineffective and relatively short life span. Several months after completion of the fort in April 1780, James Colbert led a large force of Chickasaws to the area, which caused settlers nearby to take refuge in the fort. The Chickasaws burned the settlers' houses and began harassment of the fort, which lasted nearly a year. Cotterill ("The Virginia-Chickasaw Treaty of 1783") describes the subsequent life of the structure as a time during which Chickasaws "swarmed around the fort, cut off its supplies, killed and captured stragglers from the garrison and at one time subjected the fort to such a close and protracted siege that only the timely arrival of reinforcements saved it from destruction." At one time during the siege, James Colbert demanded surrender of the soldiers and civilians or he would put them all to death when he took the fort. As he waited outside the fort after making this demand, Colbert received the answer in an unexpected way, as described later: "[S]ome Indians, who were friends [of the Americans], fired on Colbert & his flag and Wounded Colbert so that he fell—the Indians finding their Commander wounded gathered all their Force and at night began a tremendous fire on the fort Advancing up from all quarters till they were crouded very close. Capt. Owen who commanded the Block houses had the Swivels loaded with Rifle and Musquet balls and leveled them amongst the crowd which Dispersed the Indians[.]" The American army retreated in June 1781, and a plan to invade the British southwest was abandoned. Chickasaw control of the area prevented any further conquest by the Americans in the direction of British West Florida.[18]

In the meantime, British West Florida had been under attack by the Spanish. In 1779 Louisiana governor de Galvez entered the area at the head of an army and captured the British Mississippi River settlements and posts at Manchac, Baton Rouge, and Natchez, along with two small outposts on Thompson's Creek and the Amite River. The Spanish also captured eight vessels on the rivers and lakes. In May 1780, de Galvez took Fort Charlotte in Mobile. With Pensacola the next Spanish objective, the British appealed to their Indian allies. The call was answered mainly by Choctaw, along with various numbers at various times of Chickasaw, Creek, Alibama, and Seminole warriors, who greatly aided in holding the town by carrying the attack to the Spaniards through frequent surprise hit-and-run raids and on some occasions going out in strength supported by artillery and British troops. According to a letter from a Spaniard, Colbert and "three of his Indian sons" captured several Spanish soldiers at Mobile on June 5, 1780. One group of Chickasaws who participated were chiefs who had come to Pensacola to obtain ammunition to use against Americans who were encroaching on their hunting grounds and building forts (that is, Fort Jefferson). At the request of the British commander, about twenty of the Chickasaws remained to assist with the defense of Pensacola. The remainder returned north, promising to send additional young warriors if they could be spared. Malcolm McGee recalled seeing the elder Colbert, as well as Mingo Houma, there at the fall of the city. Prior to the surrender, Chickasaw commissary John McIntosh, Jr., and James Colbert witnessed the written text of a talk from the principal Choctaw chief to Cameron. The Chickasaw and other Indians at Pensacola were highly valued by most of the British officers, as illustrated by statements of Alexander Cameron, who bemoaned the fact that lack of provisions for the Chickasaw had necessitated their temporary exodus to hunt at a time when the Spaniards had tentatively planned an assault. If the attack had not been cancelled, it would have been disastrous in the absence of the Chickasaws. After the fall of Pensacola in May 1781, the Choctaws and Chickasaws were led out of the lines and back to their respective nations on foot by commissaries Farquhar Bethune and John McIntosh, Jr.; other Indians returned to their homes during the surrender negotiations. Because British West Florida effectively no longer existed, the Chickasaw were faced with an immediate economic dilemma and an extended political one.[19]

Meanwhile, the British agents had succeeded in inciting Chickasaw raids on the recently established Cumberland settlement in present-day Tennessee. Apparently, the Indians who in April 1780 attacked some of the inhabitants of Renfroe's settlement, located about forty miles northwest of Nashville bluff on a tributary of the Cumberland named Red River, were Chickasaws. The alarmed residents were trying to find safety by moving to French Lick (present-day Nashville) when they were attacked at their campsite on a creek now known as Battle Creek. Between twelve and twenty men, women, and children were killed, which was apparently almost the entire party. Again, in January 1781, a large party of Chickasaws made a surprise night attack on the stockade at Freeland's Station, where James Robertson, founder of the Cumberland settlement, was staying with his family. After many shots were fired on both sides, the Chickasaws, who killed one white man and one black man, withdrew with the loss of at least one warrior. This was the last attack by Chickasaws against the Cumberland settlement during and subsequent to the Revolutionary War.[20]

According to an early nineteenth-century history of Tennessee, about sixty Delaware Indians moved south through the Cumberland settlement area in January 1780 to establish a village on Bear Creek south of the Tennessee River and the Muscle Shoals, and from there they later allegedly launched attacks against American settlers. These Indians supposedly accomplished this incursion into the Chickasaw domain without obtaining permission from that tribe. In any case, the Delaware were still there in November 1783, at which time the Chickasaw agreed to expel them, as discussed below.[21]

By the time of the fall of Pensacola, most of the post-1779 battles of the Revolutionary War had been fought. These included Camden, King's Mountain, and Cowpens in South Carolina and Guilford Courthouse in North Carolina. In October 1781, major hostilities ceased when General Cornwallis surrendered to General Washington after the Battle of Yorktown, Virginia.[22] The British–Indian allies war with the Americans was over, but the Chickasaw soon found themselves threatened with hostilities by Britain's other southwest foe, the victorious Spanish.

With the loss of their European ally and primary supplier of trade goods, the Chickasaw now had no choice but to soften their belligerent stances toward the Spanish and Americans. As always when the Chickasaw were forced to deal with two or more non-Indian governments, factionalism played an important but sometimes divisive role in their political affairs. Chickasaw leaders such as Paya Mattaha had begun to be tolerant of the Spaniards even prior to the ouster of the British. The chief told Alexander Cameron that the talks he had recently received from the Spaniards were not bad ones, but he also stated that he would never take the Spaniards by the hand during the remainder of his life. However, after the fall of West Florida, Paya Mattaha was already looking to the future by speaking ambivalently to both the Spanish and the Americans, and before his death he had become the leader of the Spanish faction, as discussed below. The Chickasaw in general sought to take advantage of both powers but, as cogently stated by Calloway (*The American Revolution in Indian Country*), "the diplomatic shuffling aggravated and crystallized factions within the nation." In March 1782 Chickasaw, Shawnee, Delaware, and Cherokee representatives carrying symbols of peace traveled to St. Louis, where they requested peace with

Spain. Later, a Chickasaw delegation consisting of six chiefs and five other tribesmen "in the name of their chief Panimataja" (Paya Mattaha) arrived in St. Louis where they requested peace and expressed the desire to become allies of the Spanish. In October two Choctaw chiefs were employed by the Spanish to send white flags and a peace letter from Governor Miro to Paya Mattaha. The messenger, upon arriving at Paya Mattaha's house, found that he was on a peace mission to the Tallapoosa Creek and the Cherokee. The messenger, flags, and Spanish letter, however, were well received, according to Pedro Piernas, by Paya Mattaha's brother, "Tascapatapo, or Red King, who is also a chief of great importance." The latter chief assured the messenger that upon Paya Mattaha's return a delegation would gather the Spanish prisoners held by the Chickasaw, travel to New Orleans, and "take the hand of the great Spanish chief."[23]

Because the Americans were at first logistically unorganized with regard to systematic trade with the Indians, the existing Spanish faction (primarily the old French party) among the Chickasaw was immediately inclined to accept the overtures of the nearby Spanish in that regard. Accordingly, Paya Mattaha asked the Spanish for a trader named Anselmo Billet, and in late 1783 Jacobo Du Breuil, commander at Fort Carlos III on the Arkansas River, sent Billet to the Chickasaw villages on the upper Tombigbee. Additionally encouraged by free Spanish merchandise in the two years following the fall of Pensacola, the faction received new adherents. Because of overtures and initiatives from the Americans, on the other hand, the old anti-French/anti-Spanish faction became the nucleus of the new American party, led partially by war chief Piomingo, also called the "Mountain Leader."[24]

Cessation of military confrontations between the main armies of Britain on the one side and those of the Americans and Spanish on the other did not totally end Chickasaw involvement in military hostilities. For all practical purposes, the British had indeed been vanquished by the fall of Pensacola, but their loyal Indian ally, the Chickasaw, had not been vanquished and was thus technically still at war with the Americans and Spanish. In January 1782 British Choctaw agent Farquhar Bethune fruitlessly suggested that he be allowed to organize a Choctaw and Chickasaw force "to distress the enemy either on the Mississippi or at Mobile or Pensacola." A futile rebellion in April 1781 against the Spaniards by Natchez District British loyalists, some of whom had migrated there after the outbreak of the Revolution, had resulted in many of the insurrectionists (possibly as many as eighty) fleeing to the Chickasaw nation. By 1782 the loyalists were among at least 100 whites of various types (possibly as many as 300) who had taken up residence there. In addition to the Natchez refugees, the non-Indians in the nation consisted of both good and unscrupulous traders (some of whom had plantations), black slaves belonging to Chickasaws and traders, and vagabonds, some of whom were escaped or wanted criminals taking advantage of the sympathetic nature of the Chickasaw.[25] A Spaniard, Franciso Bouligny, referred to the vagabonds as follows: "The greater part of these vagabonds, dregs of Europe and America, are men abandoned to all vices and capable of committing any crime. These are the ones who have devastated this district with their continual thefts of horses, mules, and Negroes. The Chickasaw and Choctaw nations, because of a humane spirit common in almost all the Indians, receive and shelter these vagabonds, sharing with them the little they have to eat, and thereby give them the means and facilities to come [to the Spanish colony] and steal."[26]

Because James Colbert found it difficult to accept the British defeat, he independently organized male refugee loyalists into a band of resistance fighters, with headquarters at Chickasaw Bluffs (Figure 1) and with the Chickasaw settlement 100 miles to the southeast as their protector. In organization of this force, Colbert was probably assisted by at least his second in command, a man identified in July 1782 as "Cilly" by one of the band's former Spanish captives. The reference is undoubtedly to Benjamin Seeley, a white trader originally from Virginia who, like Colbert, had been among the Chickasaw since childhood, according to Malcolm McGee. From Chickasaw Bluffs the raiders harassed and assaulted American and Spanish settlements and American and Spanish vessels on the Mississippi River. D. C. Corbitt ("James Colbert and the Spanish Claims to the East Bank of the Mississippi") describes the first major event associated with "Colbert's raiders."

> During the last days of April, 1782, the keel-boat of Silvestre L'Abadie [Silbestre Labadia] was making its way up the Mississippi loaded with Indian goods, clothes for the garrison at St. Louis, and 4,900 pesos for the subsistence of the garrison. Anicanora Ramos [*sic*], the twenty-seven year old wife of Lieutenant-Colonel Francisco Cruzat, governor of St. Louis, and her four children were on board.
>
> About 11:00 A.M. on May 2, while passing the Chickasaw Bluffs, L'Abadie's boat was hailed from the west bank of the river by one Thomas Prince, who inquired in French if the boat belonged to Senor L'Abadie. Upon receiving an affirmative reply, he said that he had some letters for Madam Cruzat from her husband. Unsuspectingly the boat was turned toward the shore and when within reach Prince seized it and ordered the occupants to surrender themselves as prisoners of the king of Great Britain. About forty Englishmen and a half-breed, armed with rifles, knives, and tomahawks, rushed from the woods, taking L'Abadie and the others in charge. The leader of the band, James Colbert, assured Madam Cruzat that as his prisoner she would be protected and sent on to St. Louis in due time. The keel-boat and the prisoners were taken to one of Colbert's

camps a short distance up the Margot or Chickasaw River [present-day Wolf River], where the oarsmen were put into a log prison. L'Abadie, Madam Cruzat, her children, and her four slaves, were secured in a cabin between the prison and the cabin which Colbert shared with a Frenchman named Francisco la Grange. Little discipline and much rum made life easy for the guards as they enjoyed the spoils of the keel-boat.

. . .

During the following days, according to Madam Cruzat's declaration, they met frequently on the boat, or at Colbert's cabin, where she heard many angry disputes which occurred because the Indians and some of the whites wanted to send Madam Cruzat and the other prisoners to the Chickasaw nation to be held until ransomed by the release of Blommart [the leader of the Natchez Rebellion] and the other Natchez rebels, who were being held in New Orleans, to which neither Colbert nor his son would agree. Colbert himself told her that but for the protection of her and her children he would leave such an insubordinate group of people.[27]

Corbitt and other historians continue by describing how the raiders were joined by about 200 Chickasaws a few days after the capture of the boat. The Chickasaws, who were given powder, brandy, and some of the booty, were led by a Chickasaw son of James Colbert, probably William, the oldest, who Madam Cruzat described as the Chickasaw group's head war chief. Apparently the son made sure that no harm or frightening experiences befell the lady and her children during the captivity period. Madam Cruzat, her children and servants, Labadia, and Frope, the boat captain, were released after nineteen days of captivity and embarked in a keel boat for New Orleans. The Colberts had treated Madam Cruzat well during the ordeal and had released her and the others on parole hoping the Spanish would reciprocate and in good faith release Blommart and eight other rebels. This desire was expressed in a "Parole of Honour" from James Colbert to Louisiana governor Estevan Miro that was delivered by Madam Cruzat. The document was drawn up on May 15 by a Colonel McGillivray, who had arrived after the boat capture, bringing possible advice from a "Monsieur Tranble" of the Chickasaw nation. As previously suggested by Roper ("The Revolutionary War on the Fourth Chickasaw Bluff"), the latter man was probably John Turnbull, a trader among the Chickasaw. Beginning with John W. Caughey in 1933, the other man has been speculated to have been the mixed-blood Alexander McGillivray, who soon thereafter became the noted principal leader of the Creek and a staunch friend of the Spanish. More likely, however, the man was the Colonel John McGillivray discussed above and below in this chapter. Upon receiving the document, Miro rejected Colbert's overture and instead took steps to curtail and defend against the rebel leader's activities. Because Colbert had threatened to launch a military campaign against Natchez, Miro moved to that city, shored up its defenses, made efforts to remove the general Chickasaw population from James Colbert's influence, and took action to obtain peace with the tribe. Emissaries from the Choctaw and Chief Anguska of the Quapaw were sent to the Chickasaw with peace messages. After the governor general of West Florida rejected Miro's suggestion that he be allowed to launch an expedition into the Chickasaw nation with a thousand regular troops, 400 frontiersmen, and an unspecified number of Indians to attack Colbert's band, Miro pursued other actions. He offered a general pardon to refugees from Natchez who returned home, hoping this would cause dissipation of Colbert's band. In light of the evolving political situation, the full-blood chiefs seemed to realize that it would be prudent to distance themselves from Colbert's partisan activities. Colbert himself seemed to have no problem with that position, stating to Miro in an October 1782 letter that he had encouraged the Chickasaw to develop peace with the Spanish and Americans and "with all the world as it is proper that no Indians ought to interfere with what Concerns None but white [people]."[28]

Despite evidence that the Chickasaw in general were not involved with Colbert's activities, Governor Miro rejected initial inclinations of undertaking punitive measures against Colbert and the rebels because they were under the tribe's protection. Although Miro spoke against sending a large force into the Chickasaw nation (taking note of the French disasters in 1736), a more logical plan was devised by Governor Cruzat. Knowing that the Kickapoo were a feared traditional enemy of the Chickasaw, he arranged a secret mission to that tribe and the Mascoutin, who were induced by a lie to begin attacking the Chickasaw in mid-1782. The attacks on the Old Town Creek area villages were greatly disturbing to the Chickasaw and caused a curtailment of hunting. As Cruzat had hoped, Chickasaw chiefs led by Paya Mattaha soon traveled to St. Louis to ask for Spanish aid in gaining relief from the Indian raids. The Spanish granted the request after obtaining a promise that the Chickasaw would no longer offer refuge to Colbert's raiders, would protect Spanish prisoners who might escape from Colbert's band and seek refuge among the Chickasaw, and would thereafter demonstrate allegiance to the Spanish. Paya Mattaha and others belonging to the Spanish faction appear to have indeed eventually played a role in curtailing Colbert's raids on Spanish vessels. In November 1783 Du Breuil reported that Paya Mattaha had promised that "he would get rid of the remainder of the pirates."[29]

Although Labadia reported that there were about 300 "white men of different nations" within the Chickasaw domain, the exiles who returned to Natchez told Miro that the total number of Englishmen among the Chickasaw capable of bearing arms was no more than 100 and that no more than thirty of the whites had belonged to Colbert's band because most were traders who did not want to participate in hostilities. As observed below, there were also some fugitive black slaves among the Chickasaw, and about 100 black slaves owned by Colbert's raiders and/or Natchez refugees and other whites were reported to be in the nation in July 1782. The returning exiles also reported that the band was breaking up, but they were mistaken. The burning of Colbert's unoccupied base camp at Chickasaw Bluffs in the summer of 1782 by a Spanish force from St. Louis looking for the boat carrying the governor's family did not discourage Colbert enough to disband his raiders. In December the band reappeared on the river and captured an American boat, followed in early 1783 by apparent capture of an American flatboat "whose crew joined him," according to Miro. In January Colbert was reported by the commander of the Arkansas post to have attacked a man named Benito Vasquez (and his boat?) with no more than twenty-five men. By 1783, the Chickasaw settlement was reported to have been the forced abode of at least fifty Spanish-affiliated captives.[30]

Finally, in early April 1783 Colbert began execution of a long-planned attack on the Arkansas post or, as correctly called by the Spanish, Fort Carlos III. The band in this incident was composed of Colbert and some of his sons and nephews, eleven Indians, five blacks, one Frenchman, and "enough English and Americans to make the number eighty-two." One of the Englishmen, Malcolm Clark, later provided details of the operation. In a nutshell, two more riverboats and two large canoes collectively loaded with rum, sugar, powder, beaver skins, and bear grease were captured as the band moved down the Mississippi River. The band's boats then ascended the Arkansas River for about fifteen leagues; the men disembarked and marched overland to the fort and Arkansas settlement. By surprise at 2:30 A.M. the raiders captured several soldiers and their families who were living outside the fort. Others escaped to the fort or the forest. A patrol attacked the raiders but, badly outnumbered, the result was two soldiers and a slave killed, one soldier wounded, and six soldiers captured. Colbert then attacked the fort with determined gunfire, which precipitated about six hours of firing between the fort and the raiders. The fort defenders also answered with about 300 rounds from cannons. Colbert then sent one of his officers, a captured Spaniard, and the Spaniard's wife to the fort with a flag of truce and a surrender demand in which Colbert stated that he "had been sent by his Superiors to take the fort." The fort commander later replied by launching an attack with a small number of soldiers and Indians. At this time Colbert decided on a voluntary retreat to the boats, from which he sent another surrender demand by some of the captured women and children. The message was loaded with obvious falsehoods included for intimidation purposes. The post commander ignored it and the band soon retreated down the river, rowing all night in a rainfall. At least one of Colbert's men was killed, and among the wounded was one of his sons, possibly William Colbert. The post commander, Captain Jacobo Du Breuil, thereafter sent the Arkansas/Quapaw great chief, Anguska, with 100 warriors and twenty soldiers from the fort to catch up with the raiders and demand release of the prisoners. The Indians and troops caught up with the band at its camp about nine miles from the mouth of the Arkansas, where an intimidated Colbert turned over nearly all of the prisoners, holding eight as insurance against a possible subsequent attack. This was an intelligent move, for Du Breuil, with Anguska's Quapaws, indeed had intended to at-tack the band after securing all the prisoners. Fearing the remaining prisoners would be killed if he ordered an attack, Du Breuil withdrew.[31]

Before Colbert's raiders reached Chickasaw Bluffs, a Spanish convoy that had visited the Arkansas post after the attack while on its way to the Illinois post had returned to the Mississippi and was moving upstream in the first part of May. The commander, Captain Joseph Valliere, was now searching for Col-bert's band, which had earlier concealed itself in a bayou until the convoy passed. About seventy to ninety miles north of the mouth of the Arkansas, Valliere's scouts found signs of the raiders. Valliere began making preparations to attack them with 100 volunteers and twenty-four Quapaw Indians who were with the convoy. A confrontation thereafter ensued with a separate group of rebels about three miles up the "Chickasaw River" (also called Margot River and Las Casas River; presently Wolf River), which Colbert and his band had ascended with hundreds of pounds of flour previously captured from boats. The rebel group was led by a man identified only as "McGillivray," who was probably the same man referred to as Colonel McGillivray in July 1782 and thus probably Colonel John McGillivray, as discussed above. In the ensuing fight on the stream, McGillivray and two other rebels were reported killed, while the remainder landed and fled into the wilderness, presumably eventually rejoining a larger group that had already set out overland with many barrels of flour. Three Spanish soldiers captured earlier managed to escape during the confron-tation. Valliere later captured a flour-laden flatboat and three large canoes at the deserted rebel camp. Colbert managed to escape with the remainder of his boats, eventually arriving home in the Chickasaw nation. This was his last op-eration, for the band thereafter dissolved and the Mississippi River became safe for Spanish and American travel.[32]

Soon after this affair, a copy of the preliminary treaty of peace (Treaty of Paris) was sent to Colbert by the Spanish governor, who pointed out that ex-change of prisoners was now appropriate. Replying by a letter dated August 3, Colbert stated that he had released the prisoners as soon as he had learned of the truce between Spain and Britain, but it appears he was untruthful on the subject. Colbert also replied that he was about to leave for St. Augustine to report to his superiors and that upon his return he would address the question of the prisoners. This was one of the last letters to be sent by Colbert, for before the end of 1783 he was dead as a result of being thrown from his horse while on his way back from St. Augustine, three days after leaving Alexander McGillivray's home in present-day south-central Alabama. At a congress with the Spanish in Mobile in 1784, the Chickasaws promised to release all prisoners. Such may well have occurred, but in October 1786, Miro requested of the Chickasaw that they release a daughter of a Madam Bautista, who was being held by relatives of Colbert's sons.[33] She, however, may not have been a captive dating to the raider period and could have been obtained by the Chickasaw from another Indian group.

Apparently, full-blood Chickasaw participation in Colbert's raids was rare, but mixed-blood participation is obvious in light of the above-discussed references to Colbert's half-Chickasaw sons. Another mixed-blood, Robert Thompson, also participated in the capture of Madam Cruzat's party, according to information received by the Spanish. A Spanish letter to Paya Mattaha in June 1782 in which the writer stated, "I am convinced that your nation has played no part in the attack lately perpetrated on the Mississippi River," seems to support a lack of generalized Chickasaw support for the raiders. According to Spanish reports, the people associated with Colbert's rebel band lived in a location about fifteen miles from the main Chickasaw settlement, which as already discussed was in the open prairie on Town Creek and its tributaries. The separate location for the raiders was, according to one report, due to Chickasaw opposition, or at least increasing pro-Spanish-faction opposition, to the band's living among them. Perhaps the band lived to the north of Old Town and the Chickasaw Old Fields in the "half breed" villages or towns located there in the last quarter of the eighteenth century, as discussed in Chapter 1, or to the west of the Chickasaw Old Fields in the woodlands of present-day Pontotoc County where many mixed-bloods and whites were living by the beginning of the nineteenth century. More likely, however, they were at Colbert's plantation in the forks of the Tombigbee River and Old Town Creek, which was indeed about fifteen miles from the Chickasaw settlements. A Choctaw named Paulous, in fact, reported to Spaniard Henrique Grimarest that Colbert was "about at the *Petit Bea* on the upper Tombigbee River." This is probably the forks, which, as discussed in an earlier chapter, Frenchmen sometimes referred to as "Petite Portage."[34]

The Americans were no less perturbed than the Spanish by the activities of the raiders. In January 1783, Governor Harrison of Virginia encouraged driving out of the Chickasaw nation the Natchez "vagabonds" who were raiding boats and capturing prisoners. Because Colbert's band was labeled "pirates" by the Spanish, even James Robertson and other officials became concerned when in 1783 the Cumberland settlement was accused of supplying some of its members. Robertson thereafter wrote, in 1783 and 1784, diplomatic letters to Spanish governor Francisco Cruzat at St. Louis, to the commandant at Natchez, and to the commandant at the Spanish military post called Lance de Grace, located on the Mississippi River below the mouth of the Ohio, in which he stated that the Cumberland settlement had no involvement in Colbert's activities and would even try to have returned to the Spanish any property or prisoners that he or other Americans might be able to seize. On November 4, 1784, Cruzat sent a diplomatic letter to then Colonel James Robertson in which he accepted the latter's statements and expressed friendship toward Robertson and the settlement, despite the fact that in late 1783 Governor Alexander Martin of North Carolina (to which the Cumberland settlement was attached at the time) had issued an arrest proclamation for thirteen men accused of joining Colbert's band. After issuance of the proclamation, however, a Lieutenant Colonel James Robinson had informed the Spanish commandant at Natchez that the men were so dispersed that their apprehension was unlikely.[35]

The accounts associated with the 1782–1783 activities of James Colbert and his raiders provide some insight into the early lives of his sons. Mentions of "Colbert's son" or "Colbert's sons" in the Spanish documents are among the earliest known contemporary references to any of his children. In the several references, it is highly probable that the two oldest sons, William and George, are the ones spoken of. William was probably the son mentioned by Madam Cruzat in her report. If born in about 1760 as stated by Malcolm McGee, William would have been about twenty-two at the time. He was, therefore, undoubtedly the son who, along with his father, openly opposed the desire of some of the rebels to hold Madam Cruzat for ransom in the Chickasaw settlement, and his position in the group demonstrates that he had already achieved leadership status. According to McGee, George Colbert was born in about 1764; he was thus about four years younger than William and only about eighteen in May 1782. That George was also active militarily by this time is suggested by an August 1782 reference to Spanish soldiers who had been captured at Mobile by James Colbert and his sons. George undoubtedly participated in the raids under discussion, for some of the band that attacked the Arkansas post in 1783 included "sons" and nephews of James Colbert. The next two sons, being younger than George, were not likely engaging in warfare that early, although there is a reference to three of the sons being at Mobile, as discussed above. McGee recalled that Samuel was killed by the northern Indians after the revolution and Joseph died while a "young man" at his brothers' early nineteenth-century ferry at the mouth of Bear Creek on the Tennessee River. The reference to nephews of James Colbert is somewhat mysterious, for there is no known documentation that he had a brother or sister among the Chickasaw, although such is entirely possible, especially if he was actually a second-generation Colbert among the Chickasaw, a possibility already discussed. Those referred to here as "nephews" could alternatively have been full-blood relatives in some manner of his first two full-blood wives, one of whom was William's mother and the second the mother of George.[36]

By 1783, the Chickasaw were faced with having to seriously address the allegiance issues. Such was complicated by the continuation of hostilities from Colbert's raiders. Confusion epitomized the political situation at the time, for while many young Chickasaws now favored the Spanish and their status-elevating trade goods, James Colbert was at the same time leading attacks on them. Colbert was a realist, however, and like the chiefs knew he could not continue being an enemy of the Americans. While Virginia commissioner John Donne was in the nation in July, therefore, Colbert gave him a letter to his governor, Benjamin Harrison, in which he stated that the Chickasaw must establish new trade relationships to replace that of the British and espoused the advantages of the Americans having the Chickasaw as an ally, one of which was that they would serve as a buffer against Spain's Indian allies in the Mississippi Valley. According to the Chickasaw chiefs, the Chickasaw had ceased giving refuge to Colbert's band by this time, which seems to have been the case, for Colbert contended to Harrison that his former military activities against the Spanish were not as a guerrilla, as some characterized him, but rather as a commissioned British officer fighting against a declared war enemy and an enemy that was also a competitor of the United States for control of the Mississippi Valley. This logic had good effect on the Americans, and Colbert was thereafter considered someone who the Americans did not want to reject because of his perceived influence with the Chickasaw. Colbert's influence may have been mostly confined to his and his sons' full-blood Chickasaw relatives. Possible future clarification of this question died with Colbert when he fell from his horse in late 1783.[37] If Colbert had not gained significant influence within the nation by the time of his death, the same cannot be said of four of his sons, who became prominent in Chickasaw affairs by the turn of the nineteenth century.

8
The Strange Road Ends

Like the Spanish, the Americans eventually began making conciliatory gestures toward the Chickasaw. As had occurred in 1778, the Americans obtained the assistance of a Kaskaskia chief named Jean Baptiste de Coigne, who this time led a successful peacemaking mission to the Chickasaw. The Chickasaw chiefs later sent out messages through Indian intermediaries, and in July 1782, King Mingo Houma, principal war chief Paya Mattaha, Tuskau Pautaupau, and Piomingo had an Englishman living in the Chickasaw nation and four warriors deliver a message and a peace flag to "the Commanders of Every different Station Between this nation and the Falls on the Ohio River." This man, Simon Burney (a refugee Natchez resident and one of Colbert's raiders), probably penned the letter for the Chickasaws. Along with most other whites in the nation, Burney undoubtedly desired to make friends with the Americans out of necessity. The message declared that the Chickasaw and Americans had never been extreme enemies and that Mingo Houma wished to "eat, drink, & smoke Together as Friends & Brothers."[1] Perhaps reflecting anxiety on the part of the British loyalists among the Chickasaw, part of the message stated, "You'l observe at the Same time, Our making a Peace with you doth not Intittle Us to fall out with Our Fathers the Inglish, for we love them, as they were the first People that Ever Supported us to Defend ourselves against our former Enimys, the French & Spaniards &, all their Indians . . . [and] We are a People that never forgets any Kindness done Us by any Nation."[2]

Because the Chickasaw were no longer receiving a consistent flow of trade goods and other European materials and were confused about their current relationship with the British, about 300 of them set out for St. Augustine in the spring of 1783 to see the beleaguered British officials. The Chickasaw and Indians from other southern tribes had been encouraged by John Stuart to form a confederation to oppose the rebels and now wanted confirmation that the British would support them. In the midst of semi-chaos caused by numerous loyalist refugees from South Carolina and Georgia, officials of the remnants of the British government in America welcomed them, as well as many Choctaws, Creeks, some Cherokees, and representatives from several tribes located north of the Ohio. Indian superintendent Thomas Brown and others did the best they could under the circumstances, reassuring them that the British withdrawal was only temporary, but that if it should become permanent the Indians would best make peace with the Americans. Brown's optimistic approach, plus distribution of presents, provisions, and firing of cannons for entertainment purposes, resulted in the Indians going home in a fairly good state of mind. The Chickasaw and other tribes were shocked, however, when they learned a few months later that the British were abandoning St. Augustine and withdrawing all support to the Indians. Most of the British-allied Indians were truly saddened and distressed by the loss of their longtime friends, and they feared for their own futures.[3] This disappointing event undoubtedly created new Spanish-faction adherents among the Chickasaw, Choctaw, and other southern Indian populations.

By July 1783 the Chickasaw had become frustrated at the failure of the United States to meaningfully respond to their peace overtures. Three days after James Colbert prepared the peace overture letter to Governor Harrison mentioned in Chapter 7, five major chiefs of the Chickasaw Old Fields prairie settlement along present-day Old Town Creek, including among others King Mingo Houma, Paya Mattaha, and Piomingo, sent a long, passionate letter to the president of the United States Congress in which they pleaded for clarification of the American position toward their people. The Chickasaw confusion and apprehension are partially reflected in the following excerpt:

> It makes our hearts rejoice to find that our great father [King of Great Britain], and his children, the Americans have at length made peace, which we may wish to continue as long as the Sun and Moon, And to find that our Brothers the Americans are inclined to take us by the hand and Smoke with us at the great Fire which we hope will never be extinguished. . . . Notwithstanding the Satisfaction all these things give us we are yet in confusion & uncertainty. The Spaniards are sending talks amongst us, and inviting our young Men to trade with them. We also receive talks from the Governor of Georgia to the same effect—we have had Speeches from the Illinois inviting us to Trade and Intercourse with them—Our Brothers, the Virginians Call upon us to a Treaty, and want part of our land, and we expect our Neighbors who live on Cumberland River, will in a Little time Demand, if not forcibly take part of it from us. . . . We are told that you are the head Chief of the Grand Council [Congress], which is above these 13 Councils: if so, why have we not had

Talks from you. . . . We hope you will also put a stop to any encroachments on our lands, without our consent, and silence all those people who sends us Such Talks as inflame & exasperate our Young Men, as it is our earnest desire to remain in peace and friendship with our Br[others]: the Americans for ever.[4]

Actually, an American response had already been initiated by George Rogers Clark, who sent a representative to hold talks with the Chickasaw. The representative, John Donne, arrived in July. James Colbert's letter and the Chickasaw letter quoted from above, in fact, were written while Donne was in the nation and were carried back to Virginia by him. In response to the Chickasaw letters, Clark sent Captain Robert George with instructions to assure the Chickasaw of the Americans' desire for peace. As a result of some spoken words of Burney, Clark got the mistaken impression that the Chickasaw were favorably inclined toward selling some of their land on the left side of the Tennessee River. He therefore instructed Captain George (without authority) to try to negotiate a sale (at a specified amount not recorded) "of a little tract of Country" somewhere between the Mississippi, Tennessee, and Ohio Rivers where a town could be established for the purpose of serving as a center for Chickasaw trade. However, the trade from such a town would not likely have been limited to the Chickasaw, as the latter undoubtedly well knew. Having already learned of the desire for a land cession, the Chickasaw spoke negatively about the subject before Captain George had time to enter into formal consultations. Because many of the Chickasaw were away on their winter hunts, George prudently did not speak of a land cession, following his directive from Clark, who had told him to refrain from doing so if "they could not collect the Council necessary in such cases." Captain George, who arrived in October, therefore dropped his plan to seek the land sale, speaking instead about peace, cooperation, and provision of American trade goods. Although knowing that the Americans wanted land, the Chickasaw put aside their distrust in favor of a prudent acceptance of the peace talks. The chiefs diplomatically, but not necessarily honestly, told George and his companion that they realized British deceit and misrepresentations were to blame for the past misunderstandings and conflicts between the Chickasaw and the Americans.[5]

After Governor Harrison appointed Joseph Martin and John Donelson to hold councils with the Chickasaw and try to conclude a firm peace, as well as obtain a land cession if such talk seemed not to agitate them, the so-called Virginia-Chickasaw Treaty was concluded in November 1783 at a large sulphur spring, said by Putnam (*History of Middle Tennessee*) to have been four miles northwest of what was then French Lick (also Nashborough, which later became Nashville, Tennessee). The conference was held after many months of complicated confusion associated with arranging it. Malcolm McGee, a white resident of the Chickasaw nation since arriving there from New York as a child in 1767, was chosen by the Americans to serve as interpreter (although unable to read and write, McGee was very intelligent and spoke Chickasaw fluently). The treaty affirmed the peace, stipulated that all prisoners held by the Chickasaw were to be released, and obligated them to expel all non-Indians in the nation who were openly hostile to the United States in addition to the Delaware Indians residing on Bear Creek. The Chickasaws demanded that the Virginians aid them in ejecting intruders and in preventing intrusions. The Virginia commissioners agreed with the Chickasaws' assertion that the northeastern Chickasaw land boundary ran along the Tennessee-Cumberland divide from the Ohio River to the Duck River mouth and along it to its source at the Cumberland River divide. Cession of land was strenuously opposed, the "king of the Chickasaws" (Mingo Houma) stating in private that he had the authority to make peace but none to sell lands. A man called the "Mountain Leader," identified in the treaty as Tushatohoa, finished by stating that "Peace is now settled, I was the first that proposed it . . . & Am in hope No more blood [will be] shed by Either party." This Mountain Leader was likely the same man known at this time by his title name of Piomingo. If so, this reveals his original name prior to consistent reference to him as Piomingo, the Mountain Leader.[6]

The site of the French Lick treaty was, according to historian Putnam, at or near James Robertson's original homestead, but there seems to be uncertainty that his log house was situated four miles northwest of Nashville, where the treaty is asserted to have been held. Putnam, however, follows by stating that this was near the same place where Robertson later built his "brick dwelling." This two-story home, finished in 1797, was located southwest of early Nashville on Richland Creek. It burned in 1902 and is now commemorated by a Tennessee historical marker located at the Charlotte Pike–Lellyette Avenue intersection in present-day west Nashville. Perhaps Putnam meant to say "southwest" rather than "northwest" with regard to the treaty site of 1783. Haywood (*Civil and Political History of the State of Tennessee*), writing many years earlier than Putnam, only states that the treaty conference was held "at Nashville." A two-story log home, situated until the 1970s about one mile north of the brick home site, is believed to have been the original home of Robertson. As discussed in Chapter 9, Robertson's log home also became the first Chickasaw-Choctaw Agency in 1792 when he was appointed United States agent to those tribes. A reconstruction of that home is now in the H. G. Hill Park on Charlotte Avenue.[7]

With both the Spanish and the United States on friendly terms with the Chickasaw or, perhaps more accurately, with their respective factions of that tribe, the stage was set for an on-going tussle between the two non-Indian nations for control of the Mississippi Valley. Actually, the American-faction adherents among the Chickasaw saw advantages in also dealing with the Spanish and vice versa with regard to the Spanish faction. Both factions were in agreement that the political policies of the Spanish were a hindrance to American land-grabbing designs, which had already been demonstrated by the words of George Rogers Clark and Governor Harrison. Moreover, in 1783 the Spanish formed a cooperative agreement with the British merchants Panton, Leslie, & Company in an attempt to dominate the Indian trade and to thus create a multitribal alliance. Because the Americans could not yet offer anything comparable, a majority of the Chickasaw were affiliated with the Spanish party by the latter half of 1783, when principal war chief Paya Mattaha turned away from the Americans. In the fall he invited Spanish traders into the nation and by the spring of 1784 was solidly in the Spanish party. On his deathbed at Chickasaw Bluffs that spring, suffering from a fever and/or the measles, the aging chief supposedly stated to trader Anselmo Billet that he considered himself a Spaniard, that he had told the young Chickasaws to stay friends with the Spaniards, and that upon his death he wished to be covered with a Spanish flag and cremated. Although Spanish Captain Jacobo Du Breuil reported that Paya Mattaha's wishes were carried out,[8] the alleged cremation should be considered suspect because such was alien to Chickasaw religious beliefs and their post-death customs.

The Chickasaw factions negotiated with both the Spanish and Americans for suitable trade rates, while the Americans and Spanish competed with one another for Chickasaw agreement to the establishment of a trading post at Chickasaw Bluffs. In June 1784 all six Chickasaw villages were represented by numerous delegates at a Spanish-Indian conference in Mobile, where separate treaties were signed with each of the southern tribes. Piomingo's Choukafalya village alone sent enough delegates to consume almost 1,000 pounds of bread and meat, along with about 1,500 pounds of rice. The Chickasaw treaty called for peaceful relations with the Spanish, entailed the prompt release of all Spanish captives, asserted that Spain would be the Chickasaw protector in exchange for that tribe's allegiance, assured continued trade, and provided for new trade tariffs. Also, those Chickasaw who signed the treaty obligated the tribe, on paper anyway, to maintain peace with all tribes except the Kickapoos and to reject all trading except that under the auspices of Spain. Spain, as Chickasaw protector, promised to work with them in expelling non-Spanish traders and to keep prices for goods at a moderate level. By the end of the summer, Panton-Leslie agents were eagerly supplying the settlement with trade goods. One of the leaders who signed the treaty would eventually become the major rival of Piomingo, but in 1784 Ugulayacabe, also called Wolf's Friend, was still somewhat obscure with regard to Chickasaw politics.[9]

Upon the death of Mingo Houma in 1784, apparently due to measles, his nephew, Taski Etoka (varied spellings; called the Hare Lipped King), succeeded him as "king" as well as leader of the Spanish faction. Because of both Mingo Houma's and Taski Etoka's attachment to the Spanish faction, leaders of the American faction were concerned that the succession of the latter to the "king-ship" would cause the Americans to fear that the Spanish alliance was becoming more deeply entrenched. Accordingly, Tuskau Pautaupau, Piomingo/Mountain Leader, and other chiefs representing both factions attended a talk with the Americans in Nashville and brought black beads (signifying Mingo Houma's death) to be sent to the governor of North Carolina with a promise that the death would in no fashion affect the established American friendship. By now war chief Piomingo was undisputed principal leader of the American faction. He had also become the most powerful Chickasaw leader in the nation, as recognized in writing in 1793 by his nemesis, Alexander McGillivray of the Creek.[10] Despite being the leader of a faction opposed by the majority of the tribe, Piomingo was highly respected by the entire nation and seemingly had the last word on most important decisions made at the national councils.

As illustrated earlier, the "king" of the Chickasaw seldom had much au-thority among the Chickasaw population as a whole with regard to interaction with whites. Although the new king, Taski Etoka, generally displayed enthusiasm in his position and received an unusual amount of attention from non-Indians as a result of his courtship with the Spanish, the two dominant personalities among the Chickasaw through the remainder of the eighteenth century were full-bloods Piomingo and Ugulayacabe/Wolf's Friend. Piomingo, whose name was a postjuvenile title signifying that the individual had become recognized as an exceptional war leader, had come of age just prior to the American Revo-lution. His original given name has been lost to history, as have the origi-nal names of nearly all native Americans who achieved title names. However, as discussed above, the original name of the Piomingo known as Mountain Leader may have been Tushatohoa. If Malcolm McGee is correct in stating that Piomingo was born about 1750 at Old Town/Chuckalissa, he would have been about thirty years old when his name first began to appear in historical docu-ments around 1782. The names of his mother and father are unknown, and the clan to which he belonged is also obscure. If McGee is correct about the ap-proximate year of Piomingo's birth, the several references to Chickasaws by that name in original documents dated prior to about 1770 are undoubtedly references to older individuals having that title name. Examples of referenced earlier Piomingos who undoubtedly were not the Mountain Leader include "Pai Mingo Euleuroy" and "Paye Mingo Belixy" (or "Paheminggo Elookse"). The latter was called by John McIntosh "that corrupted villain" and "Common Disturber of the Peace of this Nation." The former is mentioned in a document dating to 1770 and the latter in documents dated 1766. This last Piomingo did not like John McIntosh and was a rival of Paya Mattaha in that year. There was a second adult Piomingo in 1783 who was head war chief of the village "Christhautra"; this spelling indicates a corrupted pronunciation of the old village of Tchitchatala. This man could have been one of the others mentioned above. A possible origin of Piomingo's nickname is suggested in a letter from Captain Zebra Pike to James Robertson in 1796: "Permit me to request you to inform the Mountain heads or the Chiefs of their [the Chickasaw] Nation of the circumstances in a manner as your superior judgement may dictate."[11]

As shown by the July 28, 1783, letter to the Continental Congress, we know that Piomingo/Mountain Leader was already one of the most prominent men of the Chickasaw. That letter is signed by him as a leading man of Choukafalya or Long Town. Three years later, in January 1786, he declared himself the "head leading Warrior to treat with all Nations." Piomingo never wavered in his solid friendship with the United States, and as illustrated below was seemingly always prepared to assist the Americans militarily. Although relatively small in size, he made up for it in character and competence and was highly respected and admired by most Indians and whites. Malcolm McGee stated that he was a Chickasaw-Chackchiuma mix, a "middle sized person," and "a great war leader." McGee added that Piomingo, like the Chackchiuma population among the Chickasaw, was of a fairer skin than the Chickasaw full-bloods. Also according to McGee, Piomingo, after a brother was killed by a Chickasaw, went to live with the Cherokee as a youth but returned just prior to the second Cherokee War with the British (mid-1770s). Affiliation with the Cherokee is indeed verified by contemporary documents. Noted Cherokee chief Bloody Fellow stated in 1793 that Piomingo was his "old friend & Can Speak my tongue as well as a Cherokee." Further confirmation of McGee's statement lies in the revelation by noted Cherokee chief Little Turkey in 1795 that Piomingo was his nephew and that the latter had a son living in the Cherokee nation. Because the Cherokee were commonly called the "Mountain Indians" by other tribes, Piomingo may have received his nickname of Mountain Leader while living among that tribe or soon after returning to the Chickasaw. On the negative side, McGee said that Piomingo "couldn't look a trader in the face" and had trouble getting credit from the traders because of not paying his debts well. In 1790, William Panton of Panton, Leslie, & Company met with Piomingo in the Chickasaw settlement and later described him in two separate letters as "a sensible talkative little Indian." A white man from middle Tennessee who apparently knew Piomingo well stated that he was "naturally one of the shrewdest of men . . . a true and good man; and . . . was among the smartest men by nature I ever saw. I have no doubt but that if he had had an education, he would have made a great statesman." More about Piomingo is incorporated in the remainder of this chapter and in following chapters.[12]

It should be pointed out here that Jack D. L. Holmes (in *Gayoso*) inexplicably confused Piomingo with a Choctaw chief named Taboca and thus presented totally erroneous data about the former. His source, a letter from Governor Manuel Gayoso to Governor Baron De Carondelet, indeed contains the data presented but clearly in relation to Taboca. Even stranger is a footnote by R. S. Cotterill (*The Southern Indians*) that states that in 1765 the Chickasaw delegation to the conference with the British at Mobile, discussed herein in Chapter 6, was led by a chief known as Opoia Mattaha (Paya Mattaha) who was "later known as Piomingo, their war chief." This, of course, is erroneous as shown by extensive documentation that Opoia Mattaha/Paya Mattaha and Piomingo were two different Chickasaws. Moreover, assuming Malcolm McGee is correct that Piomingo/Mountain Leader was born in about 1750, he would have only been about fifteen years old in 1765 and, of course, much too young to have been the leader of a Chickasaw delegation to a major Indian conference with the British. Incidentally, verifiable McGee recollections regarding events and dates are correct or close to correct on a consistent basis.[13]

With regard to new Chickasaw king Taski Etoka, Major John Doughty of the United States army had this to say about him in 1790: "a dissipated character, to be bought for a small Price. He succeeded his Uncle, the Red King; [he] cares but little for his own Dignity or for that of his Nation." However, it should be kept in mind that this description was probably repeated from one of the American-faction Chickasaws and should be considered biased against that Spanish-faction king. Taski Etoka may have been easily manipulated, as indicated by the following statement of merchant William Panton with regard to his rude behavior at the home of Governor Baron De Carondelet in Pensacola in 1793: "Your Excellency however cannot be ignorant of the Person who was at the bottom of the business [John Turnbull], and who prompted him [Taski Etoka] to say what he did—The poor old fellow was merely an Actor on that occasion, and was paid for acting—His threatening to go to the Americans in case you did not comply with his request was a meer [*sic*] delusion put into his head by his employers [John Turnbull and associates in trade]." However, the jealous Panton may have misinterpreted Taski Etoka's actions. Perhaps, in fact, the Chickasaw king was manipulating the Spaniards to get better trade rates than those offered by Panton. No matter what the character of Taski Etoka, he was not lazy and often traveled hundreds of miles on behalf of his nation. The proposals he made and assertiveness exhibited by him at the conference with the Spanish in New Orleans in late 1792 led Cotterill (*The Southern Indians*) to state that Taski Etoka "was making himself the spiritual heir of Dragging Canoe."[14]

Little more is known about Ugulayacabe/Wolf's Friend. Unlike Piomingo, he does not appear to have been active militarily, at least in the 1780s and 1790s after achieving political notoriety. There appears to be no evidence, in fact, that he ever directly participated in war activities, which indicates that he had always been a peace chief. An insertion by an American commissioner into the record of a conference in Nashville in 1792 described Wolf's Friend as "a great man; in council ranks among the first of his nation; has a considerable property, is a large man, of a dignified appearance." At the conference he wore a scarlet coat with silver lace (probably obtained from the Spanish) and carried "a large crimson silk umbrella" to protect himself from the sun or rain. According to Malcolm McGee, in the late eighteenth century Wolf's Friend was a resident of Post Oak Grove Town (old Tchitchatala in a new location on Coonewah Creek). The approximate year of his birth is unknown, but it may be assumed that he and Piomingo were of the same generation.[15] More about Wolf's Friend follows in this and other chapters.

Piomingo was well aware that the Americans desired Indian land; he vigorously opposed selling it to them, but he apparently believed this was not a serious problem and that all would be fine as long as the Indians rejected land purchase overtures while the Americans and Spaniards continued to optimistically court them with goods and munitions. He thus responded favorably to overtures from land-grabber John Sevier and his breakaway "state" of Franklin (in present-day Tennessee). In July 1785 he and other Chickasaws visited Sevier at his home on the Nolachucky River for the purpose of obtaining trade and aid against the Creek. While there he made a favorable impression, as illustrated by a letter from a citizen to a newspaper: "He seems to be a man endowed with more than ordinary prowess of mind and humanity, for an Indian. In his speeches, he delivered himself fluently and with great force of argument, disclosing a clear knowledge of the strength and interest of the Southern tribes, and of the causes and effect of the late Revolution. These people [the Chickasaw] are more comely in their persons and kindlier in their dispositions than any of the nations I have been acquainted with."[16]

Cognizant of the fact that the Spanish had made alarming progress in winning over the Creek, Chickasaw, Choctaw, and others, including negotiation of the 1784 treaty with the Chickasaws' Spanish faction at Mobile, the American Confederation Congress soon passed a resolution providing for a commission to negotiate treaties. When United States officials requested a conference of Chickasaw, Cherokee, Choctaw, and Creek, Piomingo naturally led the cooperative Chickasaw delegation to the treaty site, Hopewell on the Keowee River in South Carolina. All the invited tribes sent delegates except the anti-American Creek under the control of Alexander McGillivray.[17]

The Chickasaw representatives who attended the 1785–1786 conference did so despite previous internal and external opposition to dealing with the Americans. Upon hearing of the American treaty initiatives, Alexander McGillivray had organized in July 1785 a conference of southern Indian leaders for the pur-pose of reinforcing the Spanish–southern Indians alliance he had helped to es-tablish. The outcome of this conference was a statement drawn up for the In-dians by McGillivray and approved by the pro-Spanish representatives from the Creek, Cherokee, and Chickasaw tribes. With the Choctaw, who were not rep-resented at the conference, the major southern tribes became known as the "Four Nations." McGillivray's statement presented at the conference, held at Little Tallassie in the Creek nation, stressed that the Treaty of Paris had indis-criminately turned over all land east of the Mississippi River to the United States and Spain, with no consideration at all made for the land rights of the Indians. The statement declared that "any title claim or demand the Ameri-can Congress may set up for or against our lands, Settlements, and hunting Grounds in Consequence of the . . . treaty of peace between the King of Great Brittain and the States of America" would be objected to and opposed. McGil-livray asserted that all of the state- and citizen-initiated land cessions obtained by the Americans after 1773 were invalid. Thus the Cumberland settlement, among others, was an encroachment on Indian land. The dominant plank in McGillivray's confederation platform was opposition to the obvious intentions of the Americans to attempt further appropriation of Indian lands. McGilliv-ray's stance was the basis for years of hostility from the Creek and Cherokee toward the Cumberland settlement and others. On paper anyway, the Chicka-saw tribe was a member of the Four Nations Confederacy despite frequent hos-tilities with the Creek and Cherokee.[18]

Despite Piomingo's aversion to sale of Chickasaw land, the well-meaning chief facilitated the first puncture of the dike at the Hopewell conference when he and the other Chickasaw chiefs agreed to a request that the United States be allowed to establish a trading post at the mouth of Ocochappo Creek (present-day Bear Creek) on the Tennessee River, a location near the present-day Mississippi-Alabama state line in the vicinity of Iuka, Mississippi, and on or near the site of the now extinct nineteenth- through early twentieth-century non-Indian town of Eastport, Mississippi (Figure 12). Thus Article 3 of the treaty, which was signed on January 10, 1786, gave to the United States a circular area five miles in diameter for a trading post site at the mouth of Bear Creek. However, after Alexander McGillivray protested the Chickasaw agreement to allow this foothold deep in the Four Nations Confederacy, the Chickasaw re-thought their action and became uncooperative with regard to allowing the United States to build the post, which the latter made no serious effort to ini-tiate anyway for several years. In the early 1790s, however, the Cumberland set-tlers and American government officials began to pursue establishment of the post, claiming it would be of great benefit to the Chickasaw, Choctaw, and Americans. Knowing how McGillivray felt about it, Piomingo steadfastly re-

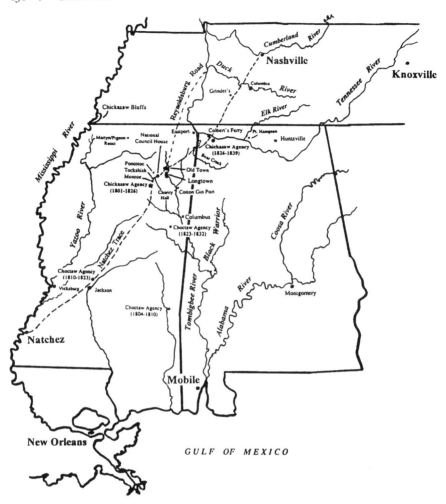

12. Locations of major late eighteenth- and early nineteenth-century Chickasaw nation sites and various cities, towns, and roads in the present-day states of Mississippi, Alabama, Tennessee, and Louisiana (by author)

fused to agree to that part of the Hopewell treaty, stating that such would certainly cause bloodshed because of Creek opposition and hostilities, which in turn would result in open war. Although in 1795 the Chickasaw finally asked for a post at the proposed site, located on the Chickasaw Trace, which meandered from present-day Nashville to present-day Tupelo, the Americans never established one there. In 1800, however, two of the Colbert brothers, Levi and George, opened a ferry there, as discussed in Chapter 11.[19]

Inaccurate wording in the Hopewell treaty regarding the proposed Bear Creek post has caused some confusion among historians not directly familiar with the geography of the old Chickasaw nation area. As mentioned above, the treaty states that the post would be located "at the lower port [*sic,* part] of the Muscle shoals, at the mouth of Ocochappo [Creek]." However, the Muscle Shoals were confined to a shallow area along the Tennessee River that is entirely in present-day north Alabama; the shoals area ends some fifty miles east of the mouth of Bear Creek. Thus statements such as that by Gibson in *The Chickasaws* that the treaty reserved a circular tract "on the lower Muscle Shoals for a trading post site" are erroneous, especially while omitting that the post was to be at the mouth of Bear Creek. Likewise, works by Cotterill (*The Southern Indians*), Calloway (*The American Revolution in Indian Country*), and Coker and Watson (*Indian Traders of the Southeastern Spanish Borderlands*) assert without mentioning Bear Creek that the post was to be established at Muscle Shoals. Calloway further asserts that because the Creek Indians claimed this land they "promptly drove off the American settlers." However, there were no American settlers on Chickasaw land at or near the mouth of Bear Creek in the late eighteenth century; Calloway's reference is to ventures opposed by the Creeks that were associated with the true Muscle Shoals in present-day Alabama, where John Donelson and Joseph Martin had illegally "purchased" a tract of land from a small group of Chickamauga/Cherokee Indians in 1783. In 1784 William Blount and others persuaded the Georgia legislature to provide for settlement of the Shoals district and organization of a county government there. Perhaps the modern historians failed to pick up on this mistake because of lack of knowledge that Ocochappo Creek was the Indian name of Bear Creek and that its mouth is actually west of Muscle Shoals. They also could have been unduly influenced by a peculiar 1792 statement by Alexander McGillivray that indicates even he had a poor understanding of the location of the mouth of Bear Creek, which was definitely never in Creek territory as McGillivray seemed to believe: "It is Bear Creek which empties into the Cherokee [Tennessee] River at the Muscle Shoals & which is in the list of Congress for an establishment. The Muscle Shoals is the passing place to my people when they go a hunting or to War & my people by my orders have frequented those places all this past Spring & Summer & they will at the end of this month swarm out there in going to attack Cumberland & the other Settlements in that quarter."[20] For this statement to have been true, the Creek would have traveled at least one hundred miles out of their way northwest to the mouth of Bear Creek in traveling to Cumberland, which was due north from the Creek settlements. McGillivray was undoubtedly referring here to the location of the Muscle Shoals as it actually existed despite his reference to the mouth of Bear Creek. Interestingly, in February 1795 while the Chickasaw and Creek were engaged in open war, twenty-eight Chickasaw chiefs sent a letter to General James Robertson, part of which requested that a garrison be established by George Washington at "the Muscle Shoals or [on] Bear Creek, or where he may think best to establish a trade."[21]

The contemporary significance of the Treaty of Hopewell concerned the official beginning of peaceful relations with the United States, and means to preserve that relationship were stated in several treaty articles. The last article began with the words, "The hatchet shall be forever buried and the peace . . . shall be universal."

The Chickasaw representatives, Piomingo, Mingotushka, and Latopoia, agreed to the wording in Article 2 that the Chickasaw were "under the protection of the United States of America, and of no other sovereign whosoever." Of course, this statement was a direct violation of the terms of the Spanish treaty signed by the pro-Spanish faction at Mobile in 1784. Almost to the point of displaying submissiveness (not intended, of course), Piomingo and the others allowed the American commissioners (Benjamin Hawkins, Andrew Pickens, Joseph Martin, Lauchlin McIntosh, and William Blount) to insert language that they did not perceive, or interpret, as harmful at the time. The treaty stated that the United States government "shall have the sole and exclusive right of regulating the trade with the Indians, and managing all their affairs in such manner as they think proper."[22] This wording and other wording similar to it enforced the previously established, unprotested practice of the English, French, and Spanish to condescendingly refer to Indians as the British/French/Spanish kings' "Red Children." The Americans continued the practice except "president," or "Great Father," replaced "king."

Although probably not in agreement with the viewpoint of Wolf's Friend and his followers, Piomingo made it clear to the Americans that he was to be in charge of Chickasaw diplomatic activities in the future, emphasizing that he was the dominant Hopewell delegate and principal war leader in the entire tribe: "You see this . . . [medal] it was worn by our great Man, he is dead and his daughter sent it for you to see it. I take place as head leading Warrior to treat with all Nations." The "great Man" reference is probably to the deceased king Mingo Houma, who had died in 1784. The medal was brought to the Hopewell conference by "Mingotushka," the nephew of the "great man." Because King Taski Etoka is documented to have been the nephew of Mingo Houma, as mentioned above, the former and Mingotushka may have been the same man.[23] Piomingo was indeed the highest ranked leader under the king in the nation, from at least the American party's and United States commissioners' viewpoints.

After learning of American satisfaction with the proceedings at Hopewell through a somewhat antagonistic letter from Benjamin Hawkins and subsequent details from another source, a perturbed Alexander McGillivray erroneously asserted that the Chickasaw "deputy" (Piomingo) was bribed to agree to the Bear Creek post concession and had offered the Americans land that actually belonged to the Creek. Piomingo and the other Chickasaws were given the usual presents and goods, but these cannot be considered bribes.[24] As already discussed, McGillivray was wrong with regard to Creek ownership of the proposed post land, and there is no known supporting documentation that Piomingo was bribed to make the concession. The statement was undoubtedly McGillivray propaganda concocted to impress the Spaniards and to discredit Piomingo.

The two parties to the treaty also agreed to various other things. One was a definition of the Chickasaw land boundary, which included a highly vague eastern Chickasaw-Choctaw boundary described as extending from the Mississippi River "as far as the Chickasaws claimed, and lived and hunted on" as of November 29, 1782. As already mentioned, the United States additionally obtained assurances that they would be given the "exclusive right of regulating trade" in the Chickasaw nation. This, of course, was unrealistic in light of the large Spanish faction in the nation and the previous similar treaty agreements made by other Chickasaws with the Spanish. In the spring of 1786, in fact, a man identified as the "great chief of the Chickasaws" arrived in Mobile for the purpose of obtaining trade goods at a cheaper rate than before; for effect, he emphasized that an American from Natchez had offered to provide the Chickasaw with all the goods they wanted if they agreed to land sales.[25] This statement by the "great chief," undoubtedly King Taski Etoka, was probably a bluff made in hopes of manipulating the Spanish with regard to goods. If such a statement by an American who was representing the American government was actually made, it would be the earliest known attempt by the United States to coerce the Chickasaw to cede land. It was probably indeed a bluff, however, for Taski Etoka later had the reputation of being a shrewd manipulator of the non-Indians.

In the meantime, Alexander McGillivray was becoming more and more agitated by the actions of Piomingo's relatively small American faction because he viewed any foothold among the Chickasaw as a threat to the security of the Creek tribe and the Four Nations Confederacy. As touched on above, he criticized Piomingo and another unnamed chief for allegedly letting the Americans delude them into giving up the five acres at the Muscle Shoals or, as called by the Indians, Chake Thlocko, again erroneously representing that the shoals was the location of the mouth of Bear Creek. An angry McGillivray wrote the Spanish governor of Pensacola, Arturo O'Neill, that "Such Conduct of the Chickasaw Chiefs has enraged Most of the rest of the Confederate Nations to attack & chastize that people." The governor thereupon wrote that the other nations "are resolved to exterminate these friends of the Americans among the Chickasaws."[26]

By early 1787, Piomingo was disturbed because little or nothing had transpired with regard to the American promise at Hopewell to look after the welfare of the Chickasaw. In a letter to Joseph Martin, Piomingo stated, "We have had nothing of goods since, only what we got by way of the Spaniards. This makes us very uneasy, and it seems that you only meant to jockey us out of our lands. The Spaniards are often sending talks to us, but we want to have nothing to say to them if we can help it, but must have trade from some place. . . . Necessity will oblige us to look to new friends if we cannot get friends otherwise."[27]

McGillivray soon demonstrated that he was not bluffing regarding military action. When a Georgian named William Davenport led a group of Americans into the Chickasaw settlements in 1786 for the purpose of cultivating that tribe to the American interest and to help organize the huge "westward to the Mississippi River" initiative and the doomed-to-failure Bourbon County that had been created by an act of the Georgia legislature, the Spanish and McGillivray became animated because it violated the 1784 Chickasaw/Four Nations treaty with the Spanish. Responding to suggestions from the Spanish, McGillivray demanded that the Chickasaw expel the Americans. When they did not do so right away, he sent a Creek "hit squad," so to speak, into the Chickasaw nation where it attacked Davenport and other Americans at trader William Kemp's house. Davenport and Kemp were killed, along with at least two other Americans, possibly including a man from Cumberland whose last name was Allen. At least six other Americans were wounded and about seventy new rifles were captured by the Creeks. When attacked, the men were at work constructing buildings, one apparently a fort, some ten miles from the Chickasaw settlement.[28] This may have occurred in present-day eastern Pontotoc County in the Pontitack settlement area where mixed-blood Kemps are documented to have lived in the nineteenth century.

The animosity between part of the Creek (and often part of the Cherokee also) and the American faction of the Chickasaw became even more acrimonious in the summer of 1789 when Piomingo's brother (Panss Fallayah, or Long Hair) and nephew were killed by a Creek war party after they and their white companions were attacked in camp west of the Clinch River (present-day Tennessee) as they traveled eastward from Cumberland to attend a conference with the Cherokee on the French Broad River. Because of a severe shortage of ammunition, the Chickasaw were unable to respond. Spanish government officials would not provide them guns and ammunition because they disapproved of warring between the Chickasaw and Creek, as well as between any of the tribes of the Four Nations, because such activities weakened Spanish control and influence and complicated trade relations. Desperate for war materials, Piomingo, other Chickasaw chiefs, and two white men set out for New York City to ask President Washington for military supplies. Upon reaching Richmond, Virginia, in mid-October, however, the group abandoned their plan to go to New York because of the weather and the urgency of the situation. Piomingo thereupon appealed to the Virginia government for powder and lead to use against the Creek, reminding the governor and others of that state's obligations under the terms of the Virginia-Chickasaw Treaty of 1783 (Treaty of French Lick). The results of the interaction of Piomingo and his companions with the Virginia legislature were reported to President Washington:

> The Chiefs of the Chickasaw Nation ([represented by] Paye Mingo) have solicited from the General Assembly a Subsidy of Munitions; the lateness of the season in this year and their desire to return to their Country because of the danger threatening their Nation, which is daily expected to commence hostilities with the Talapuches or Creeks, has led them to decide to stop here without going to New York their first destination. The resolution which we have the honor to enclose to Your Excellency will be executed in their favor, and we are confident that our conduct, because of the peculiar circumstances of the case, will meet with Your Excellency's approbation and with that of the Congress of the United States, and that being approved, we will be repayed what we have spent on this matter.

A subsequent request from Piomingo for "about 40 Gallons of rum to serve them on their route down the Ohio" was likely honored also. On the way back to present-day northeast Mississippi, the group hesitated in Kentucky long enough to also obtain ammunition from that state. By 1791, the United States had sent no soldiers to aid the Chickasaw, and the war was continuing. Frustrated and infuriated, Piomingo, William Colbert, William Glover, George Colbert, Thomas Brown, and several full-bloods again appealed to the United States government (through sympathetic James Robertson) for military aid against the Creek, pointing out that United States protection had been promised them by the Treaty of Hopewell.[29] The government, however, continued to remain neutral.

As in all societies, segments of the Creek and Cherokee populations were more belligerent and prone to violence than the society as a whole. Encouraged directly and indirectly by McGillivray's acrimonious attitude toward Piomingo, his Chickasaw faction, and the Americans, many of the independent-minded, adventuresome, energetic young warriors of the anti-American faction among the Creek and Cherokee took advantage of the political climate to further their own economic interests and warrior statuses, a social ill closely paralleled by the behaviors of modern-day inner-city youth gangs. Thus warrior raids on the Chickasaw and the Cumberland Americans (both white and black) were directly ordered by McGillivray while others occurred independently but were encouraged by him through anti-Chickasaw and anti-American rhetoric. The primary result of this malicious and vicious mischief was terrorized men, women, and children among the American settlers on both sides of the Cumberland River. The settlers were looked upon by many of the Creek and Cherokee leaders as American intruders of the most dangerous kind, for these tribes had already lost much land to the "white blight," so to speak. During this period of mixed terrorism and organized warfare, many horses and other property were stolen, primarily at the hands of Creeks but also by Cherokees; sometimes Chickasaw, Creek, Cherokee, and American lives were lost, often in horrible, obscene ways.[30]

The Chickasaw nearly always retaliated for a Creek or Cherokee affront, and in 1787 the terrorized American settlers on the Cumberland decided that they must do likewise (an average of about thirty men, women, and children were being murdered every year). Under the leadership of a frustrated and angry General James Robertson, therefore, his militia and volunteer force from the Cumberland settlement, guided by two Chickasaw warriors, marched south to the Chickasaw Trace at Duck River, crossed it, and proceeded to Blue Water Creek, a tributary of the Tennessee. They thereafter came to the Tennessee near the lower end of the Muscle Shoals, moved upriver, and attacked a small Creek village/French trading post identified earlier by the guides as the source of raiding parties that had taken the lives of many settlers. The Cave Spring, or Coldwater Creek, village in the present Tuscumbia, Alabama, area was destroyed after most of its French and Indian occupants were killed during the surprise attack. Unfortunately for the Cumberland settlers, the Coldwater raid did not result in peace negotiations with the Creek and Cherokee. Instead, surprise raids on the settlers increased. Discouraged but determined, James Robertson tried another approach to lessen the hostilities. He appealed to the Spanish governor, Estevan Miro: "The United States afford us no protection. The district of . . . [Cumberland] is daily plundered and its inhabitants murdered by the Creeks, and Cherokees, unprovoked. Your removing the latter . . . would bind us, ever to remain a gratefull people."[31]

The Americans, meanwhile, continued to make attempts to obviate the influence of the Spaniards among the Chickasaw, primarily by supplying them with goods and ammunition. The Chickasaw, of course, welcomed such overtures, for their strategy for survival at this particular time was to get all they could from both the Americans and the Spanish. In this respect, Piomingo's American party seems to have been viewed with tolerance by the Spanish-party inhabitants, the majority, who were primarily in the large prairie villages. The duplicity of the Chickasaw in this regard is best illustrated by the words of a Spanish-affiliated trader named Alexander Fraser, who wrote in a manner similar to that of twentieth-century novelist William Faulkner, but minus the latter's correct grammar and clarity:

Tuskapotapa received his Presents but told me when he went to his land that he Should Send the Americans a Talk not to send any more talks to them & that he has taken fast hold of the Spaniards by the hand & that he has been avisiting a Peopel who he looks upon to be the Same as he used to visite at Mobile formerley when the English was there and that he See agreat many English and that they Seemed to be one peopel & I believe Piomingo of the Chickeasaws Received the same Presents as Tuskpotapa, but as for Franchemastabie [Choctaw chief] I suppose he had the same presents as the others but Toboca [Choctaw chief] having Landed at the Mouth of Wolf River Could not bring them to him and when Piomingo Sent for his brought them in & has made away with them all but 1 coat 1 pr. Shoes 1 pr. Stockings & his plums of feathers . . . [which] Taboca him Self Brought him, And as to Indians receiving Presents they will . . . let it Come from any Power when sent them. . . . I understand from the Chickesaws that Piomingo of Chuckafalla is agoing to send or has Sent off for 15 Horse Load Ammunition that is [at Cumberland] for that Nation.[32]

Calloway (*The American Revolution in Indian Country*) emphasizes that the seemingly harmless Chickasaw duplicity was the source of inadvertent complications within the society:

The surface appearance of a unified and somewhat duplicitous Chickasaw foreign policy obscures more complex realities of division and disunity that both limited and expanded diplomatic choices. As British, American, and Spanish officials tried to cut through multiple and shifting Chickasaw foreign policies, they saw only the tips of intratribal politics as one party or another extended feelers and solicited their trade. The Americans represented one source of trade and protection, but only one, and the advantages offered by American allegiance were always tempered by American land hunger.[33]

Although there must have been a degree of disunion among the Chickasaw occasioned by the pro-American and pro-Spanish factions, there is no evidence that internal violence or estrangement occurred between the members of the factions, although there is documentation of at least one serious "quarrel" between King Taski Etoka on one side and Piomingo and Wolf's Friend on the other. The society, in fact, seems to have been operating as democratically as any in the world at that time. Alexander McGillivray's anger toward Piomingo because of his bucking the ideological pro-Spanish Indian confederation was not directed militarily at the American faction only. The Creek war with the Chickasaw involved both factions indiscriminately, a circumstance that angered the pro-Spanish Chickasaw chiefs such as Taski Etoka and Wolf's Friend and caused them to militarily stand alongside Piomingo's followers with equal vigor against the Creek. With regard to war and cultural survival, at least, the Chickasaw were indeed unified, a position adhered to by all but a few since first European contact.[34]

There is probably one dominant reason Piomingo and his followers stood in opposition to most of the tribe, the Spanish, and the other major southeastern tribes. The American faction undoubtedly disliked the Spaniards because they had earlier instigated Kickapoo and other northern Indian hostilities against the Chickasaw, but perhaps their position was not entirely emotional. I have the impression that Piomingo, at least, was an astute analyzer of recent history and had observed that the non-English-speaking foreign nations had never actually controlled more than relatively small areas of the southern land claimed east of the Mississippi River. He had observed the French lose all their land and saw that the British and Spanish thereafter possessed the former southern French lands east of the river. It was probably inevitable to Piomingo, therefore, that Spain was next in line to lose all its land in southern North America. Why, then, should he make an enemy of the nation that he believed would eventually be the only non-Indian governmental entity in the southeastern part of the continent? To make friends with Spain at the expense of the Americans would have been an act of foolishness in his eyes, for such would have meant that the same disruptions of trade, political alliances, and other relationships that occurred regarding the Chickasaw after the Revolutionary War would occur again when Spain's colony was no more. Piomingo probably realized that his nation would thereafter have to deal with American land-grabbing designs anyway, so his American friendship in the 1780s and 1790s was not incompetence reflecting lack of concern for his people but rather a position taken by a realist. Piomingo, in fact, was always at the forefront in opposing land acquisition at conferences with American officials, invariably carrying his Hopewell treaty land map and after July 1794, as discussed in the following chapter, a confirming proclamation of the Chickasaw land boundaries given him by President Washington. Except for the very small Bear Creek land reserve concession to the United States in 1786 (which was never fulfilled) and a later small cession of land at Chickasaw Bluffs to the Spaniards by Wolf's Friend without Piomingo's consent, not a single acre of land was promised to, or obtained by, non-Indians while Piomingo lived.

9
A Short but Dangerous Road

By 1790 non-Indian descriptions and depictions of the Chickasaw settlements were basically similar to those of earlier times, but significant alterations had occurred. An update, therefore, is appropriate at this point. For this discussion late eighteenth-century maps are valuable, but a single written account by Major John Doughty of the United States army is invaluable. As discussed by Colton Storm, the editor of the published account, Doughty had been sent on a mission to the Indian tribes south of the Ohio to deliver a message from President Washington for the purpose of improving relations and establishing more consistent and viable commercial intercourse, possibly by obtaining permission to set up American trading posts on Indian land. After arriving at the mouth of the Tennessee River on February 28, 1790, Doughty's small command eventually made its way to the Chickasaw villages, having survived almost being wiped out by a band of Creek, Cherokee, and Shawnee on the Tennessee River downstream from the mouth of Ocochappo (Bear) Creek.[1]

Although there had been some reconfiguration of the Chickasaw villages as they existed in the first three quarters of the eighteenth century, the general settlement area was still the same in 1790. Since 1763 the Chickasaw population had been steadily growing and in 1790 comprised between 450 and 550 warriors, with an estimated total population of at least 3,000 men, women, and children predominantly residing in the Black Belt prairie portion of present-day Lee County, Mississippi. The exodus of the French and peace with the Choctaws had allowed a relaxation of the former constrictions of the villages. By 1790 some of the smaller old French-period villages had lost their identities and had become extinct within the settlements that formerly constituted the three prairie village clusters, or towns, in the Chickasaw Old Fields. The most important French-period village names to pass into apparent extinction were Ackia, Apeony, and Falatchao. Apeony probably gradually merged with Choukafalya and Falatchao with neighboring Tchitchatala. Ogoula Tchetoka, the apparent primary village of Big Town/Chuckalissa during most of the eighteenth century, apparently retained its identity to at least 1793, in which year the Spanish Chickasaw agent referred to "the Great Village named Ogoula Tchito," a moderately altered rendition of the name of the old village so often harassed by the French and Choctaw in the early part of the eighteenth century. The most famous village attacked by the French, Ackia, appears to have become extinct many years prior to 1790. Perhaps the most intriguing village name to appear in a late eighteenth-century document is that of "Yanacha." If this is a continuation of use of the name for the early eighteenth-century village identified by Adair as Yaneka, which he said was the first settlement of the Chickasaw in the upper Tombigbee drainage, its 1793 appearance in a letter from the Spanish agent is the only known eighteenth-century reference to the name other than that by Adair. Because the name does not appear in documents and on maps prior to 1793, the village called Yanacha probably has no connection with the one discussed by Adair. As discussed in Chapter 1, Adair's pre-1723 Yaneka has been archaeologically identified on Yaneka/Chiwapa Creek.[2]

The major towns by 1790 were still in the same places as they had been in the 1730s, but with altered spellings and pronunciations. Doughty's recorded reference to Chuckalissa/Big Town in the large prairie, for example, was transcribed by Storm as "Chickalpoo, or Big Town, the residence of Tuskatukoh, or the Hair Lipped King" (perhaps the word was actually written "Chickalsoo" considering that early writers sometimes rendered the letters s and p similarly). This is vaguely similar to Joseph Purcell's 1773 recording of "Chicalaia," which appears to be his name for Chuckalissa/Big Town (see Chapter 6). Of course, alien white persons' spellings of a Chickasaw village name did not necessarily reflect accuracy. For example, in 1783 a letter from Piomingo and other village chiefs referred to the Indian name of Big Town in its original form, "Chuck-ul-issah our Great Town," and at the Spanish-Chickasaw treaty conference in Mobile in 1784 it was spelled "Choculiza." The more accurate renditions were undoubtedly spelled by people who were more familiar with the villages, such as traders and interpreters. On the other hand, temporary visitor Bernard Romans correctly rendered it "Chucalissa" in 1771. Longtime resident Malcolm McGee apparently pronounced the name accurately in 1841, for it was spelled "Chukwillissa." (This spelling and others below for villages named by McGee are not his but rather those of Lyman C. Draper, his interviewer.) Strangely, longtime resident James Adair's spellings of the major Chickasaw towns diverge significantly from both the earlier and later spellings: his rendering in about 1768 of Chuckalissa is "Chookheereso."[3] This and other of Adair's and other English-speaking men's spellings with the letter r in them are peculiar because this sound is not present in the Chickasaw or Choctaw language.

In the records of the 1784 Mobile conference, Choukafalya is spelled "Chuckafala," while Doughty refers to it as "Chickarallai, or Long Town." In contrast, Adair's earlier spelling was "Chookka Pharaah." Doughty's writing, combined with period maps, shows that both Big Town and Long Town were still where they had been since at least the early eighteenth century, but the third major town of the early period, Tchitchatala, was found by Doughty to be far removed from its former location in the large prairie; he stated that "Chettalai" was eight miles slightly southwest of Big Town rather than the former one mile south of Big Town. Adair's "Shatara" is probably the same town. In 1784, the village was spelled "Chatala," which is similar to the way Doughty spelled it six years later. Undoubtedly a village referred to by Malcolm McGee as "Tashatulla or Post Oak Grove" is the same village. Like Doughty, McGee also located this village southward of Big Town (but four miles rather than eight) on "Coppertown," or Tashatulla, Creek. This is undoubtedly present-day Coonewah Creek. Either eight miles (Doughty) or four miles (McGee, more likely correct) south of Big Town would place the new location of this old village on present-day southeast-running Coonewah Creek, which is where the town may have been originally located prior to the post-1723 settlement consolidations discussed in Chapter 1 (see Coonewah Creek on Figure 4). The de Crenay map of 1733, although configured somewhat out of step with reality regarding the creeks, does show "Tchichatala" southwest of the Chuckalissa villages on Old Town Creek; it appears to be between Kings and Coonewah Creek, which is where it is shown on the 1737 de Batz map. In the 1790s, Wolf's Friend, with Spanish agent Benjamin Fooy as his writer, composed letters at a place that is probably the same as this village. In 1794, Wolf's Friend, under his real name of Ugulayacabe, sent a letter to Gayoso from "Thisatera" or "Thishatare." Because Malcolm McGee recalled that Wolf's Friend lived at a village he called "Post Oak Grove" or "Tashatulla," the latter is likely an alternate, and more accurate, rendition of "Thisatera."[4]

Of all the other early villages discussed in Chapter 1 (Amalata, Taskaouilo, Etokouma, Achoukouma, Ackia, and Apeony), Doughty reports only one possible conformity. Doughty states that in 1790 "Tuskatville," the only Chickasaw village (he calls the others "towns"), was about six miles southwest of Big Town (six miles is probably too far) and had no chief. This is probably the same as old Taskaouilo or, as spelled in 1784, "Tascahuilo." Thus it was no longer in the large prairie south of present-day Old Town Creek, its new location being indicated by Doughty on either Coonewah Creek upstream from Doughty's "Chettalai" or on Little Coonewah Creek (see Figure 4). Draper rendered McGee's pronunciation of the village as "Tuskaroilloe"; its location, however, was not stated. Two other of the villages of the early 1700s survived into the 1790s. Amalata of the large prairie was spelled "Malata" at the 1784 Mobile treaty conference and Achoukouma of the large prairie was spelled

"Achucuma." McGee spoke of a village he pronounced "Hummalala," which is probably Amalata, and another pronounced "Hussinkoma" is probably the same as Achoukouma. Another village recalled by McGee, "Shiokaya," could be the same as the old small prairie village of Ackia. Unfortunately, McGee failed to discuss these three villages with regard to locations or other physical features.[5]

By 1794, a new settlement occupied primarily by whites and mixed-bloods had joined Pontitack as the only other settlement west of the Chickasaw Old Fields. Holkey, as it was called, originated on the Natchez Trace on a watershed divide known now as the Pontotoc Ridge, which separates the Tombigbee and Mississippi River drainages. The earliest known record of the settlement, located in present-day northern Chickasaw County, dates to March 16, 1794, when new Spanish agent Benjamin Fooy wrote a letter to Gayoso from Holkey. Because most or all of Fooy's subsequent letters were written from Holkey, the place was undoubtedly the location of his residence. One or more of the traders affiliated with the Spanish probably had establishments and residences there prior to Fooy's arrival. The settlement was the adult home of trader and interpreter Malcolm McGee, and in 1801 the first United States Indian agency among the Chickasaw was established near his farm, as discussed in Chapter 11. After removal of the agency to Alabama in 1826, "Hulka," as it had come to be spelled, had a United States post office for about three years. Today the modern town of Houlka is just west of the original site. Houlka, therefore, is the oldest surviving settlement in north Mississippi.[6]

By the end of the 1790s, a few other Chickasaw settlement habitations had come into existence, but unfortunately no data other than their names and general locations have come to light. The Collot map of about 1796 shows a place not entirely legible labeled "Corn ——" on Old Town Creek and northwest of Old/Big Town (labeled "Great Village of the Chickasaws") and a "Salle Bernaby Village" upstream from "Copper Town" (Doughty's Chettalai) on what appears to be present-day Chiwapa Creek but is more likely Coonewah Creek inasmuch as these two creeks are combined as one on the map. I agree with Cook, Palmer, and Riley ("Historic Chickasaw Village Locations") that the Salle Bernaby village may be the same as Doughty's "Tuskatville," discussed above. The origin of the name "Salle Bernaby" has not been ascertained. It would appear to be a person's name, perhaps that of one of the British loyalists who chose to remain in the nation after the Revolutionary War. As discussed in Chapter 1 regarding the mixed-blood settlements of the late eighteenth century, the Collot map shows a "Half Breed Settlement" northwest of the Great Village on the upper reaches of Old Town Creek. This habitation could have had its roots earlier in the second half of the eighteenth century.[7]

By 1790 many other aspects of the Chickasaw nation had undergone pronounced changes. Whereas the early Chickasaw had subsisted largely on dishes emanating from cultivation of corn, squash, beans, and other cultivars and from the products of animals obtained by hunting, fishing, and other forms of capture, European interaction had resulted in a much more diversified sustenance landscape. According to Doughty,

> Of late years [the Chickasaw] have done less [hunting] then ever, for Want of Traders to purchase of them. They possess a great many Horses & some families have Negroes & Cattle. They live in Plenty in their Towns. Their Provisions [include] Hogs, Poultry, Eggs, Beans, Corn & the finest Potatoes I ever saw. The Chickasaws appear to be verging fast towards the State of farmers. Game is getting scarce. [They] kill Bear, Otter, Deer, & some Beaver. The Chickasaws & Choctaws dress their skins to make them more valuable. They dispose of large Quantities of Bear Oil for the Orleans Markett.[8]

Of interest here are some enlightening recollections of Malcolm McGee. As shown in earlier chapters, the Chickasaw had long been in possession of horses, which they kept and bred in the prairies near their towns and villages in present-day Lee County. The first document to mention the presence of cattle in the Chickasaw nation, however, dates to the 1760s with regard to ownership of some by British agent John McIntosh and Paya Mattaha. That period for the introduction of cattle is credibly supported by the recollections of McGee, who lived with McIntosh as a young man:

> [In earlier years] some [Chickasaws] kept swine, & plenty dunghill fowls, [but] no cattle of any kind. John McIntosh, who was appointed Chickasaw Agt. just after the French War, & brought cattle into the nation from Mobile about 1770, & soon after old James Colbert from the same region—& others were subsequently brought from Natchez & Nashville. What few hogs they had in '68, the owners kept up in pens & fed them on weeds during the summer. They were kept up to keep them out of the corn—& so the owners of horses had to watch them to prevent their intruding upon the corn—for it was a law that the squaws had a right to kill all hogs & horses thus intruding; & sometimes horses were either killed or crippled by the squaws hatchets. . . . For the large fields had no fences. The horses wd. be hitched by ropes to feed upon cane along the branches; & when they had eaten all within their reach, then remove them to a new spot.[9]

Of interest also is McGee's recollection regarding the guns used by the Chickasaw: "In '68 they had nothing but old fusees [fusils, smoothbore muskets], made for the African trade, the stocks fantastically decorated with painted designs—then soon after rifles, first introduced by John McIntosh, the agent, who gave an Indian a good English rifle for a live young buffalo some six months old."[10]

With the heyday of the Chickasaw trade for deer hides long in the past as a result of extensive reduction in numbers of that overhunted animal, the economic situation within the settlement is undoubtedly epitomized by the following recording of conversations Doughty had with Chickasaw leaders:

> Both Piomingo & Alaitamoto [Piomingo's brother] received me with the most sincere Professions of friendship on their Parts & on the Part of their Nation. They inform me that their People never before were in such Distress for Want of Powder, Lead, Blanketts, Strouds, &c, that they always looked up to their old father (the English) for these Articles & never were disappointed, that they & the Choctaws were the only Nations of Indians who had sought the friendship of the Children of their old father that they had been promised at Hopewell in 1786 by the American Commissioners & before that by Genl Clark at the falls of Ohio, that Traders should be sent amongst them to supply them with Powder & Lead to hunt, & with Goods to cloth their Women & Children, but as yet they had received nothing but promises, & their Distresses were so great that many of their People were obliged to go to the Spaniards. . . . I am led to believe that the Chickasaws & Choctaws are really in a very distressed situation.[11]

Continuing, Doughty emphasized that in violation of the Hopewell treaty, the United States was not protecting the Chickasaw from exploiters, most of whom were American citizens. He wrote that "not an American is seen amongst them with a view to assist them, nor is one of respectable Character to whom they can listen without being deceived." As one example, he related a story about a man who came into the nation in need of horses and assistance to go to Natchez. Pretending to be the son of George Washington, he delivered a speech to the Chickasaw, after which the trusting Indians assisted him to the Choctaw nation. George Washington, of course, had no documented children. The Chickasaw saw him no more and were never paid for their assistance. As a second example, Doughty related that a group of men from Kentucky had pretended to be emissaries sent by General George Rogers Clark to hold a council with the Chickasaw. The latter sold them on credit a number of valuable horses to be paid for later in salt. The men and the salt were "never heard of since." Concluding his comments on the subject of American exploitation and abuse, Doughty wrote: "Such Disceptions as these have been frequent & when added to the Non-performance of the Promises made by our Commissioners at Hopewell have served to lessen us very much with these people."[12]

The 1790s saw a great deal of political interaction among the Chickasaw, the Spanish, the Americans, and other native Americans. Both Spanish and American agents worked to promote their respective country's influence and to undermine that of the other. By Congressional resolution Colonel Joseph Martin had been appointed American agent to the Cherokee and Chickasaw on June 20, 1788, while the Spanish thereafter appointed Juan de la Villebeuvre to serve as agent to the Choctaw and Chickasaw. Martin never resided among the Indians and did very little to justify his appointment. De la Villebeuvre, however, lived among the Choctaw and provided valuable intelligence about both the Choctaw and Chickasaw.[13]

In May 1790, Choctaw and Chickasaw delegates attended a conference with the Spanish at Natchez. The Spanish goal was to further strengthen friendship with the Spanish factions of the Chickasaw and Choctaw and to obtain clear title to the area in which they had already established Fort Nogales at Walnut Hills (present-day Vicksburg). The Spanish believed that official cession of this area, located near the general, vague boundary between the two tribes, required agreement of both. The primary Chickasaw representative was Tascaotuca, "King of the Chickasaw nation." This man was undoubtedly Taski Etoka. On May 14, he and the Choctaw great chief, Franchimastaba, agreed to a "Treaty of Friendship" with the Spaniards, which included relinquishment of the area in which Fort Nogales and Natchez were located. It is not surprising that Taski Etoka agreed to this cession in light of the fact that all of it was within the territory claimed by the Choctaw.[14]

Meanwhile, the United States continued to strengthen its alliance with the American faction of the Chickasaw. Following Major John Doughty's visit to the Chickasaw settlement in early 1790, Piomingo received a personal letter from President Washington in which he stressed that the United States would not violate the terms of the Treaty of Hopewell and did not "want any of your lands."[15] Perhaps this fib provides the best evidence that the cherry tree story related by Parson Weems was indeed a concoction.

Violent conflicts with Indians in and outside the Chickasaw nation varied between sporadic and frequent, depending on political situations. The Creek and Cherokee were not the only native Americans to interact violently with the Chickasaw during the late eighteenth century. A Chickasaw custom of hunting west of the Mississippi River had begun in the mid-1700s as a result of reduction of game east of the river (caused by the commercial deer-hide trade and the introduction of firearms). This, of course, resulted in territorial conflicts, for other native Americans were also forced to seek better hunting grounds west of the river. Like other groups, therefore, the Chickasaw by 1780 were in the habit of hunting where they pleased, consequently infringing on the hunting lands of resident groups west of the river. Conflicts also occurred between groups hunting west of the river who resided east of the river. In addition to the native trans-Mississippi Quapaw (Arkansas) of present-day Louisiana, Arkansas, and east Texas and the Osage of present-day Missouri, Oklahoma, Arkansas, and Kansas, the Chickasaw squabbled with the Kickapoo, Piankeshaw, Miami, and Illinois, all of whom were striving to survive in the face of disruption caused by over a hundred years of European intrusion.[16]

Despite Piomingo's strong affiliation with the Americans, the Spanish continued to attempt to bring him into the fold. Meanwhile, the Creek-Chickasaw War that had begun in 1787 had not ended. In December 1791 the Spanish were informed that the Chickasaw had recently completed "a large fort" and were expecting to be attacked at any time. This new, additional fort was probably constructed at Long Town. Piomingo was invited by Governor Manuel Gayoso to visit him in Natchez, but he declined, continued his pro-American position, and opposed the intertribal alliance espoused by Alexander McGillivray and Spain. At the same time, Wolf's Friend and Alexander McGillivray worked to undermine Piomingo by the use of spies and agents, and the former individuals kept the Spanish informed of his actions. These irritating activities actually made Piomingo even more opposed to the Spanish.[17]

The primary supplier of goods to traders doing business in the Four Nations was the firm of Panton, Leslie, & Company, which operated out of St. Augustine, Pensacola, and Mobile under the approval and protection of the Spanish government. Aware of the hindrance Piomingo and his American faction was posing to Spanish trade domination, William Panton decided in 1790 to tour the Creek, Choctaw, and Chickasaw nations for the purpose of encouraging allegiance to the Spanish and rejection of the Americans. In his report of travels to Governor Miro, Panton complained that the traders to the Choctaw and Chickasaw were charging more for goods than those who traded with the Creek. He also lamented the unfortunate effects of the traders' dealing whiskey to the Indian nations: "Another reform that is much wanted in all the nations is to prevent such amasing quantitys of Spirits being carried amongst them as is the daily practize—The evil consequence of that pernicious liquor to Indians is dreadful—No less than twelve youths lost their lives while I was among the Choctaws killed by one another in a rum drinking—not a month passes that the same thing does not happen and Such a waste of humane creatures is shocking when a person reflects that they are our Brothers altho' of a different hue."[18]

Panton's description of his visit with the Chickasaw is informative in that it illuminates the prevailing political and economic situation of the tribe at the time:

> [O]n my arrival in the Chickesaws I went to see Piomingo (the Mountain Leader) who has hithereto been a great favourer of the Americans—He had been into Virginia last winter, had obtained a present of ammunition from General Washington and an additional quantity was sent after him by Major Doughty. . . . The Chickesaws having refused to permit the Americans to take Post at Bear Creek it was proposed to make an establishment at the Fork [mouth] of Cherokee [Tennessee] river where the old French Fort stood—to this the Mountain Leader assented but he had not the voice of the Nation on his side—Great Promises of cheap Trade was made them by a merchant of Richmond in Virginia named David Ross who has stores in Kentucky and on the Rivers Holstein and at French Broad. . . . [Piomingo] is a sensible, talkative little Indian—I had much conversation with him, and I did what I could to open his Eyes to his real interest. . . . His influence however does not extend beyond his own Town Called Long Town which contains about 150 warriors—Taskabucka or Hair Lipped King the Principal of the Chickasaws with the rest of the Chiefs and the Nation in general are well enough satisfyed to live under your protection, and to take their Supply [of goods] from Mobille.[19]

The final part of Panton's report to Governor Miro is important with regard to further clarification of the details of the long-standing historical mistake in the published literature already discussed in Chapter 6. By 1800 a man named John McIntosh lived on the old Natchez Trace in present-day southwest Pontotoc County at a locale that had come to be called McIntoshville or Tockshish. As a result of incomplete research, nonscholars and scholars alike have erroneously assumed that this location had been the site of John McIntosh's British commissary, which it was not. As discussed in Chapter 7, John McIntosh, Jr., was appointed British commissary after the death of his father in 1780, at which time John Jr. was undoubtedly still living in or near the commissary house of his father, not yet having moved down the Natchez Trace to the area that would become known as Tockshish (see Figure 12). Panton's 1790 reference to John McIntosh, Jr., is quoted below, both for clarification purposes regarding the McIntoshes as well as to illustrate the degree of interest William Panton and the Spanish had in nurturing the latter's alliance with the Chickasaw:

> I advise you also to appoint an Agent or deputy Superintendent for the Chickasaws & Choctaws—such a person is much wanted (particularly for

the Chickesaws) whose appointment should at once be made respectable by a liberal Sallary and who ought occasionally to command a few Presents for the chiefs. . . . There is a Gentleman of the Name of John McIntosh who lives in the Chickesaws and has a considerable stock of Horses and Cattle there, who in my opinion has it in his power to serve the Government in that capacity—he is a Son to the late John McIntosh Esquire who was agent for the English—I had some conversation with him on the subject and I asked him if such an offer was made him whiter he would accept of a commission from you—He told me that he would have no objection provided a provision or Sallary was annexed to the appointment equal to the trouble he would have.[20]

John McIntosh, Jr.'s settlement had become a white and mixed-blood enclave within the nation by 1803, in which year it was visited by a Reverend Patrick Wilson, who wrote: "On the trace through the Chickasaw nation, in the neighborhood of McIntosh's (named after a British Agent resident there before the American Revolution) observed a horse grist mill, large fields and provisions in great plenty. There we bought from the Indians the best cured and sweetest bacon we found on the whole road. There are a great many white people in this neighborhood, among whom the Agent acts as a Magistrate according to the laws of the United States. The half breeds called Colberts have great property in cultivated lands and negroes in this nation."[21]

In 1791 an opportunity arose for Piomingo to demonstrate his loyalty to the United States and, in turn, further obligate the Americans to provide more military assistance to his nation. Since 1790 several tribes of northern Indians had been confederated for the purpose of forcibly keeping the Americans out of their territories. The War Department solicited the aid of the Chickasaw in the United States war with the confederation through General Robertson; thereafter Piomingo, with forty or fifty Chickasaws, according to nineteenth-century historian A. W. Putnam, assembled at Robertson's home southwest of Nashville on Richland Creek, "where they were equipped and instructed." The Chickasaws traveled north to join General Arthur St. Clair's American army north of the Ohio at Fort Washington (present-day Cincinnati). Some of the Chickasaws among them, probably including Piomingo and William Colbert, were planning to eventually go on to Philadelphia to ask Congress for assistance in the war with the Creek; the trip was apparently canceled as a result of subsequent events. The decision of these Chickasaws to join in the war was made easier by the fact that most of the foe consisted of the Wabash tribes, old enemies who had been sicced on them by the French earlier in the century.[22]

All or part of the Chickasaws arrived shortly before October 29, on which day St. Clair sent on an extended reconnaissance patrol a detachment of Chickasaws led by Piomingo and William Colbert. This detachment may have been composed of all the Chickasaws present. The men were outfitted with hand-kerchiefs with an attached single red plume, which were to be worn around their heads so they could be distinguished from the hostile Indians. The Chicka-saw detachment was instructed to capture a prisoner for interrogation pur-poses, even if it took ten days. The Chickasaw volunteers were not present at the fierce battle that occurred on November 4 in the present state of Ohio when St. Clair's American army was attacked and horribly decimated by the northern Indians under the leadership of Little Turtle and Blue Jacket. The Chickasaws, primarily led by Piomingo, William Colbert, and George Colbert, arrived after-ward and perhaps witnessed the most ghastly aftermath of a battle that any of them had ever seen. According to Malcolm McGee, St. Clair intentionally kept the Chickasaws away from the fighting in fear that they would be confused with the northern Indians during the heat of battle and fired on by the Ameri-can soldiers.[23] Perhaps the disastrous St. Clair defeat would not have occurred if the Chickasaws had been attached to the main army at the time. On the other hand, if the Chickasaws had been present, Piomingo and both William and George Colbert might have been killed.

As a result of a United States congressional act in 1790 passed for the purpose of establishing better control of American-Indian interactions, James Robert-son was appointed first United States Chickasaw agent by territorial gover-nor William Blount on May 16, 1792, with instructions to also serve the Choc-taw. Robertson had led some of the first white settlers into the Cumberland River country in 1779 and established French Lick, later called Nashborough and finally renamed Nashville. His log home, located on Richland Creek and southwest of the original Nashville settlement, became the first United States Chickasaw Agency house, as well as the first Choctaw Agency house.[24]

In 1792 an event occurred that eventually came to be described errone-ously in some of the historical literature. Prior to August of that year, Gover-nor Blount had been told that prominent Cherokee chief Double Head, other Cherokees, Creeks, and northern Indians numbering about forty people in to-tal had made a settlement on Chickasaw hunting land near the south side of the Tennessee River close to its mouth at the Ohio River in northwest Ken-tucky. At a conference in Nashville, Governor Blount accused them of launch-ing attacks in which Americans had been killed and requested of the Chicka-saws that they either drive them away or give the United States permission to do so. Further documentation of this alleged settlement does not seem to exist, but elaborations and alterations by historians have occurred nonetheless. The first to convolute Blount's assertion, Albert Goodpasture, wrote in 1918 that the forty Cherokees, Creeks, and northern Indians had made the settle-ment at Muscle Shoals on the Tennessee River in present-day northern Alabama rather than near the mouth of the Tennessee River as Blount stated. He based this assertion on a statement made years later in 1805 by James Robertson: "George Colbert asserts that doublehead settled at the Shoals by his permition [*sic*]." With Goodpasture's identification firmly embedded in the literature, Nina Leftwich wrote in 1935 that Doublehead's village was in present-day Colbert County, Alabama, on the "Tennessee just east of where George Colbert later established his ferry." This location contradicts Goodpasture's, for as discussed in Chapter 8, Muscle Shoals is located over forty miles to the east of Colbert's ferry site. Leftwich seems to have been influenced by the presence of a spring or springs in that general location called by 1935 "Doublehead's Spring" (originally "Double Head Springs"?). In reality, the settlement near the mouth of the Tennessee in Kentucky, if it ever actually existed, was probably vacated as a result of the Chickasaw appeasing Governor Blount and other Americans. In any case, Double Head established, in 1792 or soon thereafter, a new settlement (the one mentioned by Robertson) at the Muscle Shoals with George Colbert's permission. According to Fairbanks's findings in his study of Royce Area 79 (an east-west strip of land disputed by the Chickasaw, Cherokee, and Creek along the south side of the Tennessee in present-day north Alabama), Double Head's village was on the south side of the Tennessee opposite the mouth of Elk River, in present-day Lawrence County, Alabama.[25]

Like the Spanish, the Americans were perturbed that they had to contend with opposing factions among the Chickasaw. Each nation ideally would have preferred approval of both factions with regard to desired Chickasaw concessions and actions, for without mutual approval the implementation of anything would be threatened by the other faction. Thus the two powers attempted to gain the cooperation of both factions. American officials of the Southwest Territory invited Wolf's Friend to come to Nashville for a conference in 1792. After initially refusing the invitation, Wolf's Friend traveled to Cumberland, where Governor Blount treated him with much diplomacy, followed by a request for permission to establish a trading post on Chickasaw land. When Wolf's Friend replied that Spain furnished all the trade goods the Chickasaw needed, Blount starred at him with "evil eyes," according to the chief. Wolf's Friend thereafter stated that if there was a war between Spain and the United States the Chickasaw would not take sides but that they would never let the Americans encroach further on their land. This middle-of-the-road position between friendship with the Spanish and the Americans is further illustrated by a report written by James Robertson in 1793. Robertson, citing hearsay, said that Wolf's Friend told the Spanish governor that his friendship with the United States was "not to be broken" and that there "was not one man in [the Chickasaw] nation that would fight the Americans." Robertson further asserted that Wolf's Friend reported that at the subsequent Nashville conference in August 1792 "he had given Governor Blount his heart, and nothing should induce him to break the friendship he then made, and that, if the Americans and Spaniards fell out, he would not interfere on either side."[26] These revelations suggest that Wolf's Friend was not anti-American but rather a realist who wanted nothing more than to preserve his nation. He and Piomingo, therefore, basically had the same goals.

There was, however, noticeable competition between the two for recognition as the most prominent leader in the nation, as illustrated by Wolf's Friend's opinion that he was Piomingo's superior. In a letter sent after the Nashville conference to the Spanish commissioner to the Choctaw, Pierre Juzan, Wolf's Friend asserted that if the Spanish governor wished he would "send him Piomingo, who has never Given his Hand to the Spaniards, that I have only to Open my Mouth, and he will obey, because he is one of my warriors." Moreover, Wolf's Friend boasted in the same letter that he had the power to remove the current king of the Chickasaws: "[Y]ou will also tell the [Spanish] chief that I have [removed] Casse Tasqueatoqua [Taski Etoka], King of the Chies [Spanish abbreviation for Chickasaws], because he is not a man of his word, who should not be heeded, and in his place has been named the brother of the king [Chinubbee], even though he may be more of a villian than King Casse, but he is a man of his word, and is peaceful."[27] These boastful statements, possibly influenced by alcohol consumption, reek with jealousy and are similar to the ones made by Mingo Houma in 1772 with regard to Paya Mattaha, his competitor for influence with the British (see Chapter 6). In both cases, however, because the boasters were members of the Chickasaw hierarchy, they indeed seem to have held higher rank than did their achieved-status rivals.

In response to a May 1792 Spanish-sponsored conference of representatives from southern tribes held at Fort Nogales (in present-day Vicksburg National Military Park) to strengthen the 1784 alliance of Choctaw, Chickasaw, Creek, and Cherokee under Spanish protection, the Americans held the above-mentioned Nashville conference in August 1792 at James Robertson's house/agency on Richland Creek southwest of Nashville as it existed at that time. The conference was attended by several hundred Chickasaws (possibly about 500) and a lesser number of Choctaws. The former included adherents of both the American and the Spanish factions, including the leaders, Piomingo and Wolf's Friend, and other prominent chiefs. Prior to attending, however, Wolf's Friend represented to the Spanish that he was going strictly for the purpose of observing and gathering information to pass on to the governor of Louisiana, which he did. Other important Chickasaws, William and George Colbert, also attended the conference. Malcolm McGee served as Chickasaw interpreter and John Pitchlynn as Choctaw interpreter.[28]

Taski Etoka, the "Hare Lipped King," chose to not attend the Nashville conference, although asked to do so by both Piomingo and Wolf's Friend. Instead, he left on a peace mission to the Tallapoosa division of the Creek, without responding to the chiefs' request. In Taski Etoka's place, therefore, his brother, Chinubbee (or "Chenumbee," "Chinibe," and various other spellings), was chosen to represent the Chickasaw as king. He was, in fact, referred to as the "King of the Chickasaws" in the official records of the conference, and the Chickasaws requested that future government correspondence be addressed to "Chenumbe, the king." As mentioned above, Wolf's Friend later claimed to have effected the replacement of Taski Etoka with a man identified by the former as the king's brother, obviously Chinubbee. This claim, however, seems to have been only braggadocio, for Gayoso stated the following in 1794 after the death of Taski Etoka: "The Brother of the King of the Chickasaw Nation will succeed him by right of blood; Fooy informs me that this man is about fifty years of age, and of very good intentions, entirely addicted to Ougoulayacabe, who is the one that follows him in the Nation in rank and preference, although on the other hand, the greatest warrior is Piomingo, but none equals Ougoulayacabe in consideration because he has more ability than the others. The name of the new King is Tinabe-Mingo [Chinubbee]." That Taski Etoka did not permanently (if at all) lose his "kingship" in 1792 due to Wolf's Friend is thus proven by this and several other Spanish documents that refer to him as king in the years 1793 and 1794.[29]

Prior to the August 1792 Nashville conference, the secretary of war had come to the conclusion that it would be prudent to recognize the contributions of Piomingo, the Colberts, and the other Chickasaws who had assisted in the 1791 campaign against the northern Indians, undoubtedly partially in light of the fact that the war was not over and solicitation of future assistance from the Chickasaw was anticipated. Accordingly, the secretary of war, Henry Knox, arranged for the indirect presentation from President Washington of large oval silver peace medals and "rich" uniforms to Piomingo, William Colbert, and George Colbert. Knox described the presentations as follows: "The President of the United States is very desirous to reward the attachment of Piomingo and the warriors who were with him at Fort Washington [at Cincinnati], and he now sends to Piomingo, and two other principal chiefs.,—great silver medals, and each a suit of rich uniform clothes; and further, he has ordered presents to be sent from Fort Washington to the Chickasaw Nation generally, of such articles as shall be useful to them." The "two other principal chiefs" are identified in a Spanish letter pertaining to the conference as "the two sons of Colbert," undoubtedly William and George.[30]

The medals, uniforms, and other articles for the Chickasaw (and others for the Cherokee and Choctaw) were sent south by way of the new Cherokee agent, Leonard Shaw, who subsequently turned the Chickasaw and Choctaw items

13. Obverse of the Washington Peace Medal probably owned by Piomingo (courtesy of Joyce Roberson Bushman)

over to territorial governor William Blount after the former's arrival in the Cherokee nation. Blount then appointed three commissioners, James Randolph Robertson, Anthony Foster, and Captain David Smith, to deliver the medals and other items to the Chickasaw and Choctaw. The three men arrived at Taski Etoka's village (Big/Old Town) on June 11, 1792. They soon continued about three miles to Piomingo's village (Long Town), where they met with the "king" and other Chickasaws. Here the commissioners presented to them Governor Blount's invitation to attend the planned Nashville conference. They presumably presented the peace medals and other gifts to Piomingo and the Colberts during their stay at Long Town, after which two of them continued to the Choctaw nation for the same purpose.[31]

The peace medals, made and engraved by hand by New England silversmiths under contract with the United States government, depicted images of George Washington and an Indian smoking a peace pipe on one side and the presidential seal of the United States on the other. In 1956, a grave containing one of these medals dated 1793 (Figure 13) was discovered by Luther L. Roberson during street construction in south Tupelo which, as discussed above, was the location of Piomingo's village, Choukafalya, or Long Town. The grave site is located on the highest point of the ridge system in the Long Town area. In addition to the skeletal remains, the grave contained at least eighty gold, silver, brass, iron, glass, and other artifacts. The grave was almost definitely Piomingo's.[32]

At the Nashville conference, Piomingo stressed that the Chickasaw boundary as established at Hopewell was still the boundary and asked for a new map showing it, which was provided two days later along with a new copy of the Treaty of Hopewell. Piomingo was very concerned that the Cherokee would unjustifiably claim and sell to the United States some of the Chickasaw land claimed in present-day Tennessee or Alabama. He stated that he was the one who had laid off the boundary on the original Hopewell map in his possession and that he had made it plain, for he knew "the fondness of the Cherokees to sell land." Wolf's Friend also emphasized the land question, stating that the Americans had "hard shoes" and would step on Chickasaw toes if they were allowed to establish a post in their nation. As mentioned above, he stated that as a warrior Piomingo ranked below him, but curiously he qualified the statement by saying that Piomingo "is my father" and that "Piomingo and myself are one," which probably meant that they respected one another and were united in opposing land cessions and in striving to maintain independence for the Chickasaw. Wolf's Friend displayed ambivalence with regard to his Spanish allegiance by presenting Governor Blount a string of white beads and stating: "I give this to you, hold it fast; I will as a token of peace and friendship. I hope peace and friendship will be perpetual; that our children may be raised up in all possible happiness."[33] As always, the Americans presented gifts to the Indians. To the Chickasaw and Choctaw in general and specifically to the pro-American Chickasaw leaders, Governor Blount stated, "The object of the present meeting is not to alter these treaties, but to strengthen and keep alive that friendship of which those treaties are the basis, and to beg you acceptance of a quantity of valuable goods, as a proof of the sincere friendship of the United States. . . . Another object is, publicly to present Piamingo, the Colberts, and their followers, who joined the arms of the United States last year, and fought against their enemies, hearty and sincere thanks for their services, and to present them each with a rifle."[34]

Perhaps as a response to the Nashville conference, Governor Carondelet called a conference in November at New Orleans with some leading chiefs of the Cherokee, Creek, Choctaw, and Chickasaw for the purpose of emphasizing that the Spanish, unlike the Americans, had the best interest of the Indians at heart. The chiefs, including the Chickasaw king, Taski Etoka, agreed with the Spanish wishes that in the spring they "would establish the permanent congress composed of three chiefs from each nation" and that the "12 envoys would be maintained by the [Spanish] King, which might cost some 2500 pesos annually, the group to be advised by the King's Commissary, who would therefore become the arbiter of those nations."[35] This proposed permanent congress does not seem to have materialized.

Despite Taski Etoka's friendship with the Spanish, Piomingo continued to reject peace with the Creek, a circumstance received with consternation by McGillivray. The sporadic hostilities became a full-scale war after a severe Creek insult occurred on February 8, 1793, when a band of Creeks attacked four Chickasaw warriors hunting near their villages, killing one of the hunters. Following scalping, they "hacked and mangled his body, and threw it into a pool of water." The infuriated Chickasaw immediately called a national council at Choukafalya to discuss escalation of the war. Coincidentally, three Cherokee chiefs (Bloody Fellow, John Taylor, and the Bold Hunter) were in the Chickasaw nation at this time, having stopped there, while on their way home from a conference with the Spanish in New Orleans, for the purpose of trying to talk the Chickasaw as a whole into joining the intertribal confederacy under the protection of the Spanish and to make peace with the Creek. The Cherokee chiefs were dismayed by the murder of the Chickasaw warrior, as evidenced by a letter from Bloody Fellow to Carondelet written from Choukafalya, in which he chastised the Creek warriors for having "killed the Warrior of Piomingo," an action, he said, that served to "spoil our way and consequently our talk." On the same day, Piomingo wrote a letter to Carondelet in reply to one he had received: "We received the Letter you sent us by Mr. [Simon] Favre and the Cherokees which have given much pleasure and we all give you the hand, but we learn with sorrow that we have just had a man killed by the Creeks who have for a long time menaced us. They receive ammunition from you and kill all the white traders in the nation and pillage anything they can lay their hands on. As there is not time to receive a message we are going to take revenge and only inform you that we have listened to your letter with pleasure."[36]

Infuriated, Piomingo declared that "he was so determined on war, that his very breath was bloody" and that the Cherokee could go home and join with the Creek if they so chose and make war on the Americans with whom they had in the past "pretended peace and friendship." The council then sent a war leader named Tatholah, "the confidant of the Mountain Leader," with forty warriors in search of the Creek band that had so horribly violated their land and fellow Chickasaw. In that same month, a Creek war party found one of Piomingo's warriors in his cabin and killed him. When Piomingo heard of the killing, he and other Chickasaws reportedly left for Natchez and New Orleans to speak to the Spanish officials, apparently to ask them to do something about the Creek aggressions. After another Creek war party went to trader Hardy Perry's house to ask for food, Chickasaw warriors located them and killed at least three, two of whom happened to be the son and nephew of the Creek's principal war chief, Fahakio, commonly called "Mad Dog." In this war, the Chickasaw were unified. Even Taski Etoka took an active part, either traveling to, or sending a messenger to, the Choctaw nation with "a bloody Knife" to urge them to join the Chickasaw in the war against the Creek. An aggravated Taski Etoka and the major chiefs of Long Town and Big Town wrote de la Villebeuvre that they hoped the Spanish would not interfere with their talks with the Choctaw, and they expressed a desire that the Spanish stop supplying the Creek with provisions and in the future give "provisions to only Good people." Because there had been much intermarriage between the Chickasaw and Choctaw by this time, the Spanish feared the Choctaw would feel obligated to join in the war, but their opposition persuaded the latter to remain neutral. At the same time, four men from Choukafalya, four from Taski Etoka's village (Old Town), and four from Wolf's Friend's village of "Chatalaya" (Tchitchatala), led by Piomingo and a mixed-blood named Babe Metife, traveled to American territory to ask for ten cannons.[37]

On February 13, Piomingo sent an impassioned letter to Chickasaw agent Robertson, informing him of the declared war and asking for United States guns and ammunition, including muskets, rifles, smoothbores, ten blunderbusses, and a gunsmith; a bombardier to operate six swivel guns was also requested. As always when Piomingo requested goods from the Americans, whiskey was an item solicited. In this instance he stated that "it is good to take a little at war talks; please send me some." Later, Robertson opined that a large Creek war party was discouraged from subsequently making intensive war on the Chickasaw after they arrived at the Chickasaw settlement to find that they had built many new forts, bringing the total to nearly thirty.[38] However, thirty forts is likely an exaggeration by Robertson's information source.

Because of the Creek hostilities against the Chickasaw and the fact that some of the former had already murdered a number of whites and stolen many horses in the Cumberland settlement during the fall and winter of 1792–1793, a concerned Robertson wrote to Governor Blount in Knoxville, enclosing Piomingo's letter. He recommended military aid to the Chickasaw, pointing out that Creek depredations against Americans had actually, in his opinion, placed the United States at war with that tribe. For emphasis he lamented that "we are yet so apprehensive of hourly receiving death from their hands, that we venture out of doors with great caution." Apparently Piomingo's and Robertson's letters were effective, for that spring Lieutenant William Clark, under the direction of the secretary of war, delivered to Piomingo at Chickasaw Bluffs munitions and goods consisting of 500 guns, 2,000 pounds of powder, 4,000 flints, 4,000 pounds of lead, 100 gallons of whiskey, 100 bushels of salt, 50 pounds of vermillion, 1,500 bushels of corn, and a gunsmith with tools. According to Benjamin Fooy, "much sugar" was also included. This was the least the War Department could do, but Robertson and Blount would continue to be disappointed by lack of attention to their requests for United States military assistance in response to the Creek and Cherokee harassment of the Cumberland settlement, harassment that had intensified after the totally one-sided victory in 1791 over the United States army by the now jubilant northern confederacy and its energized Indian supporters in the south. Much to the chagrin of Robertson and others, the United States mostly turned a deaf ear to the pleas of the southern Americans, for carrying on the war with the northern Indians was its priority; besides, two wars at once would have been too expensive.[39] An illustration of Indian animosity toward Americans in 1792 was recorded by Spanish-affiliated John McDonald while he was in the Cherokee nation: "A Considerable body [of Cherokee and Creek] have turned out to war against Cumberland; their plan was to attack and distroy the City of Nashville, they have been gone about fifteen days and I have waited with Impatience till now to hear the issue of their expidition . . . their number was between three and four hundred." This quotation is related to the unsuccessful Cherokee-Creek attack on Buchanan's Station (blockhouses within a stockade), located four miles south of Nashville, on September 30, 1792. The figure of three or four hundred attackers is independently reported by Governor Blount.[40]

By January 1793, the Chickasaw were in dire straights as a result of a crop failure the year before, as reported by commissary/agent de la Villebeuvre: "The two hundred bushels of corn which [James] Robertson sent to Piomingo are completely used up, while the Chickasaws have not profited by this food and are dying of hunger." Earlier, Carondelet had informed Gayoso and de la Villebeuvre that the Spaniards should likewise provide corn for the hungry Chickasaw. The latter commented in agreement: "If you furnish corn to the nation, as you indicate to me, it will be the biggest favor you can do them in the scarcity that troubles them this year, and will gain us a lot of merit." Afterward, the Spanish indeed supplied greatly appreciated corn to the desperate Chickasaw. Despite the corn supplied by the Americans and Spanish that winter, many of the Chickasaw men still had to hunt for game and many of the women had "to dig wild potatoes to Save them from dying with hunger."[41] Although some livestock must have been slaughtered for food, the majority of the Chickasaw had few or no cattle and hogs.

Spanish opposition to the war and their intervention resulted in a Creek-Chickasaw peace in mid-1793, a peace perhaps partially aided by the sickness and subsequent death of Alexander McGillivray in Pensacola on February 17, 1793. Prior to the peace, however, Chickasaw king Taski Etoka became irritated with the Spanish for preventing Choctaw assistance, curtly telling de la Villebeuvre in one letter that since "you are in a borrowed land Your Self I don't See that you have any rite to inter fair [interfere], for it is not Our Seeking that the dispute was brought on." As a result of the war, Piomingo and Taski Etoka became unified, as shown by the words of de la Villebeuvre: "Today the Chickasaw King is a great friend of Piomingo, as is Olacta Opaye, or [William] Glover, and it seems to me that they put a lot of trust in help from the Americans. . . . Piomingo is a better politician than the others without any doubt and has won them over. Ougoulayacabe is not of the same opinion and has written me that he will die a Spanish chief, but he is almost alone and is obliged to espouse the Cause of his nation since his nephew has been burned lately by the Creeks and he weeps continually."[42]

Wolf's Friend was also perturbed at the Spanish for dissuading the Choctaw. Extremely distraught and angry at the Creek for burning his nephew, Wolf's Friend had sent the Choctaw "three red knives . . . asking them to declare war also on the Creeks."[43]

Nevertheless, de la Villebeuvre managed to arrange for a Choctaw-Chickasaw-Spanish agreement at a conference in the Choctaw village of Boucfouca in May, which paved the way for a Choctaw effort to terminate the war.[44] Meanwhile, the late Alexander McGillivray's white military "general" and brother-in-law, Louis le Clerc Milfort, made plans to launch a massive attack against the Chickasaw despite opposition of the Spanish:

A party of our warriors will start on the 18th instance to go to the Chickasaws. [They] have made for themselves a sort of stockade, that they call a fort, in the middle of a great prairie. They have a great number of Cattle and I have recommended to the Chiefs of the [force] that they eat their animals and to force them to surrender or die of hunger. I recommend to them that in case of surrender to take the women and children prisoners. And even if they surrender unconditionally they should only kill the group of the Mountain Leader since the others always said that they wanted to stay friends with the Creeks.[45]

Milfort thereafter started a Creek army of about 800 warriors on May 16 but soon received a letter from Governor O'Neill (sent via a runner by William Panton) informing him that a peace emissary had been sent to the Chickasaw. Milfort immediately sent word for the force to return, with the exception of two Creeks who were instructed to continue to the Chickasaw settlement with peace overtures. Return of the Creek army was fortunate for the Chickasaw, considering that Piomingo and a great many of his warriors were at Chickasaw Bluffs awaiting 400 bushels of corn being delivered on a flatboat by Elijah Robertson, son of James Robertson. The Chickasaw, represented primarily by Wolf's Friend, accepted the peace overtures and sent peace beads and a written message back to the Creek army "to assure the Creeks that they ask nothing better than to live at peace with them." On June 1 at Piomingo's house in Long Town, with trader Benjamin James from the Choctaw nation serving as Spanish representative, Choctaw emissaries presented to Chickasaw Mucklesaw Mingo a belt of beads as a symbol of peace from the Choctaw. After completion of his speech and much ceremony, the Choctaw speaker, Tuscoonopoy, presented to Mucklesaw Mingo a belt of wampum sent by the Creek chiefs Peomingo of the Cowittas and Offey Hago of the Tuckabatchees. Mucklesaw, after pointing out that the late Paya Mattaha was his forefather, made a speech declaring peace and stated that their beloved man "Hylaycabby" (Wolf's Friend) had already sent a message of peace to the Creek, as mentioned above. Following more ceremony, Mucklesaw handed the Creek belt to Piomingo, who made a long speech filled with bitterness and misgivings about accepting the peace (he even called the Creek "thieves and murderers"). He did, however, accept the peace, having been encouraged earlier to do so by an apparent important Chickasaw named Mongoulachamingo and the Colbert brothers, who, according to de la Villebeuvre, led "the largest party," apparently in opposition to Piomingo. As becomes a great person of character and integrity, Piomingo ended his peace acceptance speech on a positive note: "And now my Warriors and Women and Children, let the dark cloud that has been over us so long be blown off, and the Sun shine clear on us, & each of you to your devotion or calling that you follow, and the Fruits that Nature sends prosper us so famished."[46]

10

The War Road Ends

Prior to the Creek-Chickasaw peace, the Spanish had been trying to arrange a conference with the Four Nations tribes for the purpose of ending the war and creating "a permanent congress composed of three chiefs of each of the four nations" in order to strengthen mutual protection and trade ties and to maintain the land boundaries of each nation. Governor Gayoso instructed John Turnbull to go to the Chickasaws, urge them to make peace, and present letters from Gayoso regarding the proposed conference to Taski Etoka, Piomingo, Wolf's Friend, and two traders affiliated with the Spanish, Hardy Perry and Benjamin Fooy. Gayoso proposed that the conference be held at "the ball ground," which was located a short distance up the Yazoo River from Walnut Hills (present-day Vicksburg). Upon being informed of the desired conference, the Choctaws demanded, as reported by Juan de la Villebeuvre, that it be held "in a place they call Scito Ayacha which is a little below the Ball Ground because the water is better there, for they fear the fever." After postponements requested by the Chickasaw and Creek, the Spanish finally decided to hold the conference at Fort Nogales in October. Wolf's Friend attended the Nogales conference, along with a number of the Spanish-faction Chickasaw consisting of Atakabeholacta, Mongulacha Mingo, Chicacha Olactaopaye, Stanapayahacho, Ufehuma, and Enehenantla. Although earlier in the year Piomingo had expressed interest in attending, he failed to show up. The Treaty of Nogales, signed on October 28, 1793, bound the southern tribes in an offensive-defensive alliance. It also provided diplomatic support from Spain regarding Indian land claims, provided for annual distributions of gifts at sites desired and/or approved by the Indians, and provided for the appointment of permanent Spanish Indian agents. With regard to the latter, trader Benjamin Fooy became the Chickasaw agent in early 1794, replacing de la Villebeuvre, who had been agent for both the Choctaw and Chickasaw.[1]

Although the Chickasaw-Creek War had officially come to an end in June

1793, the animosities and misunderstandings did not end. Both Piomingo and Mad Dog had lost close relatives, and the former, at least, could not let it go. On the first day of September, Piomingo sent a long letter to Mad Dog through the hands of James Seagrove, United States Indian agent to the Creek, in which he pleaded for clarifications as to why his nation disliked the Chickasaw. Like a person seeking closure after being surprised by rejection in a personal relationship, Piomingo articulated to Mad Dog his bewilderment and lack of understanding for the past Creek animosities. He closed the letter by almost begging a response from Mad Dog: "I have given you my thoughts in full and Expect you will not hide your own from me."[2] If Mad Dog received the letter and responded, his letter does not seem to have survived. In any case, the peace was to be of short duration.

The end of the Chickasaw-Creek War did not terminate depredations against the Cumberland settlement by Creek radicals, a circumstance that greatly distressed General Robertson. Between May 20 and July 20, at least eleven white people were murdered and five whites and a black man were wounded by Creek marauders in the Cumberland settlement, by then called the Mero District. Detailed examples of the attacks that occurred in August alone include the killing of Samuel Miller at Joslin's Station; the killing in Tennessee County (present-day area of Robertson, Montgomery, Cheatham, and Dickson Counties) of the widow Baker and all her "numerous" children except two who were old enough to manage to escape; and the killing in the same county of Robert Wells's wife and two children while he was away from home.[3]

In late August, with peace between the Creek and Chickasaw concluded, Piomingo felt comfortable enough to set out with four other Chickasaw chiefs on a journey to Philadelphia, apparently at the invitation of the U.S. president. The trip, however, was terminated in southwest Virginia after Governor Blount happened to encounter them there. After Blount informed them that a fever epidemic was raging in Philadelphia, the group decided to cancel their trip and accompany Blount back to Knoxville.[4]

In the meantime, the United States army was recouping from the St. Clair disaster of 1791. Now Major General Anthony Wayne was in command of a United States army bent on revenge. Again the Chickasaw were solicited to help, this time by agent Robertson under a directive from the secretary of war. Even prior to the Nashville conference of August 1792, some Chickasaws were prepared to march north when summoned. While General Wayne was building up and training his army, United States officials were at the same time trying to negotiate a peace settlement with the confederation. Knowing that some of the pro-American Chickasaw were prepared to march north as early as July while the negotiations were in progress, Secretary of War Henry Knox became concerned. In a letter to General Wayne dated July 13, he stated, "It will be necessary that you should send an express to Nashville to prevent the Chickasaws from joining at Fort Washington. To have them repair to that post and to keep them in Idleness would be a monstrous evil . . . [but] if the [hostile] Indians should refuse our offers and fall upon the frontiers, then you would require the assistance of the Chickasaws."[5]

In response, General Wayne wrote to Knox on July 20 that he was "really at a loss to know what to do respecting the Chickasaw Indians—however I will endeavour to stop & support them at Nashville until further orders." By July 27, Wayne still had not sent a messenger to Nashville because he could not find a "proper Officer" suitable for the task. On that date, Knox sent a letter to Wayne restating his earlier opinion regarding near-future use of the Chickasaw but elaborating somewhat in stating that because it was too late to make preparations for an offensive operation that could be concluded before winter weather set in, "it will not be proper to endeavour to obtain a body of the Chickasaws to join our army—Should they be brought to Fort Washington with the expectation of seeing there a large army for offensive operations and find it otherwise, disgust would ensue." Knox followed, however, with the suggestion that perhaps Wayne might want to encourage the Chickasaw "to make a stroke by themselves." Knox continued: "In this however they cannot be indulged unless the negociations should be at an end and it shall be discovered that the War must progress."[6] Following the Nashville conference, the Chickasaws there returned to their Tombigbee River basin homes, having received no summons to join General Wayne's army.

Knox, however, kept up his communication with the Chickasaw in anticipation of asking for their military aid because the negotiations with the northern Indians did not look promising. In April 1793, Knox sent a message for the Chickasaw to Wayne, along with a schedule specifying the nature of goods to be delivered them with the message. The goods apparently were to partially consist of about 1,053 used and repaired arms currently on hand at Fort Washington. In this letter, Knox made it clear that the arms were being sent to the Chickasaw to be used in their war against the Creek, "who are represented by Governor Blount to be extremely troublesome to the Cumberland settlements and other parts of his Government—But as it is the policy of the Government to endeavour to preserve a peace with the Creeks, the Articles [to be] forwarded [to Chickasaw Bluffs] are put upon the footing of [payments for] services rendered to the United States." On May 27, Wayne acknowledged Knox's order with a qualification, stating, "due attention shall be paid your orders respecting the Arms, Ammunition & stores for the Chickasaws as enumerated in the schedule sent me, as far as will be in my power to procure them!" The irritated General Wayne obviously did not assign as much importance to the Chickasaw as did Knox, stating toward the end of the same letter that because of the non-arrival at Fort Washington of even a portion of the stores and articles necessary for his campaign against the Indian confederacy, "those furnished from the Magazines at this place for the Chickasaws, I trust will be immediately replaced."[7]

Apparently in May or June, General Wayne placed Lieutenant William Clark in charge of the Chickasaw munitions and sent him off downriver with them, but Wayne cautioned Knox that this operation was extremely dangerous inasmuch as the convoy would have to pass by a Spanish post about eighty miles below the mouth of the Ohio and the Spanish there might attempt to seize the arms and ammunition, suspecting that they were intended for Frenchmen in Louisiana (Spain and France were at war). To reduce the chances of this happening, Wayne ordered Clark to quietly pass by the post in the night. The munitions and other items gathered by Wayne, detailed in the latter part of the previous chapter, were those delivered by Clark at Chickasaw Bluffs in the spring of 1793 in response to the pleadings of Piomingo and Robertson, but they included only about half the guns stated in Knox's letter. By September 17, 1793, Clark had returned to Fort Washington, having completed his mission, according to Wayne, "with a promptitude & address that does him honor & which merits my highest approbation!" Accompanying Clark were a Chickasaw chief named Underwood and eight warriors who were "determined and anxious for action." Clark also brought copies of letters from Piomingo to General Robertson and originals from Robertson to Wayne.[8] Clark, incidentally, was the William Clark of the future Lewis and Clark expedition to the Pacific Ocean in the early nineteenth century.

The first part of 1794 was relatively uneventful with regard to the Chickasaw. Of interest, however, is a confrontation in March between Piomingo and the secret Spanish agent living at Holkey, Benjamin Fooy. Apparently Piomingo had become angry with some unspecified news Fooy had reported by letter to the Spanish governor. When Piomingo learned that Fooy and "young Frazer" were building a residence, Piomingo ripped off a letter to Fooy in which he accused him of coming there "as a Ruler amongst the Red people," chastised him, and stated that he was "determined that no more Comisary shall ever Remain in the Nation" and "[r]esolved as we are yet people to our Selves not to have any more Commishon men with us no more at present." Fooy did not choose to vacate the nation, however. Instead he asked Gayoso to encourage William Colbert to provide him protection. Piomingo must have cooled down, for Fooy was still at Holkey in early July. He was still there in March 1795 but by mid-April had apparently moved to an island, later named for him, west of the lower Chickasaw Bluffs where he had a trade store and served the Spanish as an interpreter.[9]

Chickasaws and Choctaws, having learned of the failure of peace negotiations and the imminent movement of General Wayne against the northern Indians, began gathering at Nashville in April 1794. For a long time, the Chickasaw and Wabash Kickapoo had been enemies and the former felt that they owed the latter a blow for past hostilities. According to de la Villebeuvre, Piomingo had induced some Choctaws to go with him to Nashville to receive presents prior to accompanying the Chickasaw northward to fight against at least the Wabash Kickapoo in concert with General Wayne. General Robertson received the first group of Chickasaw on April 7 at his agency house, where they were provisioned by Bennet Searcy, United States "agent of Indian supplies," by authority of purchase orders issued by Robertson. Piomingo, other Chickasaws, and a larger group of Choctaws (about seventy individuals) arrived as a single group at Nashville on May 11 with the intention of joining General Wayne's army. That Piomingo and other Chickasaws were traveling with the larger Choctaw group is supported by Malcolm McGee, who recalled that Piomingo "may have joined the Choctaws & went to Wayne's army—but not the Colberts." He was correct regarding William Colbert, who had left the nation at the head of 100 warriors before being called back because of a report that a large Creek force was on its way to the Chickasaw villages. Piomingo did not go to join Wayne either but went to Philadelphia instead, as discussed below. On May 24 a number of Chickasaw chiefs arrived at Wayne's headquarters at Greenville, where they presented Wayne a letter from General Robertson that reported that the Chickasaw nation was greatly divided by the "promises, presents, & intrigues" of the Spanish and that the inhabitants of Big Town had "declaired in their favor." These may have been the seventeen Chickasaws who left Nashville on April 16 and were escorted to General Wayne's camps by James Donelson. Piomingo and George Colbert were still in Nashville on May 15. Most of the Chickasaws and Choctaws apparently went north in April and June; some left as late as June 30. During this period, Piomingo's 1793 request of General Robertson that a rifle be made for him was fulfilled. At the time of the request, Blount told Robertson that the chief "must have the gun from Simpson [because] It is essential to keep him in good humour with the United States." Thomas Simpson of Nashville finished the rifle on June 30, but Piomingo had already left Nashville for Philadelphia by then. This rifle may have been fashioned after one owned by a popular middle Tennessee frontiersman named Kasper Mansker, as per Piomingo's 1793 request, but such is undocumented. In any case, this gun could be the Pennsylvania-Kentucky long rifle found in the south Tupelo grave discussed in Chapter 9 that possessed the Washington Peace Medal.[10]

Sometime after May 15, Piomingo, George Colbert, "Mucklisha," and between seventeen and twenty other chiefs set out for Philadelphia. After their embarkation, William Glover and Taski Etoka, having learned that the Creek of Tuckabatchee had committed a war-starting offense against the Chickasaw, sent an express rider after Piomingo and his party to urge their return to the nation. The express apparently failed to catch up to the party, which on July 11 was received by President Washington, who delivered a short address to Piomingo and the other chiefs; he then "smok'd the peace-pipe, eat, drank, &c. and then retir'd." In Washington's welcoming address he expressed friendship and thanked them for their military assistance in 1791. He also told them that the government would cover the expense of teaching any of their sons to read and write who desired to learn to do so. A subsequent Chickasaw conference with the secretary of war resulted in preparation of a document by the president in which the eastern boundary of the Chickasaw domain in present-day Mississippi, Alabama, Kentucky, and Tennessee was explicitly stated. This unusual document, signed by Washington and his secretary of state on July 21, 1794, also stated the legal rights of the Chickasaw as owners of their settlements and hunting grounds and forbade citizens of the United States to directly or indirectly purchase Chickasaw land. Occurrences of trespass and molestation committed by citizens were to be protected by United States laws.[11] In canceling out several previous and current encroaching land speculation schemes initiated by eastern states and individual Americans, this document was, in effect, the equivalent of a quit-claim deed.

The president, through the secretary of war, presented the Chickasaws with many gifts. Gayoso was told the following, partly at least through Wolf's Friend, who did not go to Philadelphia but obtained the information upon return of the delegation.

> The President gave . . . [Piomingo] a present of some consideration as follows: one thousand pesos [dollars] for himself; complete suits of clothing even to hose and boots for those that accompanied him, with added presents for their families, for they had the prolixity to tell him the number of old persons, women, and children they had left at home, so that . . . [some] received a very large package of presents, but were not satisfied because they were not given vermillion and other items that Indians use. Also, to each one of those present he gave thirty pesos to purchase in the stores whatever they wanted; and Piomingo also received several presents for persons whom he recommended who had remained in the Nation.[12]

Before finishing the letter from which the above is taken, Gayoso was informed by someone that Wolf's Friend was mistaken with regard to the one thousand pesos to Piomingo, the correct amount supposedly being 600 pesos. During the conference with President Washington, Piomingo and his group were promised that the Chickasaw would receive annual presents worth $3,000.

Secretary of War Timothy Pickering expressed concern that these annual presents might not be distributed fairly and suggested that the chiefs be asked to ensure that only the most needy in the nation receive shares of them. This $3,000 annuity, affirmed by congressional acts on February 25, 1799, and March 3, 1835, was paid to the Chickasaw until 1903.[13]

While Piomingo and the others were in the north, the Creek-Chickasaw dispute was evolving toward open war, which was the case by the end of January 1795. By mid-February, only Long Town in the southern part of the Chickasaw Old Fields was directly involved, but precautions were taken in the northern part of the settlement by moving scattered inhabitants there into "the large old field of the big town." Big Town warriors had been prevented from warring through the efforts of Wolf's Friend, William Glover, and King Chinubbee. During the second half of 1794, Wolf's Friend had been in charge of dealing with the situation because of Piomingo's absence in the north. In a letter to Gayoso in July 1793, Wolf's Friend had complained that guns and ammunition were scarce in the nation and that he had lost the confidence of his people and warriors. He had requested that the Spanish try to prevent further Creek hostilities, which he blamed on a man named Tahayo the Elder of Tuckabatchee, the only town "that had lifted up their weapons against me." Wolf's Friend went on to say to Governor Gayoso, "As I am not a person that has as yet taken up arms against any people, for which reason I have never been supplied with ammunition but the others [the Creek and Cherokee] have and I expect always will be, so it will seem as if it was the Spaniards that hates us."[14]

According to Benjamin James, the second Creek-Chickasaw War began after the Chickasaw assumed that a man found dead at the mouth of Wolf River had been killed by Creeks. Benjamin Fooy explained that it was unclear whether the Chickasaw was killed or died naturally, but because a three-man emissary to the Creek to inquire into the matter had not returned, the assumption was (in mid-February) that Creeks had killed them. In January 1795, James Robertson reported that the Chickasaw had killed five Creeks and had brought their scalps to the Cumberland settlement, an incident discussed further below.[15]

After finishing the Chickasaw nation business in Philadelphia, most or all of Piomingo's group returned to the Old Southwest. Some, however, may have traveled west to join the Chickasaws who had come up from Nashville to join General Wayne, but direct documentation appears to be lacking. George Colbert did not travel to present-day Ohio to join General Wayne; by August 31 he was in Knoxville with two other Chickasaws and Piomingo's horses. Because the goods pledged by the secretary of war and President Washington were to be received in Knoxville, Piomingo and the other Chickasaws waited there for them to be accumulated. Finally, by November 3, the goods were presented. The Spanish later received information that "the Chickasaw Indians of Piomingo's

Party are not satisfied with the present from President Washington." Almost one year later, an assortment of goods consisting of "Calicoes, Woolens, Lead, Powder, etc.," apparently the second of the annual payments promised by President Washington, was loaded on a boat diplomatically named the *Opoiamingo,* commanded by Captain John Gordon, who was to deliver the goods down the Cumberland, Ohio, and Mississippi Rivers to Chickasaw Bluffs. Gordon was instructed to afterward sell the boat "for the most she will fetch and credit the United States for the same."[16]

Related to Gordon's delivery of goods to Chickasaw Bluffs is a mysterious circumstance regarding some cannons that seemingly had been authorized by the secretary of war for delivery to the Chickasaw. Accordingly, David Henley, government agent at Knoxville, instructed Robertson to have them delivered. In May 1794, the six cannons were described as three and one-half inch howitzers; 100 rounds for each, including twenty-five grape shot rounds, accompanied them. However, in August 1795 Governor Blount wrote Robertson to "forebear to forward to the Chickasaws the six howitzers . . . ordered from Fort Washington for their use by the Secretary of War," because the Creek appeared to have declared a peace with the Chickasaw (a peace had not been declared, however). Apparently the letter from Blount remained undelivered by the time James Gordon set off down the Cumberland to Chickasaw Bluffs, for Blount was later informed that Robertson had sent the howitzers along with the goods carried by Gordon. The perturbed Blount, fearing that delivery of the howitzers to the Chickasaw would affect a potential Creek-Chickasaw peace, immediately sent John McKee to the bluffs with written "instructions," which partially may have authorized him to take possession of the howitzers and return them to Nashville. McKee's primary mission, however, was to deliver a stern protest message from Blount to Gayoso with regard to the Spanish establishment of Fort San Fernando de las Barrancas at Chickasaw Bluffs, a circumstance addressed below. A few days after sending McKee to Chickasaw Bluffs, Blount informed Robertson that he had been made aware that the secretary of war had not intended for the howitzers to be given to the Chickasaw in the first place. McKee delivered the message to Gayoso, but further reference to the cannons in contemporary documents does not seem to exist. This probably means that McKee was able to return the cannons to Nashville.[17]

Sometime in 1794, apparently not much before October and while Piomingo and the others were in the north, death took the aged king of the Chickasaw, Taski Etoka, who was succeeded by his brother Chinubbee, as discussed in Chapter 9. Although from the same town (Long Town) as Piomingo and the Colberts at the time, Chinubbee was affiliated with the Spanish faction.[18]

Meanwhile, General Wayne was finalizing preparations for military confrontation with the northwest Indian confederacy, made up of native Americans from the Delaware, Shawnee, Miami, Wyandot, Ottawa, and Chippewa populations. The first major battle in which troops under Wayne were engaged occurred at the site of St. Clair's 1791 defeat. The Americans had subsequently built a fort there, which they optimistically named Fort Recovery. Early on June 30, 1794, a supply escort force of 140 men was vigorously attacked near the fort by over 1,000 northern Indians, followed by an assault from every direction on the fort itself and subsequent fighting that lasted all day. Repulse of a second assault on the morning of July 1 caused the northern Indians to withdraw. Many Americans and northern Indians were killed and wounded in the fighting.[19]

Prior to the attack on Fort Recovery, General Wayne had sent two parties of Chickasaws toward Grand Glaize and the White River (in present-day Indiana) to capture prisoners for the purpose of obtaining intelligence. A third party, made up of Choctaws and ten of Wayne's best scouts, searched toward a place called Girty's Town. This time for identification purposes the Indian scouts were instructed to tie yellow ribbons to the hair on the crowns of their heads. The Choctaw party encountered a large group of northern Indians and subsequently discovered that there were many white men with them. Greatly outnumbered, the Choctaws withdrew and reported what they had seen to General Wayne at his Greenville headquarters on June 28. The two Chickasaw parties trailed other "hostile" Indians as the large force converged southward on Fort Recovery along various trails. One of the Chickasaws, Jimmy Underwood, undoubtedly a mixed-blood, entered the Fort Recovery garrison and excitedly reported the signs of the numerous northern Indians that he and other Chickasaws had observed in the vicinity of the Wabash. He also reported that many armed white men believed to be British soldiers and officers were traveling in the rear of the Indian army. Shortly thereafter the hostilities discussed above began. The intelligence from the Chickasaws confirmed Wayne's and others' previous intelligence that the British were encouraging and participating in the Indian war in hopes of claiming that area or parts of it.[20]

Angered by the attack on Fort Recovery and loss of a number of his best officers, General Wayne was eager to engage the enemy in a major confrontation, but because of circumstances such did not occur until August. On July 28 Wayne put his 3,000-plus force, called the Legion of the United States, in motion. From Fort Recovery the determined and spirited Americans marched northeastward to the Maumee River, where fortifications named Fort Defiance were constructed. On August 15 the legion resumed its march, crossed to the north side of the Maumee, followed it northward, and on August 20 came upon the waiting Indian force (which had retreated) at a place where a storm had blown down many trees, a place thereafter known as Fallen Timbers. Little Turtle, realizing the unlikely continuation of military success against the Americans, had resigned as leader of the confederacy on August 14. The Americans were victorious at the subsequent Battle of Fallen Timbers. The battle led to the Treaty of Greenville, signed a year later at Wayne's 1794 headquarters. Britain's ambition to add part or all of the region to its Canadian territory was destroyed, and the Indians would no longer pose a serious military threat in the northwest.[21]

As in 1791 the Chickasaws apparently had not been allowed to participate in the fighting at Fallen Timbers. Their assistance as scouts, however, had again been valuable. The Treaty of Greenville was especially beneficial to the Chickasaw, for the United States peace with the northern Indians and eventual alliance of the Chickasaw and Choctaw with the United States generally put an end to the long-duration hostilities (intensified by the French) between the Chickasaw and most native Americans residing north of the Ohio.

The Chickasaws and Choctaws who aided General Wayne must have been gratified with regard to their participation in the successful defeat of the northern Indians. They likewise must have felt unappreciated and betrayed when they were attacked on their return south by a group of white American citizens in Cincinnati on September 8 and 9. Several of the Indians were seriously injured in three separate assaults on their camp by the club-swinging and stone-throwing men. The militia was called out by Winthrop Sargent, acting governor of the Northwest Territory, to suppress the volatile situation. A Cincinnati grand jury later indicted two of the major participants, one of whom escaped. The other was tried and acquitted. Sargent attributed the assaults to lingering affinity to the British cause and to general animosity toward all native Americans, no matter what tribe, in that frontier area.[22]

A false report about Piomingo prior to his return from Philadelphia is significant because of its repercussions. Prior to the Battle of Fallen Timbers, General Wayne received a message that "the Mountain Leader" had been killed. This false report apparently bounced around for the next two months, eventually resulting in a rumor that he, as well as his companions, had been killed by a party of Cherokees, who with some of the Creek had allied with the northern Indians in the war with the United States. The rumor that Cherokees had killed Piomingo and his party reached a group of Chickasaws camped at the mouth of Bear Creek, who were there awaiting Piomingo's return from Knoxville. Angered, William and George Colbert formed two Chickasaw forces on each side of the Tennessee River to cut off a band of Cherokees that was moving to the Mississippi River to escape the violence occurring in their nation. At this time, a third brother of the Colberts, Levi, made his appearance on the documentation scene: Robertson and interpreter John McCleish reported that he talked his older brothers out of doing harm to the Cherokee band, urging that they needed more information first. William and George listened to their brother and let the Cherokee band pass unharmed. Afterward, however, another Cherokee canoe occupied by one man, two women, and two children appeared coming down the river. When William Colbert ordered them to come on shore, they instead turned away, which was a drastic mistake. An infuriated "Bill" (or "Billy") Colbert, as McCleish, other Americans, and even some of the Spaniards sometimes called him, and other Chickasaws went after the terrified Cherokees, chased them into the woods, and caught all five of them. Colbert tomahawked and scalped the male, who though purposefully unnamed by Robertson must have been a man of importance. Levi Colbert afterward went to Nashville and told McCleish that if the Cherokee retaliated William planned to "cry havoc! and let loose the dogs of war."[23]

On November 6, Levi Colbert and another Chickasaw left Robertson's house in an attempt to find Piomingo, obviously having learned that the report of his death was erroneous. On November 7, Piomingo arrived in Nashville from Knoxville. Upon learning of the misunderstandings and the killing of the Cherokee man by Colbert, Piomingo asked McCleish to dispatch word to his people at Bear Creek to wait there for him and his party with patience and to go after any who had gone home. Soon thereafter, Levi Colbert reappeared and took McCleish's written instructions from Piomingo to Bear Creek. Little is known about the events that followed, but the Chickasaws under William Colbert continued patrolling the Tennessee-Duck River area in search of Creek parties. On January 2, 1795, Colbert's warriors, co-led by Captain James Underwood, Captain Mucklishapoy the elder, and the Old Counselor, came upon the camp of a Creek band near the Duck River, attacked it at daybreak the next morning, and killed and scalped all five of its members, including Shotlatoke, the leader, and his brother. Colbert's force of about 100 Chickasaws arrived at Robertson's house in a few days. They proudly showed the scalps of the five Creeks to Robertson. The group included Colbert's Creek wife, all his children, and six African Americans, presumably slaves, who Colbert planned to use in putting in a crop. Robertson reported that "entertainment" was to be provided for Colbert's group at his house the next day and that the Chickasaws were planning to have a war dance at night. According to the secretary of war, this was a "scalp dance." At this time, William Colbert informed Robertson that he had been away from home since early fall of 1794.[24]

While the Creek-Chickasaw hostilities were firing up again, the Spanish and Americans continued to compete for acquisition of Chickasaw permission to build a fort at Chickasaw Bluffs. Earlier, the Spanish had cultivated a relationship with John Turnbull, a trader who had fathered two children with a Chickasaw woman and who had established a trading store on the lower Yazoo River by July 1793. Erroneously believing that the Americans were on the verge of coming downriver to occupy the bluffs, Governor Carondelet increased pressure on Wolf's Friend to allow Spanish occupation there and establishment of a trading post to be operated by either William Panton or Turnbull. Without having confirmed consent of the Chickasaw, Carondelet instructed Gayoso to go to Chickasaw Bluffs and occupy that strategic locale in the name of the Spanish crown, even if Chickasaw acquiescence had not been obtained by the time he got there.[25]

After Gayoso arrived at a Spanish encampment on the west side of the river opposite the bluffs, he was told that Wolf's Friend and his warrior companions were ready to meet with him at their camp on the east side of the river. Gayoso crossed on a boat and hiked to the camp, where Wolf's Friend spoke, through interpreter Benjamin Fooy, in favor of the Spanish fort but before making a decision opted to first discuss it in council with other Chickasaw chiefs not present. Gayoso thereupon persuaded Wolf's Friend to allow immediate Spanish occupation of the fort site area (the entire lower bluff) and to permit commencement of clearing of vegetation by the Spanish soldiers. This did not require much persuasion, however, for Wolf's Friend had earlier voiced to Pedro Rousseau a willingness to allow the fort. On May 25, Wolf's Friend and his warriors broke camp and returned home, undoubtedly because they heard that a Creek war party was threatening the Chickasaw villages, as discussed below. Clearing continued until the 29th, and on May 30, 1795, Gayoso formally took possession of the site selected for the fort. Construction began the next day without a formal cession of land from the Chickasaw and apparently without Wolf's Friend having yet consulted with the American faction. Gayoso named the fort San Fernando de las Barrancas (Figure 14), in honor of the person next in line for ascendency to the Spanish throne. Finally, on June 13, forty Chickasaw warriors led by chiefs William Glover and Payehuma arrived and went into camp. The former carried a message from King Chinubbee and the latter a message from Wolf's Friend. The next day Gayoso met with the Chickasaws, who apparently voiced no objections to the activities of the Spaniards. However, Gayoso was embarrassed to have to report that the ship carrying presents for them had not yet arrived from New Orleans. Despite continued delay of the boat, official cession of the fort land was accomplished on June 20 with signing of a treaty document by Gayoso, ten other Spaniards, chief William Glover, and chief Payehuma. Interpreter Fooy signed underneath as witness to the marks made next to the written names of the Chickasaw chiefs. Gayoso then lit his personal pipe and passed it to the chiefs, who were thereafter saluted with seven cannon blasts followed by firing of all artillery at the fort.

On June 25, William Glover and some of the warriors returned to their villages, while Payehuma stayed with the remainder to await the boat carrying their presents, which finally arrived on July 6. Eight days later, Wolf's Friend, with his wife and children and a large party of other Chickasaws, arrived at

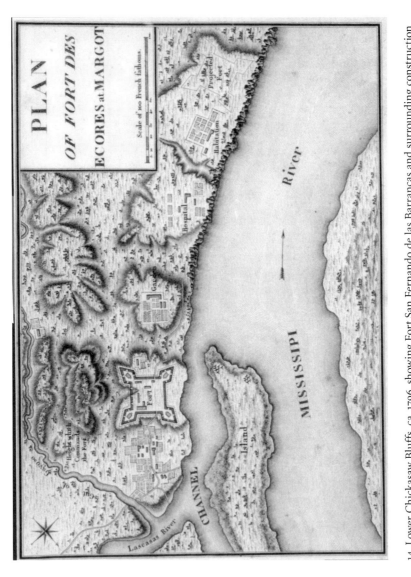

14. Lower Chickasaw Bluffs, ca. 1796, showing Fort San Fernando de las Barrancas and surrounding construction (from atlas accompanying Victor Collot's *Voyage in North America*, 1826; courtesy of W. S. Hoole Special Collections Library, University of Alabama)

the fort and camped nearby. That night Wolf's Friend and most or all of the Chickasaw males, at least, became, as Gayoso related, "inebriated, for which reason Chief Ugulayacabe could not come [to see him the next day]." By August 4, various Chickasaws had visited the fort, including William Glover's son and another man, four curious men from Piomingo's faction (who were probably there as observers), three unnamed men and a woman, and, finally, King Chinubbee with 166 men, 84 women, and 35 children, who were saluted by the Spaniards with artillery as Gayoso and Chinubbee sat under a brush arbor made for that purpose under the instructions of Gayoso.[26] Apparently Chinubbee had overruled objections to the fort by Piomingo's faction.

Panton and Forbes Trading Company was awarded the Chickasaw Bluffs concession by Carondelet; their post was later established about one mile south of the fort. With Gayoso's support, John Turnbull also established a trading operation in the vicinity, but it was short-lived.[27]

Thus the Spanish-American rivalry for control of the Old Southwest region continued unabated, but the Spanish had leaped ahead with establishment of Fort San Fernando de las Barrancas. As part of Gayoso's plan to establish the fort he had urged Carondelet, in late 1794, to provide Wolf's Friend with an annual payment of 500 pesos (same as $500 at that time) in recognition of his loyalty and service and to further ensure his fidelity, to which Carondelet agreed. That the first payment was apparently made in the first half of 1795 while the Spaniards were trying to persuade Wolf's Friend to agree to construction of the fort is no coincidence, and it undoubtedly influenced the chief to allow pretreaty initiation of construction in May and to finally sign a land cession treaty with Gayoso in June. Wolf's Friend received this payment until 1802, at which time Secretary of War Dearborn reported that on a visit to the Spanish governor, the chief was highly offended "and in his passion relinquished a pension of 500 Dollars which he has heretofore received annually from that Government."[28]

The determined Piomingo with King Chinubbee, Wolf's Friend, and other full-blood chiefs who supported him to various degrees, plus mixed-bloods William and George Colbert, William Glover, John Brown, Thomas Brown, and others, braced themselves for another possible extended war with the Creek, who eventually launched attacks on Choukafalya/Long Town, where most of the members of Piomingo's faction lived. Evidently, the arms and ammunition brought to the Chickasaw nation from Fort Washington in 1793 by Lieutenant William Clark had been stockpiled with other arms and supplies at Long Town. In addition, General Robertson had supplied the Chickasaw with a small brass swivel gun in April 1793 on the same boat that carried the corn taken to Chickasaw Bluffs by Elijah Robertson for relief of the famine-stricken people, as discussed previously. This piece, observed by a Spaniard when the boat stopped at New Madrid, was described to him by Elijah Robertson as "a species of small howitzer of about a three pounder size." A possible larger caliber cannon, however, was supplied Piomingo at Nashville in early 1794. The cost of that cannon, six dollars, was charged to the United States by Robertson. One of the two was undoubtedly the cannon on hand at Long Town when the Creek invasions discussed below occurred in 1795.[29]

Two major attacks on Long Town were planned and initiated by the Creek in 1795, one in the summer and another in the fall. Becoming aware of the impending first Creek campaign against his people, William Colbert, who was still bivouacked with his force near Nashville for the purpose of providing protection for the settlement, found General Robertson amicable to providing military assistance to the Chickasaw. Robertson "sanctioned and encouraged the enlisting of two companies to go to their relief," and other settlement inhabitants concurred. When Governor Blount became informed of the expedition, he also agreed that it was a prudent thing to do under the circumstances. Captain David Smith and William Colbert, with other Chickasaws and between fifteen and twenty Cumberland volunteers, marched down the Chickasaw Trace to the Chickasaw villages, reaching Long Town on about May 1. At the same time, Colonel Kasper Mansker and Captain John Gwyn, commanding another party, went most of the way by boats, reaching Long Town on about May 10. Governor Blount heard that a total of about 100 white men were involved; he admitted that this was only hearsay, but Captain Smith alone was reimbursed in 1818 for his expense in outfitting forty-five men for the expedition. At Long Town, Captain Smith turned over his command to Colonel Mansker and served in a company led by a Chickasaw war leader named Captain George. When the Creek force appeared near the town, supposedly on about May 28, the Chickasaw and white defenders under Piomingo, William Colbert, and Mansker were ready for them. However, the sight of several well-made forts on the high ridge bordering the Old Town Creek floodplain and the presence of the Americans caused the Creeks to lose spirit and confidence. The situation was very similar to that of 1736 when Bienville also looked upward to see forts on top of that same ridge system. Unlike the imprudent Bienville, however, the Creeks decided to forego a concerted attack that they knew could only result in loss of many Creek lives. With no attack occurring, Captain Smith proposed to make a sortie, but William Colbert would not agree to it, stating that such could result in the Creeks drawing the warriors away from the forts and then rushing in upon the women and children inside. Eventually, however, a few Chickasaws, who were relatives of some women who had been caught by surprise in the woods and killed prior to detection of the presence of the Creek force, left the fortifications to seek revenge. When one was killed and scalped, Colbert changed his mind and ordered a sortie to aid the men, which frightened the Creeks into retreating, with Chickasaws snapping at their heels, so to speak, killing and wounding perhaps twenty-six of them with few or no losses themselves. Satisfied that all or most of the Creeks had returned to their nation, Colonel Mansker and the settler force returned to Cumberland after about ten days. About two months later, Governor Blount falsely claimed to Creek agent Alexander Cornell that the whites had not gone to the Chickasaw nation with the intention of assisting them against the Creeks and that the occurrence of the Creek attack while they were there was a coincidence. He also claimed that "a considerable part of them belonged to the states East of the Mountains." Cornell must have found these statements incredulous since Blount offered no alternate explanation for the group's visit to the Chickasaw nation.[30]

With the Creek offensive in the past and there being no indication that another would be undertaken, William Colbert and others decided to visit President Washington in Philadelphia to plead for United States aid for the Chickasaw in the war with the Creek. Other Chickasaws who went to the American capital included mixed-bloods William McGillivray and John Brown, accompanied by interpreter Malcolm McGee. A white man from the Cumberland settlement, Colonel Robert Hays, conducted the group. A man called by Blount "the Chickasaw Red Shoes" returned after reaching Knoxville, having complained to Blount that he had not been receiving as many presents as Colbert and the other Chickasaws in the group, mentioning specifically "a saddle, Bridle and Saddle bags." A second party, consisting of both Chickasaws and Choctaws under James Kemp, was conducted by Captain John Chisholm. Kemp's party arrived prior to William Colbert's party and had left Philadelphia after an audience with the president in June. Fortunately, war leaders Piomingo, George Colbert, and William Glover were at home when another Creek force attacked Long Town in September.[31]

In reply to the talks of the separate Chickasaw delegations, during which William Colbert complained that U.S. army officers had not been supplied to aid in the war with the Creeks, President Washington delivered an address on August 22 in which he expressed regret for the "difficulties in which you are involved by the mistaken opinions which have been entertained of the intentions and obligations of the United States towards their friends the Chickasaws." He continued by stating that the United States did not intend for the Chickasaw to get the impression that they would be assisted militarily in their war with the Creek and that General Robertson was wrong to give them that impression. He explained that the United States never intended to "interfere in the disputes of the Indian Nations among one another, unless as friends to both parties to reconcile them," and he stated that "I shall do every thing in my power to serve the Chickasaw Nation." A second subject addressed by Washington is interesting in that it probably explains the origins of some or all of the Chickasaw military titles: "It seems, also, that the commissions which were given to a number of the Chickasaw chiefs were not truly interpreted. They were expressly confined to operations against the Indians north-west of the Ohio." According to McGee, during this visit to Philadelphia William Colbert tried to talk Washington into publicly recognizing him as the Americans' preferred war leader among the Chickasaw rather than Piomingo, to which Washington replied that he had no authority to do such a thing; to placate Colbert, McGee said, Washington commissioned him a major general. He was indeed known thereafter as General Colbert. Governor Blount later recorded that William Colbert and James Kemp returned to Knoxville in bad moods as a result of being dissatisfied with what the president and secretary of war had to say.[32]

By the first of September, Piomingo had learned from some Choctaws that the Creek were planning to again attack Long Town. Earlier, on August 9, Governor Blount had directed James Robertson to travel with a militia escort to the Chickasaw villages to assist in effecting a peace between the Creek and Chickasaw and to attempt relinquishment of Creek prisoners in order to appease that tribe. After consultations with Piomingo and others at Long Town in early September, Robertson returned to Nashville, apparently without the Creek captives. Shortly thereafter the second Creek invasion of the Chickasaw settlement occurred.[33] This time the people of Big Town, probably alarmed by the size of the force, came to the aid of their fellow citizens at Long Town, as described by Piomingo in a letter to Robertson: "About a thousand Creeks came to destroy the Chickasaw nation. They had some white people with them; they came with drums, and had ammunition, and preparations to make a siege and capture of Long-Town, and of other places. A great many came on horseback. The Chickasaw warriors of Big-town fell on them, put them to rout, pursued them about five miles, took all their baggage and clothing—except their flaps. The baggage consisted of their blankets, leggins, and other articles . . . their ammunition, kettles, and their provisions."[34] In his interviews with Draper, Malcolm McGee furnished a similar sketchy recollection of the event, which McGee learned about upon returning from Philadelphia in October:

> George Colbert . . . [and] Wm Glover, a half breed, were chief leaders—the day was a drizzly rain—the Chickasaws dashed into the action with great spirit, & drove their enemies, who—so sure of taking the town, had brought their packs with them, now dropped them & ran—these were temptations to the Chickasaws, who seized the plunder and made back for the town, some on foot & others mounted. George Colbert was sick at the time, but fought bravely & had a horse killed under him. Had it not

been for the love of plunder, the victory wd have been still more bloody, as it was, some forty Creeks were slain, & not more than five Chickasaws. Piomingo was blamed for remaining in town with the cannon—they thought he so great a warrior, ought to have brought forth the "big gun" to the battle field.[35]

Upon learning of the second repulse of the Creeks, General Robertson became confident that this event would initiate the death knell of the Creek-Chickasaw War, which indeed eventually transpired, although there were sporadic violent incidents and horse thefts into 1798. Primarily through the efforts of John Chisholm, James Robertson, John McKee, and, more importantly, Benjamin Hawkins, who in August 1796 had been appointed by President Washington to the position of United States agent to the Creek and overall superintendent of Indian affairs for the territory south of the Ohio River, the Indians began to return prisoners and stolen horses, and leaders from each of the Four Nations tribes began to exchange communications regarding peace. As their ambassador, the Creek appointed Mucclassee Hoopoie, who delivered peace talks to the Chickasaw chiefs in October 1797. This resulted in cessation of serious hostilities between the two tribes. Creek hostilities against the Americans also ended during the mid-1790s.[36]

In the meantime, United States diplomats were negotiating with the Spanish court regarding the northern boundary of Spanish West Florida. Because of a number of factors, including feared war with Britain, Spain reluctantly agreed to a treaty negotiated by Thomas Pinckney at San Lorenzo in the fall of 1795. Under the treaty, Spain recognized the 31st parallel as the northern boundary of West Florida, the Mississippi River was officially opened to U.S. navigation, and cooperation was established between the two countries in preventing Indian attacks along one another's frontier. The first of these terms, of course, necessitated the abandonment of Fort San Fernando de las Barrancas at Chickasaw Bluffs, which occurred but not until the spring of 1797 because of attempts by Spain to renege on its treaty commitments. The fort was destroyed and the bluffs evacuated by the Spanish military after it learned that an American force under Captain Isaac Guion was moving south to take possession of the Spanish military posts on the east side of the river north of the 31st parallel. Panton and Forbes continued operating at the bluffs until 1799 when U.S.-inspired Chickasaw harassment persuaded abandonment of the store.[37]

A military cantonment and fort originally named Fort Adams, which name was afterward changed to Fort Pike, was established by Captain Guion at the lower bluff of the Chickasaw Bluffs in July 1797 with William Colbert's permission. (A new fort named Fort Pickering was later built two miles to the south.) In August 1797 an Irishman in the service of Spain named Colonel

Charles Howard arrived with a Spanish force at the military post across the river. Soon afterward Wolf's Friend and a contingent of Chickasaws arrived at the bluff, followed two days later, on August 13, by Piomingo, who was in "bad health." With regard to Wolf's Friend and his people, Guion stated that they were "a very disorderly, turbulent and troublesome clan." Apparently thinking he was being backed up by Colonel Howard's Spaniards, Wolf's Friend began to give Guion "all the trouble he could or dared to offer, constantly objecting to our remaining on this ground, even at the moment of his receiving his part of the presents from us." Guion opined with regard to controlling Wolf's Friend that "a few hundred dollars" would be "the best 'talk' for him." Because of spoilation of salt meat brought with him, Guion was forced to purchase from James Allen, "a white man living in the nation, a drove of beef cattle." This man was probably the son or brother of a Benjamin Allen who lived at Chickasaw Bluffs by 1805.[38]

In order to participate in negotiations with the Creek, both Piomingo and Wolf's Friend soon went home, finally returning to the lower bluff on October 12. By now Wolf's Friend, who Guion described as "a warm partisan of the Spaniards, and a cunning, mischievous fellow," was even more belligerent, partially as a result of having told Colonel Howard of the Spanish force that he would not permit the Americans to remain at the bluff, thus obligating himself to try to keep his word. Accordingly, he told Guion that he wished to make a talk, with Colonel Howard in attendance. Guion thereafter set October 16 for the meeting in order to give both Piomingo and William Colbert time to make arrangements to attend. In anticipation of Wolf's Friend's design, Colbert made a preemptive strike by quickly making the following "bold and animated talk," which he directed at the chief and secondarily at the Spanish colonel: "I know your object is to expel the Americans and bring back your friends, the Spaniards. But this shall not be while I live. The works now being built here were begun with my consent. I, and my people, gave our consent and our promise, and I would like to see the man or the chief who can make that promise void. The Americans may go away if they choose to go, but they shall not be forced to go. I hear you talk of force. You will do well to count the warriors of this nation. Before you can drive the Americans, you must first kill me, and my warriors, and bury us here." While Wolf's Friend sat silent and moody, and with his Spanish-faction companions disconcerted, Piomingo stood and made a similar speech. If the humiliated Wolf's Friend replied to the speeches, this was not mentioned by Guion.[39] If he did reply, it made no difference. The Spanish, as had the French and British, were by necessity abandoning the Chickasaw. The viability of both Wolf's Friend and his Spanish faction was now greatly disabled. Neither would recover.

The power that William Colbert had achieved in the Chickasaw nation is cogently illustrated by his assertive rebuke of Wolf's Friend. What Gibson (*The Chickasaws*) referred to as the "Twilight of the Full Bloods" had begun at Chickasaw Bluffs on that late summer day. In another of the letters in which Colbert's rebuke of Wolf's Friend was reported, Captain Guion prophetically articulated what would indeed be the future means of United States–Chickasaw communication and interaction: "The friendship shown us by [Colbert] and Piomingo, but more particularly Colbert, deserves some distinct attention from our government. I have lately heard from them and all is quiet."[40]

About a year after the Spanish finally withdrew and lost influence with the Chickasaw, the former's most determined native American nemesis in North America passed into history. Within a few months of October 20, 1798, when he was mentioned in a letter from General Robertson, Piomingo died of unknown causes and was buried at his home in Long Town. Surviving him were his wife, said to be named Molletulla, and two offspring, a daughter and a son, who may have been called "Mountain Leader Tippo" by 1796. According to Haywood, a son of Piomingo in 1787 was called "Batterboo" (perhaps pronounced and spelled more accurately "Ba-tabee"?), who may or may not have been the son who survived Piomingo. This man may have been the son of Piomingo who lived among the Cherokee, as discussed in Chapter 8. Wolf's Friend would live several more years as a respected Chickasaw but one whose support of the Spanish and influence in the nation had fallen by the wayside at Chickasaw Bluffs in August 1797.[41]

11

The Road West Begins

By the turn of the nineteenth century the Chickasaw had unknowingly begun to move down a road that they were destined to never retravel. The trek had begun in the 1790s when the United States government realized that methods had to be formulated to facilitate centralized and standardized control regarding vast areas possessed by native Americans within its domain. The Indian Trade and Intercourse Act of 1790 was the first formal legislative step toward this goal. In competition with Spain, the United States' initial objective, as in the past, was to obtain hegemony over these lands and their native populations. The 1790 act, somewhat similar to the previous British Proclamation of 1763, set a precedent for enforcing the American treaties previously made with the various tribes by providing for licensing of traders and punishment for crimes committed by whites against Indians; it also voided private purchases of Indian lands. Refinements of the act were thereafter passed in 1793, 1796, 1799, and 1802. The means of enforcement already touched on in Chapters 8 and 9, the appointment of Indian agents to interact with the various tribes, was first motivated on a limited basis by the 1790s act. Over the period between James Robertson's appointment as Chickasaw agent in 1792 and the final act in 1802, United States Indian policy evolved into a formal set of principles. In abbreviated form, the objectives of the principles were to protect Indian rights to their land, restrict white entrance into their land, deny the right of private individuals or local governments to acquire Indian land, regulate the Indian trade, control liquor traffic, provide for punishment of crimes committed between whites and Indians, and promote "civilization" and education among the Indians so they might eventually be amalgamated into non-Indian society.[1]

By the end of 1798, with the Spanish confined to below the 31st parallel and the area west of the Mississippi River, the United States government was pursuing a more focused approach to its dealings with the Chickasaw and other tribes. The Indian Trade and Intercourse Act of 1793 had authorized the president to "appoint such persons, from time to time, as temporary agents, to reside among the Indians, as he shall think proper." Because James Robertson did not live among the Chickasaw and therefore had not been in a suitable position to enforce trade regulations and other terms of the act, and because he would not move into the nation as required by the 1793 act, he was removed in June 1797 by Colonel Benjamin Hawkins, who had been appointed principal agent for the Four Nations by President Washington in August 1796. Despite his dismissal, however, Robertson on occasion illegitimately authorized and distributed goods to Chickasaws, who had come to expect them when visiting the Cumberland settlement. After Robertson furnished goods and provisions to Wolf's Friend and his party on their way to pay an unannounced visit to President John Adams in October 1798, the secretary of war lectured Robertson regarding the impropriety of doing so, stating that in the future such unauthorized accounts would not be honored. He was especially irritated at Robertson because a replacement officially authorized to provide goods, attorney Samuel Mitchell of Hamilton District, Tennessee, had been appointed Choctaw and Chickasaw agent by Hawkins on August 12, 1797, at a salary of $500 per year. William McClish, who had previously interpreted for the Americans and Chickasaw, was assigned to serve as Mitchell's Chickasaw interpreter and John Pitchlynn as his Choctaw interpreter and assistant in that nation.[2]

The visit to President Adams by Wolf's Friend in October 1798 is enlightening with regard to changing political directions occasioned by the Spanish withdrawal and opening of the Mississippi River to unrestricted American travel. The timing of the trip may also be significant in light of the fact that October is the last month for which there is record of Piomingo. As mentioned in Chapter 10, Piomingo had been in poor health on a visit to Chickasaw Bluffs the year before. Thus the latter may have been on his deathbed in October. If so, Wolf's Friend may have been making a move to replace Piomingo as the Americans' best friend among the Chickasaw by paying a visit to the president. General James Wilkinson of the United States army was instrumental in motivating and encouraging Wolf's Friend to visit Philadelphia, which suggests that Wilkinson was the first to recognize the importance of nurturing American friendship with that chief. James Robertson may have also foreseen the imminent end of Piomingo's reign as the Americans' most influential Chickasaw ally. On his way to Philadelphia, Wolf's Friend conversed with Robertson at his home, whereupon Robertson wrote a letter to President Adams that Wolf's Friend hand-delivered for him. Although stating in this letter that Piomingo had always shown "a warm attachment to the interest of the U. States," Robertson described Wolf's Friend as "one of the greatest and [most] influential characters in the Chickasaw Nation." He also asserted that Wolf's Friend always had more influence in the nation than Piomingo, writing, "I suppose at this time [he] lead[s] three fourths of the Nation, & sensible I am he is much the most useful Chief in the Nation." Robertson continued in his praise of Wolf's Friend:

> I think him to be one of the best disposed men I ever knew of the color. He has ever endeavored to keep his Nation at peace with the whole world, and particularly with neighboring people and States, and although he has been greatly caressed by another government, I am pretty well informed that he has at all times answered them that he was determined to be at peace with the United States, and if white people fall out, the Chickasaws would be Neutral. From my knowledge of him, I expect he calculates on being noticed by you and the officers of the Government. This Sir, I drop you as a hint.[3]

There seems to be no significant extant record of the proceedings that transpired at the meeting between Wolf's Friend and President Adams. Of interest is that George Colbert (referred to as "Major Colbert" by Robertson) was a member of the group that accompanied Wolf's Friend. His presence is perhaps the most significant aspect of the visit. As discussed in Chapter 10, Captain Isaac Guion had realized the importance of dealing with William Colbert in future interactions with the Chickasaw. Since by now George Colbert had also achieved respect and influence within the Chickasaw nation, his face-to-face meeting with the president probably added to the growing awareness that perhaps the key to future political subjugation of that tribe was through certain influential mixed-bloods.[4]

As mentioned, one of the objectives of the trade and intercourse acts was "civilization" of the Indian tribes. In other words, the Americans desired to "re-educate" them, so to speak, to conform with typical American customs and values, means of subsistence, and other American lifestyles and eventually lead them away from their ancient religions to the typical American one, Christianity. Achievement of the first of these goals, conformity to American customs and values, would effect dissolution of tribal land ownership, followed by amalgamation of the Indians into a general population occupying all lands under the domain of the United States government. Accomplishment of the latter ambitious goal, however, was to be abandoned because of the slowness of such an evolutionary process. Land-hungry Americans had no patience for something that was not going to occur in their lifetimes.

The United States undertook the "plan of civilization" by allocating large sums every year for that purpose. The various Indian agents were to use part of their respective allocations for teaching the American methods of spinning and weaving and to give the Indians spinning wheels and looms. The agents were instructed to encourage the establishment of family farmsteads having cattle and hogs in addition to the horses already possessed. Cultivation techniques that used wooden plows with iron shares pulled by horses and oxen were encouraged by providing the Indians with such implements. Blacksmiths to make and repair agricultural tools and equipment for the Indians were eventually stationed at the agencies or appropriate places elsewhere in the nation. Although the plan of civilization encompassing these things on a consistent and general scale did not occur in the Chickasaw nation until the first two years of the 1800s, the Chickasaw had been receiving iron hoes and other "tools of husbandry" for many years through trade. Under the new plan of civilization, James Robertson was authorized by the secretary of war to provide gifts of cultivation tools for a party of Chickasaws in late 1796 or early 1797.[5] Acquisition of plows by trade or gift from the government prior to 1799, however, was rare. In March 1799, Chickasaw and Choctaw agent Samuel Mitchell reported to Mississippi Territory governor Winthrop Sargent: "I have advised the Indians to settle out separately or in small villages, farm their fields and turn their minds to agriculture and the raising of stock for the support of their families . . . a number of half breeds and some Indians in this quarter have settled out for the purpose of raising of stock."[6]

Mitchell's reference to "settling out" concerns the first significant change in Chickasaw settlement patterns since 1723 when the Chickasaw constricted their villages and confined their occupation area to Town Creek and its primary upper tributaries. By this Mitchell meant that the Chickasaw had begun to take the agent's and others' advice with regard to establishing discrete family farmsteads outside of the old towns and thus often outside of the Black Prairie in which the towns were located. Initially, stock raising seems to have been the primary reason for "settling out." George Colbert appears to have been instrumental in effecting this population dispersal, as indicated by Benjamin Hawkins in October 1801:

> The Chickasaws are settling out from their old towns and fencing their farms. They have established and fenced within two years nearly two hundred. All of these farmers have cattle or hogs and some of the men attend seriously to labour. Major [George] Colbert, who ranks high in the government of his nation . . . has laboured at the plough and hoe during the last season, and his example has stimulated others. Several of the families have planted cotton, which grows well, and some of the women spin and weave. As they cannot count, they cannot warp without aid, but they know the process and perform with exactness when the threads are counted for them. They begin to have a taste for individual property, and are acquiring it by every means in their power.[7]

Because Samuel Mitchell had been appointed both Choctaw and Chickasaw agent, with the Choctaw the primary focus, he first moved into that nation. Probably because of criticisms of Mitchell by Governor Winthrop Sargent, to whom he was required to report, a second Choctaw agent, Colonel John McKee, was appointed in early 1799. Mitchell asked for permission to move to the Chickasaw nation, and his request was granted by the secretary of war through Benjamin Hawkins on February 22, 1801. By July Mitchell's Chickasaw agency operation was under way. He chose a site for the agency house on the old Natchez Trace where it ran north-south along the Pontotoc Ridge, in present-day northern Chickasaw County east of present-day Highway 15 and about one mile southeast of present-day Houlka, Mississippi (Figure 12). At a cost of $791, Mitchell built his agency house, a corn house, a potato house, a meat house, a loom house, a kitchen, and a wheelwright/carpenter shop. He wanted to build a blacksmith shop but the War Department refused to let him hire a blacksmith; one was hired, however, in 1807, at which time a shop was built.[8] In 1805 Dr. Rush Nutt described the agency, the site of which has been archaeologically located: "Altho' the agency house is in a fine & elevated situation, free from stagnat & noxious poisons from marshes or standing water, & having good water is yet very sickly. . . . Near the agency house on high & beautiful situations are six farms in a high state of cultivation. Those are made by white men having Indian families & by Chactaw half breeds who have settled here by permission of this nation. In this settlement travelers are mostly supplied with grain & provisions—here would admit of a large settlement."[9]

The frame agency house built by Mitchell was apparently thirty feet in length with porches nine feet deep on the front and rear that extended the length of the house. It had a central chimney with back-to-back fireplaces for its two main rooms. The house, therefore, was built in a style known as a "saddlebag." Later, in 1810 and 1811, a new agency house was built nearby by agent James Neelly, but the old one was preserved as an employee residence until sometime after late 1812, when it was extensively repaired by agent James Robertson. The second frame house was about fifty-four feet in length with a porch all the way across the rear and a porch centered on the front (north) side that was fourteen by nine feet in size. The house was probably about thirty-four feet in width, and its two chimneys were probably located on each end.[10]

The same activities associated with the American plan to "civilize" the Chickasaw were occurring in other native American groups. In concert with increasing cultivation of cotton, some Choctaw chiefs, in 1800, requested of Choctaw and Chickasaw agent John McKee that the United States establish a cotton gin in their nation. McKee subsequently gained approval from the secretary of war for a gin. He purchased the gin works in Natchez in December 1800, but for reasons uncertain the gin was rejected by chiefs of the Choctaw nation. McKee thereafter opted to build it in the Chickasaw nation, undoubtedly with consent of that tribe. The location, on the west side of the Tombigbee River and about one mile south of the forks of the Tombigbee River and Old Town Creek, gave rise to the name Cotton Gin Port, and from there Chickasaw nation inhabitants and traders shipped their furs, cotton, and other products to Mobile. Apparently the gin was under the proprietorship of George or Levi Colbert, probably the former. In March 1810 Tennessee governor Willie Blount referred to it as "Colberts Cotton Gin, at the head of navigable waters on the Tombigbee river." The gin was burned by a band of Choctaws prior to September 1811, perhaps because of jealousy caused by its having been erected in the Chickasaw nation rather than the Choctaw nation as that tribe had first requested.[11]

Because of the dispersal of much of the Chickasaw population from the Chickasaw Old Fields that began in the mid-1790s, new hamlets in the hardwood forests bordering the prairie on the west were established. In 1805, Philadelphia physician Rush Nutt visited the Chickasaw on his way north from Natchez. Fascinated by the Chickasaw and the region, he stayed long enough to acquire a good understanding of the settlement configurations, the geography of a large area surrounding the settlement, the flora, fauna, and soils of the area, and many Chickasaw customs and beliefs. His ethnographic account is invaluable. With regard to the old and new settlements, he recorded the following:

> This nation is divided into four Districts, viz., Pontatock, Cheshatalia, Chucanfaliah (or Long Town), & Big-town (Chuguilisa). Pontatock lies . . . on a small creek of the same name running into Yannabba [Old Town Creek] one of the main branches of Tombigbee; this village or settlement contains ninety three men, 99 women, & 67 Children agreeable to the numbers given in last August, when receiving their annual Stipend . . . [but] not more than 8 families remain in or near the village, they have settled 50 or more miles around promiscuously through their country. . . . Most of these Indians have horses, cattle & hogs, & have settled out for the benefit of their stock.
>
> North about 50 [degrees] east 12 miles from Pontatock is the village called Chishataliah [Chitchatala], situated in a large prairie on Hatchalio [Falatchao] Creek [present-day Coonewah] a branch of Yannabba. This district contains 179 men, 258 women & 106 Children. All except two families have removed from the village.
>
> East 4 miles from Chishataliah, & north 30 [degrees] from the agency-house 19 miles is Chucaufaliah (or long town) situated in a prairie near 15 miles in length & from one to two in width on Yannabba Creek. . . .

This District contains 166 men, 197 women, 43 boys, 30 girls, & 35 children; agreeable to their last returns. For the convenience of the range, water & timber all the Indians have removed out of long-town, & settled in different parts of the country; & have turned their attention to farming, manufacturing & raising of stock.

North 4 miles from long town, & on the same creek & in the same prairie is Big-Town (Chaguiliso), a high and beautiful situation, was formerly the residence of the whole nation, but at present not more than 8 or 10 families remain in the old fields. They have settled out & made tolerable farms with worm fences. The men attend to the farm, while the women employ themselves in spinning &c. This district contains 205 men & 270 women & girls. The children are not ascertained. There are many families who do not attend the delivery of the annual stipend that are not numbered in either district.

Nutt goes on to say that in "the year 1797 the whole nation was contained (or nearly so) in these old towns [referring to Long Town, Big Town, and Chitchatala], but by the advice of the agent & other officers of government, they have settled out, made comfortable cabins, enclosed their fields by a worm fence, & enjoy the benefits of their labor, & stock, and are measurably clothed by their own industry." Nutt's statement regarding the population of the old towns is verified by the Reverend Joseph Bullen, who stated in May 1799 that Big Town alone "consists of two hundred houses."[12]

In addition to the above villages/towns, Nutt recorded the presence of some new, small hamlets: "S. 10 deg—west 3 miles from the agency house is a small village call'd Chuguillaso, containing six comfortable Cabins inhabited by Chactaws & Chickasaws. This village is on the head waters of Hoolky (running in Tombigbee) in the most fertile part of the country, watered by a number of fine springs, they have their fields fenced with a worm fence, raise a plenty of hogs & cattle."[13]

The similarity will be noticed between the name of this small village and the original name for Big Town on Old Town Creek to the east, called "Chaguiliso" by Nutt. The similar name strongly suggests that the small village three miles from the agency house was settled by former residents of Big Town, or Chuckalissa. A previous published study concluded that the small new village was located about three miles southwest of the agency and present-day Highway 15 and, as stated by Nutt, on the headwaters of Houlka Creek. The presence of Choctaws at this village and in the agency area in general is explained by Nutt in the quoted passage above regarding the agency. The Choctaw presence is, in fact, documented in some detail by Samuel Mitchell, who provided goods for Edmond Folsom, "a Choctaw half breed, for himself and two other familys of Choctaws that live north or near him. The reason Mr. Dinsmoor [Choctaw agent] requested me to furnish the articles, those famalies live near me, and upwards of one hundred miles from him; therefore I furnished the articles and took Folsom's receipts for the same which I forward."[14]

Although the agency location area came to be called "Hoolkie" or "Hulca," a small Indian village south of the agency visited by Nutt was also identified by that name, which he spelled "Holka." General James Wilkinson's survey map of about 1802 of the old Natchez Trace identifies the village as "Wholkey, a small village of Chactaws." His map places it south of the agency on the old Natchez Trace. The study mentioned in the previous paragraph concluded that this village was at a prehistoric mound site now called Thelma Mounds, located about three miles south of the agency site and on the old Natchez Trace. At least one of the original mounds was a pyramidal type with an observable earthen ramp. Nutt's description of the location of this Holka or Wholkey village identifies it as an ancient mound site with multiple mounds, the origin of which the Chickasaw had no knowledge. Among earlier prehistoric pottery types, historic period Choctaw sherds also have been recovered there. Types identifiable as Chickasaw-made have not been recovered, but there is good evidence that iron and copper trade vessels had almost totally replaced native Chickasaw pottery by 1805. Because the Wilkinson map only identifies it as a Choctaw village, perhaps no historic period Chickasaws ever lived there. This village may be the "Holkey" at which Benjamin Fooy wrote letters in the 1790s (see Chapter 9).[15]

Nutt mentions two other small villages or hamlets inhabited by Chickasaws. Both were undoubtedly extended-family farmsteads. He describes one as being located in the first twenty-five miles of country lying in a northwest direction from the agency and "on a small creek a branch of Tallahatchee, called Oaktockopullo containing 10 families." Continuing, Nutt states: "The country around Oaktockopullo is high broken pine land, very little fit for cultivation. The Indians have settled it for the benefit of range, as they have horses, cattle & hogs." This village was probably the origin of present-day Toccopola, Mississippi, situated at the northwestern boundary of present-day Pontotoc County. The second outlying settlement was on Pigeon Roost Creek "four miles N.W. of Tallahatchee (Yazoo) in some rich prairies [where] many families of Indians have settled & are making good improvements." This settlement was in the vicinity of present-day Holly Springs, Mississippi, in Marshall County. As discussed in Chapter 12, a Presbyterian mission was established there in 1826.[16]

Apparently the Pontitack settlement, which had originated in the 1760s with establishment of John McIntosh's commissary, was the first locale to receive a significant exodus from the old fields in the late 1790s and first two or three years of the 1800s. Although also mostly "settled out" for as much as fifty miles (undoubtedly to the north, west, and south), the Pontitack district had 260 people claiming affiliation in 1805, as reported by Dr. Nutt.[17] Thus the districts reported by Nutt would have contained most of the scattered native American can occupants of small hamlets/villages and separate family-unit farmsteads. At the time, most were located in present-day Lee, Prentiss, Tishomingo, Itawamba, Monroe, Clay, Pontotoc, Union, Lafayette, Marshall, and Chickasaw Counties and perhaps the northern part of present-day Calhoun County. By 1834, Chickasaws were also occupying the other Mississippi counties now in the old Chickasaw nation.

By 1799 a somewhat isolated family occupation had been established around the mouth of Bear Creek at the crossing of the Chickasaw Trace over the Tennessee River. There is an intimation that the site had been the residence of Levi Colbert since at least 1794, as suggested by a statement of William McCleish (McClish) in October of that year that he met at Cumberland with "Levi Colbert, from the mouth of Bear Creek." However, Levi and brothers George and Joseph were definitely living in the Long Town area in May 1799. In any case, Levi Colbert opened a ferry at the mouth of Bear Creek in early 1800, as documented by the following statements by David Henley: "[O]ne of the Colberts is at this place [Knoxville], he is come to purchase a large boat to load with corn and to establish himself at the mouth of Bear Creek where he intends to have a ferry and a public house for travelers, which will be of great convenience and use. I, therefore, am attending to his request in getting supplies for him which he purchases with his own money. He seems to be a well disposed Half-breed Indian, his name is Levi Colbert."[18]

A few days later, Henley sent a letter to Wolf's Friend, William Colbert, and George Colbert (who were also in Knoxville) in which he stated that "I have received your letter and have assisted [Levi] Colbert as I could, who you recommend, and wish his adventure may be fortunate. . . . Our Great Father Genl. Washington is dead, for which all the white people are in mourning." Henley had already negotiated a contract with Taylor Townsend and James Coulter from Knoxville to "deliver to the said Levi Colbert three hundred bushels [of] corn . . . and also agree to deliver a large flatt Boat thirty feet in length and seven and [one] half feet in breadth at thirty five dollars, the boat being sound and able to carry the above corn." Although Levi paid one-third of a dollar per bushel for the corn, Henley charged the cost of the boat and all other expenses incurred by Levi and the others to the War Department. The flatboat was undoubtedly used as the ferry boat after its arrival at the mouth of Bear Creek, as suggested by an item in the invoice: "A flat bottom boat for the use of his ferry [—]$35." Both Levi and George Colbert owned the Bear Creek Ferry, but by December 1800 the latter Colbert was its operator, as reported by a traveler at that time.[19]

Long before 1800 the typical Chickasaw dress had changed to accommodate the white man's cloth and metal jewelry. In 1797, the Reverend Joseph Bullen recorded the following observation:

> The Chickasaw men are very effeminate and dressy—the head is, in a hot summer day, bound with a handkerchief, over it a thick binding of fulled cloth, covered with broaches; to the nose hang six bobs, one in each ear, the outer curl of which is slit, and enraped in silver and beads, the hair of a deer's tail coloured red; this hangs over the face and eyes: the face is painted with streaks and spots of red and black; the beard is pulled out; the neck adorned with a dozen strings of beads of different sorts, besides a silk handkerchief; the arms and wrists adorned with silver bands; the body and arms covered with a calico shirt; the dress of the lower limbs is various. The women have no covering or ornament on the head but that of nature, unless a little paint, and the hair clubbed behind with binding. The men have a bunch of white feathers fastened to the back part of the neck, and if a person of note, a black feather; and lest the dress or colouring should be discomposed, carries his glass [mirror] in his pocket, or hanging to his side.[20]

Because of isolation of the important Natchez District from the main American settlements, the United States began encouraging the Chickasaw and Choctaw to allow the Americans official right of passage through their vast territories. A few months prior to Samuel Mitchell's move to the Chickasaw nation in the first half of 1801, an act of Congress had provided for establishment of a post road from Nashville to Natchez. After initiation of improvements and rerouting of the old Chickasaw Trace by the United States military in Tennessee and the northwest corner of present-day Alabama, the Chickasaw agreed to negotiations regarding further development of the post road through their core land in present-day north Mississippi. By now the Americans also wanted the road widened to accommodate wagons. At Chickasaw Bluffs, in October 1801, King Chinubbee, with consent of the other chiefs present, agreed to the primary wishes of the United States represented by commissioners General James Wilkinson, Benjamin Hawkins, and Andrew Pickens, who had assured the Chickasaw that cession of land was not involved and that the improvements would also benefit the inhabitants of their nation. The commissioners also requested that Americans be allowed to establish wayside inns, or "stands" as they were called, for the accommodation of travelers. After postnegotiation consultations with George Colbert and the other Chickasaws on October 21 and further discussions on the twenty-second, Chinubbee responded, through speaker George Colbert, to the Americans the next day: "I am very glad to hear the commissioners hold such language that does not require the cession of land or any thing of that kind; I consider the propositions to be made for the benefit of our women and children." The Chickasaw council finalized the agreement, made in consideration of only $700 in goods, by stating through George Colbert, who was "fully empowered by the council" to do so, that "The nation agrees that a waggon road may be cut thro' this land, but do's [does] not consent to the erection of houses for the accommodation of travelers. We leave that subject to future consideration, in order that time may enable our people to ascertain the advantages derived from it. In the meantime travelers will always find provisions in the nation sufficient to carry them through."[21]

The Choctaw also gave permission for the Choctaw nation road improvements and right of passage by the Treaty of Fort Adams near Natchez in that same year. Strangely enough, the United States was engaged in "laying out" the road through Chickasaw land prior to the Treaty of Chickasaw Bluffs. Between July 28 and August 31, 1801, Lieutenant Colonel Thomas S. Butler and General Wilkinson had supervised surveyor Edmund P. Gaines's "running of a line from Nashville, Tennessee to the Mouth of Bear Creek for the purpose of laying out a road leading to Natchez by order of Col. Strong." After the treaty, agent Mitchell participated in survey of a guide line by Gaines and laying out of the road "from 26 miles S.W. of Nashville to the crossing of the Tennessee River." During the interval between August 31 and March 7, 1802, the route was altered from a crossing at the mouth of Bear Creek to a new crossing some twenty miles to the east (Figure 12). George Colbert had apparently suggested the relocation of the crossing. At the new location an army cantonment was established by Colonel Butler. By agreement between General Wilkinson and George Colbert, a two-story frame "house of accommodation" was constructed for Colbert, but not entirely finished, by army personnel while stationed at the ferry. Use of the ferry by the troops resulted in deterioration of the ferry boat, presumably the one obtained by Levi Colbert in 1800. As a result, the army replaced it with one built by the soldiers, but because of the use of green wood, the boat rotted within a year. In 1804 when an army command under Colonel George Doherty was ordered to New Orleans to oversee transfer of the Louisiana Purchase land to the United States, Gilbert C. Russell was directed to build two ferry boats for the use of the army. These boats may have been turned over to George Colbert for use in his ferry operation. The house mostly built by the army troops in 1801 was finished (probably in 1805) by George Colbert at a cost of $650. The house stood until about 1929, when it burned. In 1811, a traveler reported that the "rich Indian" who lived at the ferry, and whose house "looks like a country palace with its abundance of glass in doors and windows," owned two ferry boats and "makes a great deal of money." Apparently the Colberts were not the only Chickasaw inhabitants of the area, for agent Samuel Mitchell reported in January 1803 that many Chickasaw families formerly from Long Town (George and Levi's original home) had settled on the Tennessee near Colbert's Ferry and at the mouth of Bear Creek in order to supply corn and meat to travelers. The Chickasaw population on Bear Creek where the Chickasaw Trace crossed were occupants of a settlement called Underwood's Village by 1800.[22]

Between March 8 and October 31, 1802, a guideline for the post and wagon route was surveyed from the Tennessee River crossing through the Chickasaw and Choctaw land to Bayou Pierre northeast of Natchez. However, the road was actually "cut out" only to about forty miles southwest of Colbert's new ferry and from the south to about forty miles northeast of Bayou Pierre, leaving about 186 miles of the old Natchez-Nashville route unimproved in between. Thus the route from the Tennessee River was initially only improved to the Chickasaw villages. This part of the improved Natchez-Nashville road (afterward called the Natchez Trace) ran to or through Big/Old Town and possibly as far as the newer Pontitack settlement (Figures 1, 4, and 12).[23]

Meanwhile, Samuel Mitchell continued to work toward his mandate of bringing the Chickasaw into the new century in a way considered the most prudent by the Americans. He appears to have begun the so-called plan of civilization among the Choctaw and Chickasaw in as suitable a manner as possible under the circumstances. In March 1799, Mitchell informed Mississippi Territory governor Winthrop Sargent that he had encouraged the Chickasaw to disperse from their old villages in family units or small villages where they could establish farm fields and raise stock for their primary sustenance.[24] Because the Chickasaw had long been purchasing their blankets and clothing from traders, most women no longer knew how to make thread and weave in the manner performed prior to European contact. To help them overcome this dependency, the plan of civilization included teaching them European methods of spinning and weaving. In 1802 Mitchell reported the following to Cherokee agent Return J. Meigs: "The [spinning] wheels and cards that I have given are used by the Indians to great advantage—great preparation is making to plant cotton this season with an expectation that government will assist them. . . . Col. Hawkins directed me to employ a weaver for a short time to weave what threading is on hand. I have employed one of the women at 15 dollars per month. I expect there is 400 yards unfinished ready for the loom. I shall employ an Indian woman to weave one month in a remote part of the nation, as she has a loom of her own and geer and understands the business."[25]

A few months later new governor William C. C. Claiborne wrote to Mitchell:

I am pleased with your efforts to advance the Happiness of the Chickasaws and I flatter myself, that the Habits of Industry and of Civil life will
soon acquire such an ascendency in the nation, as to banish from the
land, that attachment to Idleness, which has hitherto, so much impeded
the progress of Civilization. While you exercise all the Means in your
power, to excite the Chickasaw Men to agricultural pursuits, you will be
equally Zealous in encouraging a spirit of Domestic Economy among the
women;—It seems to me advisable that you should continue to supply them with wheels and Cards and also to retain in your employ the
weaver.—If you could induce a few young Indian Girls to pass some time
with the Weaver, and he would undertake to teach them, an adequate
compensation for his trouble, may be made him.—It would also be a prudent measure to place a few active Indian Lads with the Wheele-maker.[26]

Soon afterward, Mitchell received an encouraging letter from the secretary
of war, to which he responded as follows with regard to the Chickasaw: "It will
be truly pleasing to the Indians to hear they are to be supplied with mechan-
icks, Cards, Ploughs &c. I had prior to the reception of your letter by advice
from Governor Claiborne a man to make fifty cotton wheels—also a man who
understands making looms, stocking ploughs & is retained and his wife who
understands weaving is also retained for the purpose of putting some Indian
lads in the care of the mechaniks who may in time become serviceable to
themselves and to their Nation."[27]

In the years up to the removal, the agencies purchased thousands of pounds
of iron and steel, which were used by the agency blacksmiths and others stationed at various places to make plowshares, hoes, spinning wheel irons, and
other tools for the Chickasaw. Residents of the nation, usually white men, were
paid to construct wooden plow stocks, looms, spinning wheels, and so on for
the Chickasaw men and women. The agency also supplied free food to Chickasaw men, women, and children who visited the agency, whether on business or
not. The free food, as well as repair of tools and other free services, is documented in detail in the Chickasaw Agency fiscal papers.[28]

Although the Treaty of Chickasaw Bluffs was not consummated until October 1801, the post office department had been sending mail through the Chickasaw nation via the Natchez Trace for several years with no apparent objection
from the Chickasaw. Because of the distance involved, establishment of relay
stations along the route became necessary. For several years, John McIntosh, Jr.'s
farmstead was the only one of these between Natchez and Nashville. In June
1801 the postmaster general decided to establish a post office in the Chickasaw
nation with McIntosh as postmaster. McIntosh, who was appointed on June 30,
had been recommended for the position by Choctaw agent John McKee on

May 24. By this time, McIntosh had moved from the Pontitack settlement and the old homestead established by his father in about 1765. He now lived farther down the trace in present-day Pontotoc County at a new homestead that came to be called Tockshish or, by the post office department, McIntoshville (Figure 12). McIntosh's new homestead, located about nine miles north of the agency, thus became the second post office to be established in what is now Mississippi (Natchez being the first). For years, McIntosh's plantation, first the one at Pontitack and then the new one, had been utilized by travelers as a place to rest or obtain food. It was also frequented by Indians, probably because it had "everything which such a country affords in the greatest abundance." In 1797, fearing an attack from the Creek, McIntosh fortified his homestead "with a regular stockade raised about twelve feet high, and formed of thick planks." McIntosh served as postmaster until his resignation or death in early 1803. In either case, he died prior to August 15, 1803, after leaving the nation for the "warm Springs west of the Mississippi" (apparently present-day Hot Springs, Arkansas). His widow, who was the former wife of James Colbert the elder and the mother of James Colbert the younger, stayed at Tockshish and continued to accommodate travelers. By April 19, 1803, the postmaster position had been filled by James Allen, a local white resident (married to a mixed-blood) who lived north of the agency, evidently at or very near Tockshish. Allen apparently did not like the pay and may have resigned. Regardless, Samuel Mitchell became postmaster on October 3, and his agency house became the Chickasaw nation post office.[29]

Following precedents set by the United States government with regard to the Cherokee, Creek, and Choctaw nations, a trading house was established for the purpose of providing regulated, fair trade to the Chickasaw. The "Chickasaw Factory" was established at Fort Pickering on the lower Chickasaw Bluffs in 1802. Its purpose was not to make a profit but to be a "means by which the Indians may be relieved, and benefited, as well in relation to their wants, as to their habits." It operated until temporarily closed during the War of 1812, after which it operated until 1820 when moved because of the financial losses of its operation as a result of competition from private traders, a Chickasaw desire to manage their own trade, and the "extreme unhealthiness of the place." The hundred-mile distance from the main Chickasaw villages undoubtedly also contributed to its eventual failure. It was reestablished on the Arkansas River to accommodate Cherokees who had migrated to the Arkansas Territory. The first Chickasaw Bluffs factor, or operator, was Thomas Peterkin; the last was Isaac Rawlins. According to visitor Francis Baily, there were five or six white settlers at the bluffs in May 1797, most of whom were allied to the Chickasaw by marriage. The factory evidently at least partially motivated the establishment of a Chickasaw habitation area located about five miles inland by 1806. Prior to that year a population of Chickasaws had apparently established a somewhat nomadic residency on the west side of the Mississippi River in present-day Arkansas and northern Louisiana. Presence of the trading house and private trading houses at the bluffs undoubtedly had much to do with the establishment of this population also. Apparently hunting and trading were extensively practiced by this group of Chickasaws, described as "vagabonds" by an English traveler named Fortesque Cuming.[30]

Upon visiting Fort Pickering in 1809, Cuming recorded rare descriptions of Indians identified by him as Chickasaw warriors who had come to receive presents from the government. Some or all may have been from the nearby inland settlement mentioned above; otherwise they could have come from the trans-Mississippi population or the main settlement in present-day north Mississippi. One individual was described as follows:

> An Indian was at the landing observing us. He was painted in such a manner as to leave us in doubt as to his sex until we noticed a bow and arrow in his hand. His natural colour was entirely concealed under the bright vermillion, the white, and the blue grey, with which he was covered, not frightfully, but in such a manner as to mark more strongly, a fine set of features on a fine countenance. He was drest very fantastically in an old fashioned, large figured, high coloured calico shirt—deer skin leggins and mockesons, ornamented with beads, and a plume of beautiful heron's feathers nodding over his forehead from the back of his head.

Cuming observed fifty warriors present at the top of the 120 square logs that formed the steps up the bluff to Fort Pickering and noted, "There was a trace of fresh [deer] blood the whole way up the stair, and on arriving at the top, we saw seated or lazily reclining on a green in front of the entrance of the stoccado [stockade], about fifty Chickasaw warriors, drest each according to his notion of finery, and most of them painted in a grotesque but not a terrifick manner. Many of them had long feathers in the back part of their hair, and several wore breast plates formed of tin [probably tarnished silver] in the shape of a crescent, and had large tin [silver] rings in their ears."[31]

By 1800, Americans were increasingly encroaching on remote, outlying Indian lands (see Figure 15). Ownership of much of the Indian land on the north side of the Tennessee River in present-day north Alabama and southern Tennessee was in dispute. Both the Cherokee and Chickasaw claimed parts of the area, although the Chickasaw claim was the stronger as a result of the preponderance of recorded historical evidence, especially the Treaty of French Lick in 1783, the Treaty of Hopewell in 1786, and the land declaration given to Piomingo by President Washington in 1794. American communications with the Chickasaw determined that the latter were amicable to ceding their claim

15. Approximate Chickasaw domain prior to the treaties of 1805, 1816, and 1818 (by author)

to the disputed land, which included the so-called Chickasaw Old Fields area south of present-day Huntsville in Madison County, Alabama. The primary reason for Chickasaw willingness to treat for the land cession was the pressure being applied to settle the large debt owed to trading houses for merchandise received over the years. According to R. J. Meigs, the Chickasaw owed nearly $50,000 to trading houses and individual traders. By early July 1805, arrangements had been made for the Chickasaw leaders to meet in the Chickasaw nation with the two appointed American commissioners, James Robertson and Choctaw agent Silas Dinsmoor. The negotiations were apparently held at a treaty ground located at or very near Big Town. The secretary of war, in fact, had instructed Robertson and Dinsmoor to hold the treaty at "the Principal Chickasaw town." The treaty ground was at or near the home of Wolf's Friend, for the commissioners were assigned quarters there for the duration of the negotiations. Malcolm McGee, who lived near the agency at "Hoolkie," served as one of the interpreters in his official position as an employee with the agency. The Treaty of Chickasaw Nation, as it was called, gave the United States a huge tract of land north of the Tennessee River in exchange for the low price of $20,000, over half of which was required to pay off the Chickasaw debt to John Forbes & Company. The disposition of the remaining $8,000 is unknown, but some or all probably went to various traders to whom money was owed. Despite a common misconception, the cession did not include all land on the right side of the river but rather just a portion that lay north of that part of the river that runs generally east-west in present-day north Alabama. References in various documents to land west of the "Big Bend" sometimes refer to that area as being "east" of the river and other times "north" of the river. Thus the Tennessee and present-day Alabama land ceded in 1805 generally consisted of the area at and northeast of the vicinity where the site of Griner's (or Grinder's) Inn was later located (about sixty-five miles southwest of Nashville) and an irregular area in a southeast-northwest direction from the Ohio River and including, on the south, land between the Tennessee River and the southern boundary of Tennessee. The latter area, combined with land ceded by the Cherokee, was designated Madison County, Mississippi Territory, in 1808. The remaining Chickasaw land north and east of the river, as discussed below, was later ceded in 1816.[32]

Reserved by the Chickasaw was one square mile of land "adjoining to and below the mouth of Duck River, on the Tennessee, for the use of the chief O'Koy [Okoye], or Tisshumastubbe" (later called Tishomingo?). Apparently this tract was later sold. Also, George Colbert and Okoye (Tishumustubbee) were granted $1,000 each "at the request of the National council, for services rendered their nation," and King Chinubbee was given "an annuity of one hundred dollars, during his natural life, granted as a testimony of his personal worth and friendly disposition." The treaty was signed by Robertson, Dinsmoor, King Chinubbee, George Colbert, Okoye/Tishumustubbee, Choomubbee, Mingo Mattaha, E. Mattaha Meko, William McGillivray, Tisshoo Hooluhta, and Levi Colbert. After the treaty was signed on July 23, Samuel Mitchell hosted a ball at the agency house on the 27th, which was attended by all or most of the whites present at the treaty, including the treaty secretary, Thomas A. Claiborne, as well as ex-Choctaw agent John McKee. Other whites, in addition to Malcolm McGee, included an army officer named R. Chamberlain, W. P. Anderson of Tennessee, John Pitchlynn, Christopher Oxberry, and William Tyrrell. Another was ex–vice president Aaron Burr, who happened to be there as he traveled up the Natchez Trace from New Orleans to Nashville.[33]

Of interest with regard to the treaty is that neither Wolf's Friend nor William Colbert is mentioned in the negotiations or appears among the signatories. Probable explanations exist for these absences. With regard to Wolf's Friend, Malcolm McGee recalled in 1841 that after the Spanish abandoned the bluffs, he "lost his influence in the nation, subsequently went to Phila. with General Wilkinson in 1799 & shot himself shortly after[ward] (having long suffered with the gravel),—on Duck River, near the mouth of Piney river, where he & Gen. [William] Colbert (and son-in-law) went to reside not long before." Thus, if McGee's recollected time of death and other facts are correct, Wolf's Friend was no longer living in July 1805.[34] The treaty commissioners probably lodged on his original home place, where members of his family probably still resided.

William Colbert had been invaluable in the late eighteenth century with regard to helping hold the Creek at bay in concert with Piomingo and other Chickasaws. Throughout his adult life, Colbert's methods had displayed political talents oriented toward solving problems through military means rather than by analytical diplomacy. He seems to have been impetuous and always eager for a fight at either real or perceived provocation. As discussed in Chapter 10 with regard to his confrontation with Wolf's Friend at Chickasaw Bluffs, he was also assertive within the tribe. He perhaps was not suited for, nor particularly interested in, working out disagreements with anybody, no matter what their race. Neither did he seem to display much concern for fulfilling financial obligations, as suggested by his defaulting on a partnership agreement with white man John Gordon in operating a stand and ferry at the Duck River crossing of the Natchez Trace in 1803. The ferry and buildings, erected by the U.S. army troops cantoned there during improvements of the Natchez Trace in that area, were given to them by the government. By 1805, Colbert had not contributed to the agreed-upon expense sharing of developing, operating, and maintaining the Duck River Ferry operation. Perhaps part of William Colbert's seemingly irresponsible behavior stemmed from his overindulgence in alcoholic beverages. Malcolm McGee reflected that he was "honest, brave, & respected—but the fire water lessened the respect entertained for him." McGee further described Colbert as a "middle sized [man], black eyes, full pleasant face, full of animation & never dulled—possesed of wit & pleasantry."[35]

With Piomingo dead by 1800, and Wolf's Friend no longer physically able or competent, the Chickasaw king and council realized that they possessed no one well qualified to effectively communicate and negotiate with the Americans regarding concessions and land cessions. Apparently at the encouragement of Benjamin Hawkins, at least, the Chickasaw decided to "appoint a head to trans-act their business." Because George Colbert had emerged as a sober, enterprising, conscientious war chief who had distinguished himself in the interest of his nation, he was by 1801 the Chickasaws' principal chief. The circa 36-year-old English-speaking Colbert was thus elected spokesman by the Chickasaw council in about 1800, according to Malcolm McGee and Benjamin Hawkins. This date is undoubtedly accurate considering that Colbert had obviously been the dominant spokesman for the Chickasaw at the Treaty of Chickasaw Bluffs negotiations in 1801 and at the Treaty of Chickasaw Nation negotiations in 1805. McGee related that thereafter George Colbert "was twelve years head chief of the Nation, & had the management of the affairs of state: Naturally the smartest man of the Colberts." A resident of Florence, Alabama, recalled that he was "tall, slender and handsome with straight black hair . . . down to his shoulders. His features were that of an Indian but his skin was lighter than that of his tribe."[36]

For reasons not entirely clear, but partially because of earlier complaints from Mississippi Territory governor Winthrop Sargent, Samuel Mitchell was replaced as agent by the secretary of war in early 1806. Mitchell afterward established a stand on the Natchez Trace north of present-day French Camp in the Choctaw nation, where he died in about 1811. His replacement, William Hill of Georgia, committed suicide before traveling to the agency. Thereafter a Quaker from Maryland, Thomas Wright, was appointed on May 27, 1806. Mitchell continued as agent and postmaster for several months while awaiting the arrival of Wright, who reached the nation in about November. Wright contracted the "Ague & fever" on August 10, 1808, and died on September 26 at the agency, where he was buried. The position went unfilled for about a year, until August 9, 1809, at which time James Neely from Nashville was appointed. When the Creek Indians became aggressive in 1812, the secretary of war replaced him with James Robertson, supposedly because of his expertise in dealing with Indians and because of his previous experience as agent during the 1790s. Robertson served until September 1, 1814, on which day he died at the agency. Robertson was buried there, undoubtedly near agent Wright's grave. By the end of September, a new agent, William Cocke from North Carolina, had been appointed. Under criticism after 1815 from James and Levi Colbert and other Chickasaws, he served until June 1818, after which Henry Sherburne from Rhode Island took charge of the agency. The sickly Sherburne resigned and returned to Rhode Island upon arrival of a new subagent, William Vans from Washington, in April 1820. Vans served as acting agent until the arrival of Robert C. Nicholas from Lexington, Kentucky, on September 17, 1820. Nicholas was fired in 1822 after complaints from Levi Colbert and others and was replaced by subagent Reodolphus Malbone, who became acting agent; he was ex-agent Sherburne's stepson and also from Rhode Island. In January 1824, a new agent, Benjamin Fort Smith, originally from Kentucky but lately from Hinds County, Mississippi, arrived at the agency, and Secretary of War John C. Calhoun fired subagent Malbone in February. In 1825 Smith was authorized to move the agency to present-day northwest Alabama, which was accomplished in 1826. Smith was eventually replaced after complaints from Levi Colbert and others, several War Department investigations of his conduct, and his subsequent abandonment of the agency in mid-1829. He was temporarily replaced by nation resident and subagent John L. Allen, who served as acting agent. Colonel Benjamin Reynolds from Tennessee, appointed on February 22, 1830, proved to be a capable agent during the trying 1830s. He served until March 3, 1839, when the Chickasaw Agency east of the Mississippi River was permanently closed. All agents except Thomas Wright and William Cocke had served as officers in the United States Army.[37] Much of the post-1800 history of the Chickasaw while east of the Mississippi River is tightly intertwined with the agency, its employees, and their federal superiors.

From the American standpoint there was one major downside to the enterprising segment of the mixed-bloods becoming dominant in affairs between the Chickasaw and Americans. In addition to the economic benefits to the Chickasaw derived from large plantations worked by black slaves possessed by some mixed-bloods, usually those whose white fathers had maintained consistent relationships with them, additional economic benefits were forthcoming through sale of merchandise within the nation by a few. Gibson (*The Chickasaws*) has emphasized that the Chickasaw refusal to allow white stand keepers, ferry operators, and similar positions along the Natchez Trace in 1801 was motivated by George Colbert's desire to monopolize such enterprises for himself and a few other mixed-bloods. Such a stance by both the full-blood and mixed-blood Chickasaws was not unfair, for they could not be blamed for wanting to keep white businessmen from flooding into the nation in pursuit of monetary rewards to the detriment of Chickasaw control over their own economy and government. However, Gibson also suggests that in the treaty of 1805 the mixed-bloods demanded payment in specie rather than goods in order to increase their sales of goods at annuity time, thus insinuating that the Chickasaw people were being exploited for the benefit of the mixed-blood merchants. He fails to mention in making this point that most or all of the $20,000 under that treaty was to be used to pay off debts incurred with whites. Regardless of the latter weak claim, Gibson convincingly demonstrates that some of the more enlightened of the Chickasaw mixed-bloods, primarily the Colberts and close relatives, were successfully able to manage the affairs of the Chickasaw by keeping exploitative whites out of the nation, unlike the situation in which whites "profited from the easy entree they enjoyed in every [other] Indian nation." Thus, as Gibson points out, the Chickasaw nation "continued as a self-governing community in the period before removal." Gibson contends that after 1800 the United States would gain no concessions from the Chickasaw without consent of prominent members of the Colbert family.[38] However, they were apparently acting according to the wishes of the majority of the mixed-bloods and full-bloods. Gibson's implied assertion that the Colberts were virtual dictators is highly unlikely.

A significant economic resource within the nation that has been overlooked by historians was the United States' Chickasaw Agency. It did not sell goods, farm products, or other items to the Chickasaw but it was responsible for circulating a great deal of federal money within the tribe every year. The agents often hired Chickasaws, usually full-bloods, to ride express with messages within and outside the nation to individuals or to post offices such as the ones at the Choctaw Agency and Columbus, Mississippi. No less than four dollars per day was paid to the riders, a significant amount in the early nineteenth century. In the first half of 1822, for example, Warpershetchu, Chistarnay, and Ushtartarubby were paid for riding express to the post office at Columbus. Other Chickasaws, both full- and mixed-bloods, were hired to use their wagons to haul wood, charcoal, building materials, and sometimes annuities from place to place, often to the agency. Others were hired to guard the annuities as they were transported to the agency or to other places of distribution. For example, in 1822 James Colbert and ten other Chickasaws under his supervision were paid $180 to guard the wagons carrying the annuity specie from the Chickasaw Bluffs to the agency. Both full- and mixed-bloods were also paid to provide hundreds of pounds of beef and vegetables for conferences and annuity distributions attended by hundreds of Chickasaws at the agency and elsewhere. Others, usually women, were paid by the agents to cook at the conferences and annuity distributions, and Chickasaw men were sometimes paid to provide the services of black slaves at these gatherings. Some mixed-blood Chickasaws were paid for the services of their slaves to work in the government-funded blacksmith shops. Sometimes both whites and Chickasaws were hired to build or repair structures at the agency or other places, such as the council house or the annuity storage house at Chickasaw Bluffs. On occasion structures were rented for boarding of American officials or for goods storage during treaty negotiations, annuity distributions, and other events. Full- and mixed-blood Chickasaws who traveled west to examine potential areas for tribal relocation were paid certain amounts per day. Of course, with their federal pay the agent and other employees purchased from Chickasaws goods, supplies, horses, and so on for the use of the agency and themselves. Some mixed-bloods even served as full-time employees of the agency, such as interpreters James Colbert and Jackson Kemp. All of these activities and others not mentioned brought many thousands of dollars into the nation between 1800 and 1838.[39]

After the opening of the War of 1812, the belligerent Red Stick faction of the Creek, having been emboldened by the rhetoric of anti-American Shawnee leader Tecumseh and his brother, "The Prophet," intensified its devastating raids on white settlers and settlements. Alarmed, the United States government appealed to the southern tribes to assist General Andrew Jackson's Army of the South in putting down the uprising. Because of the visit of Tecumseh (and possibly The Prophet also) to the Chickasaw in 1811, the U.S. government became fearful that they had influenced the Chickasaw to join their confederacy. When the Chickasaw allowed some marauding Creeks carrying stolen American property, white scalps, and a captured white woman to pass through the nation with impunity in the summer of 1812, Andrew Jackson became alarmed and sent a stern letter to George Colbert in which the Chickasaw were warned against future abetting. George Colbert soon put American fears to rest by writing letters to Tennessee governor Willie Blount. In the first he stated that "[t]he white people have a suspicion on us we the Chickasaws having concern with The Prophet's business, but there is nothing of it—We know that we are not able to make war with the United States." James Robertson, who had been appointed new Chickasaw agent on June 4, 1812, began to encourage the Chickasaw to furnish the requested military aid. After a major Chickasaw council called by Robertson in August 1812 and another in early 1813, Robertson reported that "[t]he Chickasaws are in a high state for war. They have declared war against the Creeks . . . and are ready to give their aid." This statement is confirmed by a January 1814 letter from George and James Colbert to Jackson, dictated to James by George, in which they expressed regret that the Chickasaw had been dissuaded by the War Department from joining Jackson's army. Continuing, the Colbert brothers stated, "If any of the Creeks attempt to pass through this nation we will kill the men & take the women & children prisoners[.] you may calculate on us doing our part, if we can have an opportunity, but it appears we are urged on by some & kept back by others[.] we start in six days to join the Chaktaws to scower the Black warrior [river]. I have got the war clubs that Mackey and his party were killed with, and will carry them along."[40]

In late 1813, George Colbert resigned as principal chief of the nation as a result of the Red Stick uprising, although he had much earlier become somewhat negligent with regard to affairs of the nation. He and William Colbert turned their attention to fighting the Creek. In November, William joined Colonel Gilbert Russell's command in present-day Alabama, and upon an attack against the Creek warriors at and near the "Beloved Ground" he recklessly rode among them and killed two warriors. William, George, Levi, and James Colbert later raised a military force of about 230 Chickasaw warriors, which left in March 1814 to join Colonel Russell at Fort Claiborne in present-day

Alabama. In addition to the Colberts, the Chickasaw leaders who joined the United States forces were William McGillivray, William Glover, James Brown, Samuel and Thomas Seeley, William Colbert, Jr., Thomas Thompson, Benjamin Duke, Tishomingo, Caryoucuttaha, and Chickwartubby.[41]

For the previous ten years or so William Colbert had mostly dropped out of sight with regard to activism within the Chickasaw nation. After moving from Tennessee back to the main settlement area in about 1805, Colbert had established a residence on the west side of the Tombigbee River a few miles north of the intersection of the Chickasaw-Choctaw border with the river at Plymouth Bluff. The Red Stick uprising, however, apparently revived his old fighting spirit displayed so often in the late eighteenth century. In late 1814 the Chickasaws attached to the command of John McKee and led by William and George Colbert attacked a Creek fortification in present-day south Alabama, destroyed it, killed several defenders, and captured eighty-five Creeks. After the war, William Colbert participated in two treaty negotiation conferences but otherwise kept a low profile. A few years prior to 1824, he and his wife, Ishtanaha, moved to the upper Chuckuatonchee Creek in present-day Chickasaw County. He died there on May 30, 1824, where he was undoubtedly buried.[42]

Fearful of Creek attacks into the Chickasaw nation, Robertson had taken defensive measures. In late 1813 he had directed the construction at the Chickasaw Agency of at least two blockhouses, reporting later to the secretary of war that his accounts were higher than usual due to "the necessity there was to prepare for the defence of this place against the disaffected Creeks. We are expected daily to be attacked. All the timbers for the Blockhouses had to be hauled nearly a mile." The feared attack on the agency and Hulka settlement never occurred, however. Without permission from the secretary of war, the aggressive Robertson also organized a Chickasaw military force, initially engaging twelve of the "most active & enterprising warriors as spies or rangers, to protect this agency, the white people living in this nation, the road & citizens who travel it." They were instructed to range about sixty miles southeast of the agency "so as to be out of the Stock range & about half way to the little Warrior Town on the Black Warrior river." He purchased from a merchant fifty pounds of powder and forty pounds of lead and contracted for 400 additional pounds of powder and 865 pounds of lead to be stored at the agency "for the defence of the Chickasaws & of the public property." By December 1814 he was commander of a force of fifty-four troops (probably Chickasaws but possibly U.S. soldiers), which he ordered to protect Colbert's Ferry, the U.S. mail, the post rider and horses, and the Natchez Trace. With regard to the latter, he had the troops escort groups of travelers through the dangerous parts of the trace. Robertson was also important as a communication link between the interior and the military and political officials, writing several informative letters to

General Jackson and others. Before the Red Stick uprising and War of 1812 were over in 1815, however, Robertson succumbed to a chronic health problem, said to be pleurisy or neuralgia, and died with severe brain inflammation at the agency on September 1, 1814, in the company of his wife and youngest son. He lay buried in the agency cemetery until 1825, in which year his remains were disinterred by the state of Tennessee and reburied in Nashville.[43]

To the numerous Americans who traveled down the Mississippi River on barges loaded with products to sell at New Orleans or Natchez, the wearisome trip back home over the Natchez Trace to Tennessee, Kentucky, and further points was an ordeal. Because of the lack of branch roads, some travelers were having to go many more miles than would have been the case otherwise. Also, there was no adequate road running southwest from the upper Tennessee that connected with the Tombigbee River, a direct shipping route to Mobile. Thus for two reasons a road was especially needed from the upper Tennessee River to the Chickasaw nation. In 1812 such a road, built by army troops, was completed. Before the road was completed, George Colbert, who opposed the road, complained to General Wade Hampton that its construction had not been approved by the Chickasaw. Hampton wrote a reply that apparently satisfied Colbert and persuaded him to drop the matter and allow construction to continue. The road became known as Gaines' Trace, after its 1807–1808 surveyor, Edmund P. Gaines. The road connected the Tennessee River at Melton's Bluff near the head of the Muscle Shoals to the head of navigation on the Tombigbee at Cotton Gin Port. From there it ran down the west side of the Tombigbee River toward St. Stephens in the Choctaw nation. Later, in May 1815, a council of headmen and warriors met with new agent William Cocke at the agency, partially to discuss a request from citizens of Tennessee to allow construction of a road to run about due south from the Tennessee River at Reynoldsburg, Tennessee, to an intersection with the Natchez Trace at Big/Old Town. George Colbert furnished 1,267 pounds of beef and thirty-five bushels of corn for this council, as well as hands to tend the cows and do the cooking. Councils were later held at King Chinubbee's house and at George Colbert's house west of present-day Tupelo. At the latter council, for which Colbert supplied 1,300 pounds of beef, "bread stuff," and salt bacon, fourteen Chickasaws signed a document granting permission for construction of the road. In March and April 1816 government and Chickasaw commissioners surveyed the road, and in 1817 the U.S. Congress appropriated $4,000 to aid Tennessee in its construction. The road as surveyed intersected the Natchez Trace "near the south end of the Chickasaw Old Town" (Figure 12). The Chickasaw commissioners, appointed by agent Cocke, were Captain James Brown and Kenncuttchee (also spelled "Cyacuttahay" and "Chigcuttalia"). Although not a well-known road now, at the time it was characterized by the U.S. commissioners as having great obvious value "to the citizens of the western part of Tennessee, Kentucky, Ohio and the Territories." George Colbert apparently did not oppose the road because of previous loss of traffic at Colbert's Ferry caused by construction of the Gaines' Trace. As a result of this and the Red Stick uprising, George had moved back to the central part of the Chickasaw nation in late 1813.[44]

Although the Chickasaw were claiming land located north and south of the Tennessee River, land-hungry Americans found it easy to encroach on these isolated areas. Patiently, the Chickasaw refrained from attacking the settlers, but they complained to the agent in expectation of their removal by United States authorities. Such was only done, however, after many had settled and after repeated and increasingly insistent complaints were made by the Chickasaw. By 1809 many white intruders had entered the outlying Chickasaw lands, some of whom were nothing more than outlaws but most of whom were people who only wanted to establish farmsteads. The agents and the War Department tended to ignore the intrusions unless crimes were committed against Chickasaws. In late 1811 and early 1812, for example, agent Neely reported that a number of hogs, cattle, and horses had been stolen from Chickasaws living near, east, and north of Colbert's Ferry and that Pitman Colbert had his house robbed of bacon, corn, a saddle, a bridle, two axes, three Bills of Exchange, eight horses, and a black slave. Some of these depredations occurred in spite of intruder removal only a few months earlier by United States troops from Fort Hampton at the mouth of Elk River (Figure 12). Agent Neely reported that upon exodus of the removal troops "the intruders is gathering faster than they did, & have settled down the Buffalow [River] near where some Indians live." The next year a Chickasaw called Factor's Son, who had a stand thirty-five miles north of Colbert's Ferry, was robbed of cattle; soon afterward the cattle and thieves were tracked by Captain David Dobbins and two other white men into Giles County, Tennessee, to the town of Pulaski. Under pressure from the Chickasaw in late 1814, agent Cocke and Captain John A. Allen, commander at Fort Hampton, acting under orders from the secretary of war, went into the area on the north side of the Tennessee River in present-day Alabama with a force of white soldiers and burned a number of farmhouses, as well as an iron works established on Shoal Creek by Nathaniel Taylor. The Chickasaw were much perturbed, however, when they discovered that Cocke and Allen had left undisturbed some intruders who had obtained permits from the United States military because of having rendered services to the army during the Red Stick uprising by furnishing meal, guarding Thomas Redush's grist mill on Elk River, and operating ferries. Cocke was later accused by a Chickasaw delegation to Washington, accompanied by a loose-cannon white man and enemy of Cocke named Wigton King, of having prevented removal of some intruders because he was connected to them by marriage, to which Cocke retorted that this circumstance had nothing to do with sparing the farms of those particular people.[45]

By 1816 the Chickasaws were adamant that all of the intruders be removed. By letter from Tishomingo and others to Opouy Hummah, George Pettygrove, and Samuel Seeley, the recipients were instructed to tell Cocke that there were at least 300 families settled on Chickasaw land and that many of them were "right in the heart of Colonel George Colbert's cow range, and are daily killing of his cattle." These, on "Stinking Bear Creek," plus an additional 100 new families attached to "Russels Settlement," were specifically mentioned. The number of families cited by Tishomingo may be overstated—but probably not. Earlier, in February, Tishomingo had threatened to go to war against them, stating that he would "go on & destroy the houses I find built on our Land and if blood should be spilt it will not be our fault." In that month, Cocke told the secretary of war that he did not have "the means of removing a single offender" and asked for his advice on what to do about them. The secretary of war responded in June that Cocke had no authority to personally order a military action against the intruders. However, by June Captain John A. Allen was again in the process of removing intruders, but on July 5 the secretary of war suspended the removals "until the results of the negotiations with the Chickasaw shall be known." He continued: "This delay will at least give them time to make their crops, and provide for the next year's subsistence."[46]

By mid-1816, the United States had persuaded the Chickasaw to enter into negotiations for the relinquishment of more land in present-day Tennessee and Alabama. The aggravating land encroachments and continued conflicting land claims with the Cherokee regarding the eastern areas south and north of the Tennessee probably partially influenced the Chickasaw to consider giving up some more of their land. Following instructions from Andrew Jackson, agent Cocke managed, despite a few problems, to arrange a conference with Chickasaw and Cherokee delegations at George Colbert's new home southwest of Old Town; his frame house, possibly similar to the one he had at Colbert's Ferry, was apparently the structure referred to as the Chickasaw Council House. A Choctaw delegation also attended, with regard to their northeastern boundary with the Creek, who were invited but did not make an appearance. American commissioners Andrew Jackson, General David Meriwether, and Jesse Franklin were successful in obtaining a treaty on September 20 that ceded to the United States all remaining land claimed by the Chickasaw on the east/north side of the Tennessee River and on the south side east of a line surveyed earlier in the year by General John Coffee. The Cherokee delegation tentatively agreed to relinquish their tribe's claims to some of the land ceded by the Chickasaw, including that on the south side of the Tennessee, which had been determined already to have been owned by the Creek. The tentative claim relinquishment

of the Cherokee was dependent on agreement of the tribe at a subsequent negotiation to be held in that nation, which indeed transpired before the end of
the year. The United States agreed to pay the Chickasaw $12,000 per year for
ten years. The eastern Chickasaw boundary south of the Tennessee in present-
day northwest Alabama and northeast Mississippi, therefore, was established
along a line running from the mouth of Caney Creek to its source, south from
there to Gaines' Trace, and along that road to Cotton Gin Port. The eastern
boundary farther south was the west bank of the Tombigbee River to an intersection with the Choctaw boundary at the mouth of Tibbee Creek.[47] Thus the
dwindling Chickasaw lands now consisted of a relatively small area in the
northwest corner of present-day Alabama, the north portion of present-day
Mississippi west of the Tombigbee River above Tibbee Creek, northwest from
the latter's headwaters to the Mississippi, the western portion of Tennessee, and
the adjoining southwestern part of Kentucky on the south side of the Ohio and
west of the Tennessee. In two years the northern portion in Tennessee and Kentucky would also be in the possession of the United States.

For the first time, the importance to the Americans of George and Levi
Colbert in obtaining land cessions was publicly exposed in the 1816 Treaty of
the Chickasaw Council House. George was awarded a generally four-by-four-
mile tract of land on the north side of the Tennessee River near his earlier
home on the south side and nearby ferry crossing. This area, located on the
west side of the Natchez Trace, had not been included in the cession of 1805.
The tract was obviously part of his extensive cattle range in that area, as indicated by part of the description of the tract: "[The tract] will include a big
spring about half way between his ferry and the mouth of Cypress [Creek], it
being a spring [branch] that a large cow path crosses . . . near where a cypress
tree is cut down." George Colbert did not live at the ferry by this time, as addressed above. He apparently continued maintaining his plantation/unfenced
cattle range on the Tennessee, probably by employing someone (his son Pitman?) to oversee it and operate the ferry. Colbert was rumored to have later
sold his treaty reservation for as much as $40,000, but there is no known docu-
mentation for this alleged transaction. However, documentation exists that
Andrew Jackson made a deal with a private citizen to provide $20,000 for pur-
chase of both George's and Levi's tracts at the treaty negotiations of 1818, as
discussed below.[48]

Levi Colbert, whose Indian name appears to have been Itawamba, and others also received reservations. Like George Colbert's reservation, some of these
were also on the east side of the Tennessee River. Sometime before 1812 Levi
had established a homestead about seven miles southwest of Colbert's Ferry on
the Natchez Trace at a place he or someone else named Buzzard Roost, where
he operated a stand until moving back to the main settlement in late 1813. He

then or soon afterward settled on the bluff on the west side of the Tombigbee River landing opposite the site of the future town of Cotton Gin Port and built a grist mill north of there on Old Town Creek. By 1816 Levi Colbert had replaced George Colbert as principal chief and spokesman of the nation, apparently as a result of George's disinterest. The treaty gave Levi two reserved tracts, containing forty acres each, that were to be about two and one-half miles south of his home, but on the east side of the river; their specific locations were to be selected by Colbert. Also, mixed-blood John McCleish (McClish), probably a son of former interpreter William McCleish, received a square-mile tract east of the Tennessee and encompassing his "settlement and improvements on the north side of Buffalo creek." The only full-blood to receive a reservation was district chief Apassantubby. His reservation, two miles square in size, was "on the north [or east] bank of the Tennessee river, and at its junction with Beach creek." [49] Perhaps it may be assumed that all four of these men were instrumental in persuading the Chickasaw to accept the terms of the treaty, especially after having obtained assurances that they would receive the reservations.

In October 1818 the United States paid the Chickasaw for improvements (land clearing, structures, and so on) made on the land ceded in 1816. Authorization for the payments for improvements, in the total amount of $4,500, was stated in Article 3 of the treaty; payments for improvements were also stipulated in the 1818 treaty, but dollar amounts were unstated. A receipt recently discovered in the National Archives is from Levi Colbert for money "to be paid into my hands as a compensation for any improvements which individuals of the Chickasaw Nation may have had on the lands surrendered to the United States agreeable to the Treaty made by Major General Andrew Jackson . . . [et al.] with the Chickasaw Nation in the year one thousand eight hundred & sixteen." Under the transaction, Levi Colbert, as chief of the nation by that time, received $2,000 for improvements on the east side of the Tombigbee River and $2,500 for improvements on land ceded on the north/east side of the Tennessee River. The unanswered question with regard to these payments concerns the disposition of the $4,500. Presumably, Levi would have distributed the money among the Chickasaws who had made the improvements. Some historians have concluded, however, that the $4,500 was nothing more than a bribe to facilitate cession of the land under consideration in 1818. This appears to be confirmed by the words of Andrew Jackson, who later stated that "presents offered to the influential chiefs, amounting to $4500, to be paid on the success of the negotiations . . . seemed to produce some sensible effect." Levi Colbert may have retained the entire $4,500 considering that his was the only name on the receipt for the money. [50]

The $4,500 paid to Levi Colbert in 1818 for the 1816 improvements thus appears to indeed have been a bribe. If not, secret cash payments given to the primary Chickasaw chiefs in 1816 certainly were. These payments, to Levi, George, William, and James Colbert and Tishomingo, probably awarded immediately after the treaty signing, were made without the knowledge of the general population, as explained by Jackson himself: "We have drawn upon the Department of War for the amount of those presents distributed to the Principal Chiefs, & which could not appear on the treaty: Secrecy was enjoined as to the names; Secrecy is necessary, or the influence of the Chiefs would be destroyed, which has been, & may be useful on a future occasion. The chiefs will accompany the Drafts, which we have no doubt will be duly honored & paid." The secret payments, in the amount of $1,000 to each of the chiefs, thus represent definite proof of bribery.[51] If the unconcealed $1,000 payments to George Colbert and Tishumustubbee in 1805 were not considered bribes by either party, the same cannot be said of the concealed 1816 payments for the same amounts.

Although the dispersal from the old fields had resulted in a loose and informal division of the Chickasaw population into four geographical areas, as reported by Nutt in 1805, formal organization came about as a result of the disorganized annuity distributions. In 1815, agent Cocke divided the nation into four districts, which at first caused objections from Tishomingo and "his party." In 1818, the annuities for 1817 and 1818 were paid by agent Sherburne to the chiefs of each of the four districts, identified by numbers. These districts encompassed all of the remaining Chickasaw land, located in present-day north Mississippi and northwest Alabama. The chiefs in 1818 were Samuel Seeley (District 1), William McGillivray (District 2), Tishomingo (District 3), and Apassantubby (District 4). In 1831, however, McGillivray was chief of District 3 and Tishomingo was chief of District 2. This switch of district numbers is confusing, but in any case Tishomingo's district was the northeast part of the nation and McGillivray's was the northwest part. A county named Tishomingo is presently located in the northeast corner of the state of Mississippi and one named Coahoma (McGillivray's Indian name) is located in the northwest part. Captain Isaac Albertson succeeded Apassantubby as chief of District 4 in or prior to 1831. District 4 appears to have been in the southeastern part of the nation (present-day Tupelo included) and District 1 in the southwestern part containing present-day Pontotoc and the Chickasaw Agency site. Prior to payment of the annuity in 1818, agent Sherburne was instructed to conduct a census of each district, which appears to have been primarily accomplished by subagent David Cook, probably with the assistance of James Colbert. This census determined that 3,625 Chickasaw men, women, and children were in the nation. Gibson (*The Chickasaws*) states that four divisions were established by the Chickasaw in 1824 "to accommodate an emerging public judicial system and to improve administration of the nation." These divisions, identified by village names located in the present-day Lee and Pontotoc Counties area, do not seem to correlate with the four larger geographical districts established for the purpose of paying annuities.[52]

The 1816 treaty also regulated the numerous non-Indian peddlers who had been "constantly traversing their nation from one end to the other." By Article 7, the agent was prohibited from issuing licenses to "entitle any person or persons to trade or traffic merchandise," in order to stop disputes, misunderstandings, and fraud. Any white person violating the regulation would forfeit his goods, which would be distributed evenly between the Chickasaw and the United States. At least one person was caught violating this provision of the treaty. In September 1818 Tishomingo seized the goods of a man trading without a license. Agent Sherburne held an auction at the agency, resulting in proceeds of $64.12, which was divided equally between the Chickasaw and the government. Tishomingo, assisted by subagent John L. Allen, did the same thing against two traders in 1831, but by that time the state of Mississippi had extended its laws over the Indian territories. The traders, John Walker and Marshall Goodman, later brought state charges against Tishomingo and subagent Allen in Monroe County, Mississippi, court, resulting in Tishomingo's temporary incarceration and a $500 judgment in favor of the traders.[53]

Not yet satisfied with regard to land acquisition, Andrew Jackson and other American officials continued to press the Chickasaw for more of their domain. By 1818 a boundary line separating the state of Tennessee from the newly admitted state of Mississippi had been surveyed by General James Winchester. The line ran west from a point about thirty-five miles downriver from Colbert's Ferry to the Mississippi River at a point south of Chickasaw Bluffs. Thus the line bisected the Chickasaw lands. In mid-1818, Andrew Jackson began to instruct agent Sherburne with regard to treaty arrangements for acquisition of the land north of the line. Despite some mistakes made with regard to logistics and other details, Sherburne arranged the conference for October 1818 at a council house located one mile east of Old Town and about three miles from George Colbert's home. The American commissioners, Andrew Jackson and Isaac Shelby, negotiated a treaty with George and Levi Colbert and others, signed on October 18, that ceded to the United States all remaining land in the states of Tennessee and Kentucky. This cession came to be called the Jackson Purchase. Although the final Tennessee-Mississippi boundary on the western end was discovered to be as much as four miles south of Winchester's line as a result of a survey error by him, the latter line was retained as the land cession boundary. In exchange for the land, the Chickasaw were granted $20,000 per year for fifteen years.[54]

Under the 1818 treaty, the Chickasaw in general received a new land reserve, on the east side of the Tennessee, and those reserves made to George and Levi

Colbert, John McClish, and Apassantubby in 1816 were confirmed. The 1818 tract to the Chickasaw, four by four miles in area on or near the Sandy River, included a salt lick spring and good timber. By a strange and cumbersomely worded clause in the treaty, the salt lick, with Levi Colbert and James Brown as trustees for the nation, was to be leased to a citizen or citizens of the United States who was to pay the Chickasaw in salt as the lease cost, but if the salt was sold for more than one dollar per bushel after two years following ratification of the treaty the entire reservation would "revert" to the United States. The Chickasaw later leased this tract to William B. Lewis and his attorney, Robert P. Currin, for the acquisition of salt, but the venture proved impractical. Later, by the treaty of 1830 at Franklin, Tennessee, the lease agreement was altered. The United States was to pay Levi Colbert and James Brown $2,000, and Lewis and Currin were to pay them on an annual basis "four bushels of salt, or the value thereof." Because that treaty was never ratified, as discussed below, the altered agreement became invalid. The U.S. Congress, in 1832–1833, declared the reservation forfeited to the United States. The Chickasaw, however, apparently protested this action, and in the Treaty of Washington in 1834 offered it to the United States at $1.25 per acre. The latter did not respond to the offer, holding the position that the Chickasaw had forfeited it. The Chickasaw, however, continued to claim the tract as late as 1852, at which time the secretary of war was instructed by the treaty of that year to take under consideration the possibility of paying them for it if he agreed that their claim was justified. Apparently he decided that the claim was unjustified. The tract reserved to Apassantubby in 1816 was to be sold to the United States for $500 after ratification of the 1818 treaty. This indeed occurred, on April 24, 1819, as documented by a receipt in the agency fiscal papers.[55]

The 1818 treaty also provided for "fair and reasonable compensation" related to improvements. Amounts were not stated and no such payments appear to have been made in addition to the $4,500 paid for improvements under the 1816 treaty, as discussed above. Agent Smith reported in 1824 that he was "repeatedly applied to by the people who had improvements on the ceded territory for the valuation of their improvements that was promised them by the government." Rumors circulating by 1826 asserted that George Colbert received and "pocketed" $20,000 for his 1816 reservation and that the 1818 reservation with the salt lick came under the control of Levi Colbert and James Brown and was sold for a large sum that Levi "pocketed." One reporter of these rumors, special U.S. agent among the Chickasaw John D. Terrell, opined that the rumor about Levi Colbert was probably false, which it was. As discussed above, that tract reverted to the United States.[56] The rumor about the $20,000, however, is verified, as indicated by the following excerpt from a letter written by Jackson to Thomas Kirkman of Philadelphia two days after the treaty was signed:

[I]t becomes necessary to raise more funds than we were authorized to draw on the Government for, to enable us to surmount the difficulties that presented themselves: to do this, it became necessary to apply to the citizens who were interested, or from principles of patriotism, would make the advance wanted on the security of the reserves secured to the Colberts by the treaty with the Chickasaw Nation of 1816. These reservations have been secured by treaty to the Colberts, their heirs and assigns, and the Deed executed to James Jackson, of Nashville, and the sum of twenty thousand dollars secured to be paid them in goods by you in Philadelphia within sixty days after the ratification of the treaty concluded with the Nation for all the lands in the States of Kentucky & Tennessee on the 18th instant . . . for which a bill has been drawn on this date on you for the sum of twenty thousand dollars, in merchandise, to be paid . . . by myself and Major William B. Lewis, of Nashville, in favor of Martin Colbert of the Chickasaw nation."

Continuing, Jackson informed Kirkman that if the government refused to pay him the $20,000, then he and James Jackson would "cheerfully pay to you the amount." He also stated that "it was the confidence in me that induced them [the Colberts] to take the draft—and it was this alone that secured to us the beneficial treaty that we have made, and the reservations are worth the money to be paid." Apparently, then, the three tracts received by George and Levi Colbert in 1816 were indeed sold to the United States on May 15, 1819, for $20,000 in goods, which were distributed as follows: George Colbert, $8,500; Levi Colbert, $8,500; James Colbert, $1,666.33; Samuel Seeley, $666.33; and William McGillivray, $666.33.[57]

In addition to the vaguely documented but apparent large amounts obtained primarily by the Colberts through special concessions and under-the-table sales of concessions, some payments to the principal Chickasaws are openly documented. Under Article 7 of the treaty, the major chiefs and military leaders of the Chickasaw were awarded $150 and $100, respectively. Accordingly, King Chinubbee, Tishomingo, Apassantubby, Samuel Seeley, William McGillivray, Levi Colbert, George Pettygrove, Immartarharmicko, James Brown, and the heirs of deceased Ickaryoucullaha were paid $150 by agent Sherburne on April 24, 1819. The ten military leaders who received $100 each were James Colbert, Cowemarthlar, Hopoyeahaummar, George Colbert, Hopoyeahaummar Junior, Immauklusharhopoyea, Tushkarhopaye, Illachouwarhopoyea, a second Immauklusharhopoyea, and Carlushahtahay on behalf of the children of deceased William Glover. The fact that the interpreter, Malcolm McGee, was also paid $150 indicates that all these payments were simply intended by the Americans to compensate the participants for their time and trouble rather than intended as bribes, as some historians have asserted. Presentation of gifts from visitors was a customary expectation of Indians of the Americas, and United States officials knew this. A separate payment to James Colbert in the amount of $1,089 to compensate him for a pickpocket theft while at a theater in Baltimore in June 1816 was interpreted by Gibson (*The Chickasaws*) to be a special concession for the purpose of obtaining his agreement to the treaty. This is also nothing more than a supposition, for it was customary for the United States to reimburse Chickasaws, whether mixed- or full-bloods, for crimes committed against them by whites.[58]

I feel that Gibson may have somewhat overstated the case in attempting to show that the mixed-bloods were in total control of the full-bloods and were running the nation as if it were their "commercial fief." For one thing, by 1830 there were hundreds of mixed-bloods representing many white trader progenitors, but the only family name Gibson mentions with regard to domination is Colbert. Moreover, besides George and Levi Colbert, he never cites the name of another Colbert as being part of this so-called "Colbert-led clique," nor does he identify other mixed-blood families of the clique. Gibson is undoubtedly correct in stating that the Colbert family was the most prominent of the mixed-bloods, but a generalized characterization such as "domination by the mixed-bloods" seems inappropriate. Perhaps "domination by the Colberts" would have been more appropriate. This is, in fact, supported by writings of some of the agents, including Robert C. Nicholas, who reported the following to the secretary of war in 1822: "[My suggestion for improvement of the quality of life in the nation] is resisted alone by Levi Colbert & his son [Martin] to whose commercial arrangements the welfare of this nation is ever made to give way—the father leans upon the son in all commercial transactions—the Chiefs lean upon the father & suffer themselves to be led by him. It is said openly & by men of respectability among them, that some of the Chiefs at least are susceptible of being bribed—of this fact I strongly suspect there are [documents] in the archives of the War Department that would be illustrative of it."[59]

The alleged elitism of all the mixed-bloods over all the full-bloods, therefore, is questionable. My research has revealed no substantial support for Gibson's insinuation that the mixed-bloods as a whole were manipulating and thus altering the general Chickasaw population's cultural, political, and social configurations.

By 1818 King Chinubbee, the titular ruler of the Chickasaw, was nearing the end of his life and reign. Less than a year after the signing of the 1818 treaty, he passed away at the age of about seventy-five on August 10, 1819. In the early 1790s he had been a resident of Long Town, as mentioned in Chapter 10. The location of his residence at the time of his death is unclear, but his probable widow is said to have lived just south of present-day Pontotoc before her death at an unknown date. A respected Chickasaw woman who was probably Chinubbee's widow, referred to as the "old and beloved" Queen Pucaunla, was given a $50 annuity in the 1832 Treaty of Pontotoc Creek. Chinubbee was succeeded by his 20-year-old nephew Chehopistee, who died soon afterward. He was succeeded by another of Chinubbee's nephews, Ishtehotopa, who would live through the removal and die in present-day Oklahoma.[60] Chinubbee's death marks the end of the period in which the foundation was laid for the final push by the Americans to end Chickasaw ownership of their ancient homeland.

12

The Road West

Because the Chickasaw were holding conferences and annuity payment assemblages at various places in the nation deemed suitable by the Chickasaw at the particular times, which gatherings were expensive and troublesome to the Chickasaws living at and near the places selected and, if held at the agency, the agent and his employees, agent Robert C. Nicholas complained to the chiefs and stated that he would no longer pay the annuities at the agency. The chiefs, therefore, decided to build a permanent council house. Nicholas supported the idea and recommended "building the house for a National purpose, when all who went could take their own provisions & thus avoid imposing on the hospitality and goodness of those who were able to feed them." The chiefs agreed and thereafter chose a site on which they built the council house (Figures 12 and 16). The site chosen was at the settlement of Pontitack on the Natchez Trace. Upon return to the nation with the 1820 annuities, Nicholas found that the house had been built, which he described and complained about: "On my return I found it up . . . [which] resulted in myself, clerk & guard being crowded into a common log cabin, one room alone of which we occupied, in size, 18 by 8 [feet], without floor, loft, doors or chimney, one side of it not chinked or daubed."[1]

Nicholas thereafter decided that he would pay the 1821 annuities at Chickasaw Bluffs, much to the consternation of the chiefs. They were insulted by rejection of the council house that they asserted to have been built for Nicholas's "accommodation at their own expense, where he paid the last annuity in." By February 1824, however, the chiefs and agent Benjamin Fort Smith had affirmed the permanent National Council House. In that month Smith paid Tookpulca for work "done in building a kitchen at [the] Council House." Alterations and improvements to the council house structure had likely been made by the chiefs prior to that time. In January 1824 Smith had paid the annuities there. Later additions were built under the direction of Smith, which

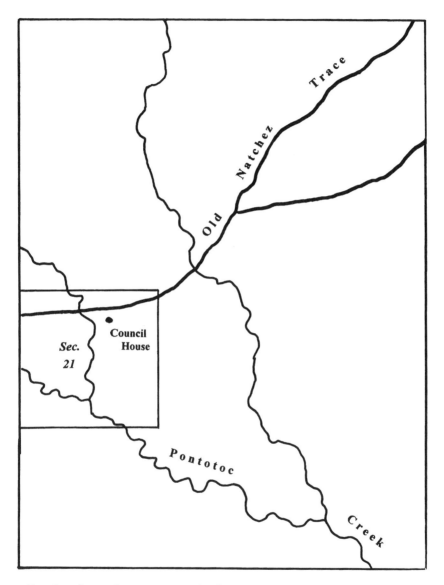

16. Drawing of part of an 1834 U.S. Land Office survey township plat showing the location of the last Chickasaw Council House north of Pontotoc Creek (by author, after copy at Mississippi Department of Archives and History)

resulted in the site becoming comparable to the agency complex. In about June 1826 Smith directed the construction of a blacksmith shop at the council house, apparently built by a man named Levi Thomas. In early 1828 Smith paid council house blacksmith A. W. Dew to build not only a new blacksmith shop but also a dwelling house for the blacksmith, a smokehouse, a corncrib, a stable, and possibly a new kitchen. The cost of construction came from the "fund appropriated by the Chickasaws for the support of a Blacksmith Shop at the Council House." The first blacksmith, assigned there by Smith in 1827, had been James Watkins, who was expelled by Levi Colbert because of excessive drinking and lack of production.[2]

Compatible with the government's "plan of civilization," conversion of the so-called "heathen" to European brands of religion began to be thrust on the Chickasaw near the turn of the nineteenth century when the missionary society of the New York Presbyterian churches sent the Reverend Joseph Bullen from Vermont to the Chickasaw. Bullen arrived in June 1799, made the purpose of his visit known to the Chickasaw leaders, obtained their cooperation, and presented several sermons. Encouraged by his hospitable reception, he left the nation with a plan to return and Christianize the Chickasaw. Upon returning with his family and another missionary, Ebenezer Rice, Bullen eagerly began to recruit people willing to listen to his explanations of Christian doctrine and principals. His son taught some to write their names and some to read and write on a rudimentary level by tutoring them in their homes through an interpreter. Bullen directed his religious teachings not only to Chickasaws but also to black slaves as well. Despite his good intentions, Bullen's visitation among the Chickasaw, which ended in 1803, was a general failure, partially because it established no organized religious infrastructure in the form of churches and schools. His work would have been significant with regard to opening the door for subsequent and consistent missionary work in the nation if any had been forthcoming in a timely manner.[3] However, eighteen years would pass before any of the denominations again made significant attempts to try to "save" Chickasaw souls in accord with ethnocentric Christian dogma.

Attempts to educate Chickasaws, however, did not always depend on the whims of missionaries. Even prior to the arrival of Bullen, education of some Chickasaws was occurring. James Colbert the younger was sent by his father to Pensacola, where he was working for the mercantile firm of Panton, Leslie, & Company in late 1783. He appears to have been taught to read and write under the care of Colbert's attorney, Anthony Hutchins of Natchez. Bullen stated in 1799 that Colbert was a "native of this country who had been baptized, reads and writes, is a man of property; one quarter Indian, is a sober man." That James the younger was indeed educated is illustrated by the fact that he sometimes served as interpreter for the Chickasaw agency in the early nineteenth century, often penned personal letters and additional letters for Chickasaw leaders who could not read and write, including his older brothers, George, William, and Levi, and witnessed with his signature Chickasaw *X* marks on various documents. As mentioned in Chapter 10, Piomingo made arrangements with James Robertson in 1795 to have his daughter educated, apparently in Nashville, at the expense of the War Department. In the very early nineteenth century, several Chickasaws were educated at the expense of the government, including Pitman Colbert, son of George. Pitman was schooled, at the request of his father, between 1803 and 1805 at Ellicott's Mills, Maryland, where he was boarded, clothed, and educated by John Ellicott. A young Chickasaw mixed-blood named J. Love also studied at Ellicott's Mills at that time. A son of Levi Colbert named Dougherty Colbert was boarded and schooled during the mid-1820s in Georgetown, District of Columbia, by Thomas L. McKenney, the superintendent of the Office of Indian Affairs. Between 1805 and 1808, James Robertson sponsored schooling in Nashville for two Chickasaw boys named J. [John?] Jefferson and James Wolf. The government reimbursed Robertson for their tuition, board, and clothing expenses, as it did in 1810 after he paid for the education in Nashville of two additional boys. These boys were the son and nephew of Miatubbe, "a respectable Chickasaw." The latter boys, evidently full-bloods, were said by Miatubbe to have learned "little but rudeness," but agent Thomas Wright found that they could "read & write tolerably." Miatubbe desired that the government furnish them additional education.[4] Some of these and other boys educated through white sponsorship became noted Chickasaw leaders in later life, such as Pitman Colbert, Dougherty Colbert, and James Wolf.

Aware that the religious sects were showing no interest in pursuing "education" of the Chickasaw, agent Robertson took matters into his own hands. Since 1803 various Chickasaw chiefs had been requesting establishment of schools in the nation, but the War Department had turned a deaf ear to their requests, submitted through agents Samuel Mitchell and James Neelly. In January 1813, however, Robertson started a school for Chickasaw children at the agency without first asking permission of the War Department. He hired Thomas Love, a white resident of the nation married to a Chickasaw, to build the schoolhouse at a cost of $50. The schoolhouse was likely a one-room log structure. The teacher, unfortunately, was a deceitful, self-serving white man named Wigton King. Apparently paid by the children's parents, King began teaching the English language, as well as reading, writing, arithmetic, geography, and bookkeeping "in order to encourage the institution & civilization in the Chickasaw country," as stated by Robertson. After construction of the schoolhouse, Robertson suggested to the secretary of war that a government allowance of $200 per year for two years would enable the teacher "to teach those children whose parents are not able to pay for their Education & would wish their children to be taught." Robertson further stated that if this was not done, the institution would likely "fall through, as the few subscribers he [King] has at present will be insufficient to support him." The school apparently indeed had a short life, for there is no evidence that the secretary of war approved funding, and prior to his death in September 1814, Robertson had for unknown reasons expelled King from the nation. After Robertson's death the ambitious King reportedly returned, stole a private letter of Robertson's, and naively wrote to the secretary of war of his desire to be appointed Chickasaw agent. Two years later, in July 1816, the apparently smooth-talking King returned again and made an enemy of Tishomingo, who demanded that agent William Cocke expel him from the nation because of "rioting, drunkardness, seditious behavior, house breaking, and entering into negro quarters disturbing the peace of families in the neighborhood."[5]

In 1819 religious sects once again turned their attention to the Chickasaw nation after the United States Congress passed a law in that year that encouraged missionary societies to participate in providing both religious and secular education for native American children. Those that chose to do so were to be supported by federal funds, which would reimburse them for providing free tuition to the students. The first sect to construct a school among the Chickasaw, the Elk Presbytery in Tennessee, Cumberland Presbyterian Association, sent Robert Bell to serve as superintendent. Bell had previously ministered among the Chickasaw during brief visits, on at least one occasion holding services at Levi Colbert's home on the bluff west of Cotton Gin Port (Figure 12). In 1820 Bell, Samuel King, and James Stewart met with Colbert and expressed their desire to build a school for Chickasaw children. Colbert called a meeting of chiefs and leaders with them at his house, resulting in approval of the establishment of the school, which, in addition to literary training, would provide instruction in the mechanical arts and agriculture. The school soon opened in Levi's house, with the Reverend Bell and his wife providing instruction. One of Bell's sons supervised the construction of temporary log buildings at the site selected, about three miles south of Colbert's house at the foot of the bluff. Later, using hired help, more substantial structures were built, including classrooms, student housing, a blacksmith shop, a saddler's shop, and a tanyard; other buildings associated with a farm operation were also established. Assistance in operating the school was provided for a time by the Reverend John C. Smith and his wife. With the continued support of Levi Colbert and most of the other Chickasaw leaders, the school, named Charity Hall, generally operated successfully. Fifteen to thirty students attended each session prior to its closing in about 1832 as a result of financial obstacles and a sharp decline in students because of disconcertion caused by removal negotiations.[6]

Beginning in 1819 the Methodists and Baptists began to pay attention to the Chickasaw on a limited basis. A Methodist circuit rider, the Reverend Alexander Deavers, visited the Chickasaw on occasion for several years beginning in 1821, usually holding camp meetings with the aid of an interpreter before moving on to another tribe. In 1827 ministry was continued by the Mississippi Conference of the Methodist Church. Efforts were mostly directed at the Choctaw, but the Chickasaw occasionally received attention from the missionaries. For a time after 1819 the Baptist Board of Foreign Missions sometimes sent the Reverends John A. Ficklin and Stark Dupuy among the Chickasaw, and in 1828 the Reverend John A. Ware apparently established a short-lived Baptist mission in the vicinity of Tockshish (Figure 12). The 1833 field notes of the Chickasaw Cession surveyors mention a "Camp Ground" church located about three miles northwest of Tockshish, which might represent this poorly documented establishment.[7]

The most active missionary society to enter the Chickasaw nation, the Presbyterian South Carolina–Georgia Synod, began to build its first mission and school in 1821 after its representatives received a positive reception from Levi Colbert and other chiefs at Colbert's home in June 1820. Soon afterward, the synod's representatives, the Reverend David Humphries and ministry candidate Thomas C. Stuart, attended a stick-ball game at George Colbert's home and plantation near present-day Tupelo, where the missionaries consulted with the Chickasaw leaders and gained written approval for a mission and school. Leaving there, the missionaries traveled to James Colbert's home at or near Tockshish, where another conference with Chickasaw leaders occurred. Stuart was soon appointed superintendent of the Chickasaw missionary activities and remained in that position until the imminent Chickasaw removal caused cessation of operations. Reverend Stuart's first mission and school, named the Monroe Mission, was located on a ridge west of the Natchez Trace in present-day southwestern Pontotoc County (Figure 12). The school/mission, student housing, and other buildings were partially constructed in 1821, at which time the mission accepted day students from the neighborhood only. Upon completion of structures in 1822, students from the entire nation began to be boarded there. In 1823, the Reverend Hugh Dickson arrived and in cooperation with Stuart established church services for Chickasaw, white, and black adults and their families, either at the Monroe Mission or at a separate location about one mile north of the mission where Stuart is shown on one of the Chickasaw Cession plat maps prepared by the U.S. Land Office to have been residing in 1833. After establishment of the Monroe Mission, the Reverend Stuart saw to the construction of more schools/missions with the aid of tribal annuity funds in the amounts of $5,000 for construction and $2,500 a year for operations. This money was subtracted from the annual annuities and passed on to Reverend

Stuart through the Chickasaw agents. The new missions/schools included one established near Tockshish in 1824. When the Monroe Mission closed in 1830, its students were transferred to Tockshish. This mission operated until 1834. In 1825 construction began on a third mission, named Martyn, located at a place called Pigeon Roost a few miles southwest of present-day Holly Springs, Mississippi, in Marshall County (Figure 12). Martyn operated until 1832. A fourth mission, also initiated in 1825, was located southeast of the new Chickasaw Agency (Figure 12) in present-day Colbert County, Alabama. It was named Cane (or Caney) Creek Mission after the nearby creek by that name. Like Martyn, it closed in 1832. Of course, additional missionaries/teachers were sent to the nation to operate the new establishments. After the exodus of the Chickasaw in the following years, Stuart continued his ministry in the area. He died in Tupelo, Mississippi, in 1882.[8]

In 1825 an Indian school was established in Scott County, Kentucky, that afforded Chickasaw parents an opportunity to obtain better and more advanced education for their children than that provided at the missions. Founded by United States senator Richard M. Johnson, the Choctaw Academy eventually accepted children from tribes other than the Choctaw. By late 1834 the U.S. Indian Department was paying from tribal funds the clothing and traveling expenses of Chickasaw boys bound for the academy. For example, in 1834 and 1835 agent Benjamin Reynolds covered expenses for John B. Love, Stephen Perry, Maxwell Frazier, William Brown, Levi Perry, John Hall, Logan Albertson, Benjamin R. Albertson, Robert Johnson, Thomas H. Benton, Shtokaway's son, Takintubby's nephew, and at least eleven other boys, all of whom were between the ages of eight and sixteen. Three of the boys, Stephen Perry, Maxwell Frazier, and John B. Love, could already either read or both read and write. These three students had probably previously been schooled at one of the mission stations, none of which was still operating. In June 1839 enrollment at the academy included twenty-four Chickasaws, twenty Choctaws, and a number of students from additional tribes.[9]

One of the primary causes for decline of the missions in the several years before Chickasaw removal was acts passed by the state of Mississippi between 1828 and 1830 that nullified tribal laws and made the Chickasaw subject to Mississippi laws. Therefore a tribal law that forbade liquor trafficking and consumption became void. According to the missionaries, this caused a significant increase in alcohol consumption as a result of unregulated peddling within the nation. Thus this "orgy of intemperance," as it was termed by Gibson, combined with the depression and demoralization caused by loss of Chickasaw rights and increasing pressure to give up their homeland to the Americans, resulted in significant loss of Chickasaw interest in the white man's religion and education. In a broader sense, the loss of tribal rights was instrumental in breaking the spirit of the Chickasaw and converting more people to a small but growing removal segment of the population.[10]

For years the Chickasaw Agency house and other buildings had been difficult to maintain, as they were in December 1824 when agent Smith recommended construction of a new house rather than repair of the "dilapidated" and "decayed and fallen to pieces" existing one. With permission of Superintendent of Indian Affairs McKenney, Smith contracted with Robert Wilson of Natchez for building of a frame house eleven feet high, forty feet long, and twenty-six feet deep, with a gallery nine feet wide in the rear and two sixteen-foot-square rooms divided by a central hallway eight feet wide containing a stairway. It also was to have a fireplace in each of the rooms and two bedrooms above the lower rooms with windows in each gable end. Thus the eleven-foot height would not have included the gabled second floor, unless it was a half-story. Much to the consternation of the chiefs, however, Smith had the new house built near the south bank of the Tennessee River not far from the Cane (or Caney) Creek Mission in present-day Colbert County, Alabama (Figure 12). Rather than build it of wood as he initially planned, Smith had it built of brick. Also, he seems to have dropped Wilson as his builder, and it is not certain that Smith followed the original plan mentioned above. Apparently, however, the final structure was a one-and-a-half or two-story house, and by mid-1826 the house and outbuildings were finished. Afterward, other structures were built, including a kitchen sixteen feet square, a smokehouse fourteen feet square, a stable and corncrib combination with a twelve-foot passage between them, and a blacksmith shop. In 1830 subagent John L. Allen added another smokehouse for his use, as well as an additional kitchen, stable, and "lumber house" for "taking care of Indian packs when visiting the Agency on public business." Evidently Allen and the agent shared the house. In 1833, agent Reynolds allowed his blacksmith, John A. Caudle, to build a dwelling house and kitchen for himself and his family. In that same year, the first blacksmith shop accidentally burned, after which Caudle built a new one.[11]

After establishment of the new agency, King Ishtehotopa and the primary chiefs submitted a petition to President John Q. Adams complaining that Smith's moving of the agency to a remote part of the nation had resulted in their being "destitute" of an agent, as well as a blacksmith. They wished to know whether the president agreed with the agency removal to that location. Already aware of the dissatisfaction of the chiefs, Smith had previously written McKenney a long justification for moving the agency, to which no objection was forthcoming. Moving of the agency appears to have been both the direct and indirect cause of most of the Chickasaw dissatisfaction with some of Smith's other activities in the years to come.[12]

By 1825 the United States was in the process of girding for a determined ef-

fort to persuade by any means at its disposal the Chickasaw to cede the remainder of their land east of the Mississippi River in exchange for land in the west.
Because of the tribe's unhappiness occasioned by the abrogation of tribal law,
white settlers pressing against its boundaries, intrusions by settlers on some
parts of its land, whiskey peddlers, frequent offenses committed against its citizens by unscrupulous whites, and the debilitating effect of being unwanted by
a people to whom it had been loyal since the Revolutionary War, federal and
state officials felt the time had finally come when the remaining Chickasaw
land could be obtained with little difficulty. At the urging of the Americans,
the Chickasaw agreed to a council in October 1826 to be held at the home of
John McClish, located about six miles eastward of the old agency site. Just prior
to the council, however, the Chickasaw leaders changed their minds and informed agent Smith that the council must be held at the National Council
House that had been established by them in 1821 at the site of Pontitack. Reluctantly, the Americans removed the supplies to the council house, where
the conference began on October 16. Following an opening statement by the
American commissioners (John Coffee and Thomas Hinds) that voiced all
the negative reasons the Chickasaw should agree to surrender their land and all
the positive reasons they would be better off in the west, Martin Colbert, son
of Levi, delivered a response from the latter and others. Interpreted by Malcolm
McGee, the speech greatly surprised and disappointed the naive and once optimistic commissioners. In part, the speech was as follows:

> We never had a thought of exchanging our land for any other, as we think
> that we would not find a country that would suit us as well as this we now
> occupy, it being the land of our forefathers, if we should exchange our
> lands for any other, fearing the consequences may be similar to trans-
> planting an old tree, which would wither and die away, and we are fearful
> we would come to the same [end] . . . We have no land to exchange for
> any other. We wish our father to extend his protection to us here. . . . Our
> father the President wishes that we should come under the laws of the
> United States; we are a people that are not enlightened, and we cannot
> consent to be under your Government. If we should consent, we should
> be likened unto young corn growing and met with a drought that would
> kill it.[13]

Information in a recently discovered document related to the 1826 negotiations, however, suggests that Levi Colbert's opposition to removal was at least
partially personal. Despite the fact that Levi had already obtained thousands
of dollars primarily through sale of his 1816 treaty reserves, he was still un-
satisfied. In consultation with John D. Terrell, special agent sent by the president

to "prepare the minds" of the Chickasaw for removal, Colbert presented the following terms to Terrell three days prior to the negotiations:

> This nation contains one hundred miles square. We must have one third more land west of the Mississippi River than we have here.
> Some six or seven dollars per head for cattle.
> A reasonable price for such articles as cannot be removed.
> A reasonable price for improvements.
> Two square miles at his home residence.
> Same at his mills.
> The same at his cowpens—And five or six square miles about Buzzard Roost for his relatives.

Colbert also related to Terrell that "very few, if any other reservations would be required." Thus Colbert wanted, in the event of a removal treaty, at least 7,040 acres reserved to him and some of his closest relatives. Although the records of the negotiations do not reflect that Colbert asked for these terms during the treaty councils, Terrell undoubtedly related them to the American commissioners prior to initiation of the official negotiations. They were probably immediately rejected by the commissioners, and word of the rejection was probably passed on to Colbert. This would explain why Colbert, in turn, rejected the idea of removal in response to the opening speech by Coffee and Hinds. Despite several additional talks on the subject from both the Chickasaws and the commissioners, the latter including William Clark, who arrived eight days late, Levi Colbert and the other primary leaders steadfastly refused to sell even a portion of their remaining land and would not consider traveling west to look at a potential new area to which to move. These resolute Chickasaws, in addition to Colbert, were King Ishtehotopa, Tishomingo, Pisiatantubbe, Samuel Seeley, William McGillivray, Emmubbee, Ashtamatutka, John McClish, Martin Colbert, and others.[14]

In a report following the treaty negotiations, Terrell stated that he believed a treaty would have been accomplished if it had not been for the white men in the nation, whom he described as "the worst enemy of the treaty." In a separate letter, he related that the rumors about George and Levi Colbert secretly receiving large sums of money from sales of their 1816 and 1818 reservations greatly influenced opposition to the treaty. To pacify the Chickasaw following Levi Colbert's earlier rejection, Terrell claimed, John Coffee had offered reservations to "almost everyone," but acceptance of this offer had to be rejected by the whites, mixed-bloods, and full-bloods because of their earlier strong opposition to a treaty. Terrell opined that if all the white men were removed from the nation a large band would remove to the Arkansas Territory within six months if land was obtained and relatives, friends, and the others would thereafter follow. He also reported that all but a few mixed-bloods and many of the whites and full-bloods later stated that they wished the treaty propositions had been accepted but had been afraid to speak out because of the earlier "outrage" against a treaty. Terrell related that Pitman and Martin Colbert, sons of George and Levi, sided with the whites in opposition to a treaty and were able to influence their fathers accordingly.[15]

Despite Terrell's opinions and Levi Colbert's initial desire to make a personal profit from a total cession of Chickasaw land, opposition to removal in 1826, according to Gibson (*The Chickasaws*), came from a unified core of mixed-bloods possessing large established income-producing farms and herds of livestock—men who would be greatly affected by the trouble and expense of relocating. This is not to say that the poorer full-bloods and mixed-bloods favored removal. Most did not, simply because they viewed as distasteful abandonment of the land of their ancestors. The more advantaged of the mixed-bloods, according to Gibson, were blamed by the embarrassed commissioners for having caused their defeat at the 1826 negotiations.[16] In reality, the majority of both full- and mixed-bloods, supported by the white men with Chickasaw families, were probably unified against removal at that time because of confusion and uncertainties caused by this first formal attempt by the government to obtain their remaining land east of the Mississippi River.

Disappointed by the rebuff and irritated at the negotiation approach used by the 1826 commissioners, Thomas L. McKenney included the Chickasaw in a tour of most of the Indian nations in 1827. By now he and most other Americans had concluded that it would be in the best interest of the Chickasaw, under the negative circumstances mentioned above, for them to remove west of the Mississippi River, where they could live in peace without interference from Americans. The purpose of his visit to the Chickasaw was to convince them of this. Avoiding contact with agent Smith, who had fallen out of favor with some of the Chickasaw chiefs, including Levi Colbert, McKenney came down the Natchez Trace to the Monroe Mission in early October 1827. He soon traveled eastward to Levi Colbert's home near Cotton Gin Port and set up camp. At a conference on October 9 in Colbert's "Council-Room" with Colbert and other leaders, and with Malcolm McGee as interpreter, McKenney delivered a sensible, sensitive talk in which he sympathized with the Chickasaw dilemma while emphasizing the future benefits to their offspring of reestablishing themselves in a new home west of the river. McKenney was gratified when Levi Colbert, Tishomingo, and William McGillivray responded in writing that they would go and look at the land west of the river, which was the first Chickasaw acknowledgment that removal would be considered. At the conference, McKenney presented vouchers that instructed agent Smith to provide cash payments to King Ishtehotopa, Levi Colbert, and other major leaders, being George Colbert, James Colbert, Tishomingo, Toopulaco, Eniataushta, Hemalota, Samuel Seeley, George Pettygrove, Pistallotubbee, Emotawahto, Stemaluta, William McGillivray, Emmubbee, Pecsarhtubby, James Brown, Byhakatubby, and Thomas Shico. Smith, who was highly offended by McKenney's snub, made the payments, which varied between $50 and $25. Malcolm McGee also received $25 by order of McKenney. In addition, McKenney purchased $245 worth of goods for the Chickasaw leaders from Cotton Gin Port merchant Stephen Daggett and directed Smith to pay him.[17]

A Chickasaw exploring party indeed set out for the trans-Mississippi territory after McKenney instructed agent Smith, on June 10, 1828, to make an estimate of the expenses of twelve Chickasaws in going to St. Louis, as well as those of John Bell of Cotton Gin Port and subagent John B. Duncan. In October Duncan conducted the first Chickasaw exploring party, led by Levi Colbert, to St. Louis, where it joined other Indian exploring parties, including a Choctaw group. There they received instructions from William Clark and spent the next few months, conducted by the Reverend Isaac McCoy and escorted by Captain G. H. Kennerly, traveling around in the lands west of the Arkansas Territory and state of Missouri observing potential areas for possible relocation. The Chickasaw group returned unimpressed with the lands they had visited because none resembled or seemed comparable to the prairies and woodlands of north Mississippi and northwest Alabama.[18]

Meanwhile, white intruders were continuing to settle on Chickasaw lands. These intruders were usually ignored by the War Department until treaty negotiations for removal of the Chickasaw became imminent. Prior to the 1826 conference at the council house, agent Smith and subagent Duncan had raised a force of white volunteers to remove intruders. Under the direction of Duncan, two companies under Captain John W. Byrn and Captain James Benham left the agency on August 26 and in fifteen days covered an area from the mouth of Caney Creek on the Tennessee River southwestward to the Tombigbee River, destroying sixteen settlements by burning the houses and fences and cutting crops. A second expedition under Benham left the agency on September 17, met Duncan at the mouth of Caney Creek, and proceeded along the whole extent of the Mississippi-Tennessee boundary to the Chickasaw Bluffs. In twelve days Duncan and Benham's force abolished twelve farm settlements using the same method as before. In May 1829, prior to the Treaty of Franklin, a man named Joel W. Winston led a group to remove additional intruders, and immediately after the treaty, subagent Allen, acting under instructions from agent Reynolds, conducted another removal of intruders, one of whom was reported to be on "Colbert's Island" (present-day Koger's Island, upstream from Colbert's Ferry). A number of intruders were arrested, including Oliver Livingston, Samuel Norris, and John Hardcastle, who were taken by Allen to prison in Huntsville, Alabama.[19]

Despite the determined antiremoval position articulated by Levi Colbert in his 1826 speech and his dissatisfaction with the lands observed west of the river, which have been interpreted as nothing more than delaying tactics for the purpose of forcing the United States to offer the best possible terms for the inevitable removal, the Chickasaws agreed to another treaty conference at Franklin, Tennessee, in August and September 1830. Realizing the importance of this conference, Andrew Jackson, now president, opted to join the commissioners, Secretary of War John H. Eaton and John Coffee. The resulting Treaty of Franklin (including a supplement) saw the Chickasaw agreeing to relinquish their land and remove west of the river if a suitable place could be found during a prompt, second exploration in the west. If no suitable place could be found, the treaty was to be null and void. Among several concessions in favor of the Chickasaw, the United States agreed to pay all expenses of the removal if suitable land could be located. Emulating the previous Choctaw treaties, the 1830 Chickasaw treaty gave individuals the option of accepting fee simple half-section or quarter-section reservations on which they could reside indefinitely under the laws "of the whites" or later move west if so desired. If they did later decide to move, the government would pay them $1.50 per acre for their reservations. The commissioners initiated the award of fee simple reservations four sections in total size to each of the principal Chickasaws, being Levi Colbert, George Colbert, Tishomingo, William McGillivray, and Samuel Seeley, Senior. In addition, James Colbert, James Brown, John McClish, and Isaac Albertson would each receive two-section reservations. Seventeen named full-bloods, two mixed-bloods, and Malcolm McGee would receive one-section reservations. In a separate article, Levi Colbert was to receive an additional section of land to be located wherever he chose. In addition, the treaty stipulated that George Colbert was to retain Colbert's Island (Koger's Island) in the Tennessee River but would relinquish it to the United States for $1,000 consideration upon his moving west. The accommodating commissioners continued to agree to personal whims, including paying off a debt of James Colbert's and reimbursing Levi Colbert for a stolen horse by giving them a single section of land that they could sell. Also, agent Reynolds was to receive five quarter sections of land and subagent John L. Allen's wife was to receive a quarter section. Articles of more substance and importance to the general population included supply of 300 rifles, 300 pounds of powder, 1,200 pounds of lead, 300 copper or brass kettles, 600 blankets, and 3,000 pounds of leaf tobacco; purchase of their stock except horses and of their farming utensils; supply of new utensils upon arrival in the west; supply of meat and corn rations for the period of a year to each family upon arrival in the west; construction in the west of a council house and two houses of public worship that could also be used for schools; a blacksmith for twenty years; a millwright for five years "to aid them in erecting their saw and grist-mills"; $2,000 a year for teaching of the Christian religion; and education of twenty boys per year at the expense of the United States. Continuing to agree to anything Levi Colbert desired, the government agreed that Levi's two youngest sons, Abijah Jackson Colbert and Andrew Morgan Colbert, would be educated under the personal care of the president of the United States. Not to be left out, George Colbert was likewise given the right to have his grandson, Andrew J. Frazier, educated in a like manner.[20]

Accompanied by agent Reynolds, the second trans-Mississippi exploration party left on October 15, 1830, again under the lead of Levi Colbert. After examining the potential lands north of the Red River, Levi Colbert and others voiced their desire to explore south of the river. A probably bewildered Reynolds undoubtedly did not agree with this, for the land south of the Red River was claimed by Mexico. Reynolds, therefore, returned to the nation, while Colbert and all or some of the other Chickasaws crossed into the Mexican territory and examined land between the Red and Sabine Rivers. Upon the group's return to the nation, Levi Colbert and thirty-six other chiefs informed President Jackson by a letter composed at a large council held in May 1831 at the Chickasaw Agency that the only suitable area inspected in the west was land between the Red and Sabine Rivers adjoining the west boundary of the state of Louisiana and that they would move there if said land could be procured.[21] The Chickasaw never attempted to negotiate with Mexico for that land, and the United States apparently made no offer to assist them in such an effort.

With no suitable land located on the exploration in 1830–1831, the Treaty of Franklin was still in limbo. Reynolds was later instructed by General John Coffee and John H. Eaton to commence consulting with the Chickasaw regarding a further attempt to find suitable land in the west. In late 1831 Reynolds hosted a large conference at the agency for the purpose of encouraging the Chickasaw to negotiate with the Choctaw for part of their land in the west already obtained after the Treaty of Dancing Rabbit Creek in 1830. Beginning about March 21, 1832, Coffee, Eaton, and Thomas Hinds, acting under directions of President Jackson, began holding negotiations with the Chickasaws and Choctaws and facilitating negotiations between the two tribes for the purpose of securing a home for the former in the western Choctaw land. Pamphlets bearing the commissioners' talks were printed and delivered to each tribe. At least Coffee was at a conference at the Chickasaw Agency in April, which "a large concourse of Indians" attended. On April 22, Coffee sent express letters by G. W. Long to Levi Colbert regarding the "subject of the proposed arrangements between the Chickasaw & Choctaw nations for a country to settle the Chickasaws west of the Mississippi." The government wanted the Chickasaw to combine with the Choctaw under one government, but the Chickasaw wished to remain separate and the Choctaw likewise objected to such a confederacy. Moreover, Levi Colbert perceived the land under consideration to be inferior to the other Choctaw land. Thus these negotiations, conducted between March 21 and May 1, 1832, failed to result in acquisition of part of the Choctaw territory, thereby nullifying the Treaty of Franklin.[22]

Despite having obtained no land in the west, the Chickasaw finally ceded all their land east of the Mississippi River to the United States by the Treaty of Pontotoc Creek on October 20, 1832. The treaty negotiations, held at the National Council House, were controversial during and afterward. In Gibson's opinion, the solitary United States commissioner, John Coffee, "drove a treaty down their throats with threats and the old government trick of withholding the Chickasaw annuity until the chiefs had signed the treaty." This statement, which Gibson did not support with explanations, is a misleading oversimplification. It also reflects negatively on the intelligence of the Chickasaw. The text of the treaty, however, was indeed complicated, technical, confusing, and verbose, and anyone past or present would have to devote much study to the document in order to understand it completely. Much of the minutia in it, however, resulted from an attempt to cover all bases presented at the negotiations by the Chickasaw representatives. After signing of the treaty, the Chickasaw found objections and loose ends, which resulted in a supplement covering the previous omissions, primarily with regard to reservations and personal wishes of some of the Chickasaws. The supplement was signed on October 22. Gibson claims that because Levi Colbert was sick and apparently not present at the negotiations, the Chickasaw had no effective voice with regard to the treaty and supplement. This assertion is questionable, for both George Colbert and his educated son, Pitman Colbert, were at the negotiations, as were Martin, Dougherty, and Alexander Colbert, all of whom were educated adult sons of Levi. Levi Colbert was definitely consulted by Chickasaw treaty delegates with regard to all items, as illustrated by National Archives documents in Record Group 75, Entry 1058, which were not consulted by Gibson. For example, before signing of the treaty but after having examined the draft, Levi Colbert sent a message to Coffee in which he stated that the terms of the treaty were liberal, "yet our expenses will be so great that we hope our father will make a small present to his Chickasaw Children, before they leave their present home." Continuing, Colbert and the other chiefs asked the government "to furnish our nation with two black smiths for twenty years, with a reasonable supply of iron and steel—and that they advance us in money, to aid in moving, and for the loss of our stock here, One hundred thousand dollars—And if it thought unreasonable to grant us so much then we will be thankful for any sum which may be offered us." These concerns were addressed in the treaty by statements that removal expenses and property compensation would be covered by the proceeds of the land sales and that obtaining blacksmiths and such appurtenances would be the responsibility of the Chickasaws and funded by them from the Chickasaw proceeds resulting from the sales.[23]

After Coffee was criticized and accused of confusing and coercing the Chickasaw to the point of exasperation in a lengthy postnegotiations letter reputed to have been dictated by Levi Colbert speaking for the nation, Coffee responded that he saw no general dissatisfaction among the Chickasaw with the treaty, except from about fifty mixed-bloods and white men with Indian families who wanted reservations but were refused them by the nation. Upon the agreement to withhold these reservations, continued Coffee, who was apparently willing to give the leaders thousands of acres of reserved land, the treaty was drafted and read to the Chickasaw delegates by mixed-blood interpreter Benjamin Love. The treaty and supplement, incidentally, provided for no reservations, not even to Levi Colbert. Coffee asserted that the treaty draft was then delivered to Levi Colbert, "with a request that he should carry it to the private national council, and have it interpreted, and explained, to all his people, until they were fully satisfied." Coffee related that Colbert and the chiefs kept the draft several days, after which it was signed by Colbert and the other Chickasaws on October 20 with the agreement that some additional articles they desired would be contained in a supplemental treaty to be examined the next day. As mentioned above, the supplement was approved on October 22 and added to the main treaty. Coffee also reported that he had been informed that the critical letter (sometimes called the "Levi Colbert Memorial") had been composed by John D. Terrell and John L. Allen (who was married to a daughter of William Colbert) and taken to Colbert and the other chiefs for addition of their signatures. Coffee further stated that the letter was "a tissue of falsehood and misrepresentation." Reynolds avowed that the letter was "acknowledged to have been written or dictated" by Terrell and Allen and that the accusations in it were "wholly incorrect." He also asserted that he remained at the treaty ground paying the annuity for four days and heard no "murmurs or complaints on the part of any one [—] all appeared to be satisfied with what had taken place." Coffee also related that he had removed from the negotiations Terrell and other white men who were not residents of the nation "on account of their secret interference endeavouring to prevent the treaty being made at that time, alledging, as I understood, to the Indians, that they could make better terms here [Washington, D.C.], provided they would then decline to treat with me, and ask permission of Govt. to send a delegation . . . to Washington." The Memorial/letter asserted that this left the confused Chickasaw "deprived of the few friends on which we could rely." Strangely, the Memorial, supposedly dictated by Levi Colbert, then criticized the mixed-bloods, as if

Colbert was not one and had never received a bribe, by saying, "They are the first of our nation to turn against what the steady old Chiefs believe. . . . They seem to calculate for their own pockets forgetful of their country." Mixed-bloods J. H. Perry and Benjamin Love and white man G. W. Long (who was married to a mixed-blood) also declared in detailed written statements that the letter, which had been hand-carried to Washington by a delegation headed by George Colbert, mostly misrepresented the facts. Others in the delegation were Pitman Colbert, Tishomingo, Ishtualutka, John L. Allen, John D. Terrell, and John A. Bynum (James Colbert the younger's son-in-law). The delegation traveled by stagecoach from Tuscumbia, Alabama, to Washington, where it stayed between late 1832 and March 1833. The diverse group went for the purpose of amending the treaty, but such did not transpire because of a lack of cooperation by United States officials, who must have been as confused as I am in trying to make sense of the convoluted situation.[24]

That Levi Colbert and the other chiefs kept the treaty draft for several days and that Colbert, although sick, was not totally incapacitated are facts verified by his words on October 18, two days prior to signing of the main treaty.

> Last evening I informed you I had been much engaged on the importance of Business for the nation, on order to give genl. satisfaction to my people and give you to understand me, that I had lost no time to get on with the Business, and thinking, that by this time, that you might think I was too long or taking up too much time, deliberating . . . I have no doubt the time appears long to you. I can only beg of you not to be unease. It appear so for as the chiefs got into the articles [they?] appears to understand so you will be so good as to allow us [a] little further time to think on it.[25]

It should be emphasized here that the second-thought, postnegotiation objections to the treaty were not to removal itself but rather to some of the terms of the treaty as originally signed in October 1832. With the Chickasaw continuing to insist on amendments, the government agreed to another conference. Headed initially by Levi Colbert, a delegation set out for Washington in March 1834. Colbert, however, fell gravely ill at the agency with a "severe disease," as he expressed it on March 31. Unable to continue, Levi appointed his brother, George, to lead the delegation to Washington. Two months later, apparently on June 2, Levi died at the home of his daughter, Mrs. Kilpatrick Carter, who may have resided by this time about one mile southeast of the agency rather than at Buzzard Roost. He was probably buried where he died but may have been taken back to his last home northwest of Cotton Gin Port for burial.[26]

In May the delegation met with American officials in Washington, where amendments suitable to the Chickasaw regarding temporary land allotments,

allotments for orphans, assistance to people considered incompetent, sales of the allotments, and other items were made to the treaty. As acknowledged in both the 1832 and 1834 agreements, the Chickasaw still had not procured a home in the west. This circumstance had given rise to the provision for temporary land allotments. Unlike the 1832 treaty, the 1834 agreement provided for the award of permanent reservations (selling optional) to certain individuals. Significantly, one such reservation (a half section) went to Margaret Colbert Allen, wife of John L. Allen, one of the dissident white men who had opposed the 1832 treaty. This reservation, on the Tombigbee River north of Columbus, Mississippi, was later settled by the Allens, resulting in the establishment of a river port town called Colbert. Other reservations were awarded by the treaty to Levi Colbert (four sections) and George Colbert, Martin Colbert, Isaac Albertson, Henry Love, and Benjamin Love (one section each). George Colbert also received a fractional section between his old house (near which was buried a previous wife) on the Tennessee River and the ferry, by then sometimes referred to as Smith's Ferry. He also received Colbert's Island. King Ishtehotopa received two sections, and the mother of Charles Colbert, Mintahoyea (one of Levi's widows), received one section. Emmubbee, Ishtimolutka, Ahtohowoy, Pistahlahtubbee, Captain Samuel Seeley, and William McGillivray also received one section each. White men who received reservations included agent Reynolds (two sections) and lawyers William Cooper and John Davis jointly (one section). The latter two men were awarded the reservations because of having been "faithful to the Indians, in giving them professional advice, and legal assistance," and they were to continue to do so while the Chickasaw remained east of the river.[27]

The Chickasaw and the United States now turned their attention once again to locating a suitable home in the west. After a fruitless negotiation between Chickasaws and government representatives (including Reynolds) with the Choctaw at their new western agency in late 1833, Reynolds was instructed to prepare another land inspection tour and to again discuss land acquisition with the Choctaw at the agency. Accordingly, he procured the services of William L. Henderson to conduct a party of five Chickasaw chiefs, with James McLaughlin as interpreter, and assistance west of the river to be provided by Captain William Armstrong of the U.S. army. The excursion, which began on October 17, 1835, produced nothing of significance. Another envoy to the Choctaw west of the river was authorized in late October 1836. This important Chickasaw group, composed of James Perry, John McClish, Pitman Colbert, James Brown, and Isaac Albertson, went to the Choctaw nation, held conferences with Choctaw leaders, and persuaded them to reverse their earlier aversion to relinquishing some of their western land to the Chickasaw. By the Treaty of Doaksville near Fort Towson on January 17, 1837, the Choctaw agreed to exchange the central and western portion (about 5,000 square miles) of their vast lands for the amount of $530,000, to be paid to them by the Chickasaw nation out of the proceeds derived from the liquidation of their remaining eastern homeland (Figure 17).[28] The bones of the ancestors were soon to be left to the uncontrollable whims of the vanquishers.

In the meantime, the government had begun the task of carrying into effect the terms of the 1832 and 1834 agreements, primarily the allocation of temporary land allotments to the individual Chickasaws and subsequent sale of allotments to non-Indians. Before the end of 1834, the U.S. Land Office had surveyed the Chickasaw Cession into townships and sections. The land office had established a branch operation one-half mile east of the center of present-day Pontotoc, thereby motivating the simultaneous birth of that Mississippi city (Figure 12). Because Reynolds had been assigned the task of allocating the land allotments, recording their sales, and taking care of related details, he opened a branch office of the Chickasaw Agency on September 1, 1835, in a Pontotoc house rented to him by Thomas C. McMackin.[29]

A verbal description of the bustling Pontotoc scene was recorded by a visitor, Edward Fontaine:

Pontotoc is a flourishing embryo town in the centre of the Chickasaw Nation: it is located in a fine salutrious [sic] region. . . . The first house was built here in June 1835; now there are 40 Stores and near 2000 inhabitants. Its present prosperity is entirely ephemeral. The extensive mercantile establishments and expensive taverns are supported almost exclusively by the crowd of speculators and adventurers who attend the land sales, and the Indians who have sold their reservations and received their value. Hundreds of these are now in the streets. Many drunk and most of them wasting their money as fast as they can. It is amusing to see their displays of finery. The dress are all of the most fanciful kinds—of every variety of cut and colour. Some of them are ridiculously gaudy, while others are rich and tasty—giving the wearer a martial and splendid appearance. As soon as the land sales are over and the money of these [Indians] is expended the glory of Pontotock will fade, and its wild novelty vanish—and it will appear but as the other respectable inland towns of our country. At present it resembles a Methodist Camp ground. Its buildings are a collection of rude ill constructed huts, with the exception of a few neat little framed painted dwellings. These are tenanted by a collection of people from every State, and from many foreign countries. In this collection is centered perhaps more shrewdness and intelligence than can be found in any other congregation of the same size.[30]

17. Chickasaw domain prior to the removal treaties of 1832 and 1834 (by author)

Assisted by clerks G. W. Long and Erasmus McDowell, with mixed-blood Jackson Kemp as interpreter, Reynolds carried on his work until September 1837, at which time he closed the Pontotoc office and returned to normal operations of the agency in Colbert County, Alabama. In March 1835, subagent John L. Allen's position had been eliminated by the War Department, and on March 3, 1839, the Chickasaw Agency east of the Mississippi River was permanently closed. By this time a new agency had been opened in the new Chickasaw territory west of the river.[31]

Despite numerous instances of unethical and illegal abuses related to purchases and resale of the individual land allotments by some of the white speculators, the Chickasaw land, including the extensive unallotted acreage, was gradually liquidated, resulting in millions of dollars being placed in a Chickasaw Nation Fund established under the terms of the treaties. The exodus of the circa 4,500 Chickasaws began in June 1837 when the first 450 Chickasaw emigrants (with their slaves), recruited by A. M. Upshaw, superintendent of the Chickasaw removal, left the nation on a long and arduous trek across the Mis-

sissippi River and through the state of Arkansas to their objective, a new and
hopefully happier life in a strange land that eventually came to be called Oklahoma. By the end of 1838, most of the Chickasaw had left the land of their
ancestors, but many had not. As late as October 1841, Benjamin Love reported
that about 500 Chickasaws were preparing to migrate. Over the next nine years
the remainder made their way west until all were gone except some mixed-
bloods and some young people who had been adopted by whites. Of course,
some of the elderly and weak Chickasaws and slaves were unable to with-
stand the rigorous ordeals of the trip, called by Gibson the "Chickasaw Trail of
Tears," and died on the way. Primary leaders who had migrated with their
families included King Ishtehotopa (the last king of the Chickasaw), George
and James Colbert, Tishomingo, William McGillivray, and Isaac Albertson. All
were deceased by the end of 1850. Although most or all of the Chickasaw people
may have initially intended to forego moving west of the Mississippi River,
nearly all had sold their allotments and reservations by the end of the early
1850s and moved to the new lands in present-day Oklahoma. Of course, Levi
Colbert had already died prior to initiation of removal, as had Samuel Seeley,
who passed away in 1835. Some of those known to have remained in Mississippi
include the Allens and the Martin Colbert family. The Chickasaw were thus the
only people of the so-called Five Civilized Tribes to totally dissolve their tribal
status east of the Mississippi River.[32]

After trying years spent adjusting to their new home, the Chickasaw per-
severed as they had always managed to do when facing extinction of their
independence. The reason for the preservation of such a small population of
people is a simple one. From 1723 until the 1790s, the period when the Chickasaw were most susceptible to extinction, they had been a unified population as
a result of living in a small area where an individual normally had to travel no
more than fifteen miles to visit another Chickasaw. Although political factions always existed among them, and some abandoned the nation, the disagreements among the remaining core population never resulted in disunion,
because of maintenance of communication occasioned by the geographical
closeness of the villages, their remoteness from the edge of the white settler
tide from the east and north, and Chickasaw realization that cooperation was
their salvation. After dispersal from the old towns and the beginning of white
pressure for land on the north around the turn of the nineteenth century, the
Chickasaw were able to maintain unity because of the district system and election of principal chiefs to speak for the entire nation in their dealings with the
United States. Even the aberrant self-serving actions of George and Levi Colbert in soliciting large compensations in exchange for land cessions turned
out to be beneficial in that a final removal agreement was delayed for eight
years after the Chickasaw population ceased condoning such activities in 1826,

thereby causing the desperate United States government to agree to better liquidation terms than would have been obtained in that year. Despite occasional abuse of power by some, Chickasaw history is characterized by a cooperative strategy that has been continued to the present, as evidenced by the close-knit, viable, and progressive Chickasaw nation in Oklahoma. The ancestors left behind under the soil of the ancient homeland would be proud.

Notes

CHAPTER 1

1. "Splendid and fertile" was a description used by French governor Bienville to describe the coveted Chickasaw lands (Dunbar Rowland and Albert G. Sanders, trans. and eds., *Mississippi Provincial Archives: French Dominion* [hereafter *MPA:FD*], 3 vols. [Jackson, Miss.: Department of Archives and History Press, 1927, 1929, 1932], vol. 3, p. 767); Patricia Galloway (*Choctaw Genesis, 1500–1700* [Lincoln: Univ. of Nebraska Press, 1995], 331) asserts that those parts of migration legends concerning a trans-Mississippi origin for the Chickasaw are explanatory responses to the Chickasaws' not being native to the upper Tombigbee Region, which she says "has now been confirmed." No elaboration on (or citation for) this unsubstantiated statement that research has proved a non-Tombigbee origin for the Chickasaw is presented. If such had been proved then the place of origin would had to have come to light also, but no such place is mentioned in her peculiar statement. For a synthesis of most of the archaeological findings in the Tombigbee River watershed to 1989, see Eugene M. Futato, *An Archaeological Overview of the Tombigbee River Basin, Alabama and Mississippi* (Tuscaloosa: Alabama State Museum of Natural History, Division of Archaeology, Univ. of Alabama, 1989). See also Ned J. Jenkins and Richard Krause, *The Tombigbee Watershed in Southeastern Prehistory* (Tuscaloosa: Univ. of Alabama Press, 1986).

2. John R. Swanton, "Social and Religious Beliefs and Usages of the Chickasaw Indians," *Forty-fourth Annual Report of the Bureau of American Ethnology* (Washington, D.C.: Government Printing Office, 1928).

3. For ethnological data on the customs and lifestyle of the eighteenth- and nineteenth-century Chickasaw and sources for those data, see Swanton, "Social and Religious Beliefs." See also James Adair, *History of the American Indians,* Samuel Cole Williams, ed. (Johnson City, Tenn.: Watauga Press, 1930, reprint of 1775 edition), from which Swanton obtained much of his data. Subsequent to Swanton's studies, the most valuable ethnological document known regarding the early Chickasaw came to light recently (see Alexander Moore, ed., *Nairne's Muskhogean Journals: The 1708 Expedition to the Mississippi River* [Jackson: Univ. Press of Mississippi, 1988]); an equally valuable document for both cultural and historical data about the Chickasaw from the second half of the eighteenth century to removal

still lies in relative obscurity (see Lyman C. Draper's interview with Malcolm McGee, 1841 [Lyman C. Draper Collection, microfilm, Wisconsin Historical Society, Madison, vol. 10, series U, pp. 108–128]; hereafter cited as McGee-Draper Narrative because of the fact that the document appears in narrative form [written by Draper] using information almost entirely obtained from McGee); see also Charles M. Hudson, *The Southeastern Indians* (Knoxville: Univ. of Tennessee Press, 1976). Archaeological data and other sources regarding Tombigbee River–related subjects, such as introductions of the bow and arrow and corn, wildlife hunted and collected, house construction methods, and so on, may be obtained by referring to Futato, *An Archaeological Overview*. For discussions and illustrations of cultural material directly related to the Chickasaw, see Jesse D. Jennings, "Chickasaw and Earlier Indian Cultures of Northeast Mississippi," *Journal of Mississippi History* 3(1941): 155–226; John D. Stubbs, "A Preliminary Classification of Chickasaw Pottery," *Mississippi Archaeology* 17, no. 2(1982): 50–57; and James R. Atkinson, "Historic Chickasaw Cultural Material: A More Comprehensive Identification," *Mississippi Archaeology* 22(Dec. 1987): 32–62. For studies of transition and evolution of Mississippian hierarchy into the historic period see Vernon James Knight, Jr., "Social Organization and the Evolution of Hierarchy in Southeastern Chiefdoms," in *Journal of Anthropological Research* 46, no. 1(Spring 1990): 1–23, and V. J. Knight, Jr., "Symbolism of Mississippian Mounds," in P. H. Wood, G. A. Waselkov, and M. T. Hatley, eds., *Powhatan's Mantle* (Lincoln: Univ. of Nebraska Press, 1989), 279–291.

4. See appropriate references in Note 2, above, and Arrell M. Gibson, *The Chickasaws* (Norman: Univ. of Oklahoma Press, 1971), 11. With regard to the "sitting position" of burials, Gibson does not present his interpretation of what that meant, but Galloway (*Choctaw Genesis,* 297), taking literally the early references to the sitting position, has suggested dubiously that the numerous Chickasaw flexed burials excavated in the Tupelo area over the years might have been interred in upright, sitting positions but due to subsequent earth pressure they somehow moved in a way not described over on their sides into flexed positions. This, of course, defies all established laws of physics. Such movement as suggested, moreover, would have resulted in a disarticulated jumble of bones, which is not the case regarding the excavated flexed burials. Moreover, of the numerous excavated Chickasaw burials, not a single one was found to have been buried in an upright sitting position.

5. Swanton, "Social and Religious Beliefs"; Gibson, *The Chickasaws;* Moore, *Nairne's Journals.*

6. For one of the numerous discussions of the Mississippian Tradition in the southeast see Bruce D. Smith, "The Archaeology of the Southeastern United States: From Dalton to De Soto, 10,500–500 B.P.," in *Advances in World Archaeology,* Fred Wendorf and Angela E. Close, eds. (Orlando: Academic Press, 1986), vol. 5. For an excellent discussion and analysis of the Mississippian Tradition along the Tombigbee see John H. Blitz, *Ancient Chiefdoms of the Tombigbee* (Tuscaloosa: Univ. of Alabama Press, 1993).

7. Janet Rafferty, *Owl Creek Mounds: Test Excavations at a Vacant Mississippian Mound Center,* Report of Investigations 7 (Starkville: Mississippi State Univ., Cobb Institute of Archaeology, 1995); Richard Marshall, "The Protohistoric Component at the Lyon's Bluff Site Complex, Oktibbeha County, Mississippi," in *The Protohistoric Period in the Mid-South: 1500–1700,* David H. Dye and Ronald C. Brister, eds. (Jackson: Mississippi Department of Archives and History Archaeological Report 18, 1986); Marc D. Rucker, *Archaeological Survey*

and Test Excavations in the Upper-Central Tombigbee River Valley: Aliceville-Columbus Lock and Dam and Impoundment Areas, Alabama and Mississippi (Starkville: Mississippi State Univ., Department of Anthropology, 1974); James R. Atkinson, "The De Soto Expedition through Northeast Mississippi in 1540–1541," *Mississippi Archaeology* 22(June 1987): 61–73; Charles M. Hudson, Marvin T. Smith, and Chester DePratter, "The Hernando De Soto Expedition: From Mabila to the Mississippi River," in *Towns and Temples along the Mississippi River*, David H. Dye and Cheryl Anne Cox, eds. (Tuscaloosa: Univ. of Alabama Press, 1990); Rufus A. Ward, "The Tombigbee Crossing of the De Soto Expedition," *Mississippi Archaeology* 21(1986): 62–68.

8. The orange sherd of Spanish affiliation was identified as such by Kathleen A. Deagan of the Florida Museum of Natural History, University of Florida (copy of letter, K. A. Deagan to Richard Marshall, March 22, 1990, Cobb Institute of Archaeology, Mississippi State Univ., Starkville; original letter in possession of Richard Marshall). The gilded metal button from an Indian site at Harmon Lake was discussed in an article by Marshall, who concluded that the item was a late eighteenth- or early nineteenth-century rosette that had been converted to a pendant by an Indian (Richard A. Marshall, "A Possible Historic Indian Pendant," *Journal of Alabama Archaeology* 24, no. 2[Dec. 1978]: 125–131). Subsequently, however, the item was determined to be a sixteenth-century Damascene button similar to some found at the Fort Center site in Florida (personal communication, James V. Knight, Jr., Univ. of Alabama, June 23, 1989).

9. Adair, *History*, 70; Jesse D. Jennings, ed., "Nutt's Trip to the Chickasaw Country," *Journal of Mississippi History* 9(1947): 34–61; map of the Cotton Gin Port Mound site, in George J. Leftwich, "Cotton Gin Port and Gaines' Trace," *Publications of the Mississippi Historical Society* 7(1903). Leftwich thought he was documenting a French fortification, but in reality his map and descriptions document the Indian structures prior to obliteration by cultivation of the earthwork surrounding the mound. The mound itself is still extant. See Jack D. Elliott, Jr., "The Buried City: History, Myth, and Mystery on the Tombigbee," *Journal of Mississippi History*, forthcoming; Moore, *Nairne's Journals*, 36–37.

10. For all known historical data about the De Soto expedition, see L. A. Clayton, V. J. Knight, Jr., and E. C. Moore, eds., *The De Soto Chronicles*, 2 vols. (Tuscaloosa: Univ. of Alabama Press, 1993).

11. Clayton et al., *The De Soto Chronicles*.

12. See Clayton et al., *The De Soto Chronicles*, vol. 1, pp. 10–13 for a short overview discussion of the recent literature that addresses the De Soto expedition's significance and impacts on the southeastern native Americans. Works include those of Mary W. Helms, John F. Scarry, Rhonda L. Majors, Janet E. Levy, J. Alan May, David G. Moore, G. R. Milner, Henry F. Dobyns, Marvin T. Smith, Ann F. Ramenofsky, and Wayne Franklyn.

13. Adair, *History*, 69, 377–378; James R. Atkinson, "The Ackia and Ogoula Tchetoka Chickasaw Village Locations in 1736 during the French-Chickasaw War," *Mississippi Archaeology* 20(June 1985): 53–72; Atkinson, "The De Soto Expedition," 61–62; Atkinson, "Historic Chickasaw Cultural Material," 33–35. The Yaneka/Chiwapa Creek settlement site, located about ten miles southward from the Old Town Creek Chickasaw settlement at which James Adair lived, was officially identified in 1985 during an intensive archaeological survey I conducted along the south side of that creek from the east side of the Natchez Trace Parkway

in Lee County for about four miles westward into the southeast corner of present-day Pontotoc County (archaeological site files, Office of Historic Preservation, Mississippi Department of Archives and History [MDAH], Jackson). I did not publicize details of my findings in order to protect the numerous habitation locales found from the destructive activities of those artifact hunters/grave robbers who did not already know about them (like the Tupelo sites, they have also been extensively looted by "treasure hunters"). In the early 1980s, John D. Stubbs had performed archaeological survey in Lee County along nearby Tubbalubba Creek (Stubbs, "Archaeological Survey in Lee County, Mississippi, 1981–1983," submitted to the Chickasaw Cultural Center, Lee County, Mississippi, 1983). In the past twenty years many archaeological investigations and related studies have been published by professional archaeologists with regard to changes in Chickasaw settlement locations between the Late Mississippian and the historic Chickasaw periods (ca. A.D. 1500–1700). The primary studies, which present controversial hypotheses, include the following: Jay K. Johnson and John T. Sparks, "Protohistoric Settlement Patterns in Northeastern Mississippi," in *The Protohistoric Period in the Mid-South,* Dye and Brister, eds., 64–81; Jay K. Johnson, Geoffrey R. Lehmann, James R. Atkinson, Susan L. Scott, and Andrea Shea, *Protohistoric Chickasaw Settlement Patterns and the De Soto Route in Northeast Mississippi* (Final Report to the National Endowment for the Humanities and National Geographic Society, Washington, D.C., 1991); Jay K. Johnson, "Aboriginal Settlement and First Contact in Northeast Mississippi," *National Geographic Research and Exploration,* vol. 7, no. 4 (1991), 492–494; Jay K. Johnson, "Settlement Patterns, GIS, Remote Sensing and the Late Prehistory of the Black Prairie in East Central Mississippi," in *Applications of Space-Age Technology in Anthropology,* Cliff Behrens and Tom Sever, eds. (John C. Stennis Space Center, Mississippi, 1991), 111–119; Jay K. Johnson, "Chiefdom to Tribe in Northeast Mississippi: A Culture in Transition," in *The Hernando de Soto Expedition: History, Historiography, and "Discovery" in the Southeast,* Patricia K. Galloway, ed. (Lincoln: Univ. of Nebraska Press, 1997); Jay K. Johnson, Susan L. Scott, James R. Atkinson, Andrea B. Shea, "Late Prehistoric/Protohistoric Settlement and Subsistence on the Black Prairie: Buffalo Hunting in Mississippi," *North American Archaeologist* 15, no. 2(1994): 167–179; Jay K. Johnson, "The Chickasaw," in *Indians of the Greater Southeast: History, Archaeology, and Ethnohistory,* Bonnie G. McEwan, ed. (Gainesville: Univ. of Florida Press, 2000), 85–121; David W. Morgan, "An Analysis of Historic Period Chickasaw Settlement Patterns," Master's thesis, Department of Anthropology (Tuscaloosa: Univ. of Alabama, 1994); David W. Morgan, "Historic Period Chickasaw Indians: Chronology and Settlement Patterns," *Mississippi Archaeology* 31, no. 1(1996): 1–39.

14. The Vicenzo Coronelli map of 1684 is in the Beinecke Rare Book Room, Yale University, New Haven, Conn., and published as plate 10 in Barbara McCorkle, *American Emergent: An Exhibition of Maps and Atlases in Honor of Alexander O. Victor* (New Haven: Yale Univ. Press, 1985). The map is also published in Galloway, *Choctaw Genesis,* 234. The eighteen villages recorded by d'Iberville are published in "Documents concernant l'histoire des Indiens de la Region orientale de la Louisiane," Le Baron Marc de Villiers, ed., *Journal de Societe des Americanistes de Paris* 14(1922): 138–140; see also Swanton, "Social and Religious Beliefs," 212, for d'Iberville's list and four subsequent ones. Regarding Chickasaws on the Wabash (Tennessee) see Richebourg G. McWilliams, trans. and ed., *Iberville's Gulf Journals* (Tuscaloosa: Univ. of Alabama Press, 1981), 174; Letter, de Sauvole to Pontchartrain, Aug. 4, 1701, in Row-

land and Sanders, *MPA:FD,* vol. 2, p. 14; P. J. Higginbotham, ed., *The Journal of Sauvole* (Mobile: Colonial Books, 1969). For discussion of the Chickasaw villages/camps depicted on the Tennessee River on the Guillaume de Lisle maps, see Charles H. Fairbanks, *Cherokee and Creek Indians—Ethnographic Report on Royce Area 79: Chickasaw, Cherokee, Creek,* Findings of the Indian Claims Commission (New York: Garland Publishing, 1974), 83–86.

15. See Patricia K. Galloway, "Henri de Tonti du Village des Chactas: The Beginning of the French Alliance," in P. K. Galloway, ed., *La Salle and His Legacy: Frenchmen and Indians in the Lower Mississippi Valley* (Jackson: Univ. Press of Mississippi, 1982), 146–175, and Galloway, *Choctaw Genesis,* 193–194. Rebuttal to Galloway's locations is presented in a letter from James R. Atkinson to Patricia Galloway, Feb. 21, 1985, copy in Atkinson Collection, Special Collections, Mitchell Memorial Library, Mississippi State University, Starkville; for a discussion of the large prehistoric/historic contact settlement apparently at least partially due to Chackchiuma occupation in the Starkville/Mississippi State University area, see James R. Atkinson, "A Historic Contact Indian Settlement in Oktibbeha County, Mississippi," *Journal of Alabama Archaeology* 25, no. 1(1979): 61–82. In addition to early eighteenth-century documents that place the Chackchiuma in the Oktibbeha County area, traditions recorded by H. B. Cushman do likewise (Cushman, *History of the Choctaw, Chickasaw, and Natchez Indians* [Greenville, Texas: Headlight Printing, 1899], 186). See also Henry S. Halbert, "The Small Indian Tribes of Mississippi," *Publications of the Mississippi Historical Society* 5(1902).

16. Moore, *Nairne's Journals,* 36. This "Hollatchatroe" is spelled "Falatchao" in the French documents.

17. Ibid., 57–58.

18. Atkinson, "The Ackia and Ogoula Tchetoka Chickasaw Village Locations," 53–72; Henry M. Lusher, "Map of the Lands in Mississippi Ceded by the Chickasaws to the United States in 1832 and 1834, from Actual Survey," 1835 (copy at MDAH); archaeological site files for Lee and Pontotoc Counties, Mississippi, at Division of Historic Preservation, MDAH.

19. See quotations of these and other Europeans in Williams's footnotes 178 and 200 in Adair, *History,* 342, 447–448; Moore, *Nairne's Journals,* 38; John F. D. Smyth, *A Tour in the United States of America,* 2 vols. (New York: Arno Press, 1968, originally published in 1784), vol. 1, p. 361.

20. Moore, *Nairne's Journals,* 43; Letter, Samuel Eveleigh to Herman Verelst, Aug. 7, 1736, in Allen D. Candler, comp., *Colonial Records of the State of Georgia* (*CRG*), 26 vols., 1904–1916 (reprinted 1970, New York: AMS Press), vol. 21, p. 204; Letter, Benjamin Fooy to Governor Manuel Gayoso, April 5, 1794, in D. C. Corbitt and Roberta Corbitt, "Papers from the Spanish Archives Relating to Tennessee," *East Tennessee Historical Society's Publications* 39(1967): 89.

21. Le Page du Pratz, *History of Louisiana . . .* (Baton Rouge: Claitor's Publishing Division, 1972, reprint of 1773 ed.), 300; John R. Swanton, "The Indians of the Southeastern United States," *Bureau of American Ethnology, Bulletin 137* (Washington, D.C.: Smithsonian Institution, 1946), 105, 147, 165, 211; Bernard Romans, *A Concise Natural History of East and West Florida,* Kathryn E. H. Braund, ed. (Tuscaloosa: Univ. of Alabama Press, 1999, reprint of 1775 ed.), 124; de Crenay map of 1733, published in John R. Swanton, "Early History of the Creek Indians and Their Neighbors," *Bureau of American Ethnology Bulletin 73* (Washington, D.C.: Smithsonian Institution, 1922); Alexander de Batz, "Plan et Scituation Des Villages Tchikachas, September 7, 1737," original map at Archives Nationales, Paris, France

(copy at Natchez Trace Parkway headquarters, Tupelo, Miss.); Lusher, "Map of the Lands in Mississippi Ceded by the Chickasaw"; Adair, *History*, 69–70, 205, 378; Atkinson, "The Ackia and Ogoula Tchetoka Chickasaw Village Locations," 53–72; Atkinson, "Historic Chickasaw Cultural Material," 33–35; a study of post-1700 Chickasaw village locations by three artifact collectors from Lee County produced location identifications sometimes in conformity with mine that are discussed in this and other chapters (Steve Cook, Buddy Palmer, and Julian Riley, "Historic Chickasaw Village Locations," 1980, unpublished paper, copy at Natchez Trace Parkway headquarters, Tupelo, Miss.).

22. McGee-Draper Narrative, 118.

23. Romans, *A Concise Natural History*, 124; de Crenay map of 1733; Captain [Charles] Roberts, "A New Map of West Florida . . . " (copies at the Birmingham, Alabama Public Library, Univ. of Auburn Library, and MDAH). The Roberts map was originally made about 1773. Known examples, however, were made soon after 1797, probably no later than 1800. Except for a few post-1797 period additions, the Mississippi area of the large map otherwise conforms to that area on other maps made in about 1773, which incorporate data obtained by Bernard Romans in 1771–1772. See Jack D. L. Holmes, "A Mystery Map of West Florida: A Cartographical Puzzle," in Ronald V. Evans, ed., *Threads of Tradition and Culture along the Gulf Coast* (Pensacola: Gulf Coast History and Humanities Conference, 1986), 216–229.

24. De Batz, "Plan et Scituation"; map signed by Ignace Francois Broutin dated March 10, 1740, and entitled "Carte Particuliere [des] Routtes faite du fort de l'Assumption au Chicachachats (pour) chercher un chemin Praticable pour les charoues en 1740," original at Service Historic de la Marine, Vincennes, France (copy at Natchez Trace Parkway headquarters, Tupelo, Miss.); Joseph L. Peyser, "1740 French Map Pinpoints Battle Site in Mississippi," *Mapline* 39(Sept. 1985): 1–4. Peyser consulted with me and used Atkinson, "The Ackia and Ogoula Tchetoka Chickasaw Village Locations," in preparation of his article. For the confines of the Chickasaw Old Fields in what was once eastern Pontotoc County but is now Lee County (created in 1866), see Lusher, "Map of the Lands in Mississippi Ceded by the Chickasaw."

25. Cushman, *History of the Choctaw, Chickasaw, and Natchez Indians*, 411. Malcolm McGee, who lived among the Chickasaw for over sixty-five years and who in 1767 became one of the first inhabitants of the "Pakitakolih" area, stated in an interview with Lyman C. Draper in 1841 that "Pouketocaula" was the original name for present-day Pontotoc (McGee-Draper Narrative, 126, 128); relying on the undocumented speculations of Cushman and the work of an amateur historian from Pontotoc named E. T. Winston and others, J. H. Malone included a partially erroneous map of the Chickasaw settlement area in his book *The Chickasaw Nation: A Short Sketch of a Noble People* (Louisville, Ky.: John P. Morton, 1922), 284–287. Malone, therefore, identified Pontotoc County as the location of the ancient Chickasaw settlement area. Unlike Cushman, who apparently was unaware of the Lusher map, Malone depicted the Chickasaw Old Fields as shown on that map. William E. Myer, "Indian Trails of the Southeast," *Forty-second Annual Report of the Bureau of American Ethnology for 1924–1925* (Washington, D.C.: Government Printing Office, 1928), repeated on a trail map Cushman's and Malone's errors regarding "Old Pontotoc" being in the center of the Chickasaw settlement area at an early time. Later, E. T. Winston cemented for many years these errone-

ous notions into the minds of lay people and professionals alike in his book *Story of Pontotoc* (Pontotoc, Miss.: Pontotoc Progress, 1931, pp. 7, 48), as exemplified by Gibson, *The Chickasaws*, 6. Writing prior to Gibson's work, Charles H. Fairbanks had also fallen victim to the erroneous notion begun by Cushman regarding the alleged antiquity of that late Chickasaw settlement area. Although identifying with no reservations the main Chickasaw settlements by 1720 as being around Tupelo, Fairbanks subsequently concluded that prior to settlement in that area the main Chickasaw towns had been located by 1715 "in the vicinity of present Pontotoc," which is located about fifteen miles west of Tupelo (Fairbanks, *Ethnographic Report on Royce Area 79*, 46–47, 50, 52–53, 91). The old entrenched notion (now a myth) thus caused this noted and gifted anthropologist to wander down the same path followed by other writers before him. More recent victims of the Pontotoc myth include Helen H. Tanner ("The Land and Water Communication Systems of the Southeastern Indians," in Wood et al., *Powhatan's Mantle*, 7), who states that the "seven Chickasaw towns" of the early eighteenth century were in a tight formation "near modern Pontotoc," and Colin G. Calloway (*The American Revolution in Indian Country: Crisis and Diversity in Native American Communities* [Cambridge: Cambridge Univ. Press, 1995], 213 n. 3), who states, adding his own embellishment, that "Americans often referred to Tchoukafala as Old Pontotoc." If this were true at least one such reference to "Old Pontotoc" would be present in the hundreds of extant pre-1795 letters having data associated with the Chickasaw. See Dawson A. Phelps, "The Chickasaw, the English, and the French," *Tennessee Historical Quarterly* 16(June 1957): 126, 130, for the first published repudiation of the Pontotoc County notion, especially with regard to Winston's dogmatic assertions that the village of Ogoula Tchetoka, where an army commanded by Pierre d'Artaguette was routed by the Chickasaw in 1736, was located at "Old Pontotoc." Perhaps the most astonishing misidentification for the location of the eighteenth- and nineteenth-century Chickasaw is that in an entry by Joyce Chaplin in a recently published encyclopedia. Chaplin asserts that "[t]he towns were concentrated in the center of the nation at Chikasahha or the Chickasaw Fields, near the present-day city of Memphis" (Joyce E. Chaplin, "Chickasaw," in Alan Gallay, ed., *Colonial Wars of North America, 1512–1763: An Encyclopedia* [New York: Garland Publishing, 1996], 124–127). The first professional archaeological excavations of the early Chickasaw settlement in Lee County, conducted in the second half of the 1930s in preparation for construction of the Natchez Trace Parkway, were reported by Jesse D. Jennings ("Chickasaw and Earlier Indian Cultures," 155–226). Jennings also reconstructed the Chickasaw Old Fields in Lee County on a map prepared using Lusher's 1835 map and the original 1833–1834 U.S. Government Land Office survey plats and field notes.

26. J. H. Easterby, ed., *Journal of the Commons House of Assembly, 1736–1757* (*JCHA*), vol. 2, Colonial Records of South Carolina (Columbia: Historical Commission of South Carolina, 1952), pp. 109, 183; Easterby, ed., *JCHA*, vol. 7 (Columbia: South Carolina Archives Department, 1958), pp. 255, 262; Easterby, ed., *JCHA*, vol. 9 (Columbia: South Carolina Archives Department, 1962), 207; *CRG*, vol. 4, p. 47; *CRG*, vol. 7, pp. 28, 189, 207, 539; *CRG*, vol. 26, p. 400; William L. McDowell, ed., *Journals of the Commissioners of the Indian Trade, September 20, 1710–August 29, 1718* (popularly called one of the "Indian Books"), vol. 1, Colonial Records of South Carolina (Columbia: South Carolina Archives Department, 1955),

p. 238; William L. McDowell, Jr., ed., *Documents Relating to Indian Affairs* (*DRIA;* also one of the "Indian Books"), Colonial Records of South Carolina, South Carolina Archives Department (Columbia: Univ. of South Carolina Press, 1958), vol. 2, p. 12; *DRIA,* vol. 3, pp. 475–476.

27. Moore, *Nairne's Journals,* 40–41; although the South Carolina Squirrel King's Chickasaw-language name was said by one early writer (Wilbur R. Jacobs, *Indians of the Southern Colonial Frontier: The Edmond Atkin Report and Plan of 1755* [Columbia: Univ. of South Carolina Press, 1954], 46) to be "Tunni Mingo," Tunni is probably a confused rendition of "Fane," which means "squirrel" in the Muskhogean language.

28. William Stephens's journal entry for June 12, 1738, relates inaccurately that after a reported Choctaw-Chickasaw peace the eastern Chickasaw in South Carolina had supposedly returned to the nation and that trader Thomas Andrews was planning to go there "to attend their Resettlement" (*CRG,* vol. 4, p. 156). The statement does, however, indicate that some Chickasaw probably returned. Edward J. Cashin, *Colonial Augusta, Key of the Indian Country* (Macon: Mercer Univ. Press, 1986), 31, 58, 100; for details of the Chickasaw-McGillivray land exchange see Edward J. Cashin, *Lachlan McGillivray, Indian Trader: The Shaping of the Southern Frontier* (Athens: Univ. of Georgia Press, 1992), 179–183; John R. Swanton, "The Indian Tribes of North America," *Bureau of American Ethnology Bulletin 145* (Washington, D.C.: Smithsonian Institution, 1952), 93; Swanton, "Indians of the Southeastern United States," 118; Swanton, "Early History of the Creek Indians and Their Neighbors," 419; Verner W. Crane, *The Southern Frontier, 1670–1732* (Ann Arbor: Univ. of Michigan Press, 1929), 190, 273; Jacobs, *The Edmond Atkin Report,* 42, 44–46; Adair, *History,* 189, 343; Robert L. Meriwether, *The Expansion of South Carolina, 1729–1765* (Philadelphia: Porcupine Press, 1974), 71; Chapman J. Milling, *Red Carolinians* (Columbia: Univ. of South Carolina Press, 1969, reprint), 197–201; John Haywood, *The Natural and Aboriginal History of Tennessee . . . to 1768* (Jackson, Tenn.: McCowat-Mercer Press, 1959, originally published in 1823), 225; Fairbanks, *Ethnographic Report on Royce Area 79,* 179, 261; Letters, R. J. Meigs to Henry Dearborn (Secretary of War), Jan. 23, 1805, and Meigs to General James Robertson, May 5, 1805, in National Archives, Office of Indian Affairs (Record Group [RG] 75; Records of the Cherokee Indian Agency in Tennessee, 1801–1835, Correspondence and Miscellaneous Records, 1801–1802), microfilm M-208, roll 1, abstracted in James R. Atkinson, *Records of the Old Southwest in the National Archives: Abstracts of Records of the Chickasaw Indian Agency and Related Documents, 1794–1840* (hereafter *Records of the Chickasaw Agency*) (Chickasaw Nation, Ada, Oklahoma, and Cobb Institute of Archaeology at Mississippi State Univ., Starkville, 1997), pp. 307, 310. With regard to the Chickasaw exodus from South Carolina, Benjamin Hawkins cites an elderly Creek nation Indian: "Some of the Chickasaws straggled off and settled near Augusta, from whence they returned and sat down near Cussetuh [Kashita] and thence back to their nation" (Benjamin Hawkins, *A Sketch of the Creek Country, in the Years 1798 and 1799* [Collections of the Georgia Historical Society, vol. 3, pt. 1, originally published in 1848, reprinted, Spartanburg, S.C.: Reprint Company, 1982], 83, and Benjamin Hawkins, *Letters of Benjamin Hawkins* [Collections of the Georgia Historical Society, vol. 3, pt. 1, originally published in 1848, reprinted, Spartanburg, S.C.: Reprint Company, 1982]); Journal of David Tait, March 27, 1772, Appendix A in K. G. Davies, ed., *Documents of the American Revolution, 1770–1783* (Dublin, Ireland: Irish Univ. Press, 1972–1981) (hereafter cited as *DAR*), vol. 5, p. 265; Benjamin Hawkins provided one of the few descriptions of the Chickasaw Old Fields on the

Tennessee River in stating, "I have once seen their old town on the Tennessee; as mentioned in the certificate [from President Washington], it is several miles above the Muscle Shoals and extended for 6 miles on the north side of the river" (Hawkins, *Letters*, 393); as part of the seemingly never-ending struggle to help stem the almost constant flow of published misinformation about the Chickasaw, I should point out here that Patricia Galloway, citing no references, attempts to strengthen a point regarding the obscure roots of the Chickasaw migration legend by erroneously stating that the "Chickasaw settlement in South Carolina . . . may have dated from Woodward's day" (late seventeenth century). See Galloway, *Choctaw Genesis*, 336.

29. Easterby, *JCHA*, vol. 2, p. 183; *CRG*, vol. 26, pp. 62–63; Milling, *Red Carolinians*, 188.

30. Jacobs, *The Edmond Atkin Report*, 46; Easterby, *JCHA*, vol. 6 (1956), pp. 190–191, 242, 244.

31. Meriwether, *Expansion of South Carolina*, 71, 189, 204, 228; Cashin, *Lachlan McGillivray*, 30; *CRG*, vol. 28, pt. 1, p. 250; Easterby, *JCHA*, vol. 3 (1953), pp. 122–123, 143, 160, 170, 201, 204–205; Williams, "Introduction," in Adair, *History*, xvi; Adair, *History*, 264–265; John R. Alden, *John Stuart and the Southern Colonial Frontier* (Ann Arbor: Univ. of Michigan Press, 1944), 128–129. With regard to the approximately 37-year-old James Colbert (sometimes spelled "Calvert") who fought in the Cherokee War in 1761, Samuel Cole Williams (*Tennessee during the Revolutionary War* [Knoxville: Univ. of Tennessee Press, 1944], 171) believed (Williams presented no documentation) that he was the son of a deceased white trader also named James Colbert. Later, Duane K. Hale and Arrell M. Gibson (*The Chickasaw* [New York: Charles House, 1991], 35) contended (with no accompanying documentation) that James Colbert was the son of a trader named James Logan Colbert. Two Colberts would explain James Adair's statement (*History*, 370) that James Colbert had resided in the Chickasaw nation since childhood, but that statement alone is insufficient. Recently, a Colbert descendant presented genealogical and historical data in demonstrating that James Logan Colbert was probably born in Virginia or North Carolina; most likely the latter (Richard A. Colbert, "James Logan Colbert of the Chickasaws: The Man and the Myth," *North Carolina Genealogical Society Journal* [May 1994 and Feb. 1995]). Richard Colbert now theorizes that James Logan Colbert's father was William Calvert/Colbert who lived by 1727 on Plum Tree Island (in the Roanoke River) in North Carolina near a man named James Logan, who could have been James Colbert's maternal grandfather (personal communication, letter, July 5, 2001). However, contemporary documentation has not been found that verifies the existence of a trader named James *Logan* Colbert. The "Logan" name first appeared in H. B. Cushman's 1899 book (*History of the Choctaw, Chickasaw, and Natchez Indians*, 414, 423), in which he refers to "Logan Colbert" but never calls him either James or James Logan. However, Cushman appears to be referring to the James Colbert under discussion here in stating that he was an early eighteenth-century trader to the Chickasaw who sired the noted Colbert brothers including William and George. Because Cushman called him "Logan," subsequent writers of history began to combine the two names, thus creating "James Logan Colbert" as the assumed full name of the early trader. As mentioned above, however, not one of the numerous eighteenth-century documents possessing James Colbert's name has come to light that includes the middle name "Logan," nor do any refer to a "Logan Colbert." Cushman may have been correct in his identification of the original trader as being named Logan

Colbert rather than James or James Logan Colbert but incorrect in identifying Logan as the father of the noted mixed-blood Colbert brothers. This would mean, then, that James Colbert was an eighteenth-century full-blood white offspring of a white trader to the Chickasaw named Logan Colbert. Richard Colbert's theory that James Colbert's father was William Colbert may well be correct. An erroneous notion in the popular literature that James Colbert was born in Scotland is disputed by Colbert's own words in a letter written by him in 1783 (also addressed by Richard Colbert), which states that he was born in the United States (see Letter, James Colbert to the governor of Virginia, July 25, 1783, in William P. Palmer, arranger and ed., *Calender of Virginia State Papers and Other Manuscripts*, vol. 3 [Richmond: Virginia State Library, 1883, reprinted, New York: Kraus Reprint, 1968], 514).

32. Easterby, *JCHA*, vol. 8 (1961), p. 401; *DRIA*, vol. 2, p. 12; *DRIA*, vol. 3, p. 475; *CRG*, vol. 7, p. 539, and vol. 28, pt. 1, p. 80; Cashin, *Lachlan McGillivray*, 179–180; Milling, *Red Carolinians*, 198.

33. McDowell, *Journals of the Commissioners of the Indian Trade*, 238; *DRIA*, vol. 2, pp. 351, 510; *DRIA*, vol. 3, pp. 301, 368, 417, 445; Easterby, *JCHA*, vol. 3, p. 313; William Bonar map, "A Draught of the Creek Nation," May 1757 (original in British Public Record Office, London, CO700/Carolina 21); Jacobs, *The Edmond Atkin Report*, 64; Adair, *History*, 18, 343; Swanton, "Early History of the Creek Indians and Their Neighbors," 283, 418n; Fairbanks, *Ethnographic Report on Royce Area 79*, 109. The reference to Breed Camp Chickasaw moving to Illinois is in Fairbanks, *Ethnographic Report on Royce Area 79*, 114; Adair's discussion of the anti-English behavior of the "Torrepine [terrapin] Chieftain" is one of the rare mentions of the Creek territory Chickasaw in his book (Adair, *History*, 310–311). This man may or may not have been a resident of the Breed Camp, however. A man called "Terrapin Leader" who visited the main Chickasaw settlement in 1772 was probably the same Chickasaw discussed by Adair, for the former man's behavior was also controversial (Letter, John McIntosh to Charles Stuart, Sept. 33, 1772, in Eron O. Rowland, "Peter Chester," *Publications of the Mississippi Historical Society*, Centenary Series, 5(1925): 163. See also Duane Champagne, *Social Order and Political Change: Constitutional Governments among the Cherokee, the Choctaw, the Chickasaw, and the Creek* (Stanford: Stanford Univ. Press, 1992), 63. Champagne asserts that the Terrapin Leader was from the Breed Camp; Galloway (*Choctaw Genesis*, 336), in the face of overwhelming evidence to the contrary, erroneously concluded that the Breed Camp was on the Tennessee River and that its location there influenced one of the Chickasaw migration legends, which asserts that the Chickasaw first went to the Tennessee River before finally settling on the Tombigbee.

34. Easterby, *JCHA*, vol. 9, p. 305; Milling, *Red Carolinians*, 192n.

35. *DRIA*, vol. 2, pp. 384–385, 509–510.

36. Victor Collot map, approximately 1796, in Edward E. Ayer Collection, Newberry Library, Chicago, published in Swanton, "Early History of the Creek Indians and Their Neighbors"; map entitled "Mississippi Territory," by S. Lewis, printed by Thomas and Andrews, Boston, 1812 (an original copy is in Special Collections, Mitchell Memorial Library, Mississippi State Univ., Starkville); "Map of Mississippi," by John Melish, 1819 (copy at MDAH); "Map of Louisiana, Mississippi, and Alabama," by A. Finley, 1826 (copy at MDAH).

37. Fairbanks, *Ethnographic Report on Royce Area 79*, 261.

38. Romans, *A Concise Natural History*, 128; Declaration of Silbestre Labadia, July 5, 1782,

in Lawrence Kinnaird, "Spain in the Mississippi Valley," *Annual Report of the American Historical Association for the Year 1945* (Washington, D.C.: U.S. Government Printing Office), vol. 3, pt. 2 (1946), 31; Wyatt F. Jeltz, "The Relations of Negroes and Choctaw and Chickasaw Indians," *Journal of Negro History* 33(Jan. 1948): 25–30; Michael F. Doran, "Negro Slaves of the Five Civilized Tribes," *Annals of the Association of American Geographers* 68(Sept. 1978): 337–338, 346, table 2.

39. Doran, "Negro Slaves of the Five Civilized Tribes," 337–342; Daniel F. Littlefield, Jr., *The Chickasaw Freedmen* (Westport, Conn.: Greenwood Press, 1980), 4–10; Jeltz, "The Relations of Negroes and Choctaw and Chickasaw Indians," 29.

CHAPTER 2

1. For comprehensive discussions of the seventeenth-century European contacts with the Choctaw, Chickasaw, and other groups, see Galloway, *Choctaw Genesis.*

2. Edward G. Bourne, ed., *Narratives of the Career of Hernando De Soto* (New York: Allerton Book Co., 1904), vol. 1; Moore, *Nairne's Journals,* 40, 62–64; Clayton et al., *The De Soto Chronicles;* Adair, *History,* 459–469; for an excellent study of Indian-European interaction in the south, see Crane, *The Southern Frontier.* Regarding the very early eighteenth-century Chickasaw, see Moore, *Nairne's Journals;* see also John D. Stubbs, Jr., "The Chickasaw Contact with the La Salle Expedition in 1682," in Galloway, *La Salle and His Legacy,* 41–48. For a general overview of English-Chickasaw-French interaction between 1699 and 1744, see Phelps, "The Chickasaw, the English, and the French," 117–133. An article dealing with the causes and repercussions of Indian attacks on French travelers on the Mississippi River in the 1740s supplements Phelps's article in that original French documents related to the northern New France colony are utilized in addition to those related to the Louisiana colony (Norman W. Caldwell, "The Chickasaw Threat to French Control of the Mississippi in the 1740s," in *Chronicles of Oklahoma* 17[1939]: 465–492). Caldwell, however, had the mistaken notion that the eighteenth-century Chickasaw were located on the upper Yazoo River; see also William M. Simpson, "Rivalry for Empire: Choctaw and Chickasaw Relations with the English in the Eighteenth Century" (Master's thesis, 1972, Department of History, Mississippi State Univ., Starkville). An overview of the 1736 French attacks on the Chickasaw villages makes use of original French documents to the total exclusion of English ones and therefore lacks comprehensiveness (Allan Cabaniss, "Ackia: Battle in the Wilderness," *Northeast Mississippi Historical Journal* 5, no. 1[Nov. 1972]: 1–15); see also a poplar article by Cabaniss, "Ackia: Battle in the Wilderness, 1736," *History Today* 25, no. 12(Dec. 1975): 799–817. For a contemporary assessment of the French-Chickasaw-English interactions in 1755 see Jacobs, *The Edmond Atkin Report.*

3. Moore, *Nairne's Journals;* Swanton, "Social and Religious Beliefs and Usages," 173–273.

4. Moore, *Nairne's Journals,* 38.

5. Ibid., 38–39; Romans, *A Concise Natural History,* 125. The nature of upper leadership among the Chickasaw by the mid–seventeenth century as illustrated by Romans's statement regarding Paya Mattaha is partially clarified by Malcolm McGee, who states: "The Head Chief, like the King was in some measure hereditary, the head chief being from the beloved family" (McGee-Draper Narrative, 122). McGee's statement seems to imply that the great

war chiefs, and possibly the kings, were members of a highly respected and elite family or clan called by the Chickasaw the "honored family." James Adair's characterization of the honored people is summarized by one writer as "a group of old beloved men or religious specialists, who argued that they deserved to be supported by the labor of others because their services prevented the young from violating the sacred customs and bringing misfortune to the community" (Champagne, *Social Order and Political Change*, 71). Patricia Galloway has speculated that honored men among the Choctaw were probably elderly men who served as councils to the primary chiefs (Galloway, "Choctaw Factionalism and Civil War, 1746–1750," *Journal of Mississippi History* 44[Nov. 1982]: 294). If so, that obviously incomplete definition may apply also to the Chickasaw honored men. Another interesting statement is that made in a 1753 letter to South Carolina by the Chickasaw head men, who stated that the South Carolina governor's English traders were his "honored men" (*DRIA*, vol. 2, p. 458), which suggests that at least some traders were considered part of the governor's ruling family, so to speak, and represented it as such in bringing goods and messages from him, carrying messages from the Chickasaw to him, and giving advice to both the Chickasaw and the governor. Also, in 1793, a prominent Chickasaw chief called Wolf's Friend referred to the Spanish Chickasaw and Choctaw agent as the "Beloved man" of the Spanish (Corbitt and Corbitt, "Papers from the Spanish Archives," 34[1962]: 87). Perhaps beloved men were those who had never participated in war or had retired from warring due to advanced years or disabilities. Thus they may have been men who advised the chiefs and the young toward solving problems in prudent ways.

6. Galloway, "Henri de Tonti," 146–175; Thomas Cooper and David J. McCord, eds., *The Statutes at Large of South Carolina* (Columbia: 1837), vol. 2, pp. 309–316; Hudson, *The Southeastern Indians*, 436.

7. Hudson, *The Southeastern Indians*, 437; Rowland and Sanders, *MPA:FD*, vol. 3, pp. 34, 37; see Galloway, "Henri de Tonti," 157. These groups were allied against the Choctaw in 1702.

8. Hudson, *The Southeastern Indians*, 437; William R. Snell, "Indian Slavery in Colonial South Carolina, 1671–1795" (Ph.D. dissertation, Univ. of Alabama, Tuscaloosa, 1972), 126; regarding postcontact disease among native Americans see Henry Dobyns, *Their Number Become Thinned* (Knoxville: Univ. of Tennessee Press, 1983); Ann F. Romenofsky, "The Introduction of European Diseases and Aboriginal Population Collapse," *Mississippi Archaeology* 20, no. 1(1985): 2–19; Romenofsky, *Vectors of Death: The Archaeology of European Contact* (Albuquerque: Univ. of New Mexico Press, 1987).

9. Rowland and Sanders, *MPA:FD*, vol. 3, p. 671.

10. The Shawnee-Chickasaw conflict tradition first appears in two secondary histories published in 1823: John Haywood, *The Civil and Political History of the State of Tennessee from Its Earliest Settlement up to the Year 1796* (Nashville: Publishing House of the Methodist Episcopal Church South, 1891, reprint of 1823 edition), 426, and John Haywood, *The Natural and Aboriginal History of Tennessee*, 206; see also Williams, *Tennessee during the Revolutionary War*, 172.

11. McWilliams, *Iberville's Gulf Journals*, 171–173; Galloway, "Henri de Tonti," 149; Pierre Margry, *Decouvertes et establissements des Francais dans l'ouest er dans le sud ed l'Amerique Septentrionale, 1614–1754*, 4 vols. (Paris, 1875–1886), vol. 4, p. 520; Rowland and Sanders,

MPA:FD, vol. 2, p. 23; Rowland and Sanders, *MPA:FD*, vol. 3, pp. 36, 52; Patricia K. Galloway, Dunbar Rowland, and A. G. Sanders, trans. and eds., *MPA:FD*, vols. 4 and 5 (Baton Rouge: Louisiana State Univ. Press, 1984), vol. 4, p. 144; B. F. French, *Historical Memoirs of Louisiana* (New York, 1853), 107. French states that after leaving Fort Tombecbe during the 1736 Ackia campaign the French "reached a fort called Tibia." Whether he got this from a document or from his imagination is unknown, but because the French force stayed a few days at the mouth of Octibia (Oktibbeha/Tibbee) Creek, it is possible that a rudimentary fort of some type was hurriedly constructed by the advance of the army and was the same one mentioned by Diron d'Artaguette in 1737 as being occupied by Chickasaws at that time (Galloway et al., *MPA:FD*, vol. 4, p. 144). According to H. S. Halbert ("The French Trading Post and the Chocchuma Village in East Mississippi," *Publications of the Mississippi Historical Society* 11[1910]: 325–329), an apparent blockhouse, which Halbert suggested may have been built by d'Iberville or Bienville, was still standing in the mid–nineteenth century on top of Plymouth Bluff near the mouth of Tibbee Creek. However, as pointed out by Jack D. Elliott, Jr., in James R. Atkinson and Jack D. Elliott, Jr., *A Cultural Resources Survey of Selected Construction Areas in the Tennessee-Tombigbee River Waterway: Alabama and Mississippi*, vol. 2 (Starkville: Mississippi State Univ., 1978), 26, and in Jack D. Elliott, "The Plymouth Fort and the Creek War: A Mystery Solved," *Journal of Mississippi History* 62, no. 4(Nov. 2000): 329–370, it is highly unlikely that an early eighteenth-century Octibia "fort," whether built by the French or the Chickasaw, would have survived that long; the structure described by Halbert was undoubtedly built in 1813 during the Creek uprising by Choctaw Agency interpreter John Pitchlynn, who lived at Plymouth Bluff. For discussions of the early Chickasaw-English-French interactions see Joel W. Martin, "Southeastern Indians and the English Trade in Skins and Slaves," in Charles Hudson and Carmen C. Tesser, eds., *The Forgotten Centuries: Indians and Europeans in the American South, 1521–1704* (Athens: Univ. of Georgia Press, 1994), 304–324; Daniel H. Unser, Jr., *Indians, Settlers, & Slaves in a Frontier Exchange Economy* (Chapel Hill: Univ. of North Carolina Press, 1992), 18–21, 78–91; Patricia D. Wood, *French-Indian Relations on the Southern Frontier, 1699–1762* (Ann Arbor, Michigan: UMI Research Press, 1979), 13–21, 45–53, 68–71, 106–109.

12. For an example of Chickasaw dissatisfaction with the English traders (resulting in the deaths of some) during the Yamasee War, see William O. Scroggs, "Early Trade and Travel in the Lower Mississippi Valley," in Benjamin F. Shambaugh, ed., *Proceedings of the Mississippi Valley Historical Association for the Year 1908–1909* (Cedar Rapids, Ohio: Torch Press, 1910), vol. 2, p. 245 n. 34; Rowland and Sanders, *MPA:FD*, vol. 2, p. 40. The chief mentioned was probably Fattalamee, the great chief in April 1708 (Moore, *Nairne's Journals*, 38).

13. Rowland and Sanders, *MPA:FD*, vol. 3, pp. 159, 161.

14. Rowland and Sanders, *MPA:FD*, vol. 2, p. 163; Rowland and Sanders, *MPA:FD*, vol. 3, p. 224.

15. Rowland and Sanders, *MPA:FD*, vol. 2, p. 219.

16. Ibid., 249.

17. For studies of culture-altering European interactions with native Americans in the south after first contact, see: Richard White, *The Roots of Dependency* (Lincoln: Univ. of Nebraska Press, 1983); J. Leitch Wright, Jr., *The Only Land They Knew: The Tragic Story of the American Indians in the Old South* (New York: Free Press, 1981); Unser, *Indians, Settlers, &*

Slaves; Wood et al., *Powhatan's Mantle;* Hudson and Tesser, *The Forgotten Centuries;* Crane, *The Southern Frontier;* Verner Crane, "The Southern Frontier in Queen Anne's War," *American Historical Review* 24, no. 3(April 1919). See also James J. Cooke, "France, The New World, and Colonial Expansion," in Galloway, *La Salle and His Legacy,* 81–92, and Glenn R. Conrad, "Reluctant Imperialist: France in North America," in Galloway, *La Salle and His Legacy,* 93–105, for discussions of the reasons for the failure of French colonialism in North America. Other works on Chickasaw-European interactions and resulting Chickasaw economic dependency include Wendy St. Jean, "The Chickasaws: Firm Friends of the English?" (Master's thesis, Department of History, Univ. of Virginia, Charlottesville, 1994), and an article by St. Jean with the same title in *Journal of Mississippi History* 68, no. 4(1996): 345–358.

18. Rowland and Sanders, *MPA:FD,* vol. 3, pp. 303, 356–357; Rowland and Sanders, *MPA:FD,* vol. 2, pp. 24, 277.

19. Rowland and Sanders, *MPA:FD,* vol. 2, p. 277; Rowland and Sanders, *MPA:FD,* vol. 3, p. 343; Adair, *History,* 69, 378.

20. Rowland and Sanders, *MPA:FD,* vol. 3, pp. 355–356.

21. Ibid., 357.

22. Ibid., 343.

23. Ibid., 457, 459.

24. Rowland and Sanders, *MPA:FD,* vol. 2, pp. 411, 537; Galloway et al., *MPA:FD,* vol. 4, p. 21; Romans, *A Concise Natural History,* 274–275.

25. Rowland and Sanders, *MPA:FD,* vol. 2, p. 573.

26. Galloway et al., *MPA:FD,* vol. 4, pp. 16, 20–22.

27. Jack D. Elliott, Jr., "The Fort of Natchez and the Colonial Origins of Mississippi," *Journal of Mississippi History* 52(Aug. 1990): 159–197; John A. Green, "Governor Perier's Expedition against the Natchez Indians," *Louisiana Historical Quarterly* 19(1936): 547–577.

28. Galloway et al., *MPA:FD,* vol. 4, pp. 18–19, 71, 122; Rowland and Sanders, *MPA:FD,* vol. 1, p. 183.

29. Rowland and Sanders, *MPA:FD,* vol. 1, p. 59; Galloway et al., *MPA:FD,* vol. 4, p. 37.

30. Galloway et al., *MPA:FD,* vol. 4, p. 37.

31. Ibid., 55, 74. The chief was probably Ymahatabe; see further references to him in following text.

32. Rowland and Sanders, *MPA:FD,* vol. 1, p. 184; Galloway et al., *MPA:FD,* vol. 4, pp. 58–61.

33. Galloway et al., *MPA:FD,* vol. 4, pp. 18, 22, 62, 148–149; Rowland and Sanders, *MPA:FD,* vol. 1, p. 183; Edmond Atkin, "Historical Account of the Revolt of the Choctaw Indians in the late War from the French to the British Alliance and of their Return Since to that of the French," Jan. 20, 1753 (British Library, Lansdowne Manuscript 809; on microfilm at MDAH).

34. Galloway et al., *MPA:FD,* vol. 4, pp. 62, 65. Regis Du Roullet, the writer of this source, stated that the four villages, according to Ymahatabe, "prefer to abandon [meaning move away from] the three villages [in the small prairie] of their nation that are listening to the word of the English rather than the supplies of the French, and that the Great Chief [of the Choctaw] granted them their request." In an article by Patricia Galloway, the Du Roullet statement is ignored as inaccurate; she contends that the small prairie villages were the ones that should have been addressed. However, there is no actual contradiction of Du Roul-

let's statement in the documents. As a result of Galloway's article, other researchers have made dubious (probably erroneous) statements and hypothesis. She states that Ymahatabe's plan to move three villages to the Choctaw nation in 1731 showed that these villages were pro-French and that they were the three villages of the small prairie (Patricia Galloway, "Ougoula Tchetoka, Ackia and Bienville's First Chickasaw War: Whose Strategy and Tactics?" *Journal of Chickasaw History* 2, no. 1[1996]: 3–10). In fact, however, they were *not* the three villages of the small prairie but, rather, the *four* villages of the *large* prairie listed by Du Roullet.

35. Galloway et al., *MPA:FD,* vol. 4, p. 126.

36. Ibid., 70.

37. Ibid., 80, 122–123, 126; Rowland and Sanders, *MPA:FD,* vol. 1, pp. 185–190.

38. Rowland and Sanders, *MPA:FD,* vol. 1, pp. 165, 185–190; Galloway et al., *MPA:FD,* vol. 4, pp. 122–123, 126.

39. Rowland and Sanders, *MPA:FD,* vol. 1, pp. 190, 198, 200; Galloway et al., *MPA:FD,* vol. 4, p. 81.

40. Clayton et al., *The De Soto Chronicles,* vol. 1, p. 106; Galloway et al., *MPA:FD,* vol. 4, pp. 121–122; Rowland and Sanders, *MPA:FD,* vol. 1, pp. 165–167; Atkinson, "A Historic Contact Indian Settlement," 61–82. As discussed in Chapter 1, the Chackchiuma were apparently at least the last occupants of a large Mississippian-Protohistoric-Historic settlement in and around the present-day city of Starkville, Mississippi, and the Mississippi State University campus. It may be here that De Soto camped in 1540–1541 or visited when he marched to "Saquechuma."

41. Rowland and Sanders, *MPA:FD,* vol. 1, p. 167. These Chackchiuma were probably from the village of Achouchouma (or "Chochouma"), which likely originated when the Chickasaw accepted a portion of that splintered tribe in the very early eighteenth century (see Atkinson, "Historic Chickasaw Cultural Material," 53–54, and Atkinson, "A Historic Contact Indian Settlement," 67).

42. Rowland and Sanders, *MPA:FD,* vol. 1, pp. 210–211; Galloway et al., *MPA:FD,* vol. 4, p. 141; for a discussion of French-Chickasaw-Choctaw interactions between 1733 and 1735, see Michael Foret, "War or Peace? Louisiana, the Choctaws, and the Chickasaws, 1733–1735," *Louisiana History* 31, no. 3(Summer 1990): 273–292.

43. Galloway et al., *MPA:FD,* vol. 4, p. 141; Gaspard-Joseph Chaussegros de Lery, Jr., "Journal De La Campagne Faite Par Le Detachement Du Canada Sur Les Chicachas En Fevrier 1740 Au Nombre De 201 Francais, Et 337 Sauvages De Canada, Illinois, Missouris Et 58 Chactas Faisant En Tout 596 Hommes" (hereafter cited as de Lery's Journal), in *Rapport de l'Archivists de la Province de Quebec pour 1922–1923* (Quebec, 1923), 164. An anonymous typescript translation is in the files of the Natchez Trace Parkway Headquarters, Tupelo, Miss.

44. Rowland and Sanders, *MPA:FD,* vol. 1, pp. 234–235.

45. Ibid., 227.

46. Ibid.

47. Ibid., 241–242.

48. Rowland and Sanders, *MPA:FD,* vol. 3, pp. 633–634; Galloway et al., *MPA:FD,* vol. 4, p. 132.

49. Rowland and Sanders, *MPA:FD*, vol. 1, pp. 229–230, 245. Diron d'Artaguette stated that this village was Tchitchatala, but that it was actually Choukafalya is shown by Bienville's statement in 1736 with regard to the village in which the Great Chief's son had been killed during the 1734 attack (see Rowland and Sanders, *MPA:FD*, vol. 1, p. 304). Bienville also stated that it was the Great Chief's uncle rather than his brother who also had been killed there. By 1736 the village of Choukafalya, which was adjacent to the village of Ackia, was located in the present-day southern city limits of Tupelo, mostly in a present-day subdivision called Lee Acres. See Atkinson, "The Ackia and Ogoula Tchetoka Chickasaw Village Locations."

50. Rowland and Sanders, *MPA:FD*, vol. 1, pp. 256–257.

51. Ibid., 266–267, 275, 288; Galloway et al., *MPA:FD*, vol. 4, pp. 147–148.

52. Rowland and Sanders, *MPA:FD*, vol. 1, pp. 273, 276.

CHAPTER 3

1. Rowland and Sanders, *MPA:FD*, vol. 1, pp. 301, 316; for a comprehensive but somewhat subscholarly study of the French attempts to conquer the Chickasaw, see John B. Harris, *From Old Mobile to Fort Assumption: A Story of the French Attempts to Colonize Louisiana, and Destroy the Chickasaw Indians* (Nashville: Parthenon Press, 1959). Following old secondary sources, Harris mislocates the sites of Ackia and other towns and presents imaginative prose.

2. Rowland and Sanders, *MPA:FD*, vol. 1, pp. 300–301.

3. Caroline Dunn and Eleanor Dunn, trans., "Indiana's First War" ("Account of the Battle Fought by D'Artaguette with the Chickasaws, March 25, 1736"), *Indiana Historical Society Publications* (Indianapolis) 8(1924): 107–109. This is a translated contemporary French account of the d'Artaguette fiasco; de Batz, "Plan et Scituation"; Atkinson, "The Ackia and Ogoula Tchetoka Chickasaw Village Locations," 65–70, fig. 2; Atkinson, "Historic Chickasaw Cultural Material," 34. The large prairie village (or villages) involved is shown on the 1740 French map (discussed in Chapter 1) that also shows the attack route taken by d'Artaguette in 1736 (Broutin, "Carte Particuliere," 1740).

4. Letter, Samuel Eveleigh to Herman Verelst, South Carolina, June 29, 1736, *CRG*, vol. 21, pp. 175–178.

5. Letter, Eveleigh to Verelst, South Carolina, Aug. 7, 1736, *CRG*, vol. 21, pp. 203–205.

6. Dunn and Dunn, "Indiana's First War," 109–113, 117; early French writers of Louisiana colony and New France history address the d'Artaguette attack and the subsequent Bienville attack, but their descriptions are usually sketchy and diverge from the contemporary reports by participants in the attacks as a result of their not having access to those written reports. Du Pratz's descriptions are the longest and contain a few interesting details not to be found in the reports, but because of other obvious inaccuracies most such details cannot be considered reliable. Du Pratz had been a resident of the French colony and wrote credible descriptions of events that he observed while there, especially with regard to the Natchez Indians, but he had been in France for two years prior to the attacks in 1736 and thus wrote without the aid of contemporary reports and without access to colony participants. See du Pratz, *History of Louisiana*, 87–96; also see Charles E. O'Neill, ed., *Charlevoix's Louisiana:*

Selections from the History and the Journal (Baton Rouge: Louisiana State Univ. Press, 1977), 127–128. Pierre F. X. de Charlevoix's multivolume work was written in and first published (1744) in Paris after he had left the New World in about 1728.

7. Dunn and Dunn, "Indiana's First War," 113–115, 125; Letter, Eveleigh to Verelst, South Carolina, June 29, 1736, *CRG*, vol. 21, pp. 175–178; Letter, Eveleigh to Verelst, South Carolina, Aug. 7, 1736, *CRG*, vol. 21, pp. 203–205.

8. Dunn and Dunn, "Indiana's First War," 115–117; Galloway et al., *MPA:FD*, vol. 4, p. 141.

9. Dunn and Dunn, "Indiana's First War," 115–117.

10. Ibid., 117; Galloway et al., *MPA:FD*, vol. 4, p. 150.

11. Dunn and Dunn, "Indiana's First War," 120–121, 125; *Richardville's Account of d'Artaguette's Attack,* Archives des Colonies, series C13C, vol. 4, ff. 202–205 (copy at MDAH translated by Patricia K. Galloway); Galloway et al., *MPA:FD*, vol. 4, p. 141; Letter, Eveleigh to Verelst, South Carolina, June 29, 1736, *CRG*, vol. 21, pp. 175–178; Letter, Eveleigh to George Morley, June 4, 1736, *CRG*, vol. 21, p. 155; Letter, Eveleigh to Verelst, South Carolina, Oct. 16, 1736, *CRG*, vol. 21, p. 214.

12. Dunn and Dunn, "Indiana's First War," 121; Letter, Eveleigh to Verelst, South Carolina, June 29, 1736, *CRG*, vol. 21, pp. 175–178; *Richardville's Account.*

13. Dunn and Dunn, "Indiana's First War," 121; Letter, Eveleigh to Verelst, South Carolina, June 4, 1736, *CRG*, vol. 21, p. 155.

14. Dunn and Dunn, "Indiana's First War," 125–127; *Richardville's Account;* Rowland and Sanders, *MPA:FD*, vol. 1, pp. 311–314; Galloway et al., *MPA:FD*, vol. 4, pp. 141–142; Letter, Eveleigh to Verelst, South Carolina, Aug. 7, 1736, *CRG*, vol. 21, pp. 203–205; Letter, Mathurin le Petit to Francis Ritz, June 25, 1738, in R. G. Thwaites, *The Jesuit Relations and Allied Documents,* 73 vols. (Cleveland: Burrows Brothers, 1896–1901), vol. 69, p. 32; Jean Delanglez, *The French Jesuits in Lower Louisiana, 1700–1763* (Washington, D.C.: Catholic Univ. of America, 1935), 307.

15. Adair, *History,* 158–162.

16. *Richardville's Account;* Letter, Eveleigh to Verelst, South Carolina, Aug. 7, 1736, *CRG*, vol. 21, pp. 203–205.

17. *Richardville's Account;* Rowland and Sanders, *MPA:FD*, vol. 1, pp. 311–314; Galloway et al., *MPA:FD*, vol. 4, pp. 141–142.

18. *CRG*, vol. 22, pt. 2, pp. 71–72, and vol. 29, p. 308; Jean-Bernard Bossu, *Travels in the Interior of North America, 1751–1762,* Seymour Feiler, trans. and ed. (Norman: Univ. of Oklahoma Press, 1962), 173; Galloway et al., *MPA:FD*, vol. 4, p. 153 n. 17.

19. Galloway et al., *MPA:FD*, vol. 4, 149.

20. Rowland and Sanders, *MPA:FD*, vol. 1, pp. 302–303, 317; French, *Historical Memoirs,* 107–108. The fort built at the portage was not necessarily a palisade type, although it probably was. Chaussegros de Lery, Sr., mentioned in 1739 that in addition to palisade construction, the French had the option of building obstacles "made of trees one on top of the other" (Joseph L. Peyser, "The Chickasaw Wars of 1736 and 1740," *Journal of Mississippi History* 44, no. 1[Feb. 1982]: 13). The official French reports, however, mention that the fort was built by cutting "piles," which implies that they were erected vertically.

21. De Marigny map, 1743, copy at Natchez Trace Parkway; de Crenay map (1733) and Purcell map (1773), reproduced in Swanton, "Early History of the Creek Indians and Their

Neighbors"; Rowland and Sanders, *MPA:FD*, vol. 1, p. 309; Captain Roberts map, ca. 1773; part of the original Romans map (in the Colonial Office, London, in 1924 but now missing) is supposedly the one redrawn and discussed in Henry S. Halbert, "Bernard Romans' Map of 1772," *Publications of the Mississippi Historical Society* 6(1902): 414; P. Lee Phillips, *Notes on the Life and Works of Bernard Romans* (Florida Historical Society, Gainesville, 1924), 119; Gideon Lincecum, "Personal Reminiscences of an Octogenarian," in *American Sportsman* (Oct. 24, 1874).

22. French, *Historical Memoirs*, 107–108; Rowland and Sanders, *MPA:FD*, vol. 1, p. 303.

23. Adair, *History*, 378.

24. Rowland and Sanders, *MPA:FD*, vol. 1, p. 303.

25. Ibid., 303–304.

26. Ibid., 304.

27. Ibid., 305, 318; Galloway et al., *MPA:FD*, vol. 4, p. 148; *DRIA*, vol. 3, p. 461. The thesis of a recent short article about the French/Choctaw and Chickasaw war concerns the obvious—that the Indians, especially the Choctaw, had their own agenda (revenge) in the two French-Indian attacks on the Chickasaw in 1736 and thus were using the French as much as the reverse (Galloway, "Ougoula Tchetoka, Ackia, and Bienville's First Chickasaw War," 3–10).

28. Galloway et al., *MPA:FD*, vol. 4, p. 121.

29. Atkinson, "The Ackia and Ogoula Tchetoka Chickasaw Village Locations," 54–61; the first researcher to suggest that the small prairie and Ackia were somewhere in south Tupelo was Henry B. Collins, archaeologist with the Smithsonian Institution, in a report dated January 14, 1939 (see Don Martini, "The Search for Ackia," *Northeast Mississippi Historical Journal* 5[Nov. 1971]: 17–31). In an unpublished appendix to this article, Martini agreed with Collins (manuscript of "The Search for Ackia," on file at Natchez Trace Parkway Headquarters, Tupelo, Mississippi). In 1980, Cook et al. ("Historic Chickasaw Village Locations," 30) were the first to suggest that Ackia and the other small prairie villages had been located on the north part of the ridge system in the area adjacent on the south to the old Tupelo High School.

30. Rowland and Sanders, *MPA:FD*, vol. 1, pp. 305, 318; Dumont du Montigny, "Attack of the French Army on the Village of the Enemy the Chickasaw the 26 May, 1736" (translation of French title), map in Montigny's "Memoire," ms. in the Edward E. Ayer Collection, Newberry Library, Chicago.

31. Rowland and Sanders, *MPA:FD*, vol. 1, p. 305.

32. Ibid., 306–307, 319; Galloway et al., *MPA:FD*, vol. 4, p. 35 n. 9.

33. Du Pratz, *History of Louisiana*, 91; Adair, *History*, 381–383.

34. Du Montigny map, "Attack of the French Army"; Ignace Francois Broutin, "Plan a l'estimate ou. Scituation de Trois villages Chicachas 1736," original map in Archives Nationales, Paris, France (copy at Natchez Trace Parkway Headquarters, Tupelo, Mississippi); Atkinson, "The Ackia and Ogoula Tchetoka Chickasaw Village Locations," 53–70; map (unknown maker), "Plan Figure des Villages Chikachas Attaquez Par les Francois le vingt six May 1736," original in *Ministere de la France D'Outremer, Depot des Plans et Fortifications*, Archives Nationales, Paris. See foregoing map in *The American Heritage History of the Thirteen Colonies* (American Heritage Publishing, New York, 1967), 222. The identifying cap-

tion added by the publisher states in error that the scene is near the Chickasaw village of "Amalahta."

35. Rowland and Sanders, *MPA:FD*, vol. 1, pp. 319, 339, 366; Letter, Eveleigh to Verelst, South Carolina, Aug. 7, 1736, *CRG*, vol. 21, pp. 203–205; Rowland and Sanders, *MPA:FD*, vol. 3, p. 690; Galloway et al., *MPA:FD*, vol. 4, p. 153; Letter, Eveleigh to Verelst, South Carolina, Dec. 1, 1736, *CRG*, vol. 21, p. 277.

36. Rowland and Sanders, *MPA:FD*, vol. 1, pp. 308–309; McGee-Draper Narrative, 115.

37. *MPA:FD*, vol. 1, pp. 307, 310, 320, 331; Letter, Bienville to the governor of South Carolina, Mobile, Sept. 2, 1736, *CRG*, vol. 21, pp. 266–269.

38. See Peyser, "The Chickasaw Wars of 1736 and 1740," 1–25; Rowland and Sanders, *MPA:FD*, vol. 3, p. 704.

39. Galloway et al., *MPA:FD*, vol. 4, p. 150; Rowland and Sanders, *MPA:FD*, vol. 1, p. 331.

40. Rowland and Sanders, *MPA:FD*, vol. 1, p. 331.

41. Ibid., 339.

CHAPTER 4

1. Rowland and Sanders, *MPA:FD*, vol. 1, pp. 332–333, 389, 404; Anonymous, "Journal of the Chickasa War," in J. F. H. Claiborne, *Mississippi as a Province, Territory and State* (Jackson: Power and Barksdale, 1880), 65, 74–75. The journal, by an unidentified officer, had been published in French in 1859 (*Journal de la Guerre du Micissippi contre les Chickachas en 1739 et finie en 1740 le 1er d'Avril par un Officier de l'Armee de M. de Nouaille* [New York, 1859]). According to Claiborne, his copy of the publication or a handwritten copy of the journal (he does not say which) was obtained in Paris by Colonel B. F. French and translated by Ferdinand Claiborne of New Orleans. It is twenty-one printed pages in length (pp. 64–85 of Claiborne's history).

2. Rowland and Sanders, *MPA:FD*, vol. 1, pp. 338, 340; Rowland and Sanders, *MPA:FD*, vol. 3, p. 694.

3. Rowland and Sanders, *MPA:FD*, vol. 3, p. 700.

4. Ibid., 702–703.

5. Ibid., 703–704.

6. Ibid., 704.

7. Ibid., 741; Galloway et al., *MPA:FD*, vol. 4, pp. 148–149.

8. Rowland and Sanders, *MPA:FD*, vol. 3, p. 704.

9. Ibid., 704–705.

10. Jennings, "Chickasaw and Earlier Indian Cultures," 166–167.

11. Rowland and Sanders, *MPA:FD*, vol. 3, p. 705.

12. For the best discussion of horses possessed by the Chickasaw and the uses made thereof, including as objects of trade, see Morgan, "An Analysis of Historic Period Chickasaw Settlement Patterns," 120–139. See also Adair, *History*, 205, 340, and Williams's footnote on latter page; in the 1770s, John F. D. Smyth reported that the Chickasaw were "remarkably handsome, and . . . have a beautiful breed of horses amongst them, which they carefully preserve unmixed" (Smyth, *A Tour in the United States of America*, vol. 1, p. 361); as a result

of intentional inbreeding, the Chickasaw horse retained its identity as such throughout the nineteenth century and even into the twentieth. My late father, of Chickasaw County, Mississippi, told me in the 1960s of having many years earlier known a man who owned one of the last "Chickasaw Ponies."

13. Easterby, *JCHA*, vol. 1 (1951), p. 560; Rowland and Sanders, *MPA:FD*, vol. 1, pp. 709–710, 718–719; Galloway et al., *MPA:FD*, vol. 4, p. 163.

14. Galloway et al., *MPA:FD*, vol. 4, pp. 149, 151; Rowland and Sanders, *MPA:FD*, vol. 3, pp. 706–707, 767; Rowland and Sanders, *MPA:FD*, vol. 1, p. 323; Bonnefoy's Narrative, in Samuel C. Williams, *Early Travels in the Tennessee Country, 1540–1800* (Johnson City, Tenn: Watauga Press, 1928), 160–162; Journal of David Tait, entry for March 27, 1772, Appendix A in *DAR*, vol. 5, p. 265; Benjamin Hawkins, *A Sketch of the Creek Country, in the Years 1798 and 1799*, 42.

15. Rowland and Sanders, *MPA:FD*, vol. 1, pp. 364, 387, 396–397, 399; Rowland and Sanders, *MPA:FD*, vol. 3, pp. 724–726; *CRG*, vol. 22, pt. 1, p. 89.

16. *CRG*, vol. 4, pp. 325–326.

17. Easterby, *JCHA*, vol. 2, p. 24.

18. Rowland and Sanders, *MPA:FD*, vol. 1, pp. 384–385; see Peyser, "The Chickasaw Wars of 1736 and 1740," for a discussion of proposed French attack plans.

19. Rowland and Sanders, *MPA:FD*, vol. 1, pp. 386, 404, 414, 434; Anonymous, "Journal of the Chickasa War," 65; for a study of the second French campaign, see Michael J. Foret, "The Failure of Administration: The Chickasaw Campaign of 1739–1740," *Revue de Louisiane/ Louisiana Review* 11(1982): 49–60.

20. Rowland and Sanders, *MPA:FD*, vol. 1, pp. 428–429.

21. Ibid.

22. Ibid., 430–432; Anonymous, "Journal of the Chickasa War," 80.

23. Galloway et al., *MPA:FD*, vol. 4, pp. 74–79.

24. Rowland and Sanders, *MPA:FD*, vol. 1, pp. 444, 450; de Lery's Journal, 157–158.

25. De Lery's Journal, 157–158; Rowland and Sanders, *MPA:FD*, vol. 1, pp. 419–420, 453–454; Rowland and Sanders, *MPA:FD*, vol. 3, p. 741; Galloway et al., *MPA:FD*, vol. 4, pp. 170–171; Anonymous, "Journal of the Chickasa War," 83.

26. Rowland and Sanders, *MPA:FD*, vol. 1, pp. 453–454; de Lery's Journal, 157–158.

27. Rowland and Sanders, *MPA:FD*, vol. 1, p. 450.

28. De Lery's Journal, 157–160.

29. Ibid., 160–161.

30. Ibid., 161.

31. Ibid., 161; Anonymous, "Journal of the Chickasa War," 79.

32. De Lery's Journal, 162.

33. Ibid., 162; see Atkinson, "The Ackia and Ogoula Tchetoka Chickasaw Village Locations"; see also Peyser, "The Chickasaw Wars of 1736 and 1740."

34. De Lery's Journal, 162–163.

35. Ibid.; according to Mingo Houma there were only about forty Natchez remaining by August 1737 (Galloway et al., *MPA:FD*, vol. 4, p. 149).

36. De Lery's Journal, 163–164.

37. Ibid.; Rowland and Sanders, *MPA:FD*, vol. 1, pp. 452–453.

38. De Lery's Journal, 163–165; Rowland and Sanders, *MPA:FD*, vol. 1, pp. 452–456.

39. Rowland and Sanders, *MPA:FD*, vol. 1, 455; de Lery's Journal, 165.

40. Rowland and Sanders, *MPA:FD*, vol. 1, p. 457.

41. See Jacobs, *The Edmond Atkin Report*, 69–70; Caldwell ("The Chickasaw Threat to French Control," 471) cites original French documents regarding the incarceration and expulsion to France of these men.

42. Galloway et al., *MPA:FD*, vol. 4, p. 148.

43. Rowland and Sanders, *MPA:FD*, vol. 1, p. 456.

44. Ibid., 456–457.

45. Ibid., 457–458.

46. Ibid., 444, 457–458.

47. Ibid., 458–459.

48. Ibid., 465; Rowland and Sanders, *MPA:FD*, vol. 3, p. 733.

CHAPTER 5

1. Rowland and Sanders, *MPA:FD*, vol. 3, p. 733.

2. Rowland and Sanders, *MPA:FD*, vol. 1, p. 465; Rowland and Sanders, *MPA:FD*, vol. 3, pp. 733–734.

3. Rowland and Sanders, *MPA:FD*, vol. 3, pp. 735, 748, 752, 754, 767, 776.

4. Ibid., 755.

5. Ibid., 741.

6. Ibid., 742.

7. Galloway et al., *MPA:FD*, vol. 4, pp. 182, 196, 200–202.

8. Easterby, *JCHA*, vol. 4 (1954), pp. 490, 499–500; Easterby, *JCHA*, vol. 5 (1955), p. 87; Easterby, *JCHA*, vol. 7, p. 70.

9. Galloway et al., *MPA:FD*, vol. 4, pp. 200–202; Phelps, "The Chickasaw, the English, and the French," 130–131; also see Adair, *History*, 382–383, for a possible reference to the affair; Easterby, *JCHA*, vol. 4, pp. 499–500.

10. Rowland and Sanders, *MPA:FD*, vol. 3, pp. 758–759, 774; Galloway et al., *MPA:FD*, vol. 4, p. 203; Caldwell, "The Chickasaw Threat to French Control," 477.

11. Rowland and Sanders, *MPA:FD*, vol. 3, p. 764.

12. Ibid., 774; Easterby, *JCHA*, vol. 3, p. 553; See Jacobs, *The Edmond Atkin Report*, 66–71, for a general discussion of the Chickasaw regarding their relationship with the French and with regard to their importance to the English colonies in 1755.

13. Galloway et al., *MPA:FD*, vol. 4, pp. 211–213.

14. Ibid., 217, 219–220.

15. Ibid., 226, 230.

16. Ibid., 232–233.

17. Ibid., 244.

18. Francois-Xavier Martin, *History of Louisiana from the Earliest Period*, 2 vols. (New Orleans: 1827), vol. 1, p. 322. For recent examples of mistaken references to such an attack, see

Gibson, *The Chickasaws*, 56, and Cashin, *Lachlan McGillivray*, 122. See Dawson A. Phelps's rebuttal to the notion in "The Vaudreuil Expedition, 1752," *William and Mary Quarterly* 15, no. 4(Oct. 1958): 483–493.

19. Galloway et al., *MPA:FD*, vol. 4, p. 253; see Adair, *History*, 71; Atkin, "Historical Account of the Revolt of the Choctaw."

20. Galloway et al., *MPA:FD*, vol. 4, p. 254.

21. Ibid., 254–255.

22. Easterby, *JCHA*, vol. 6, p. 173.

23. See Galloway, "Choctaw Factionalism and Civil War," 289–327, for an in-depth analysis of the Choctaw civil war. See also a revised version, Patricia K. Galloway, "Choctaw Factionalism and Civil War, 1746–1750," in Carolyn K. Reeves, ed., *The Choctaw before Removal* (Jackson: Univ. Press of Mississippi, 1985), 120–156; Galloway et al., *MPA:FD*, vol. 4, p. 260.

24. Galloway et al., *MPA:FD*, vol. 4, p. 307.

25. Adair, *History*, 338–340, 354–355; R. Nicholas Olsberg, ed., *JCHA*, vol. 10, Colonial Records of South Carolina (Columbia: Univ. of South Carolina Press, 1974), pp. 108, 178; Galloway et al., *MPA:FD*, vol. 4, p. 298; Atkin, "Historical Account of the Revolt of the Choctaw."

26. Easterby, *JCHA*, vol. 7, p. 216. Despite considerable lobbying Adair was unable to obtain reimbursement from the Commons House of Assembly (Adair, *History*, 375–376).

27. Galloway et al., *MPA:FD*, vol. 4, p. 298; Galloway, "Choctaw Factionalism and Civil War" (journal version), 309.

28. Galloway et al., *MPA:FD*, vol. 5, pp. 33–35; Adair, *History*, 344, 351. Adair gives a date of spring 1747 for this incident, but he is obviously in error. His account is similar to the 1749 account by Governor Vaudreuil, and no incident of this sort is reported in the French documents for 1747.

29. Adair, *History*, 356; Galloway et al., *MPA:FD*, vol. 5, p. 35.

30. Adair, *History*, 360.

31. Ibid., 364–365; Galloway et al., *MPA:FD*, vol. 5, p. 44. These may be the French prisoners purchased from the Chickasaw by trader John Pettycrew, reimbursement for whom he petitioned the House of Commons in March 1753 (Terry Lipscomb, ed., *JCHA*, vol. 12, Colonial Records of South Carolina [Columbia: Univ. of South Carolina Press, 1983], p. 132).

32. *DRIA*, vol. 2, pp. 6–7, 36–37, 39.

33. Ibid., 458.

34. Ibid., 365, 458; see Phelps, "The Vaudreuil Expedition, 1752."

35. "Audience of the Chickasaws at Savannah in Georgia July 1736 [with] James Oglethorpe Esqr.," July 13, 1736, typed transcript copy of a manuscript, in William R. Coe papers, South Carolina Historical Society, Charleston. A copy of the transcript was sent to me by Alexander Moore in 1987.

36. *DRIA*, vol. 3, pp. 110–113, 414, 459–461. This Pyomingo, possibly the one living at Amalata in 1746, is not the same man who achieved Chickasaw fame as a pro-American war leader during the last quarter of the eighteenth century. Born in about 1750, that Piomingo would thus have been only about six years old in 1756 (McGee-Draper Narrative, 111).

37. *DRIA*, vol. 3, pp. 458–460.

38. *DRIA*, vol. 2, pp. 512–513.

39. Ibid., 511–514.

40. Fairbanks, *Ethnographic Report on Royce Area 79*, 260–261; with regard to the traditional Cherokee attack on the Tennessee River "Chickasaw Old Fields," see Letter, R. G. Meigs to James Robertson, May 5, 1805, in James Robertson, "Correspondence of General James Robertson," *American Historical Magazine* 5, no. 2(1900): 171.

41. *DRIA*, vol. 2, p. 512.

42. Ibid., 366, 368, 384–385, 402; *DRIA*, vol. 3, pp. 109, 292.

43. Lipscomb, *JCHA*, vol. 12, pp. 295, 308, 372; Lipscomb, *JCHA*, vol. 14 (1989), p. 50; *DRIA*, vol. 2, p. 511; *DRIA*, vol. 3, p. 114.

CHAPTER 6

1. Gary B. Nash, John R. Howe, Allen F. Davis, Julie Roy Jeffrey, Peter J. Frederick, and Allan M. Winkler, *The American People: Creating a Nation and a Society*, 2 vols. (New York: Harper and Row, 1990), vol. 1, pp. 134–139.

2. Ibid., 138; Gibson, *The Chickasaws*, 57.

3. Meriwether, *Expansion of South Carolina*, 245; Cashin, *Lachlan McGillivray*, 218–223; Williams, "Introduction," in Adair, *History*.

4. "Proceedings at the Congress at Mobile with the Chickasaws and Choctaws," March–April 1765, in Dunbar Rowland, ed., *Mississippi Provincial Archives, 1763–1766: English Dominion* (hereafter *MPA:ED*) (Nashville: Press of Brandon Printing, 1911), 215–255; Gibson, *The Chickasaws*, 59–61; Cashin, *Lachlin McGillivray*, 227; Alden, *John Stuart*, 202.

5. *MPA:ED*, "Proceedings at the Congress at Mobile," 246.

6. Alden, *John Stuart*, 314–315.

7. J. Russell Snapp, *John Stuart and the Struggle for Empire on the Southern Frontier* (Baton Rouge: Louisiana State Univ. Press, 1996), 74, 78, 85, 98–99; Alden, *John Stuart*, 212, 225; McGee-Draper Narrative, 120; Letter, Alexander Fraser to General Haldimand, May 4, 1766, in C. W. Alvord and C. E. Carter, eds., *The New Regime, 1765–1767*, Collections of the Illinois Historical Society, vol. 11 (Springfield: Illinois State Historical Library, 1916), 231; James A. Padgett, ed., "Minutes of the West Florida Assembly," Jan. 30, 1769, *Louisiana Historical Quarterly* 23, no. 1(Jan. 1940): 35; Gibson, *The Chickasaws*, 61–62; Romans, *A Concise Natural History*, 128, 273; the first commissary to the Choctaw, Elias Legardere, served about three years, dying in April 1770 while commissaries were temporarily suspended (see Alden, *John Stuart*, 212–213 n. 90).

8. Purcell, "New Map of West Florida . . . ," 1773, published in Swanton, "Early History of the Creek Indians and Their Neighbors"; Roberts, "A New Map of West Florida," ca. 1773 (copied in ca. 1800). Although there seems to be no extant copy of a map made by Roberts in the 1770s, one was obviously compiled and available for copying around the turn of the century when the copy cited was made with additions related to post-1797 events. Jack D. L. Holmes's research on this map has shown that Roberts was probably Charles Roberts, who was a master in the Royal Navy until captured by the Americans in April 1776, and that a map referred to by Governor Peter Chester in 1772 was probably the "New Map of West Florida" under discussion here (Holmes, "A Mystery Map of West Florida: A Cartographical Puzzle," 217–218); McGee-Draper Narrative, 120; Harry Warren, "Missions, Missionaries,

Frontier Characters and Schools," *Publications of the Mississippi Historical Society* 8(1904): 585. Dawson A. Phelps ("Tockshish," *Journal of Mississippi History* 13[1951]: 138–145) and Gibson (*The Chickasaws*, 65, and "The Colberts: Chickasaw Nation Elitism," in H. G. Jordan and T. M. Holm, eds., *Indian Leaders: Oklahoma's First Statesmen* [Oklahoma City: Oklahoma Historical Society, 1979], p. 81) repeat Warren's erroneous statements; Henry S. Halbert, "Bernard Romans' Map of 1772," *Publications of the Mississippi Historical Society* 6(1902): 415–439; James R. Atkinson, *History of the Chickasaw Indian Agency East of the Mississippi River* (Starkville, Miss.: privately printed, 1998), 30–31.

9. Purcell, "New Map of West Florida," 1773; Roberts, "A New Map of West Florida"; "Minutes of the Congress Held at Mobile in December 1771 and January 1772," in Eron O. Rowland, "Peter Chester," 135, 143–144; Letters, Charles Stuart to John Stuart, June 12 and Dec. 26, 1770, in *DAR*, vol. 2, pp. 105, 303; Letter, Charles Stuart to John Stuart, Dec. 12, 1774, in *DAR*, vol. 7, p. 237; McGee-Draper Narrative, 125, 128; Letter, Governor Miro and Navarro to Valdes, April 1, 1788, in Corbitt and Corbitt, "Papers from the Spanish Archives," 14(1942): 97; Calloway, *The American Revolution in Indian Country*, 223, 234; Letter, Charles Stuart to John Stuart, June 12, 1770, in *DAR*, vol. 2, p. 105; James Colbert, John Highrider, and John McBean appear on a list of twenty-nine English traders and packhorsemen to the Chickasaw by January 22, 1766 (Colonial Office Records, series 5, no. 67 [British Public Records Office, Kew, England]); a letter written to "Messrs. McGillivray & Strothers" (probably John McGillivray and Arthur or William Strother) suggests that these individuals were still partners in the Indian trade in 1775 (Letter cited in Robert V. Haynes, *The Natchez District and the American Revolution* [Jackson: Univ. Press of Mississippi, 1976], 163 n. 18); Padgett, "Minutes of the West Florida Assembly," Jan. 30, 1769, p. 34. That John McGillivray was a trader among the native Americans by 1769 is evidenced by an entry in the minutes of the Council of West Florida that year (see James A. Padgett, ed., "Minutes of the Council of West Florida," June 5, 1769, *Louisiana Historical Quarterly* 23, no. 2[April 1940]: 379); Don Martini (*The Indian Chiefs of the Southeast* [Ripley, Mississippi: 1991], 106) states with no documentation that Pitman Colbert's actual name was Sam B. Colbert and that he was an adopted son of George Colbert. This speculation may or may not be factual. Collot map, ca. 1796–1800; another plantation, not shown on maps, was operated in 1771 by a man supposedly named Caldwell, who was said to have had the largest stock of cattle in the nation (Romans, *A Concise Natural History*, 128).

10. See appropriate references in Notes 8 and 9, above; the main, east fork of Old Town Creek was called Yannubbe Creek in the early days. Sometimes the west fork (Old Town) was also referred to as Yannubbe by whites.

11. Letters, Farmar to John Stuart, Dec. 16, 1765, Stuart to the Lords of Trade, July 10, 1765, and Farmar to General Thomas Gage, Dec. 16–19, 1765, in Alvord and Carter, *The New Regime*, 127–128, 130, 132.

12. Snapp, *John Stuart and the Struggle for Empire*, 35, 38, 91, 97–98; both John and Alexander McIntosh had served as members of the Commission of the Peace in British West Florida in 1769. Alexander had been a resident of British West Florida since the "Commencement of the Government" (see Padgett, "Minutes of the Council of West Florida," April 27, 1769, p. 368). See also Padgett, "Minutes of the Council of West Florida," p. 403, regarding Alexander McIntosh's residency in British West Florida.

13. Letter, John McIntosh to Richardson, April 15, 1766, in Alvord and Carter, *The New Regime,* 214–215.

14. Snapp, *John Stuart and the Struggle for Empire,* 85–86; Alden, *John Stuart,* 323; *MPA: ED,* "Proceedings at the Congress at Mobile," 254; "Minutes of the Congress Held at Mobile," in Rowland, "Peter Chester," 146.

15. Snapp, *John Stuart and the Struggle for Empire,* 85–86.

16. Ibid.; Alden, *John Stuart,* 323; "Minutes of the Congress Held at Mobile," in Rowland, "Peter Chester," 134–160; Calloway, *The American Revolution in Indian Country,* 234–235; Francis P. Prucha, *Indian Peace Medals in American History* (Madison: State Historical Society of Wisconsin, 1971), i–xiv; "Paya Mattaha" was a title name. Calloway (*The American Revolution in Indian Country,* 220), citing personal communication with Patricia Galloway, contends that the name (specifically that of the man under discussion) signified "war prophet." Calloway states that the name was derived from "Hopaii imitaha," meaning "war prophet" in the Choctaw language. Cyrus Byington's "Dictionary of the Choctaw Language" (*Bureau of American Ethnology, Bulletin 46,* Washington, D.C.: Government Printing Office, 1915) indeed states that "Hopaii" means "prophet," but it also lists alternate meanings, including "military leader or captain; a captain-general; a general; a war chief." Calloway's identification is further suspect because Byington's "Dictionary" defines "imitaha" (actually spelled *imalhtaha*) as "maintained; ministered; satisfied; prepared; stored; supplied; sustained." Despite the seemingly incongruous nature of the last part of the name, the full name undoubtedly actually signifies "war leader." Malcolm McGee, who knew the Paya Mattaha under discussion, stated in 1841 that this chief's alternate name in English was "White Man Killer" and that he belonged to the "beloved family" (McGee-Draper Narrative, 117). The latter is verified by James Adair, who mentions "Pa-Yah-Matahah and other beloved warriors" (Adair, *History,* 357). Apparently the few holy men among the Chickasaw were from the beloved "family" and were known as "Hopaiis" (Gibson, *The Chickasaws,* 12), but the latter word's inclusion as part of the name of a man belonging to the beloved "family" did not automatically mean that he was a "holy man" or "prophet." The beloved men and the beloved family were probably not people who necessarily shared a blood relationship but rather people with a fraternal relationship, with war exploits being the prerequisite for lifelong membership; they made up a membership of respected inactive elderly warriors who, having achieved spiritual status, counseled and advised the active leaders and warriors (see Swanton, "Social and Religious Beliefs," 215, 237–238, 263). In this regard, McGee stated that the meaning of "Paya Mattaha" (spelled *Pimataha* by his interviewer) is "one who has attained the highest character for war exploits." McGee also recalled Paya Mattaha's previous name, Nuholubbee (as spelled by his interviewer), and gave its meaning as "he killed a white man." Byington's "Dictionary" indeed identifies "white man" or "white people" as "Na hollo" and "kill" or "to kill" as "abi." McGee, incidentally, related that when Paya Mattaha was a very young man he "fought the [French] invaders & probably there first distinguished himself" (McGee-Draper Narrative, 117); see C. C. Jones, *The History of Georgia* (Boston: Houghton, Mifflin, 1883), 283–285, for John Wesley's interview with chiefs "Mingo Mattaw" and Paustoobee at Savannah on July 20, 1736.

17. Letter, Charles Stuart to John Stuart, June 12, 1770, in *DAR,* vol. 2, p. 105; Alden, *John Stuart,* 255, 260–261, 318–319, 323; Snapp, *John Stuart and the Struggle for Empire,* 74, 78.

18. R. S. Cotterill, *The Southern Indians: The Story of the Civilized Tribes before Removal* (Norman: Univ. of Oklahoma Press, 1954), 34; Padgett, "Minutes of the Council of West Florida," April 27, 1769, p. 368; Letters, John Stuart to Earl of Hillsborough, Dec. 2, 1770, General Thomas Gage to Earl of Hillsborough, Sept. 8, 1770, and Gage to John Stuart, Sept. 19, 1770, in *DAR*, vol. 2, pp. 179, 217, 281–282; the circumstances and time of McIntosh's apparent reappointment with pay are somewhat unclear as a result of a statement by Governor Chester in September 1771 that a commissary should be appointed to the Chickasaw. However, McIntosh was present at his Chickasaw nation home and serving as commissary when Chester wrote the foregoing, as verified by Bernard Romans who was in the nation at that time (Letter, Governor Chester to John Stuart, Sept. 10, 1771, in *DAR*, vol. 3, p. 180; Romans, *A Concise Natural History*, 128, 273). During his second tenure, McIntosh also served for a time as Choctaw commissary, as shown by a few references to such in British documents and by the following identification in the minutes of the 1771–1772 Mobile conference: "John McIntosh Commissary of Indian Affairs for the Chickasaw and Chactaw Nations" ("Minutes of the Congress Held at Mobile," in Rowland, "Peter Chester," 135). Prior to April 1778, Farquhar Bethune became Choctaw commissary (Letter, John Stuart to Lord Germain, April 13, 1778, in *DAR*, vol. 15, p. 95).

19. Romans, *A Concise Natural History*, 128.

20. "Minutes of the Congress Held at Mobile," in Rowland, "Peter Chester," 135–139, 142. Chester's reference to the eagle feathers as a calumet is interesting in that a calumet has come to mean a ceremonial smoking pipe. The calumet (pipe) ceremony, however, often involved eagle feathers attached to the long, wooden (usually cane) stem that was inserted into the stone or clay bowl (see Ian W. Brown, "The Calumet Ceremony in the Southeast and Its Archaeological Manifestations," *American Antiquity* 54, no. 2[April 1989]: 311–331). Perhaps Chester was confused.

21. "Minutes of the Congress Held at Mobile," in Rowland, "Peter Chester," 142–146. The talks of the Indians were first explained by Frenchmen serving as interpreters to Charles Stuart, who then recorded them on paper in English ("Minutes of the Congress Held at Mobile," in Rowland, "Peter Chester," 159).

22. Letter, Governor Chester to John Stuart, Sept. 10, 1771, in *DAR*, vol. 3, pp. 179–180.

23. Letter, Charles Stuart to John Stuart, Dec. 26, 1770, in *DAR*, vol. 2, pp. 303–304.

24. Letter, Undersigned Citizens of Kaskaskia to John Todd, Magistrate, May 21, 1779, in Clarence W. Alvord, ed., *Kaskaskia Records, 1778–1790*, Collections of the Illinois State Historical Society, vol. 5 (Springfield: Illinois State Historical Library, 1909), 90.

25. Gibson, *The Chickasaws*, 70–71.

CHAPTER 7

1. Calloway, *The American Revolution in Indian Country*, 222.

2. Ibid.; Gibson, *The Chickasaws*, 71; Helen L. Shaw, *British Administration of the Southern Indians, 1756–1783* (Lancaster, Pa.: Lancaster Press, 1931), 111–121; Letter, John Stuart to Henry Stuart, Oct. 24, 1775, in *DAR*, vol. 11, p. 163; Letter, Governor Peter Chester to Lord George Germain, Dec. 26, 1776, in *DAR*, vol. 12, p. 277.

3. Talk at Mobile, John Stuart to Chickasaws and Choctaws, May 14, 1777, in *DAR*,

vol. 14, pp. 79–82; Letter, John Stuart to Lord Germain, June 14, 1777, in *DAR*, vol. 14, pp. 112–115; Calloway, *The American Revolution in Indian Country*, 223, citing Colonial Office Records, series 5, vol. 78: 143, 153, 205, and Library of Congress Colonial Office transcripts, 5/78:197–204. See also Cotterill, *The Southern Indians*, 44. According to Cotterill, war chief Piomingo was at this conference and, Cotterill implies, was referred to in the records of it by his common nickname of "Mountain Leader." If this were true, it would be the first definite documentation of this Chickasaw, but it is not so. Somehow Cotterill got the erroneous notion that Paya Mattaha and Piomingo were the same person, as he directly states in a footnote on page 33. The most serious case of mistaken identity regarding Piomingo was that made by nineteenth-century historian Samuel G. Drake (*Biography and History of the Indians of North America, from Its First Discovery* [Boston: Sanborn, Carter, & Bazin, 1857]), who thought he was the same as William Colbert, oldest son of James Colbert, thereby obscuring for many years the historical importance of the full-blood Piomingo. Albert V. Goodpasture ("Indian Wars and Warriors of the Old Southwest, 1730–1807," *Tennessee Historical Magazine* 4, nos. 1–4[1918]: 108) first discussed Drake's mistake, pointing out that this intermeshing diminished the historical significance of both men. Probably related to Drake's confusion is the assertion that the two Chickasaws were the same person in Frederick W. Hodge, ed., "Handbook of American Indians North of Mexico" (*Bureau of American Ethnology Bulletin 30*, pt. 1 [1907], 322, and pt. 2 [1910], 257 [Washington, D.C.: Government Printing Office]). Although Drake's reason for the assertion apparently stemmed from a speculation by him, he would have been more justified if he had known about a Spanish letter that erroneously states that one of the Colbert brothers had been given the title name "Piomingo": "these are the two mestizos named Colbert, persons of means, and one of which is also called Piomingo" (Letter, Manuel Gayoso de Lemos to Baron de Carondelet, Oct. 18, 1793, in Corbitt and Corbitt, "Papers from the Spanish Archives," 36[1964]: 70). As discussed later, application of that title name to an exceptional Chickasaw warrior was not an uncommon occurrence, but there seems to be no supporting evidence that a Colbert received it, although there were several "Piomingos" at any given time among the Chickasaw, at least in the eighteenth century. In any case, there was only one Piomingo nicknamed Mountain Leader.

4. Letters, Henry Stuart to John Stuart, May 7 and Aug. 25, 1776, in *DAR*, vol. 12, pp. 130, 132, 191, 194, 197, 208; Williams, *Tennessee during the Revolutionary War*, 35; Cotterill, *The Southern Indians*, 42–43; McGee-Draper Narrative, 109. A detailed discussion of the Cherokee-American battle at Island Flats is presented by J. G. M. Ramsey, *The Annals of Tennessee to the End of the Eighteenth Century* (Kingsport, Tenn.: Kingsport Press, 1926, originally printed in 1853), 150–155.

5. George Rogers Clark's Memoir, written to John Brown, ca. 1791, in James A. James, ed., *George Rogers Clark Papers*, Collections of the Illinois State Historical Library, Virginia Series, vol. 3 (Springfield: Illinois State Historical Library, 1912), 260–261; Calloway, *The American Revolution in Indian Country*, 223, citing Colonial Office Records, 5/558:675–678, 683–686, Library of Congress Colonial Office transcripts, 5/558:517–519, 5/78:186, and 5/79:29; Letters, John Stuart to Lord George Germain, Aug. 27, 1777, and Oct. 6, 1777, in *DAR*, vol. 14, pp. 169, 195.

6. James E. Roper, "The Revolutionary War on the Fourth Chickasaw Bluff," *West Ten-*

nessee Historical Society Papers 29(Oct. 1975): 8–9; Robert V. Haynes, "James Willing and the Planters of Natchez," Journal of Mississippi History 37, no. 1(Feb. 1975): 24–25; Letter, Hardy Perry to Farquhar Bethune, Feb. 4, 1778, in DAR, vol. 13, p. 246; Letters, John Stuart to Lord Germain, April 13, 1778, and May 2, 1778, in DAR, vol. 15, pp. 96, 112; Letter, Charles Stuart to John Stuart, July 1, 1778, in DAR, vol. 15, p. 157; Calloway, The American Revolution in Indian Country, 223–224; George C. Osborn, "Relations with the Indians in West Florida during the Administration of Governor Peter Chester, 1770–1781," Florida Historical Quarterly 31, no. 4(April 1953): 263–264; McGillivray and Stuart blamed widespread Chickasaw consumption of alcohol for their indifferent attitude with regard to accompanying the former's corps to Natchez, but this is not likely accurate. As discussed below in this chapter, Paya Mattaha stated during the summer of 1778 that the Chickasaw were not inclined to fight English-speaking white people who until recently had been British subjects; for information about Osage interactions with the Chickasaw and other groups during the eighteenth century and early nineteenth century see Gilbert C. Din and A. P. Nasatir, The Imperial Osages: Spanish Indian Diplomacy in the Mississippi Valley (Norman: Univ. of Oklahoma Press, 1983); Willard H. Rollings, The Osage: An Ethnohistorical Study of Hegemony on the Prairie-Plains (Columbia: Univ. of Missouri Press, 1992); and W. David Baird, The Quapaw Indians: A History of the Downstream People (Norman: Univ. of Oklahoma Press, 1980).

7. Letter, John Stuart to Lord Germain, Aug. 10, 1778, in DAR, vol. 15, pp. 183–184; Calloway, The American Revolution in Indian Country, 224.

8. Calloway, The American Revolution in Indian Country, 224; Letter, Stuart to Germain, Aug. 10, 1778, in DAR, vol. 15, pp. 183–184.

9. Letter, Stuart to Germain, Aug. 10, 1778, in DAR, vol. 15, pp. 183–184; Calloway, The American Revolution in Indian Country, 224; Letter, Governor Peter Chester to Lord Germain, Aug. 21, 1778, in DAR, vol. 15, p. 188.

10. Calloway, The American Revolution in Indian Country, 225; Letter, John Stuart to John McIntosh, Sept. 19, 1778, in DAR, vol. 13, p. 395; Letter, John Stuart to William Knox, Oct. 9–Nov. 26, 1778, in DAR, vol. 15, p. 212; Osborn, "Relations with the Indians in West Florida," 267.

11. Calloway, The American Revolution in Indian Country, 225, citing Papers of the Continental Congress, 1774–1789, National Archives, microfilm M-247, reel 104, item 78, vol. 24, p. 435; the commission is published in William P. Palmer, arranger and ed., Calendar of Virginia State Papers and Other Manuscripts, vol. 1 (Richmond: Virginia State Library, 1875), 391; Goodpasture, "Indian Wars and Warriors," 106; Letter, Henry Stuart to John Stuart, May 7, 1776, in DAR, vol. 12, p. 132; Williams (Tennessee during the Revolutionary War, 35) erroneously states that Colbert was a British "sub-agent in the Chickasaw Nation" in 1776 and was deputy Chickasaw agent in 1779. Cotterill (The Southern Indians, 43, 47) asserts that he was the "British commissary" in 1777. James H. O'Donnell, III (Southern Indians in the American Revolution [Knoxville: Univ. of Tennessee Press, 1973], 74) states that Colbert was the British "departmental deputy" to the Chickasaw until he "resigned for no apparent reason" in 1778. Walter H. Mohr (Federal Indian Relations, 1774–1788 [Philadelphia: Univ. of Pennsylvania Press, 1933], 43) implies that James Colbert was the Chickasaw deputy agent and John McIntosh the Choctaw agent. To the contrary, John McIntosh was the only Chickasaw deputy

agent/commissary between 1765 and early 1780, when he died at his home in the Chickasaw Nation, after which his son, John, was appointed to act in his place rather than James Colbert because the latter was "illiterate and very extravagant." Although the elder McIntosh was referred to as commissary of the Choctaw in a 1774 letter from Governor Peter Chester, he was primarily the Chickasaw commissary (Letter, Chester to Earl of Dartmouth, March 7, 1774, in *DAR*, vol. 7, p. 55). There is no evidence that the middle-aged James Colbert ever held a deputy agent/commissary position among the Chickasaw. However, when the Choctaw became difficult to manage in late 1779, Colbert was apparently unofficially appointed, by Alexander Cameron or Charles Stuart, to assist Choctaw commissary Farquhar Bethune. This appears to have been a temporary duty. See Letter, Charles Stuart to Alexander Cameron, Dec. 20, 1779, in *DAR*, vol. 16, pp. 238–239, and Letter, Cameron to Lord Germain, July 18, 1780, *DAR*, vol. 18, p. 125.

12. Declaration of Don Silbestre Labadia, July 5, 1782, in Kinnaird, "Spain in the Mississippi Valley," vol. 3, pt. 2, pp. 32, 60; McGee-Draper Narrative, 110, 113.

13. Calloway, *The American Revolution in Indian Country,* 225, citing Library of Congress Colonial Office transcripts 5/80:243–245.

14. Calloway, *The American Revolution in Indian Country,* 226; "Chickasaw Talk to the Rebels" (through Isaac Shelby), May 22, 1779, Papers of the Continental Congress, reel 65, item 51, vol. 2, pp. 41–42 (published in Colin G. Calloway and Alden T. Vaughan, eds., *Revolution and Confederation* [Bethesda, Md.: Univ. Publications of America, 1994], 262–263); Letter, John Todd, Jr., to Thomas Jefferson, June 2, 1780, in James, *George Rogers Clark Papers,* vol. 3, p. 423; because "Tuskau" is part of Tuskau Pautaupau's name, possibly he was the same man as the future "king" of the Chickasaws, Taski/Taska Etoka, sometimes called the "Hare Lipped King"; Letters, John Stuart to Lord Germain, Jan. 11, 1779, and Commissioners for Indian Affairs to Lord Germain, May 10, 1779, in *DAR*, vol. 17, pp. 29, 122; Letter, Charles Stuart to Lord Germain, May 6, 1779, in *DAR*, vol. 16, p. 95.

15. "Chickasaw Talk to the Rebels," in Calloway and Vaughan, *Revolution and Confederation,* 262–263; Calloway, *The American Revolution in Indian Country,* 226; Letter, Alexander Cameron and Charles Stuart to Lord Germain, April 10, 1779, in *DAR*, vol. 17, p. 98; Letter, Commissioners for Indian Affairs to Lord Germain, May 10, 1779, in *DAR*, vol. 17, p. 121; Letter, Thomas Jefferson to the Speaker of the House of Delegates, June 14, 1780, in *DAR*, vol. 17, p. 427.

16. Nash et al., *The American People,* 173–180; Calloway, *The American Revolution in Indian Country,* 227; Osborn, "Relations with the Indians in West Florida," 266; Atkinson, *History of the Chickasaw Indian Agency,* 65–66; Alden, *John Stuart,* 212n; Letter, Alexander Cameron to Lord Germain, July 18, 1780, in *DAR*, vol. 18, p. 125; Malcolm McGee, who lived with McIntosh for several years as a youth, recalled in 1841 that he died in March 1780 "at a little fort" (the British commissary) on the old Natchez Road a "little below the union of Pontotoc & other creeks" and was buried there (McGee-Draper Narrative, 120). McGee may be correct that McIntosh died in March rather than February, for it will be noted that Cameron's letter cited above is dated July 18, long enough after the fact to cause an error in his information; Letter, Alexander Cameron to Germain, August ?, 1780, in *DAR*, vol. 16, p. 392.

17. Calloway, *The American Revolution in Indian Country,* 227; Letter, Alexander Cameron to Lord Germain, July 18, 1780, in *DAR,* vol. 18, p. 121, and vol. 16, p. 367 (Paya Mattaha's talk to the Spanish and Spanish Governor Bernardo de Galvez's talk to him are enclosed with this letter).

18. Robert S. Cotterill, "The Virginia-Chickasaw Treaty of 1783," *Journal of Southern History* 8, no. 4(Nov. 1942): 484; *Letters of Thomas Jefferson,* vol. 2 of H. R. McIlwaine, gen. ed., *Official Letters of the Governors of the State of Virginia* (Richmond: Virginia State Library, 1928), 36, 93; Kathryn M. Fraser, "Fort Jefferson: George Rogers Clark's Fort at the Mouth of the Ohio River, 1780–1781," *Register of the Kentucky Historical Society* 81, no. 1(Winter 1983): 12; Calloway, *The American Revolution in Indian Country,* 227; Gibson, *The Chickasaws,* 72–73; Letter, Thomas Jefferson to George Rogers Clark, Jan. 29, 1780, in Alvord, *Kaskaskia Records, 1778–1790,* 147; Guy B. Braden, "The Colberts and the Chickasaw Nation," *Tennessee Historical Quarterly* 17, no. 3(Sept. 1958): 223–224.

19. Albert W. Haarman, "The Spanish Conquest of British West Florida, 1779–1781," *Florida Historical Quarterly* 29(July 1960–April 1961): 111, 113, 126; Osborn, "Relations with the Indians in West Florida," 270; John W. Caughey, "The Natchez Rebellion of 1781 and Its Aftermath," *Louisiana Historical Quarterly* 16(1933): 70; J. Barton Starr, *Tories, Dons, and Rebels: The American Revolution in British West Florida* (Gainesville: Univ. Presses of Florida, 1976), 177–179; McGee-Draper Narrative, 108; Letter, Major General John Campbell to Lord Germain, Nov. 26, 1780, in *DAR,* vol. 18, p. 234; Talk from Franchumastabie (Choctaw) to Alexander Cameron, April 1, 1781, in *DAR,* vol. 19, p. 113; on July 11, 1780, Pierre Juzan's messenger reported that "Colbert is coming [to Pensacola] with a party of Chickasaws" (Letter, P. Juzan to Governor Galvez, July 11, 1780, in Kinnaird, "Spain in the Mississippi Valley," vol. 2, pt. 1 [1949], p. 383); Letter, Cruzat to Miro, Aug. 8, 1782, Kinnaird, "Spain in the Mississippi Valley," vol. 3, pt. 2 (1946), 51 (see also page 33 regarding capture of the five soldiers). If indeed three sons were present at Mobile, the third must have been Samuel, whom McGee recalled as having been killed by northern Indians after the Revolution (McGee-Draper Narrative, 113); Letter, Farquhar Bethune to Lieutenant-General Alexander Leslie, Jan. 19, 1782, in *DAR,* vol. 21, p. 29; Letters, Alexander Cameron to Lord Germain, Feb. 10, 1781, and May 27, 1781, in *DAR,* vol. 20, pp. 60, 150.

20. Goodpasture, "Indian Wars and Warriors," 46–49; Williams, *Tennessee during the Revolutionary War,* 172–175; for one of the best discussions of the founding of present-day Nashville and the Cumberland settlement see S. J. Folmsbee, R. E. Corlew, and E. L. Mitchell, *History of Tennessee* (New York: Lewis Historical, 1960), 139–143.

21. Williams, *Tennessee during the Revolutionary War,* 165, citing John Haywood, *The Civil and Political History of Tennessee* (Knoxville: Heskill and Brown, 1823), 125.

22. Nash et al., *The American People,* 178–181.

23. Calloway, *The American Revolution in Indian Country,* 227–228; Louis Houck, ed., *The Spanish Regime in Missouri,* 2 vols. (Chicago: Donnelley, 1909), vol. 1, pp. 209–210; Letter, Governor Cruzat to Governor Miro, Aug. 8, 1782, in Kinnaird, "Spain in the Mississippi Valley," vol. 3, pt. 2, p. 52; Pedro Piernas's account of Choctaw Messenger, Oct. 24, 1782, and Letter, Piernas to Governor Miro, Oct. 28, 1782, in Kinnaird, "Spain in the Mississippi Valley," vol. 3, pt. 2, pp. 61–62. Piernas's reference to Tascapatapo being called the "Red King" is somewhat confusing in light of the fact that Mingo Houma was still alive at this time and

still the Chickasaw king. However, some whites interpreted "Mingo" to mean "chief" while others interpreted the word to mean "king."

24. Calloway, *The American Revolution in Indian Country,* 228; Letter, Du Breuil to Governor Miro, Nov. 8, 1783, in Kinnaird, "Spain in the Mississippi Valley," vol. 3, pt. 2, pp. 89–91.

25. Letter, Farquhar Bethune to Lieutenant General Alexander Leslie, Jan. 19, 1782, in *DAR,* vol. 21, pp. 29–31; Caughey, "The Natchez Rebellion of 1781," 57–68; see Snapp, *John Stuart and the Struggle for Empire,* 26–40, for discussion of non-Indian residency in the Chickasaw and other Indian territories in the mid to late eighteenth century.

26. Letter, Franco Bouligny to Governor Miro, Aug. 22, 1785, in Kinnaird, "Spain in the Mississippi Valley," vol. 3, pt. 2, p. 137.

27. D. C. Corbitt, "James Colbert and the Spanish Claims to the East Bank of the Mississippi," *Mississippi Valley Historical Review* 24, no. 4(March 1938): 458–459. Corbitt obtained nearly all of his data about Colbert's band from Spanish documents in a collection called by him the Archivo Nacional de Cuba, Floridas, legajo 3, no. 8, located in Seville, Spain. Other historians have obtained additional data from Spanish documents in Archivo General de Indias, Seville, Papeles Procedentes de Cuba and other collections. Calloway (*The American Revolution in Indian Country,* 229–230) and other writers deviate from Corbitt's rendition of Madam Cruzat's first name, writing it in full as "Senora Nicanora Ramos de Cruzat." Other secondary accounts include John Caughey's article "The Natchez Rebellion of 1781," 69–83; Gilbert C. Din's article "Arkansas Post in the American Revolution," *Arkansas Historical Quarterly* 40, no. 1(1981): 14–30; Din's chapter entitled "Loyalist Resistance after Pensacola: The Case of James Colbert" in W. S. Coker and R. R. Rea, eds., *Anglo-Spanish Confrontation on the Gulf Coast during the American Revolution* (Pensacola: Gulf Coast History and Humanities Conference, 1982); James E. Roper's article "The Revolutionary War on the Fourth Chickasaw Bluff," 5–24; and Robert V. Haynes's book *The Natchez District and the American Revolution,* 142–152. Part of the original documentation (Spanish declarations, letters, and so on) regarding Colbert's raiders is published. See Kinnaird, "Spain in the Mississippi Valley," vol. 3, pt. 2, pp. 15–16, 21–34, 49–54, 60, 89–91 (see especially the Declaration of Silbestre Labadia, July 5, 1782, on pages 21–34 and his references to "Cilly" on pages 28 and 32). See also Houck, *The Spanish Regime in Missouri,* vol. 1, pp. 211–233, which includes the account of Madam Cruzat (pp. 221–231). Regarding my identification of Cilly as probably Benjamin Seeley, see McGee-Draper Narrative, 115. With regard to James Colbert, Labadia returned to New Orleans with the following information, as recorded by Labadia's interviewers: "[A] man of some sixty years, but in good health, with a strong constitution, active and capable of enduring the greatest hardships in war and possessing a violent temper. He has been known for more than forty years among the Chickasaws, Choctaws, and various other nations of Indians. He is settled in the nation of the Chickasaws, where he has a very fine house, with some hundred and fifty Negroes, according to what he himself told the witness." Colbert was also somewhat loose-tongued, as illustrated by Labadia's relation that Colonel McGillivray had to interrupt Colbert to stop him from divulging their plans with regard to future military operations against the Spaniards. According to Labadia, Colbert told Madam Cruzat that her husband the governor had "escaped from me when he recently came up from the capital and I was coming down from the Iron Mine [or Iron Banks, a post on the Mississippi River], where, while making an attack upon that American fort with five

hundred Indians, I received three wounds, which you see here (showing them to her)" (Declaration of Don Silbestre Labadia, July 5, 1782, in Kinnaird, "Spain in the Mississippi Valley," vol. 3, pt. 2, pp. 32–33).

28. Corbitt, "James Colbert and the Spanish Claims," 461–464; Calloway, *The American Revolution in Indian Country*, 229; John W. Caughey, *McGillivray of the Creeks* (Norman: Univ. of Oklahoma Press, 1938), 16; Din, "Loyalist Resistance after Pensacola," 162–164; Declaration of Don Silbestre Labadia, July 5, 1782, and Letter, Governor Cruzat to Governor Miro, Aug. 8, 1782, in Kinnaird, "Spain in the Mississippi Valley," vol. 3, pt. 2, pp. 21–34, 49–54; Letter, James Colbert to de Galvez, May 15, 1782, in Houck, *The Spanish Regime in Missouri*, vol. 1, p. 219; Colbert's letter to Miro, dated Oct. 6, 1782, is published in Kinnaird, "Spain in the Mississippi Valley," vol. 3, pt. 2, p. 60; Roper, "The Revolutionary War on the Fourth Chickasaw Bluff," 17; Caughey, "The Natchez Rebellion of 1781," 71–78. Caughey cites the declaration of Labadia for the information about the author of the "Parole of Honour" being Alexander McGillivray. Because Labadia only states "McGillivray," Caughey obviously assumed the first name of Alexander. Caughey repeated the assertion in his book *Bernardo De Galvez in Louisiana, 1776–1783* (Berkeley: Univ. of California Press, 1934), 232. Other writers to subsequently repeat Caughey's assumption that the man was Alexander McGillivray rather than the more likely man, Colonel John McGillivray, are Haynes (*The Natchez District and the American Revolution*, 146) and Din, "Loyalist Resistance after Pensacola," 163. Din, like Corbitt in "James Colbert and the Spanish Claims" (p. 471), states (apparently mistakenly) that in May 1783 a "McGillivray" was Colbert's second in command rather than "Cilly" as discussed above. Both writers also state that this McGillivray was subsequently killed in a skirmish near Chickasaw Bluffs. If so, and if he was the same McGillivray as the one who wrote the "Parole of Honour," he could not have been Alexander McGillivray as asserted by Caughey. In addition to "Cilly" (probably Benjamin Seeley), Colonel McGillivray, Thomas Prince, and Colbert's sons, some of the more important of Colbert's raiders included (partially written in Spanish) "Simon Burney, Ziblan Mathews, James Clonketin, Juan Hosten [Holston], Ricardo Hall, Betnigo Swallen, Patricio Rogers, Joel Starn, James Mchim, William Windrigth, and Patrico Marr" (from Caughey, "The Natchez Rebellion of 1781," 81, and *Bernardo De Galvez in Louisiana*, 240, citing Declaracion de Henoc Wales, April 9, 1783, Archivo General de Indias, Seville, Papeles Procedentes de Cuba [hereafter AGI, PC], legajo 196). Also, Madam Cruzat insinuated that Farquhar Bethune, the Choctaw's British commissary (she thought Chickasaw), was a participant by stating that "a person named Bethun, commissary of the Nation Chicachas" had "stirred up" the rebels to make their attacks (Houck, *The Spanish Regime in Missouri*, vol. 1, p. 230). This statement by Madam Cruzat has been totally ignored by historians. Perhaps Bethune had an unrecognized prominent role in organizing "Colbert's Raiders."

29. Calloway, *The American Revolution in Indian Country*, 229–230; Corbitt, "James Colbert and the Spanish Claims," 464–465; Letter, Governor Cruzat to Governor Miro, Aug. 8, 1782, and Letter, Du Breuil to Governor Miro, Nov. 8, 1783, in Kinnaird, "Spain in the Mississippi Valley," vol. 3, pt. 2, 49–54, 89–91; Letter, Governor Miro to de Galvez, June 5, 1782, in Houck, *The Spanish Regime in Missouri*, vol. 1, p. 214–215.

30. Corbitt, "James Colbert and the Spanish Claims," 464–465; Letters, Cruzat to Miro, Aug. 8, 1782, and Du Breuil to Miro, Nov. 8, 1783, in Kinnaird, "Spain in the Mississippi

Valley," vol. 3, pt. 2, pp. 49–54, 89–91; Declaration of Silbestre Labadia, July 5, 1782, in Kinnaird, "Spain in the Mississippi Valley," vol. 3, pt. 2, p. 32; Din, "Arkansas Post in the American Revolution," 14–22.

31. Din, "Arkansas Post in the American Revolution," 22–25.

32. Ibid., 26–30. As discussed above, John Stuart commissioned in 1778 a Lieutenant Colonel John McGillivray to command a provincial corps of whites and Indians soon after Willing's raid. A John McGillivray who was a Spanish prisoner in Havana in 1781 most likely was that man, and he was probably captured at Mobile or Pensacola. A memorandum from Captain Alexander Shaw of the 60th Regiment asked for McGillivray's release because of his great influence with Indians (see letter regarding undated Memorandum by Captain Alexander Shaw [1781], in *DAR,* vol. 19, p. 238). Perhaps he was indeed released, after which he joined Colbert's band. Unless Valliere was mistaken in saying that the raider McGillivray was killed, the latter could not have been the Alexander McGillivray who Caughey says wrote the "Parole of Honour" in 1782, unless he was not the same man who later became principal chief of the Creek. McGillivray the raider may be the same as the "McGillwray" discussed in Chapter 6 who had a half interest in a plantation in the Chickasaw Nation by 1771. The latter was probably John McGillivray. Whoever he was, the McGillivray reported killed in 1783 was likely related to William McGillivray, an early nineteenth-century Chickasaw district chief whose Indian name was Coahoma. According to a white man from Cotton Gin Port, J. N. Walton, who knew William McGillivray, he was a full-blood, despite his English name (Letter, J. N. Walton to Lyman C. Draper, June 25, 1882, in Draper Collection, vol. 10, series U, pp. 140/6–140/7). According to Malcolm McGee, a McGillivray who was with George Colbert's Chickasaw group under General Arthur St. Clair in 1791 was related to Alexander McGillivray, the mixed-blood Creek chief mentioned above. The man with St. Clair was probably William McGillivray, but he may have been an unidentified brother, half-brother, or other relative. For a discussion of the tributaries at Chickasaw Bluffs, see Jack D. L. Holmes, "Spanish-American Rivalry over the Chickasaw Bluffs, 1780–1795," *East Tennessee Historical Society's Publications* 34(1962): 26–27. Apparently another stream called by the Spanish the Carondelet River is present-day Nonconnah Creek. Erroneous is one of two footnotes by Corbitt and Corbitt. One identifies the Chickasaw River as present-day Nonconnah Creek and the other, in agreement with Holmes, states that the Carondelet River is present-day Nonconnah Creek (Corbitt and Corbitt, "Papers from the Spanish Archives," 34[1962]: 91, 96).

33. Calloway, *The American Revolution in Indian Country,* 232; Corbitt, "James Colbert and the Spanish Claims," 469, 471–472; Letter, Governor Miro to Don Pedro Favrot, Oct. 3, 1786, in Corbitt and Corbitt, "Papers from the Spanish Archives," 10(1938): 148. While in St. Augustine, Colbert became seriously ill but then recovered well enough to attempt the return journey, which he planned to undertake in mid-November. Apparently, his sickness made him aware that his life might not last much longer because of danger from illness as well as his "exasperated enemies." Before leaving for home he asked his attorney, by letter drafted for him by Anthony Hutchins, to make sure that his youngest son, James Colbert, receive all funds from his estate if he should die (Letter, James Colbert, St. Augustine, to John Miller, Nov. 12, 1783, in May Wilson McBee, *The Natchez Court Records, 1767–1805: Abstracts of Early Records* [Baltimore: Genealogical Publishing Co., 1979], 257–258). Malcolm

McGee (McGee-Draper Narrative, 109) related a common rumor that circulated concerning the death of Colbert—that he had been murdered by his black slave servant named Cesar, who apparently was the only person with him on his return. Cesar thereafter returned to the Nation and reported that Colbert had been thrown from his horse and killed. The latter is exactly what Alexander McGillivray reported in a letter to the Spanish in early January 1784 (Caughey, "The Natchez Rebellion of 1781," 82, citing Letter, McGillivray to O'Neill, Jan. 7, 1784, AGI, PC, legajo 197). The letter is published in Caughey, *McGillivray of the Creeks,* 68. It is improbable that the servant killed Colbert; if he had, returning to the Nation would have been an unlikely, foolish thing to do. If Colbert was murdered, a more likely suspect would have to be Alexander McGillivray, who by this time was embracing the Spanish and angry with the anti-Spanish faction among the Chickasaw. Such a possibility is enhanced by the fact that his letter to O'Neill was the second written to him after the death of Colbert. McGillivray claimed to have forgotten to mention this important event in the first letter. Interestingly, McGee's recollection that Cesar was taken to Natchez by William Colbert and sold is documented in the Natchez court records. The slave, whose name was indeed Cesar, was sold by Colbert in about 1787 (McBee, *The Natchez Court Records,* 101). Apparently Colbert did not believe that Cesar killed his father. If he had, Cesar would not likely have been in his possession for those four years.

34. Din, "Arkansas Post in the American Revolution," 20, citing Letter, Villars to Miro, July 6, 1782, AGI, PC, legajo 2359; Letter, Bouligny to Miro, Dec. 12, 1785, in Kinnaird, "Spain in the Mississippi Valley," vol. 3, pt. 2, pp. 158–159; some former Spanish prisoners of the Chickasaw reported that at least six chiefs opposed giving further aid to the raiders and were in favor of expelling them from the Chickasaw territory (see Haynes, *The Natchez District and the American Revolution,* 149); Letters, Henrique Grimarest to Paya Mattaha, June 11, 1782, and Grimarest's Report of Paulous's Mission to the Chickasaw, Sept. 1782, in Kinnaird, "Spain in the Mississippi Valley," vol. 3, pt. 2, pp. 20, 57.

35. Letter, Governor Harrison to Joseph Martin, John Donelson, and Isaac Shelby, Jan. 11, 1783, in *The Letters of Thomas Nelson and Benjamin Harrison,"* vol. 3 (1929) of McIlwaine, *Official Letters of the Governors of the State of Virginia,* 425–426; A. W. Putnam, *History of Middle Tennessee, or Life and Times of Gen. James Robertson* (Knoxville: Univ. of Tennessee Press, 1971, reprint of 1859 edition), 191, 216–217, 222 (Cruzat's letter to Robertson is published on pages 216–217). Robinson's letter to the commandant at Natchez, dated Dec. 7, 1783, is published in Kinnaird, "Spain in the Mississippi Valley," vol. 3, pt. 2, p. 93.

36. Corbitt, "James Colbert and the Spanish Claims," 457–472; Caughey, "The Natchez Rebellion of 1781," 70; McGee-Draper Narrative, 112–113.

37. Calloway, *The American Revolution in Indian Country,* 232; Letter, James Colbert to the Governor of Virginia, July 25, 1783, in Palmer, *Virginia State Papers,* vol. 3, pp. 513–514.

CHAPTER 8

1. Calloway, *The American Revolution in Indian Country,* 230–231; Stanley Faye, "Illinois Indians on the Lower Mississippi, 1771–1782," *Journal of the Illinois State Historical Society* 35, no. 1(March 1942): 70–72; Letter, Message from the Chickasaw/Paya Mattaha, et al. to U.S. Commanders, July 9, 1782, in Palmer, *Virginia State Papers,* vol. 3, pp. 278–279 (also published

in James, *George Rogers Clark Papers,* vol. 4 [1926], pp. 73–75). A copy of the original letter, made by John Bowman, is in The Tennessee Papers (papers of William and Joseph Martin), Draper Collection, vol. 1, series XX, pp. 50+; see also Letter, Major John Bowman to Benjamin Harrison, Aug. 30, 1782, in James, *George Rogers Clark Papers,* vol. 4, pp. 99–100; O'Donnell, *Southern Indians in the American Revolution,* 125; transcription spellings of the names of the four Chickasaw chiefs vary, and secondary works citing the transcriptions present them differently also. For example, James's works on George Rogers Clark spell the head war chief's name "Poymau Tauhaw" (Paya Mattaha). Palmer, *Virginia State Papers,* has them Poyman Tauhaw (Paya Mattaha), Mingo Homan, Turkaw Potapo, and Poymingo. Citing this source, Goodpasture ("Indian Wars and Warriors," 106) spells them Poymace Tankaw, Mingo Homaw, Tuskon Patapo, and Piomingo. In his discussion of a Simon Burney, Harry Warren ("Some Chickasaw Chiefs and Prominent Men," *Publications of the Mississippi Historical Society* 8[1904]: 569) appears to be describing a mixed-blood Simon Burney rather than the British loyalist by that name who had lived near Natchez until about 1780, for he states that Burney was an "Indian" who was "refugeed to the whites." Documentation of a mixed-blood Simon Burney, the son of a Colonel David Burney who apparently lived among the Chickasaw in the early nineteenth century, is present in the Draper Collection, George Rogers Clark Manuscripts, vol. 28, Series J, pp. 68–69. Blood relationships, if any, between the aforementioned white Simon Burney who delivered the Chickasaw message in 1782, white Colonel David Burney, and mixed-blood Simon Burney are unclear. To confuse matters more, by 1840 a white Simon Burney (aged between 60 and 70) was living in Chickasaw County, as was his probable son (also white), David Burney, aged between 20 and 30 (U.S. Census, Chickasaw County, Mississippi, 1840; Tax Assessment List, Chickasaw County, 1840, at MDAH). This Simon Burney would not have been the man who delivered the Chickasaw message in 1782, for he would have been no older than twelve in that year. The former owned twenty-three slaves in 1840. By the early 1830s, a David Burney lived in a part of Chickasaw County that was later separated in 1872 to form present-day Clay County, Mississippi. This location for a David Burney is depicted on one of the 1834 United States township plats of the Chickasaw Cession lands and mentioned in the field notes of the survey. However, a Simon Burney and a David Burney are recorded in the U.S. Land Office documents as having come into possession of adjacent tracts of land in what is still Chickasaw County (near present-day Trebloc) as a result of the Chickasaw land cession treaties of 1832 and 1834 (see Don Martini, "Chickasaw Empire: The Story of the Colbert Family," copy of typescript [revised], 1986, Special Collections, Mitchell Memorial Library, Mississippi State Univ., Starkville, map 4). By the end of 1841, no Burneys appear on the Chickasaw County tax rolls or the census records for that county. Despite the confusion surrounding these various Burneys, all appear to have been related because of the common use of the surnames Simon and David.

2. Letter, Message from the Chickasaw/Paya Mattaha, et al. to U.S. Commanders, July 9, 1782, in Palmer, *Virginia State Papers,* vol. 3, pp. 278–279.

3. Calloway, *The American Revolution in Indian Country,* 233; O'Donnell, *Southern Indians in the American Revolution,* 129–130; J. Leitch Wright, *Florida in the American Revolution* (Gainesville: Univ. Presses of Florida, 1975), 133–134.

4. Letter, Mingohoma, Pyamathahaw, Kushthaputhasa, Pyamingoe of Christhautra,

and Pyamingo of Chuckaferah to His Excellency the President of the Honorable Congress of the United American States, "Done at Chuck-ul-issah our Great Town the 28th Day of July, 1783," in Palmer, *Virginia State Papers,* vol. 3, pp. 515–517. The "Kushthaputhasa" chief is probably the same man as "Tuskau Pautaupau." "Pyamingo of Chuckaferah [Choukafalya]" is the noted "Mountain Leader," for he is well documented to have resided there. His rise to power in the Chickasaw nation had begun.

   5. Calloway, *The American Revolution in Indian Country,* 231; Letter, George Rogers Clark to Governor Harrison, Oct. 18, 1782, in Palmer, *Virginia State Papers,* vol. 3, pp. 345–347 (also in James, *George Rogers Clark Papers,* vol. 4, pp. 135–137); Letter, Governor Harrison to the Speaker of the Virginia House of Delegates, Dec. 7, 1782, in James, *George Rogers Clark Papers,* vol. 4, p. 166; Letter, Clark to Governor Harrison, March 8, 1783, in James, *George Rogers Clark Papers,* vol. 4, p. 213; Talk to the Chickasaw at a council in the Chickasaw nation from Captain Robert George and James Sherlock, Oct. 24, 1782, in Palmer, *Virginia State Papers,* vol. 3, pp. 356–357; Answer from the Chickasaws at council to Captain George and Sherlock, Oct. 24, 1782, Palmer, *Virginia State Papers,* vol. 3, pp. 357–358. A Talk from Governor Harrison to the chiefs and warriors of the Chickasaw Nation, Dec. 19, 1782, in *The Letters of Thomas Nelson and Benjamin Harrison,*" vol. 3 of McIlwaine, *Official Letters,* pp. 407–408 (see additional correspondence regarding land sales in the same source); the Chickasaws attending the council were Paya Mattaha, Mingo Houma, Piomingo, Chambeau, and "The Red King and Several Other Sachims [Sachems, leaders or chiefs] and Warriors." The mention of the "Red King" is undoubtedly a reference to Paya Mattaha's brother, Tascapatapo/ Tuskau Pautapau, who was also called Red King and described as "a man of great importance" (Pedro Piernas's account of Choctaw Messenger, Oct. 24, 1782, in Kinnaird, "Spain in the Mississippi Valley," vol. 3, pt. 2, pp. 61–62).

   6. Calloway, *The American Revolution in Indian Country,* 232, 234; Gibson, *The Chickasaws,* 75–76; Treaty of French Lick, 1783, in The Tennessee Papers (papers of William and Joseph Martin), Draper Collection, vol. 1, series XX, pp. 65+. This document is actually a record of proceedings and the treaty in combination. Names at the bottom include those of Martin and Donelson and the Chickasaw chiefs. The Chickasaw names are "[hole in paper]goamaw [Mingo Houma?]—The Red King" and "Tushatohoa The mountain Leader," along with "Beticio"(?), "Tontontoba"(?), "Tobonoloby," and "Toashoway." Below the chiefs' names are the words "Jn. [John or Jonathan] Betford a half breed." Clerks/witnesses were John Brown and [document torn] Donelson; Letter, John Donelson and Joseph Martin to Governor Harrison, Dec. 16, 1783, in Palmer, *Virginia State Papers,* vol. 3, p. 548; Letter, Joseph Martin to Governor Harrison, May 3, 1784, Palmer, *Virginia State Papers,* vol. 3, p. 581; Calloway and Vaughan, *Revolution and Confederation,* 374–376; Cotterill, *The Southern Indians,* 59–60; the complicated, laborious details of the events leading to the treaty are presented in Cotterill, "The Virginia-Chickasaw Treaty," 487–496; see McGee-Draper Narrative, 121, regarding Malcolm McGee's early years among the Chickasaw. Among other historians of the nineteenth and twentieth centuries, Putnam (*History of Middle Tennessee,* 167, 196) presents confused information about the Treaty of French Lick. Putnam states that it was signed in June rather than the accurate month of November. He and others also state that thousands of acres of land in present-day Tennessee were ceded to the United States by the Chickasaw and confirmed by the Treaty of Hopewell in 1786. Actually, not a single acre of land was

obtained by the United States under either of these treaties, although the right for the United States to establish a trading post at the mouth of Bear Creek was granted by the Chickasaw in the latter treaty, as discussed below in this chapter. For the apparent origin of the land cession confusion see Letter, Governor William Blount to the Secretary of War, Nov. 8, 1792, in *American State Papers* (hereafter *ASP*) (Indian Affairs), vol. 1, 1832, pp. 325–326. Blount stated with regard to the alleged Chickasaw cession of the Cumberland settlement land: "And so they did by a treaty held at Nashville, in the year 1783 . . . two years prior to the treaty of Hopewell. . . . This treaty, probably, never was reported to Congress." Blount was correct that the treaty was never acted on by Congress. It appears to me that the Americans considered the absence of a Chickasaw claim to the Cumberland River area as confirmation that they did not, in fact, consider it part of their territory. Cotterill ("The Virginia-Chickasaw Treaty," n. 35) was the first to address the mistake. Actually, the Cumberland settlement land was ceded to the Colonel Richard Henderson/Transylania Company of land speculators by the Cherokee in March 1775 (see Archibald Henderson, "Richard Henderson: The Authorship of the Cumberland Compact and the Founding of Nashville," *Tennessee Historical Magazine*, no. 3 [Sept. 1916], reprinted in *Tennessee Old and New* [sponsored by the Tennessee Historical Commission and the Tennessee Historical Society, Kingsport, Tenn: Kingsport Press, 1946], vol. 1, pp. 93–111; see also Folmsbee et al., *History of Tennessee*, 139–143). Neither the Cherokee nor the Chickasaw protested initiation of white settlement at French Lick in 1779.

7. Putnam, *History of Middle Tennessee*, 196; Haywood, *Civil and Political History of Tennessee*, 288; personal communication, Sue Maszaros, Tennessee State Library, July 23, 2001.

8. Calloway, *The American Revolution in Indian Country*, 234–235, and Din, "Loyalist Resistance after Pensacola," 171, citing Letter, Du Breuil to Miro, April 20, 1784, in AGI, PC, legajo 107; Malcolm McGee recalled in 1841 that Paya Mattaha died of the measles in 1784 (McGee-Draper Narrative, 116).

9. Calloway, *The American Revolution in Indian Country*, 235; Gibson, *The Chickasaws*, 77, 81; Cotterill, *The Southern Indians*, 60; Jack D. L. Holmes, "Spanish Treaties with West Florida Indians, 1784–1802," *Florida Historical Quarterly* 48(July 1969–April 1970): 143; the six villages represented at the Mobile Treaty were (as spelled in the Spanish document) Choculiza, Chatala, Tascahuilo, Malata, Achucuma, and Chucafala (Rations Given to Indians at Congress of Mobile, June 24, 1784, in Kinnaird, "Spain in the Mississippi Valley," vol. 3, pt. 2, p. 102). The treaty proceedings may be found in unpublished translated transcripts of Spanish documents in "Mississippi Provincial Archives: Spanish Dominion," vol. 2, pp. 162–170 (copies of documents at MDAH); "Ugulayacabe" was pronounced and spelled "Ugly Cub" by some Americans who apparently thought such was accurate (see Jack D. L. Holmes, *Gayoso: The Life of a Spanish Governor in the Mississippi Valley, 1789–1799* [Baton Rouge: Louisiana Univ. Press, 1965], 149). Some of the older secondary works possess inaccurate data about Wolf's Friend. John Haywood's *Civil and Political History of Tennessee*, 352, for example, states that he was a Cherokee and resident of the Cherokee nation in 1792. Except for this and other rare mistakes, Haywood's detailed writings published in the early nineteenth century about the Chickasaw are remarkably accurate. He conducted extensive research in historical documents and consulted with a number of the actual participants in events of the 1780s and 1790s.

10. Calloway, *The American Revolution in Indian Country*, 234–235; Letter, Alexander McGillivray to Carondelet, Jan. 15, 1793, in Caughey, *McGillivray of the Creeks*, 351; "The substance of a talk held at Nashville with some of the Chickasaws" (1784), in Walter Clark, collector and editor, *The State Records of North Carolina* (Goldsboro, N.C.: Nash Brothers, 1899), vol. 17, pp. 85–87; other chiefs besides Piomingo and Tuskau Pautaupau who attended the talk in Nashville included the new king (Taski Etoka), Paya Mattaha, and William Glover; both Paya Mattaha and King Mingo Houma died during a measles outbreak among the Chickasaw in 1784, according to Malcolm McGee, who also recalled that the outbreak took the lives of nearly half the population of Long Town (McGee-Draper Narrative, 116). Paya Mattaha died after the Nashville talk, apparently between about September and the end of the year.

11. McGee-Draper Narrative, 111; Cotterill, *The Southern Indians*, 44–45; Letter, Mingo-homa et al. to the president of the U.S. Congress, July 28, 1783, in Palmer, *Virginia State Papers*, vol. 3, pp. 515–517; regarding Paye Mingo Belixy see a document by James Adair entitled "A Memorandum of some Material Heads of what was lately transacted in the Chickasaw Nation," Feb. 26, 1766, in Colonial Office Records 323/24(1)/73. Paye Mingo Belixy is also mentioned by Bernard Romans, who spelled his name "Opaya Mingo Luxi" (Romans, *A Concise Natural History*, 128); regarding "Pahemimggo Elookse," see Letter, John McIntosh to acting Deputy Superintendent of Indian Affairs, April 15, 1766, in Alvord and Carter, *The New Regime*, 214; Letter, Captain Zebra Pike to Robertson, June 5, 1796, in Robertson, "Correspondence," 4, no. 3(July 1899): 283.

12. Letter, Panton to Carondelet, Jan. 1, 1793, in D. C. Corbitt, trans. and ed., "Papers Relating to the Georgia-Florida Frontier, 1784–1899," *Georgia Historical Quarterly* 23, no. 2(June 1939): 198–199; Records of the Proceedings of the Treaty of Hopewell, Jan. 9, 1786, in *ASP* (Indian Affairs), vol. 1, 1832, p. 51; McGee-Draper Narrative, 111, 112a; Letter, Bloody Fellow to Carondelet, Feb. 1793, in Corbitt and Corbitt, "Papers from the Spanish Archives," 29(1957): 156; Letter, Little Turkey and Black Fox to General James Robertson, April 10, 1795, in Robertson, "Correspondence," 4, no. 2(April 1899): 192; D. C. Corbitt, trans. and ed., "Some Papers Relating to Bourbon County, Georgia," *Georgia Historical Quarterly* 19, no. 3(Sept. 1935): 261; John Carr, *Early Times in Middle Tennessee* (Nashville: Parthenon Press, 1958, originally published in 1857), 18, 97; Gibson (*The Chickasaws*, 80), citing a typescript of part of the Draper Collection, wrote that Malcolm McGee said Piomingo was "tall." I have failed to find such a reference in the Draper Collection. It is definitely not in the Draper papers series cited by Gibson (Series X, 25–28).

13. Holmes, *Gayoso*, 148–149 n. 31; Letter, Gayoso to Carondelet, July 21, 1792, in Corbitt and Corbitt, "Papers from the Spanish Archives," 27(1955): 90; Cotterill, *The Southern Indians*, 33 n. 31.

14. Cotterill, *The Southern Indians*, 97; Colton Storm, ed., "Up the Tennessee in 1790: The Report of Major John Doughty to the Secretary of War," *East Tennessee Historical Society's Publications* 17(1945): 130; Letter, William Panton to Baron De Carondelet, Jan. 1, 1793, in Corbitt, "Papers Relating to the Georgia-Florida Frontier," 198–199.

15. Record of the Nashville Conference, August 1792, in *ASP* (Indian Affairs), vol. 1, 1832, pp. 284–285. The conference record states that "Mooleshawsek" was Wolf's Friend's Indian name. Nowhere else known to me does that name appear in association with him, in con-

trast to the commonly appearing name "Ugulayacabe," which is undoubtedly correct. Incidentally, neither name translates to the words "Wolf's Friend"; McGee-Draper Narrative, 112a, 112b.

16. Samuel C. Williams, *History of the Lost State of Franklin* (New York: Press of the Pioneers, 1933), 264, citing *Pennsylvania Packet*, Sept. 30, 1785. See also Williams's discussion on pages 264–265.

17. Gibson, *The Chickasaws*, 77–79.

18. Ibid., 78; Calloway, *The American Revolution in Indian Country*, 235; Statement, McGillivray for the Chiefs of the Creek, Chickasaw, and Cherokee Nations, July 10, 1785, in Caughey, *McGillivray of the Creeks*, 90–93; A. P. Whitaker, "Alexander McGillivray, 1783–1787," *North Carolina Historical Review* 5, no. 2(April 1928): 193.

19. Treaty of Hopewell, 1786, in Charles J. Kappler, compiler and ed., *Indian Affairs: Laws and Treaties* (Washington, D.C.: Government Printing Office, 1904), vol. 2, pp. 14–16; the treaty is also published in Clark, *The State Records of North Carolina*, vol. 18 (1900), pp. 493–495; Record of the Proceedings at the Treaty of Hopewell, Jan. 9, 1786, in *ASP* (Indian Affairs), vol. 1, 1832, p. 51; Welcome speech of Governor William Blount to the Headmen and Chiefs of the Chickasaws and Choctaws, Nashville Conference, Aug. 7, 1792, in *ASP* (Indian Affairs), vol. 1, 1832, p. 285; Record of Proceedings at the Nashville Conference, August 7, 1792, in *ASP* (Indian Affairs), vol. 1, 1832, p. 287.

20. Gibson, *The Chickasaws*, 79; Cotterill, *The Southern Indians*, 59, 69; Calloway, *The American Revolution in Indian Country*, 236; W. S. Coker and T. D. Watson, *Indian Traders of the Southeastern Spanish Borderlands: Panton, Leslie & Company and John Forbes & Company, 1783–1847* (Pensacola: Univ. Press of Florida, 1986), 85, 99; A. P. Whitaker, *The Spanish-American Frontier* (Gloucester, Mass.: Peter Smith, 1962), 55; Letter, McGillivray to Governor Carondelet, Sept. 3, 1792, in Caughey, *McGillivray of the Creeks*, 336.

21. Letter, The Chickasaw Chiefs to James Robertson, Feb. 13, 1795, in *ASP* (Indian Affairs), vol. 1, 1832, p. 443. The first two signatures on this letter are those of mixed-bloods John Brown and Thomas Brown. The others are not listed in its publication.

22. Gibson, *The Chickasaws*, 79.

23. Record of the Proceedings at the Hopewell Treaty, Jan. 9, 1786, in *ASP* (Indian Affairs), vol. 1, 1832, p. 51. Mingotushka stated that "Our two old leading men are dead, and we two come as their successors in business. . . . Although our old king and leading man is dead, we wish their friendly talks may live." The medal referred to by Piomingo may have been either a Spanish or British one, for the first known United States peace medal dates later—to 1789 (see Bauman L. Belden, *Indian Peace Medals Issued in the United States* [New Milford, Conn.: N. Flaydeman, 1966, reprint], 6). However, there is a reference to United States silver medals being awarded to Cherokees by James Martin in 1787 or 1788 (Prucha, *Indian Peace Medals in American History*, 6, 8). Thus it is possible that the Chickasaw medal spoken of by Mingotushka and Piomingo was one of these "mystery medals," so to speak. These unaccounted-for medals may have carried the legend "Friendship & trade without end," for a supposedly American medal with these words had come into the hands of the Spanish in New Orleans by 1793 (see Letter, Jaudenes and Viar to Thomas Jefferson, May 25, 1792 [*sic*, 1793], in *ASP* [Foreign Affairs], vol. 1, 1833, p. 263). See Whitaker, *The Spanish-American Frontier*, 170, for comments regarding the alleged award of the mysterious American medal.

24. Letters, Benjamin Hawkins to Alexander McGillivray, Jan. 11, 1786, and Alexander McGillivray to Governor Miro, May 1, 1786, in Corbitt and Corbitt, "Papers from the Spanish Archives," 10(1938): 128, 135; Record of the Proceedings at the Treaty of Hopewell, Jan. 12, 1786, in *ASP* (Indian Affairs), vol. 1, 1832, p. 52; Piomingo's presents and goods were stolen by two Cherokees, but after the American commissioners offered a reward for apprehension of the culprits, the items were quickly recovered.

25. Kappler, *Laws and Treaties*, vol. 2, pp. 14–16; Letter, Miro to Favrot, July 6, 1786, in Corbitt and Corbitt, "Papers from the Spanish Archives," 10(1938): 141; Letter, Favrot to Miro, May 30, 1786, in Kinnaird, "Spain in the Mississippi Valley," vol. 3, pt. 2, p. 173; Gibson, *The Chickasaws*, 79; Calloway, *The American Revolution in Indian Country*, 236.

26. Calloway, *The American Revolution in Indian Country*, 236–237; Letters, McGillivray to Arturo O'Neill, May 12, 1786, and O'Neill to Galvez, May 20, 1786, in Corbitt and Corbitt, "Papers from the Spanish Archives," 10(1938): 137–139.

27. Letter, Piomingo to Joseph Martin, Feb. 15, 1787, in Palmer, *Virginia State Papers*, vol. 4 (1884), p. 241.

28. Calloway, *The American Revolution in Indian Country*, 237; Whitaker, *The Spanish-American Frontier*, 59–61; Letter, McGillivray to Governor O'Neill, July 25, 1787, in Caughey, *McGillivray of the Creeks*, 158–159; Letter, William Panton to Governor Miro, April 18, 1790, in Corbitt, "Some Papers Relating to Bourbon County, Georgia," 257–262; Letters, Benjamin James to John Joyce, July 23, 1787, and McGillivray to Governor Miro, July 25, 1787, in Corbitt and Corbitt, "Papers from the Spanish Archives," 11(1939): 87–88; Arturo O'Neill, in a letter to Miro dated Aug. 3, 1787 (Corbitt and Corbitt, "Papers from the Spanish Archives," 11(1939): 91), made the statement that Davenport and the others were attacked half a day's journey from a Chickasaw town "at a place called Wolfcreek, four day's journey from the Mississippi [River] where the Americans are making a large settlement." Jack D. L. Holmes, in "Spanish-American Rivalry over the Chickasaw Bluffs," 32, apparently believed O'Neill's reference to "Wolfcreek" indicated the present-day Wolf River at the bluffs, despite other data to the contrary. Perhaps Holmes thought O'Neill was referring to a rumored establishment of a trading post at Chickasaw Bluffs by Choctaw trader Turner Brashears. O'Neill reported the false rumor that Brashears was joined there by twenty to thirty vagrants from the Chickasaw nation (see Letters, O'Neill to Miro, Sept. 8, 1787, and Miro to O'Neill, Sept. 25, 1787, in Corbitt and Corbitt, "Letters from the Spanish Archives," 12[1940]: 100–102). In any case, O'Neill undoubtedly intended to convey that the potential "large settlement" was a four-day journey (eastward) from the Mississippi River.

29. Letters, McGillivray to Governor Miro, June 24, 1789, and McGillivray to William Panton, Aug. 10, 1789, in Caughey, *McGillivray of the Creeks*, 239, 248. In addition, see Ramsey, *Annals of Tennessee*, 484, with regard to the deaths of Piomingo's brother (Long Hair) and nephew, as well as Cotterill, *The Southern Indians*, 83, citing Piomingo's talk to Joseph Martin, Sept. 20, 1789, in Edward E. Ayer Collection, no. 722, Newberry Library, Chicago; Coker and Watson (*Indian Traders*, 178) assert that the people attacked by the Creek war party were "a group of marauding Anglo-American frontiersmen above the Chickamauga villages" and that they "were returning home from a mission to the U.S. capital." The accuracy of this information about "marauding" Americans, apparently obtained by Coker and

Watson from a cited Spanish letter (in AGI, PC, legajo 202, doc. Q, WP), should be discounted in the absence of verifying documentation; confusion in the Spanish letter with another incident seems likely. With regard to the trip north by Piomingo and his party, see Letters, General James Wilkinson to Governor Miro, Jan. 26, 1790, and Miro to Alexander McGillivray, April 7, 1790, in Corbitt and Corbitt, "Papers from the Spanish Archives," 22(1950): 137, 144–145. General Wilkinson, who was secretly communicating in a treasonable manner with the Spanish at this time, posed the following question to Governor Miro with regard to Piomingo's obtaining the goods from Kentucky: "Cannot you acquaint [Alexander] McGillivray of this circumstance & have this troublesome fellow cut off?"; the quoted report to President Washington by the Virginia legislature was published in an issue of the *Kentucky Gazette* dated Jan. 16, 1790; see also Resolution of the House of Delegates for the relief of the Chickasaw, Oct. 23, 1789, and Letter, Major E. Langham to Governor Beverly Randolph, Nov. 2, 1789, in Palmer, *Virginia State Papers,* vol. 5 (1885, W. P. Palmer and Sherwin McRae, eds.), pp. 43–44, 51–52; report of B. Lincoln, C. Griffin, and D. Humphreys, Nov. 1789, in *ASP* (Indian Affairs), vol. 1, 1832, p. 77; Cotterill (*The Southern Indians,* 83) mistakenly states that Piomingo's group went all the way to New York; see communications from Piomingo et al. to Robertson in The Tennessee Papers, Draper Collection, vol. 5, series XX, pp. 27–28 (the source comprises separate letters in one document from Piomingo, William Glover, and William Colbert to James Robertson [apparently], April 29, 1790 or 1791); Letter, Piomingo, Thomas Brown, George Colbert, Pis Micko, Muklusaw Tuskaw, Muklusaw Mingo, Tushau Hopoi, and Poy Emauba to Brigadier General James Robertson, no date, in The Tennessee Papers, Draper Collection, vol. 5, series XX, pp. 27–28. Written in the first person, this letter is obviously the words of Piomingo.

30. See Haywood, *Civil and Political History of Tennessee,* and Putnam, *History of Middle Tennessee,* for detailed narration regarding specific incidents of American-Indian violence of the 1780s and 1790s; see also various documents in John Haywood Papers, Accession Number THS 448, Tennessee State Library and Archives, Nashville; Thomas L. Connelly, "Indian Warfare on the Tennessee Frontier, 1776–1794: Strategy and Tactics," *East Tennessee Historical Society's Publications* 36(1964): 3–22; for a detailed contemporary discussion of the causes and motives of the Indian–Cumberland settlement hostilities, see Letter, Governor William Blount to Secretary of War, Nov. 8, 1792, in *ASP* (Indian Affairs), vol. 1, 1832, pp. 325–327.

31. Haywood, *Civil and Political History of Tennessee,* 230–235; Ramsey, *Annals of Tennessee,* 465; Putnam, *History of Middle Tennessee,* 257–264; Goodpasture, "Indian Wars and Warriors," 121–122, 124–127; Letter, Robertson to Cruzat(?), 1787, in Robertson, "Correspondence," 1, no. 1(Jan. 1896): 79–80. The French men and women at the Coldwater trading camp were from the Detroit area via the Wabash River; Letter, James Robertson to Governor Miro, Sept. 2, 1789, in Corbitt and Corbitt, "Papers from the Spanish Archives," 21(1949): 89. The letter is also published in Kinnaird, "Spain in the Mississippi Valley," vol. 3, pt. 2, p. 279.

32. Letter, Alexander Fraser to Governor Miro, April 15, 1788, in Corbitt and Corbitt, "Papers from the Spanish Archives," 14(1942): 99. The letter was written at the Choctaw village named Yazoo.

33. Calloway, *The American Revolution in Indian Country,* 233–234.

34. Mention of the nonviolent quarrel between King Taski Etoka on one side and Pio-mingo and Wolf's Friend on the other is in a letter from Juan de la Villebeuvre to Governor Gayoso, Sept. 10, 1792, in Kinnaird, "Spain in the Mississippi Valley," vol. 4, pt. 3 (1946), 79–80. As discussed further in Chapter 9, the subordinate chiefs wanted Taski Etoka to go with them to Nashville to confer with the Americans, but Taski Etoka gave them the silent treatment and went instead on a peace mission to the Tallapoosas in the Creek territory.

CHAPTER 9

1. Storm, "Up the Tennessee in 1790: The Report of Major John Doughty," 119–132. The original report is in the Josiah Harmar Papers, Clements Library, University of Michigan, Ann Arbor. For related documentation of the Doughty expedition see letters from a Lieutenant Melcher in Corbitt and Corbitt, "Papers from the Spanish Archives," 24(1952): 108–110.

2. Storm, "Up the Tennessee in 1790: The Report of Major John Doughty," 130. Major Doughty estimated about 500 warriors for the Chickasaw, a figure that generally conforms with late eighteenth-century estimates (see Swanton, "Indian Tribes of North America," 179). More recently, Peter H. Wood has concluded that the entire population was about 3,100 in 1790 ("The Changing Population of the Colonial South: An Overview of Race and Region, 1685–1790," in Wood et al., *Powhatan's Mantle*, 69; "Yanacha" is mentioned in Letter, de la Villebeuvre to Carondelet, April 18, 1793, in Corbitt and Corbitt, "Papers from the Spanish Archives," 32(1960): 76.

3. Storm, "Up the Tennessee in 1790: The Report of Major John Doughty," 131; Adair, *History*, 378; Romans, *A Concise Natural History*, 124; Purcell, "New Map of West Florida," 1773; Francisco Blache's tabulation, Rations Given to Indians at Congress of Mobile, June 24, 1784, in Kinnaird, "Spain in the Mississippi Valley," vol. 3, pt. 2, p. 102; McGee-Draper Narrative, 110; for one of the discussions of Adair's book regarding his cultural observations, see Charles Hudson, "James Adair as Anthropologist," *Ethnohistory* 24(Fall 1977): 311–328.

4. Storm, "Up the Tennessee in 1790: The Report of Major John Doughty," 131; Adair, *History*, 378; Rations Given to Indians at Congress of Mobile, June 24, 1784, in Kinnaird, "Spain in the Mississippi Valley," vol. 3, pt. 2, p. 102; McGee-Draper Narrative, 110, 118; de Crenay map, 1733; archaeological site data from the Coonewah Creek area in Lee County show conclusively that early eighteenth-century Chickasaw village habitations were on the south side of the creek; these remains probably represent the pre-1723 location of Tchi-tchatala, at least (see Atkinson, "The Ackia and Ogoula Tchetoka Chickasaw Village Locations," and "Historic Chickasaw Cultural Material"). As a matter of fact, all eighteenth-century villages and town areas have been determined through sixty-five years of amateur and professional archaeological investigations to lie on the consistently higher ground/prairie soils on the south sides of Old Town Creek and its tributaries; see Letters, Ogoulayacabe to Gayoso, Thisatera, March 15, 1794, March 26, 1794, and July 2, 1794, Thishatare, in Corbitt and Corbitt, "Papers from the Spanish Archives," 38(1966): 78, 82, and 40(1968): 110; as discussed below in the text, agent Fooy apparently wrote most or all of his own letters from the new settlement of "Holkey" located on the Natchez Trace in present-day northern Chicka-

saw County, Mississippi; for a short but less than comprehensive discussion of some various late renditions of the village called "Shatara" by Adair, see H. S. Halbert, "Shatala: Notes on a Chickasaw Town Name," in Milo M. Quaife, ed., *Proceedings of the Mississippi Valley Historical Association for the Year 1914–1915* (Cedar Rapids, Iowa: Torch Press, 1916), 93–94.

5. Storm, "Up the Tennessee in 1790: The Report of Major John Doughty," 131; Rations Given to Indians at Congress of Mobile, June 24, 1784, in Kinnaird, "Spain in the Mississippi Valley," vol. 3, pt. 2, p. 102; McGee-Draper Narrative, 110.

6. With regard to Pontitack, discussed in Chapter 6, the name of this recent settlement was spelled "Pantelook" or "Pantclock" by a few white residents in the 1790s (Letters, Malcolm McGee to Gayoso, Feb. 27, 1795, and Benjamin Fooy to Gayoso, Feb. 27, 1795, in Corbitt and Corbitt, "Papers from the Spanish Archives," 43[1971]: 110–111); Letter, Fooy to Gayoso, Holkey, March 16, 1794, in Corbitt and Corbitt, "Papers from the Spanish Archives," 38(1966): 79. See other 1794 letters written from Holkey in the same source, vol. 39 (1967), 87, 89, 94, and vol. 40 (1968), 111. For a detailed discussion of Holkey/Holka/Wholkey/ Hoolkie/Hulca/Houlka see Atkinson, *History of the Chickasaw Indian Agency,* 48–49 n. 15.

7. Victor Collot, "Chart of the Sources . . . ," ca. 1796; Cook et al., "Historic Chickasaw Village Locations," 22. Because these writers overlooked the data that document the location of the now-extinct late eighteenth/early nineteenth century settlement of Pontitack in present-day Pontotoc County, they speculated without supporting documentation that the Salle Bernaby/Tuskatville village moved to that location and became known as Pontitack sometime after preparation of the Collot map. This is obviously erroneous in light of the pre-1796 documentation of the presence of the Pontitack Chickasaw village.

8. Storm, "Up the Tennessee in 1790: The Report of Major John Doughty," 131.

9. McGee-Draper Narrative, 118–119.

10. Ibid., 119–120.

11. Storm, "Up the Tennessee in 1790: The Report of Major John Doughty," 124.

12. Ibid.

13. Mohr, *Federal Indian Relations,* 164–165; Whitaker, *The Spanish-American Frontier,* 167.

14. A "Treaty of Friendship" with the Choctaw and Chickasaw, in *ASP* (Foreign Relations), vol. 1, 1833, p. 280.

15. Letter, George Washington to "Piomingo, or the Mountain leader, Head Warrior and first Minister, and the other Chiefs and Warriors of the Chickasaw Nation," Dec. 30, 1790, in Clarence E. Carter, compiler and ed., *The Territorial Papers of the United States,* vol. 4, *The Territory South of the River Ohio* (Washington, D.C.: Government Printing Office, 1936), 41. Washington also stated: "In the meantime hold fast the Chain of friendship, and do not believe any evil Reports against the justice and integrity of the United States."

16. For some of the trans-Mississippi interactions between Chickasaw and other native Americans, see Arrell M. Gibson, *The Kickapoos* (Norman: Univ. of Oklahoma Press, 1963); Din and Nasatir, *The Imperial Osages;* Rollings, *The Osage;* Baird, *The Quapaw Indians.* See also Michael N. McConnell, *A Country Between: The Upper Ohio Valley and Its People, 1724– 1774* (Lincoln: Univ. of Nebraska Press, 1992).

17. Calloway, *The American Revolution in Indian Country,* 238; Holmes, *Gayoso,* 14; Cotterill, *The Southern Indians,* 104–107; in March 1793, James Robertson reported that the

Spaniards sent Piomingo a horse and saddle to induce him to visit them, "but he, at all times, has refused any connexion with them" (Letter extract, Robertson to Governor Blount, March 12, 1793, in *ASP* [Indian Affairs], vol. 1, 1832, p. 442).

18. Letter, William Panton to Governor Miro, April 18, 1790, in Corbitt, "Some Papers Relating to Bourbon County, Georgia," 257–262.

19. Ibid., 261. "Taskabucka" is one of the many contemporary written variations of the name of the king of the Chickasaws, spelled herein "Taski Etoka."

20. Ibid., 262; Phelps, "Tockshish," 138–145. Apparently John McIntosh, Jr., was not offered the Spanish position or, if so, did not accept it. As mentioned in Chapter 7, John McIntosh, Jr., had replaced his father as British commissary to the Chickasaw.

21. Stayce Hathorn and Robin Sabino, "Views and Vistas: Traveling through the Choctaw, Chickasaw, and Cherokee Nations in 1803," *Alabama Review* 54, no. 3(2001): 218. Although Wilson stated that the settlement was named after John McIntosh, Sr., it was more likely named after John McIntosh, Jr., or possibly the former's widow. See further discussion in Chapter 11.

22. Wiley Sword, *President Washington's Indian War: The Struggle for the Old Northwest, 1790–1795* (Norman: Univ. of Oklahoma Press, 1985), 168; Putnam, *History of Middle Tennessee*, 362–363. Putnam says that twenty Chickasaws were sent home by Piomingo because of a message received that the settlements were threatened by the Creek. However, the earlier history by John Haywood attributes this incident to the 1794 United States campaign against the northern Indians (Haywood, *Civil and Political History of Tennessee*, 425). Haywood is probably correct.

23. Sword, *President Washington's Indian War*, 166, 168–200; McGee-Draper Narrative, 109.

24. Regarding Robertson's appointment as Chickasaw agent, see Letter, Secretary of War to Governor Blount, April 22, 1792, in Carter, *Territorial Papers of the United States*, vol. 4, p. 141, and the same letter in *ASP* (Indian Affairs), 1832, vol. 4, p. 253. Robertson was informed of the appointment by a letter from Governor Blount dated May 8, 1792 (Robertson, "Correspondence," 2, no. 1[Jan. 1897]: 60); R. A. Billington, *Westward Expansion: A History of the American Frontier*, 3rd ed. (New York: Macmillian, 1967), 184; for references to Robertson's homes see Putnam, *History of Middle Tennessee*, 196, 257, 295, 385, 388, 524. Writing in the late 1850s, Putnam related (p. 196) that Robertson's brick home on Richland Creek was still standing "and yet remains in good preservation." According to Harriette S. Arnow (*Flowering of the Cumberland* [New York: Macmillan, 1963], 12), Robertson was living in this area by 1784 in "a forted station." As discussed in Chapter 8, he built the brick home just mentioned about a mile from the log home in 1797; Atkinson, *History of the Chickasaw Indian Agency*, 1–2.

25. Goodpasture, "Indian Wars and Warriors," 263; Letter, Robertson to unnamed recipient, April 26, 1805, in Robertson, "Correspondence," 5, no. 1(Jan. 1900): 81; Nina Leftwich, *Two Hundred Years at Muscle Shoals being an Authentic History of Colbert County [Alabama], 1700–1900* (Birmingham: Multigraphic Advertising, 1935), 12. Governor Blount stated regarding the settlement near the mouth of the Tennessee that "We have reason to believe that a chief called Double-head, of the Cherokees . . . with some other Cherokees, and some Northwards and Creeks, in all about forty, have settled on the south side of the Tennessee, near the mouth, on your lands" (Introduction by Governor Blount to the Head men and

Chiefs of the Chickasaws and Choctaws at the Nashville Conference, August 7, 1792, in *ASP* [Indian Affairs], vol. 1, 1832, p. 285); Fairbanks, *Ethnographic Report on Royce Area 79*, 202–203, 271.

26. Letter, Ogoulayacabe to Pierre Juzan, 1790 (*sic*, 1792), in Corbitt and Corbitt, "Papers from the Spanish Archives," 22(1950): 146–147; Ugulayacabe's relation of his journey to Cumberland (1792), in *ASP* (Foreign Relations), vol. 1, 1833, p. 281; Letter, General James Robertson to General Daniel Smith, July 20, 1793, in *ASP* (Indian Affairs), vol. 1, 1832, p. 465; see also Carondelet to Aranda, Nov. 8, 1792, in Corbitt and Corbitt, "Papers from the Spanish Archives," 28(1956): 135; Calloway, *The American Revolution in Indian Country*, 239.

27. Letter, Ogoulayacabe to Juzan, 1790 (*sic*, 1792), in Corbitt and Corbitt, "Papers from the Spanish Archives," 22(1950): 146–147. Of interest with regard to Wolf's Friend's power claims is reference to him as "the Great Chief of the Chickasaws" by the drafter of the above-cited letter from Wolf's Friend to Juzan, as well as in written instructions from Carondelet to Pedro Rousseau (Jan. 15, 1794, Corbitt and Corbitt, "Papers from the Spanish Archives," 37[1965]: 93).

28. Records of the Nashville Conference in August 1792, in *ASP* (Indian Affairs), vol. 1, 1832, pp. 284–287; Letter, Carondelet to Alexander McGillivray, Sept. 14, 1792, in Caughey, *McGillivray of the Creeks*, 337–338; Ugulayacabe's relation of his journey to Cumberland (1792), in *ASP* (Foreign Relations), vol. 1, 1833, p. 281; Haywood, *Civil and Political History of Tennessee*, 348–351; the Spanish-Indian conference at Nogales is documented in Manuel Serrano y Sanz, *Espana y los Indios Cherokis y Chactas en la segunda mitad del Siglio XVIII* (Seville: Tio. de la Guia Oficial, 1916), 48–62, 90; Putnam, *History of Middle Tennessee*, 196, 257, 385, 388.

29. Letter, Ogoulayacabe to Juzan, 1790 (*sic*, 1792), in Corbitt and Corbitt, "Papers from the Spanish Archives," 22(1950): 146–147; Letter, Gayoso to Carondelet, Oct. 10, 1794, in Corbitt and Corbitt, "Papers from the Spanish Archives," 41(1969): 110; Malcolm McGee lends support to Ugulayacabe/Wolf's Friend's and Gayoso's statements regarding the brother relationship by also stating that Chinubbee was a brother to the Hare Lipped King (see McGee-Draper Narrative, 117). For 1793 letters that document Taski Etoka's continuing status as king, see Corbitt and Corbitt, "Papers from the Spanish Archives," 29 and 30; except for Gayoso's and one other known contemporary reference (Corbitt and Corbitt, "Papers from the Spanish Archives," 41[1969]: 114) to the new king's being named Tinabe, his name appears in documents numerous times from 1792 until his death in 1819 as either Chinumbe or Chinubbee, or slight variations thereof. In January 1795, Chinubbee was reported by Gayoso to be a resident of Long Town (Corbitt and Corbitt, "Papers from the Spanish Archives," 42[1970]: 101). Some modern historians have stated that Chinubbee was Taski Etoka's nephew rather than his brother. Such a matrilineal hereditary progression of the position was indeed the custom under normal circumstances, but in this case, such undoubtedly did not occur. See further discussion of Chinubbee in this and following chapters.

30. Letter, Message to "Piomingo, the Mountain Leader," and the other chiefs and warriors of the Chickasaw Nation, from Henry Knox, Secretary of War, Feb. 17, 1792, in *ASP* (Indian Affairs), vol. 1, 1832, p. 249. The original document is in National Archives, Records of the Office of the Secretary of War (RG 107; Correspondence of the War Department Relating to Indian Affairs), microfilm M-1062, 1 roll. Identification of the Colbert brothers is

in Letter, Juan de la Villebeuvre to Governor Carondelet, Sept. 12, 1792, in Kinnaird, "Spain in the Mississippi Valley," vol. 4, pt. 3, p. 83.

31. Letter, Governor Blount to Robertson, May 8, 1792, in Robertson, "Correspondence," 2, no. 1(Jan. 1897): 59; Letters, Message to "Piomingo, the Mountain Leader," from the Secretary of War, Feb. 17, 1792, Instructions to Leonard Shaw from the Secretary of War, Feb. 17, 1792, and Blount to Piomingo, April 27, 1792, all in *ASP* (Indian Affairs), vol. 1, 1832, pp. 247–249, 265–266. Blount stated to Piomingo that "to these gentlemen I commit the medals and clothing mentioned in the letter of the Secretary of War, to deliver to you, and three pounds of vermillion as a present from myself to you"; Letters, Governor Blount, Knoxville, to Secretary of War, Sept. 20, 1792, and Anthony Foster, Nashville, to Governor Blount, July 29, 1792, both in *ASP* (Indian Affairs), vol. 1, 1832, pp. 282–284; Haywood (*Civil and Political History of Tennessee*, 348) erroneously identified the son of Robertson who accompanied Foster and Smith as James A. rather than James Randolph as stated by Blount and others.

32. Belden, *Indian Peace Medals Issued in the United States*, 16–17; Prucha, *Indian Peace Medals in American History*, 6–8; Luther L. Roberson, "The Seeds of Spain" (1978), carbon copy of unpublished manuscript in possession of Joyce Roberson Bushman, copy made available to me by Ms. Bushman. Detailed discussion of the grave discovery and the artifacts recovered is presented by J. R. Atkinson, "Death of a Chickasaw Leader: The Probable Grave of Piomingo," *Mississippi Archaeology* 35, no. 2(Winter 2000): 124–172; although it is possible that other Chickasaws besides Piomingo and the Colbert brothers eventually received Washington Peace Medals, one of which could be the specimen found by Roberson, such is not likely the case. If the medal was indeed Piomingo's, the 1793 date on a medal presented in 1792 could be due to postdating, perhaps because of uncertainty as to when it and others would be awarded. The matter is complicated, however, by the mid-1930s discovery north of Tupelo of a second, very similar peace medal made by the same silversmith (initials "JL") and also dated 1793. The second medal probably did not belong to one of the Colbert brothers inasmuch as George died and is buried in present-day Oklahoma and William is documented to have died at his last home in present-day northern Chickasaw County, Mississippi. However, the circumstances of the second medal's discovery are undocumented; it may not have been in a grave and therefore possibly could have been lost by its owner, who could have been George or William Colbert or another individual. A gold epaulet and associated metal French button found at the left shoulder of the grave occupant may have been a separate gift from President Washington. In 1790 the President gave two "very handsome epaulets" to Alexander McGillivray. According to McGillivray, the epaulets had been presented to the President by General Lafayette as gifts from the court of France (see General Louis Milfort, *Memoirs or a quick Glance at my various Travels and my Sojurn in the Creek Nation*, B. C. McCary, trans. and ed. [Kennesaw, Ga.: Continental, 1959, originally published in 1802], 93). Thus it is possible that the President also gave one or more similar epaulets to Piomingo.

33. Record of the Nashville Conference, in *ASP* (Indian Affairs), vol. 1, 1832, pp. 284–287. An erroneous notion that a treaty was signed at the Nashville conference appears to have originated with Gibson (*The Chickasaws*, 87).

34. Welcome speech of Governor William Blount to the Headmen and Chiefs of the Chickasaws and Choctaws, Nashville Conference, Aug. 7, 1792, in *ASP* (Indian Affairs), vol. 1,

1832, p. 285. A large quantity of goods was presented to the Indians, including the Chicka-saws "who joined General St. Clair's Army and some other Chiefs." These gifts included powder, lead, blankets, cloth of various types, binding, hats, suits of clothes, scarlet, needles and thread, and "Scalping Knives" (See Invoice and Memorandum, Governor Blount to General Robertson, 1792, in Robertson, "Correspondence," 1, no. 3[July 1896]: 283). See also Letter, Report of the Secretary of War to the President, Jan. 17, 1792, in Carter, *Territorial Papers of the United States,* vol. 4, p. 114.

35. Letter, Governor Carondelet to Aranda, Nov. 28, 1792, in Corbitt and Corbitt, "Papers from the Spanish Archives," 28(1956): 139–141.

36. Letter, Governor William Blount to Leonard D. Shaw, March 23, 1793, in *ASP* (Indian Affairs), vol. 1, 1832, p. 441; Letters, Bloody Fellow to Governor Carondelet, Tchoukafala, Feb. 11, 1793, and Piomingo et al. to Carondelet, Feb. 11, 1793, in Corbitt and Corbitt, "Papers from the Spanish Archives," 29(1957): 154–155. The other Chickasaw signatories to the latter letter are, as spelled therein, Taskato, Olantenatla, Astabe, Mingo Taksatabe, Jorg [George] Colbert, Pichon, Captain [William] Glover, and Parliot. The man named Favre mentioned by Piomingo is undoubtedly trader Simon Favre because his father, Choctaw interpreter John Favre, had died in about 1781 (Account for cash advanced "John Favre, deceased," dated Feb. 24, 1781, in *DAR,* vol. 19, p. 42); according to after-the-fact stories told to Gayoso, the escalation of war resulted from an incident on the frontier of the Cumberland settlement in the fall of 1792. One of two Creek warriors who were there for reasons unstated coveted the gun of the other, killed him to obtain it, and to cover up his crime claimed upon return-ing home that the deed was done by Chickasaws. Thereupon the relatives of the murdered Creek "took vengeance by killing the first warrior of Piomingo, from which resulted the animosity that exists today" (Letter, Gayoso to Carondelet, June 8, 1793, in Corbitt and Cor-bitt, "Papers from the Spanish Archives," 33[1961]: 67).

37. Letter, Governor Blount to Leonard D. Shaw, March 23, 1793, in *ASP* (Indian Affairs), vol. 1, 1832, p. 441; Letters, de la Villebeuvre to Carondelet, July 7, 1794, and Lanzos to Caron-delet, April 25, 1793, in Kinnaird, "Spain in the Mississippi Valley," vol. 4, pt. 3, pp. 152, 315; Letters, de la Villebeuvre to Carondelet, Jan. 16, Feb. 27, and Feb. [28?], 1793, in Corbitt and Corbitt, "Papers from the Spanish Archives," 29(1957): 145, 156–159; Letter, Taskihatoka and others to de la Villebeuvre, March 10, 1793, in Corbitt and Corbitt, "Papers from the Spanish Archives," 30(1958): 98–99. The Chickasaw chiefs whose names were affixed to this letter are, as spelled, Popyemano [Piomingo] "and all the leaders of his town" and (from Big Town) Potoattenahto, Muckhsamingo, Captain William Glover, Tuskahopoy, Pawahogo, Tobaw, and Muckhahopoy. The first signature, that of the king, was written "Tuskahatogur Mingo" (Taski Etoka Mingo). Wolf's Friend's name is noticeably absent, perhaps because of the par-tially critical nature of the letter; Letter, de la Villebeuvre to Gayoso, Aug. 30, 1793, in Corbitt and Corbitt, "Papers from the Spanish Archives," 35(1963): 86.

38. Letter, The Chickasaw Chiefs [actually dictated by Piomingo] to General Robertson, Feb. 13, 1793, in *ASP* (Indian Affairs), vol. 1, 1832, p. 442; Letter, General Robertson to General Daniel Smith, July 20, 1793, in *ASP* (Indian Affairs), vol. 1, 1832, pp. 465–466.

39. Letter abstract, General Robertson to Governor Blount, March 12, 1793, in *ASP* (In-dian Affairs), vol. 1, 1832, pp. 441–442; the goods sent to Chickasaw Bluffs are listed in Letter, Secretary of War to Governor Blount, May 14, 1793, in *ASP* (Indian Affairs), vol. 1, 1832,

pp. 429–430. The same letter is also published in Carter, *Territorial Papers of the United States,* vol. 4, p. 258. See also Account, Supply for the Chickasaw, War Department, April 27, 1793, in Robertson, "Correspondence," 2, no. 4(Oct. 1897): 363; Letter, de la Villebeuvre to Gayoso, Aug. 30, 1793, in Corbitt and Corbitt, "Papers from the Spanish Archives," 35(1963): 86; Haywood's and Putnam's year-by-year discussions of settler-Indian interactions in the late eighteenth century are characterized by a central theme—that with the exception of occasionally sending arms and ammunition to the Chickasaw, the United States government shamefully neglected that tribe and the southern American settlements in Tennessee and elsewhere, thus condoning the murder of American citizens by Creek and Cherokee malcontents. The United States, incidentally, had supplied the Creek and Cherokee with "large quantities" of goods just prior to agreeing to send some to the Chickasaw (Letter, Secretary of War to Governor Blount, Feb. 16, 1792, in *ASP* [Indian Affairs], vol. 1, 1832, p. 246).

40. Letter, John McDonald to William Panton, Oct. 6, 1792, in Corbitt, "Papers Relating to the Georgia-Florida Frontier," 196–198; see a description of the attack on Buchanan's Station in Blount's letter to Secretary of War, Oct. 10, 1792, in *ASP* (Indian Affairs), vol. 1, 1832, pp. 294–295. James Robertson's account of the attack, dated Sept. 30, 1792, was enclosed in the letter; see also discussion, largely obtained from Haywood's *Civil and Political History of Tennessee,* in Putnam, *History of Middle Tennessee,* 394–396.

41. Letters, de la Villebeuvre to Carondelet, Jan. 16, 1793, and Feb. 28, 1793, and Gayoso to Carondelet, Jan. 8, 1793, in Corbitt and Corbitt, "Papers from the Spanish Archives," 29(1957): 142–143, 160. The corn sent by Robertson to Chickasaw Bluffs in early 1793 was brought back to the villages by Piomingo and his companions in February; Letter, de la Villebeuvre to the Chickasaw Nation, March 22, 1793, in Corbitt and Corbitt, "Papers from the Spanish Archives," 30(1958): 98–99; Letter, Gayoso to William Blount, July 21, 1793, in Corbitt and Corbitt, "Papers from the Spanish Archives," 34(1962): 91; Letter, Carondelet to Gayoso, Dec. 18, 1792, in Kinnaird, "Spain in the Mississippi Valley," vol. 4, pt. 3, p. 105.

42. Letter, Taskihatoka to de la Villebeuvre, April 2, 1793, in Corbitt and Corbitt, "Papers from the Spanish Archives," 30(1958): 102–103; Letters, de la Villebeuvre to Carondelet, April 18, 1793, and April 28, 1793, in Corbitt and Corbitt, "Papers from the Spanish Archives," 32(1960): 75, 78–79.

43. Letter, de la Villebeuvre to Carondelet, April 18, 1793, in Corbitt and Corbitt, "Papers from the Spanish Archives," 32(1960): 75.

44. Message of Carondelet to Choctaws and Chickasaws, [May] 1793 (delivered at Boukfouka by de la Villebeuvre), in Kinnaird, "Spain in the Mississippi Valley," vol. 4, pt. 3, 140–141, and Kinnaird's "Introduction" in the same, p. xxviii.

45. Letter, Milfort to Carondelet, Tuckabatchee, April 9, 1793, in Corbitt and Corbitt, "Papers from the Spanish Archives," 31(1959): 79–80. The "great prairie" mentioned by Milfort is undoubtedly the large prairie, or possibly both the large and small ones, in the Chickasaw Old Fields in present-day Lee County.

46. Letters, Milfort to Carondelet, May 26, 1793, and Carondelet to Gayoso, June 17, 1793, in Kinnaird, "Spain in the Mississippi Valley," vol. 4, pt. 3, pp. 160–161, 175–177; Indian Speeches made at Long Town recorded by Benjamin James, June 1, 1793, in Kinnaird, "Spain in the Mississippi Valley," vol. 4, pt. 3, pp. 164–167; Letter, Governor Blount to Secretary of War, Aug. 13, 1793, in Carter, *Territorial Papers of the United States,* vol. 4, p. 298; Letters,

Thomas Portell to Carondelet, May 7, 1793, and de la Villebeuvre to Gayoso, May 25, 1793, in Corbitt and Corbitt, "Papers from the Spanish Archives," 32(1960): 80, 90.

CHAPTER 10

1. Proposals for Indian Congress, by Carondelet, Feb. 26, 1793, in Kinnaird, "Spain in the Mississippi Valley," vol. 4, pt. 3, pp. 141–142; Letter, Carondelet to Luis de las Casas, March 9, 1793, in Corbitt and Corbitt, "Papers from the Spanish Archives," 31(1959): 66–67; Letters, Gayoso to John Turnbull, Taski Etoka, Piomingo, Ogoulayacabe, Benjamin Fooy, and Hardy Perry, all dated April 7, 1793, in Corbitt and Corbitt, "Papers from the Spanish Archives," 31(1959): 72–77; Letters, de la Villebeuvre to Carondelet, April 28, 1793, and de la Villebeuvre to Gayoso, May 25, 1793, in Corbitt and Corbitt, "Papers from the Spanish Archives," 32(1960): 78, 91; Letter, Gayoso to Carondelet, July 25, 1793, in Corbitt and Corbitt, "Papers from the Spanish Archives," 34(1962): 94; the text of the Treaty of Nogales is in Kinnaird, "Spain in the Mississippi Valley," vol. 4, pt. 3, pp. 223–227; Ben Fooy was assigned to the Chickasaw in January 1794 as an interpreter but also secretly as the Spanish agent. As discussed in the text with regard to the village of Holkey, Fooy apparently lived in that recently established settlement area. Juan de la Villebeuvre had been agent-commissary to the Chickasaw during part of 1792 and most of 1793. He also served in that capacity to the Choctaw. He lived in the latter nation at Boucfouca (see letters and editors' footnotes in Corbitt and Corbitt, "Papers from the Spanish Archives," 29, 30, and 37).

2. Letter, Piomingo to Mad Dog through James Seagrove, dated Long Town, Sept. 1, 1793, in Corbitt and Corbitt, "Papers from the Spanish Archives," 35(1963): 90.

3. "List of murders committed by Indians in Mero District, since the 20th of May, 1793," an inclusion in Letter, Robertson to General Daniel Smith, July 20, 1793, in *ASP* (Indian Affairs), vol. 1, 1832, pp. 465–466.

4. Piomingo and his companions, including John McKee and John McCleish (Chickasaw Agency interpreter under Robertson), turned back at Abingdon, Virginia (see Letters, Daniel Smith to Secretary of War, Sept. 27, 1793, and Governor Blount to Secretary of War, Oct. 5, 1793, in Carter, *Territorial Papers of the United States,* vol. 4, pp. 305–307; the latter is also published in *ASP* [Indian Affairs], vol. 1, 1832, p. 458); see also Letter, Governor Blount to Robertson, Oct. 11, 1793, in Robertson, "Correspondence," 2, no. 4(Oct. 1897): 373.

5. Richard C. Knopf, transcriber and ed., *Anthony Wayne: A Name in Arms—The Wayne-Knox-Pickering-McHenry Correspondence* (Pittsburgh: Univ. of Pittsburgh Press, 1960), 33.

6. Ibid., 45, 49, 52, 102.

7. Ibid., 227, 242–243.

8. Ibid., 246–247, 274; for Spanish concerns regarding the military force under Lieutenant William Clark traveling the Mississippi River and delivering the goods at Chickasaw Bluffs, see Letters, Gayoso to Carondelet, July 19 and July 25, 1793, in Corbitt and Corbitt, "Papers from the Spanish Archives," 34(1962): 90, 96, and Letters, de la Villebeuvre to Gayoso, Aug. 30, 1793, and Gayoso to Carondelet, Sept. 12, 1793, in Corbitt and Corbitt, "Papers from the Spanish Archives," 35(1963): 86, 93; see also Letter, Secretary of War to General Wayne, April 27, 1793, in Robertson, "Correspondence," 2, no. 4(Oct. 1897): 362; picking up

the mistake from the old literature already discussed, Knopf (*Anthony Wayne*, 274 n. 89) erroneously identified Piomingo as an alternate name for William Colbert and thus attributed a post-1794 activity of the latter to Piomingo. The chief named Underwood was probably one of the mixed-blood descendants of a British trader, Francis Underwood, whose name first appears in records during the 1750s (see Chapter 1). The man was probably James Underwood, whose name was preceded by "Captain" in a 1795 letter from General Robertson to Governor Blount (*ASP* [Indian Affairs], vol. 1, 1832, p. 556).

9. Letters, Benjamin Fooy to Gayoso, March 16, 1794, Holkey, and Piomingo to Fooy, March 15, 1794, in Corbitt and Corbitt, "Papers from the Spanish Archives," 38(1966): 79–81; Letter, Fooy to Gayoso, July 3, 1794, Holkey, in Corbitt and Corbitt, "Papers from the Spanish Archives," 40(1968): 111; Letter, Pierre Rousseau to Carondelet, April 24, 1795, in Corbitt and Corbitt, "Papers from the Spanish Archives," 46(1974): 113 n. 35.

10. McGee-Draper Narrative, 109; Knopf, *Anthony Wayne*, 333; Haywood, *Civil and Political History of Tennessee*, 425; Letter, de la Villebeuvre to Carondelet, June 9, 1794, in Kinnaird, "Spain in the Mississippi Valley," vol. 4, pt. 3, pp. 297–298; Piomingo's request for a rifle "like Colonel [Kasper] Mansker's" is in his letter to General James Robertson, June 17, 1793, in *ASP* (Indian Affairs), vol. 1, 1832, p. 466; see also Letter, Governor Blount to Robertson, Nov. 29, 1797 (*sic*, 1793), in Robertson, "Correspondence," 3, no. 1(1898): 82; Atkinson, "Death of a Chickasaw Leader," 153–155; Purchase Orders and Invoices, April 7–June 30, 1794, in National Archives, Records of Accounting Officers of the Department of the Treasury (RG 217), 2nd Auditor, Entry 525A (Settled Indian Accounts and Claims, Unnumbered Accounts, 1796–1811), microfilm, roll 3 (see abstracts in Atkinson, *Records of the Chickasaw Agency*, 205–208). One of the purchase orders from Robertson to Searcy, dated May 10, 1794, reads as follows: "Sir, Tomorrow morning there will be upwards of one hundred Chickasaw & Choctaw Indians at my house, and I am informed that upwards of Seventy of the Choctaws intend to [go] to General Wayne's Camps. You'l please to lay in a quantity of Beef, Pork, loin, meal, Bacon, & salt & a quantity of Whiskey besides other necessaries they may want. I am also informed by the runner [that] Piomingo & several other chiefs are along. I expect they will stay at my house several days." In another dated May 15 he wrote: "Piomingo & several other chiefs will stay with me until I start for Holstun. You'l send me a Keg of the Best Whiskey, a Bag of meal, and about fifty pounds of Bacon for the use of them Indians. You'l also let George Colbert & other Indians with him have such goods as they want. Also send out some Tobacco."

11. John C. Fitzpatrick, ed., *The Writings of George Washington*, vol. 33 (Washington, D.C.: Government Printing Office, 1940), p. 423, citing Journal of the Proceedings of the President, July 11, 1794; Draft of a Speech to the Chickasaw Indians (delivered by President Washington at Philadelphia), July 11, 1794, in Carter, *Territorial Papers of the United States*, vol. 4, pp. 349–350; Haywood, *Civil and Political History of Tennessee*, 424; Letter, Benjamin Fooy to Gayoso, July 3, 1794, Holkey, in Corbitt and Corbitt, "Papers from the Spanish Archives," 40(1968): 114; Letter, John Pitchlynn to de la Villebeuvre, July 16, 1794, in Kinnaird, "Spain in the Mississippi Valley," vol. 4, pt. 3, p. 319; reliable documentation regarding the Washington land declaration presentation to Piomingo is to be found in Carter, *Territorial Papers of the United States*, vol. 3, *The Territory Northwest of the River Ohio, 1787–1803* (Washington, D.C.: Government Printing Office, 1934), 421–424, 426–427. A copy of the land dec-

laration is in National Archives, Records of the Bureau of Indian Affairs (RG 75; Letters Sent by the Secretary of War Relating to Indian Affairs, 1800–1824), microfilm M-15, roll 3. Two copies of the document are published in Robertson, "Correspondence," 3, no. 4(Oct. 1898): 350–351, and 4, no. 1(Jan. 1899): 94–95. See also Letter, Secretary of War to [President Washington?], May 9, 1795, in Robertson, "Correspondence," 4, no. 3(July 1899): 261. A copy supplied to the Spanish by the Chickasaw is published in Kinnaird, "Spain in the Mississippi Valley" ("A True Copy of the Limits of the Chickasaw Lands Granted them by America," July 21, 1784, vol. 4, pt. 3, p. 326). Another copy of the declaration, possibly copied from Piomingo's original, is included in the journal of Lieutenant James Gardner, Secretary of the Commissioners for the Chickasaw Treaty of 1816, in Andrew Jackson Papers, microfilm roll 62, Library of Congress. The original was signed by the President and Secretary of State Edmund Randolph on July 21, 1794, and made official by attachment of the "seal of the United States of America." Evidently Piomingo's original has not survived.

12. Letter, Gayoso to Carondelet, Jan. 8, 1795, in Corbitt and Corbitt, "Papers from the Spanish Archives," 42(1970): 100–101.

13. Ibid., 105; Letter, Secretary of War Timothy Pickering to [President Washington?], May 9, 1795, in Robertson, "Correspondence," 4, no. 3(July 1899): 261–262; Letter, J. M. Stewart, U.S. Director of Lands, to Charles J. Kappler, July 10, 1939, in Kappler, *Laws and Treaties*, vol. 5 (1941), pp. 709–710; Haywood, *Civil and Political History of Tennessee*, 427; Goodpasture, "Indian Wars and Warriors," 285; Cotterill, *The Southern Indians*, 111n.

14. Letter, Ugulayacabe to Gayoso, July 2, 1794, Chashathasa (or "Thishatare"), in Kinnaird, "Spain in the Mississippi Valley," vol. 4, pt. 3, pp. 313–314, and also translated in Corbitt and Corbitt, "Papers from the Spanish Archives," 40(1968): 110–111; Letters, Ougoulayacabe to Gayoso, Feb. 17, 1795, Benjamin Fooy to Gayoso, Feb. 18, 1795, and Joseph Stiggins to William Panton, Feb. 24, 1795, in Corbitt and Corbitt, "Papers from the Spanish Archives," 43(1971): 105–109.

15. Letter, Benjamin James to de la Villebeuvre, Feb. 12, 1795, in Corbitt and Corbitt, "Papers from the Spanish Archives," 43(1971): 103; Letter, Benjamin Fooy to Gayoso, Feb. 18, 1795, in Corbitt and Corbitt, "Papers from the Spanish Archives," 43(1971): 108; Letter, James Robertson to John Pitchlynn, Jan. 22, 1795, in Corbitt and Corbitt, "Papers from the Spanish Archives," 42(1970): 106–107.

16. Letter, Governor Blount to Robertson, Aug. 31, 1794, in Robertson, "Correspondence," 3, no. 4(Oct. 1898): 356; Letter, David Henley to Captain John Gordon, Sept. 26, 1795, in Robertson, "Correspondence," 3, no. 4(Oct. 1898): 358; Letter, Carondelet to de la Villebeuvre, May 6, 1795, in Corbitt and Corbitt, "Letters from the Spanish Archives," 47(1975): 147; Haywood, *Civil and Political History of Tennessee*, 427; Muckleshamingo, at least, was given a captain's commission in Philadelphia by order of the president on July 19, 1794 (see the commission in H. B. Cushman's *History of the Choctaw, Chickasaw, and Natchez Indians*, 391). With his honorary captain's commission, Muckleshamingo may have traveled west with some of the other Chickasaws to join General Wayne's army.

17. Letter, David Henley to Robertson, July 9, 1794, in Robertson, "Correspondence," 3, no. 4(Oct. 1898): 376–377; Letter, Governor Blount to Robertson, Aug. 11, 1795, Ibid., 3, no. 4(Oct. 1898): 388; Letter, Governor Blount to Robertson, Nov. 11, 1795, Ibid., 4, no. 1(Jan. 1899): 78–79; Letter, Governor Blount to Robertson, Nov. 12, 1795, Ibid., 4, no. 1(Jan. 1899):

79. The latter letter, delivered by McKee, was accompanied by McKee's instructions. After reading the instructions, Robertson was to seal and return the document to McKee. According to Jack D. L. Holmes ("The Ebb-Tide of Spanish Military Power on the Mississippi: Fort San Fernando De Las Barrancas, 1795–1798," *East Tennessee Historical Society's Publications* 36[1964]: 28–29, 32), Piomingo actually received the cannons along with other goods, but this may be inaccurate.

18. Letter, de la Villebeuvre to Carondelet, Feb. 14, 1795, in Corbitt and Corbitt, "Letters from the Spanish Archives," 43(1971): 104; Letter, Gayoso to Carondelet, Jan. 8, 1795, in Corbitt and Corbitt, "Letters from the Spanish Archives," 42(1970):101.

19. Sword, *President Washington's Indian War,* 269–274; Knopf, *Anthony Wayne,* 347–348.

20. Knopf, *Anthony Wayne,* 347–348; Sword, *President Washington's Indian War,* 269–274; Jimmy Underwood was probably the Captain James Underwood mentioned by General Robertson in a letter to Governor Blount in January 1795 and probably the Chickasaw chief called "Underwood" who returned from Chickasaw Bluffs with Lieutenant William Clark in 1793.

21. Sword, *President Washington's Indian War,* 279–324.

22. See documents related to the Cincinnati affair in Carter, *Territorial Papers of the United States,* vol. 3, pp. 421–424, 426–427.

23. Sword, *President Washington's Indian War,* 269–274. Sword apparently did not know that "Mountain Leader" was Piomingo's nickname, for he allowed the report to go unquestioned. It was an erroneous report, barring the unlikely possibility that another Chickasaw besides Piomingo had the nickname "Mountain Leader." With regard to the rumor and the Chickasaw attack on the Cherokees, see Letter, General Robertson to Governor Blount, Nov. 7, 1794, in *ASP* (Indian Affairs), vol. 1, 1832, p. 539; Letter, William McCleish to Governor Blount, Nov. 7, 1794, in *ASP* (Indian Affairs), vol. 1, 1832, p. 540; a peculiar reference to "Billy Colbert" appears in a 1795 Spanish letter that on the surface seems to suggest that "Billy" was not William Colbert: "Three days ago Billy Colbert and his father, with a Great Chief of their Nation, and a number of warriors arrived [at Chickasaw Bluffs] from their village." William Colbert's father, of course, had been dead since 1783. Because all other references to "Billy Colbert" appear to relate to William Colbert, the Spaniard was probably mistaken about the relationship of the two men (see Letter, Rousseau to Carondelet, April 24, 1795, in Corbitt and Corbitt, "Papers from the Spanish Archives," 46[1974]: 112). However, the possibility exists that at least one of the documentary mentions of "Billy" Colbert refers to a son of one of the Colbert brothers. If so, the man could have been the William Colbert who lived near Tockshish as late as 1836 (see church records in E. T. Winston, *"Father" Stuart and the Monroe Mission* [Meridian, Mississippi: Press of Tell Farmer], 1927); Atkinson, *History of the Chickasaw Indian Agency,* 164 n. 139.

24. Letter, William McCleish to Governor Blount, Nov. 7, 1794, in *ASP* (Indian Affairs), vol. 1, 1832, p. 540; Letter, General Robertson to Governor Blount, Jan. 13, 1795, Ibid., p. 556. An apparent rough draft of the latter document, as suggested by variations in the text, is published in Robertson, "Correspondence," 4, no. 2(April 1899): 163–165; Letter, Governor Blount to Robertson, Jan. 20, 1795, in Robertson, "Correspondence," 4, no. 2(April 1899): 165–167; Letter, Secretary of War to Governor Blount, March 23, 1795, in Robertson, "Correspondence," 4, no. 2(April 1899): 181 (also published in Carter, *Territorial Papers of the United*

States, vol. 4, pp. 386–393); William Colbert's wife in August 1795 is identified as Jessie Moniac in Letter, Governor Blount to James Robertson, Aug. 11, 1795, in Robertson, "Correspondence," 3, no. 4(Oct. 1898): 388, and as Jacksie Moniac in Letter, Governor Blount to Alexander Cornell, Aug. 12, 1795, in Robertson, "Correspondence," 3, no. 4(Oct. 1898): 391. At the time (August), she was with Robertson in Nashville, probably awaiting return of her husband from Philadelphia. Apparently a mixed-blood Creek, she had a brother named Samuel Moniac. In about 1788 an unidentified son of James Colbert married a sister (whose name was not recorded) of the Creek wife of Alexander McGillivray (see Letter, O'Neill to Miro, Dec. 22, 1788, in Caughey, *McGillivray of the Creeks*, 212). This son may have been William Colbert but could just as well have been George or Levi Colbert; if William Colbert, and unless he had taken a second Creek wife after 1788, this lady may have been Jessie/Jacksie Moniac. Further confusing the matter is an April 1794 reference to William Colbert's apparent wife, named therein "Wayther," who always went with him to war or elsewhere (Letter, Benjamin Fooy to Gayoso, Holkey, April 5, 1794, in Corbitt and Corbitt, "Papers from the Spanish Archives," 39[1967]: 89). More likely, then, Wayther was Colbert's wife at the time under discussion here (January 1795). Perhaps she and Jessie/Jacksie Moniac were the same person, or perhaps he had more than one wife at the same time. As discussed in Chapter 12, neither of these names matches the name of the wife William had at his death in 1824.

25. For studies of the strategic importance of the Chickasaw Bluffs and establishment of the Spanish fort, see Holmes, "Spanish-American Rivalry over the Chickasaw Bluffs," 26–57; Holmes, "Fort Ferdinand of the Bluffs, Life on the Spanish-American Frontier," *West Tennessee Historical Society's Publications*, 13(1959): 38–54; Holmes, "The Ebb-Tide of Spanish Military Power on the Mississippi," 23–44; Abraham P. Nasatir, *Spanish War Vessels on the Mississippi, 1792–1796* (New Haven: Yale Univ. Press, 1968), 65–115, which includes extensively footnoted publication of Gayoso's diary of his expedition on the ship *La Vigilante* (pp. 253–325); Coker and Watson, *Indian Traders*, 197–199; Jack Holmes's articles listed above should be used with a critical eye because of his occasional misinterpretations of Spanish documents. An example is his contention in "Spanish-American Rivalry over the Chickasaw Bluffs" (p. 32) that William Davenport and others were killed in 1787 at a fort they were building at Chickasaw Bluffs. As discussed in Chapter 8 herein, this event undoubtedly actually occurred near the Chickasaw settlement on Old Town Creek. By March 1793, John Turnbull was living on the lower Yazoo River in the Choctaw territory at or near present-day Satartia, Mississippi, at a place called "the Pumpkin Patch" (see Deposition of James Allen, April 16, 1819, Monroe County, Mississippi Deed Book 1, pp. 112–121 [Courthouse, Aberdeen, Mississippi]; also Harriet DeCell and JoAnne Pritchard, *Yazoo: Its Legends and Legacies* [Yazoo Delta Press, 1976], 63). In March the Chickasaw gave Turnbull permission to establish a secondary trading post farther up the river: "The Chickasaw have Consented for Turnbull to put up a trading post at a place not exactly on Chickasaw Bluffs, but thirty leagues from his Home, at the place named Yagano Patasadye or the flat grounds. If things change one could suggest a fort to them" (Letter, de la Villebeuvre to Carondelet, March 8, 1793, in Corbitt and Corbitt, "Papers from the Spanish Archives," 30[1958]: 97). Turnbull established a trading station at this location, to which he sometimes carried goods from his store on the lower Yazoo to trade to the Chickasaw. In March 1793 de la Villebeuvre told the Chickasaw that he would inform Carondelet about their being in favor of Turnbull coming "up the

yawsow river as far as the Yockeny Petafa to bring you a Convenient trade." The location, which probably had at least one small structure used during times of trade, was evidently at the mouth of the tributary usually spelled at the time "Yockeny Petafa," "Yakony Patafan," or "Yockeney Petaffa," being "in English the Splitt Ground a Creek that runs in the yawsow about 50 or 60 miles from the Chekesaw towns" (Letter, Benjamin Fooy to Gayoso, Feb. 25, 1793, in Corbitt and Corbitt, "Papers from the Spanish Archives," 31[1959]: 64). This place was identified in June 1793 as the place "where Turnbull will soon have his store" (Letter, Gayoso to Carondelet, June 8, 1793, in Corbitt and Corbitt, "Papers from the Spanish Archives," 33[1961]: 69). This is undoubtedly the original name of the stream presently called the Yocony River, whose intersection with the east fork of the Yazoo River (the Tallahatchie River) is in present-day Quitman County, Mississippi. A reference to Turnbull's main store on the lower Yazoo is in a letter from Gayoso to Carondelet, dated July 18, 1793, in Corbitt and Corbitt, "Papers from the Spanish Archives," 34(1962): 89.

26. "Diary of Gayoso de Lemos' Expedition on *La Vigilante*," in Nasatir, *Spanish War Vessels on the Mississippi*, 253–276; See also Letter, Gayoso to Carondelet, May 23, 1795, in Corbitt and Corbitt, "Papers from the Spanish Archives," 48(1976): 134–137.

27. Coker and Watson, *Indian Traders*, 197–199.

28. Calloway, *The American Revolution in Indian Country*, 239–240; Holmes, "Spanish-American Rivalry over the Chickasaw Bluffs," 53–57; with regard to the payments to Wolf's Friend, Gayoso made it clear that they were to be secretly paid on an annual basis: "[Wolf's Friend] instructed Fooy to inform me of everything, charging me particularly about his annual present of five hundred pesos which he wants placed in [John] Turnbull's hands to keep his Nation from knowing about this distinction which he has" (Letter, Gayoso to Carondelet, Oct. 10, 1794, in Corbitt and Corbitt, "Papers from the Spanish Archives," 41[1969]: 110). For other documentation of the payment through Turnbull, see Letter, Carondelet to Gayoso, Oct. 31, 1794, in Corbitt and Corbitt, "Papers from the Spanish Archives," 41[1969]: 114, Letter, Gayoso to Carondelet, Jan. 8, 1795, in Corbitt and Corbitt, "Papers from the Spanish Archives," 42(1970): 103–104, and Letters, Gayoso to Carondelet, March 14, 1795, and Gayoso to Ignacio Delino, March 16, 1795, in Corbitt and Corbitt, "Papers from the Spanish Archives," 44(1972): 109, 113. In 1797, Piomingo told Chickasaw agent Samuel Mitchell that he had long suspected that Wolf's Friend was "under pay by the Spaniards, but was now convinced that they gave him an annual salary of five hundred dollars for his friendship and interest in this nation" (Letter, Samuel Mitchell, Encampment near Long Town, to Colonel David Henley, Nashville, Oct. 30, 1797, in David Henley Papers, 1791–1800, Rare Book, Manuscript, and Special Collection Library, Duke Univ., Durham, North Carolina); Letter, Secretary of War to James Wilkinson, Sept. 14, 1802, in Carter, *Territorial Papers of the United States*, vol. 5, *The Territory of Mississippi, 1798–1817* (Washington, D.C.: Government Printing Office, 1937), 177.

29. Calloway, *The American Revolution in Indian Country*, 239–240; Letter, Captain Thomas Portell to Carondelet, May 7, 1793, in Corbitt and Corbitt, "Papers from the Spanish Archives," 32(1960): 80. The owner of the flatboat, John Hinds, later claimed that at Cumberland he saw four small cannon loaded on the boat along with the brass swivel gun/howitzer (Letters, Gayoso to Carondelet, May 31, 1793, and June 3, 1793, in Corbitt and Corbitt, "Papers from the Spanish Archives," 33[1961]: 62–64). No further mention of these

alleged cannons appears in known documents. With regard to the swivel gun, see also Putnam, *History of Middle Tennessee,* 438–440, 521; in March 1795, Gayoso referred to William Glover (Oulataopika) as "the famous Glover" (Letter, Gayoso to Carondelet, March 14, 1795, in Corbitt and Corbitt, "Papers from the Spanish Archives," 44[1972]: 109). Gayoso also stated that William Glover was the principal warrior under Piomingo and Wolf's Friend and "has as much influence as Piomingo himself, but is our friend" (Letter, Gayoso to Carondelet, Oct. 10, 1794, in Corbitt and Corbitt, "Papers from the Spanish Archives," 41[1969]: 110). In another letter, Gayoso related information that is a misinterpretation of a statement made earlier by Wolf's Friend about "Payahayo," who Gayoso thought was the same man as Piomingo. Actually, Payahayo was the Indian name Wolf's Friend often called William Colbert (see Letters, Gayoso to Carondelet, Oct. 19, 1794, and Ougoulayacabe to Gayoso, Aug. 23, 1794, in Corbitt and Corbitt, "Papers from the Spanish Archives," 41[1969]: 104 n. 31, 110). However, Colbert's Indian name was identified as "Chooshemataha" at the Nashville conference (Records of the Nashville Conference, August 7, 1792, in *ASP* [Indian Affairs], vol. 1, 1832, p. 284); according to Benjamin Fooy, John Brown was the son of a mixed-blood Chickasaw woman and a mixed-blood man and although "not of great speach, is of great Consequence and the greatest Warrior heare" (Letter, Fooy to Gayoso, March 16, 1794, in Corbitt and Corbitt, "Papers from the Spanish Archives," 38[1966]: 79–80). Thomas Brown, probably closely related to John Brown, was described by Fooy in July 1794 as Piomingo's "Right hand Man" (Letter, Fooy to Gayoso, July 3, 1794, in Corbitt and Corbitt, "Papers from the Spanish Archives," 40[1968]: 114); regarding presentation of the six-dollar cannon to the Chickasaw in 1794, see Purchase Order, James Robertson to Bennet Searcy, Jan. 8, 1794. The order instructed Searcy to "furnish the Chickasaw Indians with one cannon"; also see Invoice, "John and George M. Deadrick to the Territory South of the Ohio," Davidson County, Tenn., a list of goods furnished the Chickasaw and Choctaw Indians between Jan. 4 and March 10, 1794. The specific item states, "a cannon supplied by Gen. James Robertson [. . . $6]." The cannon is also listed in Account, "Payments made by Bennet Searcy, agent for procuring supplies [etc.] for the Chickasaws and Choctaws," Jan. 1, 1794, to March 10, 1794. All three documents are in National Archives, RG 217, Entry 525A (Settled Indian Accounts and Claims, Unnumbered Accounts; unnumbered James Robertson accounts), roll 3, and abstracted in Atkinson, *Records of the Chickasaw Agency,* 204–206.

30. Letter, Governor Blount to President Washington, April 20, 1795, in Robertson, "Correspondence," 4, no. 3 (July 1899): 252; Haywood, *Civil and Political History of Tennessee,* 448–450, 453, 460; Putnam, *History of Middle Tennessee,* 519–520; Chickasaw Treaty of 1818, in Kappler, *Laws and Treaties,* vol. 2, p. 175; Haywood contends that James Robertson was present at this engagement, but such is not confirmed by contemporary documentation. Haywood apparently confused this conflict with the second a few months later, as discussed below (however, Robertson was not present at that one either). Malcolm McGee's recollections of the Creek invasion closely parallel the report or reports and probable recollections of participants consulted by Haywood. McGee related to Draper that Piomingo refused to let Colonel Mansker's approximately forty men and his own warriors pursue the retreating Creeks for fear that they would be led into an ambush. He also recalled that two Chickasaw women were killed and that the Chickasaw man reported killed was a mixed-blood named Underwood. McGee recalled that the enemy force consisted of only "a small party" of

Creeks (probably an understatement), about three of whom were killed in the skirmish (McGee-Draper Narrative, 112b). Haywood, however, contends that there were about 2,000 Creeks. Haywood again may have confused the first invasion with the second, which occurred a few months later, as discussed below, for he states that between 1,000 and 2,000 Creeks were present at that conflict also; Letter, Governor Blount to Alexander Cornell, Aug. 12, 1795, in Robertson, "Correspondence," 3, no. 4(Oct. 1898): 391; after the Cumberland whites left for the Chickasaw nation, Governor Blount had second thoughts about the propriety of the expedition in light of a letter he had received from the irritated secretary of war in March, and he admonished Robertson for allowing it to occur (Letter, Blount to Robertson, May 4, 1795, in Robertson, "Correspondence," 4, no. 3[Jan. 1899]: 259); the American military assistance is partially documented in a few Spanish letters; for example: "I have been assured that within ten or twelve days the son of [James] Colbert will arrive at the Chickasaws with an American companion, a captain and a lieutenant, and somebody says that they are descending by water as far as Chickasaw Bluffs accompanied by Chickasaws and by nineteen Choctaws" (Letter, de la Villebeuvre to Carondelet, April 30, 1795, in Corbitt and Corbitt, "Papers from the Spanish Archives," 47[1975]: 142). See also Letters, Carlos Grand-Pre to Carondelet, June 5, 1795, and Thomas Portell to Gayoso, June 5, 1795, in Corbitt and Corbitt, "Papers from the Spanish Archives," 49(1977): 141–142. A letter from de la Villebeuvre to Carondelet dated June 16, 1795 (Corbitt and Corbitt, "Papers from the Spanish Archives," 49[1977]: 150) appears to refer to the Creek-Chickasaw fight at Long Town in late May: "[T]hree parties of Creeks returned the first of June, having killed three Chickasaw women and a man, as well as a Negro . . . those who were with them were safe in the fort and had raised a white flag which seemed to indicate peace. . . . They [the Creeks] have killed and stolen a quantity of stock and horses." In the Chickasaw nation, John Forbes gave information to Spaniard Pedro Rousseau, who reported in a May 22(?) letter that "the Creeks numbering eight hundred had attacked the Chickasaws, and . . . the Chickasaws had attacked the Creeks with three hundred men, [and] the Chickasaws had beaten the Creeks, having killed 26 of their men, and the Chickasaws only lost five men and one woman" (Letter, Pedro Rousseau to Carondelet, May 22(?), 1795, in Corbitt and Corbitt, "Papers from the Spanish Archives," 48[1976]: 133). If the fight actually occurred on about May 28, this report cannot refer to that incident (if the approximate date given is accurate). The day of the month on Rousseau's letter may have been misread by the transcribers; perhaps the original letter actually says May 29. With regard to the number of Creek warriors, John McKee reported that "Mr. Campbell of Will's Town" (in the Creek nation) had told him the Creek force "was supposed to be near three hundred" (Letter, John McKee to President Washington, June 9, 1795, in Robertson, "Correspondence," 4, no. 3[July 1899]: 269). Blount, however, was informed that the Chickasaws had estimated between 800 and 1,000 and that a Mr. Campbell had estimated 3,000, a number that Blount hoped was erroneous (Letter, Governor Blount to Robertson, June 10, 1795, in Robertson, "Correspondence," 4, no. 3[July 1899]: 272); it obviously was if John McKee's report is accurate.

31. Letters, Governor Blount to Robertson, Aug. 24, 1795 (two), Sept. 10, 1795, and Oct. 2, 1795, in Robertson, "Correspondence," 4, no. 1(Jan. 1899): 66–68, 72–74; Letter, Governor Blount to Robertson, Aug. 2, 1795, Ibid., 3, no. 4(Oct. 1898): 382; Invoice, John Chisholm to the United States, undated, "Expenses of the Chickasaw & Choctaw Indians on a visit to the President of the United States, at Philadelphia between the 22nd day of July and the 23rd

day of Oct. 1795," in National Archives, RG 217, Entry 525A (Settled Indian Accounts and Claims, Unnumbered Accounts; unnumbered James Robertson accounts), roll 1. A receipt and a comprehensive account of expenses, both dated Nov. 12, 1795, also document the trip to Philadelphia. For abstracts of these three documents, see Atkinson, *Records of the Chickasaw Agency,* 204.

32. President Washington's talk to Major Colbert, "John Brown the Younger," William McGillivray, and Malcolm McGee on Aug. 22, 1795, is published in Robertson, "Correspondence," 3, no. 4(Oct. 1898): 393–394. See also Letter, Secretary of War to President Washington, Aug. 16, 1795, in Carter, *Territorial Papers of the United States,* vol. 4, p. 398; McGee-Draper Narrative, 109–110, 112b; Letter, Governor Blount to Robertson, Sept. 10, 1795, in Robertson, "Correspondence," 4, no. 1(Jan. 1899): 72–73.

33. Letter, Piomingo to Robertson, Sept. 1, 1795, in Robertson, "Correspondence," 4, no. 1(Jan. 1899): 68; Letter, Governor Blount to Robertson, Aug. 11, 1795, in Robertson, "Correspondence," 3, no. 4(Oct. 1898): 387. See also Letter, Governor Blount to Alexander Cornell, Aug. 12, 1795, in Robertson, "Correspondence," 3, no. 4(Oct. 1898): 391; there seems to be a scarcity of available documentation regarding Robertson's apparent trip to the Chickasaws, although Haywood (*Civil and Political History of Tennessee,* 457, 461) asserts that he indeed went, arriving on September 8. Haywood continues that on September 7 some Creeks had attempted to kill Chickasaws. Provoked by this, the Chickasaw refused to release their Creek prisoners to Robertson. Haywood states that Robertson was there when the second major Creek attack occurred in September, but Putnam (*History of Middle Tennessee,* 526–527) asserts that Robertson had already returned to Nashville. Putnam appears to be correct, for he (as well as Haywood) had access to a letter Piomingo sent to Robertson on September 29, in which the attack was described (Letter from Piomingo to Robertson, Sept. 29, 1795, partially quoted in Putnam, *History of Middle Tennessee,* pp. 526–527). This letter may have been in the Robertson family papers in the first half of the nineteenth century when Haywood and Putnam wrote their books, but if so it has since been lost.

34. Putnam, *History of Middle Tennessee,* pp. 526–527.

35. McGee-Draper Narrative, 112b–112c. According to McGee, a Colonel James White later visited the Creek nation and learned that the force numbered between 1,100 and 1,200 warriors. With regard to the nonuse of the cannon, Piomingo had probably realized that only one such gun would likely not have inflicted much damage. It could, however, have been effective in intimidating the Creeks, for during the first half of the eighteenth century, at least, southern Indians were much afraid of artillery and would rarely attack a fort so armed. According to McGee, the cannon was a four pounder. McGee's account of casualties somewhat agrees with that provided by Haywood (*Civil and Political History of Tennessee,* 461), who states that the Chickasaw had six men and one woman killed and that at least twenty-six Creek men died. Haywood's data with regard to the deaths of twenty-six Creeks and the Chickasaw deaths, however, sound suspiciously like the data provided by John Forbes to Pedro Rousseau with regard to the summer conflict, as discussed above. It is possible here that McGee had been partially influenced by the information in Haywood's book, which was published in 1823.

36. Putnam, *History of Middle Tennessee,* 527; Letter, Governor Blount to Robertson, Nov. 13, 1795, in Robertson, "Correspondence," 4, no. 1(Jan. 1899): 80; Letter, Governor Blount to Robertson, March 29, 1795 (*sic,* 1796), in Robertson, "Correspondence," 4, no.

3(July 1899): 279; Letter, Governor Blount to Robertson, April 11, 1796, in Robertson, "Correspondence," 4, no. 3(July 1899): 280; Letters, Benjamin Hawkins to James McHenry (Secretary of War), Oct. 23, 1797, and Hawkins to Alexander Cornell, Oct. 31, 1797, Summary of Hawkins's talks to the Creek at Coweta (Oct. 27, 1797), and Speech of the Cowetas, Cussetas and other lower towns to the Chickasaw (Oct. 28, 1797), all published in Hawkins, *Letters*, 208–209, 211–217 (see also pp. 226–227, 489–494); Tussekiah Mico, a second Creek emissary to Chickasaw king Chinubbee in 1797, reported that none of the head chiefs he met with were the same as the ones he had known in the past. These chiefs were "Fan Omingo, Tusscuppatapa Omingo, Whelocke Emautau, Insuchelah, and the Chickasaw Mico" (Speech of Tussekiah Mico, Coweta Square, Oct. 28, 1797, in Hawkins, *Letters*, 212–214); Letter, Secretary of War to the President, Sept. 11, 1795, in Carter, *Territorial Papers of the United States*, vol. 4, p. 400; unless the "Chickasaw Mico" (Mingo/chief/king) was Piomingo or Wolf's Friend, neither of these leaders was present at this particular counsel.

37. Holmes, "The Ebb-Tide of Spanish Military Power on the Mississippi," 36–44; Coker and Watson, *Indian Traders*, 200–201; Gibson, *The Chickasaws*, 88–90.

38. Samuel C. Williams, *Beginnings of West Tennessee in the Land of the Chickasaws, 1541–1841* (Johnson City, Tenn.: Watauga Press, 1930), 59–60; Letter, Captain Isaac Guion to General James Wilkinson, Chickasaw Bluffs, Sept. 2, 1797, in "Letters of Capt. Isaac Guion," in *Seventh Annual Report of the Director of the Department of Archives and History of the State of Mississippi from October 1, 1907 to October 1, 1908*, Dunbar Rowland, director (Nashville: Press of Brandon Printing, 1909), 42–43; Holmes, "The Ebb-Tide of Spanish Military Power on the Mississippi," 36–44; Letters, Captain Isaac Guion to General James Wilkinson, Aug. 14, 1797, and Isaac Guion to Secretary of War, Oct. 22, 1797, in Claiborne, *Mississippi as a Province, Territory and State*, 182–183; James E. Roper, "Fort Adams and Fort Pickering," *West Tennessee Historical Society Papers* 24 (1970): 15–17; regarding Benjamin Allen and "young James Allen" see Diary of John McKee, 1804–1805, entries for July 6, 10, and 13, 1805, original in Southern Historical Collection, University of North Carolina Library, Chapel Hill (microfilm copy at MDAH).

39. Claiborne, *Mississippi as a Province, Territory and State*, 183.

40. Letter, Captain Isaac Guion to General James Wilkinson, Chickasaw Bluffs, Sept. 2, 1797, in "Letters of Capt. Isaac Guion," 43; Gibson, *The Chickasaws*, 80.

41. Martini ("Chickasaw Empire," 21 n. 38, 91) concluded that Piomingo died in November 1798, but he offers no documentation to support that specific month and year. He only points out that the last known mention of him in writing is in a letter from James Robertson dated Oct. 20, 1798, which indeed seems to be the case (Letter, James Robertson to Secretary of War, Oct. 20, 1798, in Robertson, "Correspondence," 4, no. 4[Oct. 1899]: 368). Thus I prefer to state that Piomingo *probably* died prior to the end of 1798 but possibly later in early 1799. Malcolm McGee (McGee-Draper Narrative, 111) thought that he died in "about" 1796 but this is obviously too soon considering his presence at Chickasaw Bluffs in September 1797 and his mention in the October 1798 letter from General Robertson. See also Don Martini, *Indian Chiefs of the Southeast*, 94; the supposed name of Piomingo's wife, Molletulla, is recorded by Putnam in his *History of Middle Tennessee* on pages 524 and 539, but he cites no source. Putnam was probably told this by an elderly individual in the Nashville area prior to 1858. With regard to the possible name of Piomingo's surviving son, a 1796 War Department purchase order refers to supplies for "Mountain Leader Tippo and his party, Chicka-

saw Indians" (Purchase Order/Certification, James Robertson to John Overton, March 24, 1796, in National Archives, RG 217, Entry 525A [Settled Indian Accounts and Claims, Unnumbered Accounts], roll 2, abstracted in Atkinson, *Records of the Chickasaw Agency*, 215). Haywood, in *Civil and Political History of Tennessee* (pp. 239–240), relates that a son of Piomingo in 1787 was named "Batterboo"; he obviously was not a juvenile inasmuch as he had rescued a white boy stolen by Creeks. The name of Piomingo's only surviving daughter is unknown, as is anything else about her. However, in 1795 Piomingo requested of the secretary of war that he make arrangements to teach her to read and write English. The secretary of war responded by informing Governor Blount that such could be undertaken after Robertson and Blount submitted an estimate of the expense that would be incurred (see Letter, Governor Blount to Robertson, Sept. 10, 1795, in Robertson, "Correspondence," 4, no. 1[Jan. 1899]: 72); as discussed above, Piomingo's probable grave was accidentally uncovered in south Tupelo in 1956. The individual was buried on his back with his head on a saddle, arms extended along his sides, and his rifle next to him on the right side; brass U.S. uniform coat buttons, a gold epaulet, several large silver ornaments, and a Washington Peace Medal (Figure 13) were in the upper part of the grave. See Atkinson, "Death of a Chickasaw Leader," 142–143; rarely appearing in the secondary historical literature is an undocumented, false assertion that Piomingo was murdered in 1799 by Creeks and Cherokees (see H. D. Moser, D. R. Hoth, and G. H. Hoemann, *The Papers of Andrew Jackson*, vol. 4 [Knoxville: Univ. of Tennessee Press, 1994], 68 n. 4).

CHAPTER 11

1. See Francis P. Prucha, *American Indian Policy in the Formative Years: The Indian Trade and Intercourse Acts, 1790–1834* (Cambridge: Harvard Univ. Press, 1962). For an excellent recent discussion of the evolution of American Indian policy see Jack D. Elliott, "Historical Overview," in John W. O'Hear, James R. Atkinson, Jack D. Elliott, Edmond A. Bordreaux III, and John R. Underwood, *Choctaw Agency, Natchez Trace Parkway: Archaeological and Historical Investigation, Madison County, Mississippi* (Starkville: Mississippi State Univ., Cobb Institute of Archaeology, 2000), 17–20; see also Martin Abbott, "Indian Policy and Management in the Mississippi Territory, 1798–1817," *Journal of Mississippi History* 15, no. 3(July 1952): 153–169.

2. Elliott, "Historical Overview," 19–20, 23; Letter, Hawkins to Robertson, June 14, 1797, in Hawkins, *Letters*, 178–179; Letters, Hawkins to Samuel Mitchell, Aug. 12, 1797, Hawkins to William McCleish, Aug. 12, 1797, and Hawkins to John Pitchlynn, Aug. 12, 1797, in Hawkins, *Letters*, 190–193; Letters, Robertson to [President Adams?], Oct. 20, 1798, and Secretary of War to Robertson, Dec. 12, 1799, in Robertson, "Correspondence," 4, no. 4(Oct. 1899): 368–371; see also Letter/Purchase Order/Certification, James Robertson to Anthony Foster & Co., Oct. 17, 1798, in National Archives, RG 217, Entry 525A (Settled Indian Accounts and Claims, Unnumbered Accounts; unnumbered James Robertson accounts), roll 2, abstracted in Atkinson, *Records of the Chickasaw Agency*, 227–228.

3. Letter, Robertson to President John Adams, Oct. 20, 1798, in Robertson, "Correspondence," 4, no. 4(Oct. 1899): 368–370.

4. George Colbert's presence among the delegation is shown by the words of James

Robertson, who stated in the October 20 letter that "Major Colbert's horse was sick and unable to travel. I have since got him a horse" (Letter, Robertson to President John Adams, Oct. 20, 1798, in Robertson, "Correspondence," 4, no. 4[Oct. 1899]: 368–370). By this time William Colbert was being referred to as General Colbert, apparently as a result of his being designated as such at the meeting with President Washington in 1795. George Colbert had come to be called Major Colbert, apparently as a result of his designation as such at a meeting with President Washington in 1794 (see Chapter 10). As was General Robertson's title, these were Southwest Territory militia titles rather than regular U.S. army titles. For confirmation that "Major Colbert" was George Colbert by 1797, see Letter/Bill of Exchange, Hawkins to James McHenry, Secretary of War, July 6, 1797, and Letter, Hawkins to Secretary of War, July 5, 1797, in Hawkins, *Letters,* 179–182.

5. Letter, David Henley to James Robertson, Jan. 29, 1797, in Robertson, "Correspondence," 4, no. 4(Oct. 1899): 337.

6. Letter, Samuel Mitchell to Governor Winthrop Sargent, March 31, 1799, in Sargent Papers, microfilm roll 5, frames 37–39, Library of Congress.

7. Letter, Hawkins to Henry Dearborn, Secretary of War, Oct. 28, 1801, in Hawkins, *Letters,* 392–394; also published in C. L. Grant, ed., *Letters, Journals and Writings of Benjamin Hawkins,* vol. 1, 1796–1801 (Savannah, Ga.: Beehive Press, 1980), 387. John McIntosh, Jr., is also credited with having been instrumental in encouraging the Chickasaw to disperse from the old towns (Warren, "Missions, Missionaries, Frontier Characters," 585).

8. Elliott, "Historical Overview," 25–26; Bill of Exchange, to Samuel Mitchell, 1804, in National Archives, Records of Accounting Officers of the Department of the Treasury (RG 217), Entry 366 (Journals of the Accountant for the War Department, 1792–1817), vol. 10 (journal L), p. 5652; Warrant, to Samuel Mitchell, March 9, 1805, in National Archives, Records of the Accounting Officers of the Department of the Treasury (RG 217), 2nd Auditor, Entry 374 (Registers of Warrants, War Department Accountant, 1795–1821), vol. 4 (book 5), p. 258 (abstracted in Atkinson, *Records of the Chickasaw Agency,* 272–273, 287); Atkinson, *History of the Chickasaw Indian Agency,* 2–3, 5.

9. Jennings, "Nutt's Trip to the Chickasaw Country," 41, 54–55.

10. Regarding the description of the original house, see Receipt for repairs, Edward Radford to James Robertson, Jan. 20, 1813, in National Archives, Records of Accounting Officers of the Department of the Treasury (RG 217), 5th Auditor, Entry 525 (Additional Settled Indian Accounts and Claims, 1817–1851), box 1, acct. 298 (abstracted in Atkinson, *Records of the Chickasaw Agency,* 238); for discussion and specific documents related to the second house, see Atkinson, *History of the Chickasaw Indian Agency,* 5–6, 23.

11. Letter, James McHenry, Secretary of War, to John McKee, May 20, 1800, in John McKee Papers, box 3, no. 9, Library of Congress; for documentation of the purchase of the gin works, see Bill of Exchange, John McKee to John Newman, Dec. 2, 1800, in National Archives, RG 217, Entry 366 (Journals of the Accountant for the War Department), vol. 8 (journal H), p. 3883, and Warrant, John McKee to A. Hunt, Dec. 2, 1800, in National Archives, RG 217, Entry 374 (Registers of Warrants), vol. 3 (book 4), p. 127. Both of these records state "for materials furnished for building a ginn in the Choctaw Nation—$400"; in 1801, a mixed-blood Choctaw named Robert McClure stated that "A gin is a thing I asked for long ago; it was once offered to my nation, and refused by our chiefs" (Communication from

Robert McClure to John McKee, Dec. 15, 1801, in *ASP* [Indian Affairs], vol. 1, 1832, p. 662). For documentation of the burning of the cotton gin, see Letter abstract possessing a list of goods requested by a Choctaw chief, from Silas Dinsmoor, Sept. 11, 1811, in National Archives, Records of the Bureau of Indian Affairs (RG 75; Records of the Choctaw Trading House, 1803–1824), microfilm T-500. The amount to be paid the Chickasaw was $1,000. See also Letter, Robert C. Nicholas to J. C. Calhoun, Jan. 2, 1822, in National Archives, Records of the Office of the Secretary of War (RG 107; Letters Received by the Secretary of War, Registered Series, 1801–1870), microfilm M-221; see undetailed early references to the gin at Cotton Gin Port in Claiborne, *Mississippi as a Province, Territory and State,* 59, Leftwich, "Cotton Gin Port and Gaines' Trace," 263, and James Hall, "A Brief History of the Mississippi Territory," *Publications of the Mississippi Historical Society* 9(1906): 542; Letter from Willie Blount, in *The Democratic Clarion and the Tennessee Gazette* (Nashville newspaper), March 16, 1810.

12. Jennings, "Nutt's Trip to the Chickasaw Country," 42–43; Dawson A. Phelps, "Excepts from the Journal of the Reverend Joseph Bullen, 1799 and 1800," *Journal of Mississippi History* 17(Jan.–Oct. 1955): 262.

13. Jennings, "Nutt's Trip to the Chickasaw Country," 41.

14. Letter, Samuel Mitchell to R. J. Meigs, Sept. 30, 1806, in National Archives, Records of the Accounting Officers of the Department of the Treasury (RG 217), 2nd Auditor, Entry 525 (Settled Indian Accounts and Claims, 1794–1894), box 21, folder 549 (abstracted in Atkinson, *Records of the Chickasaw Agency,* 63). Samuel Mitchell had been married to mixed-blood Sally Folsom, sister of future chief of the Choctaws David Folsom. The Edmond Folsom mentioned by Mitchell, therefore, may have been a brother to Sally and David Folsom. However, this Edmond Folsom may have been the son of white man Edmond Folsom, brother of Nathaniel (David's and Sally's father), Ebenezer, and Israel Folsom. The Folsom family, except for Nathaniel at least, lived in the Chickasaw nation for a time in the latter half of the eighteenth century. Young David Folsom lived with the Mitchells at the agency for about three years until his sister, Sally Mitchell, died there (Czarina C. Conlan, "David Folsom," *Chronicles of Oklahoma* 4[1926]: 340; Cushman, *History of the Choctaw, Chickasaw, and Natchez Indians,* 326, quoting Nathaniel Folsom's recollections, 1823). Sally Folsom Mitchell died at the agency in 1802 (see Letter, Silas Dinsmoor to Return J. Meigs, July 31, 1802, in National Archives, RG 75, microfilm M-208 [Records of the Cherokee Indian Agency in Tennessee], roll 1, abstracted in Atkinson, *Records of the Chickasaw Agency,* 298–299). For the previous study mentioned see James R. Atkinson, "The Location of the Nineteenth Century Choctaw Village of Wholkey in Chickasaw County, Mississippi," *Mississippi Archaeology* 21, no. 1(1986): 70–72.

15. Jennings, "Nutt's Trip to the Chickasaw Country," 52; James Wilkinson, "A Survey of the route proposed for the highway from Nashville in the State of Tennessee to the Grindstone ford of the Bayou Pierre in the Mississippi Territory," ca. 1802, copy at Natchez Trace Parkway Headquarters; because of vagueness of Nutt's locations of both Chaguiliso and "Holka," possibly the two were actually the same village, despite the fact that the two were discussed in separate places in his account. In an earlier article on the Chickasaw Agency site, in fact, I had concluded that Chaguiliso was probably at the Thelma Mounds, but upon becoming aware of the "Wholkey" village on the Wilkinson map, a change of opinion oc-

curred (see James R. Atkinson, "A Surface Collection from the Chickasaw Agency Site," *Mississippi Archaeology* 20, no. 2[1985]: 57, and Atkinson, "The Location of the Nineteenth Century Choctaw Village of Wholkey," 70). The Thelma Mounds site is now on the National Register of Historic Places.

16. Jennings, "Nutt's Trip to the Chickasaw Country," 45. The present town of Toccopola was in existence by 1837 (Winston, *Story of Pontotoc,* 91).

17. Jennings, "Nutt's Trip to the Chickasaw Country," 42.

18. Letter, William McCleish to Governor Blount, Nov. 7, 1794, in *ASP* (Indian Affairs), vol. 1, 1832, p. 540; Phelps, "Excerpts from the Journal of the Reverend Joseph Bullen," 263; Letter, David Henley to Secretary of War, Jan. 28, 1800, in National Archives, Records of Accounting Officers of the Department of the Treasury (RG 217), 2nd Auditor, Entry 495 (Letters Sent by David Henley, Agent for the War Department, Letterbook) (abstracted in Atkinson, *Records of the Chickasaw Agency,* 230); according to Malcolm McGee, Joseph Colbert, Levi's younger brother, died while a young man at the Bear Creek ferry where he was assisting in its operation (McGee-Draper Narrative, 113). He thus would have died between February 1800 and the end of 1802, in which year the ferry was relocated upriver, as hereafter discussed.

19. Letter, David Henley to Wolf's Friend, William Colbert, and George Colbert, Feb. 1, 1800, in National Archives, RG 217, Entry 495 (Letters Sent by David Henley); Contract, Taylor Townsend and James Coulter with David Henley, Feb. 14, 1800, and Invoice, Townsend to Henley, Jan. 31, 1800, both in National Archives, RG 217, Entry 525A (Settled Indian Accounts and Claims, Unnumbered Accounts; David Henley accounts), roll 3 (abstracted in Atkinson, *Records of the Chickasaw Agency,* 210–211, 230); Dawson A. Phelps, "Colbert Ferry and Selected Documents," *Alabama Historical Quarterly* 25, nos. 3 and 4(1963): 219; Hall, "A Brief History of the Mississippi Territory," 541.

20. Phelps, "Excerpts from the Journal of the Reverend Joseph Bullen," 273.

21. "A treaty of reciprocal advantages and mutual convenience between the United States and the Chickasaws," Oct. 24, 1801, in *ASP* (Indian Affairs), vol. 1, 1832, pp. 648–649. Although only $700 in goods were stipulated in the treaty, $2,696 worth of goods were distributed at the conference, as well as 200 gallons of whiskey and 1,000 pounds of tobacco (Letter, Commissioners to Secretary of War, Oct. 24, 1801, in *ASP* (Indian Affairs), vol. 1, 1832, p. 651; the treaty is also published in Kappler, *Laws and Treaties,* vol. 2, pp. 55–56, and in Hawkins, *Letters,* 389–390; Minutes of a Conference held at Chickasaw Bluffs, Oct. 21–24, 1801, in Hawkins, *Letters,* 387–389; Letters, Hawkins to Secretary of War Dearborn, Oct. 25 and Oct. 28, 1801, in Hawkins, *Letters,* 390–394; Chickasaw signers of the treaty included King Chinubbee, George and William Colbert, William McGillivray, William Glover, Thomas Brown, James Underwood, and ten full-bloods lacking documented personal data. The interpreter was white man Malcolm McGee, the full-time agency interpreter, who was appointed by John McKee to replace William McCleish, who Hawkins fired because of his having been appointed in "the Indian Department under auspices of people who should have no connection with it." Hawkins described McGee as follows: "I find McGee to be well qualified; he has a good memory, but cannot read; he is deemed honest; a man of great probity, and much confided in by the nation, where he has lived six and thirty years"

(Letter, Hawkins to Secretary of War, Oct. 28, 1801, in Hawkins, *Letters*, 393). According to agent James Neely, McGee considered "himself and is considered by the natives as one of the nation" (Letter, Neely to Secretary of War Eustis, April 16, 1811, in National Archives, RG 107, microfilm M-221 [Letters Received, Secretary of War], roll 39).

22. Account, Lieutenant E. P. Gaines, entered July 18, 1804, in National Archives, RG 217, Entry 366 (Journals of the Accountant for the War Department), vol. 9 (journal K), p. 5382; Bill of Exchange, Andrew Jackson to Gilbert C. Russell, April 5, 1804, in National Archives, RG 217, Entry 374 (Registers of Warrants), vol. 4 (book 5), p. 183; Letter, Samuel Mitchell to R. J. Meigs, April 2, 1802, in National Archives, RG 75, microfilm M-208 (Records of the Cherokee Indian Agency in Tennessee), roll 1 (all abstracted in Atkinson, *Records of the Chickasaw Agency*, 282–283, 297); Letter, George and Levi Colbert to James Robertson and R. J. Meigs, June 23, 1806, published in Phelps, "Colbert Ferry and Selected Documents," 221 (see also pages 213–214); Atkinson, *History of the Chickasaw Indian Agency*, 9; Elizabeth H. West, trans. and ed., "Diary of Jose Bernardo Gutierrez de Lara, 1811–1812," *American Historical Review* 34, no. 1(Oct. 1928): 63; Letter, Samuel Mitchell to Governor W. C. C. Claiborne, Jan. 23, 1803, in Papers of the Mississippi Territorial Governors, MDAH, Record Group 2, vol. 22; Underwood's Village, evidently located at the old Chickasaw Trace crossing of Bear Creek, is first documented on maps made in the early nineteenth century (S. Lewis, "Mississippi Territory," 1812; John Melish, "Map of Mississippi," 1819; A. Finley, "Map of Louisiana, Mississippi, and Alabama," 1826); in 1811, de Lara reported that he spent the night at Bear Creek where a "rich Indian" possessing many peacocks and having slave cabins arranged in a village appearance lived in a house "several stories high." Despite the reference to Bear Creek, de Lara seems to be referring to George Colbert's home at the post-1801 new location of the Natchez Trace. One of the perpetuated myths related to Colbert's Ferry is the ridiculous, unsubstantiated notion placed in the literature by Samuel R. Brown (*The Western Gazateer or Emigrants Directory* [Auburn, New York, 1817]) that George Colbert charged the United States $75,000 for provisions, horses and ferriage during the War of 1812. Unless recently removed, a sign erected by the National Park Service at Colbert's Ferry Park states this as fact. Actually, George Colbert was indeed complained of for charging too much. His fees were 50 cents for an individual and one dollar for both a man and a horse (see John S. Bassett, ed., *Correspondence of Andrew Jackson* [Washington, D.C.: Carnegie Institution of Washington, 1926], vol. 1, 323 n. 1). At these prices, therefore, the U.S. government would have been charged no more than a few thousand dollars.

23. Account, Lieutenant E. P. Gaines, entered July 18, 1804, in National Archives, RG 217, Entry 366 (Journals of the Accountant for the War Department), vol. 9 (journal K), p. 5382; Bill of Exchange, Andrew Jackson to Gilbert C. Russell, April 5, 1804, in National Archives, RG 217, Entry 374 (Registers of Warrants), vol. 4 (book 5), p. 183.

24. Letter, Mitchell to Sargent, March 31, 1799, Winthrop Sargent Papers, microfilm roll 5, frames 37–39, Library of Congress.

25. Letter, Mitchell to Meigs, April 2, 1802, in National Archives, RG 75, microfilm M-208 (Records of the Cherokee Indian Agency in Tennessee), roll 1.

26. Letter, Claiborne to Mitchell, Oct. 4, 1802, in Dunbar Rowland, ed., *Official Letter Books of W. C. C. Claiborne*, vol. 1 (Jackson: MDAH, 1917), 194–196; the agency weaver and

instructor of weaving mentioned by Claiborne was Thomas McCoy, who had been employed earlier in 1802. His wife at the time of his death at the agency in 1817 was named Sally
(Atkinson, *History of the Chickasaw Indian Agency,* 36).

27. Letter, Mitchell to Secretary of War, Jan. 19, 1803, in Papers of the Mississippi Territorial Governors, MDAH, Record Group 2, vol. 22.

28. See various documents in National Archives, RG 217, Entry 525 (abstracted in Chapters 2 and 5 of Atkinson, *Records of the Chickasaw Agency*).

29. Letters, J. Habersham, postmaster general, to John McKee, June 27, 1801, and Habersham to John McIntosh, June 27, 1801, in Ruth E. Butler, R. B. Truett, and O. T. Hagen (Na-
tional Park Service historians), "A Calendar of Letters in the Letterbooks of the Postmaster
General Pertaining to the Opening and Use of the Natchez Trace as a Mail Route," ca. 1935,
pp. 30–32 (typed manuscript at Natchez Trace Parkway Headquarters); Note, J. Habersham,
June 30, 1801, in Butler et al., "A Calendar of Letters in the Letterbooks," 32; Francis Bailey,
Journal of a Tour in the Unsettled Parts of North American in 1796 & 1797 (London: Baily
Brothers, 1856), 371; Joseph Bullen, "Extract from the Rev. Mr. Bullen's Journal," *New York
Missionary Magazine* 1(1800): 267; Phelps, "Tockshish," 138–145. As mentioned in Chapter 6,
Phelps, who overlooked many pertinent historical sources, mistakenly surmised that Tock-
shish was the old British commissary. Inexplicably, Phelps stated in 1949 without citing a
source that McIntosh "seems to have continued to reside at Tockshish until shortly before
his death which occurred at Hot Springs, Arkansas, in 1812" (Phelps, "Stands and Travel Accommodations on the Natchez Trace," *Journal of Mississippi History* 11, no. 1[Jan. 1949]: 39).
He obviously later realized the mistake, for his "Tockshish" article of 1951 acknowledges that
McIntosh died in 1803; Letter, G. Granger, postmaster general, to James Allen, July 8, 1803,
in Butler et al., "A Calendar of Letters in the Letterbooks," 38; Letter, Granger to Postmaster
at Nashville, Oct. 3, 1803, Butler et al., "A Calendar of Letters in the Letterbooks," 40; Arrell
Gibson ("The Colberts: Chickasaw Nation Elitism," 81) asserts with no stated documentation but with some imagination that Tockshish was a "Chickasaw town" that became "the
model for other mixed-blood settlements as this growing community separated itself more
and more from the primitive fullbloods." There were, however, several mixed-bloods and
white men operating farms in the vicinity, making this area a favorite respite for Natchez
Trace travelers (Jennings, "Nutt's Trip to the Chickasaw Country," 41). After, and perhaps
before, the death of John McIntosh, Jr., in 1803, James Colbert lived with or very near his
mother at Tockshish (see Phelps, "Tockshish," 142–143). In this identification, Phelps cor-
rected a mistake in his earlier "Stands and Travel Accommodations" article (p. 41) in which
he located Colbert's Stand as "a mile north of Allen's," which he also located in the wrong
place. Regarding James Allen apparently living in the Tockshish area, see Martini, *Indian
Chiefs of the Southeast,* 101. Local historians and some professionals have confused James
Allen with John L. Allen, the Chickasaw Agency subagent in the late 1820s and 1830s (see,
for example, Phelps, "Stands and Travel Accommodations," 41). Phelps assumed that the
"J. L. Allen" residence depicted on the 1833 plat map for Township 10 South, Range 3 East
was the location of James Allen's "stand." James Allen had been a resident of the nation since
1786 (Journal of the 1816 Chickasaw Treaty, Deposition of James Allen, in Jackson Papers,
roll 62, Library of Congress).

30. Ora B. Peake, *A History of the United States Indian Factory System, 1795–1822* (Denver:

Sage Books, 1954), 13–15; Aloysius Plaisance, "The Chickasaw Bluffs Factory and Its Removal to the Arkansas River, 1818–1822," *Tennessee Historical Quarterly* 11(1952): 41–56; Letter, Secretary of War Dearborn to Governor W. C. C. Claiborne, July 28, 1802, in Rowland, *Official Letter Books of W. C. C. Claiborne*, 181–182; Fortesque Cuming, "Cuming's Tour to the Western Country (1807–1809)," in Reuben G. Thwaites, *Early Western Travels, 1748–1846*, vol. 4 (New York: AMS Press, 1966, reprint), 294–295; S. C. Williams, *Beginnings of West Tennessee*, 54, 58–59, 63, 66–67. Williams's research identified three of the whites at the bluffs during this period as Benjamin Fooy, Kenneth Ferguson, and William Mizell. By 1805 another resident was Benjamin Allen, a man who had earlier lived in the present-day Pontotoc County part of the Chickasaw settlement area. James Allen, probably his son or brother, was residing south of the old Benjamin Allen place in July 1805 (see Diary of John McKee, entries for July 10 and 14, 1805, and Aug. 18, 26, and 27, 1805); Gibson, *The Chickasaws*, 142–143.

31. Cuming, "Cuming's Tour to the Western Country," 293–294. Cuming's description is intriguing in that it conjures a presumably false image of something similar to Aztec sacrifice or a scene from the movie *Apocalypse Now*. The Indian with the bow and arrow is especially intriguing considering that muskets had long ago replaced this native weapon. Perhaps some type of religious ceremony/ritual or festival had occurred or had been interrupted by Cuming's arrival. Upon talking to the commandant, future president Zachary Taylor, Cuming learned that the Chickasaws were enjoying "a jubille or gala day, on account of their having just received presents from the United States government."

32. Letter of Instruction, Secretary of War Dearborn to Robertson and Dinsmoor, March 20, 1805, in *ASP* (Indian Affairs), vol. 1, 1832, p. 700; "Articles of Arrangement" made with the Chickasaws, July 23, 1805, in *ASP* (Indian Affairs), vol. 1, 1832, p. 697. The treaty is also published in Robertson, "Correspondence," 5, no. 2(1900): 164–166, and in Kappler, *Laws and Treaties*, vol. 2, pp. 79–80; Journal of the Commissioners to Treat with the Choctaw and Chickasaw Indians, July 6–25, 1805, in National Archives, Records of the Bureau of Indian Affairs (RG 75; Documents Relating to the Negotiations of Ratified and Unratified Treaties with Various Indian Tribes, 1801–1869), microfilm T-494; see Carter, *Territorial Papers of the United States*, vol. 5, p. 214 n. 89, for sources related to the Indian debts; President James Madison, "Proclamation of Public Land Sales," April 5, 1809, in Carter, *Territorial Papers of the United States*, vol. 5, pp. 724–725; the general location of the treaty ground and Wolf's Friend's house being at or very near Big Town is supported by an 1800 entry in the journal of the Reverend Joseph Bullen, who then resided at or near Pontitack: "Disappointed of an interpreter to go with me to Wolfe's friend and Big-Town" (Phelps, "Excerpts from the Journal of the Reverend Joseph Bullen," 274, 277). Also, John McKee recorded that on his return from Chickasaw Bluffs he "came to Mr. [Thomas] Love's and after refreshing a few minutes went on to the treaty ground where I remained till the 26 when after the Treaty was concluded & signed I returned [to] Malcolm McGee's" (Diary of John McKee, summary entry for July 15-26, 1805). Thomas Love apparently lived east of the Pontitack settlement area, as suggested in statements by Bullen in 1799. Bullen refers to having ministered to Love's and Levi Kemp's children as a group on May 31, which is an indication that the two men lived in the same vicinity. Because Kemp is documented to have lived east of Pontitack by 1826, the treaty ground McKee "went on to" would have been farther east toward Big Town (Phelps, "Excerpts from the Journal of the Reverend Joseph Bullen," 266, and n. 33);

witnesses to the treaty were Claiborne, McKee, Mitchell, Chamberlain, Anderson, McGee, and Oxberry. The latter temporarily replaced McGee as agency interpreter on October 1, 1805, but died on January 4, 1806 (see Atkinson, *History of the Chickasaw Indian Agency,* 47 n. 8); Griner's Inn was the site of Meriwether Lewis's suicide in October 1809 (see Stephen P. Ambrose, *Undaunted Courage: Meriwether Lewis, Thomas Jefferson, and the Opening of the American West* [New York: Simon & Schuster, 1996], 471–478). The sites of Griner's Inn and Lewis's grave are now in a park on the modern Natchez Trace Parkway.

33. After the party at the agency, John McKee and Aaron Burr lodged at the nearby home of Malcolm McGee (Diary of John McKee, entry for July 27, 1805; Atkinson, *History of the Chickasaw Indian Agency,* 11). The $1,000 payments to Colbert and Tishumustubbee were not made until August 1807 (Bills of Exchange, Aug. 2 and 3, 1807, in National Archives, RG 217, 2nd Auditor, Entry 525 [Settled Indian Accounts and Claims], box 19, folder 470; abstracted in Atkinson, *Records of the Chickasaw Agency,* 67). This illustrates the beginning of a general tendency for the government to sometimes be late in fulfilling both personal and tribal treaty obligation payments, which caused much consternation among the Chickasaw. An extreme case of a late payment concerns the 1819 annuity. Although $3,000 of it was paid in 1820, most was not, and a final payment totaling $52,000 was made in 1829 for both the remainder of the 1819 annuity and the 1829 annuity (Receipt, Chiefs and Warriors to Smith, May 14, 1829, in National Archives, RG 217, 2nd Auditor, Entry 525 [Settled Indian Accounts and Claims], box 77, folder 1688; abstracted in Atkinson, *Records of the Chickasaw Agency,* 148). Usually, however, payments had been no more than two years in arrears. I have concluded that the Chickasaw named Okoye or Tishumustubbee was probably the same man who later came to be called Tishomingo, which is a title name meaning "speaker for the king or chief" or "speaker chief." Tishumustubbee was identified by Dr. Rush Nutt in 1805 as "the speaker of the nation," a "very good man," and one who "fills the place of George Colbert, who has for some time declined attending to business." Significantly, the man called Tishomingo had become a district chief by 1818 and was also the speaker of the nation for the king, Chinubbee. He was usually referred to as "speaker," but one white man called him "Tishomingo the national orator" in 1826 (see Jennings, "Nutt's Trip to the Chickasaw Country," 47, and Letter, John D. Terrell to William Clark, Thomas Hinds, and John Coffee, Oct. 16, 1826, in National Archives, Records of the Bureau of Indian Affairs (RG 75), Entry 1058 (Records of the Chickasaw Agency, 1806–1841). The latter is abstracted in Atkinson, *Records of the Chickasaw Agency,* 322). The name Tishumustubbee does not appear in documents after the name Tishomingo appears in about 1813.

34. McGee-Draper Narrative, 112a.

35. Ibid., 110; John Gordon, Memorial, in "Pioneer Documents," *American Historical Magazine* 2, no. 4(Oct. 1897): 351–353; the exact location of Colbert's and Gordon's Duck River Ferry stand was archaeologically discovered in 1985 (James R. Atkinson, "The Search for and Apparent Discovery of the Duck River Cantonment/Colbert-Gordon Stand Site, Maury County, Tennessee, Natchez Trace Parkway," Southeast Archeological Center, National Park Service, Tallahassee, Florida, April 1985); by a stipulation in the 1818 treaty discussed below, Gordon was paid $1,115 regarding the Duck River Ferry for "the full amount of a debt due said John Gordon, from General William Colbert . . . which the commissioners of the United States, at the requests of the Chiefs . . . agreed to pay the said John Gordon,

under Article 3" (Receipt, Benjamin Smith for John Gordon to Henry Sherburne, April 23, 1819, in National Archives, RG 217, 2nd Auditor, Entry 525 [Settled Indian Accounts and Claims], box 7, folders 106–107; abstracted in Atkinson, *Records of the Chickasaw Agency,* 86). Gordon's brick home, on the Natchez Trace Parkway, still stands near the ferry site.

36. Letter, Hawkins to Secretary of War, Oct. 28, 1801, in Hawkins, *Letters,* 393; McGee-Draper Narrative, 112c, 122; some of the contemporary characterizations and descriptions of George Colbert are compiled in Dawson Phelps's article on Colbert's Ferry. An ethnocentric Methodist minister who met him not surprisingly reported that he was a "very shrewd, talented man and withal very wicked. He had two wives." Dr. Rush Nutt recorded in 1805 that he was "the greatest of the Chickasaws, displays genius and talent . . . but is an artful designing man." Cherokee agent R. J. Meigs opined that he was "extremely mercenary, miscalculates his importance, & when not awed by the presence of the officers of Government takes upon himself great airs" (Phelps, "Colbert Ferry and Selected Documents," 212–213); see also Braden, "The Colberts and the Chickasaw Nation," 229–231.

37. For details about the agents, subagents, and events related to the Chickasaw Agency and Chickasaw nation activities, see Atkinson, *Records of the Chickasaw Agency* and *History of the Chickasaw Indian Agency;* in addition to data in Putnam's *History of Middle Tennessee* and other histories and sources, see a somewhat glorified sketch of James Robertson by E. C. Lewis, "James Robertson, Nashville's Founder," in *Tennessee Old and New, 1796–1946* (sponsored by the Tennessee Historical Commission and the Tennessee Historical Society, Kingsport, Tenn: Kingsport Press, 1946), 84–92. However, this article, reprinted from the *American Historical Magazine* of July 1903, repeats a mistake begun by nineteenth-century Tennessee historians—that the Chickasaw Agency was located at Chickasaw Bluffs (Lewis says "in West Tennessee"); for a short biography of William Cocke, see William Goodrich, "William Cocke—Born 1749, Died 1828," *American Historical Magazine* 1, no. 3 (July 1896): 224–229; for data about Benjamin F. Smith, see May Wilson McBee, "Benjamin F. Smith," in Ron Tyler, Douglas E. Barnett, Roy R. Barkley, Penelope C. Anderson, and Mark F. Odintz, eds., *The New Handbook of Texas,* vol. 5 (Austin : Texas State Historical Association, 1996), 1091–1092. See also Dunbar Rowland, ed., *Mississippi* (Spartanburg, S.C.: Reprint Company, 1976), vol. 2, p. 694; subagents employed at the two agency locations between 1818 and 1835 were David G. Cook (1818, the first subagent; accompanied Sherburne from Rhode Island), William Vans (1819–1821), Reodolphus Malbone (1822–1824), Gabriel W. Long (1824–1826), John B. Duncan (1826–1829), and John L. Allen (1829–1835). A man named Michael Davidson from Lincoln County, Kentucky, accepted the subagent position to replace Long in November 1825 after the latter and agent Smith had a falling out, but because there is no mention of Davidson among the agency fiscal records, he appears to have withdrawn his acceptance (Letter, Michael Davidson to Secretary of War, Nov. 25, 1825, in National Archives, Records of the Bureau of Indian Affairs [RG 75; Letters Received by the Office of Indian Affairs, 1824–1881], microfilm M-234, roll 135, frames 0108–0109); John L. Allen, son of David Allen, became a Chickasaw nation resident in about 1796 and lived there until appointed postmaster at Paris, Tennessee, in 1826. He then moved back to the nation after accepting the subagent position; he was William Colbert's son-in-law. Regarding the name of his father, see Letter, John L. Allen to T. L. McKenney, Oct. 16, 1829, in National Archives, RG 75, microfilm M-234 (Letters Received, Office of Indian Affairs), roll 135.

38. Gibson, *The Chickasaws,* 149–153, and Gibson, "The Colberts: Chickasaw Nation Elitism," 82–88; agent Nicholas estimated in 1822 that there were 200 to 300 slaves in the Chickasaw nation (Letter, Nicholas to Secretary of War, July 12, 1822, in National Archives, RG 107, microfilm M-221 [Letters Received, Secretary of War], roll 96).

39. For numerous examples of the various types of expenditures of the Chickasaw Agency see especially Chapters 2 and 5 in Atkinson, *Records of the Chickasaw Agency.*

40. Cotterill, *The Southern Indians,* 168–169; Letters, George Colbert to Governor Willie Blount, Feb. 7 and April 9, 1812, in National Archives, RG 107, microfilm M-221 (Letters Received, Secretary of War), roll 42; escorted by Kickapoos, Tecumseh is said to have visited the Chickasaw nation, where he delivered oratory at Chuckalissa/Old Town but was told by George Colbert and other Chickasaw leaders that they were at peace with the Americans. Tecumseh and the Kickapoos then traveled to the Choctaw nation, supposedly with a mounted Chickasaw escort (Gibson, *The Chickasaws,* 96–98); because there is no direct, contemporary documentation regarding the visit of Tecumseh and his party to the Chickasaw, some uncertainties exist. Much later accounts dating to the early 1880s assert that Tecumseh, with no mention of The Prophet, visited the Chickasaw. However, George Colbert wrote to Governor Blount in February 1812 that the Chickasaw were not listening to the words of The Prophet, with no mention of Tecumseh (Letter, George Colbert to Blount, Feb. 7, 1812, in National Archives, RG 107, microfilm M-221 [Letters Received, Secretary of War], roll 42). Of interest is a later account citing a recalled earlier conversation in about 1841 with Malcolm McGee, who supposedly related that both Tecumseh and The Prophet visited the Chickasaw in 1811 (Letter, Mrs. M. J. Stuart Stewart [daughter of the Rev. T. C. Stuart], Tupelo, Miss., to Lyman C. Draper, Nov. 6, 1882, Draper Collection, vol. 10, series U, p. 1). It is possible that Tecumseh did not visit the Chickasaw but rather The Prophet, or perhaps both did; Letter, Secretary of War to Robertson, June 4, 1812, in National Archives, RG 75, microfilm M-15 (Letters Sent), roll 3; the following in Bassett, *Correspondence of Andrew Jackson,* vol. 1: Letter, Andrew Jackson to George Colbert, June 5, 1812, pp. 226–227; Letter, James Robertson to Jackson, Sept. 16, 1813, pp. 319; and Letter, Thomas Pinckney to Jackson, Feb. 17, 1814, pp. 464–465; Letter, George and James Colbert to General Andrew Jackson, Chickasaw Nation, Jan. 10, 1814, in Jackson Papers, roll 22, Library of Congress.

41. Gibson, *The Chickasaws,* 98; Letters, James Robertson to Secretary of War, Dec. 29, 1813, Feb. 1, 1814, and April 30, 1814, in National Archives, RG 107, microfilm M-221 (Letters Received, Secretary of War), roll 56; after the treaty of 1805 in July, George Colbert had begun to be complacent with regard to affairs of the nation, as reported by Dr. Rush Nutt at the time: "George Colbert, altho he has declined sitting in council has more the ear of the nation & more weight than any of his people. He is an artful designing man more for his own interest, than that of his nation" (Jennings, "Nutt's Trip to the Chickasaw Country," 48); Martini, *Indian Chiefs of the Southeast,* 80, citing roster of Chickasaw troops discharged at Mobile on February 28, 1815; regarding Caryoucuttaha and Chickwartubby, see Receipt, James Colbert in behalf of Elijah Jefferson to Henry Sherburne, Dec. 31, 1818, and Receipt, James Colbert in behalf of Charles Jefferson to Sherburne, Dec. 31, 1818, in National Archives, RG 217, 2nd Auditor, Entry 525 (Settled Indian Accounts and Claims), box 7, folders 106–107 (abstracted in Atkinson, *Records of the Chickasaw Agency,* 85).

42. Gibson, *The Chickasaws,* 98; William Colbert's death date is documented by Receipt,

Ishtanaha to B. F. Smith, July 15, 1824, in National Archives, RG 217, 2nd Auditor, Entry 525 (Settled Indian Accounts and Claims), box 31, folder 748. His residency on the Tombigbee River was recalled by Malcolm McGee (McGee-Draper Narrative, 110) and is confirmed in a contemporary letter from Captain Hugh Young to Andrew Jackson dated Dec. 4, 1816 (in Jackson Papers, roll 22, Library of Congress). His move to present-day Chickasaw County and death there were recalled by McGee. McGee was one year off with regard to the year of his death, stating "in the autumn of 1823" (McGee-Draper Narrative, 110). Another man by the name of William Colbert has been confused with General Colbert in the local literature. This man, possibly a son, belonged to the Monroe Church after 1824, causing some to speculate that General Colbert lived at Tockshish and died in 1827 (Martini, *Indian Chiefs of the Southeast*, 96) or 1836 (Winston, *Story of Pontotoc*, 79). According to Warren, who realized that he was not General Colbert, the man was a grandson of the elder James Colbert rather than his noted son (Warren, "Missions, Missionaries, Frontier Characters," 584).

43. Receipt, James Lyons to Robertson, Jan. 21, 1814, in National Archives, RG 217, 2nd Auditor, Entry 525 (Settled Indian Accounts and Claims), box 14, folder 352; Receipt, Thomas McCoy to Robertson, Jan. 1, 1814, Receipt, James Lyon to Robertson, Sept. 16, 1813, and Letter, Robertson to Secretary of War, Jan. 1, 1814, all in National Archives, RG 217, 5th Auditor, Entry 525 (Additional Settled Indian Accounts and Claims), box 1, acct. 298 (all four of the above abstracted in Atkinson, *Records of the Chickasaw Agency*, 72, 240–241); Letter, Governor Willie Blount to Robertson, July 11, 1814, in Robertson, "Correspondence," 5(1900): 286; Letters, Robertson to Secretary of War, Sept. 23, Oct. 20, and Dec. 29, 1813, and April 30, 1814, in National Archives, RG 107, microfilm M-221 (Letters Received, Secretary of War), roll 56; McGee-Draper Narrative, 120; Putnam, *History of Middle Tennessee*, 605–606. Putnam states that Robertson suffered from neuralgia and, quoting a newspaper obituary, died from brain inflammation, but McGee recalled that he died of pleurisy. In any case, inflammation of the brain (stroke?) was undoubtedly the culprit.

44. Jack D. Elliott, Jr., "Leftwich's 'Cotton Gin Port and Gaines' Trace' Reconsidered," *Journal of Mississippi History* 42, no. 4(1980): 348–361; the following in National Archives, RG 75, microfilm M-15 (Letters Sent), roll 3: Letters, Secretary of War to R. J. Meigs, March 27 and May 25, 1811; Letters, Secretary of War to Neelly, March 29 and May 25, 1811; Letter, Secretary of War to William Cocke, March 6, 1815; Letter, Secretary of War to Willie Blount, Sept. 14, 1815; Letter, Secretary of War to Cocke, Dec. 29, 1815; and Letter, Acting Secretary of War to Joseph McMinn, Dec. 29, 1815; Letter, Neelly to Secretary of War, July 17, 1811, in National Archives, RG 107, microfilm M-221 (Letters Received, Secretary of War), roll 39; Gibson, *The Chickasaws*, 149. Gibson's reference to construction in 1811 of a road leading from "Runnolds Ferry" to the Chickasaw Agency is a mistake. Gibson misinterpreted references regarding a suggested road route from the Tennessee at Runnold's Ferry to the nation (possibly to the agency), which was never built. The Chickasaw, in fact, "positively refused" to approve it, as reported by Neelly in his July 17, 1811, letter cited immediately above; Letter, George Colbert to General Wade Hampton, Nov. 20, 1811, and Letter, Hampton to George Colbert, Jan. 12, 1812, both in National Archives, RG 75, microfilm M-15 (Letters Sent), roll 44; the following in National Archives, RG 75, microfilm M-15 (Letters Sent): Letter, Captain James McDonald to Secretary of War, March 5, 1812, roll 47; Letters, Cocke to Secretary of War, May 25, 1815, Aug. 10, 1815, and Aug. 11, 1815, roll 60; Agreement, Headmen and Warriors

of the Chickasaw Nation, Aug. 5, 1815, roll 60; Cocke, Talk delivered the Chickasaws at Council in August 1815, roll 60; and Letter, Cocke to Secretary of War, Feb. 9, 1816, roll 68; the following in National Archives, RG 217, 5th Auditor, Entry 525 (Additional Settled Indian Accounts and Claims), box 2, acct. 287: Receipt, George Colbert to William Cocke, May 7, 1815; Invoice and Bill of Exchange, George Colbert to Cocke, and Cocke to Secretary of War, Aug. 6, 1815; and Receipts, James Brown to Cocke and Captain Cya-cutta-hay to Cocke, June 2, 1816 (National Archives RG 217 documents abstracted in Atkinson, *Records of the Chickasaw Agency,* Chapter 5); Letter, U.S. Road Commissioners Thomas Johnson and Michael Dickson to Secretary of War, May 15, 1816, in *ASP* (Miscellaneous), vol. 2, 1834, p. 402; Natchez Trace Parkway Survey, *A Report of a Survey of the Old Indian Trail, Known as the Natchez Trace,* 76th Congress, Senate Document No. 148 (Washington, D.C.: Government Printing Office, 1941), 49; George Colbert's move of himself and family from the ferry to the main settlement is documented by a letter from him and James Colbert to Andrew Jackson dated January 10, 1814 (in Jackson Papers, roll 22, Library of Congress). Additional documentation is present in Letter, James Robertson to Secretary of War, Dec. 29, 1813, in National Archives, RG 107, microfilm M-221 (Letters Received, Secretary of War), roll 56.

45. Letters, James Neely to General Wade Hampton, Nov. 22 and 29, 1811, in National Archives, RG 107, microfilm M-221 (Letters Received, Secretary of War), roll 44; Letters, James Neely to Secretary of War, May 13 and June 12, 1812, ibid., roll 47; Letter, James Robertson to Secretary of War James Monroe, Feb. 14, 1813, ibid., roll 56; Letter, Captain John A. Allen to William Cocke, Nov. 14, 1814, ibid., roll 60; Letter, Cocke to Secretary of War, July 5, 1815, ibid., roll 60; Bills of Exchange and Receipts, from Neely, John C. Smith, and Kilpatrick Carter, June 8 and 9, 1812, in National Archives, RG 217, 5th Auditor, Entry 525 (Additional Settled Indian Accounts and Claims), box 2, acct. 300; Permit to Thomas Redus from Captain G. W. Sevier, Fort Hampton, Nov. 24, 1811, and Bond proclamation, Thomas Redus and others, Dec. 26, 1814, both in National Archives, RG 75, Entry 1058 (Records of the Chickasaw Agency) (Entry 525 and 1058 documents abstracted in Atkinson, *Records of the Chickasaw Agency,* 234, 316–317).

46. Letter, Cocke to Secretary of War, Jan. 2, 1816, Letter, Cocke to Secretary of War, July 20, 1816, "Talk of Tishomingo in reply to the Agent of the U.S. delivered at Tockshish . . . the 24 February 1816," Letter, Cocke to Secretary of War, Feb. 26, 1816, and Letter, Lewis Winston to Andrew Jackson, July 2, 1816, all in National Archives, RG 107, microfilm M-221 (Letters Received, Secretary of War), roll 68 (the latter also in National Archives, RG 75, Entry 1058 [Records of the Chickasaw Agency]); Letter, Tissue Mingo, Appcoun Tubbie, and William Colbert to Opouy Hummah, George Pettygrove, and Samuel Seeley, Colbert's Ferry, April 10, 1816, in National Archives, RG 107, microfilm M-221 (Letters Received, Secretary of War), roll 68 (Entry 1058 documents abstracted in Atkinson, *Records of the Chickasaw Agency,* 319–320); Letter, Cocke to Andrew Jackson, July 19, 1816, typescript in Natchez Trace Parkway library; Letter, Malcolm McGee to Cocke, April 19, 1816, typescript in Natchez Trace Parkway library; Letter, Secretary of War to Cocke, June 26, 1816, in National Archives, RG 75, microfilm M-15 (Letters Sent), roll 3; Letter, Secretary of War to Andrew Jackson, July 5, 1816, in *ASP* (Indian Affairs), vol. 2, 1834, p. 102.

47. Treaty with the Chickasaws, 1816, in Kappler, *Laws and Treaties,* vol. 2, pp. 135–137; the treaty is also published in *ASP* (Indian Affairs), vol. 2, 1834, pp. 92–93; Letter, Jackson, Meri-

wether, and Franklin to Secretary of War, Sept. 20, 1816, in *ASP* (Indian Affairs), vol. 2, 1834, pp. 104–105; Letter, Jackson to John Coffee, Sept. 19, 1816, in Bassett, *Correspondence of Andrew Jackson*, vol. 2 (1927), 260; Letter, Jackson to James Monroe, Oct. 23, 1816, in Bassett, *Correspondence of Andrew Jackson*, vol. 2 (1927), 261; Letter, Jackson to President-elect James Monroe, Oct. 23, 1816, in Moser et al., *Papers of Andrew Jackson*, vol. 4, p. 69; Cotterill, *The Southern Indians*, 199–201; Letters, Secretary of War to the Commissioners, June 15, 1816, in National Archives, RG 75, microfilm M-15 (Letters Sent), roll 3; Letter, Secretary of War to William Cocke, June 26, 1816, in National Archives, RG 75, microfilm M-15 (Letters Sent), roll 3; Letter, Cocke to Secretary of War, Sept. 21, 1816, in National Archives, RG 107, microfilm M-221 (Letters Received, Secretary of War), roll 68; Letter, John L. Allen to Secretary of War, April 26, 1816, in National Archives, RG 107, microfilm M-221 (Letters Received, Secretary of War), roll 68; Letter, Wigton King to Andrew Jackson, Feb. 12, 1816, Jackson Papers, roll 20, Library of Congress; documentation that the treaty negotiations were held near Old Town at George Colbert's home is present in a letter written to the President after the treaty was signed (Letter, John Rhea to President James Madison, Sept. 24, 1816, in J. A. Padgett, ed., "Letters from John Rhea to Thomas Jefferson and James Madison," *East Tennessee Historical Society's Publications* 10[1938]: 122–123). Rhea reported that the commissioners "set out on last Saturday morning from the Council House, namely George Colberts in the Chickasaw Nation." See also Letter, John Rhea "At the house of Coll. George Colbert in the Chickasaw Nation" to James Madison, Sept. 6, 1816, in Padgett, "Letters from John Rhea to Thomas Jefferson and James Madison," 122–123; the Old Town area is confirmed in another letter written over a year later (Letter, Martin Colbert to Secretary of War, Feb. 1, 1818, in National Archives, RG 107, microfilm M-221 [Letters Received, Secretary of War], roll 77). Located about one mile west of the present city limits of Tupelo and north of Highway 6, this home of Colbert's is evidently the one shown on an 1834 U.S. Land Office plat map of the Chickasaw Cession; a modern home is presently on the site. The Chickasaws who signed the treaty included King Chinubbee, George, Levi, James, and William Colbert, Apassantubby, William McGillivray, Tishomingo, Samuel Seeley, Captain Rabbit, William Glover, James Brown, George Pettygrove, and ten additional full-bloods. James Colbert and Malcolm McGee served as interpreters; also under the 1816 treaty, General William Colbert was granted a $100 per year annuity for life "as a particular mark of distinction and favor for his long services and faithful adherence to the United States government."

48. Treaty with the Chickasaws, 1816, in Kappler, *Laws and Treaties*, vol. 2, pp. 135–136; Gibson ("The Colberts: Chickasaw Nation Elitism," 88) states without citing a source that the rumored sale amount was $40,000. Although not cited by Gibson, Malcolm McGee's recollection of 1841 appears to be the written source of this rumor (McGee-Draper Narrative, 112c); the treaty also provided cash gifts to the leading chiefs and military leaders ($150 and $100, respectively). The chiefs were King Chinubbee, Tishomingo, William McGillivray, Apassantubby, Samuel Seeley, James Brown, Levi Colbert, Ickaryoucullaha, George Pettygrove, and Immartarharmicko. Malcolm McGee also received $150. The military leaders were William Glover, Colonel George Colbert, Captain Rabbit, Hoparyeahoummar, Immoukelusharhopoyyea, Hoparyea, Houllartir, Tushkarhopaye, Hoparyeahoummar Junior, a second Immoukelusharhopoyyea, James Colbert, Coweamarthlar, and Illachouwarhopoyea. The actual payments are documented in Receipts, Chickasaw chiefs to Henry Sherburne,

Oct. 20, 1818, and Military Leaders to Sherburne, Oct. 20, 1818, in National Archives, RG 217, 5th Auditor, Entry 525 (Additional Settled Indian Accounts and Claims), box 10, acct. 582 (abstracted in Atkinson, *Records of the Chickasaw Agency,* 267–268). By October 1818, Ickaryoucullaha was deceased. His payment was received by James Colbert on behalf of his heirs.

49. Apparently Levi Colbert moved to the Cotton Gin Port landing area in late 1813 or in 1814. In late 1813 both he and George were reported by agent Robertson to have "moved their families into the heart of the nation." The impetus for the move appears to have been fear of the Red Sticks, but because construction of the Gaines' Trace to the crossing there had caused a diversion of revenue-producing traffic from that part of the Natchez Trace where Buzzard Roost and Colbert's Ferry were located, this circumstance also came into play (see Letter, Robertson to Secretary of War, Dec. 29, 1813, in National Archives, RG 107, microfilm M-221 [Letters Received, Secretary of War], roll 56); Levi thereafter apparently operated a ferry and provided travel accommodations at Cotton Gin Port. His mill is shown on a huge map made by John La Tourette ("An Accurate Map or Delineation of the State of Mississippi with a large portion of Louisiana and Mississippi [Mobile, Alabama, 1845, originally prepared before 1839], copy in Mississippi Collection, Univ. of Mississippi Library). The Buzzard Roost farmstead/stand was afterward operated by Colbert's white son-in-law, Kilpatrick Carter, and family (see Phelps, "Stands and Travel Accommodations," 43). By the end of 1833, Colbert had abandoned his home on the bluff opposite Cotton Gin Port, having moved to a new location in the prairie about six miles to the northwest on the road leading westward from the town (U.S. Land Office, plat map for Township 12 South, Range 6 East; B. L. C. Wailes, "Transformation of Names," *American Historical Magazine* 3[1859]: 223; Letter, J. N. Walton to L. C. Draper, Oct. 2, 1882, published in *Itawamba Settlers* 17[1997]: 94). Walton's original letter is in the Draper Collection, vol. 10, series U, pp. 140/1–140/21; Levi Colbert's election as principal chief to primarily deal with the United States in place of George was recalled by Malcolm McGee (McGee-Draper Narrative, 122); McGee (McGee-Draper Narrative, 126) related that Itawamba meant "wooden bench" but did not associate the name with Levi Colbert. J. N. Walton only stated that Levi Colbert's Indian name was Itawamba, meaning "Sitting King." This traditional Indian name for Levi Colbert is inferred by a white man who knew him well ("Autobiography of Gideon Lincecum," in *Publications of the Mississippi Historical Society* 8 [1904]); Leftwich ("Cotton Gin Port and Gaines' Trace," 270) stated that Itawamba was actually Levi Colbert's herdsman, but this is likely incorrect. J. N. Walton, a white man from Cotton Gin Port who knew Levi Colbert well, recalled that at one time he owned 4,000 head of cattle and at the time of his death had about 300 horses, about 40 slaves, and an unstated quantity of hogs, sheep, and other livestock. Walton, who may have been somewhat unobjective, also had the following to say about him:

> [Levi Colbert] had an intellect far superior to the common mass of people without regard to color or nationality, he was shrewd and influential among his tribe, in fact his words or advice was the law among them, his people loved him, the Chiefs, Captains, with their King, looked up to him, his speeches in their councils would electrify them and throw them almost into ecstasies . . . he was kind and affectionate to his family, although he had a number of wives (only three) and two of them sisters, they lived as cordial and affectionately as so many sisters. They would laugh and joke each

other as though they were wives of different men, and no discord ever happened among them. (Letter, J. N. Walton to Lyman C. Draper, June 25, 1882, in Draper Collection, vol. 10, series U, pp. 140/6–140/7)

50. Kappler, *Laws and Treaties*, vol. 2, p. 135; Receipt, Levi Colbert to Henry Sherburne, Chickasaw Treaty Ground, Oct. 12, 1818, in National Archives, RG 217, 5th Auditor, Entry 525 (Additional Settled Indian Accounts and Claims), box 10, acct. 582 (abstracted in Atkinson, *Records of the Chickasaw Agency,* 266); Cotterill, *The Southern Indians,* 200; Letter, Jackson, Meriwether, and Franklin to Secretary of War, Sept. 20, 1816, in *ASP* (Indian Affairs), vol. 2, 1834, pp. 104–105. This letter is also published in Moser et al., *Papers of Andrew Jackson,* vol. 4, pp. 65–67.

51. Moser et al., *Papers of Andrew Jackson,* vol. 4, pp. 67, 68 n. 9.

52. Documentation that agent Cocke set up the district organization is in Letter, Cocke to Secretary of War, Sept. 22, 1816, in *ASP* (Indian Affairs), vol. 2, 1834, p. 106; the population determined by the 1818 census is recorded in Letter, Henry Sherburne to William Lee, 2nd Auditor, March 11, 1820, in National Archives, RG 217, 2nd Auditor, Entry 525 (Settled Indian Accounts and Claims), box 9, folder 169 or 170. A copy of this census is at Oklahoma Historical Society, Oklahoma City, and a typed transcript of that copy is at Natchez Trace Parkway, Tupelo; Receipts (four), William McGillivray, Samuel Seeley, Tishomingo, and Apassantubby to Henry Sherburne, Oct. 19 and 20, 1818, in National Archives, RG 217, 5th Auditor, Entry 525 (Additional Settled Indian Accounts and Claims), box 10, acct. 582; the following in National Archives, RG 217, 2nd Auditor, Entry 525 (Settled Indian Accounts and Claims): Receipts, Chiefs and Kings to R. C. Nicholas, Dec. 17 and 22, 1821, box 15, folder 365; Receipt, Kings and chiefs to B. F. Smith, Jan. 28, 1824, box 31, folder 748; Receipt, King and chiefs to B. F. Smith, May 14, 1825, box 48, folder 1073; Specie Annuity List, Aug. 9, 1831, box 112, folders 2495 and 2496; and Specie Annuity List, Aug. 31, 1833, box 145, folder 3994 (see abstracts of the RG 217, Entry 525 receipts and other items in Atkinson, *Records of the Chickasaw Agency,* Chapters 2 and 5); Gibson, *The Chickasaws,* 153; Atkinson, *History of the Chickasaw Indian Agency,* 24.

53. Sales Account, Henry Sherburne, Chickasaw Agency, Sept. 19, 1818, in National Archives, RG 217, 5th Auditor, Entry 525 (Additional Settled Indian Accounts and Claims), box 10, acct. 582 (abstracted in Atkinson, *Records of the Chickasaw Agency,* 265); Letter, L. Pennebecker to the Office of the Secretary of War, March 22, 1838, in National Archives, RG 75, microfilm M-234 (Letters Received, Office of Indian Affairs), roll 137; Gibson, *The Chickasaws,* 174–175.

54. Letters, Jackson to Isaac Shelby, Aug. 11 and Aug. 25, 1818, in Bassett, *Correspondence of Andrew Jackson,* vol. 2, pp. 387–388, 391–392; Letter, Jackson to George W. Campbell, Oct. 5, 1818, in Bassett, *Correspondence of Andrew Jackson,* vol. 2, p. 395; Letter, Jackson and Shelby to John C. Calhoun, Oct. 30, 1818, in Bassett, *Correspondence of Andrew Jackson,* vol. 2, pp. 399–401; Treaty of Old Town, 1818, in *ASP* (Indian Affairs), vol. 2, 1834, pp. 164–165; Treaty of Old Town, 1818, in Kappler, *Laws and Treaties,* vol. 2, pp. 174–177; Robert Butler's Journal of the Chickasaw Treaty of 1818, Sept.–Oct., 1818, in National Archives, RG 75, microfilm T-494 (Documents Relating to Negotiations), roll 1. Butler recorded that prior to initiation of negotiations, Jackson, Shelby, and others traveled on September 29 three miles from the

treaty ground to George Colbert's house, where they spent the night. As discussed earlier, the latter had been the location of the 1816 treaty. The location of the 1818 treaty site being "one mile east of Old Town" is reported by Andrew Jackson (Letter, Jackson to John C. Calhoun, Secretary of War, Oct. 4, 1819, in National Archives, RG 217, 2nd Auditor, Entry 525 [Settled Indian Accounts and Claims], box 7, folder 105 [original letter signed by Jackson is transcribed in Atkinson, *Records of the Chickasaw Agency,* 81]). An abstract of the letter is in National Archives, Records of the Office of Secretary of War (RG 107; Register of Letters Received by the Office of the Secretary of War, Main Series, 1800–1870), microfilm M-22; unaware that George Colbert had moved away from the Tennessee River by this time, Samuel Cole Williams erroneously identified the Treaty of Old Town as being held "near Tuscumbia, Alabama" (Williams, *Beginnings of West Tennessee,* 87); the Chickasaw signers of the treaty included King Chinubbee, Levi, George, and William Colbert, Samuel Seeley, Tishomingo, William Glover, William McGillivray, Apassantubby, James Brown, George Pettygrove, and James Colbert. Malcolm McGee, the interpreter, signed as a witness along with nine other whites and Martin Colbert, a son of Levi.

55. Treaty of Old Town, 1818, in Kappler, *Laws and Treaties,* vol. 2, p. 175; Treaties of Franklin (1830), Washington (1834), and Washington (1852), ibid., pp. 424, 596, 1040; Receipt, Apassantubby to Henry Sherburne, Chickasaw Agency, April 24, 1819, in National Archives, RG 217, 2nd Auditor, Entry 525 (Settled Indian Accounts and Claims), box 7, folders 106–107; after 1818, John McClish, who had a white wife in that year, apparently sold his reserve and moved to the main settlements in present-day northeast Mississippi, where he, at least, was living by 1826. It is unlikely that Apassantubby ever resided on his reserved tract.

56. Letter, Benjamin Smith to John C. Calhoun, Secretary of War, Jan. 30, 1824, in National Archives, RG 217, 2nd Auditor, Entry 525 (Settled Indian Accounts and Claims), box 31, folder 748; Letter report, John D. Terrell to Thomas L. McKenney, Jan. 6, 1827, in National Archives, RG 75, Entry 1058 (Records of the Chickasaw Agency) (both abstracted in Atkinson, *Records of the Chickasaw Agency,* 87, 119, 322); the date of payment to the Colberts for their 1816 reservations is present in Charles C. Royce, compiler, "Indian Land Cessions of the United States," *Bureau of American Ethnology, Eighteenth Annual Report,* pt. 2 (Washington, D.C.: Government Printing Office, 1899), 695.

57. Letter, Andrew Jackson to Thomas Kirkman, Treaty Ground, Chickasaw Nation, Oct. 20, 1818, in Andrew Jackson, "Valuable Letters of Andrew Jackson," *American Historical Magazine* 4, no. 2(April 1899): 99–100; regarding the recipients of the $20,000 in goods, see Memorandum, Jackson and William B. Lewis, Oct. 17, 1818, in Jackson Papers, Library of Congress, and in National Archives, RG 75, microfilm T-494 (Documents Relating to Negotiations) (published in Williams, *Beginnings of West Tennessee,* appendix, p. 296); Cotterill, *The Southern Indians,* 207; in a letter to John C. Calhoun, Andrew Jackson stated that "the difficulties that the commissioners had to surmount to obtain the concession contained in the treaty, the means they had to resort to, to raise the funds absolutely necessary, to weld the chiefs to obtain the object of that treaty; we were not authorized by you to draw for the amount <u>necessary,</u> and were compelled to resort to the means of raising the necessary funds out of the property reserved at a former treaty to the Colberts" (Letter, Jackson to Calhoun, Oct. 4, 1819, in National Archives, RG 217, 2nd Auditor, Entry 525 [Settled Indian Accounts and Claims], box 7, folder 105 [transcribed in Atkinson, *Records of the Chickasaw Agency,*

81]). For other previous discussions of the 1818 treaty see Williams, *Beginnings of West Tennessee*, 84–93, and Braden, "The Colberts and the Chickasaw Nation," 245–247.

58. Receipt, James Colbert and other military leaders to Sherburne, April 24, 1819, and Receipt, King, Chickasaw chiefs, and interpreter to Sherburne, April 24, 1819, in National Archives, RG 217, 2nd Auditor, Entry 525 (Settled Indian Accounts and Claims), box 7, folder 105; Receipt, James Colbert to Sherburne, April 23, 1819, ibid., box 7, folders 106–107 (all abstracted in Atkinson, *Records of the Chickasaw Agency*, 78, 86). Spellings of the full-blood chiefs' names vary from document to document; by Article 3 of the treaty, mixed-blood John Lewis was granted $25 for a saddle lost while "in the service of the United States" and white man David Smith of the Cumberland settlement was paid $2,000 to compensate him for the expense of provisioning a force of forty-five soldiers to assist the Chickasaw against the Creek in 1795 (see Chapter 10). This item would seem to have had nothing to do with obtaining agreement to the treaty, except for the fact that the chiefs requested the compensation for Smith.

59. Letter, R. C. Nicholas to Secretary of War, May 14, 1822, in National Archives, RG 107, microfilm M-221 (Letters Received, Secretary of War), roll 96; by 1823 Martin Colbert was operating a mercantile establishment at the Pontitack settlement of the Chickasaws (Invoice/Receipt, Martin Colbert to B. F. Smith, "Pontotock Chickasaw Nation," Aug. 30, 1826, in National Archives, RG 217, 2nd Auditor, Entry 525 [Settled Indian Accounts and Claims], box 54, folder 1245; abstracted in Atkinson, *Records of the Chickasaw Agency*, 134). He later moved to near present-day Horn Lake, Mississippi, in De Soto County, where he died in 1840 leaving an estate valued at $33,197, including 2,340 acres of land, twenty-seven slaves, and a large quantity of livestock (Martini, *Indian Chiefs of the Southeast*, 100–101). Some of the other identified mixed-blood families by the early nineteenth century who had farms with cattle herds include the Loves, Browns, Seeleys, McClishs, Gunns, Burneys, Underwoods, Perrys, Bynums, Moores, McGillivrays, Albertsons, Kemps, Glovers, Fraziers, Carters, Thompsons, and Campbells. A small minority of these and other mixed-blood families had members who were traders or merchants. None of the families, however, are documented to have been politically active with regard to external affairs or dominators of the full-bloods, although they did generally represent a more visible segment of the social strata; for an excellent alternative view of the position espoused by Gibson regarding the full-blood/mixed-blood dichotomy, see Champagne, *Social Order and Political Change*, 111–113, 281 n. 46.

60. Chinubbee was reported to be about fifty years old in 1794 (see Letter, Gayoso to Carondelet, Oct. 10, 1794, in Corbitt and Corbitt, "Papers from the Spanish Archives," 41[1969]: 110); Chinubbee's death date is documented in Receipt, Malcolm McGee to Henry Sherburne, Sept. 30, 1819, in National Archives, RG 217, 2nd Auditor, Entry 525 (Settled Indian Accounts and Claims), box 7, folder 106 or 107, and Account of Henry Sherburne, Jan. 22, 1821, in National Archives, RG 217, 2nd Auditor, Entry 525 (Settled Indian Accounts and Claims), box 7, folder 105 (both abstracted in Atkinson, *Records of the Chickasaw Agency*, 83, 88). The receipt and account are related to the final payment of Chinubbee's $100 annuity granted him under the 1805 treaty; McGee-Draper Narrative, 120; with regard to Queen Pucaunla, see Warren, "Some Chickasaw Chiefs and Prominent Men," 568, and Treaty of Pontotoc Creek, 1832, in Kappler, *Laws and Treaties*, 360. Cushman (*History of the Choctaw*,

Chickasaw, and Natchez Indians, 404) states that Pucaunla was the widow of an invalid ex-king of the Chickasaw named Tushkaapela. However, there is no documentation for a king by that name. Perhaps Cushman meant to refer to Chehopistee, or perhaps McGee was in error. The latter, however, was more likely correct, for Cushman's relations about the Chickasaw are laced with partially or completely erroneous statements.

CHAPTER 12

1. Letter, R. C. Nicholas to Secretary of War, May 14, 1822, in National Archives, RG 107, microfilm M-221 (Letters Received, Secretary of War), roll 96.

2. Ibid.; Letter, Levi Colbert to Secretary of War, Jan. 28, 1822, ibid., roll 92; the following in National Archives, RG 217, 2nd Auditor, Entry 525 (Settled Indian Accounts and Claims): Receipt, Benjamin Smith to the United States, March 20, 1824, box 31, folder 748; Receipt, Levi Thomas to Smith, June 15, 1826, box 54, folder 1245; Receipt, A. W. Dew to Smith, March 1, 1828, box 66, folder 1451; and Receipt, James Watkins to Smith, Oct. 6, 1827, box 66, folder 1451; the following in National Archives, RG 75, microfilm M-234 (Letters Received, Office of Indian Affairs), roll 135: Estimated Expenses, Chickasaw Agency, Smith to T. L. McKenney, Oct. 15, 1826; Letter, Smith to Samuel Hamilton, Oct. 7, 1827; and Deposition, John Gattis to B. F. Smith, Oct. 16, 1828 (the RG 217, Entry 525 documents are abstracted in Atkinson, *Records of the Chickasaw Agency,* Chapter 2). These data, of course, contradict the previous notions espoused by H. B. Cushman, E. T. Winston, and others that the council house at Pontitack was "ancient" and even dated to the De Soto expedition of 1540–1541. Because of incomplete research, the information in the text about the origin of the National Council House is absent from an article about it by Dawson A. Phelps ("The Chickasaw Council House," *Journal of Mississippi History* 14[1952]: 170–176); as a result, he associates some pre-1821 activities to the National Council House. With regard to the Chickasaw named Tookpulca who built the council house kitchen, a statement by Cushman (*History of the Choctaw, Chickasaw, and Natchez Indians,* 428) is significant. Although he cites no source, Cushman relates that the Treaty of Pontotoc Creek in 1832, signed at the National Council House, was held at the house of "Topulkah." The council house and Tookpulca's house were probably in close proximity, or perhaps Tookpulca occupied the council house as its caretaker. The exact location of the National Council House site is shown on the U.S. General Land Office's Chickasaw Cession survey map of Township 10 South, Range 4 East, dated 1833.

3. Gibson, *The Chickasaws,* 106–107; Phelps, "Excerpts from the Journal of the Reverend Joseph Bullen," 263–276; William L. Hiemstra, "Early Presbyterian Missions among the Choctaw and Chickasaw," *Journal of Mississippi History* 10(Jan. 1948): 11; Dawson A. Phelps, "The Chickasaw Mission," *Journal of Mississippi History* 13 (Oct. 1951): 226–235.

4. Phelps, "Excerpts from the Journal of the Reverend Joseph Bullen," 270; Letter, James Colbert the elder to Anthony Hutchins, Nov. 12, 1783, St. Augustine, in McBee, *The Natchez Court Records,* 257–258; Letter, R. J. Meigs to George Colbert, May 2, 1803, in National Archives, RG 75, microfilm M-208 (Records of the Cherokee Indian Agency in Tennessee), roll 2. Meigs stated to George Colbert that his son Pitman was "a fine lad. I should have been glad to have him stay with me some time. . . . You may rely on it that he will be treated with

the greatest Kindness by Our Father the President, and by the Secretary of War. I hope in proper time you will receive him again highly improved by Education, and that he will be a blessing to your family"; Bills of Exchange to Lewis Morin and John Ellicott, 1803–1805, for tuition, etc. for Pitman Colbert and J. Love, in National Archives, RG 217, Entry 374 (Registers of Warrants), vol. 4 (book 5), pp. 47, 242, 245, 260; Receipts, etc., James Corcoran to T. L. McKenney, Expenses for education of Dougherty Colbert, 1826 (several documents), in National Archives, RG 217, 2nd Auditor, Entry 525 (Settled Indian Accounts and Claims), box 47, folder 1059; see also B. F. Smith to T. L. McKenney, Estimated Expenses of the Agency for the year ending Feb. 28, 1827, in National Archives, RG 75, microfilm M-234 (Letters Received, Office of Indian Affairs), roll 135; Bill of Exchange, War Department to James Robertson, 1808, for tuition, etc. for J. Jefferson and James Wolf, in National Archives, RG 217, Entry 366 (Journals of the Accountant for the War Department), vol. 14 (journal P), p. 7765; Bill of Exchange, James Robertson to George Rice & Co., Sept. 6, 1810, for tuition, etc. for two Chickasaw boys, in National Archives, RG 217, Entry 374 (Registers of Warrants), vol. 6 (book 9), p. 40 (RG 217 documents abstracted in Atkinson, *Records of the Chickasaw Agency,* 196, 285, 294–295); Letter, Thomas Wright to Secretary of War, Feb. 18, 1808, in National Archives, RG 107, microfilm M-221 (Letters Received, Secretary of War), roll 15; Thomas L. McKenney, *Memoirs, Official and Personal, with Sketches of Travels Among the Northern and Southern Indians,* vol. 1 (New York: Paine and Burgess, 1846), 158; Letters, Robertson to Secretary of War, May 15 and Oct. 4, 1806, in Robertson, "Correspondence," 5(1900): 179, 183; James Colbert the younger later became the stepson of John McIntosh, Jr., who also may have assisted with his education (Letter, Reverend T. C. Stuart to "Brother," Sept. 7, 1861 [published in E. T. Winston, *"Father" Stuart and the Monroe Mission,* 86]).

5. Atkinson, *History of the Chickasaw Indian Agency,* 17; Receipt, Thomas Love to Robertson, Jan. 20, 1813, in National Archives, RG 217, 5th Auditor, Entry 525 (Additional Settled Indian Accounts and Claims), box 1, acct. 298; Expenses of the Chickasaw Agency, 1812–1814, in National Archives, RG 217, 2nd Auditor, Entry 525 (Settled Indian Accounts and Claims), box 14, folder 352 (abstracted in Atkinson, *Records of the Chickasaw Agency,* 73, 238); the following in National Archives, RG 107, microfilm M-221 (Letters Received, Secretary of War), roll 56: Letter, Robertson to Secretary of War, Jan. 20, 1813; Letter, John L. Allen to Secretary of War, April 26, 1816; and Letter, William Cocke to Secretary of War, July 20, 1816; for additional data on Wigton King, see Martini, "Chickasaw: A History, 1540–1856" (unpublished, 1971, copy at Special Collections, Mitchell Memorial Library, Mississippi State Univ., Starkville), Martini, "Chickasaw Empire," 36–37, and Martini, *Indian Chiefs of the Southeast,* 121.

6. For detailed discussions regarding establishments, operations, problems, and other information about the Charity Hall Mission and others discussed herein, see B. W. McDonald, *History of the Cumberland Presbyterian Church* (Nashville: 1888), 128–134, Gibson, *The Chickasaws,* 109–137, Percy L. Rainwater, "Indian Missions and Missionaries," *Journal of Mississippi History* 28(Feb. 1966): 15–39, and Phelps, "The Chickasaw Mission," 226–235.

7. Gibson, *The Chickasaws,* 108–109.

8. See references in this chapter, Note 6; also Letter, T. C. Stuart to "Brother," June 17, 1861, in Winston, *"Father" Stuart and the Monroe Mission,* 66–69; copies of some documents related to United States payments and assistance to the missions are in the RG 217, Entry 525 records in the National Archives (see abstracts in Atkinson, *Records of the Chickasaw Agency,*

Chapter 2). One of these documents is an undetailed invoice submitted by James Colbert for $72 regarding his "expenses incurred in furnishing provisions [to] the council assembled for the purpose of hearing the Missionaries sent to this nation" (Invoice, Colbert to United States, June 30, 1820, in National Archives, RG 217, 2nd Auditor, Entry 525 [Settled Indian Accounts and Claims], box 17, folder 417); the exact location of the Monroe Mission is depicted (by six structures labeled "Monroe Missionary Station") on the 1833 U.S. General Land Office map of Township 11 South, Range 3 East. The Reverend Stuart's home (and possible original Monroe Church) is shown a little over a mile north of the Mission. The church, however, was more likely at the mission, as suggested by a statement by missionary James Holmes in 1828: "I would remark that he [John Gattis] has been for several months a member in full communion in the Mission Church at Monroe" (Deposition of James Holmes, included on deposition of John Gattis, Oct. 16, 1828, in National Archives, RG 75, microfilm M-234 [Letters Received, Office of Indian Affairs], roll 135); because of confusion by Winston and others, current historic interpretation media in Pontotoc County have the Monroe Mission site located several miles north of both places. Stuart's gravestone in the Pontotoc Cemetery, incidentally, erroneously states that he died in 1883; Martyn Mission, located five miles southwest of present-day Holly Springs on the west side of Pigeon Roost Creek, is shown on an 1834 U.S. Land Office survey plat of the Chickasaw Cession. See Robert M. Winter, *Shadow of a Mighty Rock: A Social and Cultural History of Presbyterianism in Marshall County, Mississippi* (Franklin, Tenn.: Providence House Publishers, 1997), 18, 27–31.

9. Carolyn T. Foreman, "The Choctaw Academy," *Chronicles of Oklahoma* 6(Dec. 1928): 452–480 and 10(March 1932): 76–114; the following in National Archives, RG 217, 2nd Auditor, Entry 525 (Settled Indian Accounts and Claims): Receipt, J. W. Henderson to Benjamin Reynolds, Tuscumbia, Ala., Nov. 13, 1834, box 183, acct. 20642; Letter, Reynolds to Secretary of War Herring, Jan. 9, 1835, box 183, acct. 20642; Receipt, Reynolds to Indian Department, Jan. 6, 1835, box 169, acct. 19840; Receipt, C. T. & A. Barton to Reynolds, June 25, 1835, box 169, acct. 19840; and Documents regarding the Choctaw Academy, box 288, acct. 3362 (all abstracted in Atkinson, *Records of the Chickasaw Agency,* 177–178, 203).

10. Gibson, *The Chickasaws,* 134–135, 170.

11. Letters, B. F. Smith to T. L. McKenney, Dec. 20, 1824, June 4, 1825, June 19, 1825, and Dec. 13, 1825, in National Archives, RG 75, microfilm M-234 (Letters Received, Office of Indian Affairs), roll 135; Article of Agreement and plan drawing, April 6, 1825, Ibid.; the following in National Archives, RG 217, 2nd Auditor, Entry 525 (Settled Indian Accounts and Claims): Receipt, Martin W. Ewing to Smith, April 6, 1825, box 48, folder 1073; Letter, J. L. D. Smith to unnamed person, Florence, Ala., Aug. 28, 1828, box 84, folder 1883; Receipt, John Wallen to Smith, Dec. 30, 1825, box 54, folder 1245; Receipt, John L. Allen to United States, Jan. 18, 1830, box 80, folder 1775; Justification of Expenses, Allen to War Dept., no date, box 80, folder 1775; Reynolds to U.S., Jan. 1, 1831, box 112, folder 2496; Receipt, John A. Caudle to Reynolds, July 26, 1833, box 130, folder 2815; and Receipt, Caudle to Reynolds, Oct. 7, 1833, box 145, folder 3993 (RG 217, Entry 525 documents abstracted in Atkinson, *Records of the Chickasaw Agency,* 126, 130, 153, 162, 170, 172, 191); as mentioned earlier in the text, agent James Robertson's remains were disinterred from the Houlka area agency cemetery after imminent removal of the agency became known. The cemetery probably contains the remains of agent Wright, agent Samuel Mitchell's wife (Molly Folsom Mitchell), weaver Thomas McCoy, and

a number of other people, including several white murder victims killed by other whites, as well as sick travelers who died at the agency or nearby on the Natchez Trace (see Atkinson, *History of the Chickasaw Indian Agency,* 35–36); regarding the Folsom family and death of Molly at the agency, see Conlan, "David Folsom," 340–355.

12. Petition, Ishtehotopa, Tishomingo, Apassantubby, Levi Colbert, Samuel Seeley, and William McGillivray to the President, Sept. 8, 1826, in National Archives, RG 75, microfilm M-234 (Letters Received, Office of Indian Affairs), roll 135; Letter, Smith to McKenney, June 10, 1825, Ibid.; Atkinson, *History of the Chickasaw Indian Agency,* 36, 39.

13. Commissioners' Opening Statement, and Response from Levi Colbert, Emmubbia, Ashtamatutka, John McClish, and Martin Colbert, Journal of the Chickasaw Council, Oct. 16 to Nov. 1, 1826, in *ASP* (Indian Affairs), vol. 2, 1834, pp. 718–720.

14. John D. Terrell's copy of a speech delivered to the Chickasaw by him at the council house on October 11, 1826, Attachment entitled "Remarks of Major Levi Colbert three days before the commencement of the Treaty," in National Archives, RG 75, Entry 1058 (Records of the Chickasaw Agency) (abstracted in Atkinson, *Records of the Chickasaw Agency,* 321–322); Journal of the Chickasaw Council, Oct. 16 to Nov. 1, 1826, in *ASP* (Indian Affairs), vol. 2, 1834, pp. 718–727.

15. Postscript written after the end of treaty negotiations on Letter, John D. Terrell to Commissioners, Oct. 16, 1826, in National Archives, RG 75, Entry 1058 (Records of the Chickasaw Agency); Letter, Terrell to T. L. McKenney, Jan. 6, 1827, Ibid. (abstracted in Atkinson, *Records of the Chickasaw Agency,* 322).

16. Gibson, *The Chickasaws,* 162–167.

17. McKenney, *Memoirs,* 158–166, 324–330; for vouchers and receipts regarding the cash and presents to the Chickasaws see National Archives, RG 217, 2nd Auditor, Entry 525 (Settled Indian Accounts and Claims), box 68, folder 1503 (abstracted in Atkinson, *Records of the Chickasaw Agency,* 142–145).

18. Gibson, *The Chickasaws,* 167–169; the following in National Archives, RG 217, 2nd Auditor, Entry 525 (Settled Indian Accounts and Claims): Letter extract, McKenney to Smith, June 10, 1828, box 68, folder 1503; Accounts, John B. Duncan, 1828, box 70, folder 1555, box 76, folder 1662, and box 80, folders 1773–1774; and Accounts, John Bell, 1828, box 75, folder 1641 (Bell was the assistant "Topographologist" on the expedition); upon McCoy taking over, Duncan was appointed a "disbursing officer" regarding $500 in traveling expenses provided the Chickasaws by McCoy. Detailed accounts of Isaac McCoy are present in National Archives, RG 217, 2nd Auditor, Entry 525 (Settled Indian Accounts and Claims), boxes 70 and 71, folders 1559–1564 (the RG 217, Entry 525 documents are abstracted in Atkinson, *Records of the Chickasaw Agency,* 143, 186, 199–200); besides Levi Colbert, the other members of the exploring party were Ishtematahka, Emmubbee, Immatahishto, Ahtocowah, Ishtayahtubba, Bahkahtubby, Thomas Seeley, Isaac Love, Elapaumba, C. Colbert (probably Charles, a son of Levi), and John McClish (see John F. McDermott, ed., "Isaac McCoy's Second Exploring Trip in 1828," *Kansas Historical Quarterly* 13, no. 7 [Aug. 1945]: 401, 423).

19. Letter, John B. Duncan to Smith, Nov. 22, 1826, in National Archives, RG 217, 2nd Auditor, Entry 525 (Settled Indian Accounts and Claims), box 54, folder 1245; Receipt, John M. Byrn to Smith, Sept. 15, 1826, Ibid.; Receipt, James Benham to Smith, Sept. 27, 1826, Ibid.; Letter, Smith to T. L. McKenney, March 5, 1826, Ibid.; Receipt, J. W. Winston to Smith, June

13, 1829, Ibid., box 77, folder 1688; Receipts, Volunteers to J. L. Allen, Oct. 6, 1830, Ibid., box 116, folder 2576; Invoice/Receipt, Allen to Reynolds, Oct. 12, 1830, Ibid.; Letter, Secretary of War to Reynolds, Sept. 10, 1830, Ibid., box 112, folder 2494; Letter, Reynolds to Allen, Sept. 13, 1830, Ibid.; Letter, Reynolds to Secretary of War, Oct. 12, 1830, Ibid. (abstracted in Atkinson, *Records of the Chickasaw Agency,* 132, 135, 149, 157, 188); an exception to intruder removals only occurring prior to treaty negotiations occurred in 1809, when Cherokee agent R. J. Meigs, under orders from the executive department, reluctantly removed 201 white families from land claimed by the Chickasaw and eighty-three from lands claimed by the Cherokee in present-day north Alabama (Letters, Meigs to James Robertson, April 18 and June 25, 1809, in Robertson, "Correspondence," 5, no. 3[1900]: 260–262, and Letter, Meigs to Acting Secretary of War John Smith, June 12, 1809, in Carter, *Territorial Papers of the United States,* vol. 5, pp. 739–741).

20. Letters, Jackson to William B. Lewis, Aug. 25 and 31, 1830, in Bassett, *Correspondence of Andrew Jackson,* vol. 4 (1929), pp. 176, 178–179; Letter, Jackson to James K. Polk, Aug. 31, 1830, ibid., 179–180; Gibson, *The Chickasaws,* 171–173; Treaty of Franklin, 1830, in Kappler, *Laws and Treaties,* vol. 2, appendix, pp. 1035–1040. Of the twenty Chickasaws who signed the treaty, the most notable were Levi, George, and James Colbert, James Brown, William McGillivray, Isaac Albertson, Topulka, and John McClish. Interestingly, neither King Ishtehotopa nor Tishomingo attended the treaty negotiations. Benjamin Love served as interpreter and witnessed the signing. District chief Samuel Seeley, Sr., son of white trader Benjamin Seeley, had been succeeded by Albertson. Samuel died about four years later on present-day Yocony River (McGee-Draper Narrative, 115).

21. Letter, Reynolds to Commanding Officer of Fort Jesup, "Shawnee Village Red River, near Choctaw Nation," Jan. 25, 1831, in National Archives, RG 217, 2nd Auditor, Entry 525 (Settled Indian Accounts and Claims), box 130, folder 2814; Letter, Chiefs and Warriors of the Chickasaw Nation to General Andrew Jackson, Chickasaw Agency, May 28, 1831, in National Archives, RG 75, Entry 1058 (Records of the Chickasaw Agency) (also in National Archives, RG 75, microfilm M-234 [Letters Received, Office of Indian Affairs], roll 136). RG 217, Entry 525 and RG 75, Entry 1058 documents are abstracted in Atkinson, *Records of the Chickasaw Agency,* 168, 323; Gibson, *The Chickasaws,* 174; the Chickasaw exploring party comprised sixteen individuals, namely Levi Colbert, Eiachetubby, Inwahhoolatubbe, Thomas Seeley, Ishtukiyakatubbe, Ahtokowah, Pitman Colbert, Newberry, James Brown, Ohhacubbe, Ishkittuha, Okelahhacubbe, Elastiukhabtubbe, Shumachah, Kinhoccha, and Henry Love (see Account Statement, 1831, in National Archives, RG 217, 2nd Auditor, Entry 525 [Settled Indian Accounts and Claims], box 112, folder 2495 [abstracted in Atkinson, *Records of the Chickasaw Agency,* 160–161]).

22. Letter, Reynolds to 2nd Auditor, Jan. 2, 1832, in National Archives, RG 217, 2nd Auditor, Entry 525 (Settled Indian Accounts and Claims), box 130, folder 2814; Accounts of John Coffee and John Eaton, 1832 (various receipts with various dates), from Samuel H. Byrne, Hogan & McMahon, Benjamin Reynolds, R. Plevin, James H. Weakley, and G. W. Long, Ibid., box 115, folder 2543 (abstracted in Atkinson, *Records of the Chickasaw Agency,* 168–169, 202–203); Braden, "The Colberts and the Chickasaw Nation," 322–323.

23. Letters, Jackson to John Coffee, Oct. 23, 1831, and Nov. 6, 1832, in Bassett, *Correspon-

dence of Andrew Jackson, vol. 4, pp. 362, 483; Treaty of Pontotoc Creek, 1832, in Kappler, *Laws and Treaties,* vol. 2, pp. 356–364; Gibson, *The Chickasaws,* 175; Message, "Levi Colbert for and in behalf of the whole Chickasaw Nation" to "Gen. John Coffee, U.S. Commissioner, now present, with the Council of the Chickasaw Nation," undated but just prior to Oct. 20, 1832, in National Archives, RG 75, Entry 1058 (Records of the Chickasaw Agency) (abstracted in Atkinson, *Records of the Chickasaw Agency,* 326); among the sixty-three Chickasaw signers of the main treaty and its supplement were King Ishtehotopa, Levi, George, and Pitman Colbert, Tishomingo, John Glover, Isaac Albertson, William McGillivray, Samuel and Thomas Seeley, James Wolf, Topulka, James Brown, Newberry, Emmubbee, and Tomchickah (Tom Chico). Benjamin Love, the U.S. interpreter, was one of the witnesses.

24. Power of Attorney to Chickasaw delegation, from King Ishtehotopa, Levi Colbert, William McGillivray, Isaac Albertson, Dougherty Colbert, Alexander Colbert, William H. Allen, Pistahlaulotubbe, Tom Chico, Ahtokomah, Cochubba, and James Colbert, Nov. 22, 1832, in National Archives, RG 75, microfilm M-234 (Letters Received, Office of Indian Affairs), roll 136; Letter, Jackson to John Coffee, Dec. 14, 1832, in Bassett, *Correspondence of Andrew Jackson,* vol. 4, p. 499; the following in National Archives, RG 75, Entry 1058 (Records of the Chickasaw Agency): Letter, John Coffee to Secretary of War, Washington City, Jan. 21, 1833; Letter, Reynolds to Coffee, Washington City, Jan. 21, 1833; Letter, J. H. Perry to Reynolds, Jan. 21, 1833; Letter, Benjamin Love to Reynolds, Jan. 21, 1833; and Letter, G. W. Long to Reynolds, Jan. 21, 1833; the following in National Archives, RG 217, 2nd Auditor, Entry 525 (Settled Indian Accounts and Claims), box 130, folder 2815: Receipt, Chickasaw chiefs to Reynolds, Washington City, Feb. 7, 1833; Receipt, George Colbert and three other Chickasaws to Reynolds, Feb. 7, 1833; and Receipts, Jesse Brown to Reynolds, Washington City, Feb. 7 and March 7, 1833; Letter, R. C. Nicholas to John C. Calhoun, May 14, 1822, in National Archives, RG 107, microfilm M-221 (Letters Received, Secretary of War), roll 96; the so-called Levi Colbert Memorial, a letter dated Nov. 22, 1832, to President Jackson and signed with marks (except Pitman Colbert) by Levi Colbert, Ishtehotopa, Tishomingo, and fifty-two others, all full-bloods except Levi and Pitman Colbert, is in National Archives, RG 75, microfilm M-234 (Letters Received, Office of Indian Affairs), roll 136 (copy in the Foreman Collection, Gilcrease Museum, Tulsa, Oklahoma). Interestingly, George Colbert was not a signer. Witnesses included Dougherty Colbert, John L. Allen, John A. Bynum, William H. Allen, John D. Terrell, and Alexander Colbert. The letter indeed does not read like one that would have been dictated by Levi Colbert or another Chickasaw, especially the opening and closing paragraphs; the RG 217, Entry 525 and RG 75, Entry 1058 documents cited and others related to the treaty are abstracted in Atkinson, *Records of the Chickasaw Agency,* 169–170, 323–328; as mentioned in discussion of the 1826 negotiations, John D. Terrell had been a special agent at that period assigned to "prepare the minds" of the Chickasaw for removal. His services as a government representative appear to have been abruptly terminated after the failure of the 1826 negotiations, an action that may have influenced him to oppose the treaty. John L. Allen, on the other hand, was still Reynolds's subagent. He had been a resident of the Chickasaw nation for many years (except while serving as postmaster in Paris, Tennessee, in the late 1820s) and was married to a daughter of William Colbert named Margaret (Atkinson, *History of the Chickasaw Indian Agency,* 39–40).

25. Note, Levi Colbert to Coffee, Oct. 18, 1832, in National Archives, RG 75, Entry 1058 (Records of the Chickasaw Agency) (abstracted in Atkinson, *Records of the Chickasaw Agency*, 325).

26. Martini, "Chickasaw Empire," 61, citing Letter, Benjamin Reynolds to Commissioner of Indian Affairs, Elbert Herring, June 2, 1834. Martini relates that a copy of this letter reporting Colbert's death was sent to him by Jane Wegener (Mrs. Dick Wegener) of Wichita Falls, Texas, on Aug. 25, 1967 (see also Don Martini, "Mice in the Wigwam: The Colberts v. [versus] Historians," *Northeast Mississippi Historical Journal* 2[July 1968]: 17); Martini also states that Levi Colbert died at the Carter home near the agency ("Chickasaw Empire," 56–57). However, he cites no source for this information. He apparently assumed that a tract of land shown a mile southeast of the agency and labeled "Carter" on the 1834 land plat for the area was the site of the residence of Colbert's daughter; he also states that a man named James Brown then owned the Buzzard Roost stand where she had lived earlier. Martini's data about the 1834 location of the home of Levi's daughter and her husband, Kilpatrick Carter, may well be correct, but a receipt has since been found that suggests that a man named Henry Cook rather than James Brown operated the mercantile establishment at Buzzard Roost in 1832 (Receipt, Henry Cook to Benjamin Reynolds, "Buzzard Roost Chickasaw Nation," Sept. 10, 1832, in National Archives, RG 217, 2nd Auditor, Entry 525 [Settled Indian Accounts and Claims], box 130, folder 2813). An adult named Thomas S. Carter apparently lived near the agency by 1832 (Account/Receipt, John L. Allen to Benjamin Reynolds, Jan. 31, 1832, in National Archives, RG 217, 2nd Auditor, Entry 525 [Settled Indian Accounts and Claims], box 130, folder 2813); he was probably a nephew of Levi Colbert and an occupant of the aforementioned apparent Carter home near the agency. The apparent home, in fact, may have been his. To confuse matters further, Malcolm McGee informed Lyman Draper in 1841 that Colbert "died near the Buzzard Roost" in 1834 (McGee-Draper Narrative, 113); Levi Colbert reported his sickness and appointment of George Colbert as his replacement in a letter written at the Chickasaw Agency (Letter, Levi Colbert to Andrew Jackson, Chickasaw Agency, March 31, 1834, in National Archives, RG 75, microfilm M-234 [Letters Received, Office of Indian Affairs], roll 136, frames 500–504); the RG 217, Entry 525 documents are abstracted in Atkinson, *Records of the Chickasaw Agency*, 165–166.

27. Chickasaw Treaty of Washington, 1834, in Kappler, *Laws and Treaties*, vol. 2, pp. 418–425. The 1834 Chickasaw delegates were George Colbert, Isaac Albertson, Henry Love, Martin Colbert, and Benjamin Love (also interpreter); Gibson, *The Chickasaws*, 176–178; George Colbert's wife by 1830 was Saleachy Colbert (see reference to her in Expenditures, Chickasaw Agency, Oct. 13, 1830, in National Archives, RG 217, 2nd Auditor, Entry 525 [Settled Indian Accounts and Claims], box 101, folder 2234) (abstracted in Atkinson, *Records of the Chickasaw Agency*, 156).

28. Gibson, *The Chickasaws*, 178; Braden, "The Colberts and the Chickasaw Nation," 327; Receipt, Reynolds to the U.S., March 21, 1834, in National Archives, RG 217, 2nd Auditor, Entry 525 (Settled Indian Accounts and Claims), box 145, folder 3994; the following in National Archives, RG 217, 2nd Auditor, Entry 525 (Settled Indian Accounts and Claims), box 236, folder 1606: Letter, Reynolds to William L. Henderson, Pontotoc, Oct. 17, 1835; Letter, Reynolds to Commissioner of Indian Affairs, Dec. 19, 1835; and Letter abstract, Commissioner of Indian Affairs to Reynolds, Oct. 29, 1836; Power of Attorney (Exhibit C), 16 Chicka-

saw leaders to Perry, McClish, Colbert, Brown, and Albertson, Pontotoc, Nov. 12, 1836, copy in National Archives, Records of the U.S. Court of Claims, 1855–1939 (RG 123), Entry 1, Court of Claims file for Case K-334, The Chickasaw Nation vs. the United States (1929–1945), and Letter (Exhibit D), Nine Chickasaw leaders to Perry, McClish, Colbert, Brown, and Albertson, Pontotoc, Nov. 12, 1836, copy in National Archives, RG 123, Entry 1 (Court of Claims file for Case K-334). George Colbert's name heads the signatories of both documents. The Exhibit C document states in part that the five men were to proceed west of the Mississippi River "to apply to our ancient Friends and brothers, the Chiefs, Head men and Warriors of the Choctaw Nation, for a tract of Country as the future Home and residence of the Indians of the Chickasaw Nation, to be held in Fee Simple forever or in Such other way as they may deem most expedient." It further states that if they should fail to secure a "Resting Place" from the Choctaw then they are authorized to secure another suitable home in any other part of the country west of the Mississippi River; the RG 217 and RG 123 documents are abstracted in Atkinson, *Records of the Chickasaw Agency,* 175, 179–180, 334–335.

29. Expenditures, Chickasaw Agency, Oct. 1, 1834, to Sept. 30, 1835, in National Archives, RG 217, 2nd Auditor, Entry 525 (Settled Indian Accounts and Claims), box 183, acct. 20642; Benjamin Reynolds's account examination by the Office of Indian Affairs, April 1838, Ibid., box 236, folder 1606; Expenditures of Benjamin Reynolds, Jan. 25, 1837, Ibid.; Letter, David Hubbard to C. A. Harris, Commissioner of Indian Affairs, Aug. 2, 1838, in National Archives, RG 75, microfilm M-234 (Letters Received, Office of Indian Affairs), roll 137; Receipt, T. C. McMackin to Reynolds, June 15, 1836, in National Archives, RG 75, Entry 1058 (Records of the Chickasaw Agency); Atkinson, *History of the Chickasaw Indian Agency,* 44–45; the RG 217, Entry 525 and RG 75, Entry 1058 documents cited and others related to Reynolds's work are abstracted in Atkinson, *Records of the Chickasaw Agency,* 180–185, 331.

30. Journal of Edward Fontaine, entry for Nov. 23, 1836, Edward Fontaine Papers, 1809–1979, folder 1 (reel 1), Special Collections, Mitchell Memorial Library, Mississippi State University, Starkville.

31. Reynolds's Account Examination, April 1838, in National Archives, RG 217, 2nd Auditor, Entry 525 (Settled Indian Accounts and Claims), box 236, folder 1606; Expenditures, Jan. 25, 1837, Ibid.; Letter extract, Commissioner of Indian Affairs to Reynolds, Aug. 19, 1835, Ibid., box 169, acct. 19840; Expenditures, April 9, 1839, Ibid., box 343, acct. 5166 (abstracted in Atkinson, *Records of the Chickasaw Agency,* 180–185); Edward E. Hill, "The Chickasaw Agency," in *The Office of Indian Affairs, 1824–1880: Historical Sketches* (New York: Clearwater Publishing, 1974), 40–41; by 1833 subagent Allen lived very near the Natchez Trace and about three and one half miles west of the National Council House, as depicted on the Township 10 South, Range 3 East plat map. His home, labeled "Sub-Agents J. L. Allen," may have been where he had lived prior to his government employment (Atkinson, *History of the Chickasaw Indian Agency,* 45).

32. For a detailed study of the liquidation of the Chickasaw land, see Mary E. Young, *Redskins, Ruffleshirts, and Rednecks: Indian Allotments in Alabama and Mississippi, 1830–1860* (Norman: Univ. of Oklahoma Press, 1961); Gibson, *The Chickasaws,* 179–215; Foreman, *The Five Civilized Tribes* (Norman: Univ. of Oklahoma Press, 1934), 101–107; Letter, Benjamin Love to Daniel Saffaron, Holly Springs, Miss., Oct. 22, 1841, in National Archives, RG 75, Entry 1058 (Records of the Chickasaw Agency) (abstracted in Atkinson, *Records of the*

Chickasaw Agency, 331); for one of the better descriptive observations of the Chickasaw Trail of Tears, see John E. Parsons, ed., "Letters on the Chickasaw Removal of 1837," *New York Historical Society Quarterly* 37(1953): 273–283; George Colbert died in the new nation west of the river on November 7, 1839, and Tishomingo on May 5, 1841. Ishtehotopa died there in late 1838 or early 1839, James Colbert in May 1842, William McGillivray in 1844, and Isaac Albertson in 1850 (Martini, *Indian Chiefs of the Southeast*, 97–99, 105–106); for detailed discussions of the actual removal to west of the Mississippi, see Gibson, "Chickasaw Trail of Tears," Chapter 8 in *The Chickasaws*, and Braden, "The Colberts and the Chickasaw Nation," 327–331; for a few of the letters, from both Chickasaws and whites, complaining about the speculators' abuses of the allotment sales and other abuses, see National Archives, RG 75, Entry 1058 (Records of the Chickasaw Agency) (abstracted in Atkinson, *Records of the Chickasaw Agency*, 329–331); regarding the Allens's settlement of Colbert, Mississippi (now extinct), see Jack D. Elliott, Jr., *A Cultural Resources Survey of Selected Construction Areas*, 49–54. Also Stephen McBride, Jan [*sic*, Kim] McBride, and Jack D. Elliott, Jr., "John L. Allen and Margaret," in *History of Clay County, Mississippi* (Curtis Media, 1988), 294. Regarding Martin Colbert's settlement in present-day De Soto County, Mississippi, see Martini, *Indian Chiefs of the Southeast*, 100–101.

Bibliography

UNPUBLISHED ORIGINAL SOURCES

Allen, James. Deposition, April 16, 1819. Monroe County, Mississippi, Deed Book 1, pp. 112–121, Courthouse, Aberdeen, Miss.

Archaeological site files. Office of Historic Preservation, Mississippi Department of Archives and History, Jackson.

Archivo General de Indias. Seville, Papeles Procedentes de Cuba.

Atkin, Edmond. "Historical Account of the Revolt of the Choctaw Indians in the late War from the French to the British Alliance and of their Return Since to that of the French," Jan. 20, 1753. British Library, Lansdowne Manuscript 809. Microfilm at Mississippi Department of Archives and History, Jackson.

Atkinson, James R. Letter to Patricia Galloway, Feb. 21, 1985. Copy in Atkinson Collection, Special Collections, Mitchell Memorial Library, Mississippi State University, Starkville.

"Audience of the Chickesaws at Savannah in Georgia July 1736 [with] James Oglethorpe Esqr.," July 13, 1736. Typed transcript copy of a manuscript. William R. Coe Papers, South Carolina Historical Society, Charleston.

Chickasaw County, Mississippi, Tax Assessment. 1840. Microfilm. Mississippi Department of Archives and History, Jackson.

Colonial Office Records. Series 5. British Public Records Office, Kew, England.

Deagan, Kathy A. Letter to Richard A. Marshall, March 22, 1990. Cobb Institute of Archaeology, Mississippi State University, Starkville. Original in possession of Richard A. Marshall.

Draper, Lyman C. Collection. 486 vols. in 50 series, 123 microfilm reels. Original papers and microfilm in Wisconsin Historical Society, Madison.

———. Interview with Malcolm McGee, 1841 (McGee-Draper Narrative). In Lyman C. Draper Collection, vol. 10, series U, pp. 108–128 (microfilm). Original papers and microfilm in Wisconsin Historical Society, Madison.

Fontaine, Edward. Journal, 1836. Fontaine Papers, 1809–1979. Original papers and microfilm in Special Collections, Mitchell Memorial Library, Mississippi State University, Starkville.

Haywood, John. Papers. Tennessee State Library and Archives, Nashville. Accession Number THS 448.

Henley, David. Papers, 1791–1800. Rare Book, Manuscript, and Special Collection Library, Duke University, Durham, North Carolina.

Jackson, Andrew. Papers. Library of Congress. Microfilm Series 1–3 (63 rolls).

McGee-Draper Narrative. See Draper, Lyman C.

McKee, John. Diary, 1804–1805. Original in Southern Historical Collection, University of North Carolina Library, Chapel Hill. Microfilm copy at Mississippi Department of Archives and History, Jackson.

———. Papers. Manuscript Division, Library of Congress.

Natchez Trace Parkway Headquarters transcripts. Historical Files. Tupelo, Miss.

Papers of the Mississippi Territorial Governors. Record Group 2. Mississippi Department of Archives and History, Jackson.

Piomingo's talk to Joseph Martin, September 20, 1789. In Edward E. Ayer Collection, No. 722, Newberry Library, Chicago.

Sargent, Winthrop. Papers. Library of Congress. Microfilm.

Stewart, Mrs. M. J. Stuart. Letter to Lyman C. Draper, November 6, 1882. In Lyman C. Draper Collection, vol. 10, series U (microfilm). Original papers and microfilm in Wisconsin Historical Society, Madison.

The Tennessee Papers (Papers of William and Joseph Martin). Letters from Piomingo et al., 1790 or 1791. In Lyman C. Draper Collection, vol. 5, series XX, pp. 27–28 (microfilm). Original papers and microfilm in Wisconsin Historical Society, Madison.

———. Letter, Chickasaw chiefs to U.S. Commanders, July 9, 1782. In Lyman C. Draper Collection, vol. 1, series XX, pp. 50+ (microfilm). Original papers and microfilm in Wisconsin Historical Society, Madison.

———. Treaty of French Lick, 1783. In Lyman C. Draper Collection, vol. 1, series XX, pp. 65+ (microfilm). Original papers and microfilm in Wisconsin Historical Society, Madison.

United States Census Records, Chickasaw County, Mississippi. 1840. Microfilm.

Wales, Henoc. Declaration, April 9, 1783. Archivo General de Indias. Seville, Papeles Procedentes de Cuba, legajo 196.

Walton, J. N. Letters to Lyman C. Draper, June 25, 1882, and October 2, 1882. In Lyman C. Draper Collection, vol. 10, series U, pp. 140+ (microfilm). Original papers and microfilm in Wisconsin Historical Society, Madison.

National Archives Government Records

Papers of the Continental Congress, 1774–1789. Microfilm M-247.

Records of the Accounting Officers of the Department of the Treasury, Record Group 217. 2nd Auditor. Entry 366, Journals of the Accountant for the War Department, 1792–1817. 22 vols.

———. 2nd Auditor. Entry 374, Registers of Warrants, War Department Accountant, 1795–1821. 11 vols.

———. 2nd Auditor. Entry 495, Letters Sent by David Henley, Agent for the War Department. Letterbook. 1 vol.

————. 2nd Auditor. Entry 525, Settled Indian Accounts and Claims, 1794–1894 (numerous folders).

————. 2nd Auditor. Entry 525A, Settled Indian Accounts and Claims, Unnumbered Accounts, 1796–1811. Microfilm (3 rolls).

————. 5th Auditor. Entry 525, Additional Settled Indian Accounts and Claims, 1817–1851 (numerous folders).

Records of the Bureau of Indian Affairs, Record Group 75. Microfilm M-15, Letters Sent by the Secretary of War Relating to Indian Affairs, 1800–1824 (6 rolls).

————. Microfilm M-208, Records of the Cherokee Indian Agency in Tennessee, 1801–1835 (14 rolls).

————. Microfilm T-494, Documents Relating to the Negotiations of Ratified and Unratified Treaties with Various Indian Tribes, 1801–1869 (10 rolls).

————. Microfilm T-500, Records of the Choctaw Trading House, 1803–1824 (6 rolls).

————. Entry 1058, Records of the Chickasaw Agency, 1806–1841 (1 folder).

————. Microfilm M-234, Letters Received by the Office of Indian Affairs, 1824–1881 (962 rolls).

Records of the Office of Secretary of War, Record Group 107. Microfilm M-22, Register of Letters Received by the Office of the Secretary of War, Main Series, 1800–1870 (134 rolls).

————. Microfilm M-221, Letters Received by the Secretary of War, Registered Series, 1801–1870 (317 rolls).

————. Microfilm M-1062, Correspondence of the War Department relating to Indian Affairs (1 roll).

Records of the U.S. Court of Claims, 1855–1939, Record Group 123. Entry 1. Court of Claims file for Case K-334, The Chickasaw Nation vs. the United States (1929–1945).

PUBLISHED ORIGINAL SOURCES

Adair, James. *History of the American Indians.* Reprint of 1775 edition. Samuel Cole Williams, ed. Johnson City, Tenn.: Watauga Press, 1930.

Alvord, Clarence, ed. *Kaskaskia Records, 1778–1790.* Collections of the Illinois State Historical Library, vol. 5, Virginia Series, vol. 2. Springfield: Illinois State Historical Library, 1909.

Alvord, Clarence W., and Clarence E. Carter, eds. *The New Regime, 1765–1767.* Collections of the Illinois Historical Society, vol. 11. Springfield: Illinois State Historical Library, 1916.

American State Papers. Foreign Relations, vol. 1, 1833.

————. Indian Affairs, vol. 1, 1832.

————. Indian Affairs, vol. 2, 1834.

————. Miscellaneous, vol. 2, 1834.

Anonymous, "Journal of the Chickasa War." In J. F. H. Claiborne, *Mississippi as a Province, Territory and State,* 64–85. Jackson: Power and Barksdale, 1880. Also published in New York, 1859, as *Journal de la Guerre du Micissippi contre les Chickachas en 1739 et finie en 1740 le 1er d'Avril par un Officier de l'Armee de M. de Nouaille.*

Atkinson, James R. *Records of the Old Southwest in the National Archives: Abstracts of Records of the Chickasaw Indian Agency and Related Documents, 1794–1840.* Mississippi State University, Starkville, and Ada, Okla.: Cobb Institute of Archaeology and Chickasaw Nation, 1997. Copies of most of the documents are on deposit at Natchez Trace Parkway Headquarters, Tupelo, Miss., The Chickasaw Nation Headquarters in Ada, Okla., and the Special Collections division at Mitchell Memorial Library, Mississippi State University, Starkville.

Bailey, Francis. *Journal of a Tour in the Unsettled Parts of North American in 1796 & 1797.* London: Baily Brothers, 1856.

Bassett, John Spencer. *Correspondence of Andrew Jackson,* vols. 1, 2, 4. Washington, D.C.: Carnegie Institution of Washington, 1926–1927 and 1929.

Blount, Willie. Letter in *The Democratic Clarion and the Tennessee Gazette* (Nashville newspaper), March 16, 1810.

Bonnefoy's Narrative. In Samuel C. Williams, *Early Travels in the Tennessee Country, 1540–1800,* 160–162. Johnson City, Tenn.: Watauga Press, 1928.

Bossu, Jean-Bernard. *Travels in the Interior of North America, 1751–1762.* Seymour Feiler, trans. and ed. Norman: University of Oklahoma Press, 1962.

Bourne, Edward G., ed. *Narratives of the Career of Hernando De Soto,* vol. 1. New York: Allerton, 1904.

Brown, Samuel R. *The Western Gazateer or Emigrants Directory.* Auburn, N.Y., 1817.

Bullen, Joseph. "Extract from the Rev. Mr. Bullen's Journal." *New York Missionary Magazine* 1(1800).

Butler, Ruth E., R. B. Truett, and O. T. Hagen. "A Calendar of Letters in the Letterbooks of the Postmaster General Pertaining to the Opening and Use of the Natchez Trace as a Mail Route." ca. 1935. Typed manuscript at Natchez Trace Parkway Headquarters Library, Tupelo, Miss.

Calloway, Colin G., and Alden T. Vaughan, eds. *Revolution and Confederation.* Bethesda, Md.: University Publications of America, 1994.

Candler, Allen D., comp. *Colonial Records of the State of Georgia* (CRG). Vols. 1–26 (1904–1916), New York: AMS Press, 1970 (reprinted); vols. 27–29 (Kenneth Coleman and Milton Ready, eds.), Athens: University of Georgia Press, 1975–1976, 1979, 1985; vols. 30–32 (Kenneth Coleman, ed.), 1985–1989.

Carr, John. *Early Times in Middle Tennessee.* Nashville: Parthenon Press, 1958, originally published in 1857.

Carter, Clarence E., comp. and ed. *The Territorial Papers of the United States.* Vol. 3, *The Territory Northwest of the River Ohio, 1787–1803.* Washington, D.C.: Government Printing Office, 1934.

———. *The Territorial Papers of the United States.* Vol. 4, *The Territory South of the River Ohio, 1790–1796.* Washington, D.C.: Government Printing Office, 1936.

———. *The Territorial Papers of the United States.* Vol. 5, *The Territory of Mississippi, 1798–1817.* Washington, D.C.: Government Printing Office, 1937.

Caughey, John W. *McGillivray of the Creeks.* Norman: University of Oklahoma Press, 1938.

Clark, Walter, coll. and ed. *The State Records of North Carolina.* Vols. 17 (1899) and 18 (1900). Goldsboro, N.C.: Nash Brothers.

Clayton, L. A., V. J. Knight, Jr., and E. C. Moore, eds. *The De Soto Chronicles.* 2 vols. Tuscaloosa: University of Alabama Press, 1993.

Collot, Victor. *Voyage in North America.* 2 vols., with separate atlas. J. Christian Bay edition. Florence, Italy: O. Lange, 1924, originally published in French and in English in Paris, 1826.

Colonial Records of the State of Georgia (CRG). See Candler, Allen D., comp.

Cooper, Thomas, and David J. McCord, eds. *The Statutes at Large of South Carolina,* vol. 2. Columbia, 1837.

Corbitt, D. C., trans. and ed. "Papers Relating to the Georgia-Florida Frontier, 1784–1800." *Georgia Historical Quarterly* 23, no. 2(June 1939): 189–202.

———. "Some Papers Relating to Bourbon County, Georgia." *Georgia Historical Quarterly* 19, no. 3(September 1935): 251–263.

Corbitt, D. C., and Roberta Corbitt. "Papers from the Spanish Archives Relating to Tennessee." *East Tennessee Historical Society's Publications* 9–49(1937–1977).

Cuming, Fortesque. "Cuming's Tour to the Western Country (1807–1809)." In Reuben G. Thwaites, *Early Western Travels, 1748–1846,* vol. 4. New York: AMS Press, 1966, reprint.

Davies, K. G., ed. *Documents of the American Revolution, 1770–1783.* 21 vols. Dublin, Ireland: Irish University Press, 1972–1981.

de Lery, Gaspard-Joseph Chaussegros, Jr. "Journal De La Campagne Faite Par Le Detachement Du Canada Sur Les Chicachas En Fevrier 1740 Au Nombre De 201 Francais, Et 337 Sauvages De Canada, Illinois, Missouris Et 58 Chactas Faisant En Tout 596 Hommes." *Rapport de L'Archiviste de la Province de Quebec pour 1922–1923.* Quebec: Ls-A Proulx, Imprimeur De Sa Majeste Le Roi, 1923. Anonymous translation at Natchez Trace Parkway, Tupelo, Miss.

Documents Relating to Indian Affairs (DRIA). See McDowell, William L., Jr., ed.

Dunn, Caroline, and Eleanor Dunn, trans. "Indiana's First War" ("Account of the Battle Fought by D'Artaguette with the Chickasaws, March 25, 1736"). *Indiana Historical Society Publications* 8(1924): 106–127. In both French and English.

Easterby, J. H., ed. *Journal of the Commons House of Assembly, 1736–1757 (JCHA),* vols. 1–9 (1951–1962). Colonial Records of South Carolina. Columbia: Historical Commission of South Carolina.

Fitzpatrick, John C., ed. *The Writings of George Washington,* vol. 33. Washington, D.C.: Government Printing Office, 1940.

Galloway, Patricia K., Dunbar Rowland, and A. G. Sanders, trans. and eds. *Mississippi Provincial Archives: French Dominion,* vols. 4–5. Baton Rouge: Louisiana State University Press, 1984.

Gayoso, de Lemos. "Diary of Gayoso de Lemos' Expedition on *La Vigilante.*" In Abraham P. Nasatir, *Spanish War Vessels on the Mississippi, 1792–1796,* 253–276. New Haven, Conn.: Yale University Press, 1968.

Gordon, John. Memorial. In "Pioneer Documents." *American Historical Magazine* 2, no. 4(October 1897): 351–353.

Grant, C. L., ed. *Letters, Journals and Writings of Benjamin Hawkins,* vol. 1 (1796–1801). Savannah, Ga.: Beehive Press, 1980.

Guion, Isaac. "Letters of Capt. Isaac Guion." In *Seventh Annual Report of the Director of the Department of Archives and History of the State of Mississippi from October 1, 1907 to October 1, 1908* (Dunbar Rowland, director), Appendix, pp. 25–113. Nashville: Press of Brandon Printing, 1909.

Hall, James. "A Brief History of the Mississippi Territory." *Publications of the Mississippi Historical Society* 9(1906): 540–575. Reprint of short book originally published in 1801.

Hathorn, Stacye, and Robin Sabino. "Views and Vistas: Traveling through the Choctaw, Chickasaw, and Cherokee Nations in 1803." *Alabama Review* 54, no. 3(2001): 208–220.

Hawkins, Benjamin. *Letters of Benjamin Hawkins*. Collections of the Georgia Historical Society, vol. 3, pt. 1 (1848). Reprinted, Spartanburg, S.C.: Reprint Company, 1982.

———. *A Sketch of the Creek Country, in the Years 1798 and 1799*. Collections of the Georgia Historical Society, vol. 3, pt. 1 (1848). Reprinted, Spartanburg, S.C.: Reprint Company, 1982.

Higginbotham, P. J., ed. *The Journal of Sauvole*. Mobile: Colonial Books, 1969.

Houck, Louis, ed. *The Spanish Regime in Missouri*. 2 vols. Chicago: Donnelley, 1909.

Jackson, Andrew. "Valuable Letters of Andrew Jackson." *American Historical Magazine* 4, no. 2(April 1899): 99–102.

Jacobs, Wilbur R. *Indians of the Southern Colonial Frontier: The Edmond Atkin Report and Plan of 1755*. Columbia: University of South Carolina Press, 1954.

James, James A., ed. *George Rogers Clark Papers*. Collections of the Illinois Historical Library, vol. 8, Virginia Series, vol. 3 (1771–1781) (1912), and vol. 19, Virginia Series, vol. 4 (1781–1784) (1926). Springfield: Illinois State Historical Library.

Jennings, Jesse D., ed. "Nutt's Trip to the Chickasaw Country." *Journal of Mississippi History* 9, no. 1(1947): 34–61.

Journal of the Commons House of Assembly, 1736–1757 (*JCHA*). Vols. 1–3 and 4–9, see Easterby, ed.; vol. 10, see Olsberg, ed.; vol. 11, see Lipscomb and Olsberg, eds.; vols 12–14, see Lipscomb, ed.

Journals of the Commissioners of the Indian Trade, September 20, 1710–August 29, 1718 (*JCIT*). See McDowell, William L., Jr., ed.

Kappler, Charles J., compiler, annotator, and ed. *Indian Affairs: Laws and Treaties*, vols. 2 (1904) and 5 (1941). Washington, D.C.: Government Printing Office.

Kinnaird, Lawrence. "Spain in the Mississippi Valley." *Annual Report of the American Historical Association for the Year 1945*, vol. 2, pt. 1 (1949); vol. 3, pt. 2 (1946); and vol. 4, pt. 3 (1946). Washington, D.C.: Government Printing Office.

Knopf, Richard C., transcriber and ed. *Anthony Wayne: A Name in Arms—The Wayne-Knox-Pickering-McHenry Correspondence*. Pittsburgh: University of Pittsburgh Press, 1960.

Labadia, Silvestre. Declaration, July 5, 1782. In Lawrence Kinnaird, "Spain in the Mississippi Valley," *Annual Report of the American Historical Association for the Year 1945*, vol. 3, pt. 2 (1946), pp. 21–34. Washington, D.C.: Government Printing Office.

Le Page du Pratz. *History of Louisiana. . . .* Baton Rouge: Claitor's Publishing Division, 1972, reprint of 1773 edition.

Lincecum, Gideon. "Autobiography of Gideon Lincecum." *Publications of the Mississippi Historical Society* 8 (1904): 443–519.

———. "Personal Reminiscences of an Octogenarian." *American Sportsman,* October 24, 1874.

Lipscomb, Terry, ed. *Journal of the Commons House of Assembly, 1736–1757 (JCHA),* vols. 12–14. Colonial Records of South Carolina. Columbia: University of South Carolina Press, 1983, 1986, 1989.

Lipscomb, Terry, and R. Nicholas Olsberg, eds. *Journal of the Commons House of Assembly, 1736–1757 (JCHA),* vol. 11. Colonial Records of South Carolina. Columbia: University of South Carolina Press, 1977.

McBee, May Wilson. *The Natchez Court Records, 1767–1805: Abstracts of Early Records.* Baltimore: Genealogical Publishing, 1979.

McDermott, John F., ed. "Isaac McCoy's Second Exploring Trip in 1828." *Kansas Historical Quarterly* 13, no. 7(August 1945): 400–462.

McDowell, William L., Jr., ed. *Documents Relating to Indian Affairs (DRIA),* vols. 2 and 3 (1750–1765). Colonial Records of South Carolina, South Carolina Archives Department. Columbia: University of South Carolina Press, 1958.

———. *Journals of the Commissioners of the Indian Trade, September 20, 1710–August 29, 1718 (JCIT),* vol. 1. Colonial Records of South Carolina. Columbia: University Press of South Carolina, 1955.

McIlwaine, H. R., gen. ed. *Official Letters of the Governors of the State of Virginia.* Vol. 2 (1928), *The Letters of Thomas Jefferson.* Vol. 3 (1929), *The Letters of Thomas Nelson and Benjamin Harrison.* Richmond: Virginia State Library.

McKenney, Thomas L. *Memoirs, Official and Personal, with Sketches of Travels among the Northern and Southern Indians,* vol. 1. New York: Paine and Burgess, 1846.

McWilliams, Richebourg G., trans. and ed. *Iberville's Gulf Journals.* Tuscaloosa: University of Alabama Press, 1981.

Milfort, General Louis. *Memoirs or a quick Glance at my various Travels and my Sojurn in the Creek Nation.* B. C. McCary, ed. Kennesaw, Ga.: Continental, 1959, originally published in 1802.

Moore, Alexander, ed. *Nairne's Muskhogean Journals: The 1708 Expedition to the Mississippi River.* Jackson: University Press of Mississippi, 1988.

Moser, H. D., D. R. Hoth, and G. H. Hoemann, eds. *The Papers of Andrew Jackson.* 4 vols. Knoxville: University of Tennessee Press, 1994.

Olsberg, R. Nicholas, ed. *Journal of the Commons House of Assembly, 1736–1757 (JCHA),* vol. 10. Colonial Records of South Carolina. Columbia: University of South Carolina Press, 1974.

O'Neill, Charles E., ed. *Charlevoix's Louisiana: Selections from the History and the Journal.* Baton Rouge: Louisiana State University Press, 1977.

Padgett, James A., ed. "Letters from John Rhea to Thomas Jefferson and James Madison." *East Tennessee Historical Society's Publications* 10(1938): 114–125.

———. "Minutes of the Council of West Florida" (April–July 1769). *Louisiana Historical Quarterly* 23, no. 2(April 1940): 353–404.

———. "Minutes of the West Florida Assembly" (August 1768–June 1769). *Louisiana Historical Quarterly* 23, no. 1(January 1940): 5–77.

Palmer, William P., ed. and arranger. *Calendar of Virginia State Papers and Other Manuscripts*, vols. 1 (1875), 3 (1883), 4 (1884), and 5 (Palmer and Sherwin McRae, editors) (1885). Richmond: Virginia State Library. Vols. 3, 4, and 5 reprinted by Kraus Reprint Corporation, New York, 1968.

Parsons, John E., ed. "Letters on the Chickasaw Removal of 1837." *New York Historical Society Quarterly* 37(1953): 273–283.

Phelps, Dawson A. "Excerpts from the Journal of the Reverend Joseph Bullen, 1799 and 1800." *Journal of Mississippi History* 17(January–October, 1955): 254–281.

Richardville's Account of d'Artaguette's Attack. Archives des Colonies, series C13C, vol. 4, ff. 202–205. Copy at Mississippi Department of Archives and History translated for the author by Patricia K. Galloway.

Robertson, James. "Correspondence of General James Robertson." *American Historical Magazine* 1, nos. 1–4 (1896); 2, nos. 1–4 (1897); 3, nos. 1, 3–4 (1898); 4, nos. 1–4 (1899); and 5, nos. 1–3 (1900).

Romans, Bernard. *A Concise Natural History of East and West Florida.* Kathryn E. H. Braund, ed. Tuscaloosa: University of Alabama Press, 1999, reprint of 1775 edition.

Rowland, Dunbar, ed. *Mississippi Provincial Archives, 1763–1766: English Dominion.* Nashville: Press of Brandon Printing, 1911.

———. *Official Letter Books of W. C. C. Claiborne, 1801–1816*, vol. 1. Jackson: Mississippi Department of Archives and History, 1917.

Rowland, Dunbar, and Albert G. Sanders, trans. and eds. *Mississippi Provincial Archives: French Dominion*, vols. 1–3. Jackson: Department of Archives and History Press, 1927, 1929, 1932.

Rowland, Eron O. "Peter Chester." *Publications of the Mississippi Historical Society*, Centenary Series (Dunbar Rowland, ed.) 5(1925): 1–183.

Royce, Charles C., comp. "Indian Land Cessions of the United States." *Bureau of American Ethnology, Eighteenth Annual Report*, pt. 2. Washington, D.C.: Government Printing Office, 1899.

Serrano y Sanz, Manuel. *Espana y los Indios Cherokis y Chactas en la segunda mitad del Siglio XVIII.* Seville: Tio. de la Guia Oficial, 1916.

Smyth, John F. D. *A Tour in the United States of America.* 2 vols. New York: Arno, 1968, originally published in 1784.

Storm, Colton, ed. "Up the Tennessee in 1790: The Report of Major John Doughty to the Secretary of War." *East Tennessee Historical Society's Publications* 17(1945): 119–132. The original report is in the Josiah Harmar Papers, Clements Library, University of Michigan, Ann Arbor.

Tait, David. Journal. Appendix A in K. G. Davies, ed., *Documents of the American Revolution, 1770–1783*, vol. 5. Dublin: Irish University Press, 1974.

Thwaites, R. G., ed. *The Jesuit Relations and Allied Documents*, vol. 69 (of 73). Cleveland: Burrows Brothers, 1896–1901.

Villiers du Terrage, Baron Marc de. "Documents concernant l'histoire des Indiens de la Region orientale de la Louisiane." *Journal de Societe des Americanistes de Paris* 14(1922): 127–140.

Wailes, B. L. C. "Transformation of Names." *American Historical Magazine* 3(1859).

West, Elizabeth H., trans. and ed. "Diary of Jose Bernardo Gutierrez de Lara, 1811–1812." *American Historical Review* 34, no. 1(October 1928): 55–77.

Winston, E. T. *"Father" Stuart and the Monroe Mission.* Meridian, Miss.: Press of Tell Farmer, 1927.

NEWSPAPERS

Democratic Clarion and The Tennessee Gazette, March 16, 1810.

Kentucky Gazette, Jan. 16, 1790.

Pennsylvania Packet, Sept. 30, 1785.

PUBLISHED AND UNPUBLISHED MAPS

Anonymous. "Plan Figure des Villages Chikachas Attaquez Par les Francois le vingt six May 1736." Original in *Ministere de la France D'Outremer, Depot des Plans et Fortifications.* Archives Nationales, Paris (published in *The American Heritage History of the Thirteen Colonies,* American Heritage Publishing, New York, 1967, p. 222).

Bonar, William. "A Draught of the Creek Nation." May 1757. Original in British Public Record Office, London, CO700/Carolina 21.

Broutin, Ignace Francois. "Carte Particuliere [des] Routtes faite du fort de l'Assumption au Chicachachats (pour) chercher un chemin Praticable pour les charoues en 1740." Dated March 10, 1740. Original in Bibliotheque du Service Historique de la Marine, Vincennes, France (published in Joseph L. Peyser, "1740 French Map Pinpoints Battle Site in Mississippi," *Mapline* 39(September 1985): 2–4).

———. "Plan a l'estimate ou. Scituation de Trois villages Chicachas 1736." Original in Archives Nationales, Paris, France. Copy at Natchez Trace Parkway Headquarters.

Collot, Victor. "Chart of the Sources of the Mobile (and) of the River Yazoo Including a part of the Course of the Mississippi From the River Margot to the Natches," ca. 1796. In atlas published in association with Collot's *Voyage Dans L'Amerique Septentrionale,* 3 vols. Paris: Arthus Bertrand, Libraire, 1826 (published in John R. Swanton, "Early History of the Creek Indians and Their Neighbors," *Bureau of American Ethnology Bulletin 73,* Washington, D.C.: Smithsonian Institution, 1922).

———. "Plan of Fort Des Ecores at Margot," ca. 1796. In atlas published in association with Collot's *Voyage Dans L'Amerique Septentrionale,* 3 vols. Paris: Arthus Bertrand, Libraire, 1826 (published in Samuel Cole Williams, *Beginnings of West Tennessee in the Land of the Chickasaws, 1541–1841,* Johnson City, Tenn.: Watauga Press, 1930).

Coronelli, Vicenzo Maria. Map of the Mississippi Valley, A.D. 1684. In Beinecke Rare Book Room (map collection), Code no. 807+1683, Yale University Library, New Haven, Conn.

de Batz, Alexander. "Plan et Scituation Des Villages Tchikachas, September 7, 1737." Original in Archives Nationales, Paris, France (most recently published in Gregory A. Waselkov, "Indian Maps of the Colonial Southeast," in Peter H. Wood, G. A. Waselkov, and

M. Thomas Hatley, eds., *Powhatan's Mantle*, 292–343, Lincoln: University of Nebraska Press, 1989).

De Crenay, Baron. Untitled map, 1733. Original in Archives Nationales, Paris (published in John R. Swanton, "Early History of the Creek Indians and Their Neighbors," *Bureau of American Ethnology Bulletin 73*, Washington, D.C.: Smithsonian Institution, 1922).

de Marigny. Untitled map, 1743. Depicts the lower Mississippi, Tombigbee, and Alabama Rivers and surrounding areas and Indian groups thereon. Copy at Natchez Trace Parkway; a copy of a fragmented very similar but not identical map lacking the maker's name and date is at Natchez Trace Parkway also. According to the Parkway accession card, the latter map was made by Broutin in 1740, but this is unconfirmed.

du Montigny, Dumont. "Attack of the French Army on the Village of the Enemy the Chickasaw the 26 May, 1736" (translation of French title). Original with du Montigny's "Memoire." Ms. in the Edward E. Ayer Collection, Newberry Library, Chicago.

Finley, A. "Map of Louisiana, Mississippi, and Alabama." 1826. Copy at Mississippi Department of Archives and History, Jackson.

La Tourette, John. "An Accurate Map or Delineation of the State of Mississippi with a large portion of Louisiana and Mississippi." Mobile, Alabama, 1845. Originally prepared before 1839. Complete copy in Mississippi Collection, University of Mississippi Library.

Lewis, S. "Mississippi Territory." Boston: Thomas and Andrews, 1812. An original copy is located in Special Collections, Mitchell Memorial Library, Mississippi State University, Starkville.

Lusher, Henry M. "Map of the Lands in Mississippi Ceded by the Chickasaw to the United States in 1832 and 1834, from Actual Survey." 1835. Copy at Mississippi Department of Archives and History, Jackson.

McCorkle, Barbara. *American Emergent: An Exhibition of Maps and Atlases in Honor of Alexander O. Victor.* Includes Vicenzo M. Coronelli map, 1684. New Haven, Conn.: Yale University Press, 1985.

Melish, John. "Map of Mississippi." 1819. Copy at Mississippi Department of Archives and History, Jackson.

Purcell, Joseph. "New Map of West Florida. . . . " 1773. Also called the Stuart-Gage Map. (Published in John R. Swanton, "Early History of the Creek Indians and Their Neighbors," *Bureau of American Ethnology Bulletin 73*, Washington, D.C.: Smithsonian Institution, 1922).

Roberts, Capt. [Charles]. "A New Map of West Florida. . . . ," ca. 1800 but copied with post-1797 additions from the Purcell map or a missing map made by Bernard Romans in 1772–1773. Copies at the Birmingham, Alabama, Public Library, University of Auburn Library, and Mississippi Department of Archives and History, Jackson.

United States Land Office. Chickasaw Cession Survey Plat Maps for Township 12 South, Range 6 East; Township 10 South, Range 4 East; and Township 11 South, Range 3 East, 1833–1834. Originals at National Archives. Copies at Natchez Trace Parkway Headquarters.

Wilkinson, James. "A Survey of the route proposed for the highway from Nashville in the State of Tennessee to the Grindstone ford of the Bayou Pierre in the Mississippi Territory," ca. 1802. Original at National Archives. Copy at Natchez Trace Parkway Headquarters.

PERSONAL COMMUNICATIONS

Colbert, Richard A. Birmingham, Alabama, July 5, 2001. Regarding James Colbert the elder.

Knight, Vernon James, Jr. University of Alabama, June 23, 1989. Regarding possible De Soto artifacts.

Maszatos, Susan. Tennessee State Library and Archives, Nashville, July 23, 2001. Regarding James Robertson's homes.

PUBLISHED AND UNPUBLISHED SECONDARY SOURCES

Abbott, Martin. "Indian Policy and Management in the Mississippi Territory, 1798–1817." *Journal of Mississippi History* 15, no. 3(July 1952): 153–169.

Alden, John R. *John Stuart and the Southern Colonial Frontier.* Ann Arbor: University of Michigan Press, 1944.

Ambrose, Stephen P. *Undaunted Courage: Meriwether Lewis, Thomas Jefferson, and the Opening of the American West.* New York: Simon & Schuster, 1996.

Arnow, Harriette S. *Flowering of the Cumberland.* New York: Macmillan, 1963.

Atkinson, James R. "The Ackia and Ogoula Tchetoka Chickasaw Village Locations in 1736 during the French-Chickasaw War." *Mississippi Archaeology* 20, no. 1(June 1985): 53–72.

——. "Death of a Chickasaw Leader: The Probable Grave of Piomingo." *Mississippi Archaeology* 35, no. 2(Winter 2000): 124–172.

——. "The De Soto Expedition through Northeast Mississippi in 1540–1541." *Mississippi Archaeology* 22, no. 1(June 1987): 61–73.

——. "Historic Chickasaw Cultural Material: A More Comprehensive Identification." *Mississippi Archaeology* 22, no. 2(December 1987): 32–62.

——. "A Historic Contact Indian Settlement in Oktibbeha County, Mississippi." *Journal of Alabama Archaeology* 25, no. 1(1979): 61–82.

——. *History of the Chickasaw Indian Agency East of the Mississippi River.* Starkville, Mississippi: privately printed, 1998.

——. "The Location of the Nineteenth Century Choctaw Village of Wholkey in Chickasaw County, Mississippi." *Mississippi Archaeology* 21, no. 1(June 1986): 70–72.

——. "The Search for and Apparent Discovery of the Duck River Cantonment/Colbert-Gordon Stand Site, Maury County, Tennessee, Natchez Trace Parkway." Southeast Archeological Center, National Park Service, Tallahassee, Florida, April 1985.

——. "A Surface Collection from the Chickasaw Agency Site, 22-Cs-521, on the Natchez Trace in Chickasaw County, Mississippi." *Mississippi Archaeology* 20, no. 2(1985): 46–63.

Atkinson, James R., and Jack D. Elliott, Jr. *A Cultural Resources Survey of Selected Construction Areas in the Tennessee-Tombigbee River Waterway: Alabama and Mississippi.* 2 vols. Starkville: Mississippi State University Department of Anthropology, 1978.

Baird, W. David. *The Quapaw Indians: A History of the Downstream People.* Norman: University of Oklahoma Press, 1980.

Belden, Bauman L. *Indian Peace Medals Issued in the United States, 1789–1889.* New Milford, Conn.: N. Flayderman & Co., 1966. Reprinted with revisions by T. O'Toole and Sons, Norwalk, Conn., 1972.

Billington, R. A. *Westward Expansion: A History of the American Frontier.* 3rd ed. New York: Macmillian, 1967.

Blitz, John H. *Ancient Chiefdoms of the Tombigbee.* Tuscaloosa: University of Alabama Press, 1993.

Braden, Guy B. "The Colberts and the Chickasaw Nation." *Tennessee Historical Quarterly* 17, no. 3(September 1958): 222–249, and 4(December 1958): 318–335.

Brown, Ian W. "The Calumet Ceremony in the Southeast and Its Archaeological Manifestations." *American Antiquity* 54, no. 2(April 1989): 311–331.

Byington, Cyrus. "A Dictionary of the Choctaw Language." *Bureau of American Ethnology, Bulletin 46.* Washington, D.C.: Government Printing Office, 1915.

Cabaniss, Allan. "Ackia: Battle in the Wilderness." *Northeast Mississippi Historical Journal* 5, no. 1(November 1972): 1–15.

———. "Ackia: Battle in the Wilderness, 1736." *History Today* 25, no. 12(December 1975): 799–817.

Caldwell, Norman W. "The Chickasaw Threat to French Control of the Mississippi in the 1740s." *Chronicles of Oklahoma* 17(1939): 465–492.

Calloway, Colin G. *The American Revolution in Indian Country: Crisis and Diversity in Native American Communities.* Cambridge: Cambridge University Press, 1995.

Cashin, Edward J. *Colonial Augusta, Key of the Indian Country.* Macon, Ga.: Mercer University Press, 1986.

———. *Lachlan McGillivray, Indian Trader: The Shaping of the Southern Frontier.* Athens: University of Georgia Press, 1992.

Caughey, John W. *Bernardo De Galvez in Louisiana, 1776–1783.* Berkeley: University of California Press, 1934.

———. "The Natchez Rebellion of 1781 and Its Aftermath." *Louisiana Historical Quarterly* 16(1933): 57–83.

Champagne, Duane. *Social Order and Political Change: Constitutional Governments among the Cherokee, the Choctaw, the Chickasaw, and the Creek.* Stanford: Stanford University Press, 1992.

Chaplin, Joyce E. "Chickasaw." In Alan Gallay, ed., *Colonial Wars of North America, 1512–1763: An Encyclopedia,* 124–127. New York: Garland, 1996.

Coker, William S., and Thomas D. Watson. *Indian Traders of the Southeastern Spanish Borderlands: Panton, Leslie & Company and John Forbes & Company, 1783–1847.* Pensacola: University Press of Florida, 1986.

Colbert, Richard A. "James Logan Colbert of the Chickasaws: The Man and the Myth." *North Carolina Genealogical Society Journal,* May 1994 and February 1995.

Conlan, Czarina C. "David Folsom." *Chronicles of Oklahoma* 4(1926): 340–355.

Connelly, Thomas L. "Indian Warfare on the Tennessee Frontier, 1776–1794: Strategy and Tactics." *East Tennessee Historical Society's Publications* 36(1964): 3–22.

Cook, Steve, Buddy Palmer, and Julian Riley. "Historic Chickasaw Village Locations." Unpublished paper, 1980, copy at Natchez Trace Parkway Headquarters.

Corbitt, D. C. "James Colbert and the Spanish Claims to the East Bank of the Mississippi." *Mississippi Valley Historical Review* 24, no. 4(March 1938): 457–472.

Cotterill, Robert S. *The Southern Indians: The Story of the Civilized Tribes before Removal.* Norman: University of Oklahoma Press, 1954.

———. "The Virginia-Chickasaw Treaty of 1783." *Journal of Southern History* 8, no. 4(November 1942): 483–496.

Crane, Verner W. *The Southern Frontier, 1670–1732.* Ann Arbor: University of Michigan Press, 1929.

———. "The Southern Frontier in Queen Anne's War." *American Historical Review* 24, no. 3(April 1919): 379–395.

Cushman, H. B. *History of the Choctaw, Chickasaw, and Natchez Indians.* Greenville, Texas: Headlight Printing, 1899.

DeCell, Harriet, and JoAnne Pritchard. *Yazoo: Its Legends and Legacies.* Yazoo Delta Press, 1976.

Delanglez, Jean. *The French Jesuits in Lower Louisiana, 1700–1763.* Washington, D.C.: Catholic University of America, 1935.

Din, Gilbert C. "Arkansas Post in the American Revolution." *Arkansas Historical Quarterly* 40, no. 1(1981): 3–30.

———. "Loyalist Resistance after Pensacola: The Case of James Colbert." In W. S. Coker and R. R. Rea, eds., *Anglo-Spanish Confrontation on the Gulf Coast during the American Revolution,* 158–176. Pensacola: Gulf Coast History and Humanities Conference, 1982.

Din, Gilbert C., and A. P. Nasatir. *The Imperial Osages: Spanish Indian Diplomacy in the Mississippi Valley.* Norman: University of Oklahoma Press, 1983.

Dobyns, Henry. *Their Number Become Thinned.* Knoxville: University of Tennessee Press, 1983.

Doran, M. F. "Negro Slaves of the Five Civilized Tribes." *Annals of the Association of American Geographers* 68(September 1978): 335–350.

Drake, Samuel G. *Biography and History of the Indians of North America, from Its First Discovery.* Boston: Sanborn, Carter, & Bazin, 1857.

Dye, David H., and Ronald C. Brister, eds. *The Protohistoric Period in the Mid-South: 1500–1700.* Archaeological Report 18. Jackson: Mississippi Department of Archives and History, 1986.

Elliott, Jack D., Jr. "The Buried City: History, Myth, and Mystery on the Tombigbee." *Journal of Mississippi History.* Forthcoming.

———. *A Cultural Resources Survey of Selected Construction Areas in the Tennessee-Tombigbee River Waterway: Alabama and Mississippi,* vol. 2 (of 2), by James R. Atkinson and Jack D. Elliott, Jr. Starkville: Mississippi State University Department of Anthropology, 1978.

———. "The Fort of Natchez and the Colonial Origins of Mississippi." *Journal of Mississippi History* 52(August 1990): 159–197.

———. "Historical Overview." In John W. O'Hear, James R. Atkinson, Jack D. Elliott, Edmond A. Bordreaux III, and John R. Underwood, *Choctaw Agency, Natchez Trace Parkway: Archaeological and Historical Investigations, Madison County, Mississippi,* 17–56. Cobb Institute of Archaeology, Mississippi State University, Starkville. Tallahassee, Fla.: Southeast Archeological Center, National Park Service, 2000.

———. "Leftwich's 'Cotton Gin Port and Gaines' Trace' Reconsidered." *Journal of Mississippi History* 42, no. 4(1980): 348–361.

———. "The Plymouth Fort and the Creek War: A Mystery Solved." *Journal of Mississippi History* 62, no. 4(Nov. 2000): 329–370.

Fairbanks, Charles H. *Cherokee and Creek Indians—Ethnographic Report on Royce Area 79:*

Chickasaw, Cherokee, Creek. Findings of the Indian Claims Commission. New York: Garland, 1974.

Faye, Stanley. "Illinois Indians on the Lower Mississippi, 1771–1782." *Journal of the Illinois State Historical Society* 35, no. 1(March 1942): 57–72.

Folmsbee, S. J., R. E. Corlew, and E. L. Mitchell. *History of Tennessee.* New York: Lewis Historical, 1960.

Foreman, Carolyn T. "The Choctaw Academy." *Chronicles of Oklahoma* 6(December 1928): 452–480, and 10(March 1932): 76–114.

Foreman, Grant. *The Five Civilized Tribes.* Norman: University of Oklahoma Press, 1934.

Foret, Michael J. "The Failure of Administration: The Chickasaw Campaign of 1739–1740." *Revue de Louisiane/Louisiana Review* 11 (1982): 49–60.

———. "War or Peace? Louisiana, the Choctaws, and the Chickasaws, 1733–1735." *Louisiana History* 31, no. 3(Summer 1990): 273–292.

Fraser, Kathryn M. "Fort Jefferson: George Rogers Clark's Fort at the Mouth of the Ohio River, 1780–1781." *Register of the Kentucky Historical Society* 81, no. 1(Winter 1983): 1–24.

French, B. F. *Historical Memoirs of Louisiana.* New York, 1853.

Futato, Eugene M. *An Archaeological Overview of the Tombigbee River Basin, Alabama and Mississippi.* University of Alabama: Alabama State Museum of Natural History, Division of Archaeology, 1989.

Galloway, Patricia K. "Choctaw Factionalism and Civil War, 1746–1750." *Journal of Mississippi History* 44(November 1982): 289–328.

———. "Choctaw Factionalism and Civil War, 1746–1750." In Carolyn K. Reeves, ed., *The Choctaw Before Removal,* 120–156. Jackson: University Press of Mississippi, 1985.

———. *Choctaw Genesis, 1500–1700.* Lincoln: University of Nebraska Press, 1995.

———. "Henri de Tonti du Village des Chactas: The Beginning of the French Alliance." In P. K. Galloway, ed., *La Salle and His Legacy: Frenchmen and Indians in the Lower Mississippi Valley,* 146–175. Jackson: University Press of Mississippi, 1982.

———. "Ougoula Tchetoka, Ackia and Bienville's First Chickasaw War: Whose Strategy and Tactics?" *Journal of Chickasaw History* 2, no. 1(1996): 3–10.

———, ed. *La Salle and His Legacy: Frenchmen and Indians in the Lower Mississippi Valley.* Jackson: University Press of Mississippi, 1982.

Gibson, Arrell M. "Chickasaw Ethnography: An Ethnohistorical Reconstruction." *Ethnohistory* 18(1971): 99–118.

———. *The Chickasaws.* Norman: University of Oklahoma Press, 1971.

———. "The Colberts: Chickasaw Nation Elitism." In H. G. Jordan and T. M. Holm, eds., *Indian Leaders: Oklahoma's First Statesmen,* 79–100. Oklahoma City: Oklahoma Historical Society, 1979.

———. *The Kickapoos.* Norman: University of Oklahoma Press, 1963.

Goodpasture, Albert V. "Indian Wars and Warriors of the Old Southwest, 1730–1807." *Tennessee Historical Magazine* 4, nos. 1–4(1918).

Goodrich, William. "William Cocke—Born 1749, Died 1828." *American Historical Magazine* 1, no. 3(July 1896): 224–229.

Green, John A. "Governor Perier's Expedition against the Natchez Indians." *Louisiana Historical Quarterly* 19(1936): 547–577.

Haarman, Alfred W. "The Spanish Conquest of British West Florida, 1779–1781." *Florida Historical Quarterly* 29(July 1960–April 1961): 107–134.

Halbert, Henry S. "Bernard Romans' Map of 1772." *Publications of the Mississippi Historical Society* 6 (1902): 415–439.

———. "The French Trading Post and the Chocchuma Village in East Mississippi." *Publications of the Mississippi Historical Society* 11 (1910): 325–329.

———. "Shatala: Notes on a Chickasaw Town Name." In Milo M. Quaife, ed., *Proceedings of the Mississippi Valley Historical Association for the Year 1914–1915*, 93–94. Cedar Rapids, Iowa: Torch Press, 1916.

———. "The Small Indian Tribes of Mississippi." *Publications of the Mississippi Historical Society* 5 (1902): 302–308.

Hale, Duane K., and Arrell M. Gibson. *The Chickasaw.* New York: Charles House, 1991.

Harris, John B. *From Old Mobile to Fort Assumption: A Story of the French Attempts to Colonize Louisiana, and Destroy the Chickasaw Indians.* Nashville: Parthenon, 1959.

Haynes, Robert V. "James Willing and the Planters of Natchez." *Journal of Mississippi History* 37, no. 1(February 1975): 1–40.

———. *The Natchez District and the American Revolution.* Jackson: University Press of Mississippi, 1976.

Haywood, John. *The Civil and Political History of the State of Tennessee from Its Earliest Settlement up to the Year 1796.* Nashville: Publishing House of the Methodist Episcopal Church South, 1891, reprint of 1823 edition published by Heskill and Brown, Knoxville.

———. *The Natural and Aboriginal History of Tennessee . . . to 1768.* Mary B. Rothrock, ed. Jackson, Tenn.: McCowat-Mercer, 1959, reprint of 1823 edition.

Henderson, Archibald. "Richard Henderson: The Authorship of the Cumberland Compact and the Founding of Nashville." *Tennessee Historical Magazine,* no. 3 (Sept. 1916). Republished in *Tennessee Old and New,* vol. 1, pp. 93–111. Sponsored by the Tennessee Historical Commission and the Tennessee Historical Society. Kingsport, Tenn.: Kingsport Press, 1946.

Hiemstra, William L. "Early Presbyterian Missions among the Choctaw and Chickasaw." *Journal of Mississippi History* 10(January 1948): 8–16.

Hill, Edward E. "The Chickasaw Agency." In *The Office of Indian Affairs, 1824–1880: Historical Sketches,* 40–41. New York: Clearwater, 1974.

Hodge, Frederick W., ed. "Handbook of American Indians North of Mexico." *Bureau of American Ethnology Bulletin 30,* pt. 1 (1907) and pt. 2 (1910). Washington, D.C.: Government Printing Office.

Holmes, Jack D. L. "The Ebb-Tide of Spanish Military Power on the Mississippi: Fort San Fernando De Las Barrancas, 1795–1798." *East Tennessee Historical Society's Publications* 36(1964): 23–44.

———. "Fort Ferdinand of the Bluffs, Life on the Spanish-American Frontier." *West Tennessee Historical Society's Publications* 13(1959): 38–54.

———. *Gayoso: The Life of a Spanish Governor in the Mississippi Valley, 1789–1799.* Baton Rouge: Louisiana State University Press, 1965.

———. "A Mystery Map of West Florida: A Cartographical Puzzle." In Ronald V. Evans, ed.,

Threads of Tradition and Culture along the Gulf Coast, 216–229. Pensacola: Gulf Coast History and Humanities Conference, 1986.

———. "Spanish-American Rivalry over the Chickasaw Bluffs, 1780–1795." *East Tennessee Historical Society's Publications* 34(1962): 26–57.

———. "Spanish Treaties with West Florida Indians, 1784–1802." *Florida Historical Quarterly* 48(July 1969–April 1970): 140–154.

Hudson, Charles M. "James Adair as Anthropologist." *Ethnohistory* 24(Fall 1977): 311–328.

———. *The Southeastern Indians.* Knoxville: University of Tennessee Press, 1976.

Hudson, Charles M., Marvin T. Smith, and Chester DePratter. "The Hernando De Soto Expedition: From Mabila to the Mississippi River." In David H. Dye and Cheryl Anne Cox, eds., *Towns and Temples along the Mississippi River,* 181–207. Tuscaloosa: University of Alabama Press, 1990.

Hudson, Charles, and Carmen C. Tesser, eds. *The Forgotten Centuries: Indians and Europeans in the American South, 1521–1704.* Athens: University of Georgia Press, 1994.

Jeltz, W. F. "The Relations of Negroes and Choctaw and Chickasaw Indians." *Journal of Negro History* 33(January 1948): 24–37.

Jenkins, Ned J., and Richard Krause. *The Tombigbee Watershed in Southeastern Prehistory.* Tuscaloosa: University of Alabama Press, 1986.

Jennings, Jesse D. "Chickasaw and Earlier Indian Cultures of Northeast Mississippi." *Journal of Mississippi History* 3(1941): 155–226.

Johnson, Jay K. "Aboriginal Settlement and First Contact in Northeast Mississippi." *National Geographic Research and Exploration* 7, no. 4(1991).

———. "The Chickasaw." In Bonnie G. McEwan, ed., *Indians of the Greater Southeast: History, Archaeology, and Ethnohistory,* 85–121. Gainesville: University of Florida Press, 2000.

———. "Chiefdom to Tribe in Northeast Mississippi: A Culture in Transition." In Patricia K. Galloway, ed., *The Hernando de Soto Expedition: History, Historiography, and "Discovery" in the Southeast.* Lincoln: University of Nebraska Press, 1997.

———. "Settlement Patterns, GIS, Remote Sensing and the Late Prehistory of the Black Prairie in East Central Mississippi." In Cliff Behrens and Tom Sever, eds., *Applications of Space-Age Technology in Anthropology,* 111–119. John C. Stennis Space Center, Mississippi, 1991.

Johnson, Jay K., Geoffrey R. Lehmann, James R. Atkinson, Susan L. Scott, and Andrea B. Shea. *Protohistoric Chickasaw Settlement Patterns and the De Soto Route in Northeast Mississippi.* Final Report to the National Endowment for the Humanities and National Geographic Society, Washington, D.C., 1991.

Johnson, Jay K., Susan L. Scott, James R. Atkinson, and Andrea B. Shea. "Late Prehistoric/Protohistoric Settlement and Subsistence on the Black Prairie: Buffalo Hunting in Mississippi." *North American Archaeologist* 15, no. 2(1994): 167–179.

Johnson, Jay K., and John T. Sparks, "Protohistoric Settlement Patterns in Northeastern Mississippi." In David H. Dye and Ronald C. Brister, eds., *The Protohistoric Period in the Mid-South: 1500–1700,* 64–81. Archaeological Report 18. Jackson: Mississippi Department of Archives and History, 1986.

Jones, C. C. *The History of Georgia.* Boston: Houghton, Mifflin, 1883.

Knight, Vernon James, Jr. "Social Organization and the Evolution of Hierarchy in Southeastern Chiefdoms." *Journal of Anthropological Research* 46, no. 1(Spring 1990): 1–23.

Leftwich, George J. "Cotton Gin Port and Gaines' Trace." *Publications of the Mississippi Historical Society* 7 (1903): 263–270.

Leftwich, Nina. *Two Hundred Years at Muscle Shoals being an Authentic History of Colbert County [Alabama], 1700–1900.* Birmingham: Multigraphic Advertising, 1935.

Lewis, E. C. "James Robertson, Nashville's Founder." In *Tennessee Old and New,* vol. 1, pp. 84–92. Sponsored by the Tennessee Historical Commission and the Tennessee Historical Society. Kingsport, Tenn.: Kingsport Press, 1946.

Littlefield, Daniel F., Jr. *The Chickasaw Freedmen.* Westport, Conn.: Greenwood Press, 1980.

McBee, May Wilson. "Benjamin F. Smith." In Ron Tyler, Douglas E. Barnett, Roy R. Barkley, Penelope C. Anderson, and Mark F. Odintz, eds., *The New Handbook of Texas,* vol. 5, pp. 1091–1092. Austin: Texas State Historical Association, 1996.

McBride, Stephen, Jan [*sic,* Kim] McBride, and Jack D. Elliott, Jr. "John L. Allen and Margaret." In *History of Clay County, Mississippi,* 294. Clay County Historical Society. Houston, Texas: Curtis Media, 1988.

McConnell, Michael N. *A Country Between: The Upper Ohio Valley and Its People, 1724–1774.* Lincoln: University of Nebraska Press, 1992.

McDonald, B. W. *History of the Cumberland Presbyterian Church.* Nashville, 1888.

Malone, J. H. *The Chickasaw Nation: A Short Sketch of a Noble People.* Louisville, Ky.: John P. Morton, 1922.

Margry, Pierre. *Decouvertes et establissements des Francais dans l'ouest er dans le sud ed l'Amerique Septentrionale, 1614–1754.* 4 vols. Paris, 1875–1886.

Marshall, Richard A. "A Possible Historic Indian Pendant." *Journal of Alabama Archaeology* 24, no. 2(December 1978): 125–131.

———. "The Protohistoric Component at the Lyon's Bluff Site Complex, Oktibbeha County, Mississippi." In David H. Dye and Ronald C. Brister, eds., *The Protohistoric Period in the Mid-South: 1500–1700,* 82–88. Archaeological Report 18. Jackson: Mississippi Department of Archives and History, 1986.

Martin, Francois-Xavier. *History of Louisiana from the Earliest Period.* 2 vols. New Orleans, 1827.

Martini, Don. "Chickasaw Empire: The Story of the Colbert Family." Copy of typescript (revised), 1986. Special Collections, Mitchell Memorial Library, Mississippi State University, Starkville.

———. "Chickasaw: A History, 1540–1856." Unpublished, 1971. Copy at Special Collections, Mitchell Memorial Library, Mississippi State University, Starkville.

———. *The Indian Chiefs of the Southeast: A Guide, 1750–1861.* Ripley, Miss.: 1991.

———. "Mice in the Wigwam: The Colberts v. [versus] Historians." *Northeast Mississippi Historical Journal* 2(July 1968): 13–20.

———. "The Search for Ackia." *Northeast Mississippi Historical Journal* 5(November 1971): 17–31. Copy of manuscript with unpublished appendix on file at Natchez Trace Parkway Headquarters.

Meriwether, Robert L. *The Expansion of South Carolina, 1729–1765.* Philadelphia: Porcupine, 1974.

Milling, Chapman J. *Red Carolinians*. Columbia: University of South Carolina Press, 1969, reprint.

Mohr, Walter H. *Federal Indian Relations, 1774–1788*. Philadelphia: University of Pennsylvania Press, 1933.

Morgan, David W. "An Analysis of Historic Period Chickasaw Settlement Patterns." Master's thesis, Department of Anthropology, University of Alabama, 1994.

———. "Historic Period Chickasaw Indians: Chronology and Settlement Patterns." *Mississippi Archaeology* 31, no. 1(1996): 1–39.

Myer, William E. "Indian Trails of the Southeast." *Forty-second Annual Report of the Bureau of American Ethnology for 1924–1925*. Washington, D.C.: Government Printing Office, 1928.

Nasatir, Abraham P. *Spanish War Vessels on the Mississippi, 1792–1796*. New Haven, Conn.: Yale University Press, 1968.

Nash, Gary B., John R. Howe, Allen F. Davis, Julie Roy Jeffrey, Peter J. Frederick, and Allan M. Winkler. *The American People: Creating a Nation and a Society*, vol. 1. New York: Harper and Row, 1990.

Natchez Trace Parkway Survey. *A Report of a Survey of the Old Indian Trail, Known as the Natchez Trace*. 76th Congress, Senate Document No. 148. Washington, D.C.: Government Printing Office, 1941.

O'Donnell, James H., III. *Southern Indians in the American Revolution*. Knoxville: University of Tennessee Press, 1973.

O'Hear, John W., James R. Atkinson, Jack D. Elliott, Edmond A. Bordreaux III, and John R. Underwood. *Choctaw Agency, Natchez Trace Parkway: Archaeological and Historical Investigations, Madison County, Mississippi*. Cobb Institute of Archaeology, Mississippi State University, Starkville. Tallahassee: Southeast Archeological Center, National Park Service, 2000.

Osborn, George C. "Relations with the Indians in West Florida during the Administration of Governor Peter Chester, 1770–1781." *Florida Historical Quarterly* 31, no. 4(April 1953): 239–272.

Peake, Ora B. *A History of the United States Indian Factory System, 1795–1822*. Denver: Sage Books, 1954.

Peyser, Joseph L. "1740 French Map Pinpoints Battle Site in Mississippi." *Mapline* 39(September 1985): 2–4.

———. "The Chickasaw Wars of 1736 and 1740: French Military Drawings and Plans Document the Struggle for the Lower Mississippi." *Journal of Mississippi History* 44(1982): 1–25.

Phelps, Dawson A. "The Chickasaw Council House." *Journal of Mississippi History* 14(1952): 170–176.

———. "The Chickasaw, the English, and the French." *Tennessee Historical Quarterly* 16(June 1957): 117–133.

———. "The Chickasaw Mission." *Journal of Mississippi History* 13(1951): 226–235.

———. "Colbert Ferry and Selected Documents." *Alabama Historical Quarterly* 25, nos. 3 and 4(1963): 203–226.

———. "Stands and Travel Accommodations on the Natchez Trace." *Journal of Mississippi History* 11, no. 1(January 1949): 1–54.

———. "Tockshish." *Journal of Mississippi History* 13(1951): 138–145.

———. "The Vaudreuil Expedition, 1752." *William and Mary Quarterly* 15, no. 4(October 1958): 483–493.

Phillips, P. Lee. *Notes on the Life and Works of Bernard Romans.* Florida Historical Society, Gainesville, 1924.

Plaisance, Aloysius. "The Chickasaw Bluffs Factory and Its Removal to the Arkansas River, 1818–1822." *Tennessee Historical Quarterly* 11(1952): 41–56.

Prucha, Francis P. *American Indian Policy in the Formative Years: The Indian Trade and Intercourse Acts, 1790–1834.* Cambridge: Harvard University Press, 1962.

———. *Indian Peace Medals in American History.* Madison: State Historical Society of Wisconsin, 1971.

Putnam, A. W. *History of Middle Tennessee or, Life and Times of Gen. James Robertson.* Knoxville: University of Tennessee Press, 1971, reprint of 1859 edition.

Rafferty, Janet. *Owl Creek Mounds: Test Excavations at a Vacant Mississippian Mound Center.* Report of Investigations 7. Mississippi State University, Cobb Institute of Archaeology, Starkville, 1995.

Rainwater, Percy L. "Indian Missions and Missionaries." *Journal of Mississippi History* 28(February 1966): 15–39.

Ramsey, J. G. M. *The Annals of Tennessee to the End of the Eighteenth Century.* Kingsport, Tenn.: Kingsport Press, 1926, originally published in 1853.

Roberson, Luther L. "The Seeds of Spain." 1978. Unpublished carbon copy manuscript in possession of Joyce Roberson Bushman. Copy made available to the writer by Ms. Bushman.

Rollings, Willard H. *The Osage: An Ethnohistorical Study of Hegemony on the Prairie-Plains.* Columbia: University of Missouri Press, 1992.

Romenofsky, Ann F. "The Introduction of European Diseases and Aboriginal Population Collapse." *Mississippi Archaeology* 20, no. 1(1985): 2–19.

———. *Vectors of Death: The Archaeology of European Contact.* Albuquerque: University of New Mexico Press, 1987.

Roper, James E. "Fort Adams and Fort Pickering." *West Tennessee Historical Society Papers* 24 (1970): 5–29.

———. "The Revolutionary War on the Fourth Chickasaw Bluff." *West Tennessee Historical Society Papers* 29(October 1975): 5–24.

Rowland, Dunbar, ed. *Mississippi.* 2 vols. Spartanburg, S.C.: Reprint Company, 1976.

Rucker, Marc D. *Archaeological Survey and Test Excavations in the Upper-Central Tombigbee River Valley: Aliceville-Columbus Lock and Dam and Impoundment Areas, Alabama and Mississippi.* Starkville: Mississippi State University Department of Anthropology, 1974.

Scroggs, William O. "Early Trade and Travel in the Lower Mississippi Valley." Benjamin F. Shambaugh, ed., *Proceedings of the Mississippi Valley Historical Association for the Year 1908–1909,* vol. 2, pp. 235–256. Cedar Rapids, Ohio: Torch, 1910.

Shaw, Helen L. *British Administration of the Southern Indians, 1756–1783.* Lancaster, Pa.: Lancaster Press, 1931.

Simpson, William M. "Rivalry for Empire: Choctaw and Chickasaw Relations with the English in the Eighteenth Century." Master's thesis, Department of History, Mississippi State University, Starkville, 1972.

Smith, Bruce D. "The Archaeology of the Southeastern United States: From Dalton to

De Soto, 10,500–500 B.P." In Fred Wendorf and Angela E. Close, eds., *Advances in World Archaeology*, vol. 5, pp. 1–92. Orlando: Academic, 1986.

Snapp, J. Russell. *John Stuart and the Struggle for Empire on the Southern Frontier.* Baton Rouge: Louisiana State University Press, 1996.

Snell, William R. "Indian Slavery in Colonial South Carolina, 1671–1795." Ph.D. dissertation, University of Alabama, Tuscaloosa, 1972.

St. Jean, Wendy. "The Chickasaws: Firm Friends of the English?" Master's thesis, Department of History, University of Virginia, Charlottesville, 1994.

———. "The Chickasaws: Firm Friends of the English?" *Mississippi Archaeology* 68, no. 4(1996): 345–358.

Starr, J. Barton. *Tories, Dons, and Rebels: The American Revolution in British West Florida.* Gainesville: University Presses of Florida, 1976.

Stubbs, John D., Jr. "Archaeological Survey in Lee County, Mississippi, 1981–1983." Submitted to the Chickasaw Cultural Center, Lee County, Mississippi, 1983.

———. "The Chickasaw Contact with the La Salle Expedition in 1682." In P. K. Galloway, ed., *La Salle and His Legacy,* 41–48. Jackson: University Press of Mississippi, 1982.

———. "A Preliminary Classification of Chickasaw Pottery." *Mississippi Archaeology* 17, no. 2(1982): 50–57.

Swanton, John R. "Early History of the Creek Indians and Their Neighbors." *Bureau of American Ethnology Bulletin 73.* Washington, D.C.: Smithsonian Institution, 1922.

———. "The Indians of the Southeastern United States." *Bureau of American Ethnology, Bulletin 137.* Washington, D.C.: Smithsonian Institution, 1946.

———. "The Indian Tribes of North America." *Bureau of American Ethnology Bulletin 145.* Washington, D.C.: Smithsonian Institution, 1952.

———. "Social and Religious Beliefs and Usages of the Chickasaw Indians." *44th Annual Report of the Bureau of American Ethnology.* Washington, D.C.: Government Printing Office, 1928.

Sword, Wiley. *President Washington's Indian War: The Struggle for the Old Northwest, 1790–1795.* Norman: University of Oklahoma Press, 1985.

Tanner, Helen H. "The Land and Water Communication Systems of the Southeastern Indians." In Peter H. Wood, Gregory A. Waselkov, and M. Thomas Hatley, eds., *Powhatan's Mantle.* 6–20. Lincoln: University of Nebraska Press, 1989.

Tennessee Old and New. Vol. 1. Sponsored by the Tennessee Historical Commission and the Tennessee Historical Society. Kingsport, Tenn.: Kingsport Press, 1946.

Unser, Daniel H., Jr. *Indians, Settlers, & Slaves in a Frontier Exchange Economy.* Chapel Hill: University of North Carolina Press, 1992.

Walton, J. N. "Letter of J. N. Walton." *Itawamba Settlers* 17(1997).

Ward, Rufus A., Jr. "The Tombigbee Crossing of the De Soto Expedition." *Mississippi Archaeology* 21(1986): 62–68.

Warren, Harry. "Some Chickasaw Chiefs and Prominent Men." *Publications of the Mississippi Historical Society* 8(1904): 555–569.

———. "Missions, Missionaries, Frontier Characters and Schools." *Publications of the Mississippi Historical Society* 8(1904): 571–598.

Waselkov, Gregory A. "Indian Maps of the Colonial Southeast." In Peter H. Wood, G. A.

Waselkov, and M. Thomas Hatley, eds., *Powhatan's Mantle,* 292–343. Lincoln: University of Nebraska Press, 1989.

Whitaker, A. P. "Alexander McGillivray, 1783–1789." *North Carolina Historical Review* 5, no. 2(April 1928): 181–203.

———. *The Spanish-American Frontier.* Gloucester, Mass.: Peter Smith, 1962.

White, Richard. *The Roots of Dependency.* Lincoln: University of Nebraska Press, 1983.

Williams, Samuel Cole. *Beginnings of West Tennessee in the Land of the Chickasaws, 1541–1841.* Johnson City, Tenn.: Watauga Press, 1930.

———. *Early Travel in the Tennessee Country, 1540–1800.* Johnson City, Tenn.: Watauga Press, 1928.

———. *History of The Lost State of Franklin.* New York: Press of the Pioneers, 1933.

———. *Tennessee during the Revolutionary War.* Knoxville: University of Tennessee Press, 1944.

Winston, E. T. *Story of Pontotoc.* Pontotoc, Miss.: Pontotoc Progress, 1931.

Winter, Robert M. *Shadow of a Mighty Rock: A Social and Cultural History of Presbyterianism in Marshall County, Mississippi.* Franklin, Tenn.: Providence House, 1997.

Wood, Patricia D. *French-Indian Relations on the Southern Frontier, 1699–1762.* Ann Arbor, Mich.: UMI Research Press, 1979.

Wood, Peter H. "The Changing Population of the Colonial South: An Overview by Race and Religion, 1685–1790." In Peter H. Wood, G. A. Waselkov, and M. Thomas Hatley, eds., *Powhatan's Mantle,* 35–103. Lincoln: University of Nebraska Press, 1989.

Wood, Peter H., G. A. Waselkov, and M. T. Hatley, eds. *Powhatan's Mantle.* Lincoln: University of Nebraska Press, 1989.

Wright, J. Leitch, Jr. *Florida in the American Revolution.* Gainesville: University Presses of Florida, 1975.

———. *The Only Land They Knew: The Tragic Story of the American Indians in the Old South.* New York: Free Press, 1981.

Young, Mary E. *Redskins, Ruffleshirts, and Rednecks: Indian Allotments in Alabama and Mississippi, 1830–1860.* Norman: University of Oklahoma Press, 1961.

Index